Slavery i

Class an(*!er*

Southern slaveholders proudly pronounced themselves orthodox Christians, who accepted responsibility for the welfare of the people who worked for them. They proclaimed that their slaves enjoyed a better and more secure life than any laboring class in the world. Now, did it not follow that the lives of laborers of all races across the world would be immeasurably improved by their enslavement? In the Old South, but in no other slave society, a doctrine emerged among leading clergymen, politicians, and intellectuals, "Slavery in the Abstract," which declared enslavement the best possible condition for all labor regardless of race. They joined the socialists, whom they studied, in believing that the free-labor system, wracked by worsening class warfare, was collapsing. A vital question: To what extent did the people of the several social classes of the South accept so extreme a doctrine? That question lies at the heart of this book.

Elizabeth Fox-Genovese (1941–2007) was Eleonore Raoul Professor of the Humanities at Emory University, where she was founding director of Women's Studies. She served on the Governing Council of the National Endowment for the Humanities (2002–2007). In 2003, President George W. Bush awarded her a National Humanities Medal; the Georgia State Senate honored her with a special resolution of appreciation for her contributions as a scholar, teacher, and citizen of Georgia; and the fellowship of Catholic Scholars bestowed on her its Cardinal Wright Award. Among her books and published lectures are *The Origins of Physiocracy: Economic Revolution and Social Order in Eighteenth-Century France*, *Within the Plantation Household: Black and White Women of the Old South*, and *Feminism without Illusions: A Critique of Individualism*.

Eugene D. Genovese is a retired professor of history. Among his books are *Roll, Jordan, Roll: The World the Slaves Made*; *The Slaveholders' Dilemma: Freedom and Progress in Southern Conservative Thought, 1820–1860*; and *A Consuming Fire: The Fall of the Confederacy in the Mind of the White Christian South*.

Fox-Genovese and Genovese co-authored *Fruits of Merchant Capital: Slavery and Bourgeois Property in the Rise and Expansion of Capitalism* and *The Mind of the Master Class: History and Faith in the Southern Slaveholders' Worldview*. In 2004 the Intercollegiate Studies Institute presented them jointly with its Gerhard Niemeyer Award for Distinguished Contributions to Scholarship in the Liberal Arts.

Publication of this book has been aided by the generosity of the Mary C. Skaggs Foundation and the Watson–Brown Foundation, Inc.

Slavery in White and Black

Class and Race in the
Southern Slaveholders' New World Order

ELIZABETH FOX-GENOVESE
EUGENE D. GENOVESE

CAMBRIDGE
UNIVERSITY PRESS

CAMBRIDGE UNIVERSITY PRESS
Cambridge, New York, Melbourne, Madrid, Cape Town, Singapore, São Paulo, Delhi

Cambridge University Press
32 Avenue of the Americas, New York, NY 10013-2473, USA

www.cambridge.org
Information on this title: www.cambridge.org/9780521721813

First published 2008

Printed in the United States of America

A catalog record for this publication is available from the British Library.

Library of Congress Cataloging in Publication Data

Fox-Genovese, Elizabeth, 1941–2007.
Slavery in White and Black : class and race in the southern slaveholders' new world order /
Elizabeth Fox-Genovese, Eugene D. Genovese.
    p. cm.
Includes bibliographical references and index.
ISBN 978-0-521-89700-6 (hardback) – ISBN 978-0-521-72181-3 (pbk.)
 1. Slavery – Moral and ethical aspects – Southern States – History – 19th century.
 2. Slavery – Southern States – Justification. 3. Slavery and the church – Southern States –
History – 19th century. 4. Working class – United States – Social conditions – 19th century.
 5. Labor – United States – History – 19th century. 6. Industrialization – United States –
Social aspects – 19th century. 7. Capitalism – United States – History – 19th century.
 8. Southern States – Intellectual life – 19th century. I. Genovese, Eugene D., 1930– II. Title.
E449.F77 2008
306.3′620775 – dc22   2008007065

ISBN 978-0-521-89700-6 hardback
ISBN 978-0-521-72181-3 paperback

For

William J. and Heather Hungeling
and
Fr. James Sextone

That non-slaveholding States will eventually have to organize labour, and introduce something so like to Slavery that it will be impossible to discriminate between them, or else to suffer from the most violent and disastrous insurrections against the system which creates and perpetuates their misery, seems to be as certain as the tendencies in the laws of capital and population to produce the extremes of poverty and wealth. We do not envy them their social condition.

—The Reverend Dr. James Henley Thornwell,
"Sermon on National Sins" (1860)

Contents

Preface

Elizabeth Fox-Genovese (1941–2007) and I intended *Slavery in White and Black: Class and Race in the Southern Slaveholders' New World Order* to stand alone, so that readers who do not know our previous work would not be placed at serious disadvantage. Those who have read *The Mind of the Master Class: History and Faith in the Southern Slaveholders' Worldview* (2005) will, however, have a richer context for the place of our argument in the trajectory of proslavery thought and, more broadly, nineteenth-century transatlantic religious and secular conservative thought.

A few clarifications: "The War" refers to the War for Southern Independence of 1861–1865. The term "free labor" is not as straightforward as it might appear; different scholars use it differently. Here, we equate it with "wage labor" as usually done in the texts we discuss. Where we have identified the author of anonymous publications, the name appears in brackets. A question mark indicates that we consider the author in brackets probable. All words placed in italics for emphasis are from original sources quoted. We use *sic* only in rare cases in which it seems indispensable.

We are deeply grateful to Christopher Luse for helping us to collect materials, checking references and quotations, and offering valuable criticisms of style and content. As Elizabeth Fox-Genovese's health was collapsing, Tina Trent's kindness and innumerable professional and personal efforts on our behalf reached heroic proportions.

For critical readings of versions of this book in draft we are indebted to Douglas Ambrose, Paul Conkin, Stanley L. Engerman, William W. Freehling, Jeannette Hopkins, Peter Kolchin, James Livingston, David Moltke-Hansen, Joseph Moore, Robert L. Paquette, Mark M. Smith, Sean Wilentz, and Clyde N. Wilson.

Manuscript Collections Cited

[* Manuscripts at the Southern Historical Collection, UNC]

Sarah Eve Adams Diary*
Samuel Agnew Diary*
Elisha Allen Collection, at Georgia Department of Archives and History (Atlanta)
Everard Green Baker Diary*
David Alexander Barnes Diary*
R. R. Barrow Residence Journal*
Mary Eliza Battle Letters, at North Carolina State Archives (Raleigh)
Mary Bethell Diary*
J. H. Bills Papers*
Keziah Brevard Diary, at USC
Iveson Brookes Papers, at Duke University
Lucy Wood Butler Diary*
Cabell-Ellet Papers, at University of Virginia
Franc M. Carmack Diary*
Mary Eliza Carmichael Papers*
Kate Carney Diary*
Eliza Clitheral Autobiography*
Cole-Taylor Papers*
Juliana Margaret Connor Diary*
John Hamilton Cornish Diary*
J. B. Cottrel Diary*
Edward Cross Papers, at University of Arkansas (Fayetteville)
Louis M. De Saussure Plantation Record Book*
Records of the Dialectic Society*
Elliott-Gonzales Papers*
Holden Garthur Evans Diary, at Mississippi Department of Archives and History (Jackson)

Lucy Muse Walton Fletcher "Autobiography," Summer, 1844, at Duke University
Albert E. Fossier Papers, at Historic New Orleans Collection
Thomas Miles Garrett Diary*
Sarah Gayle Diary*
Julia A. Gilmer Diary*
James H. Greenlee Diary*
John Berkeley Grimball Diary*
Meta Morris Grimball Journal*
William Hooper Haigh Diary and Letters*
Herndon Haralson Papers*
Gustavus A. Henry Papers*
George Frederick Holmes Letterbook, at Duke University
Susan Nye Hutchinson Papers*
Jackson–Prince Papers*
Mitchell King Papers*
Thomas Butler King Papers*
Carl Kohn Letter Book, at Historic New Orleans Collection
Francis Terry Leak Diary*
Liddell Papers at LSU
John Berrien Lindsley Papers, at Tennessee State Library and Archives (Nashville)
Louis Manigault Diary, at Duke University
Basil Manly Papers*
Basil Manly, Jr., Papers*
Jason Niles Diary*
H. C. Nixon Collection, at Alabama Department of Archives and History (Montgomery)
Dr. James Norcom Papers, at North Carolina State Archives (Raleigh)
James H. Otey Papers*
Palfrey Papers, at LSU
William Porcher Miles Papers*
William Campbell Preston Papers, at USC
John A. Quitman Papers*
Walker Reid Papers*
Roach-Eggleston Papers*
Edmund Ruffin Papers*
Henry Ruffner Papers, at Washington and Lee University (Lexington)
William Ruffin Smith Papers*
Alonzo Snyder Papers, at LSU
Frank F. Steel Papers*
Francis Taylor Diary*
Ella Gertrude Clanton Thomas Diary, at Duke University
Thornwell Papers, at USC

William D. Valentine Diaries*
John Walker Diary*
Henry Young Webb Diary*
[Wake County], Resolutions and Address of the Wake County Working-Men's
    Association (Electronic ed.; Chapel Hill, N.C., 2002 [1859])
Calvin H. Wiley Papers*

Abbreviations

AJP	*The Papers of Andrew Johnson*, ed. LeRoy P. Graf and Ralph W. Haskins (Knoxville, Tenn., 1967–)
DBR	*De Bow's Review*
DD	Robert Lewis Dabney, *Discussions: Evangelical and Theological*, ed. C. R. Vaughan, 3 vols. (Carlisle, Pa., 1982)
DNCB	*Dictionary of North Carolina Biography*, ed. William S. Powell, 6 vols. (Chapel Hill, N.C., 1979–1994)
ERD	*The Diary of Edmund Ruffin*, ed. William Kaufman Scarborough, 3 vols. (Baton Rouge, La., 1972–1989)
HLW	*Writings of Hugh Swinton Legaré* [ed. Mary S. Legaré], 2 vols. (Charleston, S.C., 1846)
JCCP	*The Papers of John C. Calhoun*, ed. successively Robert Lee Meriwether, Edwin Hemphill, and Clyde N. Wilson, 26 vols. (Columbia, S.C., 1959–2003)
JDP	*The Papers of Jefferson Davis*, ed. Haskell M. Monroe, Jr., James T. McIntosh, et al., 11 vols. (Baton Rouge, La., and Houston, Tex., 1971–2004)
JHTW	*The Collected Writings of James Henley Thornwell*, ed. John Adger and B. M. Palmer, 4 vols. (Carlisle, Pa., 1986)
JSH	*Journal of Southern History*
LCL	Loeb Classical Library
LSU	Louisiana State University
QRMCS	*Quarterly Review of the Methodist Church, South*
RM	*Russell's Magazine*
SLM	*Southern Literary Messenger*
SPR	*Southern Presbyterian Review*
SQR	*Southern Quarterly Review*
SR	*Southern Review*
UNC	University of North Carolina [Southern Historical Collection]
USC	University of South Carolina

Slavery in White and Black

Class and Race in the Southern Slaveholders' New World Order

Introduction

> In everything, it is the nature of the human mind to begin with necessity and end in excess.
>
> —Pliny the Elder[1]

Elizabeth Fox-Genovese and I long insisted that the presuppositions of the southern defense of slavery ended with Slavery in the Abstract – the doctrine that declared slavery or a kindred system of personal servitude the best possible condition for all labor regardless of race. Proslavery logic cast enslavement, broadly defined, as necessary and proper for much of the white race, as well as for practically all of the black race. A vital question has remained unanswered: To what extent did so extreme a doctrine take root among slaveholders and nonslaveholders?

The expression "Slavery in the Abstract" roiled southern politics. It had several meanings, the most intriguing of which referred to a social system abstracted from race and best for whites as well as blacks. We here follow that meaning, but the principal alternative requires identification and explanation. A good many Southerners used the term to distinguish between support for specifically black slavery and support for slavery in principle. They rejected the resort to philosophical abstractions as akin to ideological special pleading. Theodore Dwight Bozeman, a gifted American historian, remarks that the Old School Presbyterians – Calvinistic Baconian advocates of induction – used words like "abstract," "theory," and "metaphysics" as "virtual obscenities." Bozeman's observation also applies to Methodist Arminians and to secular intellectuals. Southern distaste for abstractions extended to all philosophic systems – Hegel's for example. John Taylor of Caroline, Virginia's prominent secular political philosopher, lauded Baconian induction and condemned abstract, deductive reasoning in natural and social science as the instrument of social oppressors.[2]

---

[1] Pliny the Elder, *Natural History: A Selection*, tr. John F. Healy (London, 1991), Bk. 26:19.

[2] Theodore Dwight Bozeman, "Inductive and Deductive Politics: Science and Society in Antebellum Presbyterian Thought," *Journal of American History*, 64 (1977), 718; John Taylor,

Seneca, a southern favorite, mentioned the common Roman belief that glad-
iators planned their fights in the ring, watching intently for something in the
adversary's glance or hand or body language: "No one will advise at long
range; we must take counsel in the presence of the actual situation." Hugh
Legaré of South Carolina – distinguished classicist and U.S. attorney general
and secretary of state *ad interim* – repeatedly spoke out against "abstractions."
Legaré invoked Quintilian's notion of "common sense," which he rendered as
"public or general opinion." He spoke of Cicero's paean to the government of
Rome as a repository of wisdom and patriotism, which "may be taken as his
protest against that pest of our times speculative politics." In opposition to the
U.S. Supreme Court's assumption of extra-constitutional powers to promote
national consolidation, Legaré sternly criticized abstractions in political theory,
complaining that Americans had "unbounded faith in forms." He expressed no
confidence in "the science of politics, theoretically considered." He preferred
to "judge the tree by its fruits."[3]

James H. Hammond of South Carolina – congressman, governor, senator,
and wealthy planter – deplored "abstractions" but knew perfectly well that the
word "abstract," as used by the advocates of Slavery in the Abstract, referred
not to philosophical abstractions or to race relations, but to the general rather
than the particular – to slavery as a normal condition of labor abstracted from
race. Hammond, disclaiming any interest in Slavery in the Abstract, repeatedly
embraced everything except the name. In 1845, he established his reputation as
an intellectually acute polemicist in eloquent, lengthy, and widely read open letters to Thomas Clarkson, the British antislavery leader, in which he unequivo-
cally endorsed the essentials of Slavery in the Abstract. And in his "Cotton Is
King" speech in the Senate on the Kansas Question in 1858, Hammond dramatically asserted that every society rested on a "mud-sill" – a servile laboring
class.[4]

An Inquiry into the Principles and Policy of the Government of the United States, ed. Loren
Baritz (Indianapolis, Ind., 1919 [1814]), 346–347. See also [Thomas Caute Reynolds], review of
Ticknor's *History of Spanish Literature*, *SQR*, 2 (1850), 95; Arnaud B. Levelle and Thomas
I. Cook, "George Fitzhugh and the Theory of American Conservatism," *Journal of Politics*, 7
(1945), 152; "Slavery in the Abstract?" *Anti-Slavery Record*, 2 (Jan. 1836), 5; Thomas Roder-
ick Dew, *Digest of the Laws, Customs, Manners, and Institutions of the Ancient and Modern
Nations* (New York, 1884 [1852]), 658.

[3] "On the Futility of Half-Way Measures," in Seneca, *Epistles*, 3 vols., tr. Richard M. Gummere
(Cambridge, Mass.: LCL, 2002), 1:22, §2. In *HLW* see "Classical Learning," 2:30 (Quintil-
ian); "Cicero De Republica," 2:253; "Kent's *Commentaries*," 2:104, 123–134, quote at 125;
"Constitutional History of Greece," 1:421 ("fruits").

[4] The texts may be found in [Clyde N. Wilson, ed.], *Selections from the Letters and Speeches
of James H. Hammond* (Spartanburg, S.C., 1978); John H. Reagan, *Memoirs with Special
Reference to Secession and the Civil War*, ed. Walter Flavius McCaleb (New York, 1906), 85.
Hammond's sleight of hand is discussed more fully in Eugene D. Genovese, *The Slaveholders'
Dilemma: Freedom and Progress in Southern Conservative Thought, 1820–1860* (Columbia,
S.C., 1991), ch. 3. Senator Henry Wilson of Massachusetts parried Hammond's indictment of
wage-slavery by boasting of northern superiority in the arts: *Are Working-Men Slaves? Speech
of the Hon. Henry Wilson, of Mass, in reply to Hon. James H. Hammond, of South Carolina*

Southerners, like Legaré, who hated "abstractions," considered South Carolina's defiant doctrine of state nullification of federal laws unworkable. In the 1850s, Thomas Walton of Mississippi argued that, unlike state sovereignty, nullification never acquired popular support since an oppressed South could hardly expect relief from so abstract a doctrine. Although he believed that state sovereignty implied nullification, he did not explain the grounds for judging the one more abstract than the other. In a similar vein George Fitzhugh of Virginia, an extreme proslavery theorist, declared the doctrine of nullification valid in principle, but meaningless in political reality. He doubtless agreed with John H. Reagan of Texas, Postmaster General of the Confederacy, who suggested that secession posed not "the abstract right of man to personal liberty" but black capacity for freedom and assimilation into white society.[5]

The projection of the divinely sanctioned continuity of slavery from biblical times to the present encouraged assimilation of all dependent (unfree) labor to slavery or – what came to the same thing – assimilation of slavery to a pattern of social subordination in which chattel slavery served as the extreme form of dependent and unfree labor appropriate to time, place, and circumstance. Southerners reasonably took for granted that the widely revered Greek and Roman slaveholding civilizations supported their ideology. They referred to Greece and Rome frequently but rarely paused to explicate their boast of an obvious continuity between ancient and modern slave systems. In medieval Europe the categories "slaves," "serfs," and "unfree," and even groups of those called "free," reflected dependencies that shaded into one another in practice. Despite considerable ambiguity, a commitment to slavery led one writer after another to uphold the southern version as a modern variant of ancient and medieval social relations and to reject the social relations of the marketplace. George S. Sawyer, among proslavery theorists, assimilated villeins to slaves, and an English spelling book used in southern schools mistakenly equated "vassals" with slaves. Thus southern slaveholders fell into a contradiction from which they could not escape: They were fighting for a future based upon dependent labor relations and, simultaneously, on a material progress that had been effected by the overthrow of those very relations.[6]

---

in the Senate, March 20, 1858, on the Bill to Admit Kansas under the Lecompton Constitution (Washington, D.C., 1858), 10.

[5] T[homas] Walton, "Further Views of the Advocates of the Slave Trade," *DBR*, 26 (1859), 64–65; George Fitzhugh, "The Valleys of Virginia – the Rappahannock," *DBR*, 26 (1859), 275; Edgar Allan Poe considered worthless a theory that could not explicate practice: Robert D. Jacobs, *Poe: Journalist and Critic* (Baton Rouge, La., 1969), 449. Yet, *Virginia Historical Register, and Literary Companion* warmly recommended H. A. Washington's *Virginia Constitution of 1776* but respectfully disagreed with his assertion that the state constitution was purely historical and not dependent on abstract theories: 5 (1852), 107–110.

[6] In support of these generalizations, see Elizabeth Fox-Genovese and Eugene D. Genovese, *The Mind of the Master Class: History and Faith in the Southern Slaveholders' Worldview* (New York, 2005), chs. 4–9; George S. Sawyer, *Southern Institutes; Or, an Inquiry into the Origin and Early Prevalence of Slavery and the Slave Trade* (New York, 1967 [1858]), 139; Thomas Carpenter, *The Scholar's Spelling Assistant* (Electronic ed.; Chapel Hill, N.C., 2001 [1861]), 49.

With or without embracing the extreme doctrine of Slavery in the Abstract, proslavery ideologists fell prey to the same substantial miscalculation that gripped the socialists. They took the brutal class warfare at loose in the industrializing countries as evidence of the imminent collapse of the free-labor (capitalist) system. Long before the Revolutions of 1848 – but especially in their wake – proslavery theorists sounded like socialists in predicting the unraveling of society in Europe and the North. But instead of expecting socialism to emerge from a general crisis of capitalism, they saw the reduction of the laboring classes to personal servitude.

A long list of prominent Southerners, including John C. Calhoun, joined Hammond in embracing the basic doctrine while denying that they were doing so. The denials amounted to expressions of regret that anyone could think of enslaving Caucasians. An astonished Thomas Colley Grattan, British consul at Boston, heard Calhoun assert, "Servitude is a necessity for civilization." Like Calhoun, most proslavery theorists, especially those with national political ambitions, routinely declined to endorse Slavery in the Abstract, and, doubtless, some were deeply hostile to it. The strongly unionist A. H. H. Stuart of Virginia considered North and South economically complementary, with slavery entirely a question of race and climate, and he ridiculed the idea that the North would ever restore slavery. Yet, Henry Augustine Washington – protégé of James Madison, friend of Thomas Jefferson, and kin to George Washington – spoke for many:

One portion of the community always has and always will live upon the labor of the other portion. In every age and country *capital* has held labor in subjection, and always must hold it in subjection, and no where has the labourer received, or is he ever destined to receive, more than a very small proportion of the products of his own labor.... Bare subsistence, together with the means of perpetuating the race, is all that simple labor has ever received or can ever expect to receive.[7]

Proslavery Southerners drifted – some sprinted – toward an extraordinary doctrine that transcended race. The many who shrunk from public advocacy of the enslavement of whites in the capitalist countries warned against the possibility, if not inevitability. Neither did they have to predict restoration of chattel slavery among whites, for their notions of racial and class stratification encouraged a belief that a milder form of personal servitude would suffice for whites. Indeed, a great many defenders of slavery argued that southern slavery itself needed considerable reformation on behalf of the blacks.[8]

For medieval Scandinavia, see Ruth Mazo Karras, *Slavery and Society in Medieval Scandinavia* (New Haven, Conn., 1988), ch. 1; and Snorri Sturlson, *Heimskringla: History of the Kings of Norway*, tr. Lee M. Hollander (Austin, Tex., 1964), 261.

[7] Thomas Colley Grattan, *Civilized America*, 2 vols. (London, 1859), 1:182–185, Calhoun quoted at 183. "Address of Hon. A. H. H. Stuart before the Central Agricultural Society of Virginia, at Richmond, Oct. 28th, 1859," *Southern Planter*, 20 (1860), 331; H. A. Washington, "The Social System of Virginia," in Michael O'Brien, ed., *All Clever Men, Who Make Their Way: Critical Discourse in the Old South* (Fayetteville, Ark., 1982), 258.

[8] Most southern commentators assimilated slavery to other systems of personal servitude. Among the exceptions, John Archibald Campbell of Alabama, associate justice of the U.S. Supreme

Southern views on Slavery in the Abstract and the "social question" (the condition of labor in free societies) have to be teased out of diverse sources. Few slaveholders outside the ranks of the social, political, and religious elites left records of their deeper social views. Besides, there is no reason to think that ordinary slaveholders – any more than ordinary capitalists in our own time or the mass of humanity at any time – stopped to work out a coherent social philosophy in the manner of a Calhoun, a Fitzhugh, or a James Henley Thornwell. Slaveholders held several views simultaneously and lived with a good many contradictions. Some of the principal lines of dissemination do, however, emerge from churches, agricultural and scientific societies, and the press. And we may glean from the slaveholders' diaries and family letters, as well as from the reports of those who observed them, evidence that the doctrine of Slavery in the Abstract was penetrating all levels of society.[9]

The strongest evidence of the spread of the doctrine among "plain folk" came indirectly. The speeches and pamphlets of the leading political spokesmen outside the plantation belts and especially in the up country spelled out the doctrine clearly, albeit discreetly. Among the more important were Andrew Johnson and Parson William G. Brownlow of Tennessee, Thomas L. Clingman of North Carolina, Joseph E. Brown of Georgia, and Albert Gallatin Brown of Mississippi. We shall discuss the views of these and other such figures in Chapter 2. If it is difficult to discern the actual attitude of their constituents, no one with an acquaintance with those tough people could believe that they heard radical messages without reacting forcefully. That was just not their style.

Hints, indecisive but valuable: Between 1840 and 1860 a technological revolution that included steam presses, railroad networks, and the telegraph created an explosion of information and propaganda. Printed material constituted, by weight, most of the material sent through the mails. An antislavery traveler found "plenty of books" in defense of slavery, especially scriptural. An irritated M. Stokes of Wilkesborough, North Carolina, complained that nine-tenths of the speeches in Congress were never delivered and were, instead, produced as pamphlets for constituents. Alexander Stephens's supporters distributed some 40,000 copies of one of his speeches, many doubtless in the North. Diaries,

---

Court, reviewing slavery throughout world history, complained that a great many Southerners mistakenly believed that slavery could exist only in the form prevalent in the South and therefore opposed salutary efforts to reform law and practice. J. A. C. [John Archibald Campbell], "Slavery throughout the World," *SQR*, n.s. 3 (1851), 317.

[9] For the implicit relation of Calhoun's political theory to Fitzhugh's, see Robert A. Garson, "Proslavery as Political Theory: The Examples of John C. Calhoun and George Fitzhugh," *South Atlantic Quarterly*, 84 (1985), 197–212. For the inability of southern judges and legal theorists to ground slave law in "race" rather than class relations, see Mark Tushnet, *The American Law of Slavery: Considerations of Humanity and Interest* (Princeton, 1981). On medical education, Steven M. Stowe writes: "Slavery and race, along with sexuality, floated obscurely throughout the curricula." *Doctoring the South: Southern Physicians and Everyday Medicine in the Mid-Nineteenth Century* (Chapel Hill, N.C., 2004), 49–52, 172–173, 208–218, quote at 51.

including those of students, from across the South indicate widespread attention to the published speeches and political writings of Calhoun and other leading southern politicians.[10]

Throughout most of the nineteenth century, printed matter accounted for half the mail in the United States – more than half by weight. The South, with fewer cities and a spread-out population, had disproportionately fewer newspapers and depended heavily on the mails. Southern – and western – newspapers, in the words of Richard B. Kielbowicz, "avidly sought" distant publications. In 1844 President John Tyler complained that postmasters abused their franking privileges by free distribution of political materials. Since many Southerners, especially in villages and rural areas, listened to readings of the newspapers as they arrived at a tavern or general store, the elite and better-off residents had a significant advantage. The more affluent could afford the subscriptions and generally had the prerogative of choosing the publications and selecting the contents to be read aloud.[11]

The proslavery theorist Henry Hughes urged the government of Mississippi to support editors, presumably by subsidies: "Now propagandism is self-preservation." Not that Hughes had much to worry about, for at least by the mid-1830s southern editors stood together in defense of slavery and hatred of abolitionism. In 1857 the propagandistic side of the newspapers got the attention of Caroline Seabury, a northern teacher in Columbus, Mississippi, who read an advertisement from a new paper published near Aberdeen that declared, "It will be free from the 'isms' of the day, in direct opposition to the spirit of all agitators – on purely southern principles." She recorded the last words of the advertisement: "Our first number will be issued as soon as we

[10] Lorman A. Ratner and Dwight Teeter, Jr., *Fanatics and Fire-Eaters: Newspapers and the Coming of the Civil War* (Urbana, Ill., 2003), 8, 11; on travelers, see, e.g., Horace Cowles Atwater, *Incidents of a Southern Tour: or, The South as Seen with Northern Eyes* (Boston, Mass., 1857), 57–58; M. Stokes to Col. Hamilton Brown, Apr. 29, 1822, in Thomas Felix Hickerson, *Echoes of Happy Valley* (Durham, N.C., 1962), 15; Rudolph R. Von Abele, *Alexander H. Stephens: A Biography* (New York, 1946), 159, n.79; Ebenezer Pettigrew to J. H. Bryan, Jan. 18, 1827, in Sarah McCulloh Lemmon, ed., *The Pettigrew Papers*, 2 vols. (Raleigh, N.C., 1971, 1988), 2:81. At UNC, see E. G. C. Thomas Diary, June 14, 1855; T. M. Garrett Diary, 1849; Agnew Diary, July 4, 1854 (Erskine); H. P. Griffith, *The Life and Times of Rev. John G. Landrum* (Charleston, S.C., 1992 [1885]), 240.

After Thornwell visited Britain in 1860, several of his articles from *Southern Presbyterian Review* were republished there, drawing favorable critical notice. For requests for copies and congratulations, see Reverend Philips H. Thompson (Presbyterian pastor at Memphis) to Thornwell, Feb. 8, 1861; N. Long [Lord?], president of Dartin [?] College; Long to Thornwell, Feb. 9, 1861; Mitchell King to Thornwell, Feb. 9, 1861; H. W. Hilliard (prominent politician in Alabama) to Thornwell, March 13, 1861; Samuel J. Harrington (of Texas) to Thornwell, March 24, 1861 – all in Thornwell Papers; also, John S. Palmer to Leora Sims, Feb. 6, 1861, in Louis P. Towles, ed., *A World Turned Upside Down: The Palmers of South Santee, 1818–1881* (Columbia, S.C., 1991), 291.

[11] Richard B. Kielbowicz, *News in the Mail: The Press, Post Office, and Public Information, 1700–1860s* (Westport, Conn., 1989), 3, 44, 71, Table 4 on 112, 114, quote at 63. See also James Stirling, *Letters from the Slave States* (New York, 1968 [1857]), 276–281.

can obtain press and paper from the North." She could not resist commenting, "Verily, we are the people & wisdom will die with us."[12]

Northern proslavery newspapers circulated in the South more widely than other northern newspapers. James Gordon Bennett's *New York Herald*, with a daily circulation of 80,000 in 1861, the largest in the world, took a political line that pleased Southerners, especially popular in the Border States. Francis Terry Leak of Mississippi, among other planters, considered *Day-Book* of New York the best publication of its kind in the Union and had it sent to fifteen of his relatives and friends in Arkansas and North Carolina. After the War, Thomas Clingman of North Carolina shrewdly remarked that sad consequences followed: Many Southerners concluded that northern opinion was a good deal less hostile to slavery than it in fact was. Measurement even of the roughest kind will probably continue to elude us, but, unquestionably, the yeomen and town and city laborers were getting large doses of Slavery in the Abstract.[13]

A clarification: William W. Freehling has offered a model for an understanding of the regionally based political differences within the South. He identifies three regions: the Border South (Delaware, Maryland, Kentucky, and Missouri); the Middle South (Virginia, North Carolina, Tennessee, and Arkansas); and the Lower South (South Carolina, Georgia, Florida, Alabama, Mississippi, Louisiana, and Texas). For our purposes, the Lower South constituted a slave society, and the Border South did not. Large portions of the Middle South and small portions of the Border South formed part of southern slave society, but substantial portions lay outside it, in effect, tolerating slavery but not dominated by it. Freehling writes, "Just as the Middle South's whitest belts contained large antisecessionist majorities, so the Border South's blackest belts displayed large secessionist pluralities." Some immensely influential individuals in each region fell under the spell of proslavery ideology, including Slavery in the Abstract, whereas some notable figures in the Lower South did not. Thus, Border State or no, Missouri harbored some prominent supporters of Slavery in the Abstract.[14]

Across the South, men committed to Slavery in the Abstract had no difficulty in speaking as democrats since their kind of "democracy" meant constitutionally limited republican government. Staunch antidemocratic conservatives, especially those in the North, rejected Slavery in the Abstract, and some rejected

---

[12] Henry Hughes to R. H. Purdom, Oct. 9, 1858, in Stanford M. Lyman, ed., *Selected Writings of Henry Hughes: Antebellum Southerner, Slavocrat, Sociologist* (Jackson, Miss., 1985), 145; Hodding Carter, *Their Words Were Bullets: The Southern Press in War, Reconstruction, and Peace* (Athens, Ga., 1969), 10–11; April 16, 1859, in Suzanne L. Bunkers, *The Diary of Caroline Seabury, 1854–1863* (Madison, Wis., 1991), 56.

[13] Leak Diary, March 26, 28, Dec. 31, 1857; *Selections from the Speeches and Writings of Hon. Thomas L. Clingman of North Carolina* (Raleigh, N.C., 1877), 233; also, W. C. Preston to George Ticknor, May 8, 1824, in Preston Papers. During the War, the Union government suppressed *Day-Book*.

[14] William W. Freehling, *The Road to Disunion*, vol. 1: *Secessionists at Bay, 1776–1854* (New York, 1990), vol. 2: *Secessionists Triumphant, 1854–1861* (New York, 2007), quote at 2:530.

slavery itself; many radical democrats, especially those in the South, embraced it. The most said safely is that flirtation with Slavery in the Abstract strengthened an antidemocratic undertow.

Support for Slavery in the Abstract – personal servitude for all laborers regardless of race – flowed from a confluence of three commonly held premises: Southern slaves fared better than most peasants and wage-workers in free societies; slavery was proving a more humane, stable, and morally responsible social system than its free-labor rival; and Christians had to accept responsibility to succor fellow human beings. The conclusion: Christians and all civilized peoples must accept some form of slavery as the solution of the conflict between capital and labor known as "the social question." This conclusion plagued southern sensibility, for Southerners, even most slaveholders – writhed under a proslavery logic that pointed to reenslavement of whites. A long-building and widely held worldview nonetheless reached flood tide in the 1850s. George Fitzhugh of Virginia and Henry Hughes of Mississippi published treatises on "sociology" and thereby surfaced as the most flamboyant exponents of Slavery in the Abstract. Slavery in the Abstract, a distinctly southern ideology, did not take root anywhere outside the South. Neither Brazil nor Cuba nor any other ancient or modern slaveholding country produced anything like it on a politically significant scale.[15]

Marcus Cunliffe and Larry Tise have demonstrated that some of the basic ideas of Slavery in the Abstract went back a long way in England and America, becoming standard fare among Anglo-American conservatives. Tise has demonstrated that more defenses of slavery were published in the North than in the South before 1840. Although he insists that the doctrine of Slavery in the Abstract was present in other slaveholding societies, neither he nor anyone else presents evidence. Tise, Cunliffe, and others mistakenly equate militant proslavery doctrine with the specific doctrine of slavery as the proper condition of labor. With deep appreciation of our colleagues' valuable work, we must insist on a crucial distinction: Slavery in the Abstract became a common theme for the dominant class of the South, whereas abroad it remained the property of marginal intellectuals. Living through the triumphant march of industrial capitalism, notable British and continental conservatives and counterparts in the northern United States recoiled from the social and cultural consequences of

---

[15] See George Fitzhugh, *Sociology for the South, or, The Failure of Free Society* (New York, 1965 [1854]); George Fitzhugh, *Cannibals All! or Slaves without Masters* (Cambridge, Mass., 1960 [1857]); Henry Hughes, *Treatise on Sociology, Theoretical and Practical* (New York, 1968 [1854]). These books appear to have been the first in America to have the term "sociology" in titles. Hughes may have scored another first in America by using "economics," rather than "political economy," in a chapter heading. On Fitzhugh, see Eugene D. Genovese, *The World the Slaveholders Made: Two Essays in Interpretation* (New York, 1969), Pt. 2; on Hughes, see Douglas Ambrose, *Henry Hughes and Proslavery Thought in the Old South* (Baton Rouge, La., 1996). For our explanation of the emergence of "Slavery in the Abstract," see Fox-Genovese and Genovese, *Mind of the Master Class*, ch. 3. See also the trenchant remarks in Peter Kolchin, *Unfree Labor: American Slavery and Russian Serfdom* (Cambridge, Mass., 1987), especially 158, 169, 179–182.

bourgeois ascendancy. Up to a point, they sounded like the proslavery theorists of the South, but they criticized prevailing social relations from the hopeless standpoint of moribund social relations that had been undermined politically and legally by the English revolutions of the seventeenth century and the French Revolution of the eighteenth. European conservatives drew much of their literary power from the critical standpoint generated by their alienation from the mainstream of their societies. In contrast, the South's leading intellectuals lived in a society that boasted one form of the organic social relations that European and even some northern conservatives lamented losing and muttered about restoring. Like literary men and scientists elsewhere, southern intellectuals often felt unappreciated, but, rather than repudiating the social system under which they lived, they held it up as a model for worldwide reformation. Although worried about the democratic tendencies that were infecting even the South, they celebrated God-ordained slavery as the best possible foundation for a civilized Christian society. By the 1820s an increasing number of Southerners – including propertied nonslaveholders – concluded that the solution to the social question lay in the formal exclusion of the unpropertied laboring classes from the benefits of individualism and their consignment to some form of personal dependency. The French Revolution consolidated previous and disparate strands of bourgeois individualism and set the terms for future battles. The struggle over the admission of Missouri as a slave state (1819–1820) drew the lines for an ideological battle that pitted self-conscious defenses of slavery and freedom against each other.[16]

Slavery in the Abstract, notwithstanding its apparent impracticality, slowly insinuated itself into the very core of the slaveholders' worldview. Since the slaveholding South was embedded in the bourgeois world of the nineteenth century – against which it waged mortal ideological, political, and economic combat – the slaveholders needed new ground on which to defend the traditional values of hierarchy, particularism, and personal dependency. In their quest, they differed among themselves in pet notions and preferred policies. Fitzhugh alone recognized that slavery – or even an industrial serfdom – could not survive in a world dominated by an expanding world market. Hence, he concluded that the world market and the capitalist system had to be razed. He never got far in his effort to make capitalism disappear without the sacrifice of its economic achievements, much of which even he sought to preserve. Hughes, considering such a project utopian, sought a compromise, although he never demonstrated how his preferred form of servile labor relation ("warranteeism") could survive in a capitalist world market, albeit with an "ethnical qualification." Fitzhugh and Hughes thus represented two poles of corporatist thinking. Fitzhugh defended the disappearing values of organically unequal relations, while espousing a tortured version of the idea of progress. Hughes,

---

[16] Larry E. Tise, *Proslavery: A History of the Defense of Slavery in America, 1701–1840* (Athens, Ga., 1988); Marcus Cunliffe, *Chattel Slavery and Wage Slavery: The Anglo-American Context, 1830–1860* (Athens, Ga., 1979); Eugene D. Genovese, "Larry Tise's 'Proslavery': A Critique and an Appreciation," *Georgia Historical Quarterly*, 72 (1987), 670–683.

too, defended those older values but strove for a system of social subordination in a modern corporate state. Between the two poles staked out by Fitzhugh and Hughes lay a vast web of variegated proslavery notions.[17]

Southern proslavery theorists intervened dramatically in the transatlantic debate over capital-labor relations. That debate – like the debate over the contemporary "Woman Question" – bared the logic of capitalism's modern individualism: Sovereignty was rooted in the individual, whose willing acquiescence alone grounded legitimate authority. In the late 1850s Barbara Leigh Smith Bodichon of England – passionate campaigner for black emancipation and women's rights – reported, "All these slave owners are very religious people" who linked abolitionism to women's rights as "allied to atheism." Alarmed proslavery Southerners, in effect, foreshadowed the conclusion advanced by Blanche Glassman Hersh in *The Slavery of Sex: Feminist Abolitionists in America* (1978): "Feminism was an almost inevitable outgrowth of a radical movement which had as its goal the emancipation of all enslaved humanity." This modern individualism directly challenged time-honored notions of organic hierarchy and inequality. In Western Europe and America's northern states it coexisted with a plethora of customary inequalities for women, children, and working people, which it slowly recognized as anomalies. "Labour cannot emancipate itself in the white skin," declared Karl Marx, "where in the black it is branded." As if paraphrasing Abraham Lincoln's "House Divided" speech, Marx maintained that the War in the United States pitted one social system against another and that one or the other would prevail in all parts of the country.[18]

---

[17] Douglas Ambrose, in an enlightening comparison of the thought of Henry Hughes and James Henley Thornwell, charts statism in the trajectory of advanced proslavery thought: "Statism in the Old South: A Reconsideration," in Robert L. Paquette and Louis A. Ferleger, eds., *Slavery, Secession, and Southern History* (Charlottesville, Va., 2000), 101–125. Chad Morgan writes: "In foreseeing that the South had to submit to a distasteful statism to protect slavery, the putatively unrealistic Fitzhugh and Hughes were the ultimate realists." Morgan, *Planters' Progress: Modernizing Confederate Georgia* (Gainesville, Fla., 2005), 29.

[18] Barbara Leigh Smith Bodichon, *An American Diary, 1857–8*, ed. Joseph W. Reed, Jr. (London, 1972), 61 (Dec. 11, 1857); Blanche Glassman Hersh, *The Slavery of Sex: Feminist Abolitionists in America* (Urbana, Ill., 1978), 74; Karl Marx, *Capital: A Critique of Political Economy*, 3 vols. (New York, n.d.), 1:301; Karl Marx, in *Die Press*, Nov. 7, 1861, in Marx and Friedrich Engels, *The Civil War in the United States* (New York, 1961); David Hecht, *Russian Radicals Look to America* (Cambridge, Mass., 1947), esp., 33, 35, 65–66, 90, 111, 115, 125; for *Uncle Tom's Cabin*, see Arnold Schrier and Joyce Story, trans. and eds., *A Russian Looks at America: The Journey of Aleksandr Borisovich Lakier in 1857* (Chicago, 1979), xxxiv. Educated Russians knew *Uncle Tom's Cabin*. Russian radicals like Alexander Herzen, Michael Bakunin, and Nicholas Chernyshevski followed American events carefully, linking slave emancipation to the emancipation of serfs and women. Russians relied on the travelogues of Frederick Law Olmsted, John Abbott, Sir Charles Lyell, and John Robert Godley.

The Impending Collapse of Capitalism

It may be, that such a slavery, regulating the relations of capital and labor, though implying some deprivation of personal liberty, will prove a better defense of the poor against the oppression of the rich, than the too great freedom in which capital is placed in many of the free states of Europe at the present day. Something of this kind is what the masses of free laborers in France are clamoring for under the name *"the right to labor."* . . . It may be, *Christian slavery* is God's solution of the problem about which the wisest statesmen of Europe confess themselves 'at fault.'

—The Reverend George D. Armstrong of Norfolk[1]

The Doctrine Emerges

That the black slaves of the South fared better than the mass of the world's free workers and peasants became gospel among southern whites of all classes. In seventeenth-century Virginia planters asserted, with some justification, that their slaves worked a shorter and less rigorous day than English herdsmen. At the beginning of the eighteenth century Robert Beverley, in his *History and Present State of Virginia*, maintained that black slaves and white servants in Virginia did not work as long or hard as husbandmen and agricultural laborers of England. In the 1720s the Reverend Hugh Jones, a professor at the College of William and Mary, acknowledging that slaves did most of the hard work, reported their food and material conditions superior to those of English woodcutters. In 1731, Governor William Gooch complained about the inhumanity often practiced toward slaves but expressed confidence that the majority received better treatment than poor laborers in England. A few years later William Byrd wrote to a friend in England, "Our poor Negroes are freemen in comparison to the slaves who till your ungenerous soil; at least if slavery consist in scarcity, and hard work." In 1764 a Virginia slaveholder claimed, "I have traveled through most parts of Scotland and Ireland; and I can safely

---

[1] George D. Armstrong, *The Christian Doctrine of Slavery* (New York, 1967 [1857]), 134.

assert that the habitants of our negroes are palaces and their living luxurious, when compared with those of the peasants of either of those countries."[2]

Thomas Jefferson observed France under the *ancien régime*. He paid scant attention to the living conditions of urban laborers, but – guided in part by a poor woman who aroused his sympathy – he sketched the appalling conditions under which peasants, especially women and children, lived under the concentration of landownership in a few hands. Educated Southerners read British political theorists and knew that some post-Lockeans had been urging the restoration of slavery as the solution to the dangerous emergence of poverty. Andrew Fletcher, the "commonwealth man," estimated that some 200,000 Scots were already enslaved – about the number of blacks enslaved in Virginia. In late eighteenth-century Charleston, leading intellectuals of conservative temperament like David Ramsay, who disliked slavery, and Alexander Garden, who defended it, agreed that slaves fared better in South Carolina than the great mass of laborers did in Europe.[3]

Early in the nineteenth century, Maria Henrietta Pinckney wrote *The Young Carolinians; or Americans in Algiers*, in which she included a black character – the first in a play by a South Carolinian. Her Cudjoe defended slavery:

I slave for true; but poor folks must work everywhere. Suppose me poor buckra; well, I serve some rich buckra, him pay me; but when Cudjoe sick, or lame, or old too much for work, him turn me away; now misses give me too much nasty stuff for cure me – plenty sweet tea to wash em down – by and bye get well again, she look pon me with one kind eye, same like a dove – glad to see old Cudjoe well again.[4]

That refrain came frequently from slaveholders in all parts of the South, including from those critical of slavery. During the War of 1812, John Randolph

[2] Hugh Jones, *The Present State of Virginia: From Whence Is Inferred a Short View of Maryland and North Carolina*, ed. Richard L. Morton (Chapel Hill, N.C., 1956), 130; on Gooch, see Pierre Marambaud, *William Byrd of Westover* (Charlottesville, Va., 1971), 172; on Robert Beverley, see Robert A. Rutland and Helen Hill Miller, *George Mason: Gentleman Revolutionary* (Chapel Hill, N.C., 1975), 13; Marion Tingling, ed., *The Correspondence of the Three William Byrds of Westover, Virginia, 1684–1776*, 2 vols. (Charlottesville, Va., 1977), 1: 356–359; Virginian quoted in William Sumner Jenkins, *Pro-Slavery Thought in the Old South* (Gloucester, Mass., 1960), 40.

[3] William Howard Adams, *The Paris Years of Thomas Jefferson* (New Haven, Conn., 1997), 275; Jefferson to Madison, Oct. 23, 1785, in James Morton Smith, ed., *The Republic of Letters: The Correspondence between Thomas Jefferson and James Madison, 1776–1826*, 3 vols. (New York, 1995), 1:389–391, and editor's remarks, 1:333–334. On Jefferson see also George Tucker, *The Life of Thomas Jefferson*, 2 vols. (London, 1837), 1:259; Dumas Malone, *Jefferson*, 2:116–117, 130, 155; Hazen, *Contemporary American Opinion of the French Revolution*, 12; Edmund Morgan, *American Slavery, American Freedom: The Ordeal of Colonial Virginia* (New York, 1995), 380; Arthur H. Shaffer, *To Be an American: David Ramsay and the Making of the American Consciousness* (Columbia, S.C., 1991), 177; Robert M. Calhoon, *Evangelicals and Conservatives in the Early South, 1740–1861* (Columbia, S.C., 1988), 24. For subsequent developments in the South, see Lewis P. Simpson, *Mind and the American Civil War* (Baton Rouge, La., 1989), 21.

[4] M. H. Pinckney quoted in Charles S. Watson, *Antebellum Charleston Dramatists* (University, Ala., 1976), 46.

of Roanoke referred to oppressed European laborers who go "supperless to bed." Dr. James Waddell Alexander of Virginia told of an invalid slave woman who would have died in an almshouse if she had been a free woman in the North, and of two blind women on his own place, who received care they could never have expected outside a slave society. Stephen Henderson of Louisiana wrote a will in which he freed his slaves despite his conviction that they were better off as slaves than the lower classes of Europe.[5]

In Milledgeville, Georgia, in 1820, when criticism of slavery could still be heard, a writer for the *Southern Recorder* scoffed at the notion that blacks preferred slavery to freedom: "Freedom is the same to the Negro as to the white man. Let us see whether *we* should not prefer freedom with poverty to the best condition of the slave." Yet even he agreed that southern slaves probably had better material conditions of life than many northern free men. The Denmark Vesey slave conspiracy of 1822 in Charleston hardened defenses of southern slavery. Edwin Clifford Holland extolled slavery as divinely sanctioned and benign, with slaves who fared well absolutely and in comparison with northern workers. Whitemarsh B. Seabrook and Edward Brown pushed the argument to the limit. Slavery, wrote Brown, consciously echoing Seabrook, "appears, indeed, to be the only state capable of bringing the love of independence and of ease, inherent in man, to the discipline and shelter necessary to his physical wants."[6]

Charles Fenton Mercer, a prominent politician, campaigned for public education in Virginia, citing the ghastly conditions of British workers – uneducated, poverty-stricken, and increasingly tempted into crime. William Seaton of Virginia, editor of the *National Intelligencer*, recalled colonial white apprenticeship as having been as rigorous as that of the Middle Ages and of slavery itself. Among many Virginians, the legendary Turner Ashby did not doubt that southern slaves lived more comfortably than European laborers. In the second decade of the nineteenth century, Morris Birkbeck, the English agriculturalist who emigrated to America, found Virginians convinced that conditions for

---

[5] "To the Freeholders of Charlotte, Prince Edward, Buckingham, and Cumberland," May 30, 1812, in Russell Kirk, *John Randolph of Roanoke: A Study in American Politics, with Selected Speeches and Letters* (Chicago, Ill., 1964), 203 (for the political context of Randolph's appeal to southern slaveholders to oppose the War of 1812, see Adam L. Tate, *Conservatism and Southern Intellectuals, 1789–1861: Liberty, Tradition, and the Good Society* [Columbia, Mo., 2005], 67–69); for Alexander, see William Cabell Bruce, *John Randolph of Roanoke, 1773–1833: A Biography Based Largely on New Material*, 2 vols. (New York, 1970 [1922]), 2:134; "Heirs of Henderson v. Rost and Montgomery, Executors," in Helen Tunnicliff Catterall, ed., *Judicial Cases Concerning Slavery and the Negro*, 4 vols. (Washington, D.C., 1919–1937), 3:605.

[6] James C. Bonner, *Milledgeville: Georgia's Antebellum Capital* (Athens, Ga., 1978), 120; [Edwin Clifford Holland], *A Refutation of the Calumnies Circulated against the Southern and Western States, Respecting the Institution of Slavery* (Charleston, S.C., 1822), and see the praise by John Belton O'Neall, who mistakenly attributed it to Benjamin Elliott: *Biographical Sketches of the Bench and Bar of South Carolina*, 2 vols. (Spartanburg, S.C., 1975 [1859]), 2:403–404; Edward Brown, *Notes on the Origins and Necessity of Slavery* (Charleston, S.C., 1826), 42.

the slaves had improved dramatically and were superior to those for British paupers. The strongly antislavery Birkbeck acknowledged a measure of truth but stressed the ability of the British poor to organize politically to improve their lives. In later years Hugh Blair Grigsby, president of the Virginia Historical Society, reiterated the claim that from the beginning of the nineteenth century the material condition of the slaves had improved and become a credit to Virginia.[7]

During the Missouri crisis, the Federalist Charles Pinckney of Charleston, supporting strong paternal governments at both the federal and state levels, determined to integrate the lower classes into a republican system under slaveholder hegemony. Disturbed by the threat to stability and property posed by the French Revolution and even more directly by the Haitian, he defended slavery as a pillar of social order. Addressing Congress, Pinckney began by citing the Bible to prove slavery divinely sanctioned. "There is," he told Congress, "not a single line in the Old or New Testament either censuring it or forbidding it.... If you say there shall be no slavery, may you not say there will be no marriage?" Pinckney appealed to experience, noting that slavery had existed throughout world history. Blacks, whose racial inferiority especially fitted them for slavery, were "the labourers and peasants of the United States." Referring to England, he said, "The comforts of the lower classes, if they have any . . . are far inferior to those of our slaves." Long before, Pinckney had confidently told the delegates to the Federal Convention, "In all ages one half of mankind have been slaves."[8]

In the 1820s Zephaniah Kingsley of Florida – wealthy slave trader, planter, and sometime official of the United States government – advanced the cause of Slavery in the Abstract by ridiculing white pretensions to racial superiority. Defending the competence of blacks, he defined slavery as a class relation. Kingsley practiced what he preached, treating several black mistresses as wives, caring for their children, and training his slaves for skilled work to demonstrate their intelligence and ability to perform as well as whites. He became a legend in the Southeast, sufficiently rich, respected, and powerful to stare down

---

[7] Charles Fenton Mercer, "Discourse on Popular Education, 1826," in Edgar W. Knight, ed., *A Documentary History of Education in the South before 1860*, 5 vols. (Chapel Hill, N.C., 1949–1953), 2:297–356; Josephine Seaton, *William Winston Seaton of the National Intelligencer. A Biographical Sketch with Passing Notices of His Friends and His Associates and Friends* (New York, 1970 [1871]), 33; Thomas A. Ashby, *Life of Turner Ashby* (New York, 1914), 42; Morris Birkbeck, *Notes on a Journey in America from the Coast of Virginia to the Territory of Illinois*, 3rd. ed. (London, 1818), 21–22; *Discourse on the Life and Character of the Hon. Littleton Waller Tazewell* (Norfolk, Va., 1860), 26.

[8] For Pinckney, see Mark W. Kaplanoff, "Charles Pinckney and the American Republican Tradition," in Michael O'Brien and David Moltke-Hansen, eds., *Intellectual Life in Antebellum Charleston* (Knoxville, Tenn., 1986), quotes at 87–88. For the original texts, see *Debates and Proceedings in the Congress of the U.S., 1789–1824* (16th Congress, 2nd Session), 1310–1329, Feb. 14, 1820; and *Niles' Weekly Register*, n.s., 5 (Feb. 19, 1820), 438; 6 (July 15, 1820), 345, 349–357. Pinckney quoted in James Madison, *Notes of the Debates in the Federal Convention of 1787* (Athens, Oh., 1966), 505.

murmuring about his violation of racial and sexual codes. His suggestively entitled treatise, *The Patriarchal or Co-Operative System of Society*, which went through new editions in 1819, 1833, and 1834, stated, "Slavery is a necessary state of control from which no condition of society can be perfectly free." No society could sustain itself without a measure of personal servitude; class interests, not race, should determine social relations; and all property holders, regardless of color, should stand together in defense of slavery. Kingsley invoked the experience of Brazil, Spanish America, and the British West Indies to call for an end to racial discrimination and for a liberal policy toward free blacks and coloreds to secure their support for the regime. In 1818 he campaigned for fair and equal treatment of free blacks, and in 1823 he did so again as a member of the Legislative Council of St. Augustine. The response was hardly encouraging. Florida proceeded to enforce a rigid two-caste system that placed free blacks under severe constraints. Kingsley thought that North Carolina, by extending the franchise to free blacks, showed the proper way for the South to go, but North Carolina reversed its policy in the mid-1830s. Thereafter, the doctrine of Slavery in the Abstract spread across the South with a racial qualification.[9]

As sidelights to Kingsley's Florida saga, the beautiful Anna Kingsley (Anta Majigeen Ndiaye), his emancipated wife, owned a dozen slaves in Florida. Having been raised in a slaveholding, polygamous society as the daughter of a wealthy African slaveholder, she had no more objection to slavery per se than she had to her husband's having plural wives. As a slaveholder she proved herself an excellent manager and businesswoman. Zephaniah Kingsley's friend and fellow Floridian, Moses Levy, father of Senator David Yulee, opposed racism too and favored miscegenation, but, unlike Kingsley, he also opposed slavery.[10]

In South Carolina the legislature grew accustomed to gubernatorial addresses that went beyond an economic and racial defense of slave labor to proclaim the superiority of slave society over a misnamed free society. In

---

9 [Zephaniah Kingsley], *A Treatise on the Patriarchal or Co-Operative System of Society, as It Exists in Some Governments, and Colonies in America, by an Inhabitant of Florida*, 2nd ed. (n.p., 1829), 11. Kingsley, a slave trader, knew Africa and kept up contact when he took to planting. Daniel W. Stowell, editor of the modern edition of *Patriarchal System as Balancing Evils Judiciously: The Proslavery Writings of Zephaniah Kingsley* (Gainesville, Fla., 2000), declares it "the first and most important formal articulation of proslavery ideology by a Floridian after Florida became an American territory in 1821" (2). Stowell indicates changes in the editions of 1829, 1833, 1834. Influential Northerners also held a similar evolutionary view: see, e.g., William B. Hayden, *The Institution of Slavery Viewed in the Light of Divine Truth* (Portland, 1861), 20. Kingsley insisted that he had married his wives properly, according to native African custom. For the extraordinary life of Anna Kingsley, Zephaniah's black wife, see Daniel L. Schaefer, *African Princess: Anna Madgigine Jai Kingsley* (Gainesville, Fla., 2003).

10 Daniel L. Shafer, *Anna Madgigine Jai Kingsley: African Princess, Florida Slave, Plantation Slaveowner* (St. Augustine, Fla., 1997); C. S. Monaco, *Moses Levy of Florida: Jewish Utopian and Antebellum Reformer* (Baton Rouge, La., 2005), 134–135, 145–146. Anna Kingsley, raised a Muslim, converted to Catholicism.

1800, Governor John Drayton confidently but cautiously replied to abolitionist criticism with assurances that the slaves had a significantly larger measure
of comfort and security than European workers and peasants had. In 1829
Governor Stephen D. Miller spoke more boldly: "Slavery exists in some form
everywhere, and it is not of much consequence in a philosophical point of
view, whether it be voluntary or involuntary." George McDuffie opened his
gubernatorial message to the legislature in 1835 by denouncing British West
Indian emancipation as sheer robbery and American abolitionism as religious
fanaticism and Jacobinism. The slaves of South Carolina, he said, lived more
comfortably and securely than the workers and peasants of Europe, and those
who would disturb their repose ought to be executed without benefit of clergy:
"Servitude in some form is one of [society's] essential constituents. No community ever has existed without it, and we may comfortably assert, none ever
will." McDuffie's message wafted across the Atlantic. The antislavery Andrew
Bell of Southampton, England, caustically referred to "a certain Governor"
McDuffie's "laboured defence of slavery in the abstract." Bell, branding as
false the claim that southern slaves fared better than European workers, feared
that "his amiable Excellency" was echoing the "prevailing sentiment of his
country." In the 1820s the claim that America's black slaves were faring better
than British white peasants had spread far enough to call forth acute reactions from British emancipationists. Thomas Clarkson felt compelled to reply
at length, stressing the cruelties of slavery but sliding over the argument from
material conditions, simply condemning them as absurd.[11]

During the 1830s, Chancellor William Harper of South Carolina wrote a
widely circulated, immensely influential essay, "Slavery in the Light of Social
Ethics," which E. N. Elliott of Mississippi reprinted in 1860 in his *Cotton Is
King, and Pro-Slavery Arguments*. Harper skirted Slavery in the Abstract but
gave its advocates powerful ammunition in his opening lines: "The institution
of slavery exists over the greater portion of the inhabited earth. Until within a
very few centuries, it may be said to have existed over the whole earth – at least
in all those portions of it which had made any advances toward civilization.
We might safely conclude then, that it is deeply founded in the nature of man
and the exigencies of human society." Man is born in sin and ignorance and
therefore to subjection. "Let it be remembered that all the great and enduring
monuments of human art and industry – the wonders of Egypt – the everlasting work of Rome – were created by the labor of slaves." Harper appealed to

---

[11] John Drayton, *A View of South Carolina* (Charleston, S.C., 1802), 148; Miller, quoted in
Jenkins, *Pro-Slavery Thought in the Old South*, 76; [George McDuffie], *Governor McDuffie's
Message on the Slavery Question* (New York, 1893 [1865]), esp. 2–3, quote at 9; Andrew
Bell [pseudonym, A. Thomason], *Men and Things in America: Being the Experience of a
Year's Residence in the United States, in a Series of Letters to a Friend* (London, 1838), 192–
192; Thomas Clarkson, *The Argument, "That the West Indian Slaves Are Better Off than
British Peasants," Answered* (London, 1823). Miller's ambiguous formulation on "voluntary
and involuntary" distinguishes between chattel slavery and supposedly free labor that suffers
from de facto servitude.

the laws of political economy and to the British poor laws to indict the primary tendency of the free-labor system. He attributed the passing of the great civilizations of Greece and Rome to the effects of emancipation, concluding: "In short, the uncontradicted experience of the world is, that in the Southern States where good government and praedial and domestic slavery are found, there are prosperity and greatness; where either of these conditions is wanting, degeneracy and barbarism." Edmund Bellinger, Jr., spoke even more bluntly to the citizens of the Barnwell District in 1835: "In all Countries and at all times *that the people are most free, prosperous, and happy under those governments which recognize Slavery.*" The laboring classes will be slaves by whatever name and whether recognized at law or not: "In all countries slavery will and must exist."[12]

The great figure in the transition from the defense of racial slavery to support for Slavery in the Abstract was Thomas Roderick Dew of Virginia, whose famous review of the 1831–1832 Virginia debates on emancipation suggested that the laws of political economy spelled geographical limitations of slavery if not its demise. Logic, political economy, and a profound study of the history of Western civilization nonetheless led Dew to predict, albeit with a heavy heart, a new world order based on personal servitude for the laboring classes. He hailed the triumph of Western civilization as proof that moral and material progress depended on the expansion of individual freedom. Like Adam Smith and Jean-Baptiste Say, Dew advocated laissez-faire, but his political economy must be read in the context of his history of Western civilization – his erudite lectures at the College of William and Mary posthumously published as the *Digest of the Laws, Customs, Manners, and Institutions of the Ancient and Modern Nations.* Dew saw slavery or some form of servitude as the foundation of civilization and as historically ubiquitous. So far, he faced no insurmountable contradiction, for, theoretically, the progress made possible by an enlargement of the free population could be reconciled with a large slave population. Dew foresaw a secular social crisis as intrinsic to capitalist development and, in the end, viewed the social system of the South as the last bulwark against Caesarism, which must inevitably follow the social revolution and anarchy about to engulf the West. The world had to choose between slavery and the dissolution of Western civilization.[13]

---

[12] William Harper, "Slavery in the Light of Social Ethics," in E. N. Elliott, ed., *Cotton Is King, and Pro-Slavery Arguments* (New York, 1969 [1860]), 549, 555, 566, 569–570, 603–604, 606, 615; Edmund Bellinger, Jr., *A Speech on the Subject of Slavery* (Charleston, S.C., 1835), 13–14, quotes at 13.

[13] For Dew's complex thought, see Elizabeth Fox-Genovese and Eugene D. Genovese, *The Mind of the Master Class: History and Faith in the Southern Slaveholders' Worldview* (New York, 2005), ch. 22; E. D. Genovese, *Western Civilization through Slaveholding Eyes: The Social and Historical Thought of Thomas Roderick Dew* (New Orleans, La., 1986); and Eugene D. Genovese, *The Slaveholders' Dilemma: Freedom and Progress in Southern Conservative Thought, 1820–1860* (Columbia, S.C., 1991), especially, Introduction. For alternative interpretations, see Alison Freehling, *Drift toward Disunion: The Virginia Slavery Debate of 1831–1832* (Baton Rouge, La., 1982), and Allen Kaufman, *Capitalism, Slavery, and Republican Values: American*

Dew did not hesitate in his choice, yet the alternatives sickened him. He visualized an end to the expansion of human freedom for the white race and to the wonderful material progress it generated. Dew left his successors the analytical bricks with which to construct a grand worldview based upon Slavery in the Abstract, although many did not share his squeamishness about the outcome. Some clung to the hope that a worldwide slavery could replicate the story of capitalism's material progress; others did not share his enthusiasm for material progress anyway. Thus Dew – usually seen as the foremost theorist of racial slavery – contributed, if indirectly, to a theory that projected enslavement of white as well as black labor. The debates in the Virginia constitutional convention of 1829–1830 rang with denunciations of the free-labor system. Even gradual emancipationists strongly disapproved of the extreme competitiveness and unbridled individualism unleashed in free-labor societies at the expense of decency and social responsibility. Considerable fear of unbridled freedom lurked in the background of the subsequent debate over emancipation.[14]

The learned Hugh Legaré of South Carolina – temperamentally and politically a moderate – placed little credence in racial theories and scriptural arguments. He described slavery as a kind of syphilis and wished it gone, but, with Burkean caution, he wanted it to pass naturally and slowly at the hands of slaveowners. A cosmopolitan of extensive experience, Legaré distinguished between the condition of European workers and of socially mobile American workers, whom he considered basically loyal to American institutions. Yet, like Dew, he worried about a future in which the fundamental tendencies of political economy caught up with America: "Such a frightful mass of evils as now exists in England – so much bodily suffering and mental anguish – so many crimes prompted by the desperation of utter want, and punished with the unrelenting rigour of a stern and necessary policy, shew that, even under the most propitious circumstances, a large portion of mankind are doomed to servitude and misery." Reviewing the history of ancient Greece and medieval Europe, Legaré concluded that ruling classes live off the labor of slaves and serfs. In 1840, he saw class war and military despotism on the agenda for Europe and feared that the United States would catch up: "Is this to be forever so? Is that slavery of the whites, which the great prophet and apostle of the poor, the Abbé de Lamennais, pronounces so much worse than the bondage of the blacks, the

---

Political Economists, 1819–1848 (Austin, Tex., 1982). See also Dew, "Essay on Slavery," in *The Pro-Slavery Argument, as Maintained by the Most Distinguished Writers of the Southern States* (Charleston, S.C., 1852). Dew drew a hundred students at a time at the College of William and Mary: J. K. Whitaker, "Early Flowering in the Old Dominion," in William J. Barber, ed., *Breaking the Academic Mould: Economists and American Higher Learning in the Nineteenth Century* (New Brunswick, N.J., 1993), 36. For Caesarism, see Fox-Genovese and Genovese, *Mind of the Master Class* (New York, 2005), passim.

[14] For the debate in Virginia, see Dickson D. Bruce, Jr., *The Rhetoric of Conservatism: The Virginia Convention of 1829–1830 and the Conservative Tradition in the South* (San Marino, Calif., 1982), 175 and passim.

unchangeable condition of things? or when, how, how far is it to be susceptible of correction? The masses in Europe are called free, yet they...are, in truth, with few exceptions, a permanently degraded *caste*, like the Helots, slaves, not of individuals, but of whole communities," which constitutes "the worst form of bondage."[15]

The doctrine of slavery as the natural and inevitable condition of the laboring masses proceeded apace in the late 1840s, rising to a crescendo in the 1850s. In 1843 the intellectually accomplished George Frederick Holmes said that Southerners supported only racial slavery and rejected the enslavement of equals in intelligence and capacity. Yet, he acknowledged that slavery had existed throughout history independent of race and that its biblical sanction was not racially specific. In ensuing years, although vaguely suggesting an anti-slavery spirit in the Gospels, he advocated a version of Slavery in the Abstract. In 1855, Fitzhugh suggested to Holmes that until recently almost no one had endorsed Slavery in the Abstract but that, thanks to their work and that of Henry Hughes, a great many now had. Two years later, J. D. B. De Bow, editor of *De Bow's Review*, the South's most influential magazine, introduced an article by Fitzhugh: "His theory is adopted by many." Holmes disliked notoriety, hyperbole, and slashing polemics; he preferred careful scholarship, close reasoning, and temperate language. Holmes shrank from Fitzhugh's flamboyance but credited him with the wit to go beyond criticism of market practices to a root-and-branch indictment of the capitalist system.[16]

Holmes, too, described the free-labor system as a thinly disguised and particularly vicious form of slavery. Although his thought underwent a long evolution in specifics, certain themes remained constant. He accepted racial inferiority as grounds for enslavement of blacks but distinguished between the narrow question of race and the larger question of labor: "The slavery question and the labor question are indeed identical." Holmes continued acerbically: "Modern abolitionism and modern political economy have but one panacea for those threatened with starvation: by the mouth of Mr. Herbert Spencer, both say, let them die or rot. With such an alternative, slavery is the more rational and the more humane." Holmes refused to agree that whites should never enslave whites: "The interests of civilization and the interests of both the dominant and subject classes may frequently sanction the perpetuation of the relation even in these circumstances." Elsewhere Holmes, who doubted the scientific character

---

[15] In *HLW*, see "Hall's Travels in North America" (1829), 2:289; and "Constitutional History of Greece," 1:430; Michael O'Brien, *A Character of Hugh Legaré* (Knoxville, Tenn., 1985), 165–166, 232–235. For the North's much greater pauperism and criminality relative to the South, notwithstanding boasts about northern education, see the perspective of Edward Ingle, *Southern Sidelights* (New York, 1896), 188–195.

[16] [George Frederick Holmes], "On Slavery and Christianity," *SQR*, 3 (1843), 253; [George Frederick Holmes], "Observations on a Passage from Aristotle Relative to Slavery," *SLM*, 16 (1850), 193–205, esp. 197–201; Fitzhugh to Holmes, Mar. 27, 1855, in Holmes Letterbook; De Bow in *DBR*, 22 (1857), 449; Holmes, "Fitzhugh's Sociology for the South," *QRMCS*, 9 (April 1855), 180–201.

of political economy, drew on David Ricardo, Thomas Malthus, and Pierre-Joseph Proudhon to speak of "the radical antagonism" of exploitive capital and legally free but viciously oppressed labor. The North faced an economic catastrophe inherent in the laws of political economy that governed capitalist society, whereas in the South slavery rendered "impossible that terrible death struggle, the contest between capital and labor."[17]

Attacks on "wage-slavery" provoked angry reactions from Northerners, who especially resented choice thrusts from nationally respected Southerners. In 1819, John W. Taylor, a New York politician, rebuked Henry Clay for comparing the condition of the South's "black slaves" favorably to that of the North's "white slaves." More irritating were remarks attributed to John Randolph of Roanoke that northern white slaves, not southern black slaves, would enable the South to rule the Union. Down to secession Randolph's taunt rankled in New England. The Reverend R. T. Stanton of Norwich, Connecticut, as well as Josiah Quincy of Massachusetts and others, recalled it angrily. "How often," Stanton asked his congregation, "are we *reminded* of Randolph's cutting words, 'We do not govern the North by our black slaves, but by their own white slaves.'" The antislavery Francis Lieber, who returned north from South Carolina in the 1850s and joined the Republican Party, judged slaves generally well treated, drawing a heated rebuke from his friend Charles Sumner. In the 1840s Lieber had written that the Poles complained of serfs as Carolinians complained of slaves – too many hands do too little work. In 1856 he wrote privately from South Carolina of a "shameless absurdity" – the notion that "all labor ought to be owned by capital," which "is running like wildfire over the South and even through sedate reviews." Lieber ranted in the wake of the bloody working-class uprising in Paris in 1848 ("The June Days"), noting the similarity of the proslavery argument with the "downright silly clamor" of the socialists for the "organization of labor." Then, in the late 1850s, Hammond's "mud-sill speech" provoked howls of rage from New England to California. A typical response: When Jefferson Davis attended commencement at Girls High School in Portland, Maine, he inquired about Sarah Ellen Hart, the young lady who, as valedictorian, read one of her poems. He was told "Oh, she is the daughter of one of our Northern mud-sills!" The young antislavery Senator David C. Broderick of California loudly responded that he was proud of his artisan parents and his own work as a mechanic.[18]

---

[17] Holmes, "Ancient Slavery," *DBR*, 19 (Nov. 1855), 560, 570. For Holmes's popularity and influence on campus, see James J. Palmer to John S. Palmer, Oct. 11, 1860, in Louis P. Towles, ed., *A World Turned Upside Down: The Palmers of South Santee, 1818–1881* (Columbia, S.C., 1996), 269.

[18] J. W. Taylor in *Annals of Congress*, 15th Cong., 2nd Sess., 1170–1179; for one version of the remarks widely attributed to Randolph, see Henry Adams, *John Randolph* (New York, 1961 [1882]), 184. R. P. Stanton, *Slavery Viewed in the Light of the Golden Rule* (Norwich, Conn., 1860), 18; Josiah Quincy, *Address Illustrative of the Nature and Power of the Slave States and the Duties of the Free States* (Boston, 1856), 18. In Thomas Sergeant Perry, ed., *The Life and Letters of Francis Lieber* (Boston, Mass., 1882), see Lieber to a Friend, April 1858 (215);

In the 1850s antislavery newspapers reprinted or quoted *in extenso* proslavery politicians. Gamaliel Bailey's *National Era* reprinted an essay from the Petersburg (Virginia) *Intelligencer* that called for a boycott of northern watering places. No boycott could succeed, Bailey sneered, since Southerners went north to taste civilization. The antislavery *New Hampshire Sentinel* printed a long excerpt from a speech by Senator Jeremiah Clemens of Alabama, apparently convinced that it would outrage northern sensibilities. *Frederick Douglass' Paper* and William Lloyd Garrison's *Liberator* reprinted proslavery articles from *Southern Cultivator* and the *Richmond Enquirer*. The *Milwaukee Daily Sentinel*, confident that Slavery in the Abstract outraged northern public opinion, published a one-page comment and three pages of excerpts from Hammond on wage-slavery. When the *California Herald* denounced the "mud-sill speech," the *Charleston Mercury* defended Hammond's "sound, sagacious and well considered views" against a "flippant" and "malevolent" attack. It praised his exposé of "the cancerous sore at the bowels of Northern free society, destined to eat out the life of its liberties by a lawless mobocracy or agrarian Fourierism." The *New Orleans Delta* and *Charleston Mercury* applauded Hammond for identifying the basic problem between North and South as "a deadly struggle between White Slavery and Black Slavery." In Georgia, the *Macon Weekly Telegraph* reprinted a bitter letter from the *Richmond Examiner*, purportedly from a workingman in New England, who supported Hammond's depiction of free laborers as white slaves.[19]

It is difficult to fathom the surprise with which northern public opinion reacted to Hammond's speech since his formulation had long been standard fare in proslavery circles. In 1825, James Barbour told the Agricultural Society of Albemarle, Virginia, "Such a [laboring] class, whether bond or free, white or black, must exist in every community, as they are the indispensable foundation of the social fabric." In 1832 the *Richmond Enquirer* declared: "He who performs the labour, and drudgery, and menial offices, even when disguised by the term *help*, is obliged to look his master or employer as his superior, altho' of the same complexion." In 1837 the *Richmond Whig* and the *Raleigh Register and North Carolina Gazette* identified "the radical weakness in the organization of

Lieber to George Howe, May 22, 1848 (291); Lieber to G. S. Hilliard, Oct. 23, 1856 (291); also, Frank Freidel, *Francis Lieber: Nineteenth-Century Liberal* (Gloucester, Mass., 1968), 250; for Poles and Carolinians, see Lieber Journal, Sept. 21–22, in Charles Mack and Ilona S. Mack, ed., *Like a Sponge Thrown into Water: Francis Lieber's European Travel Journal of 1844–1845* (Columbia, S.C., 2002), 74; Caroline E. Vose, "Jefferson Davis in New England," *Virginia Quarterly Review*, 2 (1926), 561; for Broderick, see Thomas Lately, *Between Two Empires: The Life Story of California's First Senator* (Boston, Mass., 1969), 169–170.

[19] Gamaliel Bailey, "A Southern View of Northern Watering Places," *National Era*, 9 (1855), 130; *New Hampshire Sentinel* (Keene), Feb. 7, 1850; Daniel Lee, "Hired Labor and Free Labor," *Frederick Douglass' Paper*, May 5, 1854; "The Border Ruffian and the Free White Laborer," *Liberator*, Apr. 25, 1856; *Milwaukee Daily Sentinel*, March 16, 1858; also "The Mud Sill Theory," Jan. 23, 1860; "Senator Hammond and the Herald," *Charleston Mercury*, July 5, 1858; *Charleston Mercury*, April 2, 1858 (reprinted from *New Orleans Delta*); "White Slavery in New England," *Macon Weekly Telegraph*, May 18, 1858.

Northern Society" as the cause of mob violence in New York: "The starvation and licentiousness, necessarily engendered by large masses not compelled to labour" required military confrontation, not ordinances and edicts to control the "miserable beings called *workies* in the free States." In Texas, Houston's *Telegraph and Texas Register* compared the condition of southern slaves favorably with that of European peasants and industrial workers.[20]

Southern women, focusing on race, commented on Slavery in the Abstract less directly than their men. They did, however, frequently mention the misery of the white laboring classes of Europe and the North and the more wholesome conditions in the South. In the 1850s, Marian Harland (Mary Virginia Terhune) wrote enthusiastically in her novel *Alone* about the contented slave who lay down at night with the knowledge that he and his family need fear no want: "Can the same be said of the menial classes in any other country under the sun?" The intellectually accomplished Margaret Junkin Preston of Virginia – born and bred in the North – countered the grim picture of slavery in *Uncle Tom's Cabin* with evidence of contented slaves before her eyes. She wrote a Northern friend about the fuss made over slave weddings and the like, contrasting the behavior of slaveholders "with the utter and entire want of interest and sympathy that exists between Northern mistresses and their domestics." Mary Howard Schoolcraft filled her book *Plantation Life* with quotations from the debates in the House of Commons on the terrible conditions of British workers and from the Reverend Nehemiah Adams and prominent northern politicians on conditions in the North. She condemned "the dens, and holes, and cellars, and tenements of the white poor of New York, and other great cities," while extolling the "thoroughly ventilated" cabins of the slaves and their comfort and security. "There scarcely ever was a time in the history of the world when man did not enslave his fellow-man, and, probably, this will continue to be practiced, more or less until the glorious season of the millennium." Schoolcraft defended slavery on racial grounds but accused abolitionists of wishing to replace de jure enslavement of blacks with de facto enslavement of whites. When the War came, Keziah Brevard of Tennessee watched her slave Jim bring wood in for his family and mused, "Perhaps if he were free he would have to buy this wood – maybe have a poor house and a dirt chimney. He had a house – brick fireplace with three rooms – one to sit in – two bed rooms." In North Carolina, Catherine Edmondston never doubted that southern slaves fared better than Europe's laboring classes or that they had as much practical freedom. In New Orleans, Julia LeGrand, chafing under wartime hardships, thought of the worse hardships that befell others: "English operatives perishing with hunger."[21]

[20] "On Slaves and Slave Labor: Extracts from a late Address of James Barbour to the Agricultural Society of Albemarle, Va.," *Daily National Intelligencer*, Nov. 24, 1825; "Free Negroes and Mulattoes," *Richmond Enquirer*, Feb. 9, 1832; *Raleigh Register and North Carolina Gazette*, Feb. 28, 1837 (reprinted from *Richmond Whig*); "Laboring Classes in Europe," *Telegraph and Texas Register*, June 6, 1837. Northern house servants insisted on being called "help."

[21] Marian Harland, *Alone* (Boston, Mass., 1856); Margaret Junkin Preston to [?], Nov. 25, 1850, in Elizabeth Preston Allan, *The Life and Letters of Margaret Junkin Preston* (Boston, Mass.,

George William Bagby of Virginia, a witty man of letters, had some fun. In a satirical projection of the world of the future, he saw incipient anarchy in the North and reduction of inferior races to slavery. He gravely suggested that a victorious Confederacy enslave Yankees along with blacks. The value of the Yankee as a slave needed assessment: "Cowardly, thievish, superstitious, fanatical, destitute of a moral sense, or any fixed idea of civil polity, he possesses all the worse and none of the better traits of the Negro, and stands more in need of a master." Bagby constructed an argument for the enslavement of western Europeans as well. In previous decades southern spokesmen had long maintained – without a trace of satire – that British workers were ready to enslave themselves. Senator John Rowan of Kentucky, intervening in the Webster-Hayne debate of 1830, scorched British capitalists for brutal treatment of their workers, which, in consequence, meant that the unemployed "may justly enslave themselves for subsistence." In the 1840s Wayne Gridley of South Carolina announced that "thousands of European operatives" would sell themselves into slavery, if they could. An editorial in the *Mississippi Free Trader and Natchez Gazette* in 1851 wept: "Alas! Poor laborers of England, we verily believe ye would be glad to exchange places with the slaves of Mississippi, but we question much whether slaves would take your places; free indeed though they might be."[22]

In South Carolina the views of unionists paralleled those of quasi-secessionists like Robert Barnwell Rhett. "The vital question of labour," the unionist William J. Grayson wrote in 1859, contained little novelty: "Something perhaps in the mode of statement, nothing more." Grayson stoutly defended John C. Calhoun for advocating the Aristotelian doctrine that democracy requires masters and slaves and for preferring that the slaves be of a different race than their masters. For Grayson, not only had labor everywhere and under every kind of government taken one of two forms, hirelings and bondmen, but both classes were, in fact, "essentially the same." After the War, former Governor Francis W. Pickens of South Carolina said that Providence willed class stratification. Every society subordinated labor to capital, which must own labor individually or collectively through the political and economic system. *De Bow's Review*, despite accepting the results of the War

---

1923), 42–43, 54; *Plantation Life: The Narratives of Mrs. Henry Schoolcraft* (New York, 1969 [1860]), 20 of "Letters on the Condition of the African Race," App., the "Letters," 35, 40–41, n., 418–422, 482, and generally, ch. 3, and in main text, see also 15, 20, 35, 73–79, 307–309, 324–329, quote at 35; Keziah Brevard Diary, Jan. 21, 1860; Edmondston Diary, June 2, 1862, in Beth G. Crabtree and James Welch Patton, eds., *"Journal of a Secesh Lady": The Diary of Catherine Ann Devereux Edmondston, 1860–1866* (Raleigh, N.C., 1979), 186–187; Kate Mason Rowland and Mrs. Morris S. Croxall, eds., *The Journal of Julia LeGrand: New Orleans, 1862–1863* (Richmond, 1911), Feb. 28, 1863 (160).

22 [George William Bagby], "Manifest Destiny of the World," *SLM*, 29 (1859), 207; Speech of Mr. Rowan, of Kentucky, on Mr. Foote's Resolution, Relating to the Public Lands, in Reply to Mr. Webster of Massachusetts (Washington, D.C., 1830), 5; Wayne Gridley, *Slavery in the South: A Review of Hammond's and Fuller's Letters, and Chancellor Harper's Memoir* (Charleston, S.C., 1845), 16; "Slavery in the Southern States as Compared with Free Labor in England," *Mississippi Free Trader and Natchez Gazette*, Mar. 8, 1851.

as irreversible, reiterated that the free-labor system exploited white labor more brutally than the slave system had ever exploited black labor and that white agricultural and industrial laborers remained virtual slaves. Rhett spoke even more bluntly: "There is but one state of society in the world where labor and capital are identical in interest; and that is where domestic slavery exists; and under this form of society alone have Republics hitherto ever been maintained." Aaron, an illiterate ex-slave, understood Calhoun much as Grayson, Pickens, and Rhett did. He admonished blacks and whites to take the measure of Calhoun's assertion of slavery as the firmest basis for the world's institutions.[23]

And then there was South Carolina's William H. Trescot – diplomat and historian of diplomacy, blessed with one of the keenest minds in America. Advocating secession during the crisis of 1850, Trescot advanced an interpretation of modern history that centered on the rivalries of national states in relation to their respective social systems. He maintained that the relation of labor to capital shaped societies in three principal forms: serfdom, slavery, and free labor. Slave and free-labor systems, intrinsically antagonistic, could not long coexist in a single nation-state. The primary problem lay in the absence of morality in the free-labor system's capital-labor relation and the attendant perpetual class struggle. Even many Southerners who, unlike Trescot, stressed the constitutional and political dimension of the sectional struggle found the root in social systems. Thus, John Scott of Virginia, writing as "Barbarossa" in a book praised by Bagby as of exceptional value, declared "Equilibrium" the ruling principle of a government that embraced "two nations, of opposite civilizations and differing interests."[24]

In South Carolina, unionists and nullifiers, cooperationists and secessionists – Harper, McDuffie, Grayson, Hammond, Seabrook, Benjamin F. Perry,

[23] [William J. Grayson], "The Dual Form of Labour," *RM*, 6 (1859), 1–18, quote at 1, republished in *DBR*, 28 (1860), 48–66; *Letter of Hon. Francis W. Pickens... Written to a Gentleman in New Orleans* (Baltimore, Md., 1866), 13; "The Two Aristocracies of America," *DBR*, 2 (1866), 461–465; also, R. J. H., "Labor Question in England," *DBR*, 2 (1866), 708–719 (*DBR* picked up its old theme: see, e.g., J. H. Gibbon, "The Institution of Slavery in Accordance with the Principles of the Moral Law," *DBR*, 17 [1854], 410); Rhett quoted in Laura A. White, *Robert Barnwell Rhett: Father of Secession* (New York, 1931), 49; *The Light and Truth of Slavery: Aaron's History* (Electronic ed.; Chapel Hill, N.C., 2000), 10–11; also, *God's Image in Ebony: Being a Series of Biographical Sketches, Facts, Anecdotes, Etc., Demonstrative of the Mental Powers and Intellectual Capacities of the Negro Race*, ed. H. G. Adams (Electronic ed.; Chapel Hill, N.C., 1999 [1854], x. See also Bernard Mandel, *Labor: Free and Slave: Workingmen and the Anti-Slavery Movement in the United States* (New York, 1955), 40 and passim.

    The terms "hireling," "wage-slavery," "slavery of wages," and "white slavery" were often used interchangeably but in fact carried different connotations. For a brief account of terms and their significance, see David R. Roediger, *The Wages of Whiteness: Race and the Making of the American Working Class* (London, 1991), ch. 4, especially 44–47, 72.

[24] William H. Trescot, *The Position and Course of the South* (Boston, Mass., 1850); also, William Henry Trescot, *The Diplomacy of the Revolution: An Historical Study* (New York, 1852), Introduction; "Barbarossa" [John Scott], *The Lost Principle or the Sectional Equilibrium: How It Was Created – How Destroyed – How It may Be Restored* (New York, 1969 [1860]), 191; [George William Bagby], *SLM*, 31 (1860), 160, 238–239.

James Henley Thornwell, Henry Timrod – all pronounced personal servitude the inevitable condition of the laboring classes and the necessary foundation for a civilized social order. Even the industrialist William Gregg conceded ground to advocates of Slavery in the Abstract. In 1845 he wrote to Amos Lawrence of Massachusetts to defend slavery simply as the basis of southern prosperity. Yet in 1851, wriggling to avoid any suggestion of wanting to enslave white workers, Gregg described slavery as "the means of giving to capital a positive control over labor, and of that kind of labor which nature seems to have adapted to agricultural pursuits." In other countries, notably the manufacturing, "Labor and capital are assuming an antagonistical position." But in the South: "It cannot be the case; capital will be able to control labor; even in manufactures with whites, for blacks can always be resorted to in case of need." *Southern Presbyterian Review* doubted that slavery would be safer in an independent South. With typically conservative reserve, it warned that no one could predict the outcome of the overthrow of "a settled order, of old and tried institutions, of an earthquake." Unionists reasoned that if the free-labor system was unraveling under the threat of all-out class war, and if some form of slavery marked the wave of the future, then good sense dictated patience, caution, and avoidance of plunges into political extremism. Similarly, Hammond, writing to William Porcher Miles in 1858, described himself as "buoyant & confident" because the South was becoming strong enough to defy the world but also because "she has convinced the world that this abolition crusade is an absurdity & the world is practically confessing this conviction." The North would willingly "accept our dictation if couched in decent terms & based on reason."[25]

Less buoyant Southerners increasingly felt trapped in a hostile world. J. D. B. De Bow cried, "The hands of all mankind seem to be against us. All the great powers of Europe menace our institutions." A low country aristocrat [probably James Porcher Miles] spoke sadly to Fredrika Bremer of Sweden: "The world is against us, and we shall be overpowered by voices and condemned without justice, for what we are, and for what we are doing on behalf of our servants."[26]

Lawyers as Social Theorists

The growing appeal of Slavery in the Abstract owed much to leaders of the bench and bar, who had a ready audience of socially and politically powerful readers. Fitzhugh and Hughes were lawyers; William Harper, Nathaniel

[25] Gregg to Lawrence, quoted in Thomas P. Martin, "The Advent of William Gregg and the Graniteville Company," *JSH*, 11 (1945), 412; William Gregg, "Address to the South Carolina Institute," *DBR*, 11 (Aug. 1851), 130; "Critical Notices," *SPR* (1851), 447; Hammond to Miles, Nov. 23, 1858, in Miles Papers; Genovese, *Slaveholders' Dilemma*, ch. 2. For unionist insistence that, in an increasingly antislavery world, the Union could protect slavery more than an independent southern confederacy could, see *Letters of Nathaniel Macon to Charles O'Conor* (Montgomery, Ala., 1860), 2, 20–22.

[26] [J. D. B. De Bow], "Rail-road Prospects and Progress," *DBR*, 12 (1852), 500; Fredrika Bremer, *Homes of the New World: Impressions of America*, 2 vols. (New York, 1853).

Beverley Tucker, and James P. Holcombe were outstanding professors of law. Social theorists who advocated or flirted with Slavery in the Abstract drew on prevailing notions of the proper relation of private property to legal theory and Christian doctrine. A sophisticated theory of property and contract developed during the Middle Ages, but Lutheranism and Calvinism changed its focus. The Reformation introduced a deep-seated shift in Christian individualism that had fateful consequences for social, political, and legal theory. As Harold Berman puts it: "Old rules were cast in a new ensemble. Nature became property. Economic relations became contract. Conscience became will and intent." In consequence, "the property and contract rights so created were held to be inviolable, so long as they did not contravene conscience. And so the secularization of the state, in the restricted sense of the removal of ecclesiastical controls from it, was accompanied by spiritualization, and even sanctification, of property and contract."[27]

For Southerners, the spiritualization of property and contract meant that the positive law of slavery – like all law – ultimately had to comply with the rectitude of individual conscience. In this respect, they remained close to the Puritan ethos, which rooted individual conscience in communities that honored the Word of God, and they saw the descendants of Puritanism in nineteenth-century New England as apostates. "Remember," the Presbyterian Reverend Dr. Thomas Smyth told his flock in Charleston, "that you hold your property, as well as your time and talents, in trust for God." For the Reverend Robert Lewis Dabney of Virginia – a formidable theologian – there could be only one Christian position on property and wealth: "*Our property is purely a trust fund, and the whole of it is to be used for the benefit of the owner.*" Property is God's, and property-owning men serve as His stewards. "The owner, as a just and benevolent man, will of course allow his steward a competent subsistence out of the estate; but the profits of the property are his, not his servant's." Dabney added pointedly, "The servant must be duly fed and clothed, in order that he may be able to work for his master" and avoid being "a dull, over-worked hack." The implications for the doctrine of Slavery in the Abstract – clear in Dabney's remarks – emerged, if anything, even more piercingly in the formulations of secular theorists who took for granted that private property constituted the foundation not merely of republican government but of civilization. For Dew, it provided "the pillars of the social edifice, marriage and property." For Fitzhugh, it destroyed the extreme personal liberty and the social equality he opposed: "Private property is a trust. If private property fails to meet its responsibilities, it ought to be abolished." In the early Republic, Virginians assumed that absolute property provided the foundation for the reconciliation of economic individualism and attachment to local community, but in time – as Christopher M. Curtis has demonstrated in depth – they moved

[27] Harold J. Berman, *Law and Revolution: The Formation of the Western Legal Tradition* (Cambridge, Mass., 1983), 30.

from an ideology based on the centrality of freeholds to one based on the centrality of slave property.[28]

Legal scholars in Louisiana wrote influential books that documented the existence of slavery throughout history. John Fletcher began and ended his massive *Studies on Slavery* (1852) with the race question, but he conceded that capital and labor must be harmonious or antagonistic. They are harmonious "only when it is true that labour constitutes capital, which can only happen through slavery." Under the free-labor system antagonism prevails because it drives wages down to the lowest possible level, generating "that morass of misery into which the worn-out, broken tools of labour are thrown, with cruel heartlessness." In *Southern Institutes* (1858), George Sawyer, a scientific racist convinced of the special fitness of blacks for slavery, nonetheless described the serfs and dependent peasants of Eastern Europe, Asia, Africa, and Latin America as virtual slaves. He criticized serf emancipation in Britain and the subsequent expulsion of peasants from the land during the enclosures. Denouncing current labor conditions in Britain, Sawyer cited the Parliamentary Reports, as well as Elizabeth Gaskell's *Mary Barton* and John Cobden's *White Slaves of England* ("this most excellent work"). Hailing slavery as a system of organic social relations that bound classes together and prevented class war, he asked, "Whoever heard of an American slave perishing from starvation, or becoming a pauper at the public charge?" In short, without specifically endorsing Slavery in the Abstract, he presented a series of arguments that allowed for no other conclusion. Southern commentators also claimed that at least seventy-five percent of the peoples of Africa were slaves, stressing peoples of various shades as Africans enslaved by other Africans. George A. Baxter, one of the more ingenious of these polemicists, argued that, therefore, emancipation would wreck the African economy.[29]

---

[28] *Complete Works of the Reverend Thomas Smyth, D. D.*, ed. J. William Flinn, 10 vols. (Columbia, S.C., 1908), 5:146; "Principles of Christian Economy," *DD*, 1:132; Thomas Roderick Dew, *Digest of the Laws, Customs, Manners, and Institutions of the Ancient and Modern Nations* (New York, 1884 [1852]), 411; George Fitzhugh, *Cannibals All!, or Slaves without Masters* (Cambridge, Mass., 1960 [1857]), ch. 28; Fitzhugh, *Sociology for the South*, 185; and among many, see also [William Gilmore Simms], "Constitution of France," *SQR*, 16 (1850), 502–536. On the shift in Virginia, see Christopher M. Curtis, "Jefferson's Chosen People: Legal and Political Conceptions of the Freehold in the Old Dominion from Revolution to Reform" (Ph.D. diss., Emory University, 2002).

[29] John Fletcher, *Studies on Slavery, in Easy Lessons* (Natchez, Miss., 1852), 219–220; George S. Sawyer, *Southern Institutes; Or, an Inquiry into the Origin and Early Prevalence of Slavery and the Slave Trade* (New York, 1967 [1858]), esp. 141, 248–280, 309, 374–381, quotes at 250, n., 318. For Fletcher and Slavery in the Abstract, see also Jenkins, *Pro-Slavery Thought*, 297. For the early citation of well-known British writers on the wretched condition of the English poor, see, e.g., [Holland], *Refutation of the Calumnies*, 59–60; also, J. K. Paulding, on "the Criminal Courts of England," in *Slavery in the United States* (New York, 1836), 255. A typical review of Eugene Sue's *Mysteries of Paris* noted the horrors of crime-infested neighborhoods: "Critical Notices," *SQR*, 5 (1844), 257–259. For the influence of Charles Dickens, Charles Kingsley, Eugene Sue, and other novelists in convincing Southerners of superiority of their own labor conditions, see Fox-Genovese and Genovese, *Mind of the Master Class*, ch. 4. On Africa

Frequently cited in the South, Oliver Goldsmith's *Deserted Village* – issued in Philadelphia in 1771 with twelve editions by 1800 – showed the influence of Pliny, Cicero, Juvenal, and Horace in protesting the destruction of rural life in Britain in the wake of commercialization. When Thomas Emerson's *Tennessee Farmer* called for a strengthened yeomanry as essential to national prosperity and greatness, it quoted *Deserted Village* on the irrevocable damage done by its disappearance. *Southern Quarterly Review* and *Southern Literary Messenger* called their readers' attention to Henry Mayhew's articles of 1851 – collected as *London Labour and the London Poor* (1861) – as they appeared: "one of the most extraordinary works of the present century"; "a complete treasure house of London social statistics." John Reuben Thompson, editor of *Southern Literary Messenger*, described himself as sickened by Mayhew's account of working-class misery. Curiously, William Gilmore Simms recommended *London Labour and London Poor* as "at once amusing and instructive." De Bow saw in Mayhew's portrayal of working-class misery a degraded race of a "superannuated civilization, ignorant alike of morality, Christianity and the language and usages of those among whom they live." De Bow – like Sawyer, Thomas R. R. Cobb of Georgia, and other proslavery Southerners – cited Cobden's *White Slaves of England* extensively as a reliable source on labor conditions that confirmed a vision of human suffering reminiscent of Dante's portrayal of hell. Cobb also drew on *Household Words*, the journal edited by Charles Dickens, and on *The Glory and Shame of England* (1841) by the antislavery Presbyterian Reverend Charles Edwards Lester of New England and New York, a descendent of Jonathan Edwards. Dr. Samuel Cartwright, advancing his scientific views in defense of southern slavery, also invoked *Glory and Shame* to stress the miserable physical conditions of British labor. And a contributor to *Southern Literary Messenger* described *Glory and Shame* as a "*spiteful* but interesting book" that exposed the risk of massive social disorder. P. C. Pendleton, who reviewed *Glory and Shame* for *Magnolia* (Savannah), and Waddy Thompson, Whig politician of South Carolina, added a fresh note: British greed and profiteering were coming down hard on the working classes at home and on colonial and semicolonial peoples abroad. After the War, the *Richmond Times* and Savannah *Daily News and Herald* continued to draw on Lester's exposé of the brutal exploitation of child labor in Britain, suggesting that conditions, if anything, had worsened. Southern polemics, grounded in British and northern exposés of the exploitation of free workers, never ceased. The Presbyterian Reverend Stuart Robinson of Kentucky, exiled by the Union Army to Canada during the War, drew upon the antiabolitionist

see, e.g., J. Jones, *A Discourse Delivered . . . to the Rome Light Guards and Miller Rifles in the Presbyterian Church of Rome, Ga., on the Sabbath Morning, the 26th of May, 1861* (Rome, Ga., 1861), 10; John W. Monette, *History of the Discovery and Settlement of the Valley of the Mississippi by the Three Great European Powers, Spain, France, and Great Britain*, 2 vols. in 1 (New York, 1971 [1846]), 1:228–229; George A. Baxter, *An Essay on the Abolition of Slavery* (Richmond, 1836), 22.

The Social Conditions and Education of the People in England and Europe (1850) by the Scots economist Joseph Kay.[30]

While concentrating on Britain and Western Europe, defenders of slavery looked eastward. John Taylor of Caroline in Virginia, William Drayton in South Carolina, and the pro-southern J. K. Paulding of New York described Polish peasants as virtual slaves of especially cruel lords who treated them much worse than southern slaveholders treated their slaves. Taylor, in fact, accused Polish lords of preferring to ruin their country rather than ease the oppression of the people. In 1840, *Southern Cabinet of Agriculture, Horticulture, Rural and Domestic Economy* published one article on Austria and "the wealth of its nobles and the oppression of its peasantry" and another on Greek poverty and oppression. In 1824 the politically moderate litterateur Isaac Harby of Charleston wrote that Russian serfs would gladly change places with more humanely treated southern slaves. *Southern and Western Literary Monthly Magazine and Review* took a different tack. It asserted that the poorer peasants of Hungary and Transylvania lived close to the edge but did not suffer "the extreme want" common among the peasants of Western Europe. It then added that the life of the Hungarian and Transylvanian country gentlemen resembled that of the southern planters.[31]

---

[30] On *Deserted Village*, see Peter Dixon, *Oliver Goldsmith Revisited* (Boston, Mass., 1991), 137 and ch. 6, and James D. Hart, *The Popular Book: A History of America's Literary Taste* (New York, 1950), 28; [Thomas Emerson], "Farmers," *Tennessee Farmer*, 1 (1835), 123, 362; [John R. Thompson], *SLM*, 17 (1851), 454–455; [William Gilmore Simms], "Critical Notes," *SQR*, n. s., 5 (1852), 268; also, *SQR*, n.s., 6 (1852), 534. On Mayhew, see "National Metropolis," *DBR*, 26 (1859), 405; J. D. B. De Bow, "Notes on Political Economy," *DBR*, 19 (1855), 429, and *DBR*, 12 (1859), 118, 405; J. D. B. De Bow, *The Industrial Resources, Statistics, &c. of the United States and More Particularly of the Southern and Western States*, 3rd ed., 3 vols. (New York, 1966 [1854]), 1:24; T. R. R. Cobb, "An Historical Sketch of Slavery," in *An Inquiry into the Law of Negro Slavery in the United States* (New York, 1968 [1858]), ch. 10; [Samuel Cartwright], "Canaan Identified with the Ethiopian," *SQR* 2 (1842), 351; "Of New Works, and Literary Intelligence," *SLM*, 7 (1841), 875; [P. C. Pendleton], "The Editor's Table," *Magnolia* [Savannah], 3 (Nov., 1841), 525; Waddy Thompson, "Speech on the War with Mexico (First Report)," Jan. 4, 1848, in *JCCP*, 25:67; "The Murder of Innocents," Savannah *Daily News and Herald*, July 31, 1866 (reprinted from the *Richmond Times*); Stuart Robinson, *Slavery, as Recognized in the Mosaic Civil Law* (Toronto, 1865), 63–66. De Bow, who respected the *Edinburgh Review*, rebuffed its antislavery by trotting out British labor conditions and British oppression of India and Ireland: *DBR*, 10 (1851), 519; 11 (1851), 344.

[31] John Taylor, *An Inquiry into the Principles and Policy of the Government of the United States*, ed. Loren Baritz (Indianapolis, Ind., 1919 [1814]), 104; [William Drayton], *The South Vindicated from the Treason and Fanaticism of the Northern Abolitionists* (Philadelphia, 1836), 251; J. K. Paulding, *Slavery in the United States* (1836), 266; see also B., "Polish Language and Literature," *Virginia Literary Museum and Journal of Belles Lettres, Arts, Sciences, Etc.*, 1 (1830), 675–677; Harby, "The Presidency," in Moise Abraham, ed., *A Selection from the Miscellaneous Writings of the Late Isaac Harby* (Charleston, S.C., 1829), 134; A Charlestonian, "Notes on European Agriculture," *Southern Cabinet of Agriculture, Horticulture, Rural and Domestic Economy*, 1 (1840), 6; S. Olin, "Greece as It Is," *Southern Cabinet of Agriculture, Horticulture, Rural and Domestic Economy*, 1 (1840), 172–177; "Paget's Hungary and Transylvania," *Southern and Western Literary Monthly Magazine and Review*, 12 (1846), 76, 78.

Without specifically endorsing Slavery in the Abstract, T. R. R. Cobb left little doubt where he stood. He prefaced his book, *The Law of Negro Slavery in the United States* – the South's strongest proslavery legal treatise – with an impressive book-length review of slavery in world history. Cobb invoked Scripture to justify the racial enslavement of blacks but went to considerable lengths to show that most of the world's peoples, white or colored, had always lived in bondage. The condition of the laboring classes of Great Britain differed from personal bondage only in the name: "There is perhaps no solution of the great problem of reconciling the interests of labor and capital, so as to protect each from the encroachments and oppressions of the other, so simple and effective as negro slavery." Societies based on wage labor were recent, unstable, and doomed: "In every organized community there must be a laboring class to execute the plans devised by wiser heads; to till the ground, and to perform the menial offices necessarily connected with social life." In free-labor societies, "The labor performed by the lower classes is servile labor. In name it is *voluntary*, in reality, it is *involuntary*, forced by a master more relentless than their feudal lords – stern necessity." Slavery in one form or another had always existed at the base of society and would continue until the millennium.[32]

The Wondrous Unity of Capital and Labor

The defense of slavery required an exposé of the evils of the free-labor system but also assurances that slavery spawned class harmony. From colonial times Southerners claimed that slavery united the interests of capital and labor through the master's direct ownership of labor. That is, the master's self-interest coincided with his sentimental attachment to those who lived within his extended household. They thus avoided the arrogance of claiming inherently superior Christian virtue and morality – of being innately better people than Northerners in the sight of God. They claimed, instead, that slave owning encouraged Christian behavior. Especially after the Missouri crisis, the notion of slavery as the unification of capital and labor pervaded southern society.

On the horrors of Russia and Eastern Europe see also T. R. R. Cobb, "Historical Sketch" in *An Inquiry into the Law of Negro Slavery* (New York, 1968 [1858]), especially cxvii; [R. S. Breck], "Duties of Masters," *SPR*, 8 (1855), 271; also *DD*, 4:293ff; "American Slavery in 1857," *SLM*, 25 (1857), 84–86; Frederick A. Ross, *Slavery Ordained of God* (Philadelphia, 1857), 67. An exception: W. C. Duncan described the Russian serfs as generally well treated: "The Empire of Russia – Part 2," *DBR*, 11 (1851), 561–562.

[32] Cobb, "Historical Sketch" in *Law of Negro Slavery*, especially xxxvi, cxvii–cxx, cxxxi–cxxxiii, ccxiv; chs. 1, 13, 14, and 17 discuss the special reasons for the enslavement of blacks. Cobb, brother of the politically powerful Howell Cobb and a devout and active Presbyterian layman, strongly invoked Scripture and, in fact, was regarded as something of a religious zealot by his friends. See, e.g., Linton Stephens to Alexander H. Stephens, April 5, 1858, in James D. Waddell, *Biographical Sketch of Linton Stephens, Containing a Selection of His Letters, Speeches, State Papers, Etc.* (Atlanta, Ga., 1877), 144. Mary Boykin Chesnut commented that Cobb was a good man but a religious fanatic: Mar. 9, 1861, in C. Vann Woodward, ed., *Mary Chesnut's Civil War* (New Haven, Conn., 1981), 21.

From the 1820s onward, prominent men – Dew, James Barbour, and M. R. H. Garnett of Virginia and R. J. Turnbull and Edwin C. Holland of South Carolina – proclaimed the happy consequences of masters' having to blend humanity with interest to promote the welfare of their slaves and thereby avoid class war. In 1858, J. L. M. Curry of Alabama, in his maiden speech to Congress, accused the abolitionists of undermining "social institutions" and extolled slavery for harmonizing the interests of labor and capital. Curry warned that the North faced riots and anarchy. In 1860 he reiterated: "Where slavery does not exist, the antagonism between labor and capital is everywhere felt." The Protestant Methodist Reverend Andrew A. Lipscomb, chancellor of the University of Georgia, ended a fast-day sermon to the state legislature by praising slavery: "And now, can capital and labor elsewhere show this advance in their inter-relations?" Dr. Richard D. Arnold, Mayor of Savannah and a prominent Unitarian layman, appealed for greater attention to the health of slaves, emphasizing the difference in the slaveholders' position relative to that of capitalists. "Servitude, as it exists with us, is the only institution in which Interests & Humanity go hand in hand together."[33]

In slightly different accents, J. T. Wiswall of Alabama spoke of the historical ubiquity of aristocracy and the slaveholding basis of the South's stable, aristocratic, conservative social order. Even Louisa McCord of South Carolina, a confirmed Manchesterian, stressed the personal interest of the slaveholder in his laborers, contrasting it with the indifference of the capitalist. And Elizabeth Randolph Preston Allan of Lexington, Virginia, said that she had never heard of or seen slaves mistreated, although she conceded the possibility of isolated cases. After the War, Edward A. Pollard blithely reiterated the claim that slavery united capital and labor. Bill Arp [Charles Henry Smith], Georgia's popular humorist, put it a bit differently: "The Anglo-Saxon race glories in owning men and it makes but little difference whether the men are their dependents or their slaves." Writing after the turn of the twentieth century, Arp linked big corporations and railroad kings with planters: "The glory is all the same if they have got them [workers] in their power."[34]

---

[33] James Barbour, "Address to the Agricultural Society of Albemarle," *American Farmer*, 7 (1825), 290; Turnbull quoted in [Holland], *Refutation of Calumnies*, 56; Thomas R. Dew, *Lectures on the Restrictive System, Delivered to the Senior Political Class of William and Mary College* (New York, 1969 [1829]), 10; [M. R. H. Garnett], *The Union, Past and Future: How It Works, and How to Save It*, 4th ed. (Charleston, S.C., 1850), 34–35; J. L. M. Curry, *Congressional Globe*, 35th Cong., 1st Sess. (Feb. 25, 1858), 819–820; Curry, "Perils and Duties of the South," in Jon L. Wakelyn, ed., *Southern Pamphlets on Secession*, Nov. 1860–April 1861 (Chapel Hill, N.C., 1996), 35–54; Andrew A. Lipscomb, *Substance of a Discourse Delivered before the Legislature of Georgia* (Milledgeville, Ga., 1860), 19–20; R. D. Arnold to Jacob McCall, Aug. 29, 1849, in Richard H. Shryock, ed., *Letters of Richard D. Arnold, M. D., 1808–1876* (Durham, N.C., 1929), 34.

[34] J. T. Wiswall, "Causes of Aristocracy," *DBR*, 28 (1860), 551–556; "Negro and White Slavery," in *Louisa S. McCord: Political and Social Essays*, ed. Richard C. Lounsbury (Charlottesville, Va., 1995), 192–193; Janet Allan Bryan, ed., *A March Past: Reminiscences of Elizabeth Randolph Preston Allan* (Richmond, Va., 1938), 80; Edward A. Pollard, *A New Southern History*

Edward Dicey, the prominent English journalist, wrote in 1860 that the slaveholders' transformation of labor into capital logically applied to whites as well as blacks: "This truth is obvious." Jefferson Davis habitually took racial ground in defense of slavery, yet in the U.S. Senate in 1848 he inadvertently rendered race marginal by asserting that southern slaves "bear the kindest relation that labor can sustain to capital" in "a paternal institution." Shortly thereafter he spoke more broadly: "The power to oppress dependents exists in all countries, and bad men everywhere abuse the power. In no relation in which labor bears to capital is such oppression better guarded against than in that of master and slave." Davis, for whom slavery breathed kindness, mused: "Slaves are capital, and, in the mind of the master, there can be no contest between capital and labor – the contest from which so much of human suffering has arisen." Davis challenged the antislavery William H. Seward of New York to admit, "Your menials are not your equals," and congratulated the South on having an inferior race to do the dirty work that Northerners compelled members of their own race to do. William Elliott, Sr. and Jr., editors of *Southern Review*, and Simms expressed sympathy for the plight of the British working class, as did Frederick Grimké, who added the French peasants. Simms and Senator R. M. T. Hunter of Virginia declared that if North and South came to blows, the South would have the advantage of not being torn by the social hatreds that besieged the North.[35]

In 1851 a contributor to *Southern Quarterly Review* pulled together leading strains of the argument for Slavery in the Abstract: "[Slavery] is sectional;

---

of the War of the Confederacy (New York, 1867), ch. 2; [Charles Henry Smith], *Bill Arp from the Uncivil War to Date, 1861–1903* (Electronic ed.; Chapel Hill, N.C.: 1998 [1903]), 48–49; also, "Choctaw," "Letter from Mississippi," *Mississippian and State Gazette*, Dec. 8, 1858.

   By the time M. R. H. Garnett was twenty-nine in 1851 – five years before his election to Congress – he was considered a rising star in Virginia politics: William A. Link, *Roots of Secession: Slavery and Politics in Antebellum Virginia* (Chapel Hill, N.C., 2003), 21. Adam L. Tate suggests that when John Taylor sought to produce contented and productive slaves by providing good food and living conditions, he was eschewing "benevolent paternalism" for economics. It seems to us, however, that Taylor advanced a version of the common southern insistence on the unity of humanity and interest: see Tate, *Conservatism and Southern Intellectuals, 1789–1861: Liberty, Tradition, and the Good Society* (Columbia, Mo., 2005), 109. For consequences of the slaveholders' loss of a material interest in their slaves and the transformation of paternalism after the War, see Peggy G. Hargis, "For the Love of Place: Paternalism and Patronage in the Georgia Lowcountry," *JSH*, 70 (2004), 825–864.

[35] Edward Dicey, *Labour and Slavery* (Ithaca, N.Y., 2006 (1860]), 8. In *JDP*, see remarks in the Senate: Apr. 20, 1848 (3:315); July 12, 1848 (3:355, 358); see also "Speech at Mississippi City," Oct. 2, 1857, in 6:147 and "Speech at Jackson," Nov. 4, 1857, in 6:158; "Reply to William H. Seward," Feb. 29, 1860, in *JDP*, 6:281; for Davis's insistence that black slavery rendered southern whites equal to each other in a manner unknown elsewhere, see, e.g., "Speech at Columbus, Miss.," Oct. 2, 1864, in 11:76; Frederick Grimké, *The Nature and Tendency of Free Institutions*, ed. John William Ward (Cambridge, Mass., 1968 [1848, 1856]), 128; [William Gilmore Simms], review of Augustus Baldwin Longstreet's *Voice of the South*, in "Critical Notes," *SQR*, 13 (1848), 262; "Speech of Mr. Hunter of Virginia," *National Intelligencer*, Feb. 14, 1860. On Simms and *SR*, see John R. Welsh, "An Early Pioneer: Legaré's Southern Review," *SLM*, 3 (1971), 79.

it is social; it has made a social basis the test of political ascendancy.... In addition to these it involves a question of race." Denouncing the condition of labor in Britain, he elaborated, "Labour lies at the foundation of all human organization." In the free-labor system, "Labour and capital are antagonistic," and in an unequal struggle, capital overwhelms labor: "The contest goes on unceasingly, and always to the disadvantage of the poor." The South has escaped this "inexorable law" because "*Where the labourer is capital*, the problem is solved." The South has "the best fed, best clad, best housed, best nursed labouring population on earth."[36]

The Divines Enter the Fray

Offering indispensable support to proslavery secular theorists, the divines advanced a "Bible argument" that buttressed the moral foundation not only of the slaveholders' worldview in general but of Slavery in the Abstract in particular. As Lincoln saw, the scriptural defense of slavery claimed too much: The Bible did not sanction racial slavery; it sanctioned slavery per se. Those who invoked the Noahic curse to prove the contrary ran into difficulty. By no means did all southern divines accept the racial interpretation of biblical slavery or identify the enslaved peoples of biblical times as black. Since the Bible sanctioned enslavement regardless of race, the Noahic curse, even if racially specific, merely placed blacks in a special case. That is, all blacks might be fit for slavery, but many whites were also. The most genuinely learned and honest southern divines read both Scripture and history as confirming God's sanction for the enslavement of whites as well as blacks. Many of the leading divines argued that since God had ordained slavery and indeed commanded the Israelites to enslave Canaanites and others, slavery would last indefinitely. In 1861 the Presbyterian Reverend J. C. Mitchell of Mobile, combining several themes, cited the Coolie trade and the disguised enslavement of laborers throughout the world as evidence of the ubiquity of slavery: "*Slavery in some form and to some extent, will continue unto the end of the world.*"[37]

It was one thing to argue that slavery would continue as one social relation among many but another to pronounce slavery the necessary and proper condition of labor. The first rendered the second theologically permissible without endorsing it as social policy. The divines had to move from theology to history, political economy, and moral and social philosophy. And secular moral and social philosophers moved to theology to justify their proposal to solve the social question by reenslaving the laboring classes. They,

---

[36] "Is Southern Civilization Worth Preserving?" *SQR*, n.s. 3 (1851), 189–225, quotes at 212, 217, 219–221.

[37] J. C. Mitchell, *A Bible Defense of Slavery and the Unity of Mankind* (Mobile, Ala., 1861), 13. Henry C. Sheldon stressed the southern divines' commitment to Slavery in the Abstract as late as 1895, when he published his *History of the Christian Church*, 5 vols. (Peabody, Mass., 1999 [1895]), 5:236.

too, refused to separate religion from society in either thought or action, but increasingly, they did so in a manner that horrified their strongest northern sympathizers.

Theologians, grounded in history and political economy, shaped the thought of the town and country preachers, who constituted a large – probably the largest – portion of the South's educators and exercised a determining influence over the educational system. Divines dominated the academies and old-field schools attended by slaveholders, as well as the Sabbath schools that provided rudimentary education for the yeomanry. They dominated secular as well as denominational colleges, and together with religiously committed laymen, they occupied almost all the chairs of history, political economy, and moral philosophy. They taught the elite and the parvenus of the political class, even if they learned history and political economy from Thomas Cooper, Thomas Roderick Dew, George Tucker, and others steeped in the work of Adam Smith, David Ricardo, Thomas Malthus, and Jean-Baptiste Say. Committed to laissez-faire policies, southern political economists saw capitalism as heading into either a Malthusian population crisis of fearful proportions or at least into a slow descent into the immiseration of the laboring classes under the impact of the so-called iron law of wages, the law of diminishing returns, and the steady accumulation of capital by fewer and fewer people. As students of the French Revolution and observers of great social struggles in Europe and, increasingly, in the North, the divines concluded that the laboring classes, rather than accept immiseration, would mount massive rebellions and initiate anarchy. The outcome: a Caesarism that destroyed liberty while offering protection and succor to the laborers to whom it appealed demagogically. The doctrine of Slavery in the Abstract resonated widely among ordinary slaveholders and nonslaveholders in no small part because leading theologians and country preachers supported one or another version.

It is written (Isaiah 1:15): "And when ye spread forth your hands, I will hide mine eyes from you: yea, when ye make many prayers, I will not hear: your hands are full of blood." In 1776 the Reverend Samuel Hopkins, pastor of the First Congregational Church in Newport, Rhode Island, and New Divinity theologian, delivered a sermon from that text, in which he denounced slavery, called for immediate abolition, and uttered a grave warning: "He that will Enslave an African would inslave an American if he could. He that will inslave one man would inslave all men if he had power" [*sic*]. By the mid-1830s, abolitionists were taking his warning to heart, challenging the southern clergy to deny that proslavery logic and policies pointed toward the enslavement of white labor, as well as black. James Gillespie Birney received reports from Northerners who settled in the slave states and came to accept the notion that laboring classes everywhere lived in some form of slavery. Harriet Beecher Stowe, in *Key to Uncle Tom's Cabin*, quoted the defense of slavery in the address of the Charleston Baptist Association to the South Carolina legislature in 1835: "The question, it is believed is purely one of political economy. It amounts, in effect, to this – Whether the operatives of a country shall be bought and sold, and themselves become property, as in this State; or whether they are to be hirelings, and their labor only become property, as in some other States." Stowe pounced on the Episcopal Reverend George W. Freeman of North Carolina for a proslavery tract that allowed for the enslavement of whites as well as blacks, and she rebuked the New England–born High Church Bishop Levi Silliman Ives of North Carolina for supporting Freeman.[38]

From the 1840s on, leading Presbyterians maintained unambiguously that the free-labor system and its social atomization threatened church and state with frightful isms, which slavery allowed the South to resist. The Reverend T. C. Thornton, president of Centenary College in Mississippi: "The history of slavery is but the history of Europe, and especially is it the history of England for all her boast of MAGNA CHARTA and British Liberty." The Reverend Samuel Cassells of South Carolina: "Yea, at this moment, the South is willing to challenge *the whole world*, to exhibit a laboring class less burdened, better provided for, or who enjoy more real happiness than the Africans who are, in the course of Providence, held slaves by her laws!" In 1850 the Reverend A. A. Porter praised Elwood Fisher's *North and South* for its exposé of northern pauperism and starvation. Porter – like Thornwell, Fisher, and Cassells – appealed to the laws of political economy to predict that the free-labor North would follow Europe into a massive social crisis. He told his congregation in Charleston that the South faced a North determined to destroy the very fabric of southern society: "It is a not a mere political contest – not a struggle with fanaticism, or a rivalry and contention for power. It is a conflict of systems – of two radically different and antagonistic forms of society."[39]

In 1850, *Southern Presbyterian Review* dryly affirmed class war inevitable in free-labor countries. In 1859 the Presbyterian Reverend John N. Waddell, a prominent educator, contrasted British free labor with southern slave labor. On the one side, "The factory operative, the half human miner in the coal pits, shut out from the light of day, and *crawling on all fours* harnessed to a coal car; or even of the pale and exhausted midnight clerk starving for fresh

---

[38] Jonathan D. Sassi, ed., "'This Whole Country Have Their Hands Full of Blood This Day': Transcription and Introduction of an Antislavery Sermon Manuscript Attributed to the Reverend Samuel Hopkins," *Proceedings of the American Antiquarian Society*, 112, Pt. 1 (2002), 92; James M. Buchanan to Birney, Feb. 7, 1836, in Dwight Lowell Dumond, ed., *Letters of James Gillespie Birney, 1831–1857*, 2 vols. (New York, 1938), 1:304–308; Harriet Beecher Stowe, *A Key to Uncle Tom's Cabin* (Washington, N.Y., 1968 [1853]), 385; see George W. Freeman, *The Rights and Duties of Slaveholders* (Raleigh, N.C., 1836). William Gilmore Simms understood Stowe's intention to throw the anticapitalist rhetoric of the Southerners back in their faces by identifying slavery with the evils of a marketplace run wild; he intended Woodcraft as a reply: see especially Lewis P. Simpson, *The Dispossessed Garden: Pastoral and History in Southern Literature* (Athens, Ga., 1975), 55–61.

[39] T. C. Thornton, *An Inquiry into the History of Slavery* (Washington, D.C., 1841), 20, and throughout; A. A. Porter, "North and South," *SPR*, 3 (1850), 348; A. A. Porter, *Our Danger and Duty* (Charleston, S.C., 1850), 8–11, quote at 11; S. J. Cassells, "Relation of Justice to Benevolence," *SPR*, 7 (1853), 91, and [S. J. Cassells], *Servitude and the Duty of Masters to Their Servants* (Norfolk, Va., 1843), 4–5.

air and exercise" caught in a "system of ceaseless toil, crushed and prostrated upon a sick-bed." On the other, "The Southern slave, moderately laboring during day-light, and left to his nine or ten hours of sleep at night, well clad, well fed, well nursed in sickness, kindly treated in health, whistling, shouting, singing, laughing for the very freedom from care, furnished with a decent and comfortable house of worship." The Reverend Benjamin M. Palmer of New Orleans – reputedly the highest paid minister in the South – pronounced slavery the solution to "this mighty conflict between capital and labor." Armstrong, replying to the antislavery New School Presbyterian Reverend Albert Barnes, stressed the slaves' cradle-to-grave security and the superiority of their living conditions over those of northern laborers.[40]

In 1855, Thornwell warned that both sides were playing loose with the issues: "A 'slaveholder' at the North is the very embodiment of evil, and an 'abolitionist' at the South an emissary of darkness. It is the trick of politicians to bandy epithets." Five years earlier he had protested that the North was hurling "every epithet of vituperation and abuse" against the South and that the abolitionists were overlooking "the evils which press around their own doors, the vices and crimes and sufferings of their own neighbours and countrymen." So long as the demand for labor outran the supply, the North would fare well, but the day of reckoning would come. In 1860 Thornwell affirmed that the South cherished slavery, which he characterized as simply a form of labor organization, "not from avarice, but from principle." He reiterated that whereas slavery protected its laborers, capital accumulation in free societies resulted in the lowest possible wage and generated insurrection and anarchy. With greater restraint, the Presbyterian Reverend Alonzo Church, president of University of Georgia, said of the North: "The social system is sadly disordered." And indeed, spurred by the Missouri agitation, southern clergymen assured their northern brethren that the slaveholders treated black slaves better than northern and European capitalists and landowners treated white laborers. By the next decade many committed antislavery ministers departed the South.[41]

---

[40] *SPR*, 3 (1850), 342; John N. Waddell, "The Lecture System – Its Influence upon Young Men," *SPR*, 12 (1859), 269–270; Palmer quoted by Stephen R. Haynes, *Noah's Curse: The Biblical Justification of American Slavery* (New York, 2002), 129; Armstrong, *Christian Doctrine of Slavery*, 92–93, and quote at the head of this chapter. See also William Hutson, "History of the Girondists," *SPR*, 2 (1848), 399–410. Armstrong became a special target of the Yankee occupiers for his proslavery writing, and when he refused to lead prayers for Lincoln, they threw him in jail.

[41] *JHTW*, 2:508, 4:400, 539–541; Alonzo Church, *A Discourse Delivered before the Georgia Historical Society, on the Occasion of Its Sixth Anniversary* (Savannah, Ga., 1845), 10. For the social question, the progress of humanity, and atheism, see "Slavery as a Moral Relation," *SLM*, 17 (1851), 405.

Thornwell, son of an overseer, was a towering figure in his own day, commanding admiration and respect even from adversaries. See especially James Oscar Farmer, Jr., *The Metaphysical Confederacy: James Henley Thornwell and the Synthesis of Southern Values* (Macon,

Among Baptists, the Reverend Patrick Mell of Georgia conceded that the North far outstripped the South in organizations for reform of public morals: "But then, they need them – and none more urgently than for the members of those societies themselves." The *Baptist Banner* in Kentucky, edited by the staunchly proslavery Reverend William C. Buck, remarked that in all ages and climes the strong have oppressed the weak and that only "some benevolent arrangement" can protect the poor and helpless. The Reverend Iveson Brookes of Georgia found slavery in existence everywhere, including in Europe where, disguised as free labor, it subjected workers to conditions worse than those endured by southern slaves: "Free and white, too, as it is boastingly called, is the fiction of abolition cant." At a debate in Cincinnati in 1846 the abolitionist Reverend J. Blanchard went for the jugular of the Reverend N. L. Rice: "Those who prove slavery to be sinless, prove it from the Bible – and the argument, if it proves anything, justifies the slavery of white people as well as black." Rice countered feebly that he opposed slavery and was discussing only its alleged sinfulness. Blanchard pressed on, quoting the reply of the *Alabama Baptist* to a newspaper editor in Vermont who had accused southern clergymen of being as rabid in the defense of slavery as fire-eating politicians. The *Alabama Baptist* returned the fire: "He says we endorse the sentiment of George McDuffie – 'slavery is the best *possible* relation between the employer and the laborer' and 'We repudiate that *old-fashioned* doctrine, that all MEN are born equal.' THIS IS EXACTLY OUR POSITION."[42]

The Reverend Thornton Stringfellow of Virginia became the most widely read proslavery Baptist. Without conceding that he accepted the enslavement of whites or explicitly endorsing Slavery in the Abstract, he preached its essentials. Maintaining that in New England one family in seven was homeless, Stringfellow accused free-labor societies of undermining the family by denying proper housing to laborers: "No right-minded man or woman, who had the means, could ever consent to have a family without a home; and no State should make wealth her boast, whose families are extensively without homes." Inveighing against the squalor, prostitution, and insecurity of the laboring classes of New England, especially the more than 30,000 paupers, Stringfellow ridiculed those

Ga., 1986). In 1847, Thornwell at age thirty-four became the youngest moderator of a National Assembly in the history of the Presbyterian Church. Southern contemporaries referred to him as "the Calhoun of the Church" – a description his enemies in the northern Presbyterian Church doubtless accepted without intending a compliment.

42 [Patrick Mell], *Slavery. A Treatise, Showing that Slavery Is Neither a Moral, Political, nor Social Evil* (Pennfield, Ga., 1844), 27; William C. Buck, *The Slavery Question* (Louisville, Ky., 1849), 13 (pamphlet version of articles in *Baptist Banner*); Iveson L. Brookes, *A Defence of the South against the Reproaches of the North* (Hamburg, S.C., 1850), 12, 45–46; Iveson L. Brookes, *A Defence of Slavery against the Attacks of Henry Clay and Alex'r Campbell* (Hamburg, S.C., 1851), 22; J. Blanchard and N. L. Rice, *A Debate on Slavery* (New York, 1969 [1846]), 17, 358. *Alabama Baptist*, launched in 1835, continued under various titles until 1865: see Rhoda Coleman Ellison, *Early Alabama Publications: A Study in Literary Interests* (University, Ala., 1947), 89.

who laid responsibility upon ignorant and vicious immigrants: "These foreigners are all from non-slaveholding countries. From their infancy they have shared the blessings of freedom and free institutions."[43]

The increasingly strong Disciples of Christ embraced pro- and antislavery men. Alexander Campbell, the Disciples' leader, became cautiously antislavery, but the Reverend James Shannon, an accomplished theologian, embraced Slavery in the Abstract along with Calhoun's political theory. A fine classical scholar trained at the University of Belfast, Shannon migrated to the United States in the 1820s and served for a time as professor of ancient languages at the University of Georgia and successively as president of the College of Louisiana, Bacon College in Kentucky, the University of Missouri, and Christian University in Missouri. During the 1850s he became a center of controversy for his militant speeches and debates with antislavery men. Shannon created a furor by calling on the South to risk civil war if the North refused to respect slavery. In a paper, "The Philosophy of Slavery as Identified with the Philosophy of Human Happiness," he praised slavery as a superior social system that recognized the fundamental inequality of human beings: "Some are incapable of making proper use of freedom." For such people, "Bondage is a blessing, and freedom an unmitigated calamity." In 1849, stressing racial slavery and the Noahic Curse, he contented himself with the usual comparison between black slave labor and white free labor: "Indeed, it may fairly be questioned, whether there exists on the face of the globe a laboring population of the same extent as happy and as well provided for in all respects as the slaves in the United States." In 1855 he went further:

This relation, when properly contemplated, is much more independent, dignified and endearing than that of the hireling. There is an identity of interest, and there frequently is, and always should be, one of sympathy, between master and slave; but no such identity exists between master and hireling.... The slave is, therefore, independent and happy. Not so the poor hireling, who is wholly dependent on his daily labor for his daily bread.[44]

---

[43] Stringfellow, "Statistical View of Slavery," in Elliott, ed., *Cotton Is King*, 529–533. Stringfellow, who owned about thirty slaves, insisted that black slaves were better satisfied with their condition than the white lower classes were satisfied with theirs: *Slavery: Its Origin, Nature, and History, Considered in the Light of Bible Teachings, Moral Justice, and Political Wisdom* (New York, 1861), 5. George Sawyer picked up Stringfellow's taunt about the origins of New England's dangerous classes in free societies: *Southern Institutes*, 366; see also B. F. Stringfellow of Missouri, *Negro-Slavery, No Evil; or the North and the South* (St. Louis, Mo., 1854), 23. Samuel M. Janney of Virginia, an outspoken antislavery Quaker, in a reply to Thornton Stringfellow, denied that Virginians supported Slavery in the Abstract: Patricia Hickin, "Gentle Agitator: Samuel M. Janney and the Antislavery Movement in Virginia, 1842–1851," *JSH*, 37 (1971), 159–190, esp. 168.

[44] [Alexander Campbell], "Our Position on American Slavery," *Millennial Harbinger*, 2 (1845), 195, 234; James Shannon, *The Philosophy of Slavery as Identified with the Philosophy of Human Happiness* (Frankfort, Ky., 1849), 9, 17; James Shannon, *An Address ... on Domestic Slavery* (St. Louis, Mo., 1855), 16–17; David Edwin Harrell, Jr., *A Social History of the Disciples of Christ. Vol. 1, Quest for a Christian America: The Disciples of Christ and American Society*

From the 1830s both the theologically liberal and orthodox took a hard line on slavery and social order. The Episcopal Reverend James Warley Miles, the most prominent theological liberal in the Southeast, preferred racial to class grounds. He staunchly defended slavery and cast a jaundiced eye on the materialism of bourgeois social relations. Miles strove mightily to reconcile science with Christianity. He advanced racial arguments drawn from "nature." Flirting with scientific racism, he distinguished between the "natural" inferiority of blacks, which fitted them for slavery, and circumstances that might condemn whites – who had the capacity to lift themselves – to slavery in time and place. Miles allowed that appeals to Scripture and history justified slavery per se and not merely black slavery. Miles opened his lecture "The Relation between the Races at the South" by declaring that the southern states had launched the Confederacy "to preserve the great principles of constitutional free government, in contradistinction to the despotism of the sectional rule of a majority," and he added, "to protect the equitable relation between capital and labor which at present exists in the Southern States, to the manifest benefit of both the white and black races." He later opposed arming the slaves, remarking, "The abolition of slavery in the South would deprive us of the great conservative element in our institutions, and we would rapidly run into the worst of all political conditions – an utter democracy."[45]

Another theological liberal, the Virginia–New School Presbyterian Reverend Frederick A. Ross of East Tennessee and then Alabama, stood out as the author of *Slavery Ordained of God*, a militant defense of slavery that implicitly endorsed Slavery in the Abstract. An enthusiastic Ross invited wrathful replies when, among his polemical swipes, he credited Christian restraint as solely responsible for keeping wives from being their husband's slaves. Hermann Bokum, an East Tennessee unionist, protested the preaching of Ross and other clergymen who anointed slavery as the indispensable foundation of a Christian social order and of political freedom.[46]

Theologically liberal Unitarians helped to radicalize proslavery thought. In 1835 the *United States Telegraph* published a five-column review of a sermon by the Unitarian Reverend Charles A. Farley of Richmond, Virginia, in which he rhetorically asked, "Of what use would be freedom to a man who would starve amidst plenty?" The startling appearance of the Reverend Theodore Clapp of

to 1866 (Nashville, Tenn., 1966), 122–126, Shannon quoted at 122–123; also Harrell, "James Shannon: Preacher, Educator, and Fire-Eater," *Missouri Historical Review*, 63 (1969), 135–170; W. C. Rogers, *Recollections of Men of Faith, Containing Conversations with Pioneers of the Current Reformation* (St. Louis, Mo., 1889), 17–18. See also Franc M. Carmac, a twenty-year-old Disciples minister and unionist, Diary, Sept. 30, 1852.

45 [James Warley Miles], *The Relation between the Races at the South* (Charleston, S.C., 1861), 3, 5–7, 9, 19.

46 Frederick A. Ross, *Slavery Ordained of God* (Philadelphia, 1857), especially 26 and 53–55 for wives; Hermann Bokum, *The Testimony of a Refugee from East Tennessee* (Electronic ed.; Chapel Hill, N.C., 1998 [1863]), 11–12; also Charles C. Ross, ed., *The Story of Rothwood, from the Autobiography of Rev. Frederick A. Ross, D. D.* (Knoxville, Tenn., 1923), 7.

New Orleans as a proslavery militant eclipsed such tame observations by cautious Unitarians. A transplanted Northerner who became the most prestigious
Unitarian minister in the Southwest, Clapp had been a popular Presbyterian
minister who had a stormy time because of his liberal theology. He provoked
fellow Presbyterians by announcing a God of love who need not be feared. In
a few words he acknowledged just how far he had departed from Calvinism:
"I cannot love a God who would permit an absolute evil; I cannot love a God,
who, having the power, would not prevent an absolute evil." Before long, he
stretched just about every tenet of Calvinism until it broke. Meanwhile, denying all charges, he asserted his orthodoxy. Clapp outraged the orthodox by
claiming that atheists could be moral men destined for salvation. Befriending
and working with Catholic priests and nuns, he risked his life to attend the
sick during the frequent and terrible epidemics in New Orleans when some
Protestant ministers ran for cover. His tolerance, courage, and lively preaching
made him a local favorite and commanded loyalty, and most of his parishioners followed him into the Unitarian fold. And there were those like Henry
Hughes who did not abandon Presbyterianism but attended Clapp's sermons
regularly. In theology and even in some of his social views Clapp ranked as an
extreme liberal. But he, too, thought that the laboring classes would be better
off under some form of slavery, and, appealing to Cicero's doctrine of natural
law, he contended that slavery promoted the happiness and best interests of the
enslaved. In the 1830s theologically liberal clergymen like Clapp joined their
theologically conservative counterparts like the Baptist Basil Manly in preaching from New Orleans to Charleston that European laborers and peasants,
especially women and children, lived on the edge of starvation, suffering much
worse privation than southern slaves did.[47]

Visiting England in the late 1840s, Clapp forced himself on Thomas Carlyle,
who expressed pleasure at assurances that southern slaves were well treated
and content. Clapp quoted the late Reverend Sylvester Larned, his predecessor
as pastor in New Orleans, as denouncing the hypocrisy of those who preached
to the poor and the afflicted but did little to allay their earthly miseries. For
Clapp, acknowledgment that the poor are always with us constituted no excuse
for ignoring them, and he worked especially hard on behalf of the rivermen
and sailors. Long convinced that God-ordained slavery had existed everywhere
and in all ages, he explained in his "Autobiographical Sketches" that he had
left New England for the South full of antislavery prejudices. Those who had
directed his education seemed unaware that "in the most civilized nations of

---

[47] *United States Telegraph*, Nov. 19, 1835; Theodore Clapp, *Slavery: A Sermon* (New Orleans,
La., 1838), 5, 42–50; Clapp quoted by George Rogers, *Memoranda of the Experience, Labors,
and Travels of a Universalist Preacher, Written by Himself* (Cincinnati, Oh., 1845), 250; Harold
Wilson, "Basil Manly, Apologist for Slaveocracy," *Alabama Review*, 15 (1962), 47. "Diary of
Henry Hughes," in Stephen Berry, ed., *Princes of Cotton: Four Diaries of Young Men in the
South, 1848–1860* (Athens, Ga., 2007), 212, 256; Clapp had northern admirers. An agricultural
editor in Philadelphia, for one, enthusiastically recommended his autobiography, dissociating
himself only from its religious views: *American Farmer's Magazine*, 11 (1858), 118.

antiquity three-fourths, at least, of their inhabitants were disfranchised, and doomed through life to endure the evils of a slavery vastly more aggravated than that which now exists in any part of the world." Shocked and dismayed at the condition of the urban and rural laboring poor in Great Britain, he congratulated southern slaveholders on their sympathy for the laborers in their charge.[48]

The Reverend William A. Smith of Virginia – floor leader for the southern contingent at the national meeting that split the Methodist Church in 1844 – provided an especially arresting example of church leaders who tried to fudge the question of Slavery in the Abstract. Smith exerted considerable influence in Virginia, where his prominence as an educator matched his prominence as a Methodist theologian and church leader. Among other accomplishments, he built Randolph-Macon College into a solid institution after inheriting a financial disaster. His success stemmed in part from his personal attention to students. In 1856, as president of Randolph-Macon College, he published lectures for his class on moral philosophy as *Lectures on the Philosophy and Practice of Slavery*. Preferring racial ground, Smith struggled to avoid the larger question. He nonetheless referred contemptuously to "the so-called free states" and described Nat Turner's revolt as a "trifling affair" in comparison with the social unrest and violence in the free-labor countries. He began: "The position I propose to maintain in these lectures is, that slavery *per se*, is right; or that the great abstract principle of slavery is right, because it is a fundamental [principle] of the social state; and that domestic slavery, as an *institution*, is fully justified by the condition and circumstances (essential and relative) of the African race in this country, and therefore equally right." Assailing Jefferson's egalitarianism, Smith described southern "domestic slavery" as one form of "the *general* system of slavery," which consisted in "*submission or subjection* to the will of another" and included British villeinage, Russian serfdom, and Mexican peonage. Moving beyond racial argument, he predicted that the United States would follow Europe into manufacturing and urbanization, with all its social evils, including the formation of "a distinct class of menial poverty." Smith issued the customary words of comfort – since the South has black slaves, it had no need for white – but he immediately ran into trouble, for he defended southern slavery as a Christianizing process to prepare blacks for emancipation and transportation to an Africa they would help to civilize.[49]

According to Smith's reasoning, white labor would eventually have to replace black labor in the South. Smith had already upheld slavery as right in principle; analytically assimilated serfdom, peonage, and other forms of

---

[48] Theodore Clapp, "Sermons," *New Orleans Daily Picayune*, Mar. 19, 1848, Mar. 25, June 24, 1849; John Duffy, ed., *Parson Clapp of the Strangers' Church of New Orleans* (Baton Rouge, La., 1957), 149–151, 158, 166–167.

[49] J. C. Granberry, "Rev. William A. Smith, D. D.," in William T. Smithson, ed., *In Memoriam* (New York, 1971), 40–41; William A. Smith, *Lectures on the Philosophy and Practice of Slavery* (Nashville, Tenn., 1856), 11–13, 18, 40, 262, quotes at 13, 40, 18 (Turner), 11–12.

personal servitude to slavery; viewed economic development as creating dangerous menial classes; and held that laborers fared much better as slaves than as wage-workers. What, then, except some version of Slavery in the Abstract, offered a Christian alternative to social catastrophe? Identifying black inferiority as the issue at hand, Smith repeatedly betrayed awareness of the logical outcome of his formulations. As enslaved peoples progressed morally, he argued, their bondage should loosen. He supported proposed reforms of the slave system that pointed toward a variety of serfdom. He expected Irish and other immigrants to replace emancipated blacks, bringing with them all the evils of the dreaded social question, yet, "No communities on earth are as free from domestic insurrections, and the disturbing influences which come up from the lower orders of society as those of the Southern States." In February 1861, Smith took off the gloves in an address to a large meeting at the Mechanics Institute in Richmond. He drew a vivid contrast between the condition of white labor in North and South, referring to northern workers as quasi-slaves. Competition in the North, he claimed, pitted four or five workers against each other for every available job and drove men into menial labor that no white man would perform in the South. Smith had come a long way since the Methodist split over slavery in 1844, when he restricted himself to constitutional and legal grounds on behalf of the southern wing of the Church.[50]

In 1845, Henry Bidleman Bascom, future Methodist bishop, similarly had tried to distance himself from proslavery and remain on constitutional and legal ground. He proved so mushy that Hammond refused to review his book and poured out his wrath in private correspondence. Yet, when Bascom discussed the place of slavery in world history and contemporary affairs, he lashed out at the British, accusing them of fostering disguised slavery in every part of their empire: "Who can help seeing that the fetters were struck from eight hundred thousand negroes, in the West Indies, only to be fastened upon as many European sufferers, of the labouring classes at home.... Plainly, the millions of the common mass of England and Ireland, are more truly slaves, than the Negroes of our Southern states." Equating serfs with slaves, he referred to forty million enslaved Russians and added countless souls in central and southern Europe. Slavery, he concluded, existed in biblical times and remained the prevalent labor system of the world. The Methodist Reverend H. N. McTyeire of Tennessee spoke more openly in an essay that won a prize offered by an interdenominational committee in Alabama in 1849 and republished a decade

---

[50] Smith, *Philosophy and Practice of Slavery*, 17–18, also 53–54; William A. Smith, "The Relations of Capital to Labor, and of Slavery to the Workingmen and Non-Slaveholders, as Called Forth by the Present Crisis," as reported in *Richmond Daily Dispatch*, Feb. 4, 1861; also, Gross Alexander, et al., *A History of the Methodist Church, South* (New York, 1894), 34. The leading southern Methodist journal agreed that southern slaves were better off than "the hireling population of the Eastern or the Western continent": see "Rivers' Elements of Moral Philosophy," *QRMCS*, 14 (1860), 187. For reports from *New York Observer* on horrible factory conditions in Europe, especially child labor, see "The American Factory System," *QRMCS*, 2 (1848), 486–487.

later. McTyeire called the conflict between labor and capital "the conflict of ages," marked by the oppressive superior strength of capital and rebellions by labor. Under the free-labor system: "Capital seeks its own, heartlessly grinding down the laborer to the lowest terms," whereas under slavery, "capital and labor are one and the same thing." And the Methodist Reverend W. J. Sasnett of Georgia, a self-styled "progressive" professor of political economy at Emory College, wrote that a dense population meant class war, demagogy, and tyranny, which America's free land would stave off but only for so long. He presented slavery as a God-ordained social order based on a frank recognition of inequality among men.[51]

John England, the great Catholic bishop of Charleston, did not endorse Slavery in the Abstract – no Catholic leader did – but he offered comfort to its advocates. In 1832, England "laid down as a maxim that no greater moral evil could be brought upon any country than the introduction of slavery," but he doubted that any country in which slavery became deeply embedded could easily or safely discard it. Prominent proslavery writers drew on Bishop England's work, attesting to his credentials as a reliable guide to the history of slavery and much else. Like the Protestant divines, he assigned slavery to the things that are Caesar's, characterizing it as a problem of social policy, not of religious principle. He reflected on the relation of slavery to the conditions of the laboring classes in general: "No labouring people upon the face of the globe have, comparatively speaking, less severe tasks, or greater physical comforts. The general treatment of the negroes in the diocese of Charleston is kind and affectionate; far, very far more so than the bulk of the Irish agricultural or other labourers." In 1829 he rebuked his friend Daniel O'Connell: "I pray you might succeed in raising the ruined population of Ireland to the level of the comforts of the Carolinian slave." England described himself as no friend to slavery, but, "When it can and ought to be abolished is a question for the legislature and not for me." But since life was more precious than liberty, slavery had advantages over free labor in guaranteeing food, clothing, and shelter. During the secession crisis, Bishop Augustine Verot of Florida – a doctrinal liberal in Catholic context – picked up the relay: Slavery offered the laboring classes "a certainty which many distressed and starving families in Europe and in the larger cities of America, would indeed appreciate highly." He contrasted the contented and cheerful slaves of the South with the gloomy and sullen white proletarians of Europe and the North and saw no reason for the South to apologize for its social relations. Bishop Francis P. Kenrick of Philadelphia, future archbishop of Baltimore, matched Bishop England's qualified defense of

---

[51] For the exchange between Hammond and Calhoun over Bascom's book, see Fox-Genovese and Genovese, *Mind of the Master Class*, 476–477; H. N. McTyeire, *Duties of Christian Masters*, ed. Thomas O. Summers (Nashville, Tenn., 1859), 74; W. J. Sasnett, "The United States – Her Past and Her Future," *DBR*, 12 (1852), 626–627; William J. Sasnett, *Progress: Considered with Particular Reference to the Methodist Episcopal Church, South*, ed. T. O. Summers (Nashville, Tenn., 1855), ch. 1.

slavery in his *Theologia Moralis*. He regretted that slavery existed but upheld it as a civil institution that required obedience to the law. Meanwhile, the Catholic bishops rejected the notion of slavery as a divine institution and specifically condemned the southern Presbyterians' support for that doctrine.[52]

Divines who tried to avoid direct confrontation with Slavery in the Abstract repeatedly tripped over themselves. The Presbyterian Reverend John Adger, a protégé of Thornwell and sometime missionary to the Near East, said that Southerners did not advocate or promote any such doctrine – that they had not investigated, much less decided whether slavery should become a universal system. Yet his own writings embraced the logic of Slavery in the Abstract:

It may have occurred to many of us, a thousand times, that equal rights to equal things for all men, is neither a possible nor a desirable form of the social state; that all communities have actually to use the involuntary labor of most classes of their people; that capital and labor are constantly carrying on their mutual struggle in every country; and that in our Northern States there are likely to arise some very peculiar embarrassments and dangers to the peace and safety of society, as soon as capital and labor have both grown somewhat bigger and stronger, and the war between these now infant giants shall have begun to be carried on in earnest; but certainly we have not undertaken to decide how these States should regulate these affairs of their own. [The South] never has meddled with such questions, because not pertaining to her.[53]

Neither could the more reticent Episcopalians escape the logic of the proslavery argument. In the mid-1830s, the northern-born Reverend Jasper Adams, president of the College of Charleston, who had seen the social fruits of industrialization firsthand in Massachusetts, tore into the exploitation of child and female labor: "Manufacturing establishments are unfavorable to health and length of life. This is to be ascribed to the severity of the confinement of the inmates, to the impure atmosphere which they breathe, to their want of opportunities for exercise, and, above all, to their being kept from the enjoyment and the invigorating influence of the open air." Discussing the ramifications of capital accumulation, Adams argued that industrial capitalism tended "to make

---

[52] John England, "A Brief Account of the Introduction of the Catholic Religion," in G. Messmer, ed., *The Works of the Right Rev. John England, First Bishop of Charleston*, 7 vols. (Cleveland, Oh., 1908), 3:257–258; England quoted and commented upon in E. S. Abdy, *Journal of Residence and Tour in the United States of North America*, 3 vols. (New York, 1969 [1835]), 3:216, 3:118; Michael V. Gannon, *Rebel Bishop: The Life and Era of Agustin Verot* (Milwaukee, Wisc., 1964), 31–34, Verot quoted at 40–44. For Kenrick, see R. R. Duncan, "Catholics and the Church in the Antebellum Upper South," in Randall M. Miller and Jon L. Wakelyn, eds., *Catholics in the Old South: Essays on Church and Culture* (Macon, Ga., 1983), 87–88. On Albert T. Bledsoe, see John B. Bennett, "Albert Taylor Bledsoe: Transitional Philosopher of the Old South," *Methodist History*, 11 (1972), 12; "Bledsoe," 192; John Fletcher, *Studies on Slavery*, 259, 267, 299, and "Study IV"; George Frederick Holmes, "Observations on a Passage from Aristotle Relative to Slavery," *SLM*, 16 (1850), 193–205; Cobb, "Historical Sketch," in *Law of Negro Slavery*, cix; John Henry Hopkins, *A Scriptural, Ecclesiastical, and Historical View of Slavery from the Days of the Patriarch Abraham to the Nineteenth Century* (New York, 1864), chs. 27–28.

[53] [John Adger], "The Revival of the Slave Trade," *SPR*, 11 (April, 1858), 103–104.

the rich richer, and the poor poorer: "A manufacturing population is divided into capitalists and labourers, owners and operatives – the former class generally small in number, and wealthy; the latter numerous, poor, and depressed. The laborers receive little, if any thing, more than a scanty subsistence, while it is in the nature of capital to augment itself." He judged the free-labor system "highly unfavorable to intellectual, moral, and social improvement." Some twenty years later, in March 1859, the editors of the *Southern Episcopalian* (Charleston) called slavery "a necessary element towards the composition of a high and stable civilization – as a thing good in itself,...the best mode in which labor and capital can stand associated."[54]

The War brought a spate of pertinent sermons and discourses. Calvin H. Wiley of North Carolina, a prominent educational reformer and Presbyterian layman, maintained that subjected peoples seek to flatter their oppressors but that for southern slaves, "The great and obvious means of pleasing the master is to be faithful to his interest," thereby guaranteeing the security of the household. Slaveholders and their apologists took Wiley's notion for granted. In 1861 the Baptist Reverend E. T. Winkler told the Moultrie Guards in Charleston that unlike antislavery Northerners, Southerners did not seek to array capital against labor. The Methodist Reverend John T. Wightman said, "The workmen of the North are drifting into agrarian licentiousness.... There is no reserve power in the hands of conservative masses to check and balance these extremes." In 1862 the bishops of the Episcopal Church issued a Pastoral Letter that described the labor systems of Europe "in many respects, more severe [than] our own," although less likely to separate families. After the War, Bishop Richard Wilmer of Alabama reiterated that the slaves of his native Virginia had fared much better than European workers and that the world had never seen a system in which laborers received fairer treatment. Southern slavery "presented the justest and fairest condition of society that I have ever seen or read of." It had "solved the most difficult question in political economy." For spice, Bishop Alexander Gregg of Texas echoed Thornwell's attack on the abolitionists as anarchists and communists. Even J. A. Lyon's wartime "Report to the General Assembly of the Presbyterian Church," which called for a humane revision of the slave codes, denounced "the mere hireling relation between master and servant, misnamed 'free labor.'" Southerners, it continued, combined the interests of capital and labor. Presbyterians carried the theme forward beyond the War.[55]

54 Jasper Adams, *Elements of Moral Philosophy* (Philadelphia, Pa., 1837), 362; *Southern Episcopalian*, quoted in Walter J. Fraser, Jr., *Charleston! Charleston! The History of a Southern City* (Columbia, S.C., 1989), 241.
55 "A Practical Treatise: On the Duties of Christians Owning Slaves" (ms.), Ch. 2:53, in Calvin H. Wiley Papers, UNC (Wiley entered the clergy after the War); E. T. Winkler, *The Duties of the Citizen Soldier* (Charleston, 1861), 9; John T. Wightman, *The Glory of God, the Defence of the South* (Charleston, 1861), 8; for the Lyon Report see SPR, 16 (July, 1863), 1–37; William A. Hall, *Historic Significance of the Southern Revolution* (Petersburg, Va., 1864); William A. Clebsch, ed., *Journals of the Protestant Episcopal Church in the Confederate States of*

As the War went badly, the preachers reiterated the message, if anything more forcefully. The Baptist Reverend J. J. D. Renfroe of Alabama, preaching to Confederate troops in August 1863, described himself as a poor man whose family had never owned slaves and who, on that account, had an even stronger attachment to slavery than the slaveholders did. Arguing that if the South did not have black slaves, it would have to reduce white laborers to practical slavery, he implored the troops to remember that poor men must depend upon employment by the rich: "In our country, color is the distinction of classes – the only real distinction." In the North, as in Europe, white laborers were virtual slaves. With emancipation, the laws of the market would drive the cost of labor to rock bottom and generate white slavery. The Baptist Reverend Isaac Taylor Tichnor told his congregation in Montgomery, Alabama, that God instituted slavery as "the best form of human society." God thereby "solved the great problem which had baffled the wisdom of man – reconciled the long conflict of capital and labor, thus giving social order and peace to the world, never again to be disturbed by the insane fanaticism of men." The Presbyterian Reverend W. A. Hall preached to Confederate troops in Virginia in 1864 that since the South had a menial class of racially inferior slaves, it faced no tumults and insurrections.[56]

With the collapse of the Confederacy, the intrepid Dabney charged that immigrants had brought to the North "the radicalism, discontent, crime, and poverty of Europe," and that "the Northern States became, like the rabble of Imperial Rome, the *colluvies gentium*." Northerners had become a people who mistook license for liberty and were turning Britain into a democracy, enthroning Red Republicanism in France, and giving "the crowns of Germany to the Pantheistic humanitarians of that race." After the War, Dabney explained that Virginians just wanted to be left alone: "We had no desire to force it on others, or to predict universal prevalence, as the best organization of society." Dabney then sang the praises of slavery as a superior form of social organization, noting the Parliamentary Reports and other evidence of a savage form of slavery among British colliers. He argued that the free-labor system necessarily impoverished the laboring classes, whereas slavery's unification of labor and capital generated a socially sound and moral result: "[Slavery] answered the question raised by the gloomy speculations of Malthus, at whom all anti-slavery

America (Austin, Tex., 1962), Pt. 3, 227; Richard H. Wilmer, *The Recent Past from a Southern Standpoint: Reminiscences of a Grandfather* (New York, 1887), 45, 222. For Gregg, see James Marten, *Texas Divided: Loyalty and Dissent in the Lone Star State, 1856–1874* (Lexington, Ky., 1990), 54. For the southern divines' identification of abolitionism with communism in general, see Donald G. Mathews, *Slavery and Methodism: A Chapter in American Morality, 1780–1845* (Princeton, N.J., 1965), 239.

[56] J. J. D. Renfroe, *"The Battle Is God's": A Sermon Preached before Wilcox's Brigade* (Richmond, Va., 1863), 9–10, 18, 19, quote at 18, and on Renfroe, see B. F. Riley, *History of the Baptists of Alabama from the Time of Their First Occupation of Alabama in 1808, until 1894* (Birmingham, Ala., 1895); I. T. Tichenor, *Fast-Day Sermon* (Montgomery, Ala., 1863), 13; Hall, *Historic Significance of the Southern Revolution*, 38.

philosophers have only been able to rail, while equally impotent to overthrow his premises, or to arrest the evils he predicts." Slavery enabled Virginia "to resist and repair the evils of over-population, vastly better than any other form of labour." For Dabney, slavery – abstracted from the race question on which he preferred to dwell – had given the world a Christian labor system that solved the painful problems created by the free-labor system.[57]

The end of the War did not bring an end to the insistence of prominent ministers on the necessity for some form of personal servitude or on the superiority of slavery as a social system that protected workers against the ravages of the marketplace. Attacking the "pestilent heresy" of abolitionism in 1867, Wilmer, in a memorial sermon on Bishop Stephen Elliott, claimed that the slaves had had a better standard of living than any comparable class of laborers in the world: "The Southern system had solved the most difficult problem in political economy." Elliott himself had viewed society as divided into laboring and thinking classes and upheld the slaveholders' right to rule. The Methodist Reverend R. H. Rivers of Wesleyan University in Alabama and the Presbyterian Reverend Benjamin Morgan Palmer confronted the issue when discretion might have called for silence. Rivers, who had defended slavery vigorously in his *Elements of Moral Philosophy* (1859), revised his discussion of the relation of capital to labor in the editions of 1872 and 1883. The definitive end of slavery, he wrote, challenged capitalists to find a way to bestow paternalistic protection to their laborers. They wanted to pay the lowest possible wages but had to accept moral responsibilities. Palmer bade "Servants" to understand that their interests corresponded to those of their "masters": "In some one of its many forms, servitude is a permanent relation in all the conditions of human society." Servitude, "evolving itself from the curse of labour, is simply one of those adjustments of Divine Providence by which the poor find relief from the pressure of their necessities."[58]

In the 1890s Dabney pondered the rise of labor unions, populism, and spreading social disorder. Never one to straddle, he had difficulty in figuring out what to do. Still reeling from the Paris Commune of 1871, he condemned labor unions for denying strikebreakers the right to work and for fruitless efforts to forget that labor is a commodity subject to the laws of supply and demand. Sympathizing with the plight of farmers, he denounced populism as a prelude to communism, the worst form of slavery, and denounced paternalistic

[57] R. L. Dabney, *Life and Campaigns of Lt. Gen T. J. (Stonewall) Jackson* (Harrisonburg, Va., 1983 [1865]), 159–160; Robert L. Dabney, *Defence of Virginia (and through Her of the South) in Recent and Pending Contests against the Sectional Party* (New York, 1969 [1867]), esp. 66–67, 295, 303ff, 307.

[58] Richard H. Wilmer, *In Memoriam: A Sermon in Commemoration of the Life and Labors of the Rt. Rev. Stephen Elliott* (Mobile, Ala., 1967), 12, 18; Virgil Sims Davis, "Stephen Elliott: A Southern Bishop in Peace and War" (Ph.D. diss., University of Georgia, 1964), 164; R. H. Rivers, *Elements of Moral Philosophy* (1st ed., Nashville, Tenn., 1859), ch. 6 of Pt. 2, and 347–349, of the 1871 and 1883 editions; B. M. Palmer, *The Family, in Its Civil and Churchly Aspects. An Essay in Two Parts* (Richmond, Va., 1876), 124.

theories of government. He approved cooperatives to regulate distribution, although he thought programs to regulate production could not work. He saw tyranny ahead and displayed much of his old hatred for big corporations. What to do? Dabney had no answer. But one thing he knew: Plantation slavery had provided a humane social system and nothing had proven superior.[59]

"Cast out the Beam"

Proslavery Southerners, pleased by their own righteousness, professed puzzlement: Why did Britons fret about the slaves of the South instead of relieving the oppression of their own poor? They recalled the words of Jesus: "Thou hypocrites, first cast out the beam out of thine own eye, and then shalt thou see clearly to cast out the mote out of thy brother's eye" (Matthew 7:5). Southern slavery, Wiswall wrote, stood as the most effective system for reining in those who would destroy liberties they themselves were unfit to exercise.[60]

In the 1840s, the southern-born Eliza Middleton Fisher of Philadelphia corresponded with Mary Herring Middleton of the South Carolina low country, who had grown up in England and spent the 1820s in Russia while her husband served as American minister. Fisher wrote that William Wilberforce and others of the "Clapham Sect" meant well but lacked knowledge of the slavery they denounced and should direct their "philanthropy" toward abolition of "the real Slavery of their own countrymen in Engd." The Presbyterian Reverend T. C. Thornton of Mississippi, taunting British abolitionists for lack of sympathy for their own poor, railed against the brutal quasi-slavery in British India. A few years later, in *Southern and Western Literary Monthly Magazine and Review* of Richmond, Samuel Henry Dickson of Charleston, noting British oppression of India and the crushing of China, cited Dickens, Eugene Sue, and other novelists on the miseries of the European poor.[61]

In the 1850s, Francis Terry Leak of Mississippi, a planter who usually discussed slavery as a racial matter, sent the editor of *Star in the West* a stiff protest

---

[59] *DD*, 295–321. For Dabney's postwar attacks on capitalism, see David H. Overy, "When the Wicked Beareth Rule: A Southern Critique of Industrial America," *Journal of Presbyterian History*, 48 (1970), 130–142; and Sean Michael Lucas, *Robert Lewis Dabney: A Southern Presbyterian Life* (Phillipsburg, Pa., 2005). Speaking to the Ladies Benevolent Society of Charleston in 1882, the Presbyterian Reverend John Girardeau stressed the mounting threat of socialism, communism, and "Lawless Radicalism" but pleaded for respect for the rights of the working classes; George A. Blackburn, ed., *Sermons by John L. Girardeau* (Columbia, S.C., 1907), 80, 109–110.

[60] J. T. Wiswall, "Southern Society and Its British Critics," *DBR*, 32 (1862), 186, 196.

[61] Eliza Middleton Fisher to Mary Herring Middleton, Aug. 26, 1844, in Eliza Cope Harrison, ed., *Best Companions: Letters of Eliza Middleton Fisher and Her Mother, Mary Hering Middleton, from Charleston, Philadelphia, and Newport, 1839–1846* (Columbia, S.C., 2001), 401; T. C. Thornton, *An Inquiry into the History of Slavery* (Washington, D.C., 1841), 125–129, 213–214; [Samuel Henry Dickson], "Difficulties in the Way of the Historian," *Southern and Western Literary Monthly Magazine and Review*, 2 (1845), 110–111; William Makepeace Thackeray, who received a royal reception on his lecture tours of the South, bolstered the southern indictment of Britain's exploitation of labor: Michael O'Brien, *Conjectures of Order: Intellectual Life and the American South, 1810–1860*, 2 vols. (Chapel Hill, N.C., 2004), 1:58–59.

against its criticism of "the so-called slavery of the South." Leak opened by arguing that the obvious inferiority of the black race made the relation necessary in a biracial society: "In that relation he is one of the *happiest, best-cared-for* & *most useful* of the world's toiling millions, but out of it, soon & necessarily he relapses into barbarism." He ended belligerently: "Please attend to your own poor, whom you always have with you – dealing justly and mercifully with them – and leave us – without denunciation, to attend to ours. And this latter injunction our Northern people might safely observe, as they must see, or ought to see, that our interests, as the owners of our labourers – fortunately for them – coincide with our obligations in that respect." Disciples of Christ Reverend Franc M. Carmack of Mississippi, a young, politically moderate schoolteacher, responded no less harshly to an abolitionist tract: "Charity begins at home. Let Englishmen devote their great benevolence to the amelioration of the condition of the thousands of their own race among themselves, which is in many instances worse than that of our Slaves, and then they will have a little more show of reason for transporting their philanthropy across the Atlantic."[62]

The charges extended to antislavery Northerners, who, according to Southerners, cared nothing about the oppression of the laboring poor. Missouri's northern-born Judge William Barclay Napton admonished northern women and clergymen who sparked abolitionism to look to the condition of their own dangerous classes. The polemically effective charges had a core of truth but obscured the complexity of abolitionist response. Many northern evangelists, notably Francis Wayland and Charles Grandison Finney, did support laissez-faire and oppose the labor movement and its demands for a ten-hour day, but some spoke out against the injustices of the free-labor system. The panic of 1819 alerted Unitarian divines in New England to the problem of pauperism, and they established such institutions as Massachusetts General Hospital and the McLean and Perkins Asylums for the Blind to help the poor, the orphaned, and the afflicted. Still, few critics of slavery gave much attention to the day-to-day plight of workers during the terrible depressions. They focused on the threat to property posed by angry workers rather than on the human suffering that provoked the anger. For the most part abolitionists sought to rein in the excesses of a capitalist system they supported. Still, among northern opponents of slavery there had long been an undercurrent of social criticism. When William Ellery Channing and Theodore Parker spoke out on poverty and the stupefying and alienating effects of the division of labor, the northern literary world took heed, although it tended to view such problems as the results of moral disorder and to seek a cure in education. Experiments with communal living and one or another form of socialism implicitly, when not explicitly, challenged the social relations of the marketplace. The severe depression that followed the panic of 1837 encouraged acute social criticism and flirtation with radical ideologies. Other important abolitionists concerned themselves with the condition of the

---

[62] Leak Diary, July 9, 1851; Carmack Diary, Sept. 30, 1852. After the war, Leak said that he had accepted slavery because he was convinced that it was in the blacks' best interest.

working class and the poor, primarily advocating reforms to broaden political participation and encourage peaceful struggles for reform. Others behaved like Henry Clarke Wright, who spent five years in Britain, including time in the Manchester that Friedrich Engels excoriated in *The Condition of the Working Class in England in 1844*, without showing much interest in the condition of the working class and the poor.[63]

Abolitionists felt pressure from Northerners who joined the southern clamor about the oppression of labor in Britain and the North. Northwestern Democrats joined Southerners in accusing the antislavery movement of shedding crocodile tears over the cruelties of slavery. In the 1850s workers in Illinois toiled eleven and twelve hours per day, and the unskilled barely made enough to stay alive. Periods of unemployment wreaked havoc; workers faced starvation during the especially bad winter of 1854. Reminding Abraham Lincoln of the biblical injunction "Judge not, lest ye be judged," Stephen A. Douglas challenged Lincoln during their debate at Quincy, Illinois, in 1858: "We have objects of charity at home – let us perform our domestic duties. Let us take care of our own poor, our own suffering, and make them comfortable and happy, before we go abroad to intermeddle with other people's business." In 1857, estimates of the number of unemployed in Philadelphia hovered around 40,000 and in New York City and Brooklyn ranged from 30,000 to 100,000, with as many as 40,000 reported homeless at one point. Even the most conservative estimates revealed suffering of staggering proportions. Cincinnati, Chicago, and other cities reeled. In Pennsylvania mine owners laid off some 20,000 workers, whereas in New England employers tried to avoid layoffs by a ten percent reduction in hours and wages. The employers meant well, but the workers took a hard blow. City governments, churches, and philanthropists had long taken a paternalistic interest in the poor and now made efforts to relieve suffering and create jobs. Their efforts demonstrated a greater concern than proslavery critics gave them credit for but did not meet the needs. The southern press had a field day, not noticing that even Nashville was suffering.[64]

---

[63] Christopher Phillips and Jason L. Pendleton, eds., *The Union on Trial: The Political Journals of Judge William Barclay Napton, 1829–1883* (Columbus, Mo., 2005), 125–126; Betty Fladeland, *Abolitionists and Working-Class Problems in the Age of Industrialization* (Baton Rouge, La., 1984); Lewis Perry, *Childbirth, Marriage, and Reform: Henry Clarke Wright, 1797–1870* (Chicago, 1980), 265–271.

[64] Harold Holzer, ed., *The Lincoln-Douglas Debates: The First Complete, Unexpurgated Text* (New York, 1994), 311; for Illinois, see Arthur C. Cole, *The Irrepressible Conflict, 1850–1865* (New York, 1934), 204; generally, Robert W. Fogel, *The Fourth Great Awakening and the Future of Egalitarianism* (Chicago, 2000), chs. 1, 3; Charles C. Cole, Jr., *The Social Ideas of the Northern Evangelists, 1826–1860* (New York, 1954), 111. In 1860, New York had almost a million people, Philadelphia a half million. The modern form of unemployment appeared in Massachusetts between the aftermath of the War of 1812 and the panic of 1837, cushioned by the large proportion of the people who remained in agriculture or were self-employed. With the burgeoning of the manufacturing sector and the Irish immigration of the late 1840s, unemployment emerged as a severe social problem. See Alexander Keyssar, *Out of Work: The First Century of Unemployment in Massachusetts* (New York, 1986), ch. 2.

Nathaniel Hawthorne denounced the hard class distinctions in Britain and the oppression of the poor, and Herman Melville, especially after 1848, followed the course of Britain's radical working-class Chartist movement. In response, some abolitionists expressed heightened sympathy with the plight of northern laborers, and, during the War, William Lloyd Garrison, Wendell Phillips, Angelina Grimké, and others committed themselves to the struggle for the rights of labor. Henry Ward Beecher, preaching in Brooklyn in January 1861, condemned northern society for its failure to suppress the same kind of corrupt passions that sustained slavery in the South. He spoke of "the grinding of the poor, the advantages which capital takes of labor, the oppression of the farm," and the treatment of colored peoples at home and abroad. "We have," he concluded, "our own account to render." Some abolitionists flirted with socialism or echoed socialist criticism of the evils of capitalism. The New England–born Swedenborgian and spiritualist Stephen Pearl Andrews, who had come of age in Louisiana and Texas, embraced Charles Fourier's socialism, vigorously opposed slavery, and even supported the entrance of Texas into the British Empire if necessary to advance emancipation. Fitzhugh called him "the Proudhon of America." Yet despite his militant opposition to slavery and his advocacy of "free love," Andrews acknowledged that slavery contained "elements of the true order of Society wholly wanting in the isolated and individual freedom" of the North. When Nathaniel P. Rogers denounced capital's buying labor "at auction," he in effect denounced "wage slavery." But more typically, antislavery Northerners argued that freedom took precedence over the specific conditions of labor. An ironic postscript: Northern radicals and conservatives slowly recognized that the War had ended their hopes for a morally rejuvenated America. The radicals thereupon dedicated themselves to women's rights, supported the labor movement, or faded. Conservatives found themselves at sea.[65]

---

[65] Charles C. Cole, Jr., *The Social Ideas of the Northern Evangelists, 1826–1860* (New York, 1954), 188–191; Henry Ward Beecher, "Peace Be Still," *Fast Day Sermons, or the Pulpit on the State of the Country* (New York, 1861), 265–280, quote at 272; Madeleine B. Stern, *The Pantarch: A Biography of Stephen Pearl Andrews* (Austin, Tex., 1968), quote at 19, and see 82–83 on free love; Madeleine B. Stern, "Stephen Pearl Andrews and the Americanization of Texas," *Southwestern Historical Quarterly*, 68 (1964), 491–523; George Fitzhugh, "The Conservative Principle," *DBR*, 22 (1857), 421; for Andrews's social views and Fitzhugh's response, see Lewis Perry, *Radical Abolitionism: Anarchy and the Government of God in Antislavery Thought* (Ithaca, N.Y., 1973), 210–212; Charles Elliott, *Sinfulness of Slavery*, 2 vols. (New York, 1968 [1850]), 2:297ff; Bertram Wyatt-Brown, *Yankee Saints and Southern Sinners* (Baton Rouge, La., 1985), 21–22. For the commitment to capitalism, see F. O. Matthiessen, *American Renaissance: Art and Expression in the Age of Emerson and Whitman* (New York, 1941), 336–337, 382–383; David Brion Davis, *Slavery and Human Progress* (New York, 1984), 272–273. For the postwar trajectory of northern radicals, see Peter Walker, *Moral Choices: Memory, Desire, and Imagination in Nineteenth-Century American Abolition* (Baton Rouge, La., 1978), chs. 12–13, and for the crisis of northern conservatism, see Lewis P. Simpson, *Mind and the American Civil War: A Meditation on Lost Causes* (Baton Rouge, La., 1989).

For the perception of socialist tendencies in abolitionism, see Anne C. Rose, *Transcendentalism as a Social Movement, 1830–1850* (New Haven, Conn., 1981), 72, 88, 91, 110–114, 129–130, 217–218; Ronald G. Walters, *The Antislavery Appeal: American Abolitionism after*

From the 1830s onward, Southerners, supported by some important Northerners, condemned northern interference with slavery. They protested that they
did not interfere with northern free labor and that the North needed southern
support against its radical workers. "When did the South ever place her hand
on the North?" Calhoun asked the Senate in 1838. "When did she ever interfere with her peculiar institutions?" When did she ever aim a blow at her peace
and security?" In 1848, Calhoun spelled out some of his assumptions, telling
a public meeting in Charleston: "The North is rich and powerful, but she has
many elements of division and weakness – Fourierites – the vote yourself a
farm men – the strife of labor with capital – a spirit of anarchy and misrule
already developed – which sooner or later will end in her overthrow."[66]

In the 1830s, a contributor to *Princeton Review* expressed disgust at abolitionists' abuse of the South: "We do not expect to abolish despotism in Russia
by getting up indignation meetings in New York." William Drayton of South
Carolina, citing the Richmond *Enquirer*, asked Northerners to suppose that
their workers rose against their exploiters. Would you not want and expect
Southerners to support efforts to preserve order? In the 1840s southern newspaper editors wondered aloud how New Englanders would feel if Southerners
formed anticapitalist societies to educate northern workers on the roots of
their suffering in the exploitation of wage-slavery. In 1845 the Macon *Georgia Telegraph and Republic* republished a piece from the *New York Globe*
that quoted a citizen of Indiana who claimed to oppose all forms of slavery:
He urged Southerners to do to the North what Northerners were doing to
them: "Is there not philanthropy enough in the South to form a society for
the abolition of northern [wage] slavery?" In Georgia a few years later, the
Rome Southerner and Macon's *Georgia Telegraph* expressed confidence that
Europe's "hirelings" would rise against their capitalist exploiters. At the end
of the 1850s, the *Weekly Raleigh Register* and the *National Intelligencer* of
Washington warned that withdrawal of substantial southern patronage from
the northern economy would spur a depression in the North, radicalize workers, and spur bread riots that would give the North an idea of the character
of the insurrections that abolitionists were encouraging in the South. In 1849,
Senator Jeremiah Clemens of Alabama asked if Northerners would tolerate a
southern campaign to liberate wage-slaves. Henry W. Hilliard of Alabama, a
Whig, asked the House of Representatives, "Suppose the South should select
a particular institution existing in the Northern States, or a particular feature
in Northern society – the labor of operatives in factories, for instance – and
undertake to denounce it and overthrow it, how would it be regarded? . . . Why

---

1830 (Baltimore, Md., 1976), 111–128; Lewis Perry, *Radical Abolitionism: Anarchy and the
Government of God in Antislavery Thought* (Ithaca, N.Y., 1973), 120–121, 211–212. Herbert
Aptheker has argued that the abolitionist movement – not merely its extreme left wing – was a
genuinely revolutionary movement: *Abolitionism: A Revolutionary Movement* (Boston, Mass.,
1989), xii.

[66] Calhoun, "Remarks," Jan. 11, 1838, *JCCP*, 14:95; "Remarks at a Public Meeting in
Charleston," Aug. 19, 1848, in *JCCP*, 26:18.

then is this course pursued toward the South?" In the wake of John Brown's raid at Harpers Ferry, the unionist Dr. John Allan Wyeth of Huntsville, Alabama, protested that the South would gradually end slavery were it not for the "insurrectionary and murderous meddlesomeness of the northern Abolitionists."[67]

Samuel M. Wolfe of Virginia, replying to the fiercely antislavery Hinton Helper of North Carolina, denied that Southerners sought to impose their social system on the North or preach class war to northern workers or call for the murder and plundering of employers. Yet, Marcus A. Bell of Atlanta came close to calling upon the northern laboring poor to rise against their exploiters, and E. J. Pringle of South Carolina, Henry Hughes of Mississippi, Edmund Ruffin of Virginia, and Robert Toombs of Georgia issued barely disguised threats. Northerners, "Amor Patriae" wrote, might consider the possibility that armed Southerners would aid rebellion among northern workers and the poor. The poor were everywhere, Pringle wrote in 1853, but Southerners did not preach crusades against the want, crime, and disease "that infect the lanes and cellars of New York and Boston." The North sooner or later would face consequences of the population pressure that was wracking Europe, he added, but the South did not try to impose its system abroad. Hughes crowed that European workers were in revolt against capitalist oppression and that the northern workers were not far behind: "Southern soldiers will be marched to New York to guard the property-holders from the laboring class." Ruffin, hearing of the massive demonstrations of the unemployed, concluded that New York would not survive the secession of the South and withdrawal of its conservative influence. Toombs, in his farewell address to the United States Senate in 1861, condemned the Republican Party for waging war on the South's "social system," insisting that Southerners did not claim the right to interfere with northern institutions. As Southerners intensified their counter-attack in the 1850s, friendly Northerners came to their aid. The Reverend Leander Ker of Pennsylvania protested that Southerners were not sending prejudiced snoops to record social conditions in the North as abolitionists were doing in the South. A lady of Massachusetts, traveling in Virginia, reported on the South's Eleventh Commandment: "Each one mind his own business."[68]

[67] "Slavery. By William E. Channing," *Princeton Review*, 8 (1836), 271; [Drayton], *South Vindicated*, 217; for Clemens see *Cong. Globe*, 31st Cong., 1st Sess., Appendix, 52–54; *Georgia Telegraph and Republic*, Nov. 11, 1845; "Freedom of the South from Dependence on the North," *Weekly Raleigh Register*, Dec. 21, 1859; *Georgia Telegraph*, Sept. 18, 1849 (from *Rome Southerner*); "Speech of Mr. Hunter of Virginia," *National Intelligencer*, Feb. 14, 1860; Speech in House of Representatives, Jan. 5, 1847, in Henry W. Hilliard, *Speeches and Addresses* (New York, 1855), 110–111; John Allan Wyeth, *With Sabre and Scalpel: The Autobiography of a Soldier and Surgeon* (Electronic ed.; Chapel Hill, N.C., 1998 [1914]), xvii.

[68] Samuel M. Wolfe, *Helper's Impending Crisis Dissected* (New York, 1969 [1860]), 33, 65; Marcus A. Bell, *Message of Love: South-Side View of Cotton Is King; and the Philosophy of African Slavery* (Atlanta, Ga., 1860), 36–38; "Amor Patriae," *The Blasphemy of Abolitionism Exposed: Servitude and the Rights of the South Vindicated: A Bible Argument*, new ed., rev. (New York, 1850), 13; [E. J. Pringle], *Slavery in the Southern States, by a Carolinian*

American Exceptionalism?

Through the early decades of the nineteenth century Southerners, including the generally sober Legaré, considered the United States free of poverty and centuries away from having to face a social crisis. By the 1850s a contingent of formidable Virginians – George Frederick Holmes, Ellwood Fisher, M. R. H. Garnett, John Randolph Tucker, Edmund Ruffin – asserted that the availability of land in the West was doing no more than buying time for the North, temporarily staving off the revolutions that were wracking Europe. They considered the deepening antagonism between capital and labor insurmountable. Ruffin, a distinguished soil scientist and secessionist firebrand, drew on *South Vindicated* (1836) by William Drayton, the South Carolina unionist who moved to Philadelphia in the 1830s. Drayton depicted the North as class-rent, with labor oppressed and in a dangerous mood. Ruffin considered the impact of Drayton's tract comparable to that of Dew's *Essay on Slavery*. R. E. Cochrane, who considered reenslavement of whites politically impracticable, warned Europe and the North to reconcile capital and labor or face working-class insurrection. Lending credence to such sweeping generalizations were cries from the North. Ezra D. Pruden of New Jersey wrote to Calhoun in 1848 about the terrible oppression suffered by working people like himself. In 1854, "A Northern Gentleman" in *De Bow's Review* invoked the scathing denunciation of the condition of the free-state poor by Dorothea Dix, one of the few northern philanthropists whom Southerners held in high regard. Meanwhile, the Democrats in the Midwest were protesting northern wage-slavery

(Cambridge, Mass., 1852), 15, 19, 50; "Reopening of the Slave Trade," in Stanford M. Lyman, ed., *Selected Writings of Henry Hughes: Antebellum Southerner, Slavocrat, Sociologist* (Jackson, Miss., 1985), 91; Nov. 9–13, 1857, *ERD*, 1:122–127; Robert Toombs, "Farewell to the Senate," in J. A. Chandler, ed., *The South in the Building of the Nation*, 12 vols. (Richmond, Va., 1909), 9:312–313; Leander Ker, *Slavery Consistent with Christianity*, 3rd ed. (Weston, Mo., 1853), 31; Misses [Sarah] Mendell and [Charlotte] Hosmer, *Notes of Travel and Life by Two Young Ladies* (New York, 1854), 163. That the South did not interfere in the North was a theme supported by men like Representative Clement L. Vallandigham: see his speech in Dayton, Ohio, in 1855: *The Record of Hon. C. L. Vallandigham on Abolition, the Union, and the Civil War* (Wiggins, Miss., 1998 [1863]), 31. Mrs. Schoolcraft was among the South Carolinians impressed by Wolfe's book: *Plantation Life: The Narratives of Mrs. Henry Schoolcraft* (New York, 1969 [1860]), 401.

John H. Reagan of Texas, postmaster general of the Confederacy, said that a great many Southerners, presumably including himself, believed that "the commercial and manufacturing interest of the North and East" would resist a war with the South. *John H. Reagan, Memoirs with Special Reference to Secession and the Civil War*, ed. Walter Flavius McCaleb (New York, 1906), 105. Nathaniel Beverley Tucker took that position: see Maude Howlett Woodfin, "Nathaniel Beverley Tucker; with a Sketch of His Life," *Richmond College Historical Papers*, 2 (1917), 33. In that spirit, at Alabama's secession convention G. T. Yelverton described the British as a calculating people who would recognize the Confederacy as a dollar-and-cents matter: William R. Smith, ed., *The History of the Convention Debates of the People of Alabama* (Montgomery, 1861), 231.

and affirming the superiority of the material condition of southern slaves relative to the poor of the free states.[69]

In the early years of the nineteenth century, especially in wake of the financial crisis of 1819, William Duane and other Northerners warned that America was moving toward a recapitulation of the class warfare that marked industrial England. During the Jacksonian era, the class-struggle rhetoric of the Democratic Party – and the Whig Party's peculiar version of it – added credibility to the proslavery vision of a North that, despite a temporary respite from the availability of western lands, was headed into social crisis. In 1834 Calhoun warned northern capitalists that their degraded laborers would use the vote to despoil them. Yet, despite the natural antagonism between the radical democratic ideology of the Loco-Focos and the conservative republicanism of the southern slaveholders, a number of the most radical of the Loco-Focos eschewed criticism of slavery, stressing the wage-slavery they perceived in the free states. The Loco-Focos in New York divided on Calhoun and on slavery and abolition. Some important northern pro-labor radicals, including the formidable Ely Moore, opposed the abolitionist's national petition campaign. For awhile in the early 1840s some northern radicals discovered the virtues of Calhoun, John Tyler, and states' rights. Fitzwilliam Byrdsall and Orestes Brownson, among others, rallied to Calhoun, in part because they opposed paper money and credit and supported strict construction of the Constitution. Byrdsall, in his *History of the Loco-Foco or Equal Rights Party*, outlined the party's principles, citing resolutions of 1835, in which strict construction of the Constitution and a defense of state rights accompanied an assault on the banks. Radicals often sounded like Fitzhugh in their denunciations of wage-slavery. In the 1840s flamboyant Michael Walsh, addressing mass meetings of working men, extolled John Tyler as a true democrat. And for Walsh: "There is no

---

[69] "Constitutional History of Greece," in *HLW*, 1:430; [Drayton], *South Vindicated*, 67–68, 110–112; *ERD*, 1:136; [George Frederick Holmes], "Observations on a Passage from Aristotle Relative to Slavery," *SLM*, 16 (1850), 198–200; [George Frederick Holmes], "California Gold and European Revolution," *SQR*, n. s., 1 (1850), 287; [Holmes], "Latter-Day Pamphlets," *SQR*, n. s., 2 (1850), 336; Ellwood Fisher, *Letters on the North and the South* (Wilmington, N.C., 1849), 31–32; [Garnett], *Union, Past and Future*, 23, 30–31; John Randolph Tucker, "The Great Issue," *SLM*, 32 (1861), 173; R. E. C. [Cochrane], "The Problem of Free Society – Part II," *SLM*, 27 (1858), 2, 12–13; see also J., "The National Anniversary," *SQR*, n.s., 2 (1850), 177; Ezra D. Pruden to Calhoun, Oct. 4, 1848, in *JCCP*, 26:77–78; [A Northern Gentleman], "Modern Philanthropy and Negro Slavery," *DBR*, 16 (1854), 263–276. See also J. T. Trezevant's statistical comparison of crime, North and South: "Education and Crime at the North and the South," *DBR*, 16 (1854), 578–581. For South Carolina's respect for Dorothea Dix, who stayed clear of antislavery agitation, see Peter McCandless, *Moonlight, Magnolias, and Madness: Insanity in South Carolina from the Colonial Period to the Progressive Era* (Chapel Hill, N.C., 1996), ch. 6, esp. 137. Dix's *Remarks on Prisons and Asylums* was being read in Montgomery, Alabama, as well as in the South's principal cultural centers: see Feb. 19, 1858, in Barbara Leigh Smith Bodichon, *An American Diary, 1857–8*, ed. Joseph W. Reed, Jr. (London, 1972), 113.

tyranny on earth so oppressive as the tyranny of wealth – and no slavery so great as the slavery of poverty." Sean Wilentz comments on Walsh's election to Congress: He "arrived in Washington as much as a northern champion of southern rights as labor's voice in the House of Representatives."[70]

The radical John L. O'Sullivan and his *Democratic Review* supported slavery on racial grounds while he condemned the supposed quasi-enslavement of white workers in the North and abroad. During the War, radicals like Christopher Gray of Massachusetts took up the cause of the working class against capitalist oppressors. He did not support some version of Slavery in the Abstract but – to the contrary – denounced all forms of slavery, including wage-slavery. He nonetheless inadvertently provided grist to the mill of those who equated chattel slavery with wage-slavery and drew opposite political conclusions. Resisting the proslavery lure, large if undetermined numbers of northern workers, while themselves attacking "wage slavery," rallied to the Free Soilers, Republicans, and even the abolitionists.[71]

The ideological chasm between proslavery Southerners and anticapitalist Northerners foreclosed an effective political coalition, notwithstanding tub-thumping rhetoric and dire threats. In the commonly expressed southern view, the availability of land in the West temporarily saved the United States from a Malthusian crisis, and the availability of American foodstuffs at least temporarily was helping Europe to stave off the worst. The hopeful speculations of proslavery Southerners were reinforced by the rhetoric of radical New Yorkers and even Russian radicals like Michael Bakunin, who saw the North's "safety valve" of western lands as a temporary phenomenon and predicted intense class warfare. Yet, contrary to socialist and proslavery predictions, American society generally maintained considerable occupational as well as generational mobility throughout the nineteenth century.[72]

---

[70] Sean Wilentz, *The Rise of American Democracy: Jefferson to Lincoln* (New York, 2005), 228–229, chs. 16–17, 333, 430, 477, 553–555, quote at 333; William Trimble, "The Social Philosophy of the Loco-Foco Democracy," *American Journal of Sociology*, 26 (1921), 712–713; F[itzwilliam] Byrdsall, *The History of the Loco-Foco or Equal Rights Party: Its Movements, Conventions and Proceedings* (New York, 1842), 27; *Sketches of the Speeches and Writings of Michael Walsh: Including His Poems and Correspondence* (New York, 1843), 19–20, 30, 93–95; see also Michael A. Bernstein, "Northern Labor Finds a Southern Champion: A Note on the Radical Democracy, 1833–1849," in William Pencak and Conrad Edick Wright, eds., *New York and the Rise of American Capitalism: Economic Development and the Social and Political History of an American State, 1780–1870* (New York, 1989), 147–167, Walsh quoted at 153.

[71] Robert D. Sampson, *John O'Sullivan and His Times* (Kent, Oh., 2003), 146–147; C. Gray, *Slavery: Or, Oppression at the North as well as the South!* (Ithaca, N.Y., 2006 [1862]); Edward Magdol, *The Antislavery Rank and File: Profile of the Abolitionists' Constituency* (Westport, Conn., 1986), especially 37, 57, 96–97, 112.

[72] [D. J. McCord], "Barhydt's Industrial Exchanges," *SQR*, 15 (1849), 468–469; David Hecht, *Russian Radicals Look to America* (Cambridge, Mass., 1947), 60; Joseph P. Ferries, *The End of American Exceptionalism? Mobility in the U. S. since 1850* ("National Bureau of Economics Working Paper Series": Research Paper No. 11324; Cambridge, Mass., 2005).

No sooner had the economic crisis of 1857–1858 passed than Thomas R. R. Cobb, advocating the secession of Georgia, predicted another devastating financial crash in the North. With secession on the horizon, Fitzhugh, still a conditional unionist, called for ending economic and cultural relations with the northern states while avoiding a political separation. We have, he wrote in *De Bow's Review*, no quarrel with the northern people as such, only with their revolutionaries, infidels, socialists, and agrarians. "Let us of the South be patient and wait for the process of subsidence and stratification in Northern society, which will be sure to put our friends uppermost; for it is as natural for *them* to ride, as it is for the *masses* to be ridden." The tide is turning the world over in our favor, he claimed with the wish father to the thought: "It is the *rolling back of the reformation!* Of reformation run mad." He explained that the South "alone has made adequate provision for the laboring man. She, alone, has a contented, moral, religious society, undisturbed by infidelity, riots, revolutions, and famine. She, alone, can say to the world, we present the model which you must imitate in reforming your institutions."[73]

Reports of misery and economic crisis in the North encouraged visualization of free-labor society in its death throes. Pickens wrote to Perry, "In part, the division now at the North is deep and bitter, and it is between capitalists and laborers, and as population increases, and becomes so dense as to press society down into its different strata, this difference will grow deeper and wider every year." Pickens had made the main points in an address to the State Agricultural Society of South Carolina in 1849, and as early as 1836, he had told the House of Representatives that class stratification inhered in the human condition and that laborers, whether called slaves or not, necessarily lived in a condition of servitude. In 1866 Pickens reiterated that the European free-labor system was much harsher than southern slavery had been: "The old system of patriarchal slavery has been changed, and the new system of modern slavery has been instituted, whereby the whites and blacks shall both be owned by capitalists and associated wealth in the shape of corporations, through the power of government."[74]

---

[73] T. R. R. Cobb, speech at Milledgeville, in William W. Freehling and Craig M. Simpson, eds., *Secession Debated: Georgia's Showdown in 1860* (New York, 1992), 27; George Fitzhugh, "Disunion within the Union," *DBR*, 28 (1860), 4–7, quotes at 5, 7.

[74] F. W. Pickens to B. F. Perry, June 27, 1857, in Stephen Meats and Edwin T. Arnold, eds., *The Writings of Benjamin F. Perry*, 3 vols. (Spartanburg, S.C., 1980), 3:169; F. W. Pickens, *Congressional Globe*, 24th Cong., Appendix 289–290 to 24C, 1st Sess., 1836, and for Pickens on the conflict of labor and capital and the coming subjection of labor in Europe, see Pickens, *An Address Delivered before the State Agricultural Society of South Carolina* (Columbia, S.C., 1849), 13–19; *Letter of Hon. F. W. Pickens to a Gentleman in New Orleans* (Baltimore, 1866), 12–17, quote at 17.

2

Hewers of Wood, Drawers of Water

> Men may grow gray, and slavery will exist, and the only question is as to the kind of slavery, white or black, voluntary or involuntary. It will exist one way or the other, growing out of the very organization of society. This conclusion cannot be resisted.
>
> —Andrew Johnson (1856)[1]

Common sense suggests that no southern politician in his right mind dared to preach Slavery in the Abstract to enfranchised, notoriously touchy, and well-armed nonslaveholders. So much for common sense. The South's foremost politicians freely expounded it to nonslaveholders and "middling folks." Increased interest in Slavery in the Abstract owed much to the influence of local leaders, whom a politically well-informed and engaged citizenry trusted and followed, especially during crises. Notably, the nonslaveholders and small slaveholders of East Tennessee heard and read speeches by two men who, before the War, hated each other and campaigned respectively for the Democrats and Whigs. Andrew Johnson, a Jefferson-Jackson Democrat, and the Methodist Reverend William G. ("Parson") Brownlow, a Hamilton-Clay Whig, fought each other but, in step with public opinion, stood together for the Union. Yet both Johnson and Brownlow accepted the essentials of Slavery in the Abstract, proclaiming slavery normal in civilized society.[2]

"And Joshua made them that day hewers of wood and drawers of water for the Congregation, and for the altar of the Lord" (Joshua 9:27).

[1] "Address to State Democratic Convention," Nashville, Jan. 8, 1856, in *AJP*, 2:352–356, words quoted at 354.

[2] Both Johnson and Brownlow had been antislavery in the 1830s but swung to the opposite extreme: See Durwood Dunn, *An Abolitionist in the Appalachian South: Ezekiel Birdseye on Slavery, Capitalism, and Separate Statehood in East Tennessee, 1841–1846* (Knoxville, Tenn., 1997), 19–22. For a probing essay on egalitarianism and Jeffersonian republicanism among southern yeomen, see Lacy K. Ford, "Popular Ideology of the Old South's Plain Folk: The Limits of Egalitarianism in a Slaveholding Society," in Samuel C. Hyde, Jr., ed., *Plain Folk of the South Revisited* (Baton Rouge, La., 1997), 205–227.

A former tailor and self-conscious representative of artisans, mechanics, and yeomen, Johnson focused on race relations, yet time and again he ended with racially qualified class relations. Accepting the vice-presidential nomination in Nashville on July 2, 1864, he blamed slavery for the nation's ills: "Experience has demonstrated its incompatibility with free and republican Governments, and it would be unwise and unjust longer to continue it as one of the institutions of the country." In October, at Logansport, Indiana, he claimed to have reluctantly tolerated slavery while living in a slave state but never to have advocated or sustained it. The War, he announced, was emancipating many more whites than blacks. Johnson had a poor memory, for he had long advocated and sustained slavery not merely in time and place but as a historical inevitability for all peoples. To be sure, throughout his career he defended white laborers against their detractors and fought to make southern whites free and prosperous. In 1853, in his first inaugural address as governor of Tennessee, he denounced academies and colleges for filling the heads of young people with antidemocratic class prejudices. Many teachers and professors were "bigoted and supercilious on account of their literary attainments and assumed superior information on most subjects." In consequence, their students, who were likely to be well-to-do and haughty, were made "to feel that the great mass of mankind were intended by their Creator to be 'hewers of wood and drawers of water.'"[3]

Speaking in Congress as early as 1844, Johnson embraced the essentials of Slavery in the Abstract. He reiterated his position in 1845 in a statement to the people of the First Congressional District of Tennessee and again in 1849 in a speech at Evans Crossroads. Slavery, he maintained, had existed since the appearance of human communities 5,000 years ago. Since every society required a menial class, the South did better than most by having it consist of an inferior race. The industrial countries reduced workers to wage-slavery. India and other countries reduced peasants to quasi-slavery. In 1856, at the Democratic State Convention in Nashville, Johnson charged the North with wanting to abolish black slavery in order to support more profitable and easily sustainable white quasi-slavery. In every society, "We find some occupying the upper positions, and others the lower positions – composing the whole and making up what men call Society.... We find also the institution of slavery (whether white or black) incorporated into this social condition of man." Slavery had always existed: "At all periods of time and in all parts of the world, we find slavery existing in society. When we go to the North, don't we find

---

[3] In *AJP*: "Acceptance of Vice-Presidential Nomination," Nashville, Tennessee, July, 2, 1864 (7:7–10; words quoted from 10); "Speech at Logansport, Indiana, Oct. 4, 1864" (7:218–230, especially 226–227); also "Speech at Louisville, Kentucky, Oct. 13, 1864" (7:237); "First Inaugural Address as Governor of Tennessee, Oct. 17, 1853" (2:172–183, quote at 175). David Warren Bowen interprets Johnson's views as incompatible with the doctrine of Slavery in the Abstract: *Andrew Johnson and the Negro* (Knoxville, Tenn., 1989), ch. 3. We agree that Johnson choked on the idea of enslaving whites, but he accepted the fundamental contention of Slavery in the Abstract as a hard fact of life.

the white man and the white woman performing the same menial service the blacks perform at the South?" How Johnson proposed to reconcile these views with his repeated celebration of humanity's progress toward democracy and equality – even if only equality among whites – he never made clear. In 1857, rapturously celebrating humanity's march toward perfection and divinity, he reiterated that slavery – not merely black slavery – had always existed and would always exist.[4]

Johnson, like others, in effect equated menial labor per se with enslavement of the laborer, but he clearly meant something more specific: Menial laborers in a free-labor society could never earn enough to do more than support a miserable existence. Only personal servitude to a protector offered a decent living. Johnson lectured the U.S. Senate in 1858: "I do not care whether you call it slavery or servitude; the man who has menial offices to perform is the slave or servant, I care not whether he is white or black. Servitude or slavery grows out of the organic structure of man.... The only question for us to discuss is, what kind of slavery we shall have.... Will you have white or black slavery?" Two months later, replying to James H. Hammond's "Cotton Is King," speech, he did not object to the reference to "mud-sills." Every society had to have some form of slavery: "In this portion of the Senator's remarks I concur. I do not think whites should be slaves; and if slavery is to exist in this country, I prefer black slavery to white slavery." Johnson suggested that in due time the North would embrace black slavery as an alternative to white.[5]

Aroused by John Brown's raid at Harpers Ferry, Johnson addressed the Senate on the underlying issue: "There is a conflict always going on between capital and labor; but there is not a conflict between two kinds of labor." Johnson, the plebeian, defended the South against the charge of aristocracy: "You talk about a slave aristocracy. If it is an aristocracy, it is an aristocracy of labor." He took the offensive: "What kind of aristocracy have you in the North? Capital and money. Which is the most odious in its operations – an aristocracy of money or an aristocracy of labor? Which is the most unyielding?

---

[4] In *AJP*: "Speech on the Gag Resolution," U.S. House of Representatives, Jan. 31, 1844 (1:133–146, especially 136, 145); "To the Freemen of the First Congressional District of Tennessee," Oct. 15, 1845 (1:252); "Speech at Evans Crossroads," May 26, 1849 (1:498–507, especially 499–501); "Address to State Democratic Convention," Nashville, Jan 8, 1856 (2:352–356; words quoted from 354; "Speech at Raleigh," July 24, 1857 (2:477); "First Inaugural Address" (2:175–177). For arguments similar to Johnson's that without black slaves, whites laborers would sink into slavery, see [M. R. H. Garnett], *The Union, Past and Future: How It Works, and How to Save It*, 4th ed. (Charleston, 1850), 38–40, and James Sloan, *The Great Question Answered* (Memphis, 1857), 221–225.

[5] In *AJP*: "Speech on Popular Sovereignty and the Right of Instruction, Feb. 23, 1858" (3:61–62); "Speech on the Homestead Bill," U.S. Senate, May 20, 1858 (3:159–202, quote at 159). In a slave society, nonslaveholders and small slaveholders live in fear of falling into slavery. See the astute remarks of William Fitzgerald, *Slavery and the Roman Literary Imagination* (Cambridge, U.K., 2000), 111. But, as Johnson saw, the restriction of slave status to blacks provided a firm barrier to that catastrophe. See also S., "Liberty and Slavery," *SLM*, 22 (1856), 382–388; *SLM*, 22 (1856), 20–25; and *Southern Planter*, 16 (1856), 148–153.

Which is the most exacting? Every man has the answer in his own mind." He elaborated: Capital at the North oppressed the laboring man and created an irrepressible conflict within the North, not between slave states and free. Until the War, Johnson acknowledged the basic premise of Slavery in the Abstract, seeking ways to prevent enslavement of whites. He told his constituents the truth as he saw it: Slave, not free, labor grounded social life. Societies that lacked black slaves inevitably enslaved whites.

Johnson's version of Slavery in the Abstract resonated in the Border States. Benjamin F. Stringfellow of Missouri defended slavery passionately, stressing racial stratification and rejecting enslavement of whites. Yet he acknowledged that society needed a menial class and expressed relief that the South had blacks to fill it. His argument aroused the ire of proslavery men who interpreted it as a thinly veiled defense of Slavery in the Abstract, which they considered politically dangerous. The cautiously antislavery Alexander Campbell, leader of the Disciples of Christ – a church with great strength in the Border States – had his own variation: "Much as I may sympathize with a black man, I love the white man more.... As a Christian, I sympathize much more with the owners of slaves, their heirs, and successors, than with the slaves which they possess and bequeath." George William Featherstonhaugh, the traveling geologist, expressed disgust at the audacity of uneducated and crude lower-class southern whites who called poor Northerners "white Niggers." Featherstonhaugh need not have been surprised. The ascendancy of white over black was the first principle of Southern life. Yeomen and aristocrats disputed many matters but united in judging blacks an inferior race, society's permanent mud-sill. The yeomen, as freeholders who claimed the republican tradition as their own, reasonably felt themselves part of a broadly construed ruling class.[6]

Parson Brownlow, Johnson's political bête noire in East Tennessee, was a fiery Whig editor, scourge of Catholics and Calvinists, and a popular Methodist minister. He, too, rewrote his personal history when he sided with the Union and subsequently became Republican governor of Tennessee. He – of course! – had always looked forward to a republic rid of both slavery and the slave-holding gentry. So he said. But he could hardly have cited any part of his long, articulate, polemical, public record as evidence. In Philadelphia in 1858, Brownlow, braving a hostile audience, debated the abolitionist Congregationalist Reverend Abram Pryne of upstate New York. Brownlow extolled the

[6] "Speech on Harper's Ferry Incident, Dec. 12, 1859," in *AJP*, 3:334, 335; Lester B. Baltimore, "Benjamin F. Stringfellow: The Fight for Slavery on the Missouri Border," *Missouri Historical Review*, 62 (1967–1968), 19–20, 23. See also B. F. Stringfellow of Missouri, *Negro-Slavery, No Evil; or the North and the South* (St. Louis, Mo., 1854). When it became clear that the free-state forces would prevail in Kansas, Stringfellow, who valued land and railroads more than slavery, defected to the Republicans. [Alexander Campbell], "Our Position on American Slavery," *Millennial Harbinger*, 2 (1845), 234; George William Featherstonhaugh, *A Canoe Voyage up the Minay Sotor*, 2 vols. (St. Paul, Minn., 1970 [1847]), 2:195. On whites as a privileged stratum, see especially Steven V. Ash, *When the Yankees Came: Conflict and Chaos in the Occupied South, 1861–1865* (Chapel Hill, N.C., 1995), 3–4 and Prologue.

chivalric civilization of the South, praising the slaveholders as a superior people. He attributed southern superiority to a divinely sanctioned slavery that had
always existed and must exist in some form as the basis for civilization: "Slavery
is an established and inevitable condition to human society.... Slavery, having
existed ever since the first organization of society, it will exist to the end of
time." Like Johnson, Brownlow defined the issue as whether the South would
have black slaves or white slaves with a pretense of freedom. In 1862 he recalled
his debate with Pryne, emphatically reiterating its essentials.[7]

The performances of Johnson and Brownlow did not tell the whole story in
East Tennessee, where Slavery in the Abstract had long been in the air. In 1842
Ezekiel Birdseye, an abolitionist, sent Gerrit Smith of New York his opinion
of the slaveholders: "Had these despots the power they would just as soon sell
our Northern laborers as slaves as the negroes." Birdseye was preaching to the
converted. In 1836, Gerrit Smith warned that if slavery were not abolished, it
would transform northern workers into "a herd of slaves."[8]

In the 1850s James Gettys McGready Ramsey – state historian and canal,
school, and bank commissioner, detested Johnson and Brownlow. Brownlow
viciously assailed Ramsey's family, and Ramsey counted Brownlow his only
personal enemy. In 1858, Ramsey offered some "speculations" in a long letter
marked "private" to L. W. Spratt of Charleston. The replacement of patriarchal agricultural slavery by modern industrial social organization ended "in
the absolute and despotic authority of the employer and the dependence of the
employee." Ramsey spoke of the "flood of immigrants made up generally of
the unworthy, the plebian, and the poor," who brought with them "pauperism
and vice." Their influx into the North carried emancipation in its trail: "Not
that slaves were not wanted but because the labor of the dependent German
and the hardy Irishman was cheaper than that of the Negro." With the growth
of northern industry based on wage-slavery, the people of the South "have
become hewers of wood and drawers of water." The progress of civilization
rested on the relation of master to servant, whatever the form. Acknowledging
that frontier life in America encouraged an "apparent" social equality, Ramsey
stressed the inevitability of inequalities of wealth and their attendant stratification: "Someone becomes so rich as to employ the daughter of a poorer
countryman to wash or scrub for his wife, or an indigent boy or a sojourner to
black his boots or do other menial services for him." Ramsey assumed black
inferiority but considered African slavery one form of a general servitude that
differed "only in the degree of its intensity, or most perfect form." Ramsey,
although professing love for the Union, supported secession. The Southern

---

[7] W. G. Brownlow and A. Pryne, *Ought American Slavery to Be Perpetuated: A Debate* (Miami,
Fla., 1969 [1858]), quotes at 18–19, see also 271 and passim; W. G. Brownlow, *Sketches of the
Rise, Progress, and Decline of Secession* (New York, 1862), 18.

[8] Ezekiel Birdseye to Gerrit Smith, Mar. 14, 1842, in Dunn, *Abolitionist in the Appalachian South*,
213; John Stauffer, *The Black Hearts of Men: Radical Abolitionism and the Transformation of
Race* (Cambridge, Mass., 2002), 117.

Confederacy, he asserted, must prevail. Failure would not only ruin the South but "blight the best hopes of man of human improvement and of freedom everywhere."[9]

Across the state line, western North Carolina resembled East Tennessee in social structure and way of life. Thomas L. Clingman, a locally powerful sometime secessionist, sounded much like the unionists Johnson and Brownlow on the historical significance of slavery. Clingman knew the middling folks of his constituency well and did not talk down to them. Intellectually pretentious, he saw himself a figure of national stature who dared not say one thing in Asheville and another in Raleigh or Washington. His most revealing speeches, published in newspapers and as pamphlets, circulated widely among high and low throughout North Carolina and beyond. Clingman, too, preferred strict racial ground. In 1858 he told the North Carolina State Agricultural Society that the white race "has in all ages controlled the destinies of the world." Yet he defended slavery as a social system abstracted from race. He attributed the fall of the Roman Empire not to slavery but to increasing emancipation, arguing that the Roman Empire reached the height of its power under slavery. He knew – and knew that his audiences knew – that Roman slavery had not been racially based.[10]

In Congress, Clingman replied to the abolitionists, invoking scriptural sanction for slavery, presenting an accurate account of slavery among the ancient Israelites, and noting that the ancient world had seen attacks on property in land but not on property in man. He rejected the term "peculiar institution" as a "misnomer": "Ours is the general system of the world, and the *free* system is the *peculiar* one." Clingman reviewed the constitutional debates of the 1780s and the struggle against agrarian social leveling, especially in states with few or no slaves. He noted that many women had stronger qualifications for voting than most men but were nonetheless, like blacks, disfranchised. On this

[9] Ramsey to L. W. Spratt, Apr. 1858, in William B. Hesseltine, ed., *Dr. J. G. M. Ramsey, Autobiography and Letters* (Knoxville, Tenn., 2002), 83–97, quotes at 83–85, 88–89, 91, 102. Written about 1870, Ramsey's autobiography was published in 1954, with valuable letters.

[10] "Annual Address Delivered before the North Carolina State Agricultural Society," Oct. 21, 1858, in *Selections from the Writings and Speeches of Hon. Thomas L. Clingman of North Carolina* (Raleigh, N.C., 1877), 92–93, 100, 102, quote at 100; also "Philalethes," "Thoughts on the Decline of Agriculture in Ancient Italy," *SLM*, 13 (1847), 476. Some 30,000 copies of one of Clingman's speeches were distributed in 1845. Thomas E. Jeffrey, *Thomas Lanier Clingman: Fire Eater from the Carolina Mountains* (Athens, Ga., 1998), 337, n. 34. Clingman, a nonslaveholder, came from a family of small slaveholders. For a summary of the work of recent historians on the politics of western North Carolina, see 25 and ch. 4; Clingman and Andrew Johnson did not think well of each other (185).

Clingman zigzagged between secessionism and unionism. He supported Stephen A. Douglas in 1860 but became a reluctant secessionist. After the War, he quickly adjusted to abolition. See Jeffrey, *Clingman*, 6, 62, 113, 185, 192, and generally, chs. 6, 11. For a strong challenge to the interpretation of western North Carolina as significantly unionist in contrast to East Tennessee, see Terrell T. Garren, *Mountain Myth: Unionism in Western North Carolina* (Spartanburg, S.C., 2006).

principle of social order the South remained safe and sound, whereas the North headed toward mass democracy and, through it, to Caesarism.[11]

Clingman repeatedly moved from racial subordination to social subordination in general. He, too, described the living conditions of the world's laboring poor as inferior to those of the southern slaves. Why, he asked, had the English wasted money on West Indian emancipation rather than relieve the victims of the Irish famine? If Northerners succeeded in penning up slavery within present limits, the South would follow Europe into a Malthusian population crisis as a growing slave population pressed upon subsistence. Cynical Northerners expected southern slavery to disappear through the starvation and destruction of the blacks. Clingman retorted in a manner reminiscent of Jonathan Swift's *Modest Proposal*: "A not less effectual mode, however, would be to put to death the infant negroes from time to time. This, too, would be more humane, probably, than the other process." Clingman tried to restrict the discussion to the fate of the black slave, but aware of the dire projections of Thomas Malthus and David Ricardo, he saw a bleak future for the laboring classes. The politically moderate Calvin H. Wiley, North Carolina's yeoman-oriented educational reformer, gave a special twist to the standard argument that slaves, unlike free workers, benefited from living and working as part of their masters' families. Wiley focused not on labor conditions but on plantation government: "Every form of Government is one under which personal servitude exists to a greater or less extent. . . . It is manifest that all who are so governed are servants: the difference is not in principle, but in the degree of servitude."[12]

Even Alexander H. Stephens of heartland Georgia, whom historians see as a high priest of white supremacy and who qualified as a premier spokesman for the yeomen and middling slaveholders, could not defend slavery solely on racial grounds. Stephens knew the Bible well and, in appealing to it, faced the implications of its sanction of slavery independent of race. A thoughtful student of history and political economy, he celebrated moral as well as material progress in human affairs but focused on the constant threat posed by inherent human sinfulness and the nature of an economic development that threatened the well-being of free labor. Stephens assured the U.S. House of Representatives in 1845, "I am no defender of slavery in the abstract." He had long criticized Thomas Jefferson on equality by insisting on the racial inferiority of blacks, and race relations constituted the context for the remarks in the House in 1856: "None of your Fourierism liberty. Constitutional liberty – 'law and order' – abiding liberty. That is the liberty they [the Founders] meant to perpetuate." He spoke

[11] "Speech on the Political Aspect of the Slave Question," U.S. House of Representatives, Dec. 22, 1847, in *Writings and Speeches of Clingman*, 202–203, 207, 209–225, quote at 203. On southern evaluations of "Caesarism," see Elizabeth Fox-Genovese and Eugene D. Genovese, *The Mind of the Master Class: History and Faith in the Southern Slaveholders' Worldview* (New York, 2005), ch. 22.

[12] In *Writings and Speeches of Clingman*: "Speech in Defense of the South," in U.S. House of Representatives, Jan. 22, 1850 (242); "Speech on Nebraska and Kansas," U.S. House of Representatives, Apr. 4, 1851 (346, 350). "A Practical Treatise: On the Duties of Christians Owning Slaves" (ms.), Ch. 2:45–46, in Wiley Papers.

specifically of African slavery and rejected the utilitarian doctrine of the greatest good for the greatest number. Taking paternalist ground, he argued that African slavery, to be defensible, must serve the interests of enslaved Africans as well as those of their masters. Stephens, as he insisted most forcefully in his renowned "Cornerstone Speech" in Savannah in 1861, wished, if possible, to restrict his defense of slavery to the relation of whites to blacks.[13]

The problem of white slavery dogged Stephens. An admirer of Thomas Carlyle, he returned again and again to the problem of white labor. In 1855 he chided northern congressmen for the hunger and unemployment in their cities. The South, he boasted, did not have thousands of workers who wailed for bread. "We have a 'Social Providence,' to use a late very appropriate designation given by the New York *Tribune*, which prevents all this. A system by which capital accumulated in the years of plenty is required to sustain labor in the years of want." Continuing to dissent from Slavery in the Abstract, Stephens criticized the Spartans for having reduced members of their own race to helotry; and, although applauding Europeans for understanding the need for social subordination, he frowned on their enslavement of white labor in disguised form. Stephens could not sustain his racial argument. The speech in which he invoked the South's "Social Providence" said more than he might have intended. It praised slavery for reconciling the interests of capital and labor. Subsequently, he wrote that if the loathsome Know Nothings had their way, "The whole *sub stratum* of northern society will soon be filled up with a class who can work, and who, though *white*, cannot *vote*." And that would mean virtual enslavement.[14]

Linton Stephens grasped the implications of his brother's argument: "This speech clearly and distinctly reveals *a new idea*; and that is, the comparative effects of free and slave labor upon all the developments and consequently upon the prosperity of a country." On reflection, Linton Stephens thought the idea not new but the "manner of illustrating it is wholly new and very striking." He explained: "The office performed by the African – menial services and manual labor – is one which, on *universal confession*, must be performed in *every country* by *somebody*: now in the view of the *philanthropist*, who looks to the

---

[13] Alexander Stephens, "Speech on the Bill to Admit Kansas as a State under the Constitution," June 28, 1856, in Henry Cleveland, *Alexander H. Stephens in Public and Private. With Letters and Speeches before, during, and since the War* (Philadelphia, Pa., 1866), 548. See 717ff for the text of the "Cornerstone Speech" and 280–302 for the speech of Jan. 25, 1845, in the House of Representatives; also 125, 129, 650, 741, 802.

[14] Henry Cleveland, *Alexander H. Stephens in Public and Private. With Letters and Speeches* (Philadelphia, Pa., 1866), 456 and 126 for his attitude toward Carlyle, 127, 465–467; the text of the letter is at 466–467, quote at 466; also, T. E. Schott, *Alexander H. Stephens of Georgia* (Baton Rouge, La., 1988), 186. The tension in Stephens' progressivism, religious views, and understanding of capitalist development is especially noted in an older work by Rudolph von Abele, *Alexander H. Stephens* (New York, 1946), 97–99. Southern Know-Nothings made good use of the figures on pauperism in New York and other northern cities to oppose immigration and sing the virtues of southern society; see *The American Text-Book: Being a Series of Letters, Addressed by 'An American,' to the Citizens of Tennessee, an Exposition and Vindication of the Principles and Policy of the American Party* (Nashville, Tenn., 1855), 27–28.

interest of *mankind*, is there any difference between confining these offices to a *class* of men defined by *blood*, or diffusing them through a *class* marked by *poverty*?" Southern slavery, he answered, confined these offices to an inferior race, thereby offering a more humane solution than alternatives. A month later he repeated: "What is done by our negroes must be done by *somebody*.... The abolitionist would simply *substitute* the white man in place of the black."[15]

After the war Alexander Stephens remained uneasy about the extent to which labor could ever really be free. He appended to his *Constitutional View of the Late War between the States* a speech by his friend and longtime political ally Robert Toombs. Invading the lion's den in Boston in January 1856, Toombs had tried to defend slavery as a matter of racial control – no advocate of Slavery in the Abstract he – but he could not hold that ground. Southern slaves, he said, fared better than free workers and peasants in Europe, but that was not all. The laws of political economy spelled immiseration-free labor in "the great conflict between labor and capital, under free competition." The free-labor system's class war meant crime, strikes, mobs, and riots. For Toombs, free societies violated natural order by veering toward the enslavement of whites: "In short, capital has become the master of labor with all the benefits, without the natural burdens of the relation." In a subsequent defense of slavery he began by declaring whites a superior race that had to subordinate blacks if the races were to live together; he ended by asserting that slavery protected laborers as no free-labor system could.[16]

Other leading politicians of upcountry Georgia, notably Joseph E. Brown and Benjamin H. Hill, arrived at similar conclusions. The deeply pious Brown emerged from nowhere in the late 1850s as a spokesman for the common man. Born and raised in a nonslaveholding family, he became a fierce partisan of slavery. He, too, argued that emancipation of blacks would drive the price of labor down so low as to transform southern whites into impoverished tenant farmers or worse. As governor, Brown addressed the state legislature in 1861 on the organic nature of southern society. "Our whole system is one of perfect homogeneity of interest, where every class of society is interested in sustaining the interest of every other class." Hill, too, did his best to confine his defense of slavery to race but quickly transcended it. "Slavery," he said in 1860, "has always existed in some form. It is an original institution.... Now people not only see the justice of slavery, but its providence too." The world depended on slavery for its clothing and food. The South offered a magnificent example of the highest Christian excellence. "She is feeding the hungry, clothing the naked, blessing them that curse her, and doing good to them that despitefully

[15] Linton Stephens to Alexander H. Stephens, Jan. 24, 1855, and Feb. 2, 1855, in James D. Waddell, ed., *Biographical Sketch of Linton Stephens, Containing a Selection of His Letters, Speeches, State Papers, Etc.* (Atlanta, Ga., 1877), 120, 122.

[16] Robert Toombs in Alexander H. Stephens, *A Constitutional View of the Late War between the States*, 2 vols. (New York, 1970 [1868, 1870]), Appendix G, 1:625–647, quotes at 640–641, see also 2:85; Robert Toombs, "Slavery: Its Constitutional Status, and Its Influence on Society and the Colored," *DBR*, 20 (1856), 581–582, 598–600.

use and persecute her." With the Confederacy near collapse in 1864, Hill called for all-out resistance to the abolitionists and a defense of an institution that treated its poor well and benefited the world at large.[17]

In Mississippi, Albert Gallatin Brown, a substantial slaveholder, commanded the allegiance of small slaveholders and nonslaveholders and never lost an election. He defended slavery as a God-ordained blessing to both master and slave and vigorously championed its expansion. He felt compelled to repel the abolitionist onslaught mounted by Hinton Helper of North Carolina, who, in *The Impending Crisis of the South*, summoned nonslaveholders to class war against the planters. Helper rebuked the slaveholders for retarding economic development and depicted nonslaveholders as the primary victims of a grossly inefficient socioeconomic system. The *Compendium* (an abridged version of *Impending Crisis*) sold more than 140,000 copies in the United States by 1860 and may well have been one of the widest selling works of secular nonfiction to that date. Everywhere in the South officials and alarmed citizens took action to prevent the circulation of Helper's fiery polemic. Brown concentrated on slavery's alleged degradation of mechanics and workingmen. He began with stock arguments. Slaveholders created markets for labor and patronized artisans and mechanics. Helper had the story backward. The northern capitalist transformed the white laborer into a despoiled wage-slave and then left him "to shift for himself or it may be to starve or beg or steal," whereas the slaveholder protected his black slaves. Brown stressed racial solidarity, arguing that the South had no need for white slaves because it had black slaves. But he was more explicit than Alexander Stephens and matched Linton Stephens's frankness. The South, like every civilized society, had to fill its menial positions with some kind of servile labor, be it black or white.[18]

Proslavery Southerners – notably, George Howe of South Carolina and Samuel M. Wolfe of Virginia – effectively criticized Helper's statistical attempt to prove the southern slave economy a failure. Helper's misuse of statistics to support his antislavery ideology and preconceived notions also took a pummeling from Professor Elias Peissner of Union College in New York, who died leading Union troops at Chancellorsville. Peissner hit a raw nerve by turning statistics provided by J. D. B. De Bow against Helper. In 1860, northern

---

[17] Ulrich Bonnell Phillips, *Georgia and State Rights* (Yellow Springs, Oh., 1968), 198; Albert Gallatin Brown, in *The Confederate Records of the State of Georgia*, 4 vols. (Atlanta, Ga., 1909–1911), 2:124; *Senator Benjamin H. Hill of Georgia: His Life, Speeches and Writings* (Atlanta, Ga., 1896), 230, 243–244, 292.

[18] Hinton Helper, *Impending Crisis of the South. How to Meet It* (New York, 1857); James Byrne Ranck, *Albert Gallatin Brown: Radical Southern Nationalist* (New York, 1937), 127, 147, 161, 197–198, words quoted from 197. For the political impact of the *Impending Crisis*, see David Brown, *Southern Outcast: Hinton Rowan Helper and the* Impending Crisis of the South (Baton Rouge, La., 2006), ch. 7; on Helper's statistical problems, see 90; on A. G. Brown, see 168–169. On the circulation of the *Compendium*, see John Spencer Bassett, *Anti-Slavery Leaders of North Carolina* (Baltimore, Md., 1898), 18. *DBR* even charged that he was really a New Englander and not a Tarheel at all: 26 (May 1859), 608.

Democrats campaigned to refute Helper's statistics from a plausible critique by Gilbert J. Beere to a screed by Louis Schade.[19]

Other political leaders who spoke for – or at least to – nonslaveholding and small slaveholding farmers routinely maintained that the South had no need for white slaves because it had black. Thus spoke governors Arthur P. Bagby of Alabama in 1840 (presumably while sober) and J. J. Pettus of Mississippi on the eve of the War. They repeatedly held up before small property holders and the propertyless the specter of their own enslavement if blacks were removed, much as they stressed biblical sanction for slavery. By conceding the fundamental premise of Slavery in the Abstract – slavery as a social given – they taught constituents that every civilized society rested on servile labor. Pettus, addressing some 2,000 citizens of Jackson in 1859, specifically defended racial slavery as he damned northern aggression against slave property, but he warned that emancipation would force the South to "set up in its stead the Yankee hireling system." These spokesmen for nonslaveholding and small slaveholding farmers had no answer to those who logically concluded that Caucasian countries would have to reduce their own laborers to personal servitude for the good of the laborers themselves. Unlike Fitzhugh or Henry Hughes, they gagged on the prospect but feared it as the way of the world. Even in Kansas, the proslavery appeal to white laborers and farmers stressed that without black slaves, white labor would face de facto enslavement and accused the abolitionists of deliberately seeking to enslave whites.[20]

In a communication to Columbia's *South Carolina Temperance Advocate and Register of Agriculture and General Literature* in 1844, J. P. C. insisted "from actual experience" that hundreds of millions of Asians, Africans, Europeans and free-state Americans depended on a mass of common laborers who suffered immeasurably more than southern slaves. In 1851, Richard T. Archer, a wealthy planter, said the same in Jackson's *Mississippian and State Gazette*: "The question then is, whether this inferior class of laborers shall be African slaves, or white men, women, and children in a state of degrading dependence on the rich, or capitalist, class that employs them." He added that the

---

[19] George Howe, "The Raid of John Brown, and the Progress of Abolition," *SPR*, 12 (1860), 798–801; Samuel M. Wolfe, *Helper's Impending Crisis Dissected* (New York, 1969 [1860]), 38–56; Elias Peissner, *The American Question in Its National Aspect. Being also an Incidental Reply to H. R. Helper's "Compendium of the Impending Crisis of the South"* (New York, 1861), 1–56; on paupers, see 20–22 (Table VI); Gilbert J. Beebe, *A Review and Refutation of Helper's Impending Crisis* (Middletown, N.Y., 1860); Louis Schade, *Appeal to the Common Sense and Patriotism of the People of the United States* (Washington, D.C., 1860).

[20] James Benson Sellers, *Slavery in Alabama* (University, Ala., 1964), 333–334; Pettus quoted in Robert W. Dubay, *John Jones Pettus, Mississippi Fire-Eater: His Life and Times* (Jackson, Miss., 1975), 28–29; Gunja SenGupta, *For God and Mammon: Evangelists and Entrepreneurs, Masters and Slaves in Territorial Kansas, 1854–1860* (Athens, Ga., 1996), 35–38. A few years later, Thomas G. Clemson reported Arthur P. Bagby as constantly drunk: Clemson to John C. Calhoun, Aug. 1, 1849, in *JCCP*, 27:6.

abolitionists wanted to replace black slave labor with more profitably exploited formally free white labor.[21]

In response to the argument that every society rested on some form of personal servitude, antislavery Northerners warned their people of a hidden proslavery agenda. In the mid-1840s, the Reverend William Goodell of New York cited the views of Thomas Roderick Dew, F. W. Pickens, John C. Calhoun, J. H. Hammond, and Benjamin Watkins Leigh to demonstrate that proslavery logic and spokesmen signaled the enslavement of laborers of every race. Before and during the War, Republican politicians, editors, businessmen, clergymen, and educators did not let Northerners forget that southern spokesmen considered slavery the natural condition of white labor as well as black. They extensively quoted Fitzhugh, the Richmond press, and other staunch advocates of Slavery in the Abstract. Significantly, they usually quoted not from original sources but from the reprinted versions and endorsements in small-town southern newspapers that reached nonslaveholders and middling folk. In 1857 the Baptist Reverend Robert Ryland, the unionist president of Virginia's Richmond College, who rejected Slavery in the Abstract, acknowledged its spread in the South. Similarly, in 1859, *Southern Episcopalian* in a declaration republished in the *Charleston Mercury* dissociated itself from Slavery in the Abstract but noted the swing of southern opinion in its favor.[22]

In 1856 the Republican Party, citing the *Richmond Enquirer*, circulated handbills to warn of southern slaveholders' plans to enslave white labor. A young Republican group in New York fired off a broadside, the title of which spoke for itself: *The New "Democratic" Doctrine: Slavery Not to Be Confined to the Negro Race, But to Be Made the Universal Condition of the Laboring*

---

[21] J. P. C. to the Editor, *South Carolina Temperance Advocate and Register of Agriculture and General Literature*, Nov. 28, 1844; Richard T. Archer to *Mississippian and State Gazette*, June 6, 1851.

[22] Lawrence R. Tenzar, *The Forgotten Cause of the Civil War: A New Look at the Slavery Issue* (Manahawkin, N.J., 1997), chs. 5–6; William Goodell, *Views of Constitutional Law, in Its Bearing upon American Slavery*, 2nd ed. (Utica, N.Y., 1845), 12; "The Issue: White Slavery," *Republican Bulletin*, No. 9 (1856); The Young Men's Fremont and Dayton Central Union, *The New "Democratic" Doctrine: Slavery Not to Be Confined to the Negro Race, But to Be Made the Universal Condition of the Laboring Classes of Society: The Supporters of This Doctrine Vote for Buchanan!* (Ithaca, N.Y., 2006 [1856]); R. Ryland, *The American Union: An Address Delivered before the Alumni Association of the Columbian College, D. C., June 23, 1857* (Richmond, Va., 1857), 10–11; *Charleston Mercury*, April 9, 1859.

In New York, Jon H. Van Evrie's *Day-Book* took the southern side on racial slavery, as did James Gordon Bennett's New York *Herald*, which claimed a record 62,000 daily readers: Howard C. Perkins, "The Defense of Slavery in the Northern Press on the Eve of the Civil War," *JSH*, 9 (1943), 503–508; also, Kathryn Teresa Long, *The Revival of 1857–58: Interpreting an American Religious Awakening* (New York, 1998), 32. Samuel M. Wolfe of Virginia reported the New York *Herald*'s comments about the oppression of northern workers as worse than that of southern slaves and reprinted an account from *Boston Traveler* of a bitter strike at Lynn, Massachusetts: Wolfe, *Helper's Impending Crisis Dissected* (New York, 1969 [1860]), 62–65, 149.

Classes of Society: The Supporters of This Doctrine Vote for Buchanan! The broadside declared a doctrine "so monstrous and shocking as almost to seem incredible" and described it as common fare in the southern proslavery press and on the stump. The broadside provided illustrative quotes from southern politicians, from the leading newspapers of Richmond and Charleston, and from small-town newspapers, which republished articles and editorials from the leading papers. The *New Hampshire Statesman* attacked the Democrats in an article on "The New 'Democratic' Doctrine – Slavery not to Be Confined to the Negro Race." The *New Hampshire Statesman* quoted pro-Buchanan newspapers not only in Virginia and South Carolina but in Alabama, Missouri, and Washington, D.C. *Farmer's Cabinet* (New Hampshire) poured its wrath over "The White Slavery Doctrine," which was "beginning to prevail at the South." On that note William H. Seward opened his speech in Rochester in 1858 and Charles D. Drake closed his in St. Louis in 1862. The pro-Union Robert Trimble, writing from Britain in 1863, claimed that the legal codes of New Mexico assigned whites to peonage: "It is the logical sequence that if slavery be right, no question of colour or of race can long be permitted to stand in the way of what is already advocated in the South, to turn all *labourers* into capital!" The respected Andrew Dickson White of New York – probably best remembered for his *History of the Warfare between Science and Theology in Christendom* (1896) – also drew on southern politicians and newspapers to warn white workers that they faced enslavement if the South won the War. Anne Royall's antislavery but antiabolitionist and pro-southern *Huntress* (Washington, D.C.) responded that northern employers already considered their employees slaves.[23]

After 1856, Republicans repeatedly attributed to the Democratic Party the doctrine of Slavery in the Abstract and the enslavement of white labor. Not satisfied with accurate quotations from the southern press, the Republicans added embellishments that made the most extreme proslavery men gag. Garrison's *Liberator* and the *Milwaukee Daily Sentinel*, among any number of other publications, pounced on the reference to "Greasy Mechanics and Small Fisted Farmers" to condemn Herschel Johnson of Georgia, who proclaimed the South's commitment to ownership of labor. The *Sentinel* called upon artisans, laborers, and farmers to take the measure of the cry in the Muscogee (Alabama) *Herald*, "Free Society! We sicken at the name. . . . Greasy Mechanics and Small Fisted Farmers." Although much quoted by historians, the citation has a few difficulties. Muscogee, Alabama, did not exist and therefore neither did the

---

[23] *New Hampshire Statesman*, Aug. 23, 1856; *Farmer's Cabinet* (Amherst, N.H.), Oct. 9, 1856; William H. Seward, *The Irrepressible Conflict* (New York, 1858), 1; Charles D. Drake, *The War of Slavery upon the Constitution* (n.p., 1862), 7; Robert Trimble, *The Negro, North and South: The Status of the Coloured Population in the Northern and Southern States of America Compared* (London, 1863), 11; "Character of the Working Men, and Their Creed," *Huntress*, 1 (Oct. 8, 1837), 2; Andrew Dickson White, *Proofs for Workingmen of the Monarchic and Aristocratic Designs of the Southern Conspirators and Their Northern Allies* (Ithaca, N.Y., 2006 [1864]), 1, 4–6.

Herald. A Muscogee County in Georgia did exist but had no *Herald*. The citation and the reference to "Greasy Mechanics and Small Fisted Farmers" appear to have been antislavery inventions. Other southern newspapers quoted the Richmond *Examiner*, which, however, did not use the much-quoted assault on mechanics and farmers.[24]

During the War, Edward L. Pierce, a firmly antislavery agent for the United States Treasury Department, filed a widely noted protest to the secretary of the treasury. Crying out against exploitation of the freedmen, he called for measures to ensure their rights, safety, and well-being:

No man, not even the best of men, charged with the duties that ought to belong to the guardians of these people, should be put in a position where there would be such a conflict between his humanity and his self-interest – his desire, on the one hand, to benefit the laborer, and on the other, the too often stronger desire to reap a large revenue, perhaps to restore broken fortunes in a year or two. Such a system is beset with many of the worst vices of the slave system with one advantage in favor of the latter, that it is for the interest of the planter to look to permanent results.[25]

Versions of Slavery in the Abstract continued long after emancipation. In Arkansas, J. H. Trulock confidently wrote to a friend that slavery would continue for centuries, maybe to the end of time "in some *colour* or *form*." Judge Junius Hillyer of Georgia kept defending slavery not only because of black inferiority but because it cared for its laborers better than any system in the world. In 1919, Robert L. Preston of Virginia, still smarting under assertions of inhuman treatment of slaves, spoke about the immeasurably worse conditions under which northern workingmen labored. Yet those who had long boasted that they cared for their slaves as capitalists did not care for wage-laborers received a rude shock during the War, when slaveholders evicted women, children, and the superannuated once their male slaves had deserted to the Union ranks or been lost through impressments. In some cases slaveholders callously drove their slaves to the Union lines, telling them that they now depended on the largesse of their new masters. In other cases slaveholders no longer had the resources to take care of their slaves and sent them wherever help might be available. At the same time, many slaves expected their old masters to provide for them and reacted bitterly when they did not. The abolitionists opposed the hierarchically structured slaveholding household by dissociating wage labor from personal dependency and associating it with personal autonomy. After the War, freedmen, drawing their own conclusions, wanted their own land and, in

[24] *Liberator*, Sept. 19, 1856; *Milwaukee Daily Sentinel*, Oct. 4, 1856; *Bangor Daily Whig & Courier*, Jan. 31, 1856. We thank Robert L. Paquette for his detective work, which exposes the fabrications of the northern press.

[25] Ira Berlin, et al., eds., *Freedom: A Documentary History of Emancipation, 1861–1867*, Ser. One: *The Destruction of Slavery*, 3 vols. (New York, 1985–1993), 2:560; 593, 612–613, 675, 689; 3:244, 585. For the text of Pierce's report, see 3:124–143, quote at 142.

effect, accepted the proslavery – and socialist – characterization of wage labor as disguised slavery.[26]

Southerners who believed that their slaves fared better than free laborers throughout the world did not automatically conclude that slavery was the best social system for all peoples. Some conceded that slavery had little more to recommend it than free labor but held that southern slaveholders treated their slaves more humanely than capitalists treated their free workers. And most who found the slave system decidedly more virtuous than the free-labor system nonetheless objected to the enslavement of whites. William Spence Grayson of Mississippi cried out in 1861, "It is wrong to enslave a white man." Men like Grayson did not advocate enslavement of European workers but did fear that the deepening crisis of the free-labor system rendered it inevitable. What remains astonishing is that by the 1850s many Southerners went the whole distance toward advocacy and that many others either stopped just short or were weighing the arguments. No, they did not want to enslave whites, but they did, in increasing numbers, accept the notion that society required some form of personal servitude for laborers.[27]

The Printed Word

European travelers to the South expressed surprise at the impact of newspapers, books, pamphlets, and printed sermons on common people as well as planters. Towns, villages, and the countryside received controversial material through the efforts of concerned individuals, supported by congressmen who used franking privileges liberally. Proslavery and southern-rights books and pamphlets sold well. Even when they did not, they were liberally passed around, reaching untold numbers who gathered at home and in public places to hear them read aloud. A special kind of proslavery literature – advice on the religious instruction of slaves – achieved a wide circulation in the 1830s, especially among planters. In 1844, Hammond exulted, "My letter to the Glasgow Free Church has had quite a run. The Printer says he cannot supply the demand for it and is about to issue a pamphlet edition." Wayne Gridley of South Carolina said that Hammond's letters to Clarkson "are in everybody's hands." In December 1846, Hammond wrote to William Gilmore Simms that he had ordered 1,000 copies of his pamphlet on economic questions: "I wish to give

---

[26] Trulock quoted in Carl H. Moneyhon, *The Impact of the Civil War and Reconstruction on Arkansas: Persistence in the Midst of Ruin* (Baton Rouge, La., 1994), 60; *The Life and Times of Judge Junius Hillyer: From His Memoirs* (Tignall, Ga., 1989), 85; Robert L. Preston, *Southern Miscellanies* (Leesburg, Va., 1919), 13; Amy Dru Stanley, *From Bondage to Contract: Wage Labor, Marriage, and the Market in the Age of Slave Emancipation* (New York, 1998), 21, 40–41; Julie Saville, *The Work of Reconstruction: From Slave to Free Labor in South Carolina, 1860–1870* (New York, 1994), 2, 3. The abolitionists, Daniel J. McInerney remarks, viewed society as an extension of the individual and with similar expectations: *The Fortunate Heirs of Freedom: Abolition and Republican Thought* (Lincoln, Neb., 1994), 155.

[27] William Spence Grayson, "Capital Punishment," *SLM*, 33 (1861), 458.

every reading *country* man a copy. Some will get to the marrow & explain to their neighbors." Everyone who was anyone in Charleston, according to James M. Legaré, was reading and talking about Hammond's "Cotton Is King" speech of 1858.[28]

In the 1830s Thomas Cooper might have had an easier time in his struggle to survive as president of the College of South Carolina if his quasi-secessionist political and heterodox religious writings had not circulated widely, infuriating unionists and the clergy. In the 1840s and 1850s political pamphlets became the rage. Augustus Baldwin Longstreet's *Voice of the South* (1847) went through eight editions in two years. The twenty-one-year-old Edward A. Pollard of Virginia, living in Washington as an obscure congressional clerk, hoped to become famous with *Black Diamonds Gathered in the Darkey Homes of the South* (1858) – and he did. The Presbyterian Reverend Dr. James Henley Thornwell's well-circulated sermons and discourses, including his "Rights and Duties of Masters" (preached in Charleston in 1852), received favorable notice in the northern and British press. Thornwell's *Our National Sins* (preached November 21, 1861, and published repeatedly in pamphlet form) drew accolades across the South. Powerful politicians as well as ministers and laymen barraged Thornwell with congratulations and requests for printed versions of his sermons and addresses. Especially during the late 1850s, he found himself swamped with speaking invitations from Virginia to Mississippi.[29]

In 1850, George Frederick Holmes of Virginia predicted that an anthology of the best proslavery essays would sell well. He was right. *The Pro-Slavery Argument, as Maintained by the Most Distinguished Writers of the Southern*

[28] J. H. Hammond, Dec. 10, 1844, in Carol Bleser, ed., *Secret and Sacred: The Diaries of James Henry Hammond, a Southern Slaveholder* (New York, 1988), 134, also Mar. 16, 1845 (145); Hammond to Simms, Dec. 31, 1846, in Mary C. Oliphant, et al., eds., *The Letters of William Gilmore Simms*, 6 vols. (Columbia, S.C., 1952–1982), 2:389, n. 4; Wayne Gridley, *Slavery in the South: A Review of Hammond's and Fuller's Letters and Chancellor Harper's Memoir on that Subject* (Charleston, S.C., 1848), 3; Curtis Carroll Davis, *That Ambitious Mr. Legaré: The Life of James M. Legaré of South Carolina, Including a Collected Edition of His Poems* (Columbia, S.C., 1971), 123. James Johnston Pettigrew's legislative report in opposition to the reopening of the slave trade quickly went into a second printing and was read aloud at crossroads and in taverns across South Carolina: Clyde N. Wilson, *Carolina Cavalier: The Life and Mind of James Johnston Pettigrew* (Athens, Ga., 1990), 105–106 and ch. 9; also *ERD*, Dec. 24, 1857 (1:139); Albert J. Raboteau, *Slave Religion: The "Invisible Institution" in the Antebellum South* (New York, 1978), 162.

[29] W. C. Whittier, Jr., "Economic Ideas of Thomas Cooper," in B. F. Kiker and Robert J. Carlsson, eds., *South Carolina Economists: Essays on the Evolution of Antebellum Economic Thought* (Columbia, S.C., 1969), 80; Augustus Baldwin Longstreet, *A Voice from the South* (Baltimore, Md., 1847), note in eighth ed. (for a favorable review of *A Voice from the South*, see *SQR*, 13 (1848), 256–264); Jack P. Maddex, Jr., *The Reconstruction of Edward A. Pollard: A Rebel's Conversion to Postbellum Unionism* (Chapel Hill, N.C., 1974), 4; Ulrich Bonnell Phillips, "Economic and Political Essays," in J. A. Chandler, ed., *The South in the Building of the Nation*, 12 vols. (Richmond, Va., 1909), 7:185 (Elliott). For Thornwell, see James Taylor Jones to Thornwell, April 1, 1852; Thornwell to Dear General [James Gillespie?], July 21, 1860, in Thornwell Papers (USC).

States, published in 1853, contained essays that flirted with Slavery in the Abstract. Fascination with the theory spread across the South. E. N. Elliott of Mississippi had reason to expect a large audience for his anthology, *Cotton Is King, and Proslavery Arguments* (1860), which included bolder observations on slavery in relation to the larger social question of capital-labor relations. In case anyone missed the point, Elliott praised the work of Henry Hughes, much as Simms did in South Carolina. In Port Gibson, Hughes's home town, the *Reveille* hailed "St. Henry" as "a bold and vigorous thinker," and in Nashville, Fitzhugh's *Sociology for the South* occasioned considerable discussion among educated citizens, as Dew's *Essay on Slavery* had done earlier.[30]

Not every able writer fared well. Nathaniel Beverley Tucker's *Partisan Leader* did not come into vogue as a prophetic work until the War despite Abel P. Upshur's unusually lengthy and enthusiastic review, which included long excerpts. Upshur lamented that probably not 200 people even knew of the existence of his own book on states' rights, which had provoked Supreme Court Associate Justice Joseph Story to include an incensed critique in a later edition of his *Commentaries on the Constitution*. Scribblers as well as serious writers assumed that proslavery tracts would sell well in the South, but having underestimated people's powers of discrimination, they often fell on their face. *Anticipations of the Future*, Edmund Ruffin's didactic political novel, never sold at all – for the reasons that those who try to read it will understand. Its political content remains interesting but might have been condensed into a pamphlet one-tenth the size of a book that, as literature, taxed patience.[31]

The use and abuse of franking privileges had a marked impact on the circulation of pamphlets and books. John Marshall's publisher expected Federalist postmasters to frank subscription solicititations for his *Life of Washington*. Francis Lieber asked William Campbell Preston to support franking privilege for perhaps 100 savants: "I cannot investigate a number of subjects with our present dear postage." Representative F. W. Bowdon of Alabama boasted in 1848 that he sent out more than a million copies of literature in support of the presidential campaign of Lewis Cass. Franking had a mounting influence on the circulation of proslavery as well as abolitionist literature. Southerners,

---

[30] G. F. Holmes, "Observations on a Passage in the Politics of Aristotle," *SLM*, 16 (1850), 193; E. N. Elliott, ed., *Cotton Is King, and Pro-Slavery Arguments* (New York, 1969 [1860]), vii–viii; for Simms, see *Port Gibson Reveille*, Nov. 14, 1857; F. Garvin Davenport, *Cultural Life in Nashville on the Eve of the Civil War* (Chapel Hill, N.C., 1941), 176–177. Arthur Middleton Manigault may have intentionally echoed Hughes when he wrote of the South's "admirable older system of labor": R. Lockwood Tower, ed., *A Carolinian Goes to War: The Civil War Narrative of Arthur Middleton Manigault* (Columbia, S.C., 1983), 14.

[31] William W. Freehling, *The Road to Disunion* (New York, 1990), 390 (Upshur); Abel Parker Upshur, "The Partisan Leader," *SLM*, 3 (1837), 73–89; Joseph Story, *Commentaries on the Constitution of the United States*, 2 vols. (2nd ed.; Boston, 1851), 1:252; for reception of *Partisan Leader* during the War, see *EC*, 936–937; [George William Bagby], *SLM*, 1862), 399–400; Emma Holmes, Feb. 14, 1863, in Marszalek, ed., *Emma Holmes Diary*, 231. June 30, 1863, *ERD*, 3:36; also, Memucan Hunt to Willie P. Mangum, June 12, 1836, in Henry Thomas Shanks, ed., *The Papers of Willie P. Mangum*, 5 vols. (Raleigh, N.C., 1955–1956), 2:373–375.

notwithstanding their furious complaints of corruption and northern manipulation, took a share of the spoils. William C. Daniell wrote to Howell Cobb from Savannah in 1850 to describe Thornton Stringfellow's scriptural vindication of slavery as the most complete he had seen. With the first edition exhausted, Cobb subscribed to a thousand copies of a planned new edition, a hundred copies of which he expected to mail under his frank. In 1857 congressmen contributed half the money for the publication of Edmund Ruffin's *Political Economy of Slavery* and mailed at least 500 copies under franks. As time went on, political returns to the South declined steadily, whereas those to the North rose. In 1859 Senators David Yulee of Florida and Robert Toombs of Georgia, in an unsuccessful attempt to curb the power of the Republicans, led a southern revolt against the franking privilege. Still, when the secession crisis broke in 1860–1861, southern congressmen made good use of it.[32]

By the 1830s militant proslavery political speeches, pamphlets, sermons, and newspaper editorials and articles, without abandoning the focus on black slavery, applauded slavery as a labor system morally and socially superior to the free-labor system and destined to prevail over it. In 1833 the *Commercial Register* of Mobile, Alabama, denounced West Indian emancipation and asked readers to reflect on the cruel treatment of British factory workers. In upcountry South Carolina the Edgefield *Carolinian* and the *Pendleton Messenger* thundered that the industrializing countries had to choose between ownership of slaves by responsible individuals and de facto ownership by callous governments.[33]

Better educated Southerners supplemented a local newspaper with one from their state capital, especially Richmond, or from, say, Charleston, New Orleans, Mobile, Natchez, or Vicksburg. The black-belt townsmen of Marion, Alabama – established in 1823 – did not have a local newspaper until 1839 but regularly got newspapers from Cahaba, Selma, and Tuscaloosa. From the early nineteenth century the newspapers of Richmond were read all over Virginia and, in time, across the South. In the Southwest, the more well-to-do residents of Virginia origin also subscribed to Richmond newspapers, and those of South

---

[32] Albert J. Beveridge, *The Life of John Marshall*, 4 vols. (Boston, Mass., 1916), 3:230; Diary, April 10, 1836, in Thomas Sergeant Perry, ed., *The Life and Letters of Francis Lieber* (Boston, Mass., 1882), 111; W. C. Daniell to Howell Cobb, Jan. 23, 1850, in Ulich B. Phillips, ed., *The Correspondence of Robert Toombs, Alexander H. Stephens, and Howell Cobb*, "Annual Report of the American Historical Association for the Year 1911: vol. 2" (Washington, D.C., 1913), 182; April 17, 24, 1857, *ERD*, 1:174, 180; William Garrett, *Reminiscences of Public Men in Alabama, for Thirty Years* (Atlanta, Ga., 1872), 563; Jon L. Wakelyn, ed., *Southern Pamphlets on Secession, Nov. 1860–April 1861* (Chapel Hill, N.C., 1996), Introduction, especially xvii–xx and editorial notes. On the effort in 1859 to curb franking, see Roy Franklin Nichols, *The Disruption of American Democracy* (New York, 1948), 237.

[33] Joe Bassette Wilkins, "Window on Freedom: The South's Response to the Emancipation of the Slaves in the British West Indies, 1833–1861" (Ph.D. diss., University of South Carolina, 1977), 55, 63, 268. For the avid reading of newspapers in early Virginia, see John R. Thompson, "Colonial Life in Virginia," *SLM*, 20 (1854), 336. Newspapers, Susan Archer Talley advised, should be read before or during breakfast and always in the family circle: [Talley], "On Reading," *SLM*, 28 (1859), 1.

Carolina origin to Charleston newspapers. Circulation figures provide a poor index of the extent of newspaper reading for they were passed along liberally and read aloud in informal gatherings at the courthouse, church, and general store. From the eighteenth century onward, single copies of Charleston's news-papers reached the backcountry, where they were passed around, read aloud, and treasured – a pattern recapitulated across the South. Town folks gathered after church on Sunday to hear one of the leading men read the newspapers aloud. In and around the smallest villages, information circulated to an extent known in only a few countries.[34]

Newspapers and magazines took up the cry against capitalist wage-slavery despite having to be careful about how to present Slavery in the Abstract to the town laborers. Often, editors did not bother to comment, settling for a steady exposure of free-labor conditions. They found necessary ammunition in the British and northern press, from which they excerpted liberally. In 1852 the Methodist *Weekly Message* of Greensboro, North Carolina, picked up a suitable item from a newspaper in Philadelphia, which reported that although expert needlewomen enjoyed better conditions than most northern workers, they worked up to sixteen hours a day, earning about three dollars a week, half of which went for food and board. *Weekly Message* made no comment. Why should it have? Its readers knew that slaves had a shorter working day. During the War, French and British travelers noticed the widespread parroting among all classes of the *Charleston Mercury* and other newspapers that dwelled on the supposedly superior living conditions of southern slaves and on the beauties of the unification of labor and capital in a safe social system. Occasionally, the press provoked hostile reactions. The editor of the *Charleston Mercury* found himself deeply embarrassed when, in response to his endorsement of Fitzhugh's implicit argument for the enslavement of all labor, Charleston's mechanics burned him in effigy. The incident bolstered Spratt's campaign to reopen the African slave trade, for he warned of a growing danger from anti-slavery agitation among Charleston's white laborers.[35]

---

34 Weymouth T. Jordan, *Ante-Bellum Alabama, Town and Country* (Tallahassee, Fla., 1957), 37; Richard Beale Davis, *Intellectual Life in Jefferson's Virginia, 1790–1830* (Chapel Hill, N.C., 1964), 74–75; Donald E. Reynolds, *Editors Make War: Southern Newspapers in the Secession Crisis* (Nashville, Tenn., 1966), vii; E. Merton Coulter, *Joseph Vallence Bevan: Georgia's First Official Historian* (Athens, Ga., 1964), 35; Joseph G. Baldwin, *The Flush Times of Alabama and Mississippi: A Series of Sketches* (New York, 1957 [1853]), 54; John Hebron Moore, *The Emergence of the Cotton Kingdom in the Old Southwest: Mississippi, 1770–1860* (Baton Rouge, La. 1988), 137; Harvey Toliver Cook, *The Life and Legacy of David Rogerson Williams* (New York, 1916), 53–54; Sept. 7, 1862, in Mary D. Robertson, ed., *Lucy Breckenridge of Grove Hill: The Journal of a Virginia Girl, 1862–1864* (Kent, Oh., 1979), 48; for politicians at local stores, see the reflections of J. L. M. Curry, *The South in Olden Time* (Harrisburg, Pa., 1901), 5–6. Sarah Mytton Maury of England wrote in the 1840s that the townsmen of Mississippi were amazed and contemptuous that Liverpool had no daily newspaper: Maury, *Englishwoman in America* (London, 1848), 193.

35 Frank Luther Mott, *A History of American Magazines, 1741–1850* (Cambridge, Mass., 1938), 461–462; Buckingham, *Slave States*, 1:213–215; *Weekly Message* (Greensborough, N.C.),

Newspaper attacks on the free-labor system *qua* system increased dramatically with the struggle over the territories and the crisis of 1850, reaching heights with the economic crisis of 1857. From Texas to the Atlantic coast newspapers picked up exposés from free-state newspapers on the brutal conditions faced by northern labor. The *Mississippi Free Trader and Natchez Gazette* and the *Texas State Gazette* (Austin) reprinted articles from New York's *Day-Book* and Philadelphia's radical *Monthly Jubilee* on the suffering, poverty, and misery of free blacks in northern cities in contrast to the security of slaves in the South. The *Texas State Gazette* considered the reformist purposes of the northern radicals hopeless: "The evil of which the free laborer complains is not an accidental one. It is chronic in all its enormities.... The South, by its slave institution, affords an outlet to labor which prevents the evils of poverty, want and disease incident to the competition and rivalry of white laborers for bread and existence." From a newspaper in New York, Georgia's *Daily Columbus Enquirer* reprinted a piece from the *Savannah Republican* that recorded the hardships of "a sewing girl named Susan Lee," who detailed inhuman working conditions and was fired for having dared to protest. In 1858 the *Baltimore Sun* summarized Lord Shaftsbury's report in the *Times of London* on the British laborers' brutally long working day and miserable working conditions. The *Baltimore Sun* asked if the condition of the most wretched of southern slaves was worse. A few months later, the *Charleston Mercury* quoted at length an article from the Liverpool *Northern Times* that expressed opposition to black slavery but acknowledged that a large portion of the world's laborers lived no better than they.[36]

The leading newspapers in Richmond, Charleston, and New Orleans reprinted each other's stories. At random: In the 1850s the New Orleans *Picayune* – in an article reprinted in the Columbia *Daily South Carolinian* – ridiculed attempts of the British press to deny that southern slaves lived better than British laborers. The *Charleston Mercury* reprinted articles from the *New Orleans Delta* that defended black slavery as preferable to white and held the free-labor system responsible for monopolists and the destitute. The *Mississippi Free Trader and Natchez Gazette* reprinted "A Remedy for Northern Pauperism" from the *Charleston Mercury*, which had drawn on *Day-Book* of New York to recommend that parents who sent their small children out to work be enslaved. In 1860 the *New York Herald* published a petition to the northern states from "tens of thousands" of Southerners that alleged de facto enslavement of white laborers in Massachusetts, New York, and Pennsylvania.

Nov. 20, 1852. For general discussion of the press, see William Sumner Jenkins, *Pro-Slavery Thought in the Old South* (Gloucester, Mass., 1960), especially 90; Arthur C. Cole, *The Irrepressible Conflict, 1850–1865* (New York, 1934), 55. On Spratt, see William W. Freehling, *The Road to Disunion*, vol. 2, *Secessionists Triumphant, 1854–1861* (New York, 2007), 2:188.

36 *Mississippi Free Trader and Natchez Gazette*, Feb. 9, 1850; "Beneficence of Slavery," *Texas State Gazette*, May 19, 1855; "The White Slaves of the North," *Daily Columbus Enquirer*, Jan. 28, 1860; "The White Slaves of England," *Baltimore Sun*, June 25, 1858; "English Laborers," *Charleston Mercury*, Nov. 3, 1858.

In 1860–1861 the *New York Herald* grew shriller in claiming the superior condition of laborers in the South relative to those in Britain and on the Continent, where free labor qualified as a white slavery. The *Herald* supported northern workers' strikes and protests against capitalist exploitation and brutality. The antislavery *Milwaukee Daily Sentinel* indignantly dubbed the *Herald* "Satanic." From the *Richmond Enquirer*, the *Charleston Mercury* reprinted a rave review of *Cannibals All!* and an article, "Aristocracy and Abolitionism," which attributed to the British aristocracy promotion of antislavery among laborers to distract them from their own exploitation. British aristocrats "are and ever have been the richest and most oppressive slave-owners in the world." It was an old southern theme. In 1843, for example, the *Mississippian* denounced the "privileged robbers" of a brutally oppressive British ruling class.[37]

Until 1840 or so, southwestern newspapers dismissed as idle propaganda the indictment of free labor as disguised slavery. The *Arkansas State Gazette* republished an article from the *Northampton Courier* (New Hampshire) that cited the fine labor conditions in the Lowell Mills in Massachusetts. Houston's proslavery *Telegraph and Texas Register* reprinted William Ellery Channing's proclamation of the steady improvement of the condition of free labor and dismissal of claims of superior conditions among the slaves.

By the mid-1850s, sentiments had shifted decisively. An oft-reprinted article in Texas newspapers claimed that nine-tenths of northern laborers were "neither more nor less than the slave of capital." The New Orleans *Daily Picayune* commented in 1859, "We seriously question whether the slavery of the South is not comfort in comparison with the slavery of poverty in the North." The *Picayune*'s rival, the *Daily Crescent*, went further. Doubting that slavery impeded economic progress, it pronounced the question beside the point: "It is undeniable that where large masses of people are assembled together in circumscribed limits, there is not only more crime and lawlessness, but more actual suffering for the common necessaries of life. We read every day of such suffering and sometimes of starvation itself, in the dense communities of the North – rarely, if ever, in the sparsely settled sections of the South." Moderates like Calvin H. Wiley, North Carolina's prominent Presbyterian educator, agreed that big cities were nests of crime and depravity and that the South had a blessed rural social life.[38]

---

[37] *Daily South Carolinian*, Oct. 29, 1853; *Mississippi Free Trader and Natchez Gazette*, Feb. 9, 1850; *New York Herald*, Oct. 18, 1860; *Charleston Mercury*, Oct. 9, 1856, Feb. 19, 1857, May 2, 1856, Apr. 27, 1857. From *New York Herald*: "The White Slaves of Free Labor," Jan. 28, 1860; "White Slavery in British Factories," April 12, 1860; "Nigger Worship and Its Consequences," Mar. 7, 1861; Jan. 13, 1860; March 8, 1860. "The Mud Sill Theory," *Milwaukee Daily Sentinel*, Jan. 23, 1860; *Mississippian*, Jan. 6, 1843. Early British antislavery arose primarily from the ranks of the Tories, whereas the Whigs accommodated to business interests that had a vested interest in it; see Christopher Hill, *Some Intellectual Consequences of the English Revolution* (Madison, Wisc., 1980), 38.

[38] *Arkansas State Gazette*, May 8, 1839; "From Dr. Channing's Letter to Mr. Clay. The Dignity of the Laborer," *Telegraph and Texas Register*, Sept. 11, 1839; Gary J. Battershell, "Upcountry Slaveholding: Pope and Johnson Counties, Arkansas, 1840–1860" (Ph.D. diss.,

In the 1850s newspapers across the South stepped up coverage of the horrors faced by laborers in free-labor countries. The *Raleigh Register* joined the more radical press in asserting that without question, southern black slaves fared incalculably better than European wage-workers. In Jackson, the *Mississippian* reprinted an article from the *Mobile Mercury* that praised slavery's succor of its laborers and protested the callousness of employers of free laborers. During the War, it devoted four columns to slavery's superiority in promotion of economic prosperity and care of laborers, reiterating the common depiction of pauperism as a necessary concomitant to the free – but not the slave – labor system. Abandoning caution in the 1850s, Richmond's newspapers promoted slavery as a model social system. John Mitchel, the temporarily transplanted Irish revolutionary who worked for Richmond's leading newspapers, sounded so much like George Fitzhugh that the authorship of some articles remains in question. The *Richmond Enquirer* stated coyly that it would not go "to the length of declaring that Slavery in the Abstract – Slavery everywhere – is a blessing to the laboring classes," but it echoed Fitzhugh's description of free society as a "little experiment" that lacked the right principle for governing labor.[39]

Other southern newspapers reprinted its articles and similar ones from the rival *Richmond Examiner*. In 1855 the *Richmond Enquirer* repeatedly breathed fire. One article ridiculed the poor laws as a humbug worthy of P. T. Barnum. It denied that the end of villeinage liberated British labor, which "suffers more abject servitude than in the time of William the Conqueror." Contributors forecast an imminent working-class revolution in England, attributing current European upheavals to struggles between capital and labor. They concentrated fire on the "concentration and aggregation of capital in few hands, and at a few centres." The *Richmond Enquirer* added that the intellectual leaders of Europe were undermining property, family, and religion.[40]

A shaken Frederick Law Olmsted quoted the *Richmond Enquirer*, which published an article ostensibly written by a Northerner: "While it is far more obvious that negroes should be slaves than whites, for they are only fit to labor, not to direct, yet the principle of slavery itself is right, and does not

University of Arkansas, 1996), 104ff; Battershell (p. 6) stresses that small farmers and townsmen drifted in and out of slaveholding and retained a strong attachment to slave property; Thomas Ewing Dabney, *One Hundred Great Years: The Story of the Times-Picayune from Its Founding to 1940* (Baton Rouge, La., 1944), 113, for the *Daily Picayune*, Jan. 26, 1859; *Daily Crescent*, June 15, 1860, in Dwight Lowell Dumond, ed., *Southern Editorials on Secession* (Gloucester, Mass., 1964), 127–128; Calvin H. Wiley, "A Practical Treatise: On the Duties of Christians Owning Slaves," ch. 1, 3–4 (ms.), ch. 2: quote at 32–33, in Wiley Papers.

39 "The Worlds Fair," *Raleigh Register*, June 21, 1851; "Slavery in Europe and America," *Raleigh Register*, July 18, 1854; "Free and Slave Labor – A Contrast," *Mississippian*, Oct. 19, 1858; "Slave and Free States as Tested in the Census," *Weekly Mississippian*, Feb. 11, 1862.

40 From the *Richmond Enquirer*: "The English Poor Laws and the Emancipation of the Villeins," June 28, 1855; Comment by J. H., July 3, 1855; April 8, May 2, May 20, 1856; "The Family," July 1, 1856; "Negro Slavery and the Constitution," reprinted in *Charleston Mercury*, Jan. 10, 1856, from the *Richmond Enquirer*.

depend upon difference of complexion. Differences of race, of lineage, of language, of habits, and of customs, all tend to render the institution more natural and durable; and although slaves have been generally whites, still the masters and slaves have generally been of different national descent." The *Enquirer* thereupon announced that Moses and Aristotle "are both authorities in favor of this difference of race, but not of color." Olmsted had reason to worry: In Alabama and well beyond, Virginia Clay, among others, considered the *Enquirer* required reading, although the *Charleston Mercury* and the *New Orleans Delta* sneered that the *Enquirer* "prefers gasconade and assertion to logical deduction."[41]

Antislavery spokesmen felt compelled to counter the *Enquirer*'s substantial influence. In 1855, Gamaliel Bailey, editor of *National Era* (Washington) responded directly to the *Enquirer*'s endorsement of George Fitzhugh's *Sociology for the South*. He had previously conceded that slaveholders believed their own propaganda and that they, like their proslavery predecessors in England, argued logically and with great polemical power. Although at first he ridiculed the argument that southern slaves lived more comfortably and securely than European workers, he later conceded the miserable conditions of Europe's laboring masses. He insisted on steady if slow progress as political freedom expanded, whereas the even worse conditions of southern slaves promised no respite.[42]

Not to be outdone by the *Enquirer*, the Richmond *Examiner* attracted national attention with a roar much quoted then and ever since: "Free Society! we sicken of the name. . . . We have got to hating everything with the prefix *free*." Probably, few Southerners worked themselves into a hatred of everything with the prefix "free," but countless numbers at least became suspicious. The *Examiner*'s onslaught continued during the War, when Basil Lanneau Gildersleeve – the young but already formidable classicist – poured out his wrath on bourgeois society and praised slavery as a safe social system.[43]

In the 1850s, the well-circulated *Charleston Mercury* led the more radical southern newspapers in an escalation of rhetoric and substance. In 1856 it republished an article from the *Richmond Enquirer*, ostensibly by a Northerner who labeled unscriptural and ahistorical the restriction of the defense of slavery to race. The South had long defended slavery racially but was now

---

[41] Frederick Law Olmsted, *A Journey in the Back Country* (New York, 1970 [1860]), quote at 456 n.; Virginia Clay-Clopton, *A Belle of the Fifties* (New York, 1905), 26; *Charleston Mercury*, June 18, 1857 (repr. from *New Orleans Delta*). See Bernard Mandel, *Labor: Free and Slave: Workingmen and the Anti-Slavery Movement in the United States* (New York, 1955), 130–131.

[42] Gamaliel Bailey, "'The Failure of Free Society,'" *National Era*, 9 (1855), 126, 130; Gamaliel Bailey, "A Remarkable Coincidence and a Strange Dissent," *National Era*, 6 (1852), 210; Gamaliel Bailey, Untitled, *National Era*, 6 (1852), 7 (1853), 34–35.

[43] *Richmond Examiner*, Dec. 28, 1855, quoted in Mandel, *Labor: Free and Slave*, 39; B. L. Gildersleeve, "The Tontine," *Richmond Examiner*, Nov. 4, 1863, "Exile," *Richmond Examiner*, Dec. 2, 1863, in Ward W. Briggs., Jr., ed., *Soldier and Scholar: Basil Lanneau Gildersleeve and the Civil War* (Charlottesville, Va., 1998), 131, 178.

shifting ground to the more consistent and justifiable position that slavery was "right, natural necessary." Northern "nominally free society" was cornered and "dumb as an oyster." The *Charleston Mercury* characterized free society as a "little experiment," declaring, "Modern free society, as at present organized, is radically wrong and rotten. It is self-destroying... has proved a failure." In 1857 it commented on the stable condition of southern slaves in contrast to the terrible hardships of unemployed northern workers. The contrast illustrated "the essential superiority of the slave States over the social system of the hireling States." In 1858 it prophesied that as free land ran out, the North would replicate all the horrors of Europe's social struggles. Not to be left behind, the *New Orleans Daily Delta* headlined an article, "The Hireling Labor System of England a Failure and a Curse."[44]

Support for Slavery in the Abstract grew steadily in the South's leading secular highbrow journals, most notably, *De Bow's Review* (New Orleans), *Southern Literary Messenger* (Richmond), and *Southern Quarterly Review* (Charleston). Increasingly, their contributors – including Andrews Pickens Calhoun, son of John C. Calhoun – referred to the North as "the hireling states." *De Bow's Review* published such well-known writers as Ellwood Fisher and George Frederick Holmes to sustain a depiction of British and northern free workers as wage-slaves, and it discussed the work of Fitzhugh, Hughes, and William J. Grayson at length, providing lengthy summaries of their theses and long quotations from their texts. G. C. Grammer criticized the excesses in Fitzhugh's *Sociology for the South* but enthusiastically endorsed its principal theses, praising its "manly, vigorous, attractive style." De Bow himself reviewed *Cannibals All!* in the same issue in which he ran Fitzhugh's "The Conservative Principle" – a ringing exposition of the doctrine of Slavery in the Abstract. De Bow described Fitzhugh as "one of the boldest and most daring thinkers of the age." Although he took exception to Fitzhugh's blanket rejection of political economy and hinted at other disagreements, he recommended *Cannibals All!* as required reading and filled much of his seven-page review with long quotations. De Bow received Hughes's "curiously metaphysical" *Treatise on Sociology* with greater restraint, apparently put off by its "sententious" style, but he applauded its "logic without ornament."[45]

[44] *Charleston Mercury*, Jan. 10, 1856 (from the *Richmond Enquirer*); Jan. 17, 1856; Nov. 15, 1857 ("A Significant Contrast"); Feb. 15, 1858; July 5, 1858; *New Orleans Daily Delta*, July 20, 1857.

[45] In *DBR*: Andrews Pickens Calhoun, see "Extracts from a Speech to the State Agricultural Society of South Carolina," 26 (1859), 477; Ellwood Fisher, "The North and the South," 7 (1849), 309; G. F. Holmes, "Ancient Slavery," 19 (1855), 617–637; G. C. Grammer, "The Failure of Free Society," 19 (1855), 29–38; De Bow, "Cannibals All!" 22 (1857), 543–549; for Hughes, see 17 (1854), 646. For a poetaster's version of Grayson's message, see J. S. Morris, *Impromptu Lines Read before the Belles Lettres Society and Adelphi Institute of Oakland College* (Port Gibson, Miss., 1858). The solution to the North's social question, Percy Roberts wrote, lay in restoration of black slavery: "African Slavery Adapted to the North," *DBR*, 25 (1858), 379–395. For free workers as "hirelings," see also John Spencer Bassett and Sidney Bradshaw Fay, eds., "The Westover Journal of John A. Selden, Esqr., 1858–1862," in *Smith*

In three issues in 1855 *De Bow's Review* reprinted long sections of Grayson's *The Hireling and the Slave*, with encomia from the northern press and its own fervent endorsement. A year later De Bow, upon publication of a new edition of *Hireling and Slave*, printed more excerpts and an account of British labor conditions. According to Benjamin F. Perry, *Hireling and Slave* won for Grayson "a wide reputation at the South, and excited much interest." But in the early 1840s in the South Carolina up country, Perry's staunchly unionist *Greenville Mountaineer* reprinted material from the *Charleston Mercury* on British industrialization's horrible cost to laborers. Sailing from Savannah to Charleston in 1858, an English traveler found two books on board – the Bible and *Hireling and Slave*. Among the applauding luminaries, James M. Legaré, Charleston's esteemed poet, associated himself with Grayson's book, and Governor R. F. W. Allston found it powerful and convincing. Other prominent men freely paraphrased Grayson's poem, although not always with direct attribution.[46]

Although *Southern Literary Messenger* published Nathaniel Beverley Tucker's rejection of the doctrine of Slavery in the Abstract in 1835, by the early 1840s a number of its articles blasted the British free-labor system. Benjamin Blake Minor of Virginia, the editor, berated the British for oppressing not only their own poor but the peoples of Africa, India, and China. James Blair Dabney wrote: "Let the capitalists and aristocracy of Britain beware." He suggested that they contain their enthusiasm for abolition and concentrate on their own Chartists and working class. "An accomplished Northern lady" condemned the North for its thinly disguised and especially brutal form of slavery – called free labor – which reduced laborers to conditions worse than those of southern slaves. She added that northern men oppressed women in a manner that reduced them to virtual slavery. "R. T. H." [R. M. T. Hunter?] drew on British sources, official and other, to document the horrible conditions to which children in the workforce were being subjected, protesting that no such horror existed on southern slave plantations. Others condemned the oppression of workers, especially of women and children, contrasting the security of poor peasants in Catholic traditionalist Spain and Austria with the appalling conditions of the laboring poor in England. "W" of Westmoreland County, Virginia, argued that throughout history capital has warred with labor; the

---

College Studies in History, 6 (Northampton, Mass., 1921), Aug. 19, 1858 (270), July 22, 1859 (299).

[46] For Grayson, see *DBR*, 18 (1855), 185–188, 459–462; Stephen Meats and Edwin T. Arnold, eds., *The Writings of Benjamin F. Perry*, 3 vols. (Spartanburg, S.C., 1980), 2:296–297; *Greenville Mountaineer*, Nov. 19, 1841; [Hiram Fuller], *Belle Brittan on Tour, at Newport and Here and There* (New York, 1858), 126; Curtis Carroll Davis, *That Ambitious Mr. Legaré: The Life of James M. Legaré of South Carolina, Including a Collected Edition of His Poems* (Columbia, S.C., 1971), 122; Anthony Q. Devereux, *The Life and Times of Robert F. W. Allston* (Georgetown, S.C., 1976), 185. For a typical invocation of the poem without mention of Grayson's name, see J. P. Holcombe, "Is Slavery Consistent with Natural Law?" *SLM*, 27 (1858), 407. See also Howard C. Perkins, "The Defense of Slavery in the Northern Press on the Eve of the Civil War," *JSH*, 9 (1943), 503–508.

laboring classes had always been subjugated; and southern slavery was proving much more humane than the disguised slavery from the British Isles to
Russia.[47]

In the 1850s *Southern Literary Messenger* stepped up comparisons and
contrasts. The author of "A Few Thoughts on Slavery" declared, "The sun
does not shine upon a happier race of laborers." For the author of "American
Slavery in 1857," southern slaves were the best-treated of laboring classes
and war between capital and labor was inherent in the free-labor system. The
author of "Some Thoughts on Social Philosophy" supported Fitzhugh. Society
had to take care of its poor and incompetent, and there were two ways to
do this – socialism, which had proven impracticable, and personal servitude,
which was withstanding all tests. Other articles maintained that European
workers and peasants, writhing in misery, would rebel against the abstractly
sound laws of political economy. John Reuben Thompson, who succeeded
Benjamin Blake Minor as editor, responded to the mind-numbing charge that
he was insufficiently committed to defense of the South: "We are not weary
of expressing our honest conviction that slavery is the happiest solution to the
difficult problem of Labour and Capital, and that the South will never permit
it to be disturbed." A reviewer [probably Thompson] of Fitzhugh's *Sociology
for the South* exuded enthusiasm, notwithstanding the usual caveats about
his idiosyncrasies and rash formulations. Thompson subsequently welcomed
Cannibals All! with a tribute to the "boldest and ablest writer" in the proslavery
offensive, whose "new views" were enlightening the South.[48]

Southern Quarterly Review, in its initial volume (1842), discussed *Edinburgh Review*'s critique of the Poor Laws and then published articles that
invoked Hammond and Chancellor William Harper to depict wage-labor as
disguised slave labor. "E. G.," citing British Parliamentary Reports, excoriated
the treatment of the working class and described slaves as the only properly
protected laborers. He endorsed Chancellor William Harper's assertion that
many British workers would accept enslavement in preference to their current
condition. One contributor announced that Britain's emancipation of blacks
in the colonies enslaved white labor at home; a second turned to Dew and

[47] In *SLM*: A Virginian [N. B. Tucker], "Remarks on a Note to Blackstone's Commentaries,"
SLM, 1 (1835), 266–270; [Benjamin Blake Minor], "French and English Propagandism," 10
(1844), 577–583; John Blair Dabney, "Capt. Marryatt," 7 (1841), 270; [A Northern Lady],
"Northern and Southern Slavery," 7 (1841), 314–315; R. T. H. [R. M. T. Hunter?], "White and
Black Slavery," 6 (1840), 193–200; Severn Teackle Wallis, "Spain: Popular Errors," 8 (1841),
311 (Spain); William Oland Bourne, "British Oppression," 9 (1843), 506–507; Muscoe Russell
Hunter Garnett, "Wilde's Austria," 9 (1843), 600; W. [of Westmoreland Co., Va.], "Slavery in
the Southern States," 9 (1843), 740.

[48] In *SLM*: "A Few Thoughts on Slavery," 20 (1854), 197; "American Slavery in 1857," 25 (1857),
84–85; "Some Thoughts on Social Philosophy," 22 (1856), 315; also [R. E. Cochrane], "The
Problem of Free Society," 26 (1858), 401–418, 27 (1858), 1–18, 81–94; *SLM*, 26 (1858), 392;
[John R. Thompson?], "Failure of Free Society," *SLM*, 21 (1855), 129–141; [Thompson], *SLM*,
24 (1857), 239. Thompson made a strong impression on George Wythe Randolph, a descendant
of Jefferson: George Green Shackelford, *George Wythe Randolph and the Confederate Elite*
(Athens, Ga., 1988), 5, 162.

Hammond to describe European laborers as "white slaves." In 1856 another contributor referred to the "acute penetration and ingenuity" displayed by Fitzhugh in the "able and sagacious" *Sociology for the South* but charged him with being overwrought in his onslaught against political economy. The author embraced the essentials of Fitzhugh's argument, concluding that the greater portion of humanity, regardless of race, was destined to slavery. That year *Southern Quarterly Review* – effecting the utmost gravity – claimed that the slaves of Mobile were offering to contribute money to alleviate the suffering of free laborers in New York.[49]

Agricultural Societies

State agricultural societies brought together planters and the few farmers who could afford the cost of admission. In the 1820s contributors to agricultural journals sternly criticized the free-labor system, insisting that slavery provided a better life for laborers. Leading journals published addresses to state and county agricultural societies at which socially and politically engaged citizens heard the message directly. James Barbour, in his presidential address to the Agricultural Society of Albemarle (Virginia), preceded Hammond's "mud-sill speech" by a quarter century: "Whether bond or free, white or black, menials must exist in every community, as they are the indispensable foundation of the social fabric." He added that the condition of southern slaves compared favorably with that of laborers in "some of the civilized countries of Europe." Charles Cotesworth Pinckney II reviewed the plight of free laborers abroad for the Agricultural Society of South Carolina, commenting: "Beyond mere animal suffering the slave has nothing to dread. His family is provided in food, shelter, and raiment, whether he live or die." Thereafter, agricultural societies and lyceums featured prominent speakers who endorsed Slavery in the Abstract or presented arguments that implicitly lent it credence. In subsequent decades these and other state societies, as well as many county societies, devoted much time to the defense and preservation of slavery; in consequence, the advocates of Slavery in the Abstract found audiences that were at least willing to listen to their point of view.[50]

In the 1830s *Southern Agriculturalist* published an account by W. W. Hazard, who told his slaves that they had legal rights and were by no means

---

[49] In *SQR*, see 1 (1842), 283–284; E. G., "Slavery in the Southern States," 8 (1845), 317–360, esp. 345–348; "Slavery and the Abolitionists," 15 (1849), 215; on Fitzhugh, see "Slavery and Freedom," n.s. (3rd), 1 (1856), 62–95, quotes at 63, 65; on the slaves of Mobile, see "Slavery and Freedom," n.s. (3rd), 1 (1856), 75. We have found no evidence for the slaves of Mobile.

[50] James Barbour, "Address to the Agricultural Society of Albemarle," *American Farmer*, 7 (1825), 290, and see "On Slaves and Slave Labor: Extract from a late Address by James Barbour to the Agricultural Society of Albemarle, Va.," *Daily National Intelligencer*, Nov. 24, 1825; Pinckney quoted in Chalmers S. Murray, *This Our Land: The Story of the Agricultural Society of South Carolina* (Charleston, S.C., 1949), 20, and for later years see ch. 2; C. W. Turner, "Virginia State Agricultural Societies, 1811–1860," *Agricultural History*, 38 (1964), 164–177.

at his mercy. Yes, he could punish them for insubordination, but the United States government did what no slaveholder could lawfully do: It executed soldiers and sailors for insubordination. And the law required him to provide for their old age – something no capitalist had to do for his wage-laborers. In 1825 future governor Whitemarsh Seabrook of South Carolina warned the Agricultural Society of St. John's Colleton that slavery faced a mounting threat from fanatics determined to overthrow it and thereby subjugate the South. In 1834 he went further in his presidential address to the Agricultural Society: "The history of every age and country attests that personal servitude has been the lot of a considerable portion of mankind. . . . Slavery, in some form, is as necessary as the division of labor itself." Edmund Ruffin, in *Farmers' Register*, urged masters not to become complacent because the living conditions of their slaves were so much better than those of Irish peasants. "A half starved hireling in Russia, Germany, or Great Britain exhibits to his employer the most degrading attitude that one portion of the species ever stood toward the other."[51]

In the 1840s R. W. Roper, speaking to the State Agricultural Society of South Carolina, referred to a "teeming North" with federal patronage to monopolize interregional trade relations and to crafty northern capitalists in "a conspiracy against us." The eminent Charleston physicians R. W. Gibbes and Samuel H. Dickson and the celebrated William Elliott addressed the South Carolina State Agricultural Society to condemn the brutalities of British and other free labor. A committee of Alabama's Barbour County Agricultural Society "challenge[d] the world to produce a laboring population more happy, better fed or cared for than our slaves." The committee declared that incidents of cruelty were becoming rare. Robert Collins, in a prize-winning essay for Georgia's Southern Central Agricultural Society, said, "History teaches the existence of Slavery from the earliest time." Divinely established and sanctioned, "It prevailed in all the greatest and most civilized nations of antiquity." Agricultural journals increased the reprinting of favorable accounts from northern counterparts. *Southern Agriculturalist, Horticulturalist, and Register of Rural Affairs* (Charleston) included an account of the low country in 1846 by the nationally prestigious agricultural publisher John S. Skinner of New York, who reported that tasked slaves worked fewer hours than most European peasants and agricultural workers. Indirect support for southern views came from northern agricultural journals like *American Agriculturalist* of New York, which reported on the ghastly conditions of the lower classes in London and New York.[52]

---

[51] W. W. Hazard, "General Management of a Plantation," *Southern Agriculturalist and Register of Rural Affairs*, 4 (1831), 350–351; Whitemarsh B. Seabrook, *A Concise View of the Critical Situation and Future Prospects of the Slave-Holding States in Relation to Their Colored Population*, 2nd ed. (Charleston, S.C., 1825), 3; Seabrook quoted in Charles Elliott, *Sinfulness of Slavery* (New York [1850]), 1:32; Edmund Ruffin, "Management of Slaves, &c.," *Farmers' Register*, 5 (May, 1837), 32.

[52] R. W. Roper, "Address Delivered in Columbia, S.C. before the State Agricultural Society," *Southern Agriculturalist, Horticulturalist, and Register of Rural Affairs*, 5 (1845), 48, and in Pt. 2 he, in effect, charged that the South was being reduced to an economic colony of the

Even *Southern Planter* of Richmond and other publications that usually eschewed political and social controversies were heard from. In 1844 it introduced the account of a tour of England by the Reverend Henry Colman of Massachusetts, noting that Colman admired the elegance and refinement of the aristocratic classes but, like other Americans, was heartsick at the degradation of the laboring classes – which the editors blamed on the political system. Colman's own report contained a graphic description of widespread misery, making a special point of the brutal exploitation of four- to six-year-old children in the countryside. In the 1850s, among other items, *Southern Planter* published William Ballard Preston's address to the Virginia State Agricultural Society, in which he vigorously defended slavery as an economic system; Albert Taylor Bledsoe's reply to criticism of his proslavery book, *Liberty and Slavery*; and from the *Boston Congregationalist* a complimentary view of the moral quality of Virginia planters. More pointedly, *Southern Planter* published addresses by Edmund Ruffin and Franklin Minor before the Virginia State Agricultural Society. Minor tried to repel the charge that slavery undermined the dignity of labor and reminded the free states that southern slaves did the work that free men had to do in the North. As early as 1836, in an address to the Philosophical and Historical Society of Virginia, Ruffin remarked, almost casually, "Nothing will make the lowest class of laborers in any county industrious but *compulsion* – whether it be presented in the form of hunger and cold, or the power of a master." In an address to the Virginia State Agricultural Society in 1852 – published in *Southern Planter* and republished as a pamphlet – Ruffin noted that "the slavery of class to class, which in one or other form, either now prevails, or soon will occur, in every civilized country, where domestic slavery is not found." Subsequently, in Charleston he delivered a vitriolic attack on northern oppression of the South in the annual agricultural *Report of the United States Patent Office*, 100,000 copies of which were distributed throughout the United States.[53]

North: 81–90; [A. B. Allen and R. B. Allen], "Agriculture Tour in England," *American Agriculturalist*, 1 (1842), 10. The texts of Gibbes, the Barbour County Agricultural Society, Collins, and of Dr. A. P. Merrill of Memphis may be found most conveniently in James O. Breeden, ed., *Advice among Masters: The Ideal in Slave Management in the Old South* (Westport, Conn., 1980), 17, 26, 179, quote at 207. Samuel H. Dickson, "Slavery in the French Colonies," *SLM*, 10 (1844), 269; William Elliott, *The Anniversary Address of the State Agricultural Society of South-Carolina* (Charleston, 1849), 45; [John S. Skinner], "Character, Habits, and Management of Southern Planters," *Southern Agriculturalist, Horticulturalist, and Register of Rural Affairs*, 6 (1846), 413.

53 "Colman's Agricultural Tour," *Southern Planter*, 4 (1844), 194–196; William Ballard Preston, "Address before the Virginia State Agricultural Society at Its Second Annual Exhibition," *Southern Planter*, 14 (1854), 1–10; A. T. Bledsoe, "Communication," *Southern Planter*, 16 (1856), Supplement, 1–5; "Compliment to Virginia Farmers," *Southern Planter*, 19 (1859), 62–63; Edmund Ruffin, "Sketch of the Progress of Agriculture in Virginia and the Causes of Its Decline," in Jack Temple Kirby, ed., *Nature's Management: Writings on Landscape and Reform, 1822–1859* (Athens, Ga., 2000), 16 [originally published in *Farmers' Register*]; Edmund Ruffin, "Address Delivered before the Virginia State Agricultural Society," *Southern Planter*, 12 (1852), 8–16, and Ruffin's pamphlet, *Address to the Virginia State Agricultural Society on the*

Garnett Andrews of Georgia's Southern Central Agricultural Society presented the argument for Slavery in the Abstract matter-of-factly, as if his audience hardly needed to be instructed. The South "has solved the difficulties of
communism, so long and so fruitlessly dreamed of by French philosophers,
because associated labor, when controlled by the governing power of a master,
economizes in consumption and augments in production. William C. Daniell,
opening the convention of the Agricultural Association of the Slaveholding
States, attributed to free societies a rapid capital accumulation and an increase
of population that reduced workers to wage-slaves and generated intense class
war: "This is the condition of those parts of the Old World which reproach
us with slavery. It is the cry of the capitalists who have prostrated labor at
their feet, and slavery would not be a burden to the planter had he the same
command of labor which the capitalists of the Old World possess."[54]

In 1850 David Flavel Jamison, an able historian who served as president of
South Carolina's secession convention, referred to the advance of the "democratic principle," warning that in time the South might follow Europe and the
North into moral decadence and political disorder: "Its dangers are yet to come.
Our people have been comparatively pure because they have, hitherto, to a great
extent, been freed from the corrupting influences of large cities." For Jamison
the fate of the South depended heavily on the "agricultural habits" of its people
but "chiefly on the existence of the institution of slavery." In 1856, Jamison,
addressing the South Carolina Agricultural Society, got specific. The North was
rife not only with "agrarianism, communism, spiritualism and Mormonism,
but infidelity, opposition to parental control, to the marriage tie, to law, and
all the usages which time has consecrated as the necessary cement of society."
Jamison concluded: "Slavery is the great preventative of all the isms."[55]

James P. Holcombe of Virginia, a prestigious professor of law at the University of Virginia and a politically influential attorney, laid out the essential
arguments in a speech that the Virginia State Agricultural Society immediately
published and circulated. He recoiled from the enslavement of whites, but reading the history of England from the Middle Ages onward, he concluded that
the enslavement of an inferior race merely complicated a broader labor question. The most recent research showed that the descendants of emancipated

Effects of Domestic Slavery (Richmond, Va., 1853), 5, also 12–13; David F. Allmendinger,
Jr., ed., *Incidents of My Life: Edmund Ruffin's Autobiographical Essays* (Charlottesville, Va.,
1990), 133; Franklin Minor, "Address Delivered before the Virginia State Agricultural Society,"
Southern Planter, 15 (1855), 373.

54 "Address of the Hon. Garnett Andrews," *Southern Central Agricultural Society Transactions*
(Macon, Ga., 1852), 100; W. C. Daniell, "An Address Delivered at the Opening of a Convention
to Organize an Agricultural Association of the Slaveholding States," *American Cotton Planter*,
4 (Apr.–May, 1854), 106–109, 134–136, quote at 107. See also, "A.," "The Influence of Slavery
upon the Progress of Civilization," *American Cotton Planter and Soil of the South*, n.s., 3 (July,
1854), 201–204.

55 "J" [David Flavel Jamison], "The National Anniversary," *SQR*, n.s., 2 (1850), 176, 179–180;
D. F. Jamison, "Annual Address," in *Proceedings of the State Agricultural Society of South
Carolina* (Charleston, S.C., 1856), 354, 355.

European serfs would welcome a master who would furnish them with food, clothing, and shelter. European capitalists treated their laborers barbarously, although "no radical distinction of race" separated capitalists from laborers. Drawing on the observations of William Thompson, a Scots weaver, Holcombe further asserted that families were broken up in Scotland more than in the American South. Holcombe dismissed as "folly" the notion that European laborers could be reenslaved but expressed confidence that if slaves of another race were found, they would be much better off than free white laborers. European wage-slavery generated a "smothered but deeply hidden fire" that could only end in a catastrophic class war. Only in the slaveholding South did the laboring poor receive the requisite food, clothing, and housing. Necessarily so: "The mutual good will of distinct classes has, in all ages, been dependent upon a well-defined subordination." A contributor to *Russell's Magazine* said much the same thing, and Dr. John Stainbach Wilson of Georgia wrote in *American Cotton Planter & Soil of the South*: "Our slave labor is the source of all our wealth and prosperity; from this we enjoy all the necessaries and luxuries of life." But he went further: "It is the basis of the most desirable social and political system the world has ever seen."[56]

The northern-born Daniel Lee split his time between New York and Georgia, where he edited the *Southern Cultivator* and taught at Franklin College (University of Georgia). Lee agreed with those who thought that the North would eventually embrace slavery. As an editor in Rochester, New York, he championed the cause of farmers and mechanics and seemed convinced that only the extension of black slavery could keep the North from instituting white slavery. In 1845 he offered the usual assurances that the slaves on an Alabama plantation he knew were well treated, contented, and happy, pointedly adding, "with little of the concern which poor people in other countries experience." His *Southern Cultivator* generally avoided politics and North-bashing, but drawing on Horace Greeley's antislavery *Tribune*, it paraded New York's appalling number of murders, rampant prostitution, and child abuse. In effect, it returned the fire of the abolitionist press, which, like the American Anti-Slavery Society's *Anti-Slavery Examiner*, regaled readers with excerpts from the southern press on the frequency of murders and personal violence among whites.[57]

[56] J. P. Holcombe, *An Address Delivered before the Seventh Annual Meeting of the Virginia State Agricultural Society* (Richmond, Va., 1858), 9, 13–16; J. P. Holcombe, "Is Slavery Consistent with Natural Law?" *SLM*, 27 (1858), 413–414, 418; J. P. Holcombe, "The Right of the State to Institute Slavery," *Southern Planter*, 19 (1859), 37–39, quote at 38; "Slavery in England," *RM*, 5 (1859), 28; J. S. Wilson, "The Peculiarities & Diseases of the Negro," in Breeden, ed., *Advice among Masters*, 136. *Southern Cultivator* claimed 10,000 readers in 1852. Accounts of southwestern as well as southeastern planters suggest widespread circulation of agricultural journals: Moore, *Cotton Kingdom of Old Southwest*, 137.

[57] E. Merton Coulter, *Daniel Lee, Agriculturalist: His Life North and South* (Athens, Ga., 1972), 91; Gov. Hill, "An Alabama Plantation," *Southern Cultivator*, 3 (1845), 148; "'Free' Society – Life in New York," *Southern Cultivator*, 15 (1857), 9; from Jan. 1, 1838, *Anti-Slavery Examiner*, see "Arkansas" (188–191), and "Alabama" (192–194).

When Dr. E. H. Barton's presidential address to the New Orleans Academy of Sciences (1855) appeared as an article in *De Bow's Review* and as a pamphlet, Olmsted thought it important enough to mention in his *Journey in the Back Country*. Barton discussed southern soil, climate, and economic progress, and attributed the terrible famines in India and Mexico to a widespread ignorance that did not plague the enlightened people of the South. Celebrating the virtues of slavery, especially its elevation of the master class and the white population as a whole, Barton tried but failed to remain on racial ground: "The slaves constitute, essentially, the lowest class, and society is immeasurably benefited by having this class, which constitutes the offensive fungus – the great cancer of civilized life – a vast burthen and expense to every community, under surveillance and control; and not only so, but under direction as an efficient agent to promote the general welfare and increase the wealth of the community." Slavery generated a leisured and cultured class that benefited from the labor of slaves: "The history of the world furnishes no institution under similar management, where so much good results to the governors and the governed, as this, in the southern States of North America." The large mass of mankind is "averse to industry and nothing but the strongest exigencies will urge them to labor.... Compulsory labor has always been and always will exist."[58]

The Rising Generation

The elementary schools and academies quietly introduced pupils to a proslavery mind-set. *Readers* designed for young pupils carried material that made slavery a part of everyday life with casual mention: "The slave found a purse in the ditch." And they carried moral imperatives: "Do not be harsh, without cause, to servants, or those over whom you have authority. It is wrong to impose upon the helpless." Since Christian morals lay at the heart of the curriculum, educators upheld slavery as divinely sanctioned without taxing immature pupils with its political subtleties. *The First Reader, for Southern Schools* spoke simply: "It is not a sin to own slaves. It is right. God wills that some men should be slaves, and some masters." Primary and secondary schools stressed geography, and the leading texts almost casually recorded the ubiquity of slavery in time and place. They denigrated blacks but did not make slavery per se racially specific. *Readers* carried biblical references on divine sanction. *Our Own Third Reader* by Richard Sterling and James D. Campbell contained a lengthy discussion of divine sanction that included a discrete treatment of "Hebrews Might Be Enslaved," which left no doubt of the nonracial character of slavery in ancient Israel. More forcefully, Adelaide Chaudron's primary school *Third*

[58] E. H. Barton, *Anniversary Discourse before the New Orleans Academy of Sciences* (New Orleans, La., 1856), 22–23; Olmsted, *Back Country*, 387 n. During the 1850s planters and merchants who dominated southern commercial conventions shifted from a main focus on economic growth to measures to shore up slavery: Vicki Vaughn Johnson, *The Men and Visions of the Southern Commercial Conventions, 1845–1871* (Columbia, Mo., 1992).

Reader – used in the public schools of Mobile and elsewhere – included: "In England, the miners know neither how to read nor how to write. Some of them, it is said, have never heard of God! What poor, unhappy slaves! Never to hear of God! Never to know that they have a Father in heaven! How thankful we should be, who, as a nation, have no such sins upon our head."[59]

Slavery in the Abstract slowly made its presence felt in the colleges. A substantial portion of the southern elite attended college, at least for a year or two, receiving a moral and philosophical instruction approved of by political, religious, and social leaders. Educators, many of them clergymen, exercised a paramount influence in Sabbath schools, old field schools, academies, and secular as well as denominational colleges. Generally, they abstained from indoctrination while promulgating essentially conservative political and religious doctrines. Educators sought to counteract a growing transatlantic revulsion that classified slavery as a moral as well as social evil. Still, only an occasional proslavery zealot sought to impose a narrow ideological or political agenda on a southern people quick to assert their right to think for themselves. Having demonstrated that the Bible sanctioned slavery and that all historical experience sustained it, educators positioned themselves to construct a worldview appropriate to slaveholding society despite considerable disagreement over specifics.

In the late eighteenth and early nineteenth centuries, many of the brightest and most articulate students, in rebellion against their parents, espoused radical notions of all kinds and perceived reigning mores as old-fashioned and repressive. In this respect the rebels resembled college students in other climes and times. For the most part, their elders, remembering their own youthful passions and follies, reminded themselves that boys will be boys. In the 1820s and especially the 1830s, campus opinion nonetheless shifted toward acceptance of slavery as divinely sanctioned and morally justified. A prolonged campus reaction gained momentum in the wake of a series of political shocks, from Missouri and Denmark Vesey to Nat Turner and militant abolitionism. Even at the relatively liberal University of North Carolina slavery increasingly became identified as a requisite of social order and southern values. College professors,

---

[59] [Anon.], *The First Reader, for Southern Schools* (Electronic ed.; Chapel Hill, N.C., 2000 [1864]), 17; R. M. Smith, *The Confederate First Reader, Containing Selections in Prose and Poetry, as Reading Exercises for the Younger Children in the Schools and Families of the Confederate States* (Electronic ed.; Chapel Hill, N.C., 2000 [1865]), 27, quote at 29; K. J. Stewart, *A Geography* (Electronic ed.; Chapel Hill, N.C., 2000 [1864]), 16; A. de V. Chaudron, *Chaudron's Spelling Book, Carefully Prepared for Family and School Use for Beginners* (Electronic ed.; Chapel Hill, N.C., 1999 [1864]); Richard Sterling and James D. Campbell, *Our Own Third Reader: For the Use of Schools and Families* (Electronic ed.; Chapel Hill, N.C., 2000 [1861]), 211–222; A. de V. Chaudron, *The Third Reader, Designed for the Use of Primary Schools* (Electronic ed.; Chapel Hill, N.C., 2001 [1864]), 109. For mention of slaves in illustrations of rules of grammar and usage, see also Epes Sargent, *The Standard Speller* (Electronic ed.; Chapel Hill, N.C., 2001[1859, 1861]), 138; Thomas Carpenter, *The Scholar's Spelling Assistant* (Electronic ed.; Chapel Hill, N.C., 2001 [1861]), 47, 49, 86, 92, 140, 145; Levi Branson, *First Book in Composition . . . Especially Designed for Southern Schools* (Electronic ed.; Chapel Hill, N.C., 1999 [1863]), 28.

whether unionist or secessionist, weighed in on the superior condition of southern black slaves relative to that of free white workers abroad. Professor Maximilian Laborde of South Carolina College spoke for many: "There is less of want, of misery, and of suffering in our slave population than among the lower orders of other countries, and the system is one of mutual blessing and obligation."[60]

The shift on slavery was the most politically volatile manifestation of a broad-based ideological campaign against religious and political radicalism – against infidelity and Jacobinism. At least until the 1840s, when professors came under ever-closer scrutiny, southern students retained some freedom to criticize slavery, and even in the 1850s a few expressed antislavery sentiments. In 1841, Edward Pringle of South Carolina, scion of an elite low-country family, publicly called for the abolition of religion as well as slavery, and his proslavery classmate, William Henry Trescot, ridiculed the southern political pieties associated with John C. Calhoun, although he did not attack Calhoun by name. At the College of Charleston in December 1858 the sixteen-year-old William Plummer Jacobs, son of a slaveholder and a future minister of some prominence, concluded, "Slavery at best is a diabolical practice." Yet generation after generation of college students moved from criticism of slavery to acceptance of a necessary evil, and on to the exaltation of slavery as a superior social system.[61]

The campuses always had a noticeable number of radical students and some professors. The rebellious impulse that drew the youth to Tom Paine, irreligion, and even antislavery during the early nineteenth century drew them to proslavery and secessionism in later years, often in continued rebellion against more cautious parents. Charles Plummer Green of Virginia doubtless engaged in wishful extrapolation from local conditions when in 1836 he crowed that

---

[60] Robert Nicholas Olsberg, "A Government of Class and Race: William H. Trescot and the South Carolina Chivalry, 1860–1865" (Ph.D. diss., University of South Carolina, 1972), 28; Kemp P. Battle, *History of the University of North Carolina*, 2 vols. (Raleigh, N.C., 1907), 1:654–657; Charles William Dabney, *Universal Education in the South*, 2 vols. (Chapel Hill, N.C., 1936), 1:65–68; M. Laborde, letter to *Daily South Carolinian* (Columbia), May 3, 1856.

[61] Thornwell Jacobs, *The Life of William Plumer Jacobs* (New York, 1918), 51. For antislavery student sentiment during the Missouri crisis, see Glover Moore, *The Missouri Controversy, 1819–1821* (Lexington, Ky., 1966), 231. Paine, Voltaire, D'Alembert, et al. were no less heroes to the elite college students in New England. See, e.g., Lyman Beecher's account of the rage of "French infidelity" at Yale and of President Dwight's successful campaign against it: Charles Beecher, ed., *Autobiography, Correspondence, Etc. of Lyman Beecher*, 2 vols. (New York, 1871), 1:43, 100. In the 1790s professed atheism was rife among Harvard students, and students at Williams College were holding mock celebrations of the Lord's Supper. As late as the 1840s students at Yale were expelled for spreading infidelity: see H. T. Tuckerman, "Joseph Stevens Buckminister," *SLM*, 24 (1857), 50–57; Frederick Rudolph, *The American College and University: A History* (Athens, Ga., 1990), 38; Brooks Mather Kelley, *Yale: A History*, (New Haven, Conn., 1974), 211; *DNCB*, 1:234–235. Students at Princeton went wild for the French Revolution in the 1790s, going out of their way to defy college regulations to celebrate Bastille Day on the Sabbath: John M. Murrin, Introduction to J. Jefferson Looney and Ruth L. Woodward, eds., *Princetonians, 1791–1994* (Princeton, N.J., 1991), xvii–xix.

the rising generation supported Calhoun and nullification, but he probably reported accurately on the attitude of the students at Randolph-Macon College. In nearby Lexington, residents considered students at Washington College and Virginia Military Institute secessionist hotheads. In 1861 students forced the unionist president of Washington College to resign.[62]

By the 1840s, notwithstanding continuing differences over partisan politics, the indictment of the free-labor system and celebration of the superiority of slavery became common themes on college campuses. With mounting stridency, students hailed slavery as a blessing and, in the words of a young Mississippian, a "most cherished institution . . . [that] gives vitality and support to the South, and wealth and employment to many other peoples of the world." To a growing number of students, slavery offered a solution to the dangerous problem of the relation of labor to capital in modern society. Alarms sounded long before the crisis of the 1850s, as students responded to Dew and Hammond, Harper and Calhoun and saw Western civilization in danger of collapse. Reflecting on the demagogy and democratic excesses of post-Jacksonian America, the twenty-year-old William Hooper Haigh wrote in his diary for 1843, a year after his graduation from college: "A period has at length arrived when the most unreasonable & foolish doctrines find abundant advocates. In these latter days the old prophecy is verified to the letter – and false prophets have arisen and deceived many. Mormonism – Millerism – & Mesmerism find too many defenders, and if we examine minutely how easily the public mind is imposed upon – how strangely susceptible it is to every thing bearing the name of philosophy or metaphysics – we will see that the world has arrived at the unhappy stage – when diseased, & lunatic, its sage inhabitants will often in striving to reach a star grasp a cloud." Gloomily, Haigh concluded, "The merest shadow of things excites the fancy – the most abominable doctrine looked upon as the child of some noble intellect. We have truly reached the summit of political impudence."[63]

In 1845, the students of South Carolina College heard Henry L. Pinckney and Edwin De Leon urge the importance of liberal education, as they linked the exploitation of uneducated poor workers to the commission of the crimes

[62] Charles Plummer Green to Willie P. Mangum, March 1, 1836, in Shanks, ed., *Papers of W. P. Mangum*, 2:402; John Bowers, *Stonewall Jackson: Portrait of a Soldier* (New York, 1989), 24, 96, for the atmosphere in Lexington. On pro-secessionism at VMI see James Lee Conrad, *The Young Lions: Confederate Cadets at War* (Mechanicsburg, Pa., 1997), 34, and Ollinger Crenshaw, *General Lee's College: The Rise and Growth of Washington and Lee University* (New York, 1969), 117–125. Lincoln's election and especially his call for troops radicalized the campuses, swinging even unionist professors and students to secession: see, e.g., Charles William Trueheart to Henry Trueheart, Mar. 25, 1861, in Edward B. Williams, ed., *Rebel Brothers: The Civil War Letters of the Truehearts* (College Station, Tex., 1995), 23; Dunaway Wayland Fuller, *Reminiscences of a Rebel* (New York, 1913), 10–11.

[63] P. K. W[hitney], "The South Defended, *Oakland College Magazine*, 3 (Dec. 1857), 2–3; William Hooper Haigh, "United States in 1843," Diary, May 11, 1843, Haigh Papers; Edwin De Leon, *The Position and Duties of "Young America"* (Columbia, S.C., 1845), 14, 16, 21, 24, quotes at 14, 16.

and outrages that disgraced the cities of Europe and the North. De Leon called Jean-Jacques Rousseau a "wretched and frenzied enthusiast" and Victor Hugo and Eugene Sue purveyors of moral degeneracy. He launched a barrage against Europe's free-labor system in which "the masses are regarded merely as beasts of burden created for the benefit of the privileged orders." He added a caveat against the destructive seductions of socialism and other isms that threatened private property.[64]

The revolutions of 1848 spurred discussion of socialism on campuses. At the University of Virginia and the College of South Carolina student papers held slavery up as a blessing because it offered a solution to the dangerous problem of the relation of labor to capital in modern society. In 1851, Jesse Harper Lindsay, Jr., in his graduation speech at the University of North Carolina, presented a commonly held view: "The late revolutions of Europe have not been of a political but of a social nature. The tendency toward equality and universal suffrage, as a political right, is not the only characteristic of the changes of the nineteenth century. Social reform and perfectibility must also be attempted." Lindsay referred to socialism as a doctrine that dated from the earliest times: "Men have been shocked and grieved at the evils which have prevailed in almost every form that society has yet assumed. Subtle and ingenious thinkers have devised model Republics in which no misery should exist – earnest and zealous philanthropists have endeavored to realize their highest imaginations and put them in operation." He wanted no part of socialism, which would plunge "the whole fabric of government in one universal and overwhelming ruin." At the same commencement, James A. Washington elaborated on the social evils that socialists vainly tried to uproot. He described the struggle for survival of hundreds of thousands poor people in London and other great cities: pleas for bread, rampant crime, widespread prostitution, frequent suicides of hopeless workingmen. Beyond the industrial and urban parts of the world, misery plagued Russia and Prussia, Austria and Poland, Ireland and India. Ireland especially concerned southern youth. "Ireland's misery," exclaimed Junius Irving Scales in 1853, "has ever been England's shame." Scales recounted the early conquest and Cromwell's ruthlessness, concluding that despite some reforms, Irish peasants were starving. The contrast of the South with Ireland lingered on into the 1890s. Among prominent Southerners, R. Q. Mallard and James B. Avirett still insisted that southern slaves had lived better than the peasants of Ireland or the urban poor of northern cities or the white slaves in the factories of both Old and New England.[65]

---

[64] Henry L. Pinckney, *The Necessity of Popular Enlightenment to the Honor and Welfare of the State* (Columbia, S.C., 1845), 20; also Phillip Alexander Bruce, *History of the University of Virginia, 1819–1919: The Lengthening Shadow of One Man*, 5 vols. (New York, 1920–1922), 3:107, also 376–379; John Barnwell, *Love of Order: South Carolina's First Secession Crisis* (Chapel Hill, N.C., 1982), 27.

[65] J. H. Lindsay, Jr., "Socialism," UNC – North Caroliniana Collection: Speeches of Graduates, 1851; J. A. Washington, "The People," 1851, and J. I. Scales, "Ireland's Misery Has Ever Been England's Shame," 1853, UNC – North Caroliniana Collection: Speeches of Graduates; R. Q.

J. Cummings, in Emory and Henry College's *Southern Repertory and College Review*, cried out on behalf of workers who wallowed in misery in crowded cities, could not find work, and were left to fend for themselves. In an "Address to the Young Men of the South," the Southern Rights Association of the University of Virginia referred to the developing crisis in free-labor societies and saw an unbridgeable gulf between the two socioeconomic systems. It was obvious to the Reverend E. J. Stearns, professor at St. John's College in Annapolis, Maryland, that the world required hard, dirty, disagreeable work, and that someone had to do it, whether black slaves in America or white laborers in Europe. The editors of *Southern Literary Messenger* noted the special value of Virginia Military Institute in protecting slavery: "Slavery is not now so generally viewed by the Southerner as a 'necessary evil.' It is a material element of Southern power and Southern polity, and to rightly defend and direct it, constitutes an important duty on the part of those who form the mind and habits of our Southern youth. There is no labor so profitable, none so free from pernicious influences to society, when properly directed and controlled, as slave labor."[66]

At the University of Alabama, Edward C. Bullock told the students of the Erosophic and Philomathic Societies that slavery under any name disappeared only when masters no longer found it profitable; that Europe's serfs became worse off after their emancipation; and that disguised slavery prevailed under the wages system. Bullock launched a bitter attack on child labor in Britain. Commenting on the desperation of unemployed workers in New York in the late 1850s, Bullock said that the free-labor system was unsustainable and crumbling. Turning to Massachusetts, he exclaimed, "Search creation round, and where on earth have been seen such evidence of a restless, unhappy, discontented people, or of a social system so inharmonious, monstrous, deformed and out of joint?" In a more general tenor, "Anti-Novelist," in *North Carolina University Magazine*, wrote of "this age of liberalism and free institutions, when freedom, so-called, has seemingly entered into and disturbed the foundation stones of everything."[67]

Mallard, *Plantation Life before Emancipation* (Electronic ed.; Chapel Hill, N.C., 1998 [1892]), 35–36; James B. Avirett, *The Old Plantation: How We Lived in Great House and Cabin before the War* (Electronic ed.; Chapel Hill, N.C.,) 1998 [1901]), 89. For the Irish and the "Irish Question" in the South, the most useful work remains David T. Gleeson, *The Irish in the South, 1815–1877* (Chapel Hill, N.C., 2001); see also Kieran Quinlan, *Strange Kin: Ireland and the American South* (Baton Rouge, La., 2005).

[66] J. Cummings, "True Dignity of Human Nature and the Evidences of Man's Progress towards It," *Southern Repertory and College Review*, 1 (1851), 146–153; Southern Rights Association of the University of Virginia, *Address to the Young Men of the South* (Charlottesville, Va., 1851), 6; E. J. Stearns, *Notes on Uncle Tom's Cabin: Being a Logical Answer to Its Allegations and Inferences against Slavery as an Institution* (Philadelphia, Pa., 1853), 22–23; "Progress of Education in Virginia," *SLM*, 24 (1857), 241–247, quote at 247.

[67] Edward C. Bullock, *True and False Civilization: An Oration Delivered before the Erosophic and Philomathic Societies of the University of Alabama* (Tuscaloosa, Ala., 1858), 16–17, 19, quote at 21; "Anti-Novelist," "Theorizing," *North Carolina University Magazine*, 1 (1852), 9.

In the 1850s, students of the University of Virginia's Dialectical Society held a series of spirited debates on the evils of the modern age, in which James McNabb, Thomas Cowan, and David Worth worried about the effects of railroads, steamships, and the telegraph. They saw lurking in all such innovations the same arrogance that lay at the root of the movements of free love, women's rights, Mormonism, spiritualism, socialism, abolitionism, and other irresponsible schemes of unfettered imaginations devoid of firm religious principles. William Watts Glover, speaking on "Is Slave Labor Beneficial," elaborated an argument that became popular even at the liberal University of North Carolina: "The great mass of mankind are naturally disposed to avoid labor and toil." True, free laborers had direct incentives to work in order to improve their condition, whereas slaves generally did not. Yet, "If we look to the laboring class of any community or to the poor of any country, we find there many poverty stricken wretches in a more deplorable and abject condition." If the slave knew how other laborers suffered, "He would have great reason to rejoice over his lot." Glover scouted emancipation as a snare: "It is under the free system of labor where we find extensive poverty and suffering." Acknowledging the superior entrepreneurship and capital accumulation of the free-labor system, he stopped short of recommending white slavery to the North but wondered where it would all end. The University of Virginia's student society's *Jefferson Monument Magazine* commented on the misery of European workers: "The free-labour system is the Pandora's box, whence have flown all these frightful calamities.... A system so constituted can not long endure." In 1857 *University Literary Magazine* hailed Fitzhugh's *Cannibals All!* as an unanswerable critique of free society.[68]

An Incident

The murder of an Irish waiter in Washington in 1856 shook public opinion in the North and in Europe, and the reaction of the southern press underscored the abolitionist nightmare of a "Slave Power" that threatened the enslavement of all labor. Thomas Keating, a worker in Willard's Hotel, refused to serve breakfast to U.S. Representative Philemon Thomas Herbert of California after the appropriate hour without a specific order from his superiors. An enraged Herbert shot and killed him. At the trial two months later, the jury, after only forty-five minutes' deliberation, acquitted Herbert on the implausible but frequently invoked grounds of self-defense. The Alabama-born Herbert was

---

[68] James Leloudis, Introduction to Lisa Tolbert, et al., eds., *Two Hundred Years of Student Life at Chapel Hill: Selected Letters and Diaries* (Chapel Hill, N.C., 1993), 6; W. W. Glover, "Is Slave Labor Beneficial?" UNC – North Caroliniana Collection, Senior Speeches, 1855; *Jefferson Monument Magazine*, 2 (1851), 200–201; "Cannibals All; Or, Slaves without Masters," *University Literary Magazine*, 1 (1857), 193–199. Recent historians, most notably Jonathan D. Martin, believe that most slaves were hired out at least once in their lifetime. That claim seems exaggerated, but there is no question about heavy slave hiring; see Jonathan D. Martin, *Divided Mastery: Slave Hiring in the American South* (Cambridge, Mass., 2004), 2, 8, 103.

generally considered a Southerner, and the southern press leaped to his defense with breathtaking lack of restraint. The *Charleston Standard* declared that no servant had a right to resent a "provocation of words" directed at him. If white men accepted menial jobs, they should do so "with an apprehension of their relation to society, and the disposition quietly to encourage both the responsibilities and the liabilities which the relation imposes." White hotel servants, principally Irish, largely replaced blacks after 1830, and Southerners tended to view them as surrogate blacks. A newspaper in Alabama airily announced, "It is getting time that workers at the North were convinced that they are servants and not gentlemen in disguise. We hope this Herbert affair will teach them prudence."[69]

An irate Olmsted responded, "Mr. Herbert, the murderer of the Irish waiter, is protected and screened by the Southern party, because killing a slave or a low Irishman is in their opinion no murder." If one must hire labor, a Virginian told the abolitionist James Redpath in another context, better that he should hire slaves rather than Irishmen for most jobs: "The Irish, when they come to this country, get above themselves – *they think they are free, and do as they have a mind to*!!" And Charles C. Jones, Jr., of Georgia, a student at Princeton, wrote to his parents, "Nearly all of the servants here who attend about the college are Irish. They are respectful and attentive in general, and are treated quite as we do ours at home." The only difference between them appeared to be that "in the one case they are white and in the other black. Some of the boys cuff them about a little, but this is entirely beneath gentlemen."[70]

---

[69] *Charleston Standard*, quoted by Bernard Mandel, *Labor: Free and Slave: Workingmen and the Anti-Slavery Movement in the United States* (New York, 1955), 39–40; the Alabama newspaper is quoted in Frederick Law Olmsted, *A Journey through Texas; Or, a Saddle-Trip on the Southwestern Frontier* (Austin, 1978 [1857]), vi, n.

[70] "Ruffianism in Washington and Kansas" (*New-York Daily Times*, July 10, 1856), in Charles Capen McLaughlin, et al., eds., *The Papers of Frederick Law Olmsted*, 2 vols. (Baltimore, Md., 1977, 1981), 2:383; James Redpath, *The Roving Editor: Or, Talks with Slaves in the Southern States* (New York, 1859), 220; Charles C. Jones, Jr., to the Reverend and Mrs. C. C. Jones, Aug. 13, 1850, in Robert Manson Myers, ed., *A Georgian at Princeton* (New York, 1976), 73.

3

Travelers to the South, Southerners Abroad

There is no country, not even the countries in which this relation [slavery] is wholly unknown to the laws, in which the difference of rank and of wealth does not put the labor of the poor at the disposal of the rich.

—Benjamin Henry Latrobe[1]

Familiarity Breeds Disquiet

Europeans and Northerners traveled to the South; Southerners traveled to Europe and the North. Supposedly, if Northerners and Southerners visited each other more, sectional antagonisms would abate. Southerners urged Northerners to see for themselves the humanity of slavery in practice. During the congressional debate of 1819–1820 on Missouri, Senator Nathaniel Macon of North Carolina wished that an antislavery northern colleague "would go home with me, or some other Southern member, and witness the meeting between slaves and the owner, and see the glad faces and the hearty shaking of hands." In Virginia in the mid-1830s, Lucian Minor and Edgar Allan Poe followed suit in *Southern Literary Messenger*. Minor concluded a series of five articles: "*The North and South need only know each other better, to love each other more*" – a theme advanced by Poe in a review of J. H. Ingraham's *The South-West. By a Yankee*. Southerners appealed to Harriet Martineau and others to stay long enough to observe slavery closely. If they stayed awhile – so went the refrain – they would embrace the southern point of view. The Reverend Adiel Sherwood, a New Englander, offered a pleasing illustration. Having become a principal figure in the Baptist Church in Georgia, he assured Northerners that

---

[1] Benjamin Henry Latrobe, *The Journal of Latrobe: Being the Notes and Sketches of an Architect, Naturalist and Traveler in the United States from 1796 to 1820* (New York, 1905), 178. William W. Stowe discusses the literature of American travelers at length: *Going Abroad: European Travel in Nineteenth-Century American Culture* (Princeton, N.J., 1994); also Foster Rhea Dulles, *Americans Abroad: Two Centuries of American Travel* (Ann Arbor, Mich., 1964).

slaves were generally well treated. After Sherwood left Georgia for Missouri, his pro-southernism hardened.[2]

An ill-omen: Minor, reflecting on his stay in New England in the mid-1820s, remained upbeat when he published in the mid-1830s. He recalled pleasant surprises and wrote glowingly of the entrepreneurial vitality of New England, praising the Unitarian influence. Minor thought that the well-educated citizens repudiated abolitionism, which was virtually dead. He judged male and female factory workers healthy and moral, but he filed a caveat. Industrialization tended to demoralize laborers, and only firm efforts by capitalists prevented social disorder. Minor doubted that virtuous capitalists would long prevail over less admirable counterparts. And a small matter provoked a big intervention by "C.," who introduced Minor's letters. The behavior of men toward women on public conveyances in New England markedly displeased Minor, who allowed that, for the most part, in the South most travelers were gentlemen, whereas in the North less well-bred men predominated. "C." further allowed that a northern gentleman would treat properly a woman he recognized as a lady, but that a southern gentleman would simply assume she was. Why the difference? "C." concluded: "Slavery in a great degree is that cause."[3]

In the 1790s John Drayton of South Carolina, having toured the Northeast, congratulated New York, Boston, and other cities for their industry and progressive spirit. By the 1850s, although continuing to applaud the North's progressive spirit, Southerners saw its destructive forms spreading southward. Still, the *Western Journal and Civilian* of St. Louis conceded, "Every intelligent mind is conscious that there is a want of homogeneity between the people of the North and South." But, it believed, the advance of industry and technology ought to bring two different peoples into harmonious and constructive relations. That hope played well in large sections of the Border States but did not advance much in the turbulent 1850s. Reading Horace strengthened the conviction of John T. Jones of North Carolina that farmers and country people were "the happiest of all others" – a conviction widespread among people raised on Virgil as well as Horace – but the message had ominous overtones for a slaveholding South at bay. For Edward C. Bullock of Alabama, the roots of Roman decline lay in the "absence of those qualities peculiarly fostered by

---

[2] [James Kirk Paulding], *Letters from the South*, 2 vols. (New York, 1819), 1:32–33; see Macon quoted in William S. Price, Jr., "Nathaniel Macon, Planter," *North Carolina Historical Review*, 78 (2001), 202; "A Virginian" [Lucian Minor], "Letters from New England – No. 5," 426; [E. A. Poe], *SLM*, 2 (1836), 122; Harriet Martineau, *Retrospect of Western Travel*, 2 vols. (London, 1838), 2:68–69; Jarrett Burch, "Adiel Sherwood: Religious Pioneer of Nineteenth-Century Georgia," *Georgia Historical Quarterly*, 87 (2003), 27, 43. See also Solon Robinson, "Negro Slavery at the South," *DBR*, 7 (1849), 382.

[3] "A Virginian" [Lucian Minor], "Letters from New England – No. 1," *SLM*, 1 (1834), especially 83–86, "No. 3," 217 (the quote from "C." at 83), "No. 4" (1835), 273; Also J. R. Lowell, ed., "A Virginian in New England," *Atlantic Monthly*, 26 (June, 1871), 676; A. J. Rosser, Jr., "Lucian Minor," in W. Hamilton Bryson, ed., *Legal Education in Virginia, 1779–1979: A Biographical Approach* (Charlottesville, Va., 1982), 435–444.

the solitude of country life, and to the fatal and overwhelming preponderance of the tastes and habits of the cities." "E. A. B." of Georgia charged that New York – America's great commercial center – was spreading its ideas, values, and taste in all directions; he was relieved that the plantation low country was offering strong resistance. There were other irritations, large and small, according to taste: Professor Edward Dromgoole Sims of Randolph-Macon College in Virginia was troubled at seeing women in New England traveling unescorted "in violation of all modesty and decency." Isaac W. Hayne of South Carolina, addressing the Erosophic Society of the University of Alabama in 1840, railed against the worship of Mammon and an attendant "bloated and corrupt prosperity," cautioning against their penetration of the South.[4]

Southern unionists and political moderates called on their countrymen to visit the North, confident that their experiences would strengthen sectional amity. At the opening of the nineteenth century St. George Tucker, fretting over mutual misunderstandings, wrote to Mathew Carey of Philadelphia to urge Southerners and Northerners to visit each other, certain that face-to-face contact would bring about harmony. William Alexander Caruthers picked up the theme in his novel *The Kentuckian in New-York*, in which two young South Carolinians overcame provincialism and fell in love with the people and culture of New York City. In 1851, Allen Eiland of Crawford, Alabama, urged his niece Mary Dean of Georgia to expand her education and outlook by spending a summer holiday in the North. Then again, Edwin Merrick, who became chief justice of Louisiana in 1855, assured his young wife Caroline that a visit to Ohio would dispel her antislavery inclinations. It did. The hard life of white workingclass women and children especially horrified her. At a school in Massachusetts, Judge Richard H. Clark of Georgia met a white servant girl who lamented the fate of slaves in Georgia. She did not know, Clark mused in his memoirs, "that our slave domestics doing the same work that she did had an easier and happier time than she."[5]

[4] John Drayton, *Letters Written during a Tour through the Northern and Eastern States of America* (Charleston, S.C., 1794), esp. 15–16, 27–28, 90; "The North and the South," *Western Journal and Civilian*, 8 (1852), 226; see also "Climate: Its Influence on Human Character," *Western Journal and Civilian*, 14 (1855), 75–82; John T. Jones to Gen. Edmund Jones, Mar. 2, 1834, in Thomas Felix Hickerson, *Echoes of Happy Valley* (Durham, N.C., 1962), 22; Edward C. Bullock, *True and False Civilization: An Oration Delivered before the Erosophic and Philomathic Societies of the University of Alabama* (Tuscaloosa, Ala., 1858), 9; E. A. B., "Essay on American Society," *SQR*, 10 (1854), 378, 380; Sims, July 7, 1834, in W. Alexander Mabry, ed., *The Diary of Edward Dromgoole Sims, June 17–August 3, 1834* (Richmond: "The John P. Branch Historical Papers of Randolph-Macon College," 1954), 14; Isaac W. Hayne, *Anniversary Address on the Formation of Individual Character, and the Causes Which Influence It* (Tuscaloosa, Ala., 1841), quote at 8.

[5] St. George Tucker to Mathew Carey, Oct. 8, 1795, in Charles T. Cullen, *St. George Tucker and Law in Virginia, 1772–1804* (New York, 1987), 153; William A. Caruthers, *Kentuckian in New-York* (New York, 1834); Vernon Louis Parrington, *Main Currents in American Thought*, 3 vols. (New York, 1927), 2:39–40; Allen Eiland to Mary Dean, Feb. 6, 1851, in Susan Lott Clark, ed., *Southern Letters and Life in the Mid 1800s* (Waycross, Ga., 1993), 61; Caroline

As northern hostility to the South rose, southern travelers chafed. In 1840 a contributor to *Southern Ladies' Book* charged that northern schools encouraged egotism and elitism and tempted southern girls and young women into a taste for the frivolous and away from the substantial education they needed. He had nothing to fear from Sarah Potts, a young lady from Arkansas at school in New Jersey in 1849. She steadily became more "southern" in response to northern attacks on the South: "Most of Northern people object to the south on account of slavery. Why should they object to having black servants when they have white ones who are treated just as we treat our slaves?" The showiness and display at Saratoga Springs in New York repelled vacationing Southerners, but before 1840 few complained of anti-southern attitudes. As late as 1847, Peter V. Daniel of Virginia, finding Saratoga Springs acceptable if overrated, noticed no anti-southern outbursts. But then, Daniel, a secessionist and a Yankee-hater, was a U.S. Supreme Court associate justice, and people probably behaved themselves in his presence. By 1860 attitudes prevalent at northern springs made Thomas J. Jackson (later "Stonewall") and his family uncomfortable. Even in the 1850s, despite sectional tensions and an increase in the popularity of southern spas, many Southerners went north for vacations, but it is doubtful that their visits improved sectional relations. On balance, Michael O'Brien plausibly concludes that southern travelers learned more about the North than northern travelers learned about the South.[6]

The southern elite continued to send significant numbers of its children to northern schools. A glance at Southerners at northern schools illustrates some difficulties. John Couper of coastal Georgia explained in 1828 that he was sending his son William to an academy in New Hampshire to acquaint himself with "a sufficient amount of Yankee cunning" and would then send him to Berlin "to unlearn roguery and gain honor – German principles." Yet, the interaction between southern students and northern professors and students

---

Elizabeth Merrick, *Old Times in Dixie: A Southern Matron's Memories* (Electronic ed.; Chapel Hill, N.C., 1997 [1901]), 20; Lollie Belle Wylie, ed., *Memoirs of Judge Richard H. Clark* (Atlanta, 1898), 65. Long afterward, some Southerners still recalled gracious receptions in the North: see, e.g., Frank Alexander Montgomery of Mississippi: *Reminiscences of a Mississippian in War and Peace* (Electronic ed.; Chapel Hill, N.C., 1999 [1901]), 16–20.

[6] "Vindex Veritatis," "Importance of Home Education," *Southern Ladies' Book*, 1 (1840), 2; Sarah Potts to Ann Potts, Jan. 23, 1849, in Joan E. Cashin, ed., *Our Common Affairs: Texts from Women of the Old South* (Baltimore, Md., 1996), 241–244, quote at 242; Maria Bryan Harford to Julia Ann Bryan Cumming, Aug. 5, 1839, in Carol Bleser, ed., *Tokens of Affection: The Letters of a Planter's Daughter in the Old South* (Athens, Ga., 1996), 253; John P. Frank, *Justice Daniel Dissenting: A Biography of Peter V. Daniel, 1784–1860* (Cambridge, Mass., 1964), 244; James I. Robertson, Jr., *Stonewall Jackson: The Man, the Soldier, the Legend* (New York, 1997), 203; R. I. Jones, "Ante-Bellum Watering Places on the Gulf Coast," *Journal of Mississippi History*, 18 (1956), 300–301; Michael O'Brien, *Conjectures of Order: Intellectual Life and the American South, 1810–1860*, 2 vols. (Chapel Hill, N.C., 2004), 1:27. John Patrick Daly fairly concludes that each section understood the evils of the other's social system better than their own: *When Slavery Was Called Freedom: Evangelicalism, Proslavery, and the Causes of the Civil War* (Lexington, Ky., 2002), 98.

promoted affection and goodwill, if not necessarily ideological harmony. A prominent example: George Ticknor, Harvard's distinguished professor of modern languages, won plaudits from southern students whom he befriended. Some of those students – Littleton Waller Tazewell of Virginia for one – became prominent men. The unionist Bishop James H. Otey of Tennessee nonetheless lamented in 1835 the lack of Episcopalian seminaries in the South, commenting, "By educating our children abroad we encourage and perpetuate a literary dependence, the continuance of which is as unnecessary as it is impolitic." By the 1840s and 1850s southern students were having a difficult time in the North. The unionist Henry Winter Davis of Maryland recalled that at Kenyon College – and not only at Kenyon – Southerners organized their own student society. At Yale heated debates on the Constitution and states' rights threw them on the defensive. At Hamilton College in New York heightened hostility discouraged their enrollment.[7]

Sectional strains provided a wonderful opportunity for southern schools to raise enrollments. In 1838, well before sectional tensions had reached fever pitch, Charles Caldwell assured Southerners that they might safely send their children to study medicine in Louisville – that the medical school and the community supported southern institutions and values. The sober and responsible Chancellor John Berrien Lindsley of the University of Nashville invoked political arguments to attract southern students to southern schools. Those who go north to study, he grumbled in 1854, either fall prey to antislavery ideas or react by becoming bigots who oppose any Christian amelioration of slave circumstances. In the wake of John Brown's raid hundreds left the northern schools in response to well-organized pleas to abandon the land of abolitionism. Southern politicians – notably Governor Henry A. Wise of Virginia – beat the drums, but so did the leaders of southern medical schools, who saw a golden chance to increase enrollments. Although the defection gave southern nationalists an enormous propaganda victory, half of the southern students in the North stayed put, and some defectors returned. What could Southerners think when men like John A. Quitman advocated secession while their sons attended northern colleges at the extraordinary expense of up to $900 for an eight-month period? Meanwhile, the anti-southern views of northern faculties were making southern students miserable. In any case, J. D. B. De Bow estimated that the South paid the North a hundred million dollars a year for travel, books, and education: "Great God! Does Ireland sustain a more degrading relation to Great Britain?" In New York, George W. Williams, a merchant, sighed, "We Southerners abuse the Yankees and come here and spend money as if it grew

[7] John Couper quoted in James E. Bagwell, *Rice Gold: James Hamilton Couper and Plantation Life on the Georgia Coast* (Macon, Ga., 2000), 32; Norma Lois Peterson, *Littleton Waller Tazewell* (Charlottesville, Va., 1983), 102–105; Bernard C. Steiner, *Life of Henry Winter Davis* (Baltimore, 1916), ch. 2; J. H. Otey, "Plan for Theological and Literary Instruction," Feb. 16, 1835, in Otey Papers; Richbourg Gaillard to John S. Palmer, Jan. 7, 1844 (Yale), Richard Furman Wilde to John S. Palmer, Aug. 10, 1848, in Louis P. Towles, ed., *A World Turned Upside Down: The Palmers of South Santee, 1818–1881* (Columbia, S.C., 1996), 89, 137–139.

on trees." Southern spending in the North accompanied a complaint against northern businessmen. Samuel Mordecai of Virginia charged that they made fortunes in Richmond but spent their money in New York, often returning to live in the North.[8]

Slaveholders deluded themselves that most northern visitors, including abolitionists, would have reacted positively, although they had some basis for their delusion. Southerners took comfort from antislavery Northerners who sent home favorable reports. The Maryland-born Charles Willson Peale, a celebrated artist who lived in Philadelphia, viewed slavery as a system that corrupted both masters and slaves, but he, too, said that the slaves on the plantations he visited in 1791 "appear happy." In later years the northern-born and raised Judge William Barclay Napton of Missouri spent time in Virginia at the time of the Nat Turner revolt and then in the plantation states and read widely on social life around the world. He concluded that southern slaves were treated much more humanely than were West Indian slaves, Mexican peons, Russian serfs, and the free workers of Europe and the North. Napton became convinced that slavery spared the South the terrible social evils that beset free societies. In similar accents, John Blair Dabney of Virginia stated in 1841 that two great parties divided European countries – one upheld established order, the other was radical and destructive; moderates, he added, counted for little.[9]

Teachers often became *plus royaliste que le roi, plus catholique que le Pape.* James Gillespie Birney, while an antislavery colonizationist, recruited Northerners to teach in Alabama. By the late 1830s, Birney and Theodore Weld learned from reports on Northerners who went south to teach that no few easily adopted southern views. Weld received notice of a number who married into slaveholding families. In Virginia the English-born D. W. Mitchell reported that well into the 1850s New England was providing "a large proportion of teachers and schoolmasters to the South." Emily Burke reported that of the nineteen female teachers she knew of in Georgia, all except one came from the North. Joseph Holt Ingraham of Portland, Maine, settled in Mississippi about 1830 and became a successful Episcopalian minister, academy and college teacher,

[8] Charles Caldwell, "A Succinct View of the Influence of Mental Cultivation on the Destinies of Louisville," *Louisville Journal of Medicine and Surgery*, 1 (1838), 1–34; John Edwin Windrow, *John Berrien Lindsley: Educator, Physician, Social Philosopher* (Chapel Hill, N.C., 1938), 49; J. O. Breeden, "Rehearsal for Secession," in Paul Finkelman, ed., *His Soul Goes Marching On: Responses to John Brown and the Harper's Ferry Raid* (Charlottesville, Va., 1995), ch. 7; Dec. 23, 1859, ERD, 1:385; Robert E. May, *John A. Quitman: Old South Crusader* (Baton Rouge, La., 1985), 125, 218, 235; [J. D. B. De Bow], "Rail-Road Prospects and Progress," *DBR*, 2 (1852), 500; E. Merton Coulter, *George Walton Williams: The Life of a Southern Merchant and Banker, 1820–1903* (Athens, Ga., 1976), 56; Samuel Mordecai, *Richmond in By-Gone Days* (Richmond, Va., 1946 [1860]), 40.

[9] David C. Ward, *Charles Wilson Peale: Art and Selfhood in the Early Republic* (Berkeley, Calif., 2004), 58, 66–67, quote at 67; Christopher Phillips and Jason L. Pendleton, eds., *The Union on Trial: The Political Journals of Judge William Barclay Napton, 1829–1883* (Columbus, Mo., 2005), 17–18, 45, 50, 126–127, 151–155, 160; John Blair Dabney, "Capt. Marryat," *SLM*, 7 (1841), 254.

and prolific writer. In 1860 he confidently asserted that with rare exceptions, northern-born teachers identified with southern mores and institutions. C. G. Parsons, too, recounting his travels, especially noted the frequency with which these northern women married into slaveholding families. Northern men, like southern men, often became teachers as a stepping-stone to some other profession or occupation and settled down in the communities in which they had become known. The perception of northern teachers as converts to southern mores and views was doubtless strengthened by the disappearance of those who did not and returned home. And there were cases like that of Caroline Seabury of Massachusetts and New York. She arrived in Mississippi to teach at a school for the daughters of the planter elite. Holding vaguely antislavery ideas but with an open mind, she was immediately struck by the apparent mildness of the slave regime and doubted the horror stories she had heard back home. Then she received a series of jolts. The unmerciful whipping of a slave girl for theft appalled her, the more so when a white student stood revealed as the thief. And her heart sank at the sight of slave sales that separated families.[10]

Joseph Cogswell of Massachusetts and Margaret Clark Griffis of Philadelphia, among antislavery Northerners who went south to teach, defended the slaveholders against charges of cruelty and denied extensive material suffering. The antislavery and anti-racist Rosalie Roos, a Swede who taught at Limestone College in South Carolina for four years, found slaves generally well treated and thought emancipation had to be gradual. Similarly, the antislavery Catherine Stewart, who lived in the South for awhile and considered slavery an abomination, thought slaves well treated. She told Northerners that if abolitionists would see for themselves, they would temper their hostility. Sarah

[10] Lydia Maria Child to Weld, Dec. 18, 1838, Abby Kelly to Weld, Jan. 1, 1839, in Gilbert H. Barnes and Dwight L. Dumond, eds., *Letters of Theodore Dwight Weld, Angelina Grimké and Sarah Grimké, 1822–1844*, 2 vols. (Gloucester, Mass., 1965), 2:726–730, 744–748; James M. Buchanan to Birney, Feb. 7, 1836, in Dwight L. Dumond, ed., *Letters of James Gillespie Birney, 1831–1857*, 2 vols. (Gloucester, Mass., 1966), 1:304–308; on Birney's recruitment see 1:12–14; J. H. Ingraham, *Sunny South; Or, The Southerner at Home* (New York, 1968 [1860]), 5; D. W. Mitchell, *Ten Years in the United States: Being an Englishman's Views of Men and Things in the North and South* (London, 1862), 48; Emily Burke, *Reminiscences of Georgia*, 182; C. G. Parsons, *An Inside View of Slavery: A Tour among the Planters* (Savannah, Ga., 1974 [1855]), 237. Also, Charles S. Sydnor, *A Gentleman of the Old Natchez Region: Benjamin L. C. Wailes* (Durham, N.C., 1938), 131–133; J. Hodges, "A Pedagogue in Georgia" [1855], in Eugene L. Schwaab and Jacqueline Bull, eds., *Travels in the Old South: Selected from Periodicals of the Time*, 2 vols. (Lexington, Ky., 1973), 2:543; and in general, Fletcher M. Green, *The Role of the Yankee in the Old South* (Athens, Ga., 1972); C. Seabury, Nov. 18, 1854; Feb. 8, 1855; Jan. 1, 1856, in Suzanne L. Bunkers, *The Diary of Caroline Seabury, 1854–1863* (Madison, Wisc., 1991), 36–41, also Cornish Diary, especially Nov.–Dec., 1839. For additional material on the adjustment of northern teachers to southern attitudes, see also George Washington Paschal, *History of Wake Forest College*, 2 vols. (Wake Forest, N.C., 1935), 1:129–130, 236–237, 381. In Towles, ed., *World Turned Upside Down*, see 113–114, 117, 134, 137–139, 148: Victoria Murden to Elizabeth Catherine Palmer, April 10, 1848, Richard Furman Wilde to John S. Palmer, Aug. 10, 1848, Dec. 18; Sarah L. Butman to Esther Simons Palmer, June 14, 1847; Samuel W. Sutherland to John S. Palmer, July 3, 1847.

Hicks Williams of New York married a North Carolinian and wrote home to her parents that masters and slaves had loving relations – more harmonious than those of Northern employers and servants. Tryphena Blanche Holder Fox, wife of a Louisiana slaveholder, wrote to her mother in Massachusetts in the 1850s that she only wished the abolitionists among whom she had been raised could see how comfortably situated the slaves really were. Elise Waeren-skjold, a Norwegian immigrant in Texas, passionately devoted to antislavery and women's rights, thought that nothing could compensate for the loss of freedom, but she acknowledged, "Much as I despise slavery, I cannot deny that the slaves are treated rather well and that numbers of them are better off in many respects than free laborers in Europe."[11]

Bishop Levi Silliman Ives of North Carolina, a New Englander, wished that the antislavery Anglican bishop of Oxford, England, could have seen masters and slaves together in prayer at the Episcopal Church's Easter service in 1846: "I could not help believing that, had some of our brethren of other lands been present, they would have been induced to change the note of their wailing over imaginary sufferings into the heartfelt exclamation: Happy are the people who are in such a case; yea, blessed are the people who have the Lord for their God." Such sentiments made the opponents of slavery bristle, but in so doing they betrayed fears of the effectiveness of the propaganda. For Aaron, a fugitive slave or the abolitionist who wrote the tract attributed to him: "A Northern man goes to the South, sits at a table loaded from the slaves' unpaid toil, who eats his cornbread in the sun, marries a slaveholder, and then finds out that slavery is a divine institution, and defends it in Southern and Northern pulpits, religious newspapers."[12]

The Reverend Joseph Stiles of Virginia complained in 1857 that northern New School Presbyterian ministers snubbed his invitation to visit the South despite assurances for their safety. He claimed that some openly admitted fear of

[11] Dec. 13, 1835, in *Life of Joseph Green Cogswell, as Sketched in His Letters* (Cambridge, Mass., 1874), 203; on Griffis, see Rosemary F. Carroll, "A Plantation Teacher's Perceptions of the Impending Crisis," *Southern Studies*, 18 (1979), 339–350; Rosalie Roos, to Olaf Gustaf Roos, Dec. 21, 1852, Apr. 4, 1853, in Rosalie Roos, *Travels in America, 1851–1855*, tr. Carl L. Anderson (Carbondale, Ill., 1982), 69, 80; Catherine Stewart, *New Homes in the West* (Nashville, Tenn., 1843), 150–152; James C. Bonner, ed., "Plantation Experiences of a New York Woman," *North Carolina Historical Review*, 33 (1956), 389; Tryphena Fox to Anna Rose Holder, September 8, 1856, in Wilma King, ed., *A Northern Woman in the Plantation South: Letters of Tryphena Blanche Holder Fox, 1856–1876* (Columbia, S.C., 1993), 39, also, Aug. 16, 1858, Dec. 27, 1861, 77, 131–132; Charles H. Russell, *Undaunted: A Norwegian Woman in Frontier Texas* (College Station, Tex., 2006), Elise Waerenskjold quoted at 86.

[12] Ives, quoted in Marshall De Lancey Haywood, *Lives of the Bishops of North Carolina from the Establishment of the Episcopate in that State Down to the Division of the Diocese* (Raleigh, N.C., 1910), 99–100; Aaron, *The Light and Truth of Slavery: Aaron's Story* (Electronic ed.; Chapel Hill, N.C., 2000 [1845]), 8. Henry E. Handerson, an antislavery Yankee tutor in Louisiana, went on to a distinguished career in medicine. He had no doubt that the planters treated their slaves well. Clyde Lottridge Cummer, ed., *Yankee in Gray: The Civil War Memoirs of Henry E. Handerson, with a Selection of His Wartime Letters* (Cleveland, Oh., 1962), especially 21–28.

having their antislavery principles subverted. William J. Grayson, who doubted that such visits would make much difference, told of a party of northern ladies caught in a rainstorm in Charleston. A servant expressed regrets at his master's absence, invited them into the house, escorted them to the parlor, and served refreshments. The ladies, upset that such a man could be enslaved, viewed him as a victim. Grayson countered by asking where else in the world they would find a black man with such manners. Catherine Edmondston had no illusions about abolitionist visits but, unlike Grayson, chose not to be playful. She doubted that abolitionists were victims of self-deception, thinking them unprincipled fanatics.[13]

In 1837 the Presbyterian William Bailey of South Carolina praised Arthur Tappan, N. S. S. Beman, and other abolitionists he knew as good, well-meaning men, but he protested their attacks on slaveholders as an invitation to all-out sectional hostility that was undermining prospects for eventual emancipation. Bailey ruefully acknowledged that abolitionists, having made themselves odious, could not expect to be allowed to speak in the South and must expect violence if they tried. Antislavery Northerners replied directly and indirectly to pleas that they see for themselves. In 1854 the Reverend E. B. Willson cried out that Northerners in fact saw slavery firsthand when Boston became an armed camp during the forced return of Anthony Burns to slavery. According to Willson, Northerners saw the brutal effects of slavery on the contorted faces of local poor whites – depraved characters naturally drawn to proslavery – who assisted the troops in carrying out that atrocity. The Reverend Irem Smith of Durham, Connecticut, wished that his parishioners had been in Savannah on March 2, 1859, to witness the giant slave sale at the race track and hear the wails of those torn from their families.[14]

Frank F. Steel, a Republican, assured his family in Ohio that the planters of Mississippi treated their slaves well. Charmed by the "smiling countenances & merry dispositions" shown by a Mr. Reid's slaves when he returned to his large plantation in Washington County, he added that except for abolitionists, Northerners traveled safely through the South. His exception ruined his assurances. A southern lady, visiting the North, was much impressed by Henry Ward Beecher's preaching and urged him to visit the South. "Madam," he replied, "my neck is short, and not handsome; but it is the only one God has given me, and I had rather retain it in its natural state than have it elongated by external appliances." Beecher knew that for decades the southern press had threatened

---

[13] Joseph C. Stiles, *Modern Reform Examined; Or, The Union of the North and South on the Subject of Slavery* (Philadelphia, Pa., 1857), 150–151; William J. Grayson, *The Hireling and the Slave, Chicora, and Other Poems* (Charleston, S.C., 1856), 158–159, n. 17; Edmondston Diary, Sept. 25, Oct. 11, 1862, in Beth G. Crabtree and James W. Patton, eds., *"Journal of a Secesh Lady": The Diary of Catherine Ann Devereux Edmondston, 1860–1866* (Raleigh, N.C., 1979), 272–273.

[14] William Bailey, *The Issue: Presented in a Series of Letters on Slavery* (New York, 1837), 31–34; E. B. Willson, *The Bad Friday. A Sermon* (Boston, Mass., 1857), 6, 10; Irem W. Smith, *American Slavery; A Prayer for Its Removal* (Middletown, Conn., 1860), 19–20.

to hang abolitionists who dared to cross the Mason-Dixon Line. And whenever James Birney, among many, thought about a trip to the plantation states, friend and foe told him that he would risk his life.[15]

Europeans and Yankees See for Themselves

Endless anecdotes favorable to slavery emerged to challenge skeptical Northerners and foreigners to see for themselves. Mary E. Moragné of South Carolina, fishing with her brother and a cousin, saw her father's slaves at their midday meal, relaxed, talking, joking: "How I wished that a fanatical abolitionist could have been there at that moment to have felt the perfect folly – to say the least of it – of his crooked & warped policy." When Jenny, a slave maid, married in 1855, Eliza Clitherall wondered, "What wou'd the Beecherstowites have said cou'd they have seen the handsome supper given by my dear Eliza & Carrie to their servant." Visitors marveled at the white young ladies of South Carolina who sent written invitations to masters and servants of neighboring plantations to attend the wedding of a favorite servant. When the delegates to the Democratic Party's convention in Charleston in 1860 attended a black church service in the evening, Mayor Randal W. McGavock of Nashville enjoyed the astonishment of Northerners who found parishioners well dressed and cheerful. In 1861, Fannie Page Hume of Virginia delighted in escorting her northern visitor to the slaves' "grand party" and "elegant supper," Miss Johnson seemed amazed at the enjoyment of "the POOR DOWNTRODDEN SLAVES." Sally Baxter, a northern young lady, married into the Hamptons of South Carolina and visited Old Lang Syne, David and Louisa McCord's upcountry plantation. The affectionate blacks' "animal faces and idiot gestures" promised a racial improvement to the level of "only a superior animal." To Amelia Akehurst Lines, a northern teacher, black "slaves or servants as I must now call them" were "as comical as I expected." She was sure that if abolitionists saw what she saw, they would give up on emancipation. Ellen and Corinna Brown, northern-born mistresses of a Florida plantation, derided blacks and chided a relative in Ithaca, New York, for ignorance of the South.[16]

[15] For Beecher, see David Macrae, *The Americans at Home* (New York, 1952 [1870]), 61; F. F. Steel to Anna Steel, Dec. 8, 1860. Yet the Methodist Reverend William Henry Milburn, a Northerner on duty in the South, rejected charges of suppression of free speech: *Ten Years of Preacher Life: Chapters from an Autobiography* (New York, 1859), 333–334; see also Eric William Plagg, "Strangers in a Strange Land: Northern Travelers and the Coming of the Civil War (Ph.D. diss., University of South Carolina, 2006), 424.

[16] Mary E. Moragné, Journal, Mar. 25, 1837, in Delle Mullen Craven, ed., *The Neglected Thread: A Journal of the Calhoun Community* (Columbia, S.C., 1951), 31; Clitherall, "Autobiography," Mar. 1, 1855, at UNC; for the response to written invitations, see FitzGerald Ross, *Cities and Camps of the Confederate States*, ed. Richard Barksdale Harwell (Urbana, Ill., 1997), 235; McGavock, April 22, 1860, in Herschel Gower et al., eds., *Pen and Sword: The Life and Journals of Randal W. McGavock, Colonel, C. S. A.* (Nashville, Tenn., 1959), 565; Hume Diary, Jan. 1, 1861; Sally Baxter to George Baxter, Apr. 15, 1855, in Ann Fripp Hampton, ed., *A Divided Heart: Letters of Sally Baxter Hampton, 1853–1862* (Spartanburg, S.C., 1980), 22;

Another northern young lady, visiting Alexander Stephens in Georgia, expected to find bloodhounds used to track runaways. She saw none and received assurance that no one on the place had ever seen one. Such assurances did not prevent Dr. Elijah Millington Walker – for one – from praising the dogs who hunted slave runaways in rural Mississippi.[17]

The aristocratic and antislavery Isabella Lucy Bird, who had barely seen the slave states, articulated a common British reaction: "Few English people will forget the impressions made upon them by the first sight of a slave – a being created in the image of God, yet the *bonâ fide* property of his fellow-man." Yet foreign travelers everywhere met assertions that black slaves fared better in the South than the white poor fared abroad. In 1828, Mrs. Basil Hall wrote to her sister Jane from Fayetteville, North Carolina, about an argument she had with a man who said that southern slaves lived more comfortably than English workers. She simply could not understand how anyone could trumpet such absurdity. At least as early as the 1820s, travelers acknowledged – grudgingly or with pleasure – that the gentleman from Fayetteville spoke the truth. In the late 1820s Frances Trollope assessed the living conditions of the southern slaves as not at all bad, adding that the slaveholders treated their slaves a good deal better than the English treated their hired white servants. Thirty years later Anthony Trollope followed suit, allowing that slaves in Kentucky and Louisiana lived better than English and European laborers. The firmly emancipationist William Faux of England courageously denounced slavery publicly in Charleston. Faux remarked on the wretched condition of British laborers but stressed that unlike southern blacks, they could not be killed with impunity. Yet, he too witnessed humanely treated slaves, "respectable, happy, and healthy." Agostino Brunias, the Italian-born English painter, among other eighteenth- and nineteenth-century artists, comforted slaveholders with his "Scene with

---

Amelia Akehurst Lines Diary, Feb. 19, 1857, Nov. 27, 1860, Dec. 22, 1865, in Thomas Dyer, ed., *To Raise Myself a Little: The Diaries and Letters of Jennie a Georgia Teacher, 1851–1886* (Athens, Ga., 1982), 170, 219, quote at 45; Ellen and Corinna Brown to Mannevillette Brown, Aug. 1, 1836, in James M. Denham and Keith L. Huneycutt, eds., *Echoes from a Distant Frontier: The Brown Sisters' Correspondence from Antebellum Florida* (Columbia, S.C., 2004), 39–40; Myrta Lockett Avery, *Dixie after the War* (New York, 1918 [1906]), 55–56; July 28, 1850, in Lynette Boney Wrenn, ed., *A Bachelor's Life in Antebellum Mississippi: The Diary of Dr. Elijah Millington Walker, 1849–1852* (Knoxville, Tenn., 2004), 70.

[17] For slaves' accounts of being pursued and torn up by bloodhounds, see, e.g., Edward Everett Brown, ed., *Sketch of the Life of Mr. Lewis Charlton, and Reminiscences of Slavery* (Electronic ed.; Chapel Hill, N.C., 2000 [?]), 2; Josephine Brown, *Biography of an American Bondman, by His Daughter* (Electronic ed.; Chapel Hill, N.C., 2000 [1856]), 30; Francis Fedric, *Slave Life in Virginia and Kentucky; Or, Fifty Years of Slavery in the Southern States of America* (Electronic ed.; Chapel Hill, N.C., 1999 [1863]), 76; *Sunshine and Shadow of Slave Life: Reminiscences Told by Isaac D. Williams to "Tege"* (Electronic ed.; Chapel Hill, N.C., 2003 [1885]), 10; Peter Randolph, *Sketches of Slave Life: Or, Illustrations of the "Peculiar Institution"* (Electronic ed.; Chapel Hill, N.C., 2000 [1855]), 24. For the use of the bloodhound image in abolitionist propaganda of a "Slave Power Conspiracy," see John Campbell, "The Seminoles, the 'Bloodhound War,' and Abolitionism, 1796–1865," *JSH*, 72 (2006), 259–302. The forthcoming work of R. L. Paquette will document the extent and significance of attack dogs.

Dancing in the West Indies" and widely circulated engravings, which showed contented, well-treated slaves in better circumstances than Africans or the European poor.[18]

In the 1830s the geologist G. W. Featherstonhaugh deluded himself that the leading gentlemen of Virginia desired eventual emancipation. Conversations in Decatur, Tennessee, jolted him. Gentlemen believed that slaveholding elevated masters, making them strong friends of public liberty, and that the highest forms of social development required slavery. At the beginning of the 1840s, the receptivity of Southerners to articles on the evils of wage-slavery and on the superiority of the southern slavery caught the attention of James Silk Buckingham, M. P., who had been reading Savannah's *Daily Georgian*. Fellow passengers on coaches in Louisiana and Mississippi boasted to Buckingham that slaves on the lovely plantations along the Mississippi River lived much better than British laborers. Everywhere he went he heard Southerners decry the horrible exploitation of English factory workers and flaunt the superior conditions of their slaves.[19]

Between 1830 and 1860 antislavery British travelers to the South recounted – often fiercely – cruelties they saw or heard about, but they often pleased Southerners with damaging concessions to the proslavery argument. To be sure, certain travelogues went unread or at least unremarked. Without the slightest effect, S. A. Farrall, a Briton, condemned American slavery without qualification and, in particular, described the slaves on Louisiana sugar plantations as "truly wretched." More likely to get at least passing notice was a travelogue like that of Hiram Fuller, an Englishman who traveled across the South from Kentucky to Louisiana to the Atlantic Coast in the 1850s. He excoriated abolitionists for misrepresentations: "I have witnessed more unkindness, more suffering, more inhumanity, in the city of New York, in one day, than I have seen in the South in three months."[20]

[18] Isabella Lucy Bird, *The Englishwoman in America*, ed. Andrew Hill Clark (Madison, Wisc., 1966), 126; Letter of Feb. 15, 1828, in Una Pope-Hennesey, ed., *The Aristocratic Journey, Being the Outspoken Letters of Mrs. Basil Hall* (New York, 1931), 205; Frances Trollope, *Domestic Manners of the Americans* (Gloucester, Mass., 1974 [1832]), 245–246; Anthony Trollope, *North America* (New York, 1863), 376; W. Faux, *Memorable Days in America: Being a Journal of a Tour to the United States* (Cleveland, Oh., 1905 [1823]), 1:65–66, 71–72, 80, 87, quote at 65–66; Hugh Honour, *The Image of the Black in Western Art*, 4 vols. (Cambridge, Mass., 1989), 4 (Pt. 1), 32–33, 146. Edgar Allan Poe defended Trollope's *Domestic Manners* as honest, accurate: [Poe], *SLM*, 2 (1836), 393–394.

[19] George William Featherstonhaugh, *A Canoe Voyage up the Minnay Sotor*, 2 vols. (St. Paul, Minn., 1970 [1847]), 2:195; J. S. Buckingham, *The Slave States of America*, 2 vols. (New York, 1968 [1842]), 2:213–215, 399, 571.

[20] S. A. Farrall, *A Ramble of Six Thousand Miles through the United States of America* (London, 1832), ch. 7, quote at 196; [Hiram Fuller], *Belle Brittan on Tour, at Newport and Here and There* (New York, 1858), 124. For travelers who stressed good living conditions for southern slaves in comparison with those of European lower classes, see James M. Woods, "In the Eye of the Beholder: Slavery in the Travel Accounts of the Old South, 1790–1860," *Southern Studies*, n.s., 1 (1990), 33–59. Woods also discusses travelers who took an opposite view.

Captain Robert Barclay Allardice, an antislavery Scots authority on agriculture, had heard chilling stories about southern slavery, but in Virginia he confronted cheerful and contented slaves in better physical condition than British factory workers. Captain Henry A. Murray, R. N., who excoriated slavery as a curse to America, believed that the agitation of fanatical abolitionists had resulted in a worsening of the circumstances of the slaves and impeded efforts toward emancipation. Sir Charles Augustus Murray thought plausible the assertion that southern slaves fared better than many free laborers abroad. James Stuart reported brutality but also many slaves who seemed deeply attached to their masters. John Robert Godley described slaves in Virginia as worse off than he had expected – adequately fed but of "very miserable appearance" – yet he doubted that they had more wretched clothing and housing than the poorest laborers in the more backward parts of Europe had. Archibald Prentice, a liberal English reformer, denounced slavery but referred to the "squalid misery" of New York's Five Points and to "our own half-starved population at home." The Reverend Robert Everest responded caustically to proslavery apologetics, but he too thought the material conditions of the slaves no worse than those of rural English laborers. The liberal Henry Ashworth – Richard Cobden's friend and collaborator in the Anti-Corn Law League – told of a minister on John's Island, South Carolina, who retained the aversion to slavery he had formed in Scotland but did not doubt that the slaves were materially better off than British laborers. In agreement, D. W. Mitchell, an Englishman who lived in the South from 1848 to 1857, scoffed at the notion that British workers had a chance to improve their lot.[21]

For proslavery Southerners perhaps the most heartening remarks came from one of their severest critics. In the mid-1840s Alexander Mackay – as highly respected a British traveler to the South as any – dedicated a three-volume travelogue to Cobden in which he charged the slaveholders of the cotton states with gross inhumanity and called for a frank discussion of emancipation. But he added a remark that cheered the advocates of Slavery in the Abstract: "How great an extent the tide is now unfortunately turning in Europe, if not in favor of slavery, at least of something very nearly approximating to it." John Finch, a British geologist, and Alexander Marjoribanks, a Scots peer,

[21] Robert Barclay Allardice, *Agricultural Tour in the United States and Canada with Miscellaneous Notices* (London, 1842), 92–95; Sir Charles Augustus Murray, *Travels in North America during the Years 1834, 1835 and 1836* (London, 1839), 2:304; James Stuart, "Bad Roads, Loose Morals, Sadism, and Racetrack Discipline, 1830," in Thomas D. Clark, ed., *South Carolina: The Grand Tour, 1780–1865* (Columbia, S.C., 1973), 162–163; Henry A. Murray, *Lands of the Slave and the Free: Or, Cuba, the United States, and Canada*, 2nd ed. (London, 1857), chs. 25–26; John Robert Godley, *Letters from America*, 2 vols. (London, 1844), 2:206–208, quote at 206; Archibald Prentice, *A Tour in the United States* (London, 1848), 13, 14; Robert Everest, *A Journey through the United States and Part of Canada* (London, 1853), 98; Henry Ashworth, *A Tour of the United States, Cuba, and Canada* (London, 1861), 41–42; D. W. Mitchell, *Ten Years in the United States: Being an Englishman's Views of Men and Things in the North and South* (London, 1862), 242.

compared southern slavery favorably to West Indian slavery, and even Joseph John Gurney, who had almost nothing good to say about the treatment of southern slaves, admitted that he found urban slaves well clad.[22]

Educated Southerners honored eminent foreigners, noting their observations and opinions, along with their accomplishments. Planters and intellectuals admired the aristocratic Alexis de Tocqueville and his *Democracy in America*, treating him as a premier historian and political philosopher. For a man who had spent little time in the South, Tocqueville intuited a great deal, some of it to southern tastes: "Slavery does not attack the American Union directly in its interests, but indirectly in its manners." Tocqueville saw Northerners as typically middle class, with knowledge, experience, common sense, and a general aptitude for modern life. Southerners he thought more impulsive, frank, clever, generous, and intellectually brilliant. Of the quintessential Kentuckian: "Money has lost a portion of its value in his eyes; he covets wealth much less than pleasure and excitement." Of the slaveholders in general: "The habit of uninhibited command gives men a certain feeling of superiority which makes them impatient of opposition and irritated at the sight of obstacles." Tocqueville presented the slaveholders as "brave, comparatively ignorant, hospitable, generous, easy to irritate, violent in their resentments, without industry or the spirit of enterprise."[23]

Tocqueville offered a provocative analysis of master-serf relations in which serfs had no natural interest in the fate of their lords yet dutifully worked for them. The lord protected all who lived on his estate, as a matter of honor born of social duty rather than humanity. In contrast, Tocqueville believed that Southerners treated their slaves barbarously. Southern commentators nevertheless applauded his stress on certain aspects of the feudal honor that the slaveholders claimed for themselves: "In some cases feudal honor enjoined revenge and stigmatized the forgiveness of insults; in others it imperiously commanded men

[22] Alexander Mackay, *The Western World; Or, Travels in the United States in 1846–1847*, 3 vols. (New York, 1968 [1849]), 2: 125, also 92; John Finch, *Travels in the United States of America and Canada* (London, 1833), 191–193, 224, and ch. 32. See also Alexander Marjoribanks, *Travels in South and North America*, 5th ed., 2 vols. (London, 1854), 1:340–341, also 209, 261–268; Joseph John Gurney, *A Journey in North America Described in Familiar Letters to Amelia Opie* (Norwich, Eng., 1841), 371, 374, 379. For some vivid descriptions of the wretched housing of European workers and peasants, see Traian Stoianovitch, "Material Foundations of Preindustrial Civilization in the Balkans," *Journal of Social History*, 4 (1971), 228–231, 239–241; Jürgen Kuczynski, *The Rise of the Working Class*, tr. C. T. A. Ray (London, 1967), 92–94; Charles Morazé, *La France Bourgeoise, XVIII–XX siècle* (Paris, 1852), 48–54; Mrs. Pember Reeves, *Round about a Pound a Week* (London, 1914), 18–19, 22, 48–49; E. J. Hobsbawm and George Rudé, *Captain Swing* (London, 1993), 53.

[23] Alexis de Tocqueville, *Democracy in America*, 2 vols., tr. Henry Reeve (New York, 1961), 1:395, 364, also 1:38; 2:51; 2:276–277, also, 2:196–200; Tocqueville, *Journey to America*, tr. George Lawrence (New Haven, 1960), 269; also, James L. Crouthamel, "Tocqueville's South," *Journal of the Early Republic*, 2 (1982), 381–401; Nathaniel Beverley Tucker, "Moral and Political Effect of the Relation between the Caucasian and the African Slave," *SLM*, 10 (1844), 477–479.

to conquer their passions, and imposed forgetfulness of self." Nathaniel Beverley Tucker expressed unfeigned admiration for Tocqueville but regretted his failure to spend time in the Southeast, where he would have seen for himself how slavery grounded genuine constitutional liberty and democracy.[24]

Tucker's remarks suggest a prime reason for Tocqueville's popularity in the South. In *Recollections*, Tocqueville wrote of the July Monarchy: "The truth – the deplorable truth – is that a taste for holding office and a desire to live on the public money is not with us a disease restricted to either party, but the great, chronic ailment of the whole nation; the result of the democratic constitution of our society and of the excessive centralisation of our Government; the secret malady which has undermined all former governments, and which will undermine all governments to come." In *Democracy in America*, he wrote that all democratic governments tended to spend freely and that, despite pretenses, the government of the United States proved no exception. Still, he marveled that the president lacked the exclusive right to appoint people to office and that the whole number of federal employees about 1830 scarcely exceeded 12,000. John C. Calhoun echoed those thoughts year after year, describing the spoils system as a disease that corrupted all governments but especially those governments under popular control.[25]

Among the eminent foreign scientists whom Southerners honored, none ranked higher than Sir Charles Lyell, the world-famous British geologist, who visited America in the early 1840s and again in the 1850s. Lyell had expected grim conditions but found the planters kind and frank and the field hands "cheerful and free from care, better fed than a large part of the labouring class of Europe." In Alabama he witnessed no maltreatment but confessed that he had not seen Louisiana's reputedly oppressive sugar plantations. Lyell, who thought he saw improvement in Virginia, observed in Charleston, "The negroes here have certainly not the manners of an oppressed race." He painted a rosy picture of the Couper plantation on St. Simon's, with its 500 slaves, concluding that the warm relation of masters to slaves resembled the relation of feudal lords to retainers. The material condition of the slaves compared favorably to those of the poor of Scotland. Beyond these common comparisons lay the more advanced defense of slavery. In South Carolina in the mid-1840s, Lyell assessed the attitude of the planters: "'Labour,' they said, 'is as compulsory in Europe as here,'" but without the cradle-to-grave security that slavery offered. Alexander Marjoribanks, sympathetic to the slaveholders, wrote that few Americans "uphold 'slavery in the abstract,' as it is termed," naming James H. Hammond

---

[24] Proslavery Southerners also quoted Tocqueville on social conditions in the North: see, e. g., [Patrick Mell], *Slavery. A Treatise, Showing that Slavery Is Neither a Moral, Political, nor Social Evil* (Pennfield, Ga., 1844), 31.

[25] J. P. Mayer, ed., *The Recollections of Alexis de Tocqueville* (London, 1948), 33; Tocqueville, *Democracy in America*, 1:134, 249, 260; Calhoun, "Discourse on the Constitution," in Ross M. Lence, ed., *Union and Liberty: The Political Philosophy of John C. Calhoun* (Indianapolis, Ind., 1992), 244, 257.

as a prominent spokesman for those who did. He thought, however, that many Southerners agreed, "Labor is as compulsory in Europe as here."[26]

Lyell's opinion on improvement in Virginia echoed that of prominent Southerners and Northerners. In the decade after the War of 1812, St. George Tucker and James Madison of Virginia and James Kirk Paulding of New York insisted that slavery in Virginia had become much more humane than it had been before the Revolution. The antislavery Lancelot Minor Blackford also insisted the Virginians treated their slaves well. Ivan Golovin, a Russian traveler, thought bad slave masters a rarity in the United States, but then, he thought the same about serf masters in Russia.[27]

The world-traveling Charles Joseph Latrobe of England and Australia – in a book dedicated to his friend Washington Irving and hailed by Edgar Allan Poe as "the best work on America yet published" – hinted darkly about the impending danger of a growing slave population. He pitied the masters rather than their slaves – "pet and spoilt children . . . far from a pitiable." John Lambert, like almost all British travelers, loathed slave auctions. Yet, despite his concern for the refined cruelty of slavery, he considered black slaves necessary for work in tropical and semitropical climates and suggested that their living situation was improving. Nothing excused or justified slavery in the minds of Emanuel Howitt of England and the poet Henry Cogswell Knight of Massachusetts, but they depicted the slaves' living conditions as much better than expected. Mead Whitman of New York wrote upon his arrival in Savannah, "The condition of the slaves is inexpressibly shocking . . . half naked and half-starved." Yet he thought free men who had to work in the southern climate would soon be degraded to the level of slaves: "Liberty would be to them only a name." The "vacant looks and ragged appearance" of the hands in the rice fields in South Carolina repelled Adam Hodgson, a strongly antislavery Scots who peppered his two-volume travelogue with grim tales and condemnations. Yet slave huts were "not unlike a poor Irish cabin, with the addition of a chimney." Hodgson wrote from Virginia, "I have been surprised with the ease, cheerfulness, and intelligence of the *domestic* slaves. Their manners and their mode of expressing themselves have, generally, been decidedly superior to those of many of the

---

[26] Sir Charles Lyell, *Travels in North America, Canada, and Nova Scotia, with Geological Observations*, 2nd ed., 2 vols. (London, 1855), 1:169, 182, 185, quotes at 160, 1:189; Sir Charles Lyell, *A Second Visit to the United States of North America*, 2 vols. (London, 1855), 1:209, 261–268, quotes at 224 and 2:60; Marjoribanks, *Travels in South and North America*, 360, 328–330, quote at 328.

[27] Philip Hamilton, *The Making and Unmaking of a Revolutionary Family: The Tuckers of Virginia, 1752–1830* (Charlottesville, Va., 2003), 153; Drew R. McCoy, *The Last of the Fathers: James Madison and the Republican Legacy* (Cambridge, Mass., 1989), 225–226, 236–239; [James Kirk Paulding], *Letters from the South*, 2 vols. (New York, 1819), 1:Letter 3; L. Minor Blackford, *Mine Eyes Have Seen the Glory: The Story of a Virginia Lady, Mary Berkeley Minor Blackford, 1802–1896, Who Taught Her Sons to Hate Slavery and to Love the Union* (Cambridge, Mass., 1954), 116; Ivan Golovin, *Stars and Stripes, or, American Impressions* (London and New York, 1856), 96.

lower classes in England." The slaves, despite their "never agreeable" circumstances, were "merry enough."[28]

Lady Emmeline Stuart-Wortley visited Richard Taylor's plantation in Mississippi and thought the slaves well fed, comfortably clothed and housed, and seemingly happy and contented. Their cabins were "extremely nice," and the slave children well cared for. All the slaves "appeared to adore Mr. Taylor, who seemed extremely kind to them, and affable with them." Acknowledging that she had probably seen southern plantations at their best – "*coleur de rose* of the business" – she was sure that, despite atrocities of which she had heard, slaves were generally well treated.[29]

Frances Kemble hardly had a good word to say about the South. Yet, although she railed against the filth of the slave cabins, she added, "The stench in an Irish, Scotch, Italian, or French hovel is quite as intolerable as any I have ever found in our negro houses, and the filth and vermin which abound around the clothes and persons of the lower peasantry of any of these countries [are] as abominable as the same conditions in the black population of the United States." In Savannah during the late 1850s, the antislavery and politically radical Barbara Leigh Smith Bodichon of England severely criticized Amelia Murray – her aristocratic countrywoman – for whitewashing southern slavery in her *Letters from the United States, Cuba, and Canada*. Bodichon protested that even the critical James Stirling – whose travelogue the abolitionist Gamiel Bailey strongly recommended – "gives too favourable a view." Yet, Bodichon added, "Not too favourable an account of the fat and merry look of the negroes – that would be impossible. They are physically better off, I believe, than the lowest classes in England or France." And then there was Sarah Mytton Maury of England – high-church Anglican and warm admirer of Calhoun – who said she would rather live in the slave states than the free: "*I like the disposition, I like the service, I like the affection of the Slave; I like*

---

[28] Charles Joseph Latrobe, *The Rambler in North America*, 2nd ed., 2 vols. (London, 1836), 2:15; Edgar Allan Poe, "Critical Notices," *SLM*, 2 (1836), 122; John Lambert, *Travels through Canada and the United States of North America in the Years 1806, 1807, and 1808*, 2 vols., 2nd ed. (London, 1814), 2:ch. 32; E. Howitt, *Selections from Letters Written during a Tour through the United States: In the Summer and Autumn of 1819* (Nottingham, U.K., 1820), 79; Arthur Singleton [Henry Cogswell Knight], *Letters from the South and West* (Boston, Mass., 1824), 74–81, but see 110–113 for harsher treatment in Mississippi than Virginia; Mead Whitman, *Travels in North America* (New York, 1820), 13–14; Adam Hodgson, *Letters from North America, Written during a Tour in the United States and Canada*, 2 vols. (London, 1824), 1:41, 45, 24, 2:95.

[29] Lady Emmeline Stuart-Wortley, *Travels in the United States, Etc., during 1849 and 1850*, 3 vols. (London, 1851), 1:118, 218–220, 223–224, quotes at 218, 220, 223. William Gilmore Simms reinforced Stuart-Wortley's self-criticism: He condescendingly referred to the "clever" Lady Wortley, who "uses rose water instead of ink" in portraying America. Simms nonetheless commended her account of Mexico. See [William Gilmore Simms], "Critical Notes," *SQR*, n.s., 5 (1852), 232. Octavia Walton Le Vert considered Lady Stuart-Wortley a woman of genius: *Souvenirs of Travel*, 2 vols. (Mobile, Ala., 1857), 1:63. John R. Thompson found her travelogue "a great delight": *SLM*, 17 (1851), 583.

the bond which exists between him and his master." Southerners occasionally turned English criticism to advantage by a self-effacement that embodied stern rebuke.[30]

The conflicted accounts of two discerning antislavery European women in the 1850s contained much to make Southerners wince but much to comfort them. Marianne Finch of England pictured the slave cabins of Virginia "nothing like the clean, pretty cottages in which some of our English peasants live" but "infinitely better than an Irish cabin, a poor lodging house, or many other of the homes of the labouring poor in Great Britain." She sadly observed that poor Irish women and children, unlike the slaves of Virginia, had no one to provide for their sustenance: "If an American planter had to maintain his slaves in England, he might find it not only *lawful*, but *expedient* to make them free." Fredrika Bremer of Sweden found that the house servants in South Carolina lived much better than "the free servants of our own country." She told the slaves on Joel Poinsett's plantation on the Peedee that they were eating better than the Swedish poor. The well-traveled Poinsett knew as much, having witnessed the stark poverty and alcoholism among Swedish peasants. He did not, however, match the venom of De Bow, who thought Stockholm probably the "most licentious city in Europe." Bremer, who understood the value of freedom, recognized that slaves could be sold like cattle and that scores suffered under bad masters; yet she granted that under good masters they lived better than the European poor. She closed the second volume of her work with a plea that indignation over slavery not blind Europeans to the fate of their own working poor, adding that their very freedom gave them a chance to improve their conditions.[31]

Other remarks by antislavery travelers provided sweet music to southern ears. Matilda Charlotte Houstoun, the English novelist, did not close her eyes to slavery's atrocities. She expected to find slaves ill-used in Louisiana and Texas; instead, she found them cheerful and cared for. She concluded that the

---

[30] Frances Kemble, *Journal of a Resident on a Georgia Plantation in 1838–1839* (New York, 1863), 24; Feb. 23, 1858, in Barbara Leigh Smith Bodichon, *An American Diary, 1857–8*, ed., Joseph W. Reed, Jr. (London, 1972), 99, quote at 117; [Gamiel Bailey], "An English View of American Slavery," *National Era* (Washington), 9 (1855), 11 (1857), 162; Sarah Mytton Maury, *An Englishwoman in America* (London, 1848), 193. Amelia Murray's *Letters from the United States, Cuba, and Canada*, 2 vols. in 1 (New York, 1968 [1856]), drew considerable interest and praise from Southerners: see, e.g., Christopher Phillips and Jason L. Pendleton, eds., *The Union on Trial: The Political Journals of Judge William Barclay Napton, 1829–1883* (Columbus, Mo., 2005), 162–163; Elizabeth Ruffin to Edmund Ruffin, Jan. 6, 1840, in Edmund Ruffin Papers; "Preston Souther," "Miss Murray's Travels," *SLM*, 22 (1856), 455–461.

[31] Marianne Finch, *An Englishwoman's Experience in America* (New York, 1969 [1853]), 294–295, 301; Fredrika Bremer, *Homes of the New World: Impressions of America*, 2 vols. (New York, 1853), 1:277, 293, 296; 2:435, 554–555; J. Fred Rippy, *Joel R. Poinsett, Versatile American* (New York, 1968), 15; [J. D. B. De Bow], "Pictures of Northern Europe," *DBR*, 26 (Mar. 1859), 286–291. Some Southerners granted that European peasants lived in proverbially neat cottages but denounced the housing of the urban workers as ghastly: "Where Are We?" *SLM*, 19 (1853), 240; "Cities of Italy," *SLM* 19 (1853), 229.

South's "*domestic* slaves are the least unhappy *menials* in the world" and "very far from being so severely worked as most of the *servants* in free countries." In Kentucky she said more than she probably intended. Certain that Kentucky would blossom economically if it eliminated slavery, she could not understand the willingness of Kentuckians to maintain the "old and incompetent slaves whom they are now obliged to support." Similarly, a "somewhat shocked" William Chambers of Scotland, getting his first look at slavery in Maryland, could not fathom "the apparently uneconomic practice of buying men at a considerable cost to labour in the fields, instead of hiring and dismissing them at pleasure." This attitude – *bourgeois par excellence* – appeared in northern antislavery circles. The growing gulf between the social and moral visions of the slaveholders and their northern critics emerged clearly in the words used by William Channing Gannett and Edward Everett Hale in 1865 in an article titled "The Freedmen at Port Royal," in *North American Review*: "In slavery not only are natural rights denied, but what is quite as injurious, necessary wants are supplied."[32]

Reports favorable to the South came from northern women, a number of whom married Southerners, accepted slavery, and labeled abolitionist accounts wild exaggerations. Mary Haines Harker and her parents, New England Quakers, visited Virginia in 1853 and distressed northern friends by insisting that the slaves were "happy." Sarah Mendell and Charlotte Hosmer of Massachusetts refused to slake northern thirst for repulsive stories about slavery, suggesting that Virginia had dissolved their prejudices. Although critical of slavery, they reported the slaves apparently "well fed and happy."[33]

Among the antislavery clergymen who traveled or sojourned in the South, Henry Benjamin Whipple, future bishop of the Protestant Episcopal Church, and the Unitarian Reverend Abiel Abbot of Massachusetts were revolted by slave auctions and instances of cruelty but judged slave circumstances on balance fairly good. In the late 1830s the Presbyterian Reverend Leander Ker of Pennsylvania, who had spent years in Florida, wrote *Slavery Consistent with Christianity* (republished in the 1850s), in which he took racial ground but granted that southern slaves were much better off than British white wage-slaves. Ker never "saw any unnecessary severity, or wanton cruelty"; he fumed

---

[32] Mrs. [Matilda Charlotte] Houstoun, *Texas and the Gulf of Mexico; or Yachting in the New World* (Austin, Tex., 1968 [1845]), 71, 75, 155, 163; Matilda Charlotte, *Hesperos: Or, Travels in the West*, 2 vols. (London, 1850), quote from Kentucky at 1:290, 2:137, 159–161, quote at 202; William Chambers, *Things as They Are in America* (London, 1854), 255; [William Channing Gannett and Edward Everett Hale], "The Freedmen at Port Royal," *North American Review*, 101 (1865), 1; Julie Saville, *The Work of Reconstruction: From Slave to Free Labor in South Carolina, 1860–1870* (New York, 1994), 47.

[33] "Journal of a Quaker Maid: From the Diary of Mary Haines Harker, May–December, 1853," *Virginia Quarterly Review*, 11 (1935), 77; Misses Mendell and Hosmer, *Notes of Travel and Life by Two Young Ladies* (New York, 1854), 185–186, 204–206, quote at 249. See also Julia M. Brown to Jonathan Ralph Flynt, Oct. 12–13, 1832, in J. E. Cashin, ed., *Our Common Affairs*, 224; James M. Denham and Keith L. Huneycutt, eds., *Echoes from a Distant Frontier: The Brown Sisters' Correspondence from Antebellum Florida* (Columbia, S.C., 2004).

that abolitionists were *"most grossly ignorant* of the condition of the slaves."
In the 1850s the Reverend Nehemiah Adams drew heavy fire from antislavery
Northerners for singing the praises of the southern labor system in a book
recommended by *De Bow's Review* and much touted throughout the South.
During the War, the Episcopalian Bishop John Henry Hopkins of Pennsylvania, who denied the sinfulness of slavery, pointedly denounced the oppression
of labor in Britain.[34]

Among laymen, William Cullen Bryant accounted the slaves of up-country
South Carolina "a cheerful, careless, dirty race, not hard worked, and in many
respects indulgently treated." Thomas Low Nichols grew up in the North
with a horror for slavery but slowly changed his mind as he spent time in
the South. Nichols did not doubt that – on average – the slaves lived better
than did the English agricultural laborers. John Abbott, the popular northern
historian, reacted with skepticism when he met a man who assured him that
southern slaves lived better than the poorer northern laborers. No northern
farmer or laborer, Abbott said, lived in – or would live in – the squalid slave
cabins. But, he added, "The condition of the slave, under a humane master, is
undoubtedly preferable to that of the prostitutes, vagabonds, and thieves at the
Five Points in New York." The Massachusetts-born J. W. Nye of upstate New
York lectured and wrote in the early 1850s on his southern experiences, saying
that masters treated their slaves humanely – much better than the British treated
their colonials. Professor Charles Eliot Norton of Harvard, too, conceded that
slaves were well treated.[35]

The formidable Duff Green – Border-State entrepreneur, political impre-
sario, and newspaper editor – buttressed the central contentions of Slavery
in the Abstract without voicing its bald formulations. A political moderate

---

[34] [Henry Benjamin Whipple], *Bishop Whipple's Southern Diary, 1843–44* (New York, 1968),
13, 29, 31; John Hammond Moore, ed., "The Abiel Abbot Journals: A Yankee Preacher in
Charleston Society, 1818–1827," *South Carolina Historical Magazine*, 68 (1967), 119–123,
135–137; also James Oscar Farmer, Jr., *The Metaphysical Confederacy: James Henley Thornwell and the Synthesis of Southern Values* (Macon, Ga., 1986), 200; Leander Ker, *Slavery Consistent with Christianity*, 3rd ed. (Weston, Mo., 1853), iv–vi, quote at 31; Nehemiah Adams, "A
Northerner's Experience in Re Southern Slavery," *DBR*, 19 (May 1855), 573, and Nehemiah
Adams, *South-Side View of Slavery; Or, Three Months at the South in 1854* (New York, 1969
[1854]); J. H. Hopkins, *A Scriptural, Ecclesiastical, and Historical View of Slavery from the
Days of the Patriarch Abraham to the Nineteenth Century* (New York, 1864), 284–300. For
attacks on Nehemiah Adams, see, e.g., Samuel Batchelder, *The Responsibility of the North in
Relation to Slavery* (Cambridge, Mass., 1856), 5, and Horace Cowles Atwater, *Incidents of a
Southern Tour: or, The South as Seen with Northern Eyes* (Boston, Mass., 1857).
[35] William Cullen Bryant, *Letters of a Traveller; Or, Notes of Things Seen in Europe and America*
(New York, 1850), 88; Thomas Low Nichols, *Forty Years of American Life* (London, 1864),
2:242, 262–263, and ch. 18; John S. C. Abbott, *South and North; or, Impressions Received
during a Trip to Cuba and the South* (New York, 1969 [1860]), 69–70, quote at 78; for
Norton, see Stow Persons, *Decline of American Gentility* (New York, 1973), 223. See also
Horace Cowles Atwater, *Incidents of a Southern Tour: or, The South as Seen with Northern
Eyes* (Boston, Mass., 1857), quotes at 7, 25, 120, see also 31 for surprisingly generous remarks
from a staunch antislavery Northerner.

and powerful businessman, he spent a good deal of time in Europe in official and unofficial capacities, observing industrial labor. A friend of Calhoun, he defended slavery on practical economic grounds and largely shunned religious and even racial arguments. Seeking sectional compromise, he implicitly accepted George Tucker's thesis of the eventual replacement of slavery by a capitalist development that would drive the price of free labor below that of slave labor. Green nonetheless defended southern slavery as humane, insisting that southern slaves fared much better than free laborers in the North as well as in Europe.[36]

The fierce abolitionist Hinton Rowan Helper recounted the housing of the peasants near Valparaiso, Chile, as inferior to the slave quarters of the South. Domingo Faustino Sarmiento, future president of Argentina, who condemned the South without having seen it, spent much of his time in the United States recounting his extensive travels in Europe: "I have seen her millions of peasants, proletarians, and mean workmen, and I have seen how degraded and unworthy of being counted as men they are. The crust of filth which covers their bodies and the rags and tatters in which they are dressed do not sufficiently reveal the darkness of their spirits." In New Orleans the liberal Russian aristocrat Aleksandr Borisovich Lakier met a German slave trader who insisted that southern slaves were better off than European laborers. Lakier scoffed that one injustice did not excuse another. Lakier doubted that the German believed what he was saying, but he did not directly contradict the assertion.[37]

Slaveholders took special comfort in John Mitchel's account of his tour of the Southwest, published in *Southern Citizen*, which he edited in Knoxville before moving to Richmond. Mitchel, a prominent Irish revolutionary, settled in the South after a brief period in New York and fell in love with its social system as well as its people. He did not go unnoticed in the North, where Henry David Thoreau denounced *Southern Citizen* in antislavery speeches. Mitchel excoriated abolitionists for crying over black slaves rather than Irish quasi-serfs. He considered class stratification inevitable, came close to a feudalist position on class relations, and, in effect, endorsed Slavery in the Abstract. With the politically radical Leonidas W. Spratt of Charleston – his "mentor in American politics" – he defended black slavery and believed that the North would eventually embrace slavery to ward off anarchy. De Bow called *Southern Citizen* "a bold, fearless, and determined advocate of everything Southern – institutions,

---

[36] W. Stephen Belko, *The Invincible Duff Green: Whig of the West* (Columbia, Mo., 2006), 4, 28, 158–159, 286–287, 380, 450. For Tucker's thesis, see *infra*, Chapter 4.

[37] Hugh C. Bailey, *Hinton Rowan Helper: Abolitionist-Racist* (University, Ala., 1965), 7; but see also David Brown, *Southern Outcast: Hinton Rowan Helper and the Impending Crisis of the South* (Baton Rouge, La., 2006). J. W. Nye, *A Lecture on African Slavery* (Elba, N.Y., 1853), 5–6; Sarmiento, quoted in trans. introd. to Michael Aaron Rockland, tr., *Sarmiento's Travels in the United States in 1847* (Princeton, N.J., 1970), 14; Arnold Schrier and Joyce Story, trans. and eds., *A Russian Looks at America: The Journey of Aleksandr Borisovich Lakier in 1857* (Chicago, 1979), 238. Abbott reported from Cuba that African slaves lived wretchedly but not so wretchedly as the Chinese coolies there: 47–50.

policy, society, law, politics and political rights!" Maunsel White of Louisiana helped finance Mitchel's journalism. Edmund Ruffin praised him as "a strong southern and pro-slavery advocate." To the politically influential A. B. Meek of Alabama, historian and man of letters, Britain's persecution of John Mitchel "is a cloud that blots half the sun of the age." Mitchel had an extraordinary career as an Irish revolutionary; an opponent of Daniel O'Connell in the nationalist movement; a thorn to the British Crown, which imprisoned and exiled him; a world traveler; a member of the British Parliament in his later years; and an exceptionally fine writer of English prose. But he laid himself open to charges of being anti-Catholic, anti-Semitic, and pro-feudal. Mitchel felt at home with George Fitzhugh, Spratt, Ruffin, and De Bow. He displayed ferocious courage in the struggle for Irish freedom, supporting slavery on grounds that raised questions about the nature of the social relations he wanted for Ireland.[38]

Reviewing concessions in foreign reportage, Southerners gloated. Letitia A. Burwell recounted the astonishment of a visiting English gentleman who saw how much more comfortable slaves in Virginia were relative to workers in Britain. Thomas R. R. Cobb of Georgia cited Benjamin Silliman's two-volume European travelogue (1810), which identified the primary freedom possessed by workers as freedom to scramble for starvation wages. Louisa McCord, Catherine Edmondston, and Mary Howard Schoolcraft welcomed the testimony of Alexander Mackay and other Britons on the qualities of southern slaveholders and the living conditions of their slaves. Rachel Mordecai Lazarus of Warrenton, North Carolina, who favored gradual emancipation, assured the novelist Maria Edgeworth that southern masters treated their slaves with kindness, adding that the condition of slaves "is far less miserable than that of the poorer classes of white people." She, in effect, echoed the pro-emancipation Henry Laurens of South Carolina, former president of the Continental Congress, who wrote to Alexander Hamilton in 1785 that his slaves were "in more comfortable circumstances than any equal number of Peasantry in Europe."[39]

---

[38] "Slavery in Massachusetts," in Henry D[avid] Thoreau, *A Yankee in Canada, with Anti-Slavery and Reform Papers* (New York, 1969 [1892]), 109; Mitchel, "Letters to the *Southern Citizen,* Jan. 1858," typescript in private possession, courtesy of Mr. Vincent Comersford; "Editorial Miscellany," *DBR,* 26 (March 1859), 353; *ERD,* 1:187, 263–264, 266; A. B. Meek, *Romantic Passages in Southwestern History* (New York, 1857), 197–198. See also William E. Robinson to W. A. Graham, Oct. 20, 1855, in J. G. DeRoulhac Hamilton, ed., *The Papers of William Alexander Graham,* 5 vols. (Raleigh, N.C., 1957–1973), 4:606–607. Not every Southerner loved Mitchel: see the harsh remarks of Frank G. Ruffin to Thomas Ruffin, Feb. 25, 1863, in *ERD,* 2:295. A Union soldier and Confederate prisoner described Mitchel as "the most rabid rebel of the whole lot": Robert Knox Sneden, Dec. 21–24, 1863, in Charles F. Bryan, Jr., and Nelson D. Lankford, eds., *Eye of the Storm: A Civil War Odyssey Written and Illustrated by Private Robert Knox Sneden* (New York, 2000), 173. Mitchel also spoke out against British imperialist oppression of India. See Jan. 25, 1858, in Bodichon, *An American Diary,* 89. On Mitchel, see Rebecca Hunt Moulder, *May the Sod Rest Lightly: Thomas O'Connor* (Tucson, Ariz., 1977), and "History of the Irish Question," *Transactions of the Royal Historical Society,* 169–192.

[39] Letitia A. Burwell, *A Girl's Life in Virginia before the War,* 2nd ed. (New York, 1895), 27; T. R. R. Cobb, *An Inquiry into the Law of Negro in the United States* (New York, 1968 [1858]),

During the War, French and British travelers recounted the widespread parroting in all classes of the *Charleston Mercury* and other newspapers about the superior living conditions of southern slaves and the advantages of uniting labor and capital in a safe social system. William Watson of Louisiana, a Scots who fought bravely in the Confederate army after years in the West Indies, scoffed at the notions of black inferiority and of slavery as a divine institution but denied the cruelties charged in abolitionist tracts. Watson added that, contrary to common belief, abolitionist literature did circulate in the South, and that its wild and abrasive exaggerations provoked mirth, ridicule, and anger, intensifying Southerners' allegiance to slavery and southern rights. Antislavery northern travelers added grist to the proslavery mill. A typical case: "G. M." of Massachusetts, who spent three years in Virginia and visited Charleston in 1831, said, "The evils of slavery are softened by humane treatment.... The evil is like the gout, one of inheritance." Concluding that a remedy no longer existed, he warmly praised Carolinians, paraphrasing without acknowledgment what he probably knew to be Edward Gibbon's tribute to the great Byzantine General Belisarius: The Carolinian's "faults are those of his institutions, his virtues are his own." Like many other Northerners, "G. M." doubted that he would ever again see "such an out-gushing of affection as I have seen on the arrival of 'young master' or mistress."[40]

Frederick Law Olmsted provided the most widely known, read, and influential of northern travelogues. Touring the Southeast in the 1850s, he recounted views expressed by thoughtful, intelligent, apparently humane slaveholders. In Virginia a kind planter near Richmond – probably Thomas W. Gee – told him, "I am satisfied, too, that our slaves are better off, as they are, than the majority of your free laboring classes at the North, . . . better off than the English

cxx; Louisa S. McCord, "Charity Which Does Not Begin at Home," *Political and Social Essays*, ed. Richard C. Lounsbury (Charlottesville, Va., 1995), 329–330; see also *Plantation Life: The Narratives of Mrs. Henry Schoolcraft* (New York, 1969 [1860]), 35, 73–75, 307–309, 324–329; Edmonston, June 2, 1862, in Crabtree and Patton, eds., *"Journal of a Secesh Lady,"* 186–187; Rachel Mordecai to Maria Edgeworth, Oct. 21, 1824, in Edgar E. MacDonald, *The Education of the Heart: The Correspondence of Rachel Mordecai Lazarus and Maria Edgeworth* (Chapel Hill, N.C., 1977), 69; Laurens to Hamilton, Apr. 19, 1785, in Harold C. Syrett et al., eds., *The Papers of Alexander Hamilton*, 27 vols. (New York, 1987), 3:605–608. J. R. Thompson approved the "good sense" of Benjamin Silliman despite tough criticism of his style: *SLM*, 19 (1853), 646. For the impact of Silliman, Paulding, the Unitarian Reverend Henry Coleman, and other Northerners who reported on the miseries of the British working class, see John F. Kasson, *Civilizing the Machine: Technology and Republican Values in America, 1776–1900* (New York, 1976), especially 58–60.

[40] Maurice Sand [son of George Sand], "Hatred Prevailed," in Belle Becker Sideman and Lillian Friedman, ed., *Europe Looks at the Civil War, An Anthology* (New York, 1960), 59–60; [Anon.], "An Englishman in South Carolina," in Schwaab and Bull, eds., *Travels in the Old South*, 2:560–561; William Watson, *Life in the Confederate Army: Being the Observations and Experiences of an Alien in the South during the American Civil War* (Baton Rouge, La., 1995 [1887]), 24, 42–44. Of Belisarius, Gibbon wrote, "His imperfections flowed from the contagion of the times; his virtues were his own, the free gift of nature or reflection." *The History of the Decline and Fall of the Roman Empire*, 3 vols., ed. David Wormersley (London, 1994), 2:686.

agricultural laborers, or, I believe, those of any other Christian country." When Olmsted demurred, the planter said that the dearness of slave labor relative to free proved his point. When Olmsted set off for the South he held moderately antislavery views and favored gradual emancipation under the guidance of the Christian slaveholders, who would be convinced to do the right thing if reasoned with in the right spirit.[41]

Olmsted underwent a change of heart, growing disillusioned as he encountered devout Christians among the strongest defenders of slavery. In his early letters to the *New York Times* he spoke favorably of the treatment of slaves and contented himself with criticism of slavery on moral principle and social policy. He conceded that the slaves lived as well as the English and Irish poor and enjoyed greater security. In France, Germany, and Ireland, Olmsted discovered the rural poor in much worse conditions. Prostitution and vice in Liverpool he judged worse than that of New York, which had been the worst he had previously seen. Faced with the brutal treatment of seamen, he concluded that their superiors had less regard for their lives than the southern slaveholders had for the lives of their slaves. The field slaves in Virginia were, except "for their dark, inexpressive faces, exactly like the poorest Irish peasantry." He quoted an article from *Southern Planter* to remind his readers that unlike the Irish poor, southern slaves could not be left to starve. And he contrasted the slaves, wretched as they were, favorably with the degraded poor whites nearby. In the heat of the slavery controversy, he shifted ground, apparently more as a political imperative than because of new information about southern life. When in *Journey in the Seaboard Slave States* and *Journey in the Back Country* he presented the condition of the slaves as worse than that of free peasants and workers elsewhere, his southern critics hurled his earlier words back at him.[42]

Olmsted filed illuminating accounts of the hardening of proslavery sentiment in the South and, specifically, of the growing tendency to defend not merely racial slavery but Slavery in the Abstract. Many gentlemen in Virginia, viewing Europe as already in social crisis, with the North on its way, proclaimed slavery a bulwark against social disintegration.

They believe there are seeds, at present almost inert, of disaster at the North, against which Slavery will be their protection; indications that these are already beginning to be felt or anticipated by prophetic minds, they think they see in the demand for "Land Limitation," in the anti-rent troubles, in strikes of workmen, in the distress of emigrants at the eddies of their current, in diseased philanthropy, in radical democracy and in the progress of socialistic ideas in general.

[41] Frederick Law Olmsted, *A Journey in the Seaboard Slave States* (New York, 1968 [1856]), 44–45.

[42] McLaughlin et al., eds., *Papers of Olmsted*, 2:69–70, 81, 86, 102, n. 6; 1:16, 90, 131, 133–134; see "Calx," "Four Eras of Agricultural Condition, in a Particular Locality," *Southern Planter*, 12 (1852), 133–135. Even in *Seaboard Slave States*, Olmsted conceded that the slave quarters he found on Louisiana and coastal Georgia plantations "were as neat and well-made as the cottages usually provided by the large manufacturing companies in New-England, to be rented to their workmen": 659–660.

Olmsted was prepared to hear such views in South Carolina, but he reacted with anger and alarm when he heard them elsewhere. Planters scorned to temper, much less hide, their true views: "It has always been the opinion of the rulers of their community that it is impossible to educate the laboring mass to a sufficiently good judgment to enable them to take part in directing affairs of state." He attributed to South Carolina's ruling class a firm belief in the subordination of all laborers and a smug conviction that they would be better off as slaves.[43]

Olmsted found attitudes similar in the Southwest. At a commercial convention at Memphis a gentleman spoke of dining on three successive days with obviously sincere slaveholders who had traveled a good deal in the North and had no doubt that their slaves lived better than northern workers. But then, those slaveholders considered the northern masses on a par with the poorest whites of the South. Olmsted and his brother John met with Samuel Perkins Allison, a southern gentleman who had been John's classmate at Yale. In a letter to Charles Loring Brace, Olmsted admitted that Allison had shaken them with thoughtful criticisms of their antislavery and defense of free society. Allison insisted that all societies contained two broadly divergent classes and that notions of equality and freedom for all were untenable. A "silenced" Olmsted confessed to Brace: "I must be either an Aristocrat or more of a Democrat than I have been – a Socialist Democrat. We need institutions that shall more directly *assist* the poor and degraded to elevate themselves. . . . The poor & wicked need more than to be let alone." In Louisiana, Meredith Calhoun, a big slaveholder, held that Providence had expressly designed the black race for servitude, but he did not stop there. He maintained that laborers were everywhere degraded and stupid but in most places lacked the protection and succor provided by masters with a pecuniary interest in them. Olmsted reported from Louisiana on the widespread view that if the blacks were emancipated, enslaved whites would have to replace them.[44]

Southerners Abroad

Well-to-do Southerners went to Europe to study or for business, as well as for pleasure.[45] In the 1840s William C. Richards's *Orion* of Penfield, Georgia, published glowing accounts by South Carolinians of the beauty and elegance of Italy. In the 1850s about 150 South Carolinians traveled to Europe, fascinated by the art and elegance. But political and economic and social life also

---

[43] Olmsted, *Seaboard Slave States*, 183–184 (Va.), 491, 492, 500, 701–702.

[44] Frederick Law Olmsted, *A Journey in the Back Country* (New York, 1970 [1860]), 390; Olmsted to Charles Loring Brace, Dec. 1, 1853, in McLaughlin, et al., eds., *Papers of Olmsted*, 2:231–234, quote at 234, 234, 229–231 (on M. Calhoun); Frederick Law Olmsted, *The Cotton Kingdom: A Traveller's Observations on Cotton and Slavery in the American Slave States* (New York, 1861), ch. 1.

[45] For overviews of southern travelers, see John Hope Franklin, *A Southern Odyssey: Travelers in the Antebellum North* (Baton Rouge, La., 1976); O'Brien, *Conjectures of Order*, 1: Book One.

drew steady comment. In the early 1820s *Western Review and Miscellaneous Magazine* of Lexington, Kentucky, expressed intense distaste at the suppression of the political rights of the Italian people but took little notice of social conditions. There is no reason to believe that most Southerners who sent home word of the oppression of the laboring classes were looking to carp. To the contrary, they generally proceeded with goodwill, often in awe of European culture. Parents sent their children to improve in gentility and refinement, not to wallow in evidence of poverty. What Foster Rhea Dulles has written about Americans holds especially for nineteenth-century Southerners: "Europe has always represented limitless opportunity for all the special joys of sightseeing – unfamiliar scenery, new cities, strange customs; castles, palaces, cathedrals and museums. It has always represented in its long historic past an antiquity that has always had an immense appeal to the American imagination, and as a great storehouse of art for which the United States even today has no real equivalent."[46]

Social criticism of European wretchedness came slowly from southern travelers. William Pinkney of Maryland, in a generally charming account of his travels through the southern French countryside in 1807–1808, told of peasants who appeared as "very poor, though contented and happy" – happy at least to have seen the last of the excesses of the Revolution and content with the Napoleonic regime. The laborers of the Italian Piedmont struck Francis Kinloch of South Carolina as "more miserable in appearance than our negroes; they are badly clothed, and scarcely eat meat from one year's end to another." To the "mere hireling," he observed, "It can be of very little importance to which country he belongs." Thomas Jefferson had counseled Americans not to visit Paris until the age of thirty, so great was the lure of brothels, gambling houses, and assorted illicit pleasures, but James H. Hammond's son, Harry, among others, did not take heed. He was so enchanted by the wines and hospitality of Bordeaux that his father warned him not to stay too long, lest he find it impossible to leave. Yet Harry Hammond, too, flinched at the "appalling" state of labor in Strasbourg: "*This, however, is not slavery Oh No!*" Southern travelers, including the less well-to-do, published accounts of the living conditions of the laboring classes and of the widespread fear of social disorder; others wrote to friends and relatives or spoke at political meetings, local churches, and literary societies. The accumulated effect of their efforts confirmed assertions that the South's social system compared favorably with that of its rivals and that only slavery could resolve the conflict between capital and labor.[47]

[46] "M" [P. C. Pendleton], "Italia la Bella," *Orion*, 3 (1843), 158–160; Rev. W. C. Dana (Charleston), "A Visit to Venice," *Orion*, 4 (1844), 153–160; "Rambles in Italy," *Western Review and Miscellaneous Magazine*, 4 (1821), 349–351.

[47] Dulles, *Americans Abroad*, 3; [William Pinkney], *Travels through the South of France, and the Interior of the Provinces of Provence and Languedoc in the Years 1807 and 1808* (London, 1809), 259 and passim; [Francis Kinloch], *Letters from Geneva and France*, 2 vols. (Boston, 1819), 1:310–311, also 386, 393, 459; Daniel Kilbridge, "Travel, Ritual, and National Identity: Planters on the European Tour," *JSH*, 69 (2003), 555; Harvey Levenstein, *Seductive Journey:*

Some slaveholders who visited England and the continent took the tourist route and gushed over the cathedrals and museums, the fine dinners, the neat tillage, and luxurious living; others like Moses Drury Hoge, who toured Europe in 1855, criticized the political reaction and the superficiality of continental life without mentioning the laboring classes. Hoge breathed deeply in England, which he saw as a free country and the motherland of American liberties. Most Southerners who traveled to Europe for pleasure, study, or business were well-to-do and strongly committed to slavery. The Atlantic crossing, even with the vast improvements in transportation, took more than a month, and a European tour, in the estimate of a Louisiana sugar planter in the 1850s, cost close to a thousand dollars even without buying sprees and gambling. Buying sprees were common but by no means always frivolous. Wealthy Southerners bought paintings, books, furniture, and anything they thought would denote a more sophisticated culture at home. Southerners found European publications that commented favorably on the work of W. J. Grayson and others who pronounced slaves better off than free workers. Southerners traveled together in groups that reinforced their attitudes.[48]

American Tourists in France from Jefferson to the Jazz Age (Chicago, Ill., 1998), 5; [Harry Hammond], "European Correspondence," *RM*, 1 (1857), 510–520, quote at 433; William Douglas Smyth, "A Southern Odyssey: South Carolinians Abroad in the 1850s," *Southern Studies*, 23 (1984), 398–411, and for J. H. Hammond's admonition, see 398. Henry Clay, Jesse Burton Harrison, and other prominent Southerners thought Paris a dangerous temptation for young men, although many more found it impossible to resist the temptation: see O'Brien, *Conjectures of Order*, 1:118–121. Even Henry James, speaking in 1861 on the Fourth of July in Newport, Rhode Island, expressed disgust at England's "hideous class-distinctions." Henry James, *The Social Significance of Our Institutions* (Ithaca, N.Y., 2006 [1861]), 12. According to Daniel Kilbride, Virginians on tour in Europe in the 1850s largely fell silent on slavery and evinced little concern. He notes that Southerners were taken aback by the misery in Naples but attributed it to the cultural ramifications of aristocracy rather than to the absence of slavery: Kilbride, "Slavery, Nation, and Ideology: Virginians on the Grand Tour in the 1850s," in Peter Wallenstein and Bertram Wyatt-Brown, eds., *Virginia's Civil War* (Charlottesville, Va., 2005), 61–71. We disagree. The principal question is the southern view of the relation of republicanism to the slavery they considered essential to sustain it.

48 Peyton Harrison Hoge, *Moses Drury Hoge: Life and Letters* (Richmond, Va., 1899), 117–118; Theodora Britton Marshall and Gladys Crail Evans, *They Found It in Natchez* (New Orleans, La., 1939), 214; Drew Gilpin Faust, *James Henry Hammond and the Old South* (Baton Rouge, La., 1982), 186–203; Clyde N. Wilson, *Carolina Cavalier: The Life and Mind of James Johnston Pettigrew* (Athens, Ga., 1990), 61.

On the resonance of Grayson and others in European literature, see M. E. Musgrave, "Literary Justifications of Slavery," 20, n. 53. Even the wealthy Louisa McCord doubted that she could afford the "enormous expense" of a trip to Europe in 1858: L. S. McCord to Langdon Cheves, Jr., Apr. 3, 1858, in Richard C. Lounsbury, ed., *Louisa S. McCord: Poems, Drama, Biography, Letters* (Charlottesville, Va., 1996), 339; also, Vincent H. Cassidy and Amos E. Simpson, *Henry Watkins Allen of Louisiana* (Baton Rouge, La., 1964), 62; William Douglas Smyth, "A Southern Odyssey: South Carolinians Abroad in the 1850s," *Southern Studies*, 23 (1984), 398–411. For travel in groups, see Maurie D. McInnis and Angela D. Mack, eds., *The Pursuit of Refinement: Charlestonians Abroad, 1740–1860* (Columbia, S.C., 1999), 16–18. For Alabamans on the Grand Tour for cultural uplift, see also Philip D. Beidler, *First Books: The Printed Word and Cultural Formation in Early Alabama* (Tuscaloosa, Ala., 1999), 55–56.

Most affluent Americans traveled according to script, guided by burgeoning travelogues, and too often fueling an early version of the "ugly American." To Anna Maria (Calhoun) Clemson, Americans in Paris were an unattractive lot, spending ostentatiously and denigrating their own country. She meant Yankees, although Charles Sumner's brother George won her respect. Long before the 1850s, when Americans swarmed over Europe, Southerners displayed a strong penchant for seeking each other out and staying together as much as possible. Self-segregation proved wise, for as the sectional crisis deepened at home, northern and southern travelers approached sword's point. The well-traveled James Johnston Pettigrew's altercations in Berlin provoked his denunciation of "the abominable Yankees" – with few exceptions – "the most despicable of the human race."[49]

London provoked gasps. At the beginning of the nineteenth century, Washington Allston of Charleston – a fine painter in whom America took pride – arrived in London with expectations of grandeur, unprepared for "the extremes of misery and splendor." Robert Mackay, a Savannah merchant, expressed admiration for the elite culture of the great English cities, but he, too, shook his head at their squalor. Charles Fenton Mercer, a Virginia Federalist, repelled by upper-class indifference to widespread poverty, feared all-out class war. During the 1820s, Southerners stepped up proslavery comparisons. Josiah Nott of Mobile, who became a prominent physician and racial theorist, toured England and Ireland in the 1830s and confessed that not even New York had prepared him for the flood of paupers and beggars and for so much human misery.

[49] Anna Maria Clemson to John C. Calhoun, July 4, 1845, in *JCCP*, 22:9–10; Wilson, *Carolina Cavalier*, 110; also H. W. Allen, *Travels of a Sugar Planter; Or, Six Months in Europe* (New York, 1861), 78; Mary Mayo Crenshaw, ed., *An American Lady in Paris, 1828–1829: The Diary of Mrs. John Mayo* (Boston, 1927), 37, 55; Pettigrew quoted in Wilson, *Carolina Cavalier*, 38–39.

   Numerous medical students were especially important among Southerners who spent years in Europe. The leading physicians of North Carolina who studied in Germany, France, England, and Switzerland included John Grammar Brodnax (1829–1907); Moses John De Rosset (1838–1881); and Christopher Happoldt: *DNCB*, 1:233; 2:57, 3:29, 5:102; Claude Henry Neuffer, ed., *The Christopher Happoldt Journal: His European Tour with the Reverend John Bachman, June–December, 1958* (Charleston, S.C., 1960), 11–28. For Dr. Joseph Adam Eve of Charleston and Augusta, see Charles C. Jones, Jr., and Salem Dutcher, *Memorial History of Augusta* (Syracuse, N.Y., 1890), ch. 24. For Representative John Perkins Ralls, see Richard N. Current, *Encyclopedia of the Confederacy*, 4 vols. (New York, 1993), 3:1302. For foreign-born distinguished physicians who studied in Paris and practiced in Georgia, see also *Dictionary of Georgia Biography*, ed. Kenneth Coleman and Stephen Gurr, 2 vols. (Athens, Ga., 1983), 1:64, 273–274, 299. Some planters sent sons to Europe ostensibly to study medicine but really to see the world. Dr. John Cheves, son of Langdon Cheves, was among those who had no intention of practicing. See Louisa M. Smythe, ed., *For Old Lang Syne: Collected for My Children* (Charleston, S.C., 1900), 4. A number of Southerners went to Europe with the intention of practicing at home, and some went on to distinction: J. A. Chandler, ed., *The South in the Building of the Nation*, 12 vols. (Richmond, Va., 1909), 11:45, 375, 502–503; John Allison, *Notable Men of Tennessee: Personal and Genealogical*, 2 vols. (Atlanta, Ga., 1905), 1:141.

James Johnston Pettigrew could hardly believe his eyes. "There is more vice in London" – he wrote in words picked up by Edmund Ruffin – "than any other city in the world: Paris, Lisbon, Naples, and New York together would make but a small show before the giant city."[50]

Even the increasingly Anglophile John Randolph of Roanoke pointedly praised the "far superior" moral and material position of southern slaves relative to those of the British lower classes. Randolph, who thought he had prepared himself for the worst before he entered Ireland, was "utterly shocked" at the condition of the poor peasants. Of London in 1826 he wrote, "One class is dying of hunger and another with surfeit. The amount of crime is fearful; and cases of extreme atrocity are not wanting." The England he loved "is Elysium for the rich; Tartaries for the poor." Paris, although "wonderfully improved" in 1824, was "still the filthiest hole, not excepting the worst parts of the old town of Edinboro, that I ever saw *out of Ireland.*" Randolph asked some Irish Tories to visit him to see for themselves how much better Virginia's slaves lived than did their own peasants. He said that John, his personal servant, who accompanied him abroad, decided that, as a Virginia slave, he had a lot to be thankful for. Randolph's half-brother, Nathaniel Beverley Tucker, rendered summary judgment: "The wrongs of Ireland are the act of the people of England."[51]

In the 1830s, James M. Walker of Charleston, an impressive legal scholar, denounced the wealthy of London and the monarchical tendency "to create that worst and meanest of aristocracies, the aristocracy of wealth." Walker lashed the wealthy landowners for exploiting the laborers who made their wealth possible. He lashed the capitalists for treating factory workers as mere instruments: "Between the capitalist in the cotton manufacture and the labourer he employs, there is no personal intercourse, no community of feeling or of interest. The master's head is always at work to discover how he can get

---

[50] Washington Allston to Charles Fraser, Aug. 25, 1801, in Nathalia Wright, ed., *The Correspondence of Washington Allston* (Lexington, Ky., 1993), 25–26, quote at 25; Mackay to Eliza Anne Mackay, August 4, 1804, in Walter Charlon Hartridge, ed., *The Letters of Robert Mackay to His Wife: Written from Ports in America and England, 1795–1816* (Athens, Ga., 1949), 129; Douglas R. Egerton, *Charles Fenton Mercer and the Trial of National Conservatism* (Jackson, Miss., 1989), 44–45, 138; Reginald Horsman, *Josiah Nott of Mobile: Southerner, Physician, and Racial Theorist* (Baton Rouge, La., 1987), 47–48; Wilson, *Carolina Cavalier*, 60–61, 115; Pettigrew criticized Madrid for its centralization and polyglot quality, which he contrasted with the Spanish authenticity of Andalusia and the provinces. See *Notes on Spain and the Spaniards* (Charleston, S.C., 1861), 103, 121; Sept. 6, 1861, *ERD* (2:125).

[51] William Cabell Bruce, *John Randolph of Roanoke, 1773–1833: A Biography Based Largely on New Material*, 2 vols. (New York, 1970 [1922]), 1:466, 499, 500; Hugh A. Garland, 2 vols. *The Life of John Randolph* (New York, 1860), 2:222–223; Randolph to John Brockenbrough, Paris, July 24, 1824, in Russell Kirk, *John Randolph of Roanoke: A Study in American Politics, with Selected Speeches and Letters* (Chicago, 1964), 237; Randolph to Brockenbrough, Oct. 13, 1826, in K. Shorrey, ed., *Collected Letters of John Randolph of Roanoke to Dr. John Brockenbrough, 1812–1833* (New Brunswick, N.J., 1988), 78–79 ("one class is dying..."); Nathaniel Beverley Tucker, "Law Lecture at William and Mary," *SLM*, 1 (1834), 152.

his business done cheaper; and the result is almost always at the expense of the labourer." Charles Osborn of North Carolina, a Quaker, visited Britain and the continent concerned largely with religious matters and the antislavery cause, but he made striking comments on social conditions. In England he "was tendered even to weeping" by the sight of "so many poor ground down by a swarm of lordly despots"; in France he was dismayed by the extent of begging. James H. Hammond, in Europe in the 1830s to regain his health, encountered peasants and laborers as stupid and unenlightened as his slaves but much less affable, contented, and comfortable in their everyday life and labor. Their dreadful condition reinforced his poor opinion of the free-labor system. Like Kinloch and other Southerners before him, Hammond blanched at the beggars of France and Italy: "It makes the heart ache to walk the streets." Dr. John Y. Bennett of Huntsville, Alabama, loved Edinburgh, but he wrote home in 1837, "O Scotland! thou land o' cakes,... thou cluster of palaces, thou modern Athens! Could you not invent any method of getting your coal out of the mine save on the backs of females!!!! It is a fact that there are women whom you call bearers, whose business it is to carry coal out of the pit."[52]

By the end of the 1830s, southern indignation exploded not merely in print, where it may be held suspect as propaganda, but in personal papers. George Tucker, who bore the sufferings of the lower classes with equanimity, visited England in 1838 and thought the organization of the police force alone enough to immortalize Sir Robert Peel: "They consist of young men of good character and manners, who are sufficiently numerous to have a supervision of every part of the metropolis, and of congregating, at a minute's notice, so as to put down any riot or disorder." The Presbyterian Reverend Robert J. Breckinridge of Kentucky and Maryland commented on the day-and-night presence of the police in London but added that they "are really amongst its chiefest comforts." Charles Dickens, notwithstanding his blistering exposés of the degrading condition of England's wage-slaves and the appalling cruelties suffered by child laborers, retained his popularity with Southerners despite his antislavery. Dickens stood with Tucker and Breckenridge, viewing aggression as inherent in human nature and warmly cheering the urban police.[53]

The Presbyterian Reverend James Henley Thornwell of South Carolina did not bear the sufferings of the lower classes with equanimity. He put the encomia

52 [James M. Walker], "Distribution of Wealth" (review of Disraeli's *Young Duke*), SR, 8 (1831), 170–192, quotes at 186, 175; *Journal of that Faithful Servant of Christ, Charles Osborn* (Cincinnati, Oh., 1854), 228, 300; Faust, *Hammond*, 189, 198, 201; Bennett quoted in William Osler, *An Alabama Student – and Other Biographical Essays* (London, 1908), 5; cf. [Kinloch], *Letters from Geneva and France*, 2:26–27, 286. Oswell Carmichael, not especially concerned with social conditions, was nonetheless forcibly struck by the "swarm of pitiable beggars" he saw in Dublin: "Diary of European Trip of Oswell E. Carmichael," June 21, 1839, in Mary Eliza Carmichael Papers.

53 "Autobiography of George Tucker," 150; Breckenridge, *Memoranda of Foreign Travel*, 2 vols. (Baltimore, Md., 1845), 1:81; Myron Magnet, *Dickens and the Social Order* (Philadelphia, Pa., 1985), intro. and ch. 1.

in perspective. Writing to his wife from Liverpool, he expressed astonishment at the widespread hunger, horrible housing, and unspeakable way of life:

The streets are narrow and crowded, and in some parts of the town, disgustingly filthy. The police is stationed, a man for about every fifty yards, along every street, so as to be within a moment's call for the purpose of suppressing mobs, riots, and all disorder. You see an immense poor population here, all ragged and dirty, and begging for alms at almost every corner you turn. Sometimes you meet a wretched, squalid woman in ragged clothes, barefooted with a sheet, or something like it, tied around her, and two or three little children fastened in it, begging for bread, or alms of some sort, and exciting your compassion by pointing to the helpless condition of her babes.[54]

Other Southerners drew on the British press to document their indictment of Liverpool. On the eve of secession Grayson, charging that the English poor, urban and rural, suffered "evils more intolerable to humanity than any the negro in America has ever been forced to endure," picked up and spread accounts of the oppression of British workers published by the reformist *Northern Times* of Liverpool.[55]

In the 1840s, P. C. Pendleton, reviewing *The Glory and Shame of England* by the Reverend Charles Edward Lester of New England, a descendant of Jonathan Edwards, added a fresh idea that became popular in the South. British greed and profiteering, Pendleton wrote in *Magnolia*, were coming down hard on the working classes at home but also on the colonial and semicolonial peoples abroad. Dr. Samuel A. Cartwright of Natchez, Mississippi, reported that the streets of Manchester and other British cities featured "the most deplorable objects of disease and deformity produced by no other cause than the long continued over-working of the laborers." J. H. Bills, a planter in Tennessee, could not have been more impressed with almost everything he saw in 1843, yet he remarked without elaboration on hearing a shipboard lecture on the misery of the European poor. And when near Manchester, Bills contrasted the cheerful homes of the middle classes with the "mere shanties thwacked with straw" of the rural laborers. James DeVeau, the Charleston artist, pronounced his indifference to politics "incurable." Incurable indifference did not restrain his anger when, in Rome in 1846, Jerome Bonaparte offered a well-received public toast to abolition. In the 1850s, Aaron Smith Willington, senior editor and proprietor of the *Charleston Courier*, focused on the charm and beauty of Europe, but after noting that Charlestonians knew all about Lyons as a great manufacturing city, he warned of a dangerous level of unemployment: "Red Republicanism and Socialism are here the order of the day." In 1851 he wrote from Genoa: "The extremes of wealth and poverty are here to be seen

---

54 Thornwell to Nancy Thornwell, June 16, 1841, in B. M. Palmer, *The Life and Letters of James Henley Thornwell* (Richmond, Va., 1875), 168.
55 [William J. Grayson], "The Dual Form of Labour," *RM*, 6 (1859), 1–18, quote at 2. For young Virginians in the 1850s on the British aristocracy, Ireland, and India and their oppression of British laborers, see Peter S. Carmichael, *The Last Generation: Young Virginians in Peace, War, and Reunion* (Chapel Hill, N.C., 2005), ch. 3.

at every step." As in British and European cities, "magnificent abodes" had a counterpoint in swarms of "the most importunate and wretched of beggars."[56]

For Edward A. Pollard of Virginia – a rising star in journalism and letters – the world of the slave plantation offered a model of the good society. Pollard defended slavery apart from race until his postwar retrospective. He denounced "abolition liberty" as an inhumane system of atomistic individualism that desolated the laboring classes. During the depression of 1857, reports of London's 30,000 starving and wretched workers sickened him. "We have all heard enough of the colliers and factory operatives of England," he wrote in 1858, "and the thirty thousand costermongers starving in the streets of London; as also of the serfs and crown-peasants of Russia." The well-traveled Pollard got a firsthand view of labor conditions in California, in Asia, and, indeed, throughout the world. He hated the free-labor system. He concluded that northern capitalists treated workers and the poor much worse than southern slaveholders would dream of treating their slaves and that Asian laborers and peasants fared much worse than southern slaves: "I have seen the hideous slavery of Asia. I have seen the coolies of China." He held that slavery was not only a positive good but a social system much superior to alternatives. During the War, he advocated an invasion of the North to confiscate capitalist property and offer it to the workers in order to tear the social system up by its roots.[57]

Former President John Tyler and Julia Gardiner Tyler, estimating that half the population of France lived in misery, were disgusted by the countryside. Robert Toombs, who spoke French well, paid close attention to social life in France, Italy, and England and expressed astonishment at the condition of the peasantry. Speaking in Boston as well as in the South, he confidently affirmed the superior condition of southern slaves. David Hunter Strother ("Porte Crayon") wrote home to Virginia on the importuning beggars of France. Paris, like London, took heavy hits. The young Leonidas Polk – future Episcopalian bishop of Louisiana and Confederate general – found Paris unspeakably wicked and related French degeneracy to its tyrannical and corrupt politics. William Brawley of South Carolina contrasted the glitter of the Parisian boulevards with the misery in evidence on the nearby streets. A correspondent for *Southern Literary Messenger* drew a grim picture of the contrast between the affluence of the Parisian bourgeoisie in the winter of 1849–1850 and the desolation of unemployed workers and a despicable *lumpenproletariat*.[58]

---

[56] [P. C. Pendleton], "The Editor's Table," *Magnolia* [Savannah], 3 (Nov. 1841), 525; Samuel A. Cartwright, *Essays...in a Series of Letters to the Rev. William Winans* (Vidalia, Miss., 1843), 18, also 25–26; J. H. Bills Diary, June 6, 1843; Robert W. Gibbes, *Memoir of James DeVeau of Charleston, S.C.* (Concord, Mass., [1846]), 42, 125; [Aaron Smith Willington], *A Summer's Tour: A Series of Letters, Addressed to the Editors of the Charleston Courier. By "A Traveller"* (Charleston, S.C., 1852), quotes at 32, 43–44, and see 52–54.

[57] Edward A. Pollard, *Black Diamonds Gathered in the Darkey Homes of the South* (New York, 1968 [1859]), 21, 95; also Jack P. Maddex, Jr., *The Reconstruction of Edward A. Pollard: A Rebel's Conversion to Postbellum Unionism* (Chapel Hill, N.C., 1874), 12, 24–27, 32, 57.

[58] Theodore C. Delaney, "Julia Gardiner Tyler: A Nineteenth-Century Southern Woman" (Ph.D. diss., College of William and Mary, 1995), ch. 1; Stovall, *Toombs*, 127, 129–139; Cecil D. Eby,

Henry Watkins Allen, a Louisiana sugar planter and later governor of Confederate Louisiana, enjoyed the Grand Tour in 1859 and generally eschewed
carping: "I have spent this day in sight-seeing and giving coppers to beggars;
for I must say there are more beggars in Liverpool than in our whole country put together." On the continent he sighed, "Poor old Pisa! full of fleas
and beggars." Rome and Naples had "less real piety, and more high-handed
unblushing wickedness than in any other two cities in Christendom" – a judgment George Wythe Randolph of Virginia rendered on Athens ("the most filthy
and execrable hole in the Mediterranean") and other Southerners spoke about
other cities. Allen, reflecting on his travels and especially on the hard life of
British workers, concluded, "Thank God, our black slaves are well-fed, they
are properly cared for in sickness and health, and when old age comes on, they
are not sent to the poor-house or to 'linger and die' but in good warm cabins,
in the midst of abundance, and under the master's eye." [59]

The intimidating presence of police and soldiers in the streets of England
and continental Europe called forth expressions of repugnance from prominent Americans. Among Northerners, the poet and editor William Cullen
Bryant flinched at the great number of soldiers seen everywhere in France and
Germany. Southerners reacted even more vigorously. In 1819 John Edwards
Holbrook, a Yankee who rose to eminence in Charleston's scientific circles,
observed the poverty in Manchester and Dublin and the presence of soldiers,
"repressing the spirits and corrupting the morals of the people." In later years,
Thomas Clemson wrote to Calhoun that standing armies absorbed all the
resources of the European states. George Henry Calvert of Maryland noted
in the early 1850s, "The European armies hang on the nations, a monstrous
idleness, a universal polluting scab.... Standing armies are the very fomenters
of darkness." Divided politically and socially by class, Europe held the laboring class in contempt as "the *vile multitude*, as M. Thiers calls them." Calvert
dismissed the prosperity of the Belgians as a myth, referring to some two million hungry and wretchedly housed semi-paupers and to another two million
workers better off but constantly struggling to survive. In 1851, F. W. Pickens,
who became the War governor of South Carolina, charged that the British
emancipated their slaves in part in order to recall troops from the West Indies
to overawe their own people. "And what has been the result? Ireland under

Jr., *"Porte Crayon": The Life of David Hunter Strother* (Chapel Hill, N.C., 1960), 37; William
M. Polk, *Leonidas Polk, Bishop and General*, 2 vols. (New York, 1915), 1:130, 235; Glenn
Robins, *The Bishop of the Old South: The Ministry and War Legacy of Leonidas Polk* (Macon,
Ga., 2006), 38; for Brawley, see Harvey Levenstein, *Seductive Journey: American Tourists
in France from Jefferson to the Jazz Age* (Chicago, 1998), 88–89; "American," "A Glance
at the Streets of Paris during the Winter of 1849–50," *SLM*, 16 (1850), 257–266. Still, in
1866, Jacob Thomson of Mississippi, a wealthy planter, prominent politician, and Confederate
official, found Paris "the pleasantest city in the world." Jacob Thomson to William Delay,
Aug. 11, 1866, in Percy W. Rainwater, "Letters to and from Jacob Thomson," *JSH*, 6 (1940),
104. For the variety of reactions to Paris, see O'Brien, *Conjectures of Order*, 1:118–125.

[59] Allen, *Travels of a Sugar Planter*, 3, 60, 186, 222, 245; George Green Shackelford, *George
Wythe Randolph and the Confederate Elite* (Athens, Ga., 1988), 14.

the British bayonet, in chains – and perishing with starvation." The celebrated Madame Octavia Walton Le Vert of Mobile testified that the rich people of Liverpool fled to their elegant country seats to escape "the misery and toil and struggle of the city life." She referred with undisguised sarcasm to the ubiquitous policemen: "Those polite 'guardians of the law.'" She thought the people must be wicked, indeed, "to require such a surveillance by night and day." She "had never seen a watchfulness like this" outside Havana. Her views reverberated in elite circles, for as Barbara Leigh Smith Bodichon of Great Britain announced, in Mobile it was *de rigueur* to meet Madame LeVert, *"the lady of the South."*

R. S. Gladney, the gin manufacturer and educational promoter, A. S. Willington, and Dr. Samuel A. Cartwright were among prominent Southerners with access to the press who railed at the presence of troops in British and European cities. In a travelogue noted in the South, Bernhard, Duke of Saxe-Weimar Eisenach, expressed revulsion at Liverpool in general and its police measures against unemployed workers in particular. A contributor to *Southern Presbyterian Review* concluded that all despotisms and even limited monarchies and oligarchies required large standing armies.[60]

The Baptist Reverend Thornton Stringfellow of Virginia claimed, "Such is the prostration of moral restraint at the North that in their cities standing armies are necessary to guard the persons and property of unoffending

---

[60] William Cullen Bryant, "Letter 52: Europe under the Bayonet," in *Letters of a Traveller; or, Notes of Things Seen in Europe and America* (New York, 1850), 426–436, esp. 426–427; for Holbrook, see Lester D. Stephens, *Science, Race, and Religion in the American South: John Bachman and the Charleston Naturalists, 1845–1895* (Chapel Hill, N.C., 2000), 80–81, Holbrook quoted at 80; Clemson to Calhoun, Sept. 24, 1849, in *JCCP*, 27:61; George H. Calvert, *Scenes and Thoughts in Europe*, 2nd series (New York, 1852), 12–13, 18, 105–109; *Speech of the Hon. F. W. Pickens, Delivered before a Public Meeting, of the People of the District, Held at Edgefield, C. H., S. C.* (Edgefield, S.C., 1851), 13; Octavia Walton Le Vert, *Souvenirs of Travel*, 2 vols. (Mobile, Ala., 1857), 1:4, 6; Feb. 17, 1858, in Bodichon, *An American Diary*, 111; Alan Smith Thompson, "Mobile, Alabama, 1850–1851: Economic, Political, Physical, and Population Characteristics" (Ph.D. diss., University of Alabama, 1979), 318; see also [John R. Thompson], *SLM*, 25 (1857), 315–318; [Aaron Smith Willington], *A Summer's Tour: A Series of Letters, Addressed to the Editors of the Charleston Courier. By "A Traveller"* (Charleston, S.C., 1852), 32, 41, 57; Cartwright, *Essays*, 58; on Gladney, see Vicki Vaughn Johnson, *The Men and Visions of the Southern Commercial Conventions, 1845–1871* (Columbia, Mo., 1992), 141–143; R. S. Gladney, "Moral Philosophy," *SPR*, 9 (1855), 124; "The Phases of Society," *SPR*, 8 (1855), 197. For a report on the police and military forces on the streets of Paris, see American, "A Glance at the Streets of Paris during the Winter of 1849–50," *SLM*, 16 (1850), 263–264.

Since state militias intervened to maintain order only when necessary, Southerners – and Americans generally – viewed them as salutary democratic alternatives to standing armies: see, e.g., Harry S. Laver, "Rethinking the Social Role of the Militia: Community-Building in Antebellum Kentucky," *JSH*, 68 (2002), 777–816. Foreign visitors to the South suffered their own shocks when they saw nightly patrols, with fixed bayonets, to overawe the black population, the slaves, much as the troops and police overawed the laboring classes in, say, Liverpool. See John Hope Franklin, *The Militant South* (Cambridge, Mass., 1956), 74–75; Sally E. Hadden, *Slave Patrols: Law and Violence in Virginia and the Carolinas* (Cambridge, U.K., 2001), especially chs. 1–2.

citizens, and to execute the laws upon reckless offenders. This state of things is unknown in the slave States." Stringfellow's indictment failed to consider contrary evidence. Although Boston and Philadelphia made some efforts, New York became the first northern city to establish a modern, uniformed, armed police force, but it did so only after Charleston and New Orleans. Foreign travelers were stunned by the semi-military aspect of the Charleston police, whose primary function was to overawe slaves and free blacks. Then too, Northerners presented alternative evaluations of the use of police power. Benjamin Silliman of Yale responded much as Thornwell did to Liverpool, Manchester, London, and the mining districts, but viewing the many slave-trade ships in Liverpool's harbor, he assigned the cause to the baleful influence of slavery. The wide gap between rich and poor and the show of police power against the workers struck him as forcefully as they had struck Thornwell, and he, too, considered repression preferable to anarchy.[61]

Free black Americans who traveled to Europe countered with their own perspectives. David E. Dorr replied to the slaveholders' challenge by stressing the freedom of choice ostensibly given even the least fortunate European workers and peasants and, more tellingly, the protection against the separation of families. William Wells Brown, a famous former slave, recalled the statements of Robert Wickliffe of Kentucky and Pickens and George McDuffie of South Carolina, who asserted that society rested on servile labor and that the world must decide whether its laborers should be white or black. Dublin's "poorest of the poor" made him heartsick. Still, Brown knew he would rather be a beggar in England than a slave in America. In several books, he emphatically denied that the material condition of English laborers approached that of American slaves. He contrasted racial attitudes of Americans and even Canadians with those of the British, who greeted colored men like himself as men and equals.[62]

---

[61] Stringfellow, "Statistical View of Slavery," in E. N. Elliott, ed., *Cotton Is King, and Pro-Slavery Arguments* (New York, 1969 [1860]), 538–539; Dennis C. Rousey, *Policing the Southern City: New Orleans, 1805–1889* (Baton Rouge, La., 1996), ch. 1; Chandos M. Brown, *Benjamin Silliman: A Life in the Young Republic* (Princeton, N.J., 1989), ch. 5. Silliman's book won the approval of John R. Thompson: *SLM*, 19 (1853), 646. Savannah organized an effective police force in the 1850s: Walter Fraser, Jr., *Savannah in the Old South* (Athens, Ga., 2003), 306–307. In 1857, William Kingsford of Canada found New Orleans civilized and attractive – well-policed, with few armed people in the streets: [Kingsford], *Impressions of the West and South* (Toronto, Ont., 1858), 53. Southern commentators ignored slave patrols in discussions of police and the stationing of troops.

[62] *The Narrative of William W. Brown, a Fugitive Slave; and a Lecture Delivered before the Female Anti-Slavery Society of Salem, 1848* (Reading, Mass., 1967 [1848]), 75–76; William Wells Brown, *The American Fugitive in Europe. Sketches of Places and People Abroad* (Electronic ed.; Chapel Hill, N.C., 2000 [1855]), 103–104; William Wells Brown, *Three Years in Europe: Or, Places I have Seen and People I have Met* (Electronic ed.; Chapel Hill, N.C., 2000 [1852]), quotes at 7, 12, and see also 91, 134–145. For an account of Dorr's *A Colored Man Round the World* and Brown's *American Fugitive in Europe*, see William W. Stowe, *Going Abroad: European Travel in Nineteenth-Century American Culture* (Princeton, N.J., 1994), 61–73.

Did southern slaves fare better than the British and continental poor? Most black abolitionists trod carefully. William Craft did not consider any white workers worse off than "degraded and trampled" southern slaves. Theodore Gross suggested that the psychic and spiritual misery of the slaves – notably, the dread of separation – outweighed all else. Generally, although black abolitionists did not grant the argument from material welfare, they stressed issues that transcended the material. Yet the degradation of the Irish peasants astounded Samuel Ringgold Ward, antislavery activist, even in comparison with that of southern slaves. The treatment of seamen dismayed Daniel Alexander Payne, future bishop of the African Methodist Episcopal Church, who visited England in 1846. Frederick Douglass grimly observed conditions in Ireland before and after the great famine. During 1845–1846, when he was residing in Britain, courted by antislavery English and Irish aristocrats, he remained silent in public about the misery he witnessed in Ireland. In private letters to William Lloyd Garrison, he admitted his disgust, likening conditions to those of southern slaves. Still, he viewed alcoholism rather than avaricious landlords as responsible for the degradation of the peasantry. Harrison Berry, a literate slave in Georgia, did not go abroad but supported the view that masters cared for their slaves in important ways that capitalists did not care for their hired workers.[63]

MacGavock sounded like other influential politicians who traveled abroad: "The poverty of this region of [Ireland] exceeds anything I have ever heard of or saw. The coach as we passed along was thronged on either side with men, women, and children, almost in a state of nudity, and the most miserable human beings I ever saw crying out in the most doleful manner, 'Mister, for God's sake, give us a penny. We are starving.'" The culture and condition of Liverpool and Manchester enchanted MacGavock, who said nothing about the lower classes. But in London, after attending church services for poor children, he spoke out:

There is nothing in our glorious land half so low, half so pitiable. Englishmen may write, talk, and preach what they please about the horrors of our peculiar institution; they may send their abolition emissaries across the water, with pockets well filled to preach a crusade against our liberty and our laws; but they had better consider the deplorable condition of their own population, one-tenth of which is now supported by charity, and whose condition both in a physical and moral point of view is far inferior to that of the slave owned by the most cruel of masters.

[63] Samuel Ringgold Ward, *Autobiography of a Fugitive Slave* (Chicago, 1970 [1855]), 244–259; John Daniel Alexander Payne, *Recollections of Seventy Years* (New York, 1968 [1888]), 88. See in C. Peter Ripley et al., eds., *The Black Abolitionist Papers*, 5 vols. (Chapel Hill, N.C., 1985–1991), speech by William Wells Brown, Croydon, England, Sept. 5, 1849, 1:169–170; speech by William Craft, London, October 14, 1859, 1:465–468, quote at 467; speech by Theodore Gross, London, Sept. 28, 1860, 1:483; Harrison Berry, *Slavery and Abolition, as Viewed by a Georgia Slave* (Electronic ed.; Chapel Hill, N.C., 2000 [1861]), 23, 33–34. For Douglass, see William S. McFeely, *Frederick Douglass* (New York, 1991), 126, also 133, 135, 141; John F. Quinn, "'Safe in Old Ireland': Frederick Douglass's Tour, 1845–1846," *Historian*, 64 (2002), 535–560, esp. 541–542, 545.

He had no doubt that southern slaves fared much better than the laborers he saw in England, across Europe, and in Africa and the Near East. The condition of Egyptian laborers disgusted him: "Our slaves are perfect lords compared to them."[64]

Suffering in Ireland had a special import for Southerners. In 1827, R. J. Turnbull of South Carolina, echoed by numerous others, cried out that the South was becoming for the North what Ireland had become to England. A typical comment in *Southern Quarterly Review* had a cruel British misrule marked by utter disregard for the rights and sensibilities of a generous people. In 1847 southern newspapers made much of $13,000 contributed by Southerners for starving Irishmen. Others reprinted articles from the Irish press, as the Tallahassee *Floridian* did from the Dublin *Nation* on "Loss of Two Millions of the Irish People by Famine." In 1851 the *Mississippi Free Trader and Natchez Gazette* protested: "To attempt an actual description of the state of the Irish laborer would be an utter failure because no language can convey an idea of the amount of human suffering, misery, and degradation experienced." After describing the indescribable: "We challenge any man to contrast slavery with the above picture." The antislavery Presbyterian Reverend Ebenezer Davies of Guiana paraphrased a southern refrain: "You are shocked at our slavery; and yet you have horrors of ten times greater magnitude in the Irish famine at your own doors." A special embarrassment for the antislavery movement: George Hays, an Alabama planter, sent supplies to Ireland during the famine and helped finance emigrant families. Ireland, John Tucker Randolph said in 1861, stood as testimony to the fate of the South, if the North prevailed. About 30,000 Irishmen fought for the Confederacy but about five times as many for the Union. Irish units were formed in eight of the eleven Confederate states, with Louisiana easily in the lead. The Irish who settled in the South especially saw a link between the British suppression of their national aspirations and the North's suppression of southern national aspirations.[65]

---

[64] Gower, et al., eds., *Pen and Sword*, 205; Randal W. MacGavock, *Letters from Europe, Africa, and Asia* (New York, 1854), 23–33, 213–214, quotes at 63, 213.

[65] [R. J. Turnbull], *The Crisis*, 21; *PENC*, 1:316; "Ireland in 1834," *SQR*, 6 (1844), 1–31; on British oppression of Ireland, see also "Critical Notices: Ireland's Welcome to the Stranger," *SQR*, 13 (1848), 242–244; "The Edinburgh Review and the Southern States," *DBR*, 10 (1851), 513; A Young American, "An Excursion in Ireland," *SLM*, 16 (1850), 89–95; William Pembroke Mulchinock, "The Irish Famine, the Fever and the Priest," *SLM*, 16 (1850), 99–100; S. L. V., "A Day or Two in Ireland," *SLM*, 18 (1852), 273–277; Henry A. Beers, *Nathaniel Parker Willis* (Boston, Mass., 1890), 118, 129, 245, 342–343; *Macon Weekly Telegraph*, June 15, 1847; *Tallahassee Floridian*, June 15, 1847; "Free Labor in Ireland. A Contrast with Slavery in the South," *Mississippi Free Trader and Natchez Gazette*, Mar. 15, 1851. The famous Harriet Jacobs worked as a servant for Willis, who bought her out of slavery (285); John Randolph Tucker, "The Great Issue," *SLM*, 32 (1861), 174; Ebenezer Davies, *American Scenes, and Christian Slavery: A Recent Tour* (London, 1849), 48; for Hays, see William Warren Rogers, Jr., *Black Belt Scalawag: Charles Hays and the Southern Republicans in the Era of Reconstruction* (Athens, Ga., 1993), 3. A Georgian was appalled by the lack of education among British laborers: [Ebenezer Starnes], *The Slaveholder Abroad* (Philadelphia, 1860), 146–147. J. P. Gannon, *Irish*

Social oppression did not exhaust southern dissatisfactions. Charles Cotesworth Pinckney and the Methodist Reverend James O. Andrew and Reverend W. P. Harrison agreed that the sexual morals of southern slave women, although censurable, were no worse than those of the women in fashionable European circles. Those charges against European societies were directed primarily against the vestiges of aristocracy, not against the bourgeoisie. In particular, they looked askew at upper-class European women. Brawley loved much of what he saw in France but not the morals of the upper classes, for whom "marriage is nothing more than authorized prostitution." Benjamin F. Perry, the up country unionist, who spent seven or eight months in Europe, associated himself with Chancellor William Harper's outrage. He "could hardly regard them as folks." While a student in Paris in 1843, William Walker – the soon-to-be filibusterer – wrote John Berrien Lindsey, his old college chum in Nashville, about the easy toleration of sexual promiscuity and marital infidelity. Walker wrote as an irritated Christian: "John, I wish you were here for a few days, in order to observe the state of society; you may read these things in books, but when you observe them, you feel them in all their force, you can enter into their full signification." Lucy Muse Walton Fletcher reacted with greater reserve. She read a biography of Madame Germain de Staël, noting that her mother had been Edward Gibbon's lover: "It is quite the fashion in France for married ladies to have lovers." In southern eyes, the good order that slavery brought to society reined in such violations of public morals.[66]

Fury directed at the Duchess of Sutherland and her abolitionist entourage highlighted the contrast between southern slave labor and British free labor. The Duchess emerged as the most prominent of antislavery British women in southern eyes in consequence of a mass meeting at Stratford House and an antislavery petition – in fact written by the Earl of Shaftsbury – signed by some half million British women. Julia Gardiner Tyler, reflecting southern public

Rebels, Confederate Tigers: The 16th Louisiana Volunteers, 1861–1865 (Campbell, Calif., 1998), iii, 321–322. See also David T. Gleeson, *The Irish in the South, 1815–1877* (Chapel Hill, N.C., 2001).

[66] J. O. Andrew, review of address by Pinckney in *Methodist Magazine and Quarterly Review*, 13 (1831), 316; William Pope Harrison, *The Gospel among the Slaves* (Nashville, Tenn., 1893), 102; Oct. 3, 1864, in *The Journal of William H. Brawley, 1864–1865*, ed. Francis Poe Brawley (Charlottesville, Va., 1970), 67; Stephen Meats and Edwin T. Arnold, eds., *The Writings of Benjamin F. Perry*, 3 vols. (Spartanburg, S.C., 1980), 2:350; Walker to Lindsley, July 15, 1843, in Appendix to John Edwin Windrow, *John Berrien Lindsley: Educator, Physician, Social Philosopher* (Chapel Hill, N.C., 1938), 179; L. M. W. Fletcher, "Autobiography," Summer, 1844 (ms.). The outrageous behavior of Parisian women was an old theme: Rosalie Stier Calvert of Maryland wrote her sister in Belgium in 1806 that "the better class" of Americans, unlike their western European counterparts, behaved virtuously. All the young men and some of the married had mistresses, but "the latter not publicly." Rosalie Stier Calvert to Isabelle van Havre, Nov. 5, 1806, in Margaret Law Callcott, ed., *The Mistress of Riversdale: The Plantation Letters of Rosalie Stier Calvert, 1795–1821* (Baltimore, Md., 1991), 150. And for the reputation of Italian women, see Eliza Cope Harrison, ed., *Best Companions: Letters of Eliza Middleton Fisher and Her Mother, Mary Hering Middleton, from Charleston, Philadelphia, and Newport, 1839–1846* (Columbia, S.C., 2001), 217, 244–247.

opinion, confused the current Duchess of Sutherland with her predecessor, Elizabeth Gordon – Countess-Marchioness-Duchess, who expelled thousands of tenants from their ancestral lands in Scotland early in the nineteenth century. The current duchess did, however, continue the family policy of pronouncing the brutal expulsions a greater good. At age twenty-four, Julia Gardiner, from a wealthy and socially prominent New York family, married President John Tyler and settled into Virginia as a plantation mistress. Rebuking Britain's women abolitionists, she denounced the treatment of the Irish and English laborers, demanding to know the grounds on which British abolitionists claimed moral superiority: "In view of your palaces, there is misery and suffering enough to excite your most active sympathies." Tyler recalled her recent trip to London, where a hundred thousand people "rose in the morning without knowing where or how to obtain their 'daily bread.'" Southern slaves lived "sumptuously" in comparison with the poor of London. The widely traveled Marjoribanks reinforced her, insisting that British emancipationists, especially the ladies, grossly exaggerated the tribulations of slavery. When former Representative Lucien Bonaparte Chase of Tennessee, having moved to New York City, published a defense of slavery in 1854, he dedicated it "To the Aristocratic Ladies of Great Britain," chiding them for their tears for the black slaves of the South and their indifference to the victims of "English Serfdom." In his Preface he referred to the oppression that has "debased the spirit, and broken the constitutions of their lower classes." To the amusement of Captain Henry A. Murray, R. N., the Duchess of Sutherland and the Stratford House antislavery meeting were the talk of New Orleans, as indignant citizens, reading the extensive newspaper accounts, poured forth their wrath.[67]

Frederick A. Porcher admonished one and all that the Duchess of Sutherland's expulsion of tenants should never be forgotten, but curiously, even some supporters of the Duchess inadvertently fed the proslavery cause. In Washington, D.C., Anne Royall's antislavery *Huntress* printed a brief account of the Stafford meeting and the address of the Duchess of Sutherland. Royall thought southern slaves well treated but nonetheless brutes since their masters deprived them of elementary education. Yet for Royall, the abolitionists were "the common enemy" of republican social order. Some northern newspapers fueled southern attacks on the Duchess of Sutherland. The *Mississippian and State Gazette* (Jackson) reprinted a bruising piece from the *Boston Post* on "Fresh Slavery Agitation – Impudence of the British Aristocracy."[68]

[67] Julia Gardiner Tyler, *A Letter to the Duchess of Sutherland and Ladies of England* (Richmond, Va., 1853), 6; Lucien Bonaparte Chase, *English Serfdom and American Slavery; or, Ourselves as Others See Us* (New York, 1854), vi; Marjoribanks, *Travels in South and North America*, chs. 6, 18; Murray, *Lands of the Slave and the Free*, 149–151.

[68] [F. A. Porcher], "Political Institutions of Sparta and Athens." *SQR*, n.s. (3rd), 2 (1856), 457; "Slavery in the United States and the Women of England," *The Huntress*, 15 (Jan. 1, 1853), 1–2; quote in "Our Union," 13 (Jan. 4, 1851), 2; Anne Newport Royall, *Letters from Alabama, 1817–1822* (University, Ala., 1969), 2, 48–49. See especially Ian Grimble, *The Trial of Patrick Sellar: The Tragedy of Highland Evictions* (London, 1962); Evelyn L. Pugh, "Women and

The essentials of Tyler's polemic recurred in the novels of Caroline Gilman, Caroline Hentz, Maria McIntosh, Mary Virginia Terhune, and Augusta Jane Evans, whose books sold well and generated impressive incomes. These women – small slaveholders themselves – attacked free-labor societies as seedbeds of the moral ills that beset the world and lauded slavery as the foundation of southern virtues. McIntosh, the well-known Georgian who lived in New York in the 1850s, replied to the British antislavery ladies much more gently but less effectively than Julia Tyler. Doing her best to fend off attacks on the laws against slave literacy and marriage, she pictured southern slavery as mild, familial, and no more oppressive than other labor systems: "Sisters! The world – the whole world – England and America, as well as India and Africa, are full of the habitations of cruelty."[69]

Foreign travelers to the South protested the rigorous fieldwork performed by white women on small farms and their lack of leisure for reading or much else. Southern travelers retorted that European women workers and peasants were immeasurably worse off than slave women. On a three-month tour of southern France in 1787, Thomas Jefferson saw peasant women "performing the heavy labour of husbandry; an unequivocal proof of extreme poverty." Thereafter, Southerners' comments grew harsher. In the 1840s the Presbyterian Reverend William T. Hamilton of Mobile, complaining about Europe's hordes of beggars and lack of schooling, recoiled from the sight of peasant women in hard labor in fields and attendant "licentiousness." Madame Le Vert, notwithstanding her love for aristocratic and grand-bourgeois Europe, reacted similarly when she saw the awful condition of the peasant women of France, Belgium, and Germany and of thousands of women cigar-makers in Spain. She wrote of "the hard lot of the female peasants" throughout Belgium and Germany: "Poor creatures! They were often without either shoes or covering for the head; and hard usage and unceasing toil have rendered them perfectly witch-like in

---

Slavery: Julia Gardiner Tyler and the Duchess of Sutherland," *Virginia Magazine of History and Biography*, 88 (1980), 186–202; *Mississippian and State Gazette*, Jan. 14, 1853. The *New York Times* and the *New York Tribune*, as well as the *Liberator*, attacked Tyler. Among the denunciations of the Duke and Duchess, see Henry Field James, *Abolitionism Unveiled; or, Its Origin, Progress, and Pernicious Tendency Fully Developed* (Cincinnati, Oh., 1856), 84; R. E. C. [Cochrane], "The Problem of Free Society – Part One," *SLM*, 26 (1858), 406; George D. Armstrong, *The Christian Doctrine of Slavery* (New York, 1967 [1857]), 134. The discriminating Madame Le Vert found the Duchess of Sutherland beautiful and a "magnificent woman" and was overwhelmed by the splendor of her mansion and estate: *Souvenirs of Travel*, 1:36, 55–57, quote at 36.

[69] See Elizabeth Moss, *Domestic Novelists, in the Old South: Defenders of Southern Culture* (Baton Rouge, La., 1992), for the novelists, see 3–5, 8, and works cited on p. 5, n. 4; for their critique of free labor and support for slavery, see espcially 90–98. Lesser novelists also contributed to the barrage against the free-labor system: see, e.g., Rhoda Coleman Ellison, *Early Alabama Publications: A Study in Literary Interests* (University, Ala., 1947), 175–177. Marie Jane McIntosh, *Letter on the Address of the Women of England to Their Sisters of America, in Relation to Slavery* (New York, 1853), 23–26, quote at 30. McIntosh came from a family of large slaveholders that lost its fortune. William Gilmore Simms praised McIntosh and her *Women in America*: [Simms], "Critical Notices," *SQR*, n.s., 1 (1850), 247.

appearance." She thanked God that she lived in a country in which women were respected and cared for.[70]

"A most complete burlesque of a republic" is how Catherine Anne Jones of Georgia reacted in 1851 when she saw French women subjected to drudgery worse than anything suffered at home. In 1861, Eastman Johnson – painter of "Negro Life at the South," renamed "Old Kentucky Home" – wrote with a lighter touch of meeting a German peasant: "I would tell her what an odd thing it seemed to me to see such a pretty girl working in the field and how nice and lazy she could live where I come from in America where all the girls do nothing but grow fat and get married and have black slaves to wait upon them." In 1865, William H. Brawley of South Carolina wrote from France that peasant women "work harder than our own negroes in the field." The sight of poor Alsatian peasant women plowing appalled the antislavery Francis Lieber: "The same had often made me sad in Carolina when I saw negro women do it as a thing belonging to slavery and now here." Yet, postwar novels by southern women decried the burdens of field labor that the emancipation of the blacks had imposed on southern white women as if white farm women had not carried those burdens before the War.[71]

In Italy, Southerners could not believe the condition of the Neapolitan poor (lazzaroni); in various spellings "lazzaroni" became the code word for wretchedly poor people prone to crime as well as idleness and begging. So widespread did the expressions of contempt for the Neapolitan poor become during the 1830s and 1840s that a southern traveler to Naples, reporting in *Southern Literary Messenger*, protested Anglo-American bias against Italians and pointedly praised the Neapolitans and their culture. "M" of Pendleton, South Carolina, simply wrote of Naples "with its glorious bay reflecting on its pure bosom, the matchless hues of heaven." Samuel Galloway of Georgia added his appreciation of the sophisticated cultural life of Naples in *Ergonomy;*

---

[70] Kenneth R. Wesson, "Travelers' Accounts of the Southern Character: Antebellum and Early Postbellum Period," *Southern Studies*, 17 (1978), 309; Mar. 17, 1787, in Roy and Alma Moore, eds., *Thomas Jefferson's Journey to the South of France* (New York, 1999), 34; William T. Hamilton, "Observations of a Traveler in Europe," *QRMCS*, 2 (1848), 310, 314–316; Le Vert, *Souvenirs of Travel*, 1:12, 141, 280, 345; for observations on the hard fieldwork of women in northern Italy, see [Willington], *A Summer's Tour*, 42.

[71] Jones, quoted in Harvey Levenstein, *Seductive Journey: American Tourists in France from Jefferson to the Jazz Age* (Chicago, 1998), 50; Johnson quoted in Honour, *Image of the Black*, 4 (pt. 1), 338, n. 95; Mar. 25, 1865, in *The Journal of William H. Brawley, 1864–1865*, ed. Francis Poe Brawley (Charlottesville, Va., 1970), 253; Lieber Journal, Sept. 10, 1844, in Charles Mack and Ilona S. Mack, ed., *Like a Sponge Thrown into Water: Francis Lieber's European Travel Journal of 1844–1845* (Columbia, S.C., 2002), 68. Writing for the *Charleston Courier* in 1851, Aaron Smith Willington reported on women who did the hardest work in the fields of northwestern Italy: [Aaron Smith Willington], *A Summer's Tour in Europe, in 1851: A Series of Letters, Addressed to the Editors of the Charleston Courier. By "A Traveller"* (Charleston, S.C., 1852), 41. For postwar literature, see Sarah E. Gardner, *Blood and Irony: Southern Women's Narratives on the Civil War, 1861–1937* (Chapel Hill, N.C., 2004), 107–108.

Or, Industrial Science. But John Izard Middleton of Charleston, like other Americans, was all the more shaken by the contrast between the poverty and swarms of beggars and the rich cultural life and what Willington called "the unsurpassing beauties of the Bay of Naples."[72]

The Reverend Mr. Hamilton contemned the lazzaroni as "an ignorant, lazy, deceitful, and treacherous race." McGavock was struck by the awful living conditions of the "poor, ignorant, and degraded" peasants of southern Italy and of the Neapolitan lazzaroni, the "degradation of our poor species." William Drayton of South Carolina invoked Naples to predict that were the slaves emancipated, southern jails and almshouses would teem with lazzaroni. J. H. Ingraham of Natchez, Mississippi, visited Buenos Aires and compared it with Naples, adding, "I am convinced that slaves, in their present moral condition, if emancipated, would be lazzaroni in everything but colour." Chancellor Harper suggested that Naples would be a much better city if black slaves replaced the lazzaroni. Brantz Mayer of Baltimore condemned the virtual profession of begging in Mexico City – one affluent beggar had a porter to carry him in a chair – referring to Naples when speaking of Mexico's poor. William Gilmore Simms ignored race, writing, "Pity it is, that the lousy and lounging lazzaroni of Italy cannot be made to labor under the whip of a severe taskmaster." Mrs. A. T. J. Bullard of St. Louis and Madame Le Vert were taken with Europe when they traveled there in the early 1850s. Yet in a series of generally pleasant letters to the *Missouri Republican* in 1850, Mrs. Bullard said of her trip from Rome to Naples in 1850, "We saw more poverty, nakedness, filth and savage wildness than ever before." Madame Le Vert remarked that when the Neapolitans said,

---

[72] "Description of Naples," *SLM*, 8 (1842), 696–700, 9 (1843), 105–108; M., "Italia la Bella," *Orion*, 3 (1843), 158; Samuel Galloway of Georgia, *Ergonomy; Or, Industrial Science* (Princeton, N.J., 1853), 188–189, 193. Susan Ricci Stebbins, "John Izard Middleton, 'Talent Enough to Be One of the First Men in America,'" in McInnis and Mack, eds., *Pursuit of Refinement*, 77; [Willington], *A Summer's Tour*, 51, 59, quote at 51; also on beautiful Naples and its Bay see [Kinloch], *Letters from Geneva and France*, 2:136, Aug. 23, 1837; *Life of Joseph Green Cogswell, as Sketched in His Letters* (Cambridge, Mass., 1874), 210; James B. Avirett, *The Old Plantation: How We Lived in Great House and Cabin before the War* (Electronic ed.; Chapel Hill, N.C., 1998 [1901]), 24. For other reports from Naples by southern travelers, see Julia Mayo Cabell, "Reminiscences of a Traveller," *SLM*, 11 (1845), 694; Brantz Mayer, *Mexico as It Was and as It Is*, 3rd ed. (Philadelphia, 1848), 56.

For the Neapolitan lazzaroni as the epitome of wretched poverty, see [George Frederick Holmes], review of Harriet Beecher Stowe's *Uncle Tom's Cabin* in *SLM*, 18 (1852), 630–638, and Holmes, review of her Key to *Uncle Tom's Cabin* in *SLM*, 19 (1853), 321–329; A. M. Keiley, *In Vinculis; or, The Prisoner of War: Being the Experience of a Rebel in Two Federal Pens* (New York, 1866), 91. The Neapolitan lazzaroni as model of the disreputable poor prevailed in the circle around Hannah More, a southern favorite: Mona Scheuermann, *In Praise of Poverty: Hannah More Counters Thomas Paine and the Radical Threat* (Lexington, Ky., 2002), 25. A traveler who much enjoyed Italy in the 1830s also commented on the annoying beggars of Naples but not without an expression of admiration for the manner in which the girls especially raised begging to an art: "Random Recollections of a Journey Through Italy by a Backwoodsman," *Southern Rose*, 6 (1838), 260.

"See Naples and die!" they did not much exaggerate its beauties. But, noticing the large number of beggars, she remarked that the lazzaroni of Rome were pathetic but carried themselves with a certain dignity, while those of Naples provoked mirth with their jaunty and ridiculous behavior. In northern Italy, she had been told that beggary was a by-no-means dishonorable profession. Elsewhere in Italy she was greeted with swarms of beggars, pleading for bread, crying, "We are all starving!"[73]

Joel Poinsett, the South Carolina unionist and fervent American nationalist who thought that economic development would eventually put an end to slavery, froze at the poverty he saw from Sicily to Sweden. His pleasure in Sicily – and Sweden – "was marred by the deep misery of the inhabitants." Poinsett found the life of the poor in Mexico even worse than in the Middle East: "I certainly never saw a negro house in Carolina so comfortless." Benjamin Mosby Smith of Virginia, no apologist for slavery, was taken aback by the poverty in Germany. Most Southerners seem to have exempted Switzerland from their tales of European horrors and pictured a pleasant middle-class life. W. C. Rives of Virginia held up the Swiss as a model of good republican citizenry and excellent agriculture. Not so Kinloch early in the nineteenth century or the Reverend Mr. Hamilton in the 1840s. Kinloch spoke of the "lower classes" of Switzerland as "reduced to penury," and Hamilton reported Switzerland full of poor people.[74]

Francis W. Pickens, writing in 1859 from Russia after a journey across Europe, sent Benjamin F. Perry, the leader of the South Carolina's up-country Unionists, his impressions of Europe: "On the surface, to a stranger, everything appears very captivating; but when I turn from these things, and think of the degradation and helplessness of the great masses, my heart sickens.... God save us from that progress which is developed under governments resting upon a 'free labor basis.'" James Bennett Allen, a planter from Warren County, Mississippi, appreciated the beauty of St. Petersburg and noted the similarities

[73] William T. Hamilton [of Mobile], "Observations of a Traveler in Europe," *QRMCS*, 2 (1848), 316; MacGavock, *Letters from Europe, Africa, and Asia*, 196–198, quotes at 197, 198; [Joseph Holt Ingraham], *The South-West. By a Yankee*, 2 vols. (n.p., 1966 [1835]), 2:124; [William Drayton], *The South Vindicated from the Treason and Fanaticism of the Northern Abolitionists* (Philadelphia, 1836), 238; Harper, in Elliott, ed., *Cotton Is King*, 604; Brantz Mayer, *Mexico as It Was and as It Is*, 3rd ed. (Philadelphia, 1848), 54–56, quote at 56; William Gilmore Simms, "Morals of Slavery," in *The Pro-Slavery Argument, as Maintained by the Most Distinguished Writers of the Southern States* (Philadelphia, 1853), 265; Mrs. A. T. J. Bullard, *Sights and Scenes in Europe: A Series of Letters from England, France, Germany, Switzerland and Italy* (St. Louis, 1852), 146–151, quote at 146; Le Vert, *Souvenirs of Travel*, 2:180–182, 1:195–196, quotes at 2:172, 209.

[74] Joel Poinsett, *Notes on Mexico* (London, 1825), 254; J. Fred Rippy, *Joel R. Poinsett, Versatile American* (New York, 1968), 13–15, 20, 97; [Willington], *A Summer's Tour*, 110–130; "Address of the Hon. W. C. Rives before the Albemarle Agricultural Society," *Southern Cultivator*, 1 (1843), 4; [Kinloch], *Letters from Geneva and France*, 1:184; William T. Hamilton, "Observations of a Traveler in Europe," *QRMCS*, 2 (1848), 310.

and differences between Russian serfdom and southern slavery. But he too gagged on the poverty he had seen on his trip across Europe. In Germany, he disliked Stettin: "It is filled full of women, children & dirt – not so much upon the Earth as upon the people." Russia loomed increasingly large in southern discussions. L. M. Keitt of South Carolina, echoed by the editors of the *State Gazette* of Austin, Texas, predicted that the rise of Russia, depicted as a quasi-slave state, and Russian development of Alaska would soon confront the free states with slave societies to its north and south. Shortly after the War, Pickens, who had served as ambassador to Russia, recalled that until the early sixteenth century most of the slaves in Europe had been white.[75]

In 1848, in a speech to the Senate on the territorial crisis, Calhoun chided the abolitionists for refusing to admit the virtual slavery of serfdom and for showing no interest in European serfs and Mexican peons. Calhoun doubtless drew on his neighbor David McCord, a legal scholar who concluded from his survey of Mexican law that the peons were substantially worse off than southern slaves both at law and in practice. Raphael Semmes of Maryland and Alabama – the Confederacy's great sea raider and naval commander – participated in the Mexican War, concluding that its peasants fared much worse than did southern slaves, who enjoyed much closer ties to their masters. Waddy Thompson, American emissary to Mexico, called peonage "a system immeasurably worse for the slave in every aspect, than the institution of slavery in the United States." Peons got even less meat to eat than French and Irish peasants did. For spice, he told Calhoun that Santa Ana praised the South for its happy and contented slaves.[76]

Like slaveholders everywhere, Southerners claimed that they ranked as the most benevolent and responsible of all slaveholding classes, past and present. The Protestant and Jewish slaveholders of Surinam outdid most others in callousness and brutality, yet they considered themselves the best of masters. Southerners, too, assured themselves that they set the highest possible standards of Christian benevolence and deserved the world's admiration. They pointed to the reports of late eighteenth- and early nineteenth-century travelers, who found much brutality and deprivation on southern slave plantations but agreed

---

75 F. W. Pickens to B. F. Perry, April 24, 1859, in Meats and Arnold, eds., *Writings of Perry*, text of letter in 3:170–176; words quoted from 175; James Allen to Elizabeth Allen, July 7, 13, 19, 1858; Francis R. Flournoy, *Benjamin Mosby Smith, 1811–1893* (Richmond, Va., 1947), 24, 55–56; *State Gazette* (Austin, Tex.), Mar. 7, 1857; *Letter of Hon. Francis W. Pickens ... Written to a Gentleman in New Orleans* (Baltimore, Md., 1866), 13.

76 Calhoun, "Speech on the Proposal to Extend the Missouri Compromise Line to the Pacific," in *JCCP*, 25:658; David J. McCord to Calhoun, Jan. 23, 1848, in *JCCP*, 25:146–148; Raphael Semmes, *Service Afloat and Ashore during the Mexican War* (Cincinnati, Oh., 1851), 17–18, 248–250; Waddy Thompson, *Recollections of Mexico* (New York, 1847), 6–7, 12, 150; Waddy Thompson to J. C. Calhoun, March 25, 1844, in *JCCP*, 18:99. For a report on primitive living conditions among rural Mexicans in Yucatan, see H. Dikehut, "Letters from Mexico, Number Three" *SLJ*, n.s., 1 (1837), 176–177.

that the condition of West Indian slaves was worse. Protestants denounced the Catholic planters of Saint-Domingue and Cuba as monsters. Catholics took a different view. In 1839, John England, Catholic bishop of Charleston, declared the Spanish colonial system the best for protecting slaves.[77]

Southerners increased their comparisons of the South with Asia and the Near East. Southern slaves, William Hobby of Georgia wrote in 1835, are better off than the European poor and immeasurably better off than the laboring classes of China and Turkey. Most American missionaries who went to the Near East reported favorably on Turkish slavery as "domestic" and mild – some strongly demurred – and the Southerners among them, John Adger and James Warley Miles, noted that both masters and slaves came from groups across the racial spectrum. The 1840s and 1850s brought a barrage of criticism on conditions in India. In the Southwest the Presbyterian Reverend T. C. Thornton and Dr. Samuel A. Cartwright railed against the brutal quasi-slavery and "iron despotism" imposed on India's sons of Shem. William Pinckney Starke, writing to Calhoun from Paris on his travels in the Near East, labeled the Egyptians an "ignorant and cowardly" race, living in mud huts much inferior to southern slave cabins. William Boulware of Virginia, Chargé d'Affaires at the Court of the Two Sicilies, disagreed with Hobby, asserting that the slaves in the Islamic Near East lived under a patriarchal regime that recalled biblical times. They were not held in contempt and appeared to be treated with kindness and consideration. Masters treated black slaves much as they treated white slaves, and racial discrimination was not in evidence. Boulware thought the laborers of Egypt more oppressed than in other parts of the Near East, and he pointedly added that poor peasants there as well as in Syria and elsewhere were worse off than southern slaves.[78]

Some Southerners published firsthand accounts of the living conditions of the laboring classes and of the widespread fear of social disorder; more privately informed friends and relatives. Especially important, they spoke at political meetings, local churches, and literary societies at which they combined ferocious criticism of the free-labor system with warm admiration for Europe's classical and Christian legacy and continuing sense of hierarchy and order. The accumulated effect of their efforts confirmed the widespread belief that the social system of the South compared favorably with that of its rivals and

---

[77] Sebastian G. Messmer, ed., *The Works of the Right Rev. John England, First Bishop of Charleston*, 7 vols., (Cleveland, Oh., 1908), 4:267.

[78] [William Hobby], *Remarks upon Slavery, Occasioned by Attempts Made to Circulate Improper Publications in the Southern States. By a Citizen of Georgia*, 2nd ed. (Augusta, Ga., 1835), 31; T. C. Thornton, *An Inquiry into the History of Slavery* (Washington, D.C., 1841), 125–129, 213–214; Cartwright, *Essays*, 6, 8, 45, quote at 6; William Pinckney Starke to John C. Calhoun, Jan. 23, 1846, in *JCCP*, 22:498; William Boulware, "Extracts from a voyage in the East in 1843," *Southern and Western Literary Monthly Magazine and Review*, 12 (1846), 169, 172–174.

critics, and it provided substantial support for those who were arguing that only slavery could reconcile the interests of capital and labor.[79]

Overwhelmingly, Southerners believed that their slaves lived better than free laborers throughout the world, but they did not automatically declare slavery the best social system for all peoples. Some took satisfaction in believing that slavery had no more to recommend it than the free-labor system, except that evidence showed southern slaveholders more humane toward their laborers. Even those who posited the one system above the other in virtue caviled at the enslavement of whites. They did not advocate the enslavement of white workers in Europe; they merely predicted that the deepening crisis of the free-labor system would render it inevitable. What remains astonishing is that by 1850 a significant if undetermined number of Southerners were taking seriously the argument that every society rested on some form of personal dependency.

Southerners Go North

Reports on the North proved no less revealing than those on Europe. Southerners who traveled to the North expressed dismay at social conditions in the large cities. In 1765, John Rutledge of South Carolina, on his first trip to New York, stiffened at the number of black beggars and learned that New Yorkers were freeing their old slaves to fend for themselves. Rutledge had never seen a beggar in Charleston. In 1817, William Shepard sounded other themes. Impressed by the gaiety and general attractiveness of New York and Philadelphia, he expressed aversion to the obsession with money as the principal measure of status. He described price-gouging inflicted upon unwary strangers as well as on artisans and laborers at the mercy of their patrons in a way their southern counterparts did not experience. For the next half century the theme resounded across the South, especially touted by Southerners with firsthand knowledge. Northern civilization, Semmes remarked, was "coarse and practical," whereas southern was "more intellectual and refined." Such generalizations came easy but followed from attempts at serious examination. Dr. William Henry Holcombe of Natchez went to Indiana in 1855 to visit his antislavery parents. He reflected: "The prevalence of great cities – hotbeds of an uneasy civilization, the crowding of population in small areas, the sterility of soil, the coldness of climate – Stimulated thought & invention – Foreign intercourse and immigration – Trade, manufacturing, &c – Riches, corruption, demagogism, &c." Holcombe commented on slavery at length in his diary. Holding blacks in low esteem, he tried to focus on racial slavery, but in his extensive remarks on the work of Ellwood Fisher and others he did not flinch from the larger implications of the proslavery argument. "He who works under a master," Holcombe

---

[79] For tourists' appreciation of European culture, see William Douglas Smyth, "A Southern Odyssey: South Carolina Abroad in the 1850s," *Southern Studies*, 23 (1984), 398–411. Our fragmentary explorations suggest that the essentials of Smyth's account of the South Carolinians would hold for southern travelers as a group.

wrote, "and receives nothing but subsistence is a slave – See all over the North and Europe.... The capitalists of the North depress labor: The Democrats of the North were therefore the Natural allies of the South as remarked by Mr. Jefferson."[80]

Southerners who observed the great cities of the North, especially New York, congratulated themselves on not having to live there. Important exceptions included rich planters who set up permanent or summer residences in Philadelphia or Newport and artists like Edgar Allan Poe or Thomas Holley Chivers, who appreciated New York and Boston and yet supported the southern social system. Planters and the well-to-do went on vacation and sojourns to Philadelphia, upstate New York, and New England or stopped in New York City on their way to Europe. A sizable number of merchants and storekeepers went to New York City on business once a year or so. Planters, politicians, and others who occasionally or periodically visited the North spoke generously about its people and strong points but reacted to the squalor much like their counterparts who traveled to Europe. Visiting Southerners often registered unfavorable accounts of the burdens on northern workers. The Baptist Reverend James Madison Pendleton of Tennessee recalled, "When I went North, nothing surprised me more than to see laborers at work in the rain and snow. In such weather, slaves in Kentucky and Tennessee would have been under shelter." He need not have restricted his remark to Kentucky and Tennessee, for it applied generally throughout the South.[81]

The famous "Lowell Girls" attracted unfavorable southern attention. In North Carolina in 1833, Rachel Mordecai Lazarus sang the praises of the Lowell girls in a letter to Maria Edgeworth, but Representative Willie P. Mangum, making his first trip north in 1834, thought differently. He admired the beauty of Boston and the New England countryside and praised the prosperity and enterprise of Lowell, which he called "the Birmingham of the United States."

[80] Richard Barry, *Mr. Rutledge of South Carolina* (New York, 1942), 104; William Biddle Shepard Pettigrew to Ebenezer Pettigrew, April 18, 1817, in Sarah M. Lemmon, ed., *The Pettigrew Papers*, 2 vols. (Raleigh, N.C., 1971, 1988), 1:562–563; John M. Taylor, *Semmes: Rebel Raider* (Washington, D.C., 2004), 20; W. H. Holcombe Diary, July 24, 1855, in UNC, also July 20, "Notes" dated Jan. 29, 1855, but obviously written in 1861 or later. Southern divines, in defending slavery, drew heavily on Ellwood Fisher's account of the misery of northern workers and the good condition in the southern slaves: see, e.g., "North and South," *SPR*, 3 (1850), 338–381; Iveson Brookes, *A Defence of Slavery against the Attacks of Henry Clay and Alex'r Campbell* (Hamburg, S.C., 1851), 31.

[81] James Madison Pendleton, *Reminiscences of a Long Life* (New York, 1891), 127–128. Southern storekeepers depended heavily on the New York trade, and those who did business worth, say, between $6,000 and $10,000 made the trip regularly. See Lewis E. Atherton, *The Southern Country Store, 1800–1860* (Baton Rouge, La., 1949), 138. Also, M. E. E. Carmichael Diary, June 26, 1844; Weymouth T. Jordan, *Ante-Bellum Alabama, Town and Country* (Tallahassee, Fla., 1957), 47; Richard L. Zuber, *Jonathan Worth: A Biography of a Southern Unionist* (Chapel Hill, N.C., 1965), 82. For the substantial community of South Carolina's richest planters who lived in Philadelphia, especially along "Carolina Row," see Daniel Kilbride, *An American Aristocracy: Southern Planters in Antebellum Philadelphia* (Columbia, S.C., 2006).

But he shrank from the sight of the women workers. He wrote to his wife about "the thousands of Girls from 12 to 18 years of age, that labor here – They look unhealthy & unhappy – & altogether, presented to my mind a melancholy & painful spectacle." Mangum's reaction to Lowell prefigured the reaction of British travelers, who spoke highly of Lowell and other mill towns but with increasing abhorrence of the treatment of female labor. In the 1830s, Mangum notwithstanding, most travelers attested to the wholesomeness of conditions and praised the young women as virtuous and churchgoing. Admiration turned to disgust during the 1850s, when the proportion of native-born workers dropped from ninety percent to thirty-five percent. Immigrants lived in a different atmosphere.[82]

The proslavery Thomas Holley Chivers, whose poetry Northerners as well as Southerners admired, published exposés of the vice and corruption of New York in Macon's *Georgia Citizen* during 1850 and 1851. He denounced the abolitionists as "traitors" who drive widows and orphans into disgusting circumstances: "Go with me to Lowell, and I will show you beautiful girls prostituted to the basest of uses. Yet, these liars call these miserable creatures *free*. Instead of setting the *white slaves* of the North free, they make use of the most roguish and unlawful means to liberate the very property they once sold to us." The abolitionists, for their part, played up every antislavery sentiment expressed by the "factory girls" of Lowell, but the "girls" spoke for themselves in various accents. Repeatedly, they likened their exploitation to that of southern slaves. In New Hampshire the *Nashua Gazette* published a letter from "A Factory Girl in the Nashua Corporation" that excoriated factory foremen for abusing female workers: They "can do with them as any passion may dictate or any caprice suggest, with perfect impunity of the law." Yet, in the 1850s Southerners reacted angrily to the spreading influence of Fourier's socialism among the workers of Lowell, Massachusetts, an abolitionist stronghold since the 1830s.[83]

---

[82] Rachel Mordecai Lazarus to Maria Edgeworth, July 18, 1833, in MacDonald, ed., *Education of the Heart*, 249; W. P. Mangum to Charity Mangum, Sept. 2, 13, 1834, in Henry Thomas Shanks, ed., *The Papers of Willie P. Mangum*, 5 vols. (Raleigh, N.C., 1950–1955), 2:194, 201; Robert W. Fogel, *Without Consent or Contract: The Rise and Fall of American Slavery* (New York, 1986), 357. Some Southerners nonetheless found much to continue to admire about Lowell: see, e.g., "The American Factory System," *QRMCS*, 2 (1848), 486–487; Kate S. Carney Diary, Sept. 15, 1859. The system of employment at Lowell was supposed to avoid creation of a proletariat by recruiting young women who would then go on to other pursuits. With the influx of immigrants, especially the Irish, in the late 1840s and 1850s, that process no longer obtained: see Kasson, *Civilizing the Machine*, ch. 2.

[83] Charles Henry Watts, II, *Thomas Holley Chivers: His Literary Career and His Poetry* (Athens, Ga., 1956), 47–48, 50–52, quote at 51–52; "Letter from a Local Factory Girl," [*Nashua (N. H.) Gazette*], Oct. 1, 1846, in Philip Foner, ed., *The Factory Girls* (Urbana, Ill., 1977), 83. For comparisons with southern slaves from women factory workers, published by the reformist *Voice of Industry* during the 1840s, see Foner, ed., *Factory Girls*, 89–90, 131, 134–138, 181–182; and from *The Mechanic* of Fall River (Nov. 2, 1844) see *Factory Girls*, 275–276; Edward

Southerners read reports of the economic distress that wracked the northern cities. Nicholas Carroll, a Whig businessman, reported to Mangum on the economic crisis in New York in 1841: "We have had no period resembling this at all – I could not depict the actual amount of suffering here, the extreme destitution of our laboring classes." Two years later William Hooper Haigh of North Carolina wrote in his diary, "Who can wander through crowded Broadway, & not feel sympathy for the poverty & wretchedness he meets there." Watching the snow fall in Washington, D.C., in February 1849, David Outlaw, Whig congressman from North Carolina, wrote to his wife, "The sufferings of the poor in the cities at such times as this are terrible. The poor are badly clothed, have no fire-wood, and have but little or nothing to eat." The very next winter he again wrote to her of the "most startling and shocking murder" of Dr. Parkman of Boston by Professor Webster. He sighed, "Truly I think we may felicitate ourselves that our destiny has not been cast in one of these large cities, where crime and corruption of all kinds grow rank and luxuriant." In 1855, Randal McGavock shook his head over the accounts of disorder in the streets of New York, where unemployment had reached massive proportions. He did not envy a community that had to face a mass demonstration of 150,000 angry, unemployed workers, although he remained puzzled at their apparent unwillingness to claim available jobs at $1.50 per day.[84]

New York never did lose its attractions. In 1824, Martha Ogle Forman, plantation mistress in Maryland, visited New York: "I was very much pleased with the City" – the elegant shops, beautiful buildings and museums, and the battery. In 1852 the young H. S. Norcom of Edenton, North Carolina, was no less overwhelmed: "New York is a great city. Broadway is ever alive & in motion always crowded & frequently impenetrable." Ellen Douglas Brownlow of North Carolina envied a friend who visited the North in 1851 and again in 1855 and only wished she could accompany her. Brownlow, locally famous as "perhaps the best read and most cultivated woman in Warrenton," surely knew about political tensions but betrayed no apprehension of a hostile reception. J. Hampden Chamberlayn, a master's student at the University of Virginia, intended a compliment when he referred to "New York, the great center of our craving, eager, restless people."[85]

Magdol, *The Antislavery Rank and File: Profile of the Abolitionists' Constituency* (Westport, Conn., 1986), 70–71; for Fourier's influence, see the letters of Mary Paul in Thomas Dublin, ed., *Farm to Factory: Women's Letters, 1830–1860*, 2nd ed. (New York, 1993), ch. 4. By the 1850s increasing numbers of girls as young as thirteen were working in Lowell's mills: Thomas Dublin, *Women at Work: The Transformation of Work and Community in Lowell, Massachusetts, 1826–1860* (New York, 1979), 181–182. See also Thornton, *Inquiry into Slavery* (1841), 86 on the Lowell girls and 120 on the exploitation of farm girls in the North.

[84] Carroll to Mangum, April 7, 1841, in Shanks, ed., *Papers of Mangum*, 3:133; Haigh Diary, Aug. 20, 1843, in UNC; David Outlaw to Emily Outlaw, Feb. 12, Dec. 4, 1849, in UNC; McGavock, Jan. 31, 1855, in Gower et al., eds., *Pen and Sword*, 314.

[85] Forman Diary, Sept. 1, 1824, in W. Emerson Wilson, ed., *Plantation Life at Rose Hill: The Diaries of Martha Ogle Forman, 1814–1845* (Wilmington, Del., 1976), 186–187; H. S. Norcom

New York City had, nonetheless, long figured in the southern mind as the prime example of the free-labor system's oppression of the poor and its attendant mobs and anarchy. "There is a perfect canaille in this city," John Berkeley Grimball of Charleston wrote in 1834, "ready for revolution or anything else you please." The common people, he thought, were ready to crown Andrew Jackson king. By the 1850s the indictment had grown harsher. "Diogenes" wrote to the *Charleston Mercury* from New York: "Probably, there is not in Christendom a city of the size more corrupt, more vicious, and demoralized, and worse governed than New York."[86]

During 1820–1840 the Northeast underwent an unprecedented urban concentration. New York City's crime rate rose four times as fast as its population. American and European cities of 50,000 had twice the death rate of rural areas. In New York and Philadelphia, impressive cultural centers, life expectancy at birth averaged twenty-four years – six years less than that for southern slaves. In the 1830s New York City spent hundreds of thousands of dollars a year on its paupers, who constituted ten percent of the population. By 1860, New York had almost one million people, and Philadelphia 500,000. There was disease, crime, violence, distressing mortality rates, and brutally overcrowded housing, which, in Robert Fogel's words, qualified as "death traps." De Bow introduced an article in *De Bow's Review* on "New York in 1852–53" with a flattering reference to the rise and growth of a great city. He thereupon coolly presented statistics on insanity and insane asylums, accounts of the problems of immigrants, unemployment, crime, liquor consumption, and the cost of welfare. A contributor to *Southern Quarterly Review* said that, unquestionably, the slave cabins, modest as they were, were much superior to the crowded tenements in which workers in New York live, often several families crowded together. Another referred to "wide spread miseries and starvation" in New York, which, thanks to slavery, did not exist in the South. John McCrady of Charleston, a scientist, found New York City crowded, dirty, and lawless and did not find Boston and Cambridge better.[87]

In 1851, Albert J. Pickett, a noted historian, expressed gratitude for living in Alabama after he saw New York's splendor, meanness, sinfulness – its destitute lower classes and "ridiculous money aristocracy." A year later William

to John Norcom, Dec. 1, 1852, in James Norcom Papers; Ellen Douglas Brownlow to Mary Eliza Battle, Jan. 5, Feb. 24, 1851, Mar. 15, 1855, in Mary Eliza Battle Letters at North Carolina State Archives (Raleigh, N.C.); J. Hampden Chamberlayn, "Essay on American Literature" (MA thesis, 1858, typescript at Unversity of Virginia).

[86] J. G. Grimball Diary, June 13, 1834; "Diogenes," *Charleston Mercury*, Feb. 15, 1858.

[87] "New York in 1852–53," *DBR*, 14 (1853), 535–556; 'Stowe's Key to Uncle Tom's Cabin," *SQR*, 8 (1853), 238; "Slavery and Freedom, *SQR*, n.s. (3rd), 1 (1856), 63; for McCrady, see Stephens, *Science, Race, and Religion*, 148; also, J. B. Ferguson, *Address on the History, Authority and Influence of Slavery* (Nashville, Tenn., 1850), 26. Between 1790 and 1850, life expectancy in the North declined by twenty-five percent and the decline in the large cities was twice as great. During the 1830s, life expectancy at birth in New York and Philadelphia averaged twenty-four years – six years less than that for southern slaves. See Robert W. Fogel, *Fourth Great Awakening and the Future of Egalitarianism* (Chicago, Ill., 2000), 58–59, 141–142, 149.

M. Bobo of South Carolina published *Glimpses of New-York City, by a South Carolinian*, which William Gilmore Simms recommended as a guide to life in America's Babylon. Without seeing New York City for yourself, "You know little of the sorrow and the wretchedness, the dreadful want that is crushing the life out of a thousand hearts around you." The exploitation of the labor of women immigrants sickened him. He saw little difference between the relations of employers to servant girls and of masters to slaves – except that servant girls could be dispensed with at will and left to starve. Bobo included a chapter on Five Points: "the filthy cellars and the malaria … the squalid females, the sottish males, the half-starved urchins." Court records showed "more cases of crime presented at its bar, in the city of New York alone, than all the South put together." Solon Robinson, Indiana's agricultural reformer who became agricultural editor of Horace Greeley's New York *Tribune* in 1853, reinforced Bobo, describing most workers in free-labor countries as wage-slaves. In 1854 Robinson published *Hot Corn*, an exposé of poverty and prostitution in New York City. Dedicated to Greeley, it sold 50,000 copies in the first six months after attracting a huge audience as articles in the *Tribune*. Robinson represented the life of the poor in New York as "revolting." Five Points, New York's "dreadful neighborhood," had countless "houseless, naked, starving" young women "sunk in misery, poverty, crime, filth, degradation, want," who turned to prostitution to survive. Having toured the South, he excoriated the abolitionists, reporting favorably on the slaveholders and their treatment of slaves.[88]

Shortly after the appearance of Bobo's book, J. Marion Sims – on his way to a nationally prominent career in medicine – witnessed distress in New York such as "can hardly be imagined." He wrote back to his wife Theresa in Montgomery, Alabama, "Several meetings of mechanics out of employ have been held in the park, and some most inflammatory speeches made, where the speakers were loudly cheered when they spoke of oppression of capital over labor, and the necessity, if it came to the worst, of bursting the doors of storehouses and taking what they want." Sims pounced on the contrast between North and South: "Here we have vagrancy and pauperism, and all its attendant ills of vice, crime, and degradation, which we never see in a slave population. Here I feel that the time may come when a man may not be secure in the accumulation or enjoyment of wealth." Sims wrote that "the great and good Peter Cooper says the millionaires of this country have much to dread from

---

[88] For Pickett, see O'Brien, *Conjectures of Order*, 1:372; [William M. Bobo], *Glimpses of New-York City, by a South Carolinian* (Charleston, S.C., 1852), quotes at 34, 93, 95, 97, 187–188, and see, in general, chs. 12–13; [William Gilmore Simms], "Critical Notes," *SQR*, n.s., 7 (1853), 527–529. For wage-slaves, see Solon Robinson, "Negro Slavery at the South," *DBR*, 7 (1849), 223–225, 379–389; Solon Robinson, *Hot Corn* (New York, 1854), quotes at 14, 32, 52; Herbert Anthony Kellar, ed., *Solon Robinson: Pioneer and Agriculturalist: Selected Writings*, 2 vols. (Indianapolis, Ind., 1936), Editor's Introduction, vol. 1, and 2:201–202, 213–214, 218, 267, 279–280, 479; see also Glyndon G. Van Deusen, *Horace Greeley: Nineteenth-Century Crusader* (Philadelphia, Pa., 1953), 130.

the popular voice; that the time may come when the masses may vote away, confiscate, as it were, their hoarded wealth." In the same vein, George Walton Williams of Charleston wrote, "I have seen more poverty and suffering among the people living in filthy cellars, not a hundred yards from Broadway, than I have ever witnessed at the South, and the district covered by the Five 'Points,' is a disgrace to the great City of New York.'" Fitzwilliam Byrdsall of New York, a left-wing radical, wrote to Calhoun, "Our Southern social system is the best that ever existed whether morally or politically considered." Declaring himself a churchgoing Christian, Byrdsall said he would "never consent to change it for the heartless, selfish, vice, misery, and crime producing social system of the North." Class hatreds existed in the North "to an extent scarcely imaginable."[89]

David Brown, author of *The Planter; Or, Thirteen Years in the South, by a Northern Man*, asked, "Are the negroes starving to death, like the poor people of Ireland and Scotland? And even of England and Germany?" He suggested that antislavery Britons and Americans, including Mrs. Charles Dickens, should read *Oliver Twist* and *Bleak House*. Invoking Thornwell's testimony, he depicted abolitionism as a stalking horse for anarchy. The great contest raged between infidelity and radicalism on the one side and Christianity and civilized liberty on the other. The slaveholding states had no starving poor, poor taxes, or poorhouses, whereas the North did. "All over the world a very large majority of the people who depend on their daily labor for their daily bread are always, and at this moment, suffering from want of sufficiency of that daily bread, and are frequently met by all the horrors of destitution and famine; and are hurrying on that awful way to the grave – *death by starvation*." Brown taunted the abolitionists with their boast that slavery was less productive than free. Very well, he countered, but then how can it be more exploitative? Turning to Horace Greeley, Brown teased: "To be consistent as a Socialist, Greely [*sic*] ought to feel kindly towards Slavery, as approaching nearer to Socialism than anything else, on a large scale, he is likely ever to see in this world."[90]

The depression that followed the crash of 1857 provided the occasion for Hammond's "Cotton is King" ("Mudsill") speech, in which he claimed, "Why

---

[89] J. Marion Sims to Theresa Sims, Dec. 23, 1854, in Sims, *The Story of My Life* (New York, 1884), 391–392; George Walton Williams, letter to the *Southern Christian Advocate*, Sept. 16, 1857, in Williams, *Sketches of Travel in the Old World and the New* (Charleston, S.C., 1871), 69; Fitzwilliam Byrdsall to Calhoun, Feb. 11, 1850, in *JCCP*, 27:172. The northern-born Episcopal Reverend William Sparrow of Richmond, too, referred to New York City as "the great Babylon of the Western Hemisphere": William Sparrow to E. H. Canfield, April 7, 1850, in Cornelius Walker, ed., *The Life and Correspondence of Rev. William Sparrow* (Philadelphia, 1876), 193. As Forrest McDonald says, the working-class response to the depression of 1857 in New York far exceeded in militancy anything that had preceded it: *States' Rights and the Union: Imperium in Imperio, 1776–1876* (Lawrence, Kans., 2000), 181.

[90] [David Brown], *The Planter; Or, Thirteen Years in the South, by a Northern Man* (Upper Saddle River, N.J., 1970 [1853]), 10, 11, 16–19, 210–221, 272.

you must meet more beggars in one day in any single street of the city of New York than you would meet in a lifetime in the whole South." Several years earlier, a contributor to *Southern Literary Messenger* chided coldhearted New Yorkers for spurning the entreaties of free black beggars. Even before the crash of 1857, Fitzhugh pointed to the sea of immigrants from Europe as evidence of the wretchedness of the laboring classes there. George Sawyer, a transplanted Yankee who made frequent trips north, wrote "from personal experience" of some 50,000 people in New York and 20,000 in Boston immeasurably more wretched than the southern slaves in 1857. Southern newspapers carried endless horror stories. In 1857 the *State Gazette* of Austin, Texas, commented on a speech by L. M. Keitt of South Carolina: "The misery and human woe exhibited in the past winter at the North among the white slaves is appalling." In 1860, Jefferson Davis chided William H. Seward on "those masses in New York" who demand "something very like an agrarian law." Davis protested "the suffering of the poor children imprisoned in your juvenile penitentiaries – imprisoned before they were old enough to know the nature of crime." In the decades before secession and during the War, foreign travelers to the cities of the North spoke and wrote much as Southerners did.[91]

Southern attention to labor unrest in the North got a big boost from extensive newspaper coverage of the religious revival of 1857–1858. In the North the revival displayed at least two new and fateful features: concentration in the cities and the rise of the laity. Most notably, businessmen pushed the ministers rather than the reverse. In September 1857, New York's businessmen held a noonday prayer meeting, which their unemployed workers doubtless thought their bosses badly needed. Southerners watched gleefully as northern preachers decided that the crisis of 1857 provided an ideal occasion to denounce the worldliness, money-grubbing, and corruption of their society. The northern revival introduced new methods of organization and attracted middle-class white Protestants, often of antislavery, nativist, anti-Catholic, and anti-Masonic bent. The economic depression, may – as many think – have spurred the enormous revival, but more attention went into denunciations of the sin of slavery and prevalence of bad men in the nation's political leadership. Not that most preachers attacked slavery: To the contrary, they tried to

[91] "Speech on the Admission of Kansas," Mar. 4, 1858, in Clyde N. Wilson, ed., *Selections from the Letters and Speeches of James H. Hammond* (Spartanburg, S.C., 1978), 319; "A Few Thoughts on Slavery," *SLM*, 20 (1854), 199; George Fitzhugh, "The Conservative Principle," *DBR*, 22 (1857), 419; George S. Sawyer, *Southern Institutes; Or, an Inquiry into the Origin and Early Prevalence of Slavery and the Slave Trade* (New York, 1967 [1858]), 246; *State Gazette* (Austin, Tex.), Mar. 7, 1857; "Reply to William H. Seward," Feb. 29, 1860, in *JDP*, 6:283. For foreign views, see Max Berger, *The British Traveller in America, 1836–1860* (Gloucester, Mass., 1964), 28; Mitchell, *Ten Years*, 144–145, 150–151. For the widespread acceptance of Hammond's mud-sill argument, see Rosser H. Taylor, "Mud-Sill Theory in South Carolina," *Proceedings of the South Carolina Historical Association* (1939), 35–43. Even during the War, Confederate troops met many Union soldiers who admitted that they enlisted to escape unemployment and to earn a little money to relieve the economic hardship on their families: Bell Irvin Wiley, *The Life of Billy Yank: The Common Soldier of the Union* (Baton Rouge, La., 1978), 38.

defuse the issue, and prayer meetings usually barred such agitation. But the formalities could not allay the rising anger at the economic distress and political corruption that antislavery politicians were laying at the doorstep of the South. Meanwhile, proslavery propaganda played up the revelations of material want that the revivals exposed. In New York, where the commercial interests depended heavily on the southern trade, spirited resistance developed against the antislavery reformers. Kathryn Teresa Long concludes that its direct impact on politics and social reform proved slight, but that in the ensuing, fateful years, the more reform-minded intensified antislavery, temperance, and anti-Catholic agitation.[92]

The crisis of 1857 brought little suffering to the northern countryside but much to the cities. A significant amount of the crime recorded in the northern cities stemmed from desperate efforts to feed families. Southerners read that in 1850 the police in New York City killed two tailors – the first time in American history that the police shed the blood of striking workers. New York City proved a deepening horror for working-class women: brutal exploitation, prostitution fed by desperation, and what amounted to an assault on working-class families besieged by unemployment, declining wages, rising rents, and sheer want. Rent gouging became the rage during the 1850s, as workers had to pay increasingly higher rents for housing that was palpably deteriorating in physical condition. In 1854, New York's 15,000 to 20,000 unemployed

---

[92] Kathryn Teresa Long, historian of the revivals of 1857, has described it as perhaps the closest thing to a truly national revival in American history: *The Revival of 1857–58: Interpreting an American Religious Awakening* (New York, 1998), 7, 59, 64–65, and, generally, chs. 2, 5, 6. For newspaper reportage of the Revival, see J. Edwin Orr, *The Event of the Century* (New York, 1989); also, Perry Miller, *The Life of the Mind in America from the Revolution to the Civil War* (New York, 1965), 89; Kenneth M. Stampp, *America in 1857: A Nation on the Brink* (New York, 1990), 236–238; Sandra Sizer, "Politics and Apolitical Religion: The Great Urban Revivals of the Late Nineteenth Century," *Church History*, 48 (1979), 82–87; Victor B. Howard, *Conscience and Slavery: The Evangelic Calvinist Domestic Missions, 1837–1861* (Kent, Oh., 1990), ch. 14; Roy Franklin Nichols, *The Disruption of American Democracy* (New York, 1948), 132–136; Louis Filler, *The Crusade against Slavery, 1830–1860* (New York, 1960), 263. John R. McKivigan makes the best case for the notion that the revival did not help the antislavery cause. He reads the evidence too narrowly but provides a good check against exaggeration of the direct ideological effects: *The War against Proslavery Religion: Abolitionism and the Northern Churches, 1830–1865* (Ithaca, N.Y., 1984), 162. For the contradictory effects of the revivals on abolitionism, see especially Ronald G. Walters, *The Antislavery Appeal: American Abolitionism after 1830* (Baltimore, Md., 1976). For the perfectionism of the Revival as a powerful impetus to social reform movements, see Timothy L. Smith, *Revival and Social Reform: American Protestantism on the Eve of the Civil War* (Baltimore, Md., 1980), ch. 4. For the impact of the revival of 1857–1858 in hardening both proslavery and antislavery attitudes along sectional lines, see also Richard J. Carwardine, *Evangelicals and Politics in Antebellum America* (New Haven, Conn., 1993), 292–296. For municipal efforts to relieve the poor during the economic crisis, see Iver Bernstein, *The New York City Draft Riots: Their Significance for American Society and Politics in the Age of the Civil War* (New York, 1990), 138, and for class divisions, see ch. 4. For the extent of unemployment in leading northern cities, see Leah Hannah Feder, *Unemployment Relief in Periods of Depression: A Study of the Measures Adopted in Certain American Cities, 1857 through 1922* (New York, 1936), 19 and ch. 21.

workers staged massive and menacing rallies. By February 1855, conditions improved, but the city was still full of soup kitchens.[93]

Thousands of unemployed workers in New York had to beg at the doors of the rich. Socialists, anarchists, and other radicals drew huge throngs to hear increasingly threatening speeches. Not until well into 1859 did the depression run its course. The crisis exacerbated widespread fears of a moral breakdown, as Americans perceived a soaring crime rate, and Southerners pointed to the unraveling of the family in the free states. Some Southerners even proclaimed Donati's comet a sign of the displeasure and wrath that God was pouring over the infidel North during the economic crisis. Even the soberest of southern merchants – relieved at the mildness of the effects of the panic in the South – looked askance at the effects in the North. For George Walton Williams, America had been blessed "with the most abundant harvest ever known," but its commercial community "was perishing in the midst of plenty." He thanked God that King Cotton "has unlocked the iron grasp."[94]

---

[93] Elizabeth Blackmar, *Manhattan for Rent, 1785–1850* (Ithaca, N.Y., 1991), 124–125, 225–227; Robert W. Fogel, Ralph A. Gallantine, and Richard Manning, eds., *Without Consent or Contract: Evidence and Methods*, 2 vols. (New York, 1992), 414–416; also Arthur C. Cole, *The Irrepressible Conflict, 1850–1865* (New York, 1934), 32.

[94] Arthur C. Cole, *The Irrepressible Conflict, 1850–1865* (New York, 1934), 32–33; Stampp, *America in 1857*, 39, 42; Coulter, *G. W. Williams*, 37; on the response to Donati's comet, see Farmer, *Metaphysical Confederacy*, 10.

4

The Squaring of Circles

> If I furnish my negro with every necessity of life, without the least care on his part –
> if I support him in sickness, however long it may be and pay all his expenses,
> though he does nothing – if I maintain him in his old age, when he is incapable
> of rendering either himself or myself any service, am I not entitled to an exclusive
> right to his time?
>
> —Bennet H. Barrow[1]

Francois Quesnay, father of Physiocracy and personal physician to Louis XV
and Madame du Pompadour, formulated the first analysis of the circular flow
of economic life. A man of genius, he ended his life in a valiant mathematical
endeavor to square the circle. The South had no such genius but did have a
number of accomplished political economists. George Tucker of Virginia contributed to the theory of economic development and – trailed by J. D. B. De
Bow of Louisiana – did valuable work in statistics, notably with his *Progress of
the United States in Population and Wealth in Fifty Years* (1855). Jacob Cardozo of South Carolina qualified as an econometrician, especially respected for
his analyses of the tariff problem. Thomas Roderick Dew of Virginia, a sound
expositor of classical political economy, doubled as an acute historian of the
power and limits of economics in human affairs. Louisa Susanna (Cheves)
McCord of South Carolina kept southern intellectuals abreast of developments
in French political economy. Alas, they all spent their lives in a pursuit reminiscent of Quesnay's. Quixotically, they tried to defend slavery through classical
political economy, only to find that at the heart of southern society and its
worldview lay a circle that could not be squared or – for those who prefer – lay
irreconcilable contradictions.[2]

---

[1] Bennet H. Barrow, "Rules of Highland Plantation," in Edwin Adams Davis, *Plantation Life in
the Florida Parishes of Louisiana, 1836–1846, as Reflected in the Diary of Bennet H. Barrow*
(New York, 1943), 407.

[2] For the southern political economists, see Paul Conkin, *Prophets of Prosperity: America's First
Economists* (Bloomington, Ind., 1980), 43–76, 135–167; Joseph Dorfman, *The Economic Mind
in American Civilization*, 5 vols. (New York, 1966), 2:527, 566, 844–952; and Dorfman's

The slaveholders found themselves awash in a world market based on free labor, which tended toward political liberalism and the principle of each man's property in himself. Defenders of slavery moved from attempts at accommodation with transatlantic bourgeois theory to projection of an alternative world order at once reactionary and new. During the first half of the nineteenth century, the legal system emerged as a central issue in economic development. Southerners struggled to make their legal system conform to a slave society in but not of an Atlantic bourgeois world. The South had an advantage in facing the challenge to establish the claims of political economy and jurisprudence to scientific status. In Tucker and Cardozo it boasted two of the best economic brains in the United States; in St. George Tucker of Virginia, Thomas Ruffin of North Carolina, and John Belton O'Neall of South Carolina it boasted an intellectually formidable legal establishment. Although southern political economists spoke authoritatively from the marrow of plantation society, they principally represented the cosmopolitan culture of the port cities and the transatlantic world of merchant capital. They remained loyal to their slave society yet kept their distance, trying with limited success to mediate between different worlds and different discourses. In consequence, political economists became tangential to proslavery thought. Their commitment to southern slave society ultimately led into a cul-de-sac just when northern political economists were beginning to influence national social and economic policy.[3]

Theories of Value

Some of the ablest southern political economists, foreseeing the demise of slavery, separated problems that their northern colleagues merged. Even the staunchly proslavery Louisa McCord remained attached to the liberal political economy of Frédéric Bastiat despite its antislavery implications. George Tucker, Cardozo, and Dew could not reconcile economic liberalism with slave society on terms acceptable to a majority of Southerners. Tucker envisaged the withering away of slavery in response to the challenge of industrial development. The forbidden subject remained labor relations. For political economists, economic development required a market in labor-power; simultaneously, social order required perpetuation of slavery. M. R. H. Garnett of Virginia ingeniously straddled by focusing on value theory. Distinguishing between absolute and relative value (value in use and value in exchange), he explored the intricacies of the labor theory of value: "Capital, in whatever form, can always be reduced to labor." Garnett stressed that wages oscillated around the cost of subsistence

Introduction to George Tucker, *The Theory of Money and Banks Investigated* (New York, 1964). George Tucker, *Progress of the United States in Population and Wealth in Fifty Years* (New York, 1964 [1855]).

[3] For an elaboration, see Eugene D. Genovese and Elizabeth Fox-Genovese, "Slavery, Economic Development, and the Law: The Dilemma of Southern Political Economists, 1800–1860," *Washington & Lee Law Review*, 41 (1984), 1–29. See also Morton J. Horwitz, *The Transformation of American Law, 1780–1860* (Cambridge, Mass., 1977).

and reproduction – understood as culturally determined and not as biologically absolute. Without a word on slavery, Garnett provided underpinnings for the defense of the slaveholders' economic relation to labor. And William Elliott of South Carolina defended a theory of value that might have made Karl Marx smile. Elliott, like Marx, conceded the indispensability of teachers, doctors, and lawyers but denied that, "economically speaking," they produced commodity value.[4]

Southern theorists debated the social consequence of the prevailing form of labor when they discussed, say, Malthus on population, but they had trouble with "value" as the cornerstone of political economy. Often, they settled for generalizations like that offered by David J. McCord: "There can be no property not derivable from labor, present or past." Southern political economists could not accept a labor theory of value without retreating from the cutting edge of their discipline. As early as 1830, contributors to *Southern Review* (Charleston) firmly rejected the labor theory of value; in particular, they rejected theories of the intrinsic exploitation of labor propagated by socialists and the radicals of the Workingman's Party. Most southern political economists joined northern political economists in accepting the new economic theory that in effect equated value with market price, as well as the new legal theory that encouraged economic development. They thereby undermined proslavery ideology. The new political economy, which, accurately or not, attributed a labor theory of value to David Ricardo, logically led to acceptance of the morality of the free-labor system against those who condemned it as heartless abandonment of laborers to misery and starvation and celebrated slavery as a paternalistic system of protection for laborers. The new theory of value proclaimed the centrality of individual desires a reflection of natural law as well as of bourgeois economic relations. Since slavery ruled out consideration of laborers' individual desires, its defenders had to consider a slave a unit of fixed capital to be bought and sold like any nonhuman commodity. But an older paternalistic ethos proclaimed the virtues of hierarchy and dependency.[5]

With the steady industrialization of the North and the nationwide advance of evangelical Protestantism, repudiation of the labor theory of value and growing formalism in legal theory proceeded, *pari passu*, with the emergence of a militant southern defense of slavery. In effect, proslavery social theorists picked up the relay from political economists doomed to choose between marginality as scientific political economists or marginality as shapers of political and

---

[4] [M. R. H. Garnett], "Progress of Political Economy," *SQR*, 14 (1848), 1–36, quote at 29; William Elliott, "Examination of Mr. Edmund Rhett's Agricultural Address," *Southern Agriculturalist, Horticulturalist, and Register of Rural Affairs*, 1 (1841), 115, also 281–289.

[5] [David J. McCord], "Barhydt's Industrial Exchanges," *SQR*, 15 (1849), 466–467; *SR*, 6 (1830), 4–5, 10; 8 (1832), 496. "To own a slave was to have access to his entire labor and to be responsible for his full maintenance. Thus a slave was a form of capital; specifically, 'fixed capital' (as opposed to 'circulating capital,' such as inventories)." Ralph V. Anderson and Robert E. Gallman, "Slaves as Fixed Capital: Slave Labor and Southern Economic Development," *Journal of American History*, 64 (1977), 24–46, quote at 25.

social opinion and policy. Economists, northern and southern, stood comfortably within the range of doctrine derived from Adam Smith and extended to the followers of Ricardo on the one side and Lord Lauderdale (James Maitland) and Samuel Bailey or even Thomas Malthus on the other. Garnett and his uncle, Senator R. M. T. Hunter, prominent Virginia Calhounites, considered Smith's labor theory of value an absurdity that led straight to socialism. Cardozo offered a sophisticated critique of the labor theory he attributed to Ricardo. The antislavery Lieber and Daniel Reaves Goodloe of North Carolina joined proslavery theorists in denouncing the labor theory of value, maintaining that commodities contained no inherent value, only value in exchange. Goodloe in fact used Smith to construct an economic argument against slavery. In *Southern Quarterly Review*, "M." began a fifty-page assault on "the American System" by granting Henry Clay's considerable gifts but condemning him as an ignoramus in political economy. "M." thereupon extolled at great length the work of Adam Smith.[6]

It was not easy for those who defended slavery to embrace state intervention in the economy. William D. Thomas, a graduate student at the University of Virginia, announced that God's order required laissez-faire and the law of supply and demand and that those who tried to avoid His laws ended badly. Thomas derided poor laws and alms for making dependents unable and unwilling to support themselves. Few Southerners took issue with that stark proposition, but no few spoke in different accents. Chief Justice Joseph Lumpkin of Georgia and George Frederick Holmes of Virginia considered futile imperial Roman attempts to help the poor during economic crises by regulating the market and setting prices. In the wake of the revolutions of 1848, Holmes and David McCord argued that the Malthusian food-population problem lay at the heart of Europe's economic difficulties and that socialist measures only made matters worse. Robert Toombs of Georgia denounced the proposal of Simon Cameron of Pennsylvania to have the government provide jobs for a half million unemployed workers. Such legislation, he steamed, would ruin the people and the country. Toombs even wanted the government to sell the post office to private enterprise. There were, to be sure, contrary voices. Among them, Brantz Meyer of Maryland extolled the ancient Chinese effort to establish an "ever-normal granary" – storage of foodstuffs during prosperous periods for distribution during periods of shortage.[7]

---

[6] Jacob N. Cardozo, *Notes on Political Economy* (New York, 1960 [1826]); [Daniel Reaves Goodloe], *Inquiry into the Causes Which Have Retarded the Accumulation of Wealth and the Increase of Population in the Southern States: In Which the Question of Slavery Is Considered from a Politico-Economical Point of View. By a Carolinian* (Electronic ed.; Chapel Hill, N.C., 2000 [1846]), 18; M., "Henry Clay and the American System," *SQR*, 10 (1846), 174–227, esp. 175. See also Appendix: "Value Theory" in this chapter.

[7] William D. Thomas, "Connection of Political Economy with Natural Theology" (MA thesis, 1854, typescript at University of Virginia); Joseph H. Lumpkin, *An Address Delivered before the South-Carolina Institute at Its Second Annual Fair* (Charleston, S.C., 1851), 19–20; [George Frederick Holmes], "California Gold and European Revolution," *SQR*, n.s. 1 (1850), 287–291;

During the 1840s and 1850s, when the proslavery argument reached high tide, its advocates usually turned to political economy – as Senator James H. Hammond of South Carolina did – to claim that the world economy depended on slave-produced staples. They did not turn to political economy – at least not effectively – to sustain the moral claims of slavery. Usually, they paraded the argument of prosouthern Northerners like David Christie and Thomas Kettel that the North was getting rich by exploiting the South and should curb abolitionism. Pleading for maintenance of the Union, Thomas Hart Benton of Missouri argued that federal economic policies hurt the South and urged the North not to kill the goose that laid the golden eggs. E. N. Elliott, in his massive *Cotton Is King, and Pro-Slavery Arguments* (1860), published Christie rather than a Southerner on political economy, whereas he chose Southerners to write on law, morals, religion, political theory, and sociology. Talent was hardly the issue. Elliott surely knew that Christie was not the equal of Tucker or Cardozo as an economist. Political economists, often with misgivings, found themselves strategically placed to bring their young and confident science to bear on the vexing question of the interrelation of economic growth, the legal system, and slavery. They defended slavery – some with passion, some without – but did not do a good job. By the 1850s the voices of political economists as a group dropped to a whisper, although as individuals, they contributed to the proslavery cause on specific questions of economic policy and on noneconomic subjects.[8]

George Tucker's Gloomy Vision

A debate over the relative cost of slave and free labor gave the proslavery side little comfort. George Tucker judged slave labor more costly than free. Immersed in the new political economy – including Malthus's population theory and the "iron law of wages" attributed to Ricardo – he concluded that as the wages of free labor would fall to the minimum cost of subsistence necessary for reproduction of the labor force, slaveholders would abandon their costly and care-laden system. From the mid-1830s, an array of talented Virginians,

[David J. McCord], "Barhydt's Industrial Exchanges," *SQR*, 15 (1849), 461–462; Pleasant A. Stovall, *Robert Toombs, Statesman, Speaker, Statesman, Sage: His Career in Congress and on the Hustings* (New York, 1982), 197–198; [Brantz Meyer], "China and the Chinese," *SQR*, 12 (1847), 46–47.

[8] J. H. Hammond, "Speech on the Admission of Kansas, under the Lecompton Constitution," in [Clyde N. Wilson], ed., *Selections from the Letters and Speeches of James H. Hammond* (Spartanburg, S.C., 1978), 301–322, esp. 312–317; Thomas Hart Benton, *Thirty Years' View; or, A History of the Working of the American Government for Thirty Years, from 1820 to 1850*, 2 vols. (New York, 1854), 2:ch. 32, esp. 130–133. See David Christie, "Cotton Is King," in E. N. Elliott, ed., *Cotton Is King, and Pro-Slavery Arguments* (New York, 1969 [1860]), and Thomas P. Kettell, *Southern Wealth and Northern Profits* (New York, 1860). See also Holt Wilson, "Cotton, Steam and Machinery," *SLM*, 27 (1858), 161–176. For the attractiveness of Kettel's argument even for militantly proslavery Southerners, see [M. R. H. Garnett], *The Union, Past and Future: How It Works, and How to Save It*, 4th ed. (Charleston, S.C., 1850), 11ff.

including Dew, Holmes, George A. Baxter, Nathaniel Beverley Tucker, and George Fitzhugh, flirted with versions of George Tucker's thesis, worrying that falling wages discouraged resort to relatively more expensive slave labor. Elsewhere, leading southern unionists like Henry Clay of Kentucky and Robert J. Walker of Mississippi agreed that economic development would compel abandonment of slavery. When proslavery theorists braced for emancipation of the Russian serfs in the 1850s, they feared a version of the economic and social process George Tucker had outlined. John Bennett Allen of Mississippi wrote from Moscow that the projected emancipation of the serfs threatened to increase exploitation of the peasantry. Edmund Ruffin predicted "bad consequences" for both lords and serfs as well as for the government and the social order.[9]

George Tucker's attitude toward slavery has provoked sharp disagreement among his interpreters. Robert Colin McLean, Tucker's biographer, views him as basically an apologist for slavery, dishonest in his expressions of distaste. In contrast, Tipton Ray Snavely, writing on Tucker's political economy, maintains that he opposed slavery on moral as well as economic grounds and honestly tried to find a conservative way to remove it. Since Tucker wrote numerous books and articles, many of which discussed slavery, perhaps we should admire his skill in befuddling intelligent readers for more than a century. McLean, a literary scholar, properly detects dissembling in Tucker's moral stance, but Snavely, an economist, correctly says that Tucker considered slavery an obstacle to economic development and wished it gone. Tucker's economic analysis provided comfort to those who settled for a defense of slavery that called for patience and nonintervention in economic laws destined to bury it in God's – and the market's – good time. But Tucker's thesis provided no comfort to those intent on repelling the mounting moral and political assault on slavery by moving to high ground. Tucker, an admirably self-critical political economist, always tried to learn from experience. His work on statistics and population trends amply demonstrated his commitment to test theory against changing reality. Yet on the politics of slavery he ended his life, much as he had lived it, in equivocation.[10]

9   Thomas Roderick Dew, *Lectures on the Restrictive System Delivered to the Senior Political Class of William and Mary College* (Richmond, Va., 1829), 32, 111–112; George Frederick Holmes, "Capital and Labor," *DBR*, 22 (1857), 260–262; George A. Baxter, *An Essay on the Abolition of Slavery* (Richmond, Va., 1836), 16; Nathaniel Beverley Tucker, "Moral and Political Effect of the Relation between the Caucasian Master and the African Slave," *SLM*, 10 (1844), 337–338; George Fitzhugh, "The Conservative Principle," *DBR*, 22 (1857), 458; E. G., "Slavery in the Southern States," *SQR*, 8 (1845), 344; on Clay and Walker, see Norma Lois Peterson, *The Presidency of William Henry Harrison and John Tyler* (Lawrence, Kans., 1989), 209, 234–235; James Bennett Allen to Elizabeth Allen, July 17, 19, 1858; *ERD*, April 19, 1857, 1:176. See also Appendix: "Political Economy" and "Tucker Thesis" in this chapter.
10 Robert Colin McLean, *George Tucker; Moral Philosopher and Man of Letters* (Chapel Hill, N.C., 1961); Tipton Ray Snavely, *George Tucker as a Political Economist* (Charlottesville, Va., 1964), and Snavely's review of McLean in *Southern Journal of Economics*, 358–359; also, Leonard C. Helderman, "A Social Scientist of the Old South," *JSH*, 2 (1936), 148–174.

In the 1850s and during the War, a rendition of the Tucker thesis appeared in newspapers in Georgia, Alabama, Mississippi, and South Carolina, stressing the cheapness of wage labor relative to slave to demonstrate the superior living conditions of southern slaves. But that rendition did not prevent moderates like the eminent jurist John Archibald Campbell of Alabama from concluding, as Tucker did, that the rising modern economy was setting slavery on the road to extinction.[11]

Labor: Paid and Unpaid

That slave labor was unpaid labor became a central abolitionist contention. James Birney referred to the "unpaid wages of the laborer – the robbery of the poor." Yet, Boston's *Abolitionist*, supported by William Lloyd Garrison, referred to free labor as cheaper than coerced labor. The *Anti-Slavery Record*, organ of the American Anti-Slavery Society, argued that if southern slaves were in fact substantially better off than free workers, slaveholders would emancipate their slaves and employ wage laborers. Slaveholders, therefore, had no claims to compensation for emancipation since, if they had been telling the truth, they could only profit from being relieved of their burden.[12]

Opinions differed in the South. Discussing the prospects for slave-based manufacturing in the South, a writer in *Virginia Literary Museum and Journal of Belles Lettres, Arts, Sciences, Etc.* for 1829 suggested that the cost of slave labor did not vary much from the cost of free labor in manufacturing, what-ever the gap in agricultural wages. But in the 1830s, referring to slaves, the *Richmond Enquirer* asked: "Where is there a labouring class in the world that enjoys so much of mere animal comfort at so cheap a price?" William Hemsley Emory of Maryland, a principal figure in the Army's exploration and develop-ment of the West, thought slavery unprofitable in the Southwest, whereas Dew cautioned about the social costs of free labor. Twenty years later the *Charleston Mercury*, reprinting a piece from the *New Orleans Delta*, said simply: "Indu-bitably, slave labor is cheaper than hireling free labor." Among prominent Virginians, H. H. Stuart, Willoughby Newton, and (more cautiously) A. A. Campbell trumpeted slave labor as the world's cheapest labor. In Georgia dur-ing America's first great gold rush in the 1839s, mine owners preferred white labor. In part, they yielded to community prejudices but did believe free labor cheaper than slave.[13]

---

[11] "Vac Victus," *Macon Daily Telegraph*, March 24, 1865; "Slave and Free States as Tested in the Census," *Weekly Mississippian*, Feb. 11, 1862 (reprinted from the *Mobile Mercury*); *Charleston Mercury*, July 29, 1857. Robert Saunders, Jr., *John Archibald Campbell: Southern Moderate, 1811–1889* (Tuscaloosa, Ala., 1997), 65. See also "The English Poor Laws and the Emancipation of the Villeins," *Richmond Enquirer*, June 28, 1855.

[12] James G. Birney, "Correspondence," *Anti-Slavery Examiner*, May 1, 1838, 28; "Advantages of Paid Labor," *The Abolitionist*, 1 (1833), 95; "Compensation," *Anti-Slavery Record*, 1 (Feb. 1835), 17–18, and "Slavery as It Is in Practice," *Anti-Slavery Record*, 2 (Oct. 1836), 1–4.

[13] *Richmond Enquirer*, Feb. 9, 1832; William H. Goetzmann, *Army Exploration in the American West, 1803–1863* (Austin, Tex., 1991), 137–138; *Charleston Mercury*, June 18, 1857, reprinted

When considering the relative costs of free and slave labor, decades of proslavery writers dismissed as foolish the familiar notion of slave labor as unpaid labor. Most declared it dearer than free labor. In 1826 a southern agricultural writer referred to "our Northern brethren, with whom labour is comparatively cheap." In 1843, Dr. Samuel A. Cartwright held that blacks could not be driven as hard as whites and were less productive – that since "wages" were the cost of subsistence, the returns to slaveholders necessarily fell below returns to employers of free workers. The Presbyterian Reverend George Junkin, president of Miami University in Ohio and soon to be president of Washington College in Virginia, agreed that slaves received "wages," as political economists understood the term. In a discourse applauded by John C. Calhoun, Junkin affirmed the cost of a slave's sustenance as a more secure functional equivalent of a free worker's wages. In 1850 a contributor to *Southern Presbyterian Review* decried the notion of uncompensated slave labor as "palpably, undeniably, outrageously false." Southern slaves "are better paid than the laboring class of any country in the world." A year later a contributor took for granted that readers of *Southern Quarterly Review* recognized slaves as better remunerated, costlier, and less productive than free laborers. The Baptist Reverends Iveson Brookes of South Carolina and Thornton Stringfellow of Virginia pressed the case during the 1850s, and it appeared in the reflections of planters like Bennet H. Barrow of Louisiana, whose words are quoted above. E. J. Stearns, replying to Harriet Beecher Stowe, identified slave maintenance as "paid" labor. If, he asked, it were a crime for planters to get rich off their slaves' labor, how much greater would be the crime committed by New England capitalists, whose workers produced much more for them?[14]

from *New Orleans Delta*; for Stuart and Newton, see C. W. Turner, "Virginia Agricultural Reform,"*Agricultural History*, 26 (1952), 86; A. A. Campbell, "Capital and Enterprise – The Bases of Agricultural Progress," *Southern Planter*, 20 (1860), 36–39. Rensi and David Williams, *Gold Fever: America's First Gold Rush* (Atlanta, Ga., 1988), 24; "The Policy of Encouraging Manufacture – No. 4," *Virginia Literary Museum and Journal of Belles Lettres, Arts, Sciences, Etc.*, 1 (1829), 77; see the reiteration as "Defensor," "Political Economy – Correction of Errors," *Virginia Literary Museum and Journal of Belles Lettres, Arts, Sciences, Etc.*, 1 (1829), 317.

[14] "Original Communications Made to the Agricultural Society of South-Carolina; and Extracts from Select Authors on Agriculture," *Carolina Journal of Medicine, Science, and Agriculture*, 1 (1826), 42 (revision of an article published in the *Charleston Mercury*); Samuel A. Cartwright, *Essays...in a Series of Letters to the Rev. William Winans* (Vidalia, Miss., 1843), 22, 32–33; George Junkin, *The Integrity of Our National Union vs. Abolitionism* (Cincinnati, Oh., 1843), 57–58; *SPR*, 3 (1850), 340–342, quotes at 340; "Is Southern Civilization Worth Preserving?" *SQR*, n.s. 3 (1851), 221–222; Iveson Brookes, *A Defence of Southern Slavery against the Attacks of Henry Clay and Alex'r Campbell* (Hamburg, S.C., 1851), 31; Thornton Stringfellow, *Slavery: Its Origin, Nature, and History, Considered in the Light of Bible Teachings, Moral Justice, and Political Wisdom* (New York, 1861), 29, and on Stringfellow's critique, see Eugene M. Scheel, *Culpeper: A Virginia County's History through 1920* (Culpeper, Va., 1982), 161; E. J. Stearns, *Notes on Uncle Tom's Cabin: Being a Logical Answer to Its Allegations and Inferences against Slavery as an Institution* (Philadelphia, Pa., 1853), 24–26. In later years, Junkin, who left Virginia for the North in 1861, protested against the long working day of northern laborers in contrast with southern slaves: George Junkin, *Sabbatismos: A Discussion and Defence of*

Justice William Gaston of the North Carolina Supreme Court, speaking in 1832 to the student societies of the state university, implicitly identified slavery's high cost of labor as the principal cause of North Carolina's economic backwardness. That argument thereafter recurred often in a variety of forms. Neither William Gilmore Simms nor Baltimore's *American Farmer* doubted that free labor was much cheaper than slave labor. In the 1850s Charles Lyell reported that increasing numbers of Alabamans considered slave labor more expensive than free.[15]

Some prominent antislavery writers, including the Congregationalist Reverend Leonard Bacon of New England, scoffed at the notion that slave labor went unpaid. Slave remuneration, wrote James Loring Baker, compared favorably with wages of white laborers. Implicitly, Baker accepted the Tucker thesis to foresee the possibility of the eventual end of slavery through economic development. Goodloe, arguing that slavery condemned the South to economic backwardness, in effect conceded that slaves received the equivalent of wages; he tried to demonstrate empirically that their labor cost more than free labor. Andrew Johnson, arguing that slavery supported high wages for northern workers, said that if the investments in slave labor shifted to wage labor, the cost of labor would fall.[16]

A critical political ramification: Replying to the claim that free labor was less costly than slave, George Fitzhugh concluded – as did Karl Marx – that, therefore, free workers suffered greater exploitation than slave. Similarly, the widely read Methodist Reverend H. N. McTyeire maintained that slave labor was more expensive than free because masters treated laborers more humanely. As an illustration of McTyeire's point, consider the cases in which slaveholders brought suit for damages in connection with accidents to hired slaves. Both the Supreme Court of North Carolina, led by Thomas Ruffin, and the Supreme Court of Georgia, led by Joseph Lumpkin, rejected as inapplicable in slave cases the fellow-servant rule, according to which an employer was not responsible to

---

the *Lord's Day of Sacred Rest* (Philadelphia, Pa., 1866), 174–175; Calhoun to Junkin, *JCCP*, 23:450–451.

[15] William Gaston, *Address Delivered before the Philanthropic and Dialectic Societies at Chapel Hill, June 20, 1832* (Electronic ed.; Chapel Hill, N.C., 2005 [1832]), 14; for slave labor as cheaper than free, see, e.g., Richard Fuller, *Our Duty to the African Race* (Baltimore, Md., 1851), 10; [William Gilmore Simms], "Slavery – No. II: Tract No. 10 Reviewed," *Southern and Western Literary Monthly Magazine and Review*, 2 (1845), 241–242; "Agriculture in the New England States, Maryland, and Virginia," *American Farmer*, 12 (1856), 177; Charles Lyell, *A Second Visit to the United States of North America*, 2 vols. (London, 1855), 2:72.

[16] Leonard Bacon, *Slavery Discussed in Occasional Essays from 1833 to 1846* (New York, 1846), 22–23; Daniel Reaves Goodloe, *Inquiry into the Causes Which Have Retarded the Accumulation of Wealth and the Increase of Population in the Southern States* (Washington, D.C., 1846), especially 23; James Loring Baker, *Slavery* (Ithaca, N.Y., 2006 [1860]), 14, 17; "Speech at Evans Crossroads, Greene County," May 26, 1849, in *AJP*, 1:499–500. In 1892, R. Q. Mallard reiterated that no tillers of the soil in ancient or modern times were as amply compensated for their labor as the slaves of the South: *Plantation Life before Emancipation* (Electronic ed.; Chapel Hill, N.C., 1998 [1892]), 36.

an employee for an accident caused by the negligence of a fellow employee. But whereas Ruffin resorted to a contract rationale to deny damages to the plaintiff, Lumpkin offered a confused version that practically set contract theory aside. Like Ruffin, Lumpkin rejected a tort rationale, but unlike Ruffin, he awarded damages anyway on the ground that "humanity" required special protection for a slave from those responsible for him at the moment. Lumpkin suggested that when a slave disobeyed an order to avoid a dangerous situation, he could not be held responsible since he lacked the appropriate intelligence and good sense to take care of himself. Thus anyone who held a slave would, if necessary, have to chain him down for his own good. Lumpkin demonstrated that slavery imparted a paternalistic sensibility to the law, but he threatened to play havoc with the law of contracts and torts. Thomas Ruffin's more careful ruling raised problems of a different order. Invoking basic economic theory, Ruffin ruled that a slave's hiring price included the cost of his insurance. None of the South's leading political economists disagreed. Dew, Thomas Cooper, George Tucker, and others who taught leaders of the southern bench and bar pointed toward the separation of the master-slave relation from the business aspects of slavery. Courts in most slave states accepted the fellow-servant rule in principle but refused to apply it to slaves. Thus in relevant respects, slaves received greater protection than free workers did.[17]

To the horror of the Presbyterian Reverend Thomas Smyth of Charleston, scientific racists like Josiah Nott drew their own conclusions and crowed that the time would come when economic development rendered blacks expendable. In 1847 the Presbyterian Reverend Henry Ruffner of Virginia, in a widely noted pamphlet, denounced the "pernicious institution" of slavery for its political and economic evils but passed over its religious or moral aspects. Ruffner endorsed the economic analysis in George Tucker's *Progress of Population* and described Virginia as in economic decline because of the low productivity of

---

[17] George Fitzhugh, *Sociology for the South, or, The Failure of Free Society* (New York, 1965 [1852]), 279; Fitzhugh, "Southern Thought, Again" *DBR*, 23 (1857), 462. For the rate of exploitation, see Robert W. Fogel and Stanley L. Engerman, *Time on the Cross: The Economics of American Negro Slavery*, 2 vols. (Boston, Mass., 1974), 1:105–157; and the critique in Elizabeth Fox-Genovese and Eugene D. Genovese, *Fruits of Merchant Capital: Slavery and Bourgeois Property in the Rise and Expansion of Slavery* (New York, 1983), 136–171. For a review of the argument over relative labor costs, see Wilfred Carsel, "The Slaveholders' Indictment of Northern Wage Slavery," *JSH*, 6 (1940), 514. H. N. McTyeire, *Duties of Christian Masters*, ed. Thomas O. Summers (Nashville, Tenn., 1859), 74; *Gorman v. Campbell*, 14 Ga., 137 (1853); *Ponton v. Wilmington & Weldon RR. Co.*, in 51 N.C. (Jones), 245. Mark V. Tushnet, *The American Law of Slavery: Considerations of Humanity and Interest* (Princeton, 1981), 49–50; Paul DeForest Hicks, *Joseph Henry Lumpkin: Georgia's First Chief Justice* (Athens, Ga., 2002), 134; Frederick Wertheim, "Slavery and the Fellow-Servant Rule: An Antebellum Dilemma," *New York University Law Review*, 61 (1986), 1112–1148; William W. Fisher, III, "Ideology and Imagery in the Law of Slavery," *Chicago-Kent Law Review*, 68 (1993), 1052–1054; Terrence F. Kiely, "The Hollow Word: An Experiment in Legal Historical Method as Applied to the Introduction of Slavery," *De Paul Law Review*, 25 (1976), 871–875; David J. Langum, "The Role of Intellect and Fortuity in Legal Change: An Incident from the Law of Slavery," *American Journal of Legal History*, 28 (1984), 1–16.

slave labor relative to free. Ruffner taught political economy at Washington College, where he followed the Manchesterian school with a whiggish twist. He does not appear to have said much directly about slavery in class, but his economic reasoning led logically to Tucker's conclusions. Dew mentioned slavery only in passing in his lectures and textbook on political economy. The economic defense of slavery – such as it was – came primarily from pamphleteers like Edward Middleton of South Carolina, who followed Dew in arguing that climate and demographics rendered slavery necessary in certain parts of the world. Middleton, too, doubted that slavery could survive the relentless development of international capitalism, but – like Edward A. Pollard of Virginia – he declared unthinkable the emancipation of an inferior race in the midst of a superior race. An able polemicist, he scored points along the way, with an argument that led nowhere. Planters, journalists, and politicians recognized in Tucker's argument the euthanasia of the slaveholding class. Henry Watson of Alabama, a transplanted Yankee and big planter, agreed that the laws of political economy doomed slavery to eventual extinction but refused to embrace the social and political implications. Edgar Allan Poe recoiled both from industrialism and social reform movements, observing ruefully, "The horrid laws of political economy cannot be evaded." And Jefferson Davis of Mississippi asked what would become of emancipated blacks in a competitive market for which they were ill-equipped and yet dependent on whites who would no longer have a personal investment in their welfare.[18]

The debate over slave maintenance as an equivalent to wages had implications for the charged debate over whether a man could rightfully sell himself into slavery. The Reverend Lemuel Haynes of New England, a black abolitionist, having written, "Liberty is equally precious to a *Black man*, as it is to a *white one*," denied that parents had a right to sell their children into slavery. In the 1840s the cautiously antislavery Henry St. George Tucker of Virginia wrote: "Natural rights are a right to his life, limbs, and liberty; to the produce of his own labor; to the common use of air, light, and water, and of the common fruits of the earth aggregated by himself for his necessary use." Such writers in effect followed John Locke and Baron de Montesquieu in denying that any man could sell himself into slavery. Some proslavery ideologues and politicians

---

[18] "Unity of the Human Races," in *Complete Works of the Reverend Thomas Smyth, D. D.*, ed. J. William Flinn, 10 vols. (Columbia, S.C., 1908), 8:75–76; James S. Richeson, "Course of Lectures Delivered on Political Economy by Henry Ruffner" (1840), in Ruffner Papers; [Edward Middleton], *Economical Causes of Slavery in the United States, and Obstacles to Its Abolition* (London, 1857); Jack P. Maddex, Jr., *The Reconstruction of Edward A. Pollard: A Rebel's Conversion to Postbellum Unionism* (Chapel Hill, N.C., 1974), 27–29; for Watson, see Charles S. Davis, *The Cotton Kingdom in Alabama* (Montgomery, Ala., 1939), 184–185; Ernest Marchand, ed., "Poe as Social Critic," *American Literature*, 6 (1934), 28–43; Poe quoted in Terrence Whalen, *Edgar Allan Poe and the Masses: The Political Economy of Literature in Antebellum America* (Princeton, N.J., 1999), 21; William C. Davis, *Jefferson Davis: The Man and His Hour* (New York, 1991), 181–182. See also Thomas Roderick Dew, *Digest of the Laws, Customs, Manners, and Institutions of the Ancient and Modern Nations* (New York, 1884 [1852]), 406.

replied that free blacks would be better off by enslaving themselves, and others that oppressed free white workers of England and the continent would do so if they could. Abel Parker Upshur, in a posthumously published essay, declared, "The very idea of a perfect right implies the right to surrender it." Albert Taylor Bledsoe denied that the slave ever had a right to the freedom he purportedly could not transfer. The Catholic Bishop Verot of Florida, viewing a master's expenditures on his slave the equivalent to a wage, asked: "A man may sell his labor and work for a day, a week, a month, or a year: why may he not sell it for all his life?"[19]

Ramifications of Economic Development

Southern political economists like most northern, viewed economic development positively and considered industrialization inevitable. De Bow, the South's most vigorous journalistic economic promoter, advocated expansion of southern manufacturing in the 1850s. But not all southern political economists applauded the industrialization they saw as inevitable. Cooper and Dew used the argument from inevitability to oppose federal support. Let manufacturing develop slowly and naturally, they argued, and the evils that must accompany it would be more easily controlled and kept to a minimum. Misguided attempts at government intervention and protection at law only intensify those evils while they in practice retard the progress of industrialization in the long run.[20]

Cardozo and Tucker, advocates of southern manufactures, assigned an important if still limited role to government but preferred to rely on market forces. They said little about general incorporation laws, for example, although they might have been expected to press for them. Cooper grudgingly conceded some role to joint stock companies but preferred partnerships. On another vital issue they again fell silent. The Old South tolerated grazing and foraging practices normal in precapitalist societies but antithetical to capitalist forms of landownership. Yet political economists, who abstractly defended bourgeois property rights, avoided the issue, and bourgeois fence laws did not

---

[19] Lemuel Haynes, "Liberty Further Extended" (1776), in Richard Newman, ed., *Black Preacher to White America: The Collected Writings of Lemuel Haynes, 1774–1833* (Brooklyn, N.Y., 1990), 19, 26; Henry St. George Tucker, *A Few Lectures on Natural Law* (Charlottesville, Va., 1844), 52–53 and, generally, Lecture One; Baron de Montesquieu, *The Spirit of the Laws*, tr. Thomas Nugent, 2 vols. in 1 (New York, 1975), 1:Bk. 15.2; Abel Parker Upshur, "The True Theory of Government," *SLM*, 22 (1856), 406; "Mr. Bledsoe's Review of His Reviewer," *SLM*, 23 (1856), 24. Verot, *A Tract for the Times: Slavery and Abolitionism* (Baltimore, Md., 1861), 3–4, 8, quote at 4; also, J. P. Holcombe, "Is Slavery Consistent with Natural Law?" *SLM*, 27 (1858), 402–403, 407; also, Holcombe, "Civil Government," *SLM* (1857), 321–329.

[20] Thomas Cooper, *Lectures on the Elements of Political Economy*, 2nd ed. (New York, 1971 [1826, 1830]), 131–132; Dew, *Restrictive System*, 105–106; and for an acute evaluation, Allen Kaufman, *Capitalism, Slavery, and Republican Values: American Economists, 1819–1848* (Austin, Tex., 1982). For pro-protectionism see also "Protectionism," *Virginia University Magazine*, 1 (1857), 224–234; see also Appendix to this chapter, "Political Economy as Taught in the South."

become general until the overthrow of the slaveholding regime. As a group, they showed little enthusiasm for struggles over controversial legal issues – except banking.[21]

No political economist condemned manufacturing or put agriculture on a pedestal. Some like Cardozo, Tucker, De Bow, and Nathaniel Ware advocated industrialization and rapid economic development. De Bow, almost alone, argued that industrialization would strengthen slavery; the others explicitly or implicitly believed that it would eventually render slave labor unprofitable. Their arguments varied and more often than not reflected some version of Malthusian population theory. In the end, they defended slavery as necessary and just in historical time and place but predicted its eventual demise. Of special interest, some political economists presented impressive critiques of Malthus without exploring the probable consequences for the future of slavery. Cardozo and Garnett dismissed Malthus's gloomy analysis of the relation between population and subsistence by positing a technological progress that would raise food production dramatically. And during the early nineteenth century scientific and technological development in Western Europe proceeded at a pace that overcame the threat projected by Malthusian theory. Garnett slighted Malthus as a "man of one idea," whose population theory promoted a half-truth and forgot the power of man's ingenuity.[22]

No significant southern commentator followed the Physiocrats in attributing exchange value solely to agricultural labor or accepted their general economic theory. In the 1820s *Carolina Journal of Medicine, Science, and Agriculture* published a revised version of a review essay from *Charleston Mercury* that began by suggesting a continuing debate on agriculture as the sole source of national wealth. *Southern Review* joined the fray with implicit criticism of Physiocracy's exclusive focus on agriculture but respect for the larger contributions of Quesnay and his followers – a stance assumed by De Bow in the 1850s. The debate waxed hotter in the agricultural press during the 1840s. Edmund Rhett declared that the Physiocrats erred in proclaiming agriculture the only source of wealth and that no one held their theory any longer. William Elliott supported Rhett, but T. J. Randolph countered in Edmund Ruffin's *Farmers' Register* that great nations and empires relied primarily on agriculture, not commerce, for sustained prosperity and security.[23]

[21] See, e.g., Cooper, *Elements of Political Economy*, 252.

[22] Cardozo, *Notes on Political Economy*, xi, 5–18; [M. R. H. Garnett], "The Distribution of Wealth," *SQR*, 11 (1847), 41–43, quote at 41; Garnett, "The Slow Progress of Mankind," *SLM*, 18 (1852), 403–411; John Komlos, "The Industrial Revolution as the Escape from the Malthusian Trap," *Journal of European Economic History*, 29 (2000), 307–331. For a Border-State prediction of a Malthusian crisis in the North, see B. F. Stringfellow, *Negro-Slavery, No Evil; or the North and the South* (St. Louis, Mo., 1854), 34.

[23] "Original Communications made to the Agricultural Society of South-Carolina; and Extracts from Select Authors on Agriculture," *Carolina Journal of Medicine, Science, and Agriculture*, 1 (1826), 39; *SR*, 1 (1828), 197–219, 5 (1830), 381, 8 (1832), 496; D. B. De Bow, *The*

Most commentators explicitly dissociated themselves from the Physiocrats. Some even criticized Adam Smith for having conceded too much ground to their insistence on the centrality of agriculture for economic development. Those who favored agriculture over commerce and manufacturing did not stress presumed economic advantages but presumed moral superiority of people who worked the land. Inflated rhetoric sometimes provoked impatient reactions. The editors of *American Agriculturalist* of New York spoke for their southern compeers when they anticipated the content of scheduled agricultural society addresses across the United States, referring to the usual "*clap-trap* about farmers being the 'bone and sinew of the nation, the foundation and superstructure of society, &c.'" Daniel Webster, campaigning for rural votes in Massachusetts, said that much. President Francis Wayland of Brown University, a leading writer of economic textbooks, sang hymns to the farmers: "Agricultural labor is the most healthy employment, and is attended by the fewest temptations. It has, therefore, seemed the will of the Creator that a large portion of the humanity should always be thus employed." He noted, however, that farmers could not practice an extended division of labor and must master a wide variety of activities. The remark was neither innocent nor complimentary, for Wayland extolled the division of labor for improving men's minds and spirits by giving them satisfaction in the completion of tasks easily mastered. Typical southern responses finessed Physiocratic doctrine. State Senator Angus Patterson of South Carolina announced that agriculture would always be "the primary source of public as well as individual prosperity." A. H. H. Stuart of Virginia vaguely identified agriculture as "the most important interest of society" and "the principal source of production," although he argued for the mutual dependency of agriculture, commerce, and manufactures. Stuart, a unionist Whig, called for rejection of William H. Seward's "irrepressible conflict" theory and recognition of the coexistence of the slave-labor and free-labor systems as the foundation of an American division of labor that guarantees national progress and prosperity.[24]

Industrial Resources, Statistics, &c. of the United States and More Particularly of the Southern and Western States, 3rd ed., 3 vols. (New York, 1966 [1854]), 2:389; Edmund Rhett, "Who Is the Producer," *Southern Cabinet of Agriculture, Horticulture, Rural and Domestic Economy*, 1 (1840), 705–716; William Elliott, "Examination of Mr. Edmund Rhett's Agricultural Address," *Southern Agriculturist, Horticulturalist, and Register of Rural Affairs*, 1 (1841), 119; T. J. Randolph, "An Essay Delivered before the Agricultural Society of Albemarle," *Farmers' Register*, 1 (1843), 29.

[24] Dew, *Restrictive System*, 1–2, 16; Cardozo, *Notes on Political Economy*, iv, 7; De Bow, *Industrial Resources*, 1:72; "Agricultural Society Addresses," *American Agriculturalist*, 2 (1843), 133; Francis Wayland, *The Elements of Political Economy*, 2nd. ed. (New York, 1838), 47, 78, quote at 47; Angus Patterson, *An Address to the Farmers' Society of Barnwell District* (Charleston, 1826), 4; A. H. H. Stuart, "Address of Hon. A. H. H. Stuart before the Central Agricultural Society of Virginia, at Richmond, Oct. 28th, 1859," *Southern Planter*, 20 (1861), 321–336, quote at 321. A book that better educated Southerners knew stressed that landed Rome proved more powerful than commercial Carthage: Baron de Montesquieu, *Considerations on the Causes*

A number of southern colleges, including the better women's colleges, assigned Wayland's *Elements of Political Economy*. Yet, Southerners distrusted the influential Wayland, who stood high as an antislavery moralist while keeping himself removed from the abolitionist movement. The strengths and weaknesses of his *Political Economy* from a southern point of view illuminated the extent of the agreement and disagreement between southern and northern conservatives. Wayland could not hold fast to his dictum that the science of political economy concerned itself with economic law, not ethics. He defended international free trade: "God intended that men should live together in friendship and harmony." And on economic progress: "Moral and religious nations grow wealthy so much more rapidly than vicious and irreligious nations.... This is one of the temporal rewards which God bestows upon social virtue." Those sentiments sat well in the South, but others did not. Political economy married moral philosophy to economic law in an implicit critique of slavery: "But it is plain, that if a man expends labor in the creation of a value, this labor gives him a right to the exclusive possession of that value." So long as men did not injure others, the economic consequences of their thirst for gain would benefit society. "By allowing every man to labor as he chooses, we very greatly increase the happiness of every individual." Wayland condemned dependency relations for destroying self-confidence and "the healthful feeling of independence." He instanced poor relief and other measures that tended toward social leveling, but the relevance of his remarks for slavery was clear enough.[25]

Southern moral philosophers sought to incorporate a defense of property rights into a doctrine that included both free-market economics and a social corporatism appropriate to a slave society. Students learned most of their political economy and political science in courses in moral philosophy. And here the South had an advantage. Virginians and other Southerners pioneered the teaching of political economy in the United States, which they established as a secular discipline, albeit one informed by religious values. Northeasterners followed in the 1820s under the leadership of their divines. Paradoxically, the theologically orthodox South generally provided much more room for secular political economists than the more theologically liberal North did. George Tucker, Cooper, Dew, and Henry Augustine Washington emerged as leading teachers of political economy and appear to have been widely read in the South. Dew demanded that the students who attended his classes a hundred at a time read texts carefully. His *Restrictive System* presented a model of close reasoning

---

of the Greatness of the Romans and Their Decline*, tr. David Lowenthal (New York, 1965, first English tr. 1734), 45. See also Appendix to this chapter, "Political Economy as Taught in the South" and for Physiocracy, see "Value Theory" in the Appendix.

[25] Wayland, *Political Economy*, Preface, 92, 114; 19, 111, 117, 124; William J. Barber, "Political Economy and the Academic Setting before 1900: An Introduction," in Barber, ed., *Economists and Higher Learning in the Nineteenth Century* (New Brunswick, N.J., 1993), 15–41; Elizabeth Barber Young, *A Study of the Curricula of Seven Selected Women's Colleges of the Southern States* (New York, 1932), 161.

and an exposition of Manchesterian economics. The preeminence of lay professors created some problems, for they tended to take utilitarian philosophy rather than theology as their starting point. They thereby pained religiously grounded proslavery theorists. In short, southern colleges taught free-market economics but rejected free-market social theory. Southern professors – unlike their conservative northern colleagues – made a case for having the one without the other since they took slavery for granted as a superior social system. Even Dew, a strong Manchesterian, did not shy away from industrialization's social costs for the working class. Uneasily, he took Jeffersonian ground in suggesting that America rely on British manufactures and remain agricultural as long as possible. Similarly, the Methodist Reverend R. H. Rivers, author of a principal text in moral philosophy, taught the responsibility of the well-to-do to care for the poor and the unfortunate "in such a way as not to encourage indolence."[26]

A positive attitude toward manufacturing did not imply a commitment to government intervention, supportive legislation, or a pro-developmental judiciary. Views differed, but few advocated strong legal regulation. In this respect, too, southern political economists turned away from the Physiocrats, who had called for absolute sovereignty without popular representation to enforce a free market through a centralized "legal despotism." Only Cooper approached Physiocratic ground – if implicitly – by denying that self-interest served the common good, but he wanted nothing to do with any version of "legal despotism." Contrary to widespread assertion, southern political economists did not hold radical versions of laissez-faire either. Most displayed caution and moderation, considerably qualifying their arguments against government intervention and for free trade. Outright interventionists and protectionists like Nathaniel Ware were rare outside the ranks of practical industrialists who occasionally wrote on economic policy. Others avoided extreme formulations and looked to Adam Smith rather than to Ricardo for guidance.[27]

At that, most conceded more than Adam Smith did to government promotion of economic development. Cardozo called for selective state aid, even suggesting that the slave states temper their constitutional scruples and accept some federal aid. He did not, however, approve of counter-cyclical government spending and, in his precocious analysis of business cycles, wanted the economy free to right itself. Tucker called for workhouses to employ honest laborers

---

[26] Michael J. L. O'Connor, *Origin of Academic Economics in the United States* (New York, 1944), 1–6, 19–29; John K. Whitaker, "Early Flowering in the Old Dominion," in Barber, ed., *Economists and Higher Learning*, 15–4; Dew, *Restrictive System*, 32, 111–112; R. H. *Rivers, Elements of Moral Philosophy* (Nashville, Tenn., 1859), 249–250.

[27] Cooper, *Elements of Political Economy*, 332. Ware himself had industrial interests. See W. Diamond, "Nathaniel Ware, National Economist," *JSH*, 5 (1939), 501–526; Eugene D. Genovese, *The Political Economy of Slavery: Studies in the Economy and Society of the Slave South* (New York, 1965), chs. 7–8. Robert Breckenridge's *Danville Quarterly Review* in Kentucky ridiculed South Carolina's free-trade doctrines as unworkable: "State of the Country," *Danville Quarterly Review*, 1 (1861), 307.

during times of acute distress. He left room for considerable government action to promote economic growth, although – apart from his extensive discussions of banking – he spoke in generalities that did not ruffle regional sensibilities. Tucker defended patent laws, legal support for socially necessary monopolies, and laws to restrict child labor. Others introduced their own qualifications. Cooper angrily assailed caveat emptor, demanding that the courts protect consumers against unprincipled sellers. And from Cooper to De Bow, political economists wanted state promotion of mass education to protect a republican polity. Even the characteristic opposition to federal – in contradistinction to state – intervention often rested on direct political or constitutional considerations. De Bow opposed homestead legislation primarily to prevent an influx of free-soilers into the South. U.S. Representative David Rogerson Williams of South Carolina, Cooper, and Dew set the tone early by their opposition to federal support for international commercial interests and, specifically, to attempts to protect American merchants on the high seas or in foreign waters. They charged that most modern wars arose from unwarranted government concern for private commercial interests, which ought to be left to assume all the risks of their profitable trade. In general, then, southern political economists held a wide range of views on the proper relation of the law to the economy and, more important, held about the same range of views as their northern colleagues, with whom they shared a commitment to a common body of theory.[28]

On the vexing tariff question, even in South Carolina political economists proved much less volatile than the politicians. In the wake of the War of 1812 the politically radical Cooper, while still living in the North, joined some leading South Carolina politicians in supporting a tariff to build up manufacturing in the interests of national defense. After his move to South Carolina, he supported nullification and asked the South to calculate the value of the Union. Free-trade economic views went hand in hand with an aversion to a strong central government, but his economic views never hardened as did his political. Thus, he called for measures to employ the poor.[29]

The complexities faced by Cooper dogged others. In 1829 in *Southern Review*, James Hervey Smith of Virginia – scion of the planter elite of Beaufort, South Carolina – published a critique of Jean-Charles-Léonard Simonde

---

[28] See M. M. Leiman, *Jacob N. Cardozo: Political Economy in the Antebellum South* (New York, 1966), 137–138, 208–209; George Tucker, *Political Economy for the People* (Philadelphia, Pa., 1859), 221–223; Tucker, *Theory of Money and Banks Investigated* (Boston, 1839), 152; Ottis C. Skipper, *J. D. B. De Bow, Magazinist of the Old South* (Athens, Ga., 1958), 63; Cooper, *Elements of Political Economy*, 197; Dumas Malone, *The Public Life of Thomas Cooper, 1783–1839* (New Haven, Conn., 1926), 99–100; Dew, *Restrictive System*, 132; Harvey Toliver Cook, *The Life and Legacy of David Rogerson Williams* (New York, 1916), 78. Rejection of caveat emptor is not incompatible with free-trade theory; see Horwitz, *Transformation of American Law*, 180–182.

[29] Drew R. McCoy, *The Elusive Republic: Political Economy in Jeffersonian America* (New York, 1980), 247.

de Sismondi's political economy, in which he staunchly defended laissez-faire despite worries about the moral and political catastrophe it invited. After reviewing the deepening class conflicts in Europe, he turned to the North: "We have already seen some symptoms of this evil in the United States, while wages are twice or three times as high as in Great Britain, and provisions more abundant; what will be the condition of our manufacturers when these circumstances shall vary – when the population in our manufacturing towns shall become dense and poor?"[30]

Dew avoided extreme ground, conceding that agriculture might deserve a measure of tariff protection and expressing some sympathy for the English Corn Laws. Although Cardozo took a leading part in mobilizing public opinion in Charleston against the protective tariff, he sided with the unionists against nullification, replying forcefully to those who were trying to force a confrontation with the federal government. Cardozo's economic and statistical analyses seemed to demonstrate that the actual costs to the agricultural states fell far short of the figures advanced by the nullifiers. Cardozo considered the tariff a bearable evil that did not justify provocation of a constitutional crisis, and he warned against the negative economic effects of too rapid a reduction in tariff rates. Modern economic theory nonetheless suggests that Calhoun and the nullifiers had a stronger case against northern exploitation than was then appreciated. De Bow, at a lower level of economic reasoning and technical analysis, followed in the laissez-faire tradition, assuring readers that he supported free trade, but he bent far enough before the sugar planters and industrialists to temper his views. Determined to promote southern manufacturing, he kept the pages of *De Bow's Review* open to debate.[31]

Although southern political economists generally supported free trade and restraint in government economic intervention, they offered a tepid defense of southern rights in comparison with that of the constitutional theorists from St. George Tucker and John Taylor of Caroline to John C. Calhoun and Alexander Stephens. Most political economists were political moderates whose economic analyses led them to doubt that federal intervention was ruining the South. The more radical Cooper and De Bow did not rest their disunionism on economic analysis, although they used economic arguments as debaters' points. An irony

---

[30] James Hervey Smith, "Sismondi's Political Economy," in Michael O'Brien, ed., *All Clever Men, Who Make Their Way: Critical Discourse in the Old South* (Columbia, Mo., 1982), 41. For Sismondi's impact on the South as a historian as well as social critic, see Elizabeth Fox-Genovese and Eugene D. Genovese, *The Mind of the Master Class: History and Faith in the Southern Slaveholders' Worldview* (New York, 2005), ch. 9. For contemporary southern views, see S. Teackle Wallis, *Leisure: Moral and Political Economy* (Baltimore, Md., 1859), 18–19; and *SLM*, 28 (1859), 311–313.

[31] Cardozo, "The Tariff: Its True Character and Effects, Practically Illustrated," Appendix II to *Notes on Political Economy*, 157–214; also Leiman, *Cardozo*, 78; Dew, *Restrictive System*, 126–127. See also William Elliott of Beaufort, South Carolina, who effectively attacked the forty-bale theory: *Address to the People of St. Helena Parish* (Charleston, S.C., 1832), 4–7; Charles W. Turner, "Virginia State Agricultural Societies, 1811–1860," *Agricultural History*, 38 (1964), 169. De Bow, "Notes on Political Economy," *DBR*, 19 (1855), 431.

from the politically moderate side: James Walker of Charleston, a prominent
legal scholar, opposed concentration of governmental power because it created artificial social classes. For Walker, the best governments governed least.
He sternly criticized Calhoun's theories of nullification and concurrent majority as impractical, dangerous, and self-defeating. In short, whether radical or
moderate on slavery and secessionism, political economists offered little to the
proslavery argument even in its narrow formulation as a neo-Jeffersonian call
for limited government and free trade. No consistent attitude toward state or
even federal economic intervention emerged from their work, nor did a consistent view of the character and function of the legal system. The exigencies of
slavery compelled them to introduce discrete qualifications into their support
for laissez-faire and limited government. The most radical of the free traders
had to call for firm government intervention to defend the slaveholding interest. From John Taylor at the beginning of the nineteenth century to Louisa
McCord in the waning years of the regime, they understood – even if they did
not wish to discuss – the necessity for shaping the legal system in a special
way. Even those who looked to the free market to guarantee property and
social safety had to advocate stern interference to secure slave property. It is
by no means obvious that they had to do so. They might have tried to restrict
government to the good old Smithian principle of intervention only against
such market obstructions as monopoly, foreign aggression, and crimes against
property. They should have had an easy time since nineteenth-century southern
jurisprudence distinguished master-slave relations from market relations.[32]

Espousal of laissez-faire left room for legislative protection of slave property. Both secessionist and unionist political economists stood well within the
proslavery camp, avoiding offense to the predominant agricultural interest.
They qualified as safe men – safe but uninspiring. They could not bring their
advanced scientific work to bear in a theoretically significant way on the
proslavery argument or its judicial corollary, which called for considerable
regulation of the labor force, free and slave. They thereby rendered themselves
largely beside the point. As political economists slid toward marginality in the
struggle for a slaveholders' worldview, proslavery theorists turned to other dis-
ciplines. In 1847 and 1848 Garnett found it necessary to defend the scientific
character of political economy. He opened lead articles in *Southern Quarterly
Review* by remarking that most intelligent Americans had long considered
political economy as speculative and of little value, but that, fortunately, they
were manifesting a new respect. Maybe so. But reluctant recognition that political economy offered inadequate support for slavery crystallized in the turn to
sociology.

Political Economy, Economics, and Claims to Science

Henry Hughes boldly reduced political economy to "economics," restricting its
laws to a modest place in his comprehensive sociology. He redefined political

---

[32] [James M. Walker], *Tract on Government* (Boston, 1853), 24, 33–40.

economy as the union of two sciences: the one concerned with human existence, the other with its security: The first end of society "is the existence of all." The second is "the progress of all." Society must assure all of "personal subsistence and personal security." He defined the economic system as "the organ of subsistence" and the political system "as the organ of security." The best form of society in which to realize the existence and progress of all "is that in which the societary power is perfectly associated, perfectly adapted, and perfectly regulated." Hughes demanded that the laboring classes, white as well as black, be "warranted" and thereby guaranteed a living. "Everything ought to be stopped until this is done." A caveat: "Everybody ought to work. Labor whether of mind or body, is a duty." That duty had to be enforced at law. State power, which Hughes placed at the center of the social system, must capitalize labor obligations, establish hours of work and rest, set wages, and regulate and supervise the whole of economic life.[33]

Like Hughes, leading participants in southern economic discussions remained chary of claims to science. Fitzhugh constantly ridiculed the scientific pretensions of political economy. The *National Intelligencer* of Washington, D.C., among other important publications, applauded Fitzhugh's *Sociology for the South* for its criticism of Adam Smith's "crudities" and political economy in general. It charged political economists with infidelity, indifference to morals, and "the various socialisms" based on their theories. The prestigious if airy Methodist Protestant Reverend Andrew A. Lipscomb of Alabama wrote, "The relation of wages to capital is indeed a perplexing subject." Even De Bow acknowledged that political economy and political science fell well short of claims to scientific status. With greater reserve, "A South Carolinian," indicting John Stuart Mill and other critics of slavery, separated the science of political economy from the errors and prejudices of those who spoke in its name. To a contributor to *Southern Quarterly Review*, however, Mill announced, "The present free-labour system is a failure."[34]

Holmes paid tribute to the scientific progress of the age, claiming only to warn against its excessive claims and to offer constructive criticisms to a young and struggling discipline: "Notwithstanding these proud achievements, there are urgent questions of the gravest importance, which no light from Physical science will enable us to solve." He did not want his strictures understood as a rejection of the social sciences: "Our sole therapeutics are contained in the Social sciences." Holmes called for a "Social Economics" to focus on industrial developments and, in particular, the condition of the masses. He subsequently

[33] Henry Hughes, *Treatise on Sociology, Theoretical and Practical* (New York, 1968 [1854]), quotes at 47, 61, 81, 95, and see also 106–110. For an excellent critical appraisal of Hughes's thought, see Douglas Ambrose, *Henry Hughes and Proslavery Thought in the Old South* (Baton Rouge, La., 1996).

[34] *National Intelligencer*, Jan. 31, 1855; A. A. Lipscomb, *The Social Spirit of Christianity, Presented in the Form of Essays* (Philadelphia, 1846), 133; De Bow, "Some Thoughts on Political Economy and Government," *DBR*, 9 (1850), 257; A South Carolinian, "Slavery and Political Economy," *DBR*, 21 (1856), 332–335, 339–340; "Is Southern Civilization Worth Preserving?" *SQR*, n.s. 3 (1851), 222.

charged that political economy had failed to solve the problems of capitalist development, most notably, the "social question"; and that the squabbling of its contending schools undermined its pretensions to science. Holmes stressed the inability of political economists to agree on definitions of labor, capital, value, and other terms. He distinguished between political economy as doctrinal support for the discretely defensible economic policies of laissez-faire and political economy as a fatal foundation for a theory of government and society. Like science in general, political economy led men toward the false hope that technology and money-making could sustain both their bodies and their souls. A furious Louisa McCord read Holmes as trashing her revered discipline and went straight to her polemical hatchet, raining down blows on poor Holmes, who, as a southern gentleman, could not return a lady's abuse. Holmes received implicit support from a surprising quarter when George Tucker sadly found "no principle of moment in this science" on which men entirely agreed, and when he criticized those who treated political economy "as if it were a mathematical instead of a moral science."[35]

Yet political economists performed yeoman service for the proslavery argument. They lent a curious kind of support to the commonplace notion that the slaveholders alone protected blacks from the extermination that awaited them if emancipated and thrown into marketplace competition. George Tucker, who quietly rejected racism and thought blacks capable of progress, expected the eventual demise of slavery but also a general immiseration of labor in the process of capital accumulation and economic development, with dreadful consequences for the emancipated. His culturally deprived blacks would fare no better than Louisa McCord's genetically inferior blacks. Cardozo, too, thought that only disaster awaited blacks who entered the labor market without white

[35] [George Frederick Holmes], "On the Importance of the Social Sciences in the Present Day," *SLM*, 15 (1849), 77–80, quotes at 78; Holmes, "Capital and Labor," *DBR*, 22 (1857), 249–265; Holmes, "Slavery and Freedom," *SQR*, 1 (1856), 62–95; [L. S. McCord], "Slavery and Political Economy," *DBR*, 21 (1856), 331–349. For Holmes's writhing over how to respond to McCord, see G. F. Holmes to J. H. Thornwell, Dec. 1, 1856, in Thornwell Papers at the University of South Carolina. See the fine study of Holmes thought: Neal C. Gillespie, *The Collapse of Orthodoxy: The Intellectual Ordeal of George Frederick Holmes* (Charlottesville, Va., 1972), 62–95, 108–109, 158–161. Holmes and the McCords had been friends when he lived in South Carolina; see Tucker, *Political Economy for the People*, iii, 79–82, 159; George Tucker, *The Laws of Wages, Profits and Rent, Investigated* (Philadelphia, 1837), 46–50.

In 1828, Charleston's *Southern Review*, foreshadowing Holmes's impatience with political economy's inability to settle on firm definitions for its central terms precisely, expressed doubt that it could ever be scientific or even coherent: "Lectures on the Elements of Political Economy. By Thomas Cooper," *SR*, 1 (1828), 192–219. Similarly, a review of Joseph Kent's *Commentaries on American Law*, 4 vols., 2nd ed. (New York, 1832), disputed the notion that politics could be made scientific: *SR*, 1 (1828), 72–113. M. R. H. Garnett defended the claims of political economy to being a science, but he too acknowledged the difficulties of defining its elements: "The Distribution of Wealth," *SQR*, 11 (1847), 1–2. For the conflict between commitments to science and ideology, see also William M. Mathew, *Edmund Ruffin and the Crisis of Slavery in the Old South: The Failure of Agricultural Reform* (Athens, Ga., 1988), 60–63, a valuable book marred by Mathew's accusation of bad faith, indeed of hypocrisy, in Ruffin's confrontation with these issues.

protection. McCord and De Bow, preferring to stand pat, ignored the implications of Tucker's reasoning. Fitzhugh and Holmes looked to the strengthening of municipal law to extend slavery and thereby protect blacks and all laboring classes from the exploitation of the marketplace. Paul Conkin observes of Tucker's view that economic development would eventually eliminate slavery by driving the price of free labor down to rock bottom: "Surely, no one ever offered a gloomier reason for eventual emancipation."[36]

Typically, the southern political economists who followed Ricardo or such anti-Ricardians as Lauderdale and Malthus wasted little time on the poor, the unemployed, or other casualties of industrialization, although they worried about a revolutionary response from the laboring classes. In the North, Wayland, acknowledging that poverty and misery might spark lower-class insurrections, remained confident that the market would guarantee a decent living to those willing to work. Meanwhile, he depicted the effects of the laws of wages and population as often "painful to contemplate." Contrasting America with Ireland, he hoped that the abundance of land would stave off immiseration. Southern political economists expressed sympathy for the plight of those who lived under the threat of misery and starvation but denied that much could be done. Tucker and Cardozo said little. Others said more but proved less consistent. Cooper's sympathy for laborers might have been expected, for he had been a social and political radical in his younger days in England and America. Even later as a proslavery disunionist, he opposed legal restraints on trade unions and called for laws to balance the power of the capitalists. Basically, he modified his laissez-faire stance by supporting legal intervention to preclude unfair advantages to either labor or capital.[37]

Others drew on their commitment to slavery and attendant critique of labor conditions in free labor societies. In implicit agreement with Hughes, De Bow wrote that all societies have "an obligation to provide for the labouring classes." De Bow opposed trade unions and government intervention in the economy but pleaded for aid to the needy: "The poor must be fed, the miserable must be relieved or humanity ceases to perform her noble mission." Untouched by Malthusian population theory, he implicitly lent support to opponents of political economy who called for legal protection of the poor, even if it entailed their quasi-enslavement. But then, De Bow, although an advocate of laissez-faire, limited government, and the market, admired and published the work of Fitzhugh, Holmes, and others, who hated all of them. Few Southerners adopted the harsh attitudes toward the poor that the new political economy encouraged. Poor laws and workhouses, Nathaniel Beverley Tucker said, were admissions that the right to property must give way when it "comes into collision with the higher right of life."[38]

[36] Conkin, *Prophets of Prosperity*, 161.
[37] Wayland, *Political Economy*, 127, 301, 311–313; Cooper, *Elements of Political Economy*, 102–103; Dorfman, *Economic Mind*, 2:950; Conkin, *Prophets of Prosperity*, 146.
[38] De Bow, *Industrial Resources*, 332, 387–388; [Nathaniel Beverley Tucker], "The Present State of Europe," *SQR*, 16 (1850), 289; Gail S. Murray, "Poverty and Its Relief in the Antebellum

Most southern political economists rejected or ignored Slavery in the Abstract, but they contributed to it through the introduction of Malthusian population theory at a time when Malthus was coming under widespread, if not always coherent, assault in the North. J. J. Spengler concludes his illuminating historical study of population theory: "Thus by the eve of the Civil War Malthus' doctrines had been woven and integrated into a perfect theoretical defense of slavery." Spengler notes that Tucker, after rejecting Malthus, adopted a Malthusian standpoint, concluding that free labor would eventually become cheaper than slave and thereby compel emancipation. Spengler also notes that many southern writers – Cooper, Dew, Edmund Ruffin, Hammond, Edward Bryan, Mathew Estes – turned Tucker's argument around. Although some believed slave labor cheaper than free and others the reverse, they agreed that slavery protected society against the projected Malthusian subsistence crisis by checking population growth relative to food supply. Spengler aptly paraphrased diverse southern writers: "Under slavery the increase of the blacks was controlled by whites who were driven by pride to control their own numbers. Where free labor prevailed, the unbridled fertility of a prideless proletariat insured over-population and mass poverty and possibly social strife." Spengler's conclusion of a "perfect" defense of slavery does not follow, and it is startling to find so able a man end with the economic ideas of Fitzhugh, who cast anathema on the whole of political economy. Nothing so clearly indicates the impasse at which southern political economy – Malthus or no – had arrived. For no matter how clever pro-Malthusian political economists were as propagandists, they could neither escape the logic of Tucker's projection of an eventual extinction of slavery nor escape the other difficulties that Malthusianism introduced into the defense of slavery.[39]

South: Perceptions and Realities in Three Selected Cities, Charleston, Nashville, and New Orleans" (Ph.D. diss., Memphis State University, 1991), 286–287. Only a few southern cities – Charleston, Savannah, Norfolk, Richmond, New Orleans – built almshouses: Murray, "Poverty and Its Relief," 158, 166. Those who preferred classical to Christian formulations could turn to Cicero: "There is no such thing as private ownership established by nature.... Property becomes private, either through long occupancy or through conquest." Cicero, *De Officiis*, tr. Walter Miller (Cambridge: LCL, 1975), Bk. 1:7.

[39] J. J. Spengler, "Malthusianism and Debate on Slavery," *South Atlantic Quarterly*, 34 (1935), 179–189, quotes at 189, 185; J. C. Hite and E. J. Hall, "The Reactionary Evolution of Economic Thought in Antebellum Virginia," *Virginia Magazine of History and Biography*, 80 (1972), 476–488. Hite and Hall begin with the sound insight that the Virginians could not swallow liberal political economy, but they trip with untenable readings of the texts. For a strong defense of slavery from Malthusian premises, see R. E. C. [Cochrane], "The Problem of Free Society – Part One," *SLM*, 26 (1858), 401–418, and "Part Three," *SLM*, 27 (1858), 81–94, esp. 85–86.

"Luxury" presented an important related issue, which we must bypass here. For arresting studies, see John Sekora, *Luxury: The Concept in Western Thought, Eden to Smollett* (Baltimore, Md., 1977). "Principles of Christian Economy," *DD*, 1:1, 7, 11, 23–24; also, Kenneth M. Startup, *The Root of All Evil: The Protestant Clergy and the Economic Mind of the Old South* (Athens, Ga., 1997), 57–63 – and see this book for a thoughtful, alternative view of the problems discussed here.

Cooper and Dew considered industrial development inevitable, but the "Malthusian" defense of slavery made sense on the assumption of a static economy that inhibited industrialization and no sense on the Ricardian "stationary state" of mature industrialization. That static economy projected slavery as a barrier to the generation of a self-expanding labor force of blacks and to the entrance of unskilled whites into the labor market. No southern political economist proceeded on that assumption, although it remained implicit in attempts to apply Malthusian reasoning. Hammond, who used Malthusian arguments to taunt the abolitionists with the deepening social crisis of the free-labor system, choked on their implications for the South. He understood, better than most, that without economic diversification the South would be doomed with or without a Malthusian crisis. Either way, it would lack the economic, political, and military wherewithal to hold its own in an increasingly hostile world. The argument, even in Spengler's careful reading, ended with Fitzhugh. Hammond and others conversant with political economy based their defense of slavery essentially on social philosophy and sociology. Fitzhugh understood that slavery's survival required conversion of the capitalist world to some form of personally dependent labor and the destruction of the world market and the economic theory based on it.[40]

The appeal to Malthusianism had other drawbacks. It assumed a South without paupers, yet southern writers urged economic diversification to absorb the landless and bare-subsistence whites. Polemicists blithely assumed that masters could, should, and would restrict slave reproduction in the social interest. How and why? Masters encouraged "marriages" among their slaves. They deeply resented the charge of deliberate slave-breeding by other than generally respectable methods designed to encourage a stable family life. They encouraged early "marriages" among their slaves for two reasons apart from Christian conscience: to promote social stability and to generate capital gains. Individual slaveholders who faced a glut in the cotton or slave market sensibly tried to increase volume to offset a decline in price. During depressed times, reductions in cotton acreage reduced cash outlay for food, but that adjustment hardly discouraged slave reproduction since it lowered the cost of rearing. And slaveholders generally believed that such interference in the life of the quarters produced fierce reactions from the slaves and disrupted plantation order and discipline.

The contention that slavery checked the growth of the black population implied massive state intervention in the master-slave relation. No responsible political economist joined Hughes in countenancing such intervention. Most condemned it. The argument, then, was a propaganda ploy, not a

[40] See Eugene D. Genovese, *The Slaveholders' Dilemma: Freedom and Progress in Southern Conservative Thought, 1820–1860* (Columbia, S.C., 1991), ch. 3; Drew Gilpin Faust, *James Henry Hammond and the Old South* (Baton Rouge, La., 1982); and, generally, E. Cocks, "The Malthusian Theory in Pre-Civil War America," *Population Studies*, 20 (1966–1967), 354–358. Malthus bore no responsibility for the "Malthusian" defense of slavery.

serious attempt to ground the defense of slavery in political economy. For good measure, if advanced seriously, it opened a broadside against the southern legal system, which was straining to protect the master-slave relation against state interference. Even those bold enough to raise these questions – Fitzhugh, Holmes, Hughes, Hammond, Simms – had to tread carefully. Malthusian theory provided a gloss on their basic notion that the welfare of the masses everywhere had to be strictly regulated. Whether bluntly with Fitzhugh, apologetically with Holmes, or ambiguously with others, proslavery theorists used Malthus as a weapon against both free-labor society and the science of political economy.

Southern political economists said next to nothing about the legal or social conditions of the laborers closest to home – the slaves. They trumpeted the slaves' legal protections, referring to provisions of the slave codes and to court decisions that prohibited cruelty and set minimum guidelines for treatment. Rarely did they venture beyond the slave standard of comfort relative to that of laboring classes elsewhere. They contrasted the comfort of slaves to that of free blacks, especially those in the North, but said little about the comfort of southern poor whites. Religious leaders and prominent jurists made futile efforts to secure legislation to protect slave families, but political economists remained quiet. Tucker did speak out against laws that restricted or prohibited emancipation. McCord and De Bow spoke out too, but they opposed legal restrictions on the power of the masters. Neither McCord nor De Bow supported proposals to tie the slaves to the land or render them inalienable for debt. Neither invoked economic principles to insist that the state had no right to interfere with slave property. Rather, each noted in a somewhat different way that the welfare of the slaves depended on their masters, and that state interference would do more harm than good. Although compatible with a laissez-faire ideology stretched to include property in man, their views placed the master-slave relation outside the purview of economic discourse. Political economy had little to say about the legal aspects of the social conditions of the slaves. It tried to view slaves – much as it viewed free laborers – as objects in the market – but it constantly ran up against the peculiarities of their anomalous status as both persons and property. It could provide guidance to the courts in matters of a strictly business nature but proved helpless in matters that transcended business relations among whites. Since the most critical problems of the master-slave relation transcended matters of business, political economists in effect announced that they had little to offer the legal system at its most exposed and vulnerable point. In jurisprudence, social theory, and socioeconomic policy, they created a void that new social theorists rushed to fill.[41]

Philosophy and Policy

In general, Southerners, clerical and lay, rejected the philosophical foundations of Manchesterian political economy while promoting Manchesterian

[41] George Tucker, *Political Economy for the People*, 83–93; Skipper, *De Bow*, 95.

laissez-faire economic policies. Frederick A. Porcher of South Carolina turned on Adam Smith for initiating a new and destructive philosophy of selfishness and exploitation and a political economy that has "caused more desolation to the heart of humanity than all other systems of philosophy together." The philosophy that sanctioned the enclosures, the expropriation of the yeomanry, and the immiseration of the laboring classes was "the offspring of the devil." Porcher focused not on the greed of capitalists but on the objective workings of capitalism's concentration of capital in a small class. He saw concentration as intrinsic to an economic system that required periodic financial panics and depressions to purge itself. Notwithstanding sympathy for protests against government's unwillingness or inability to prevent mass immiseration, he criticized radical movements like Chartism for threatening anarchy. Porcher expressed confidence in the South's alternative but also expressed forebodings: "We whose destinies place us rather on the outskirts of the social system of Christendom and are not yet engulphed in the great maelstrom caused by the workings of political philosophy, may view calmly the condition of the rest of the world." That condition consisted primarily of making nations and capitalists richer while making the laboring classes poorer. Grimly acknowledging that Manchesterian political economy was sweeping all before it, Porcher remarked caustically – as Holmes had done – that, for all its pretensions to science, its devotees could not agree on a definition of terms or distinguish rent from profit. And more: "The whole fabric of [southern] society is based upon slave institutions, and yet our conventional language is drawn from scenes totally at variance with those which lie about us." In consequence: "The philosophy of the North is a dead letter to us. The doctrines of political economy are not true here."[42]

In 1847, Garnett judged the production and amount of wealth less important to a nation than its distribution among classes. He assailed the socialistic notion, attributed to Adam Smith, that profits are a deduction from wages and that capitalists and laborers faced each other in fundamental antagonism. Since, according to that theory, the level of subsistence, which determines wages, is determined culturally rather than absolutely, he dismissed the reasoning as circular. Yet, invoking Roman experience, he warned of the tendency of the rich to oppress the poor and justified political intervention to curb it. Thus, staunch proslavery men, no matter how much attached to free-trade economics,

---

[42] F. A. Porcher, "Conflict of Labour and Capital," *RM*, 3 (1858), 289–298, quotes at 289, 290; F. A. Porcher, "Southern and Northern Civilization Contrasted," *RM*, 1 (1857), 100, 107; Hughes, "Reopening of the African Slave Trade" in Stanford M. Lyman, ed., *Selected Writings of Henry Hughes: Antebellum Southerner, Slavocrat, Sociologist* (Jackson, Miss., 1985), 73–101, especially 82–83. For analyses of the work of Porcher and Hughes, see Charles J. Holden, *In the Great Maelstrom: Conservatives in Post-Civil War South Carolina* (Columbia, S.C., 2002), 22–29, and Ambrose, *Henry Hughes*, 146–147. For a dissection of the contradiction between Dabney's adherence to Manchesterian economics and his defense of slavery and critique of capitalism, see Andrew E. Roesell, "The Hobbesian Transformation of America, as Seen through the Eyes of Three Southern Conservatives (John C. Calhoun, Robert L. Dabney, and David Davidson)" (M.S. thesis, University of Mississippi, 1997), 50–73.

recoiled from the pontification of Francis Lieber: "Free trade is nothing more than the Christian's peace and good will toward men." To be sure, encomia for laissez-faire continued whenever southern spokesmen felt it necessary to defend the cotton interest. As South Carolina's Commissioner to the Universal Exhibition at Paris in 1857, William Elliott praised free trade in cotton as the means to peace, prosperity, and "all the inestimable blessings of civilization" for all of the world's peoples. The more common view in the South nonetheless asserted the contrary. An article on labor in *Southern Quarterly Review* cited the horrible conditions in free-labor countries, concluding, "The principles of Christianity are precisely opposed to the principles of our industrial system." Shortly thereafter the editors of *Southern Quarterly Review*, announcing that they intended to spend more time on the slavery question, pilloried Europe's free-labor countries for brutal treatment of the peasants and praised slavery for assuring the laborer of a fair share of the returns from production.[43]

The increasingly loud denunciation of the treatment of peasants and workers in free-market societies had to be squared not only with support for free-trade economics and opposition to tariffs but also with a property holder's aversion to autonomous movements of the laboring classes. Dew repeatedly warned that the working class – the big loser in marketplace struggles – would resort to violence to protect itself. Hughes, too, thought the free-labor system inherently prone to provoke rebellion by driving the price of labor to bare subsistence. In effect, Porcher cried that only southern society protected its laboring class against capitalist exploitation and, simultaneously, against its own violent and nihilistic tendencies.

During the War, Bishop Stephen Elliott of the Episcopal Church of Georgia revealed his disenchantment with free-trade policy, protesting that it condemned Southerners to be hewers of wood and drawers of water for the North. The South lacked the resources to defend itself: "The principles of unrestricted commerce are abstractly true, but they cannot be put into practice without peril, so long as nation will make war upon nation, and people will rise up against people." The Presbyterian Reverend Joel W. Tucker of Fayetteville, North Carolina, condemned market mentality. He denounced Jacob for Esau's having sold himself for a mess of pottage. "If it be true that in trade everything is worth what it will bring in market, then there is not such thing as extortion." The Golden Rule, not "the fluctuating market," provided the standard for men to buy and sell. If immutable laws of trade, specifically the law of supply and demand, regulated price, a man in trade would lose all moral agency: "He would be irresponsible. There could be no more morality in buying and selling

---

43 "M. R. H. G" [Garnett], "Distribution of Wealth," *SQR* 11 (1847), 2–3, 10, 15, 28, 32; "Labor," *SQR* 11 (1847), 77–89, quote from 85; Daniel C. Gilmore, ed., *The Miscellaneous Writings of Francis Lieber*, 2 vols. (Philadelphia, Pa., 1881), 1:292; *SQR*, 11 (1847), no. 22, i–xii; William Elliott, *Address to the Imperial and Central Agricultural Society of France* (Columbia, S.C., 1855), 10. For earlier criticism of Adam Smith for propagating a labor theory of value, see *SR*, 8 (1832), 496.

than in the flow of the river, or the fall of an earthquake. Virtue and vice, in commercial and mercantile matters would be impossible." Wages could not be left to supply and demand, for, then, the families of workingmen would risk starvation. "This sin is punished by the conflict it produces between different classes of society."[44]

Bifurcation of the Law

The contradiction between the commitment to science and the commitment to slavery appeared dramatically in the proslavery attitude toward the law. During the first half of the nineteenth century the legal profession and the as-yet unorganized economics profession struggled to take scientific ground. Many political economists, as well as their social critics, had been trained at law. George Tucker, a notably successful lawyer, paid tribute to the legal profession: "The profession of the law, in countries where the knowledge of civil and political rights is much cultivated, especially fits men for public employments." The law instilled high moral values: "In the higher departments of the profession, no class of men have a more exalted sense of honor, or the obligation of conscience."[45]

Appeals to honor, morals, and justice did not impel southern political economists to support traditional notions of just price and equity. To the contrary, most celebrated slavery as the unification of labor and capital. Like other proslavery theorists, they favored a will theory of contract and the further separation of contract law from extra-market moral considerations. However paternalistic the master-slave relation, the slave economy had proven preeminently commercial throughout world history. The South produced cotton and other exportable commodities that impelled the rise of an American national economy. Earlier than other American producers and despite particular antagonisms, southern planters and the merchants allied to them needed the kind of reliable and uniform pricing system that the world market offered. They appreciated the uses of contract to protect them against sudden changes within that dynamic system of uniform pricing. At the least, they showed little inclination to support the introjection of ethical and other noneconomic considerations into the pricing of commodities. Their commitment to international free trade biased them toward laissez-faire in general.[46]

The growth of a slave society in the midst of a rapidly expanding transatlantic capitalist world compelled a bifurcation of southern law – as if to render economic relations unto Caesar and social relations unto God. Mark Tushnet

---

[44] Stephen Elliott, *"Samson's Riddle": A Sermon Preached in Christ Church, Savannah* (Macon, Ga., 1863), 19–21, quote at 20; Joel W. Tucker, *The Guilt and Punishment of Extortion: A Sermon* (Fayetteville, N.C., 1862), 5–6, 7, 12.

[45] Perry Miller, *The Life of the Mind in America from the Revolution to the Civil War* (New York, 1965), 156–164; Tucker, *Political Economy for the People*, 121, 122.

[46] Douglass C. North, *The Economic Growth of the United States, 1790–1860* (New York, 1966), remains a succinct and lucid discussion of the southern export sector in the national economy.

demonstrates in his seminal *The American Law of Slavery* that jurists struggled mightily to isolate the master-slave relation from common-law considerations of contracts and torts, which concerned relations among the free whites.
They failed, or rather, scored limited success that exposed and exacerbated the
deep contradictions within the social order. The attempt to make the southern
legal system conform to a slave society in but not of a transatlantic capitalism
occurred during the first half of the nineteenth century when the role of the legal
system emerged as a central issue in American economic development and party
politics. During the late eighteenth and early nineteenth centuries the full significance of slavery for southern society remained hidden. The southern economy,
like the northern, remained predominantly agricultural with an export sector
controlled by northern merchants, factors, and bankers. Southern jurisprudence attempted to remove slavery from the market relations that constituted
the point at which law and political economy intersected. Slavery, the dominant
form of labor, supposedly belonged to domestic relations. Alas, reality proved
messier than myth. The myth nonetheless approximated reality close enough
to make the theoretical distinction plausible and to permit southern thinkers
considerable latitude to follow the advanced theoretical developments without
directly calling into question the social relations on which their society rested.
Their work did not depart radically from that of their northern colleagues, who
were also operating within the assumptions of merchant capital and not yet
within the assumptions of industrial capital and who also harbored deep but
different qualms about the labor question.[47]

No more in the North than in the South did law and political economy
proceed in tandem. Yet during the first third of the nineteenth century, notions
of the moral dimensions of legal relations gave way to an impersonal and
ultimately formalistic understanding of the law. Once thought of as protective,
regulatory, paternalistic, and as a paramount expression of the moral sense of
the community, law came to be valued for its facilitation of individual desires
and recognition of the exigencies of economic power. The 1820s constituted
a watershed in the emergence of a wage-labor force and factory production in
New England. However much northern law and political economy, like their
southern counterparts, tried to contain the labor question within the vestiges
of paternalism and community ethos, the rise of industrial capitalism, with
its inevitable corollary of landless wage-laborers, propelled northern thinkers
down new paths. Southern jurists faced the implications of a bifurcated legal
system. Southern law developed in response to the challenge posed by the dual
character of the slave as chattel and person, and it came to recognize that that
dual character of the slave as chattel had to be accepted notwithstanding legal
fictions. By the 1820s, especially in response to growing sophistication in the
formulation of the laws of the market and to the growing practice of hiring out

---

[47] See especially Tushnet, *American Law of Slavery*; also Fox-Genovese and Genovese, *Fruits of
Merchant Capital*, 337–387.

slaves, the question of the agency of slaves and the liability of masters became more common, complex, and acute.[48]

Planters talked a good deal about laissez-faire and limited government but usually meant little more than a revenue tariff and low taxes. When they needed protection at law, they expected to get it. As debtors, they generally approved of usury laws designed to keep interest rates low. *De Bow's Review* published articles on an increasingly hot topic. M. C. Givens tried to ground support for usury laws in economic theory, arguing that the formation of the interest rate constituted an exception to the laws of supply and demand. Proponents of usury laws turned to the Bible to bolster their case. For "An Alabaman," biblical prohibitions hurt only commerce that encouraged greed and moral decadence. Dew chided the devil for quoting Scriptures. Condemning "a big-oted interpretation of a municipal provision in the Jewish Code," he announced that Moses and Jesus had actually defended the taking of interest: "'Thou shalt not lend,' says the law of Moses 'upon usury to thy brother.'" Dew interpreted the passage as extending only to Jews, noting that ancient Israel understood the Mosaic Law as justifying the taking of interest from Gentiles. Subsequently, the Christian Church condemned usury but during the Middle Ages, as Dew knew, its scholastic doctors distinguished between usury as interest per se and usury as extortion. Hugh Legaré, opposing government intervention in economic life, cited the Athenian experience to attack the doctrine of "eminent domain," the abuse of which, he feared, was being embraced by the American people.[49]

From western Virginia came strong Presbyterian voices: George Junkin appealed for a proper understanding of ancient Jewish law to distinguish between just interest and interest-taking that violated the Golden Rule and oppressed those in need. He rejected American usury laws as self-defeating economic nonsense. Henry Ruffner joined in the rejection of usury laws in his course on political economy at Washington College. No political economist of note supported the anti-usury laws. Dew, Tucker, Cardozo, De Bow, and others tried to convince planters and farmers that such laws were not enforceable nor in debtors' long-term interest. Tucker criticized the laws in his classroom at the University of Virginia, as Dew did at the College of William and Mary. Tucker softened the blow by saying that repeal of the usury laws – like the

---

[48] On the shift in the law, see Horwitz, *Transformation of American Law*; on the emergence of a wage-labor force in New England, see K. L. Sokoloff, "Industrialization and the Growth of the Manufacturing Sector in the Northeast, 1820–1850" (Ph.D. diss., Harvard University, 1982). Jonathan D. Martin, *Slave Hiring in the American South* (Cambridge, Mass., 2004).

[49] M. C. Givens, "Should Our Usury Laws Be Repealed?" *DBR*, 26 (1859), 445–447; "Usury Laws," *DBR*, 28 (1860), 327–329; T. R. Dew, *Essay on the Interest of Money and the Policy of Laws against Usury* (Shellbanks, Va., 1834), 22; Jacob Neusner, *Economics of the Mishnah* (London, 1999), 99–102; "Public Economy of Athens," in *HLW*, 2:5016–5017. Joseph A. Schumpeter, *History of Economic Analysis*, ed. Elizabeth Boody Schumpeter (New York, 1954), 103–105, 328. Also John T. Noonan, *The Scholastic Analysis of Usury* (Cambridge, Mass., 1957).

laws themselves – would have little effect since the market determined interest rates. And indeed, Harriet Martineau reported in the 1830s that moneylenders in Mobile were getting twice the legal eight percent rate of interest. Two decades later James Stirling, an acute Englishman, observed with dismay that Kentucky's usury laws directed capital into the Chicago market. Accordingly, the governor of Louisiana vetoed a planter-supported usury bill. Once again, political economy had little to offer those slaveholders who sought a strong legal hand to protect their interests.[50]

Caveat emptor presented another difficulty for those who wished to have both slavery and the free market. Concern about the penetration of bourgeois values surfaced in southern resistance to the principle of caveat emptor, which was sweeping the North. Here too, southern jurists displayed a penchant for falling back on civil law as well as common-law equity in defense of the slaveholders' interests. Notwithstanding the obvious Latinity of the term "caveat emptor," neither the substance nor the phrase itself can be traced to Roman law or to an earlier period than the commercial revolution of the sixteenth century. No Roman or medieval writer used the term, the content of which challenged the very spirit of the civil law. It emerged on common-law foundations with the early appearance of laissez-faire economic thought. Its greatest triumph came in the northern United States during the first half of the nineteenth century. Louisiana, a bastion of civil law, and South Carolina, the cockpit of proslavery ideology, resisted caveat emptor. The courts proved solicitous of the concerns of slave buyers, although the slave-exporting states made efforts to balance them against the concerns of slave sellers. To protect slave buyers Louisiana appealed to the Roman concept of *redhibitia* (cancellation of slave sales due to hidden defects) and incorporated the Roman system of implicit warranty intact into its civil law. In South Carolina, theorists and judges condemned caveat emptor as a "disgrace." Thomas Cooper and John Belton O'Neall, usually at odds on politics and social policy, advocated protection for the buyer.[51]

---

[50] See Junkin, *Sabbatismos*, 74–75; James S. Richeson, "Course of Lectures Delivered on Political Economy by Henry Ruffner," 64, in Henry Ruffner Papers; Tucker, *Wages, Profits and Rent*, 83–91; also Dorfman, *Economic Mind*, 2:856–857 (on Cardozo); De Bow invoked the Parable of the Talents (Matt. 25:14–30) to undermine opponents' appeals to the Bible: "Usury Laws and the Value of Money," *DBR*, 7 (1849), 123–128, also *DBR*, 28 (1860), 612; Martineau, *Society in America*, 3 vols. (New York, 1834), 2:65–66; James Stirling, *Letters from the Slave States* (New York, 1969 [1837]), 44–45; Richard Holcombe Kilbourne, Jr., *Louisiana Commercial Law: The Antebellum Period* (Baton Rouge, La., 1980), 50.

[51] Hamilton, "Ancient Maxim of Caveat Emptor," 1156–1157, 1178, 1183; Andrew Fede, "Legal Protection for Slave Buyers in the U.S. South: A Caveat Concerning Caveat Emptor," *American Journal of Legal History*, 31 (1987), 354–358; Judith K. Schafer, "Guaranteed against the Vices and Maladies Prescribed by Law: Consumer Protection, the Law of Slave Sales, and the Supreme Court in Antebellum Louisiana," *American Journal of Legal History*, 31 (1987), 308–309; Dorfman, Introduction to Thomas Cooper, *Lectures on Political Economy*, 6; Belton O'Neall, *Biographical Sketches of the Bench and Bar of South Carolina*, 2 vols. (Spartanburg, S.C., 1975 [1859]), 1:26; Lawrence M. Friedman, *A History of American Law* (New York, 1973), 232–235. For the reaction against caveat emptor in the North, see Horwitz, *Transformation*

Cooper, in annotating Justinian's *Institutes*, advanced the sellers' knowledge of the hidden defects of a slave as an example of the illegitimacy of the principle of caveat emptor. Commitment to the values of slave society led at least some political economists to persist in eighteenth-century attitudes longer than their northern colleagues. When Cooper opposed caveat emptor in 1818, he did not depart radically from views that prevailed in North or South. When he did so again in 1841, he opposed dominant northern views and praised the South Carolina bench for having "revolted" at the doctrine. Cooper, who prided himself on his opposition to medieval superstitions, reached back to medieval precedent, for caveat emptor did not qualify as a respectable principle during the Middle Ages.[52]

Southern hostility to bourgeois values did not imply hostility to commerce, which, Hugh Legaré said, had everywhere proven "a mighty humanizer" that dissolved class rigidities and prevented ossification of the power of old families. Nathaniel Beverley Tucker ridiculed those who derided commerce, merchants, and the credit system. Merchants, he argued, were the staunchest defenders of property rights and, as such, natural allies of slaveholders. Following Thomas Carlyle, De Bow pronounced commerce, not cotton, king. Southerners generally lauded commerce as the natural handmaiden of agriculture and by no means assailed commercial values per se. Hughes took a positive view of the commercial revolution and of merchants, who represented a new idea of government and a new ruling class. James Chesnut declared that slavery provided the "chief earthly impulse" to commerce, culture, and Christianity, and Augusta Jane Evans had a character in *Macaria* casually refer to "commerce and agriculture" as the foundation of southern self-reliance. A student at Washington College paraphrased Henry Ruffner as saying, "It was intended by the Creator that different nations should have interchange of commerce." But Southerners, especially divines, espied vicious tendencies in commerce, which had to be curbed. The Presbyterian Reverend Thomas Smyth, preaching in Charleston, devoted much time to a Christian defense of commerce as a civilizing force, while he called on merchants to repel the rapacious spirit that commerce – if uninformed by Christian ethics – could breed. The Episcopal Reverend Jasper Adams, president of the College of Charleston, added a

---

of American Law, 180–181, 198–199. Southern courts rejected caveat emptor in slave sales, supporting those who demanded rescission of sale when a slave proved defective: William W. Fisher, III, "Ideology and Imagery in the Law of Slavery," *Chicago-Kent Law Review*, 68 (1993), 1051–1052. During the nineteenth century North and South Carolina were the only slave states to legislate protection of purchasers of slaves through implied warranties. Even civil-law Louisiana favored buyers, although favoritism ebbed after 1840: Thomas D. Morris, *Southern Slavery and the Law, 1619–1860* (Chapel Hill, N.C., 1996), 104–113.

[52] Thomas Cooper, ed., *Institutes of Justinian, with Notes* (Philadelphia, Pa., 1812), 608, 610–611; also Dorfman, Introduction to Cooper, *Elements of Political Economy*. Walton H. Hamilton, "The Ancient Maxim Caveat Emptor," *Yale Law Journal*, 40 (1931), 1136–1138, 59–62. Caveat emptor ("let the buyer beware") places the burden on the buyer rather than the seller if the merchandise is deficient, except in cases of fraud.

cautionary note, citing Cicero's approval of large-scale commerce but contempt for petty trading.[53]

Qualms accompanied accolades. In the 1830s George Tucker moaned that the prospect of high tobacco profits had led Virginians to import African slaves: "It is the spirit of commerce, which, in its undistinguishing pursuit of gain, ministers to our vices no less than to our necessary wants." Dew, citing Persia and Egypt, posited as universal law the moral degeneration of barbarian conquerors who established great empires: "A rude, ignorant people, suddenly acquiring immense wealth, are sure to indulge every extravagance and vice; they can only enjoy their possessions as *sensualists* – all self-government is lost – the most shameless extravagance prevails." But Dew, perhaps knowingly, reiterated the position of William Vans Murray of Maryland – Federalist state legislator and diplomat – by denying that luxury derived from honest labor necessarily led to corruption. While a young law student at Middle Temple, Murray wrote *Political Sketches Inscribed to His Excellency John Adams* in praise of representative republican democracy. With it, America could escape from the commonly observed cycle and prevent affluence from generating corruption and decadence. From the beginning, the divines worried about the proclamation of the kingdom of cotton or commerce, and during the War they howled. Bishop Elliott declared on behalf of all denominations, "It is not that cotton is King, but that God has given our statesmen wisdom to use a great advantage aright."[54]

Southern political economists had little to say about the bearing of political economy on problems that slavery created for the judicial system, but they contributed, if indirectly, to the tendency to categorize slave law apart from

---

53 "Constitutional History of Greece," in *HLW*, 1:423; Nathaniel Beverley Tucker, *A Series of Lectures on the Science of Government* (Philadelphia, 1845), 410–411; Henry Hughes, ms. of speech on "The New Governing Class," 1:298; Augusta Jane Evans, *Macaria; Or, Altars of Sacrifice* (Baton Rouge, La., 1992 [1864]), 366; James S. Richeson, "Course of Lectures Delivered on Political Economy by Henry Ruffner," 9, in Ruffner Papers; see in *Works of Thomas Smyth*: "Commercial Benefit of Christianity," 10:449–460; "Design and Motive of Worldly Business," 10:463–481; Jasper Adams, *Elements of Moral Philosophy* (Philadelphia, Pa., 1837), 310.

54 George Tucker, *The Life of Thomas Jefferson*, 2 vols. (London, 1837), 1:6; Dew, *Digest*, 18, 26, 28, 31, 94, 116, 143; Stephen Elliott, *God's Presence in the Confederate States* (Savannah, Ga., 1861), 116; also [Rev.] C. C. Pinckney, *Nebuchadnezzar's Fault and Fall* (Charleston, S.C., 1861), 11 [1861].

Dew developed Edward Gibbon's insight: "Europe," Gibbon wrote, "is secure from any further irruption of Barbarians; since, before they can conquer, they must cease to be barbarous." See *The History of the Decline and Fall of the Roman Empire*, 3 vols., ed. David Womersley (London, 1994), quote at 2:514. [William Vans Murray], *Political Sketches Inscribed to His Exellency John Adams . . . by a Citizen of the United States* (London, 1787), esp. ch. 2; also, Alexander DeConde, "William Vans Murray's Political Sketches: A Defense of the American Experiment," *Journal of American History*, 41 (1955), 623–640, esp. 635–636. See also George Fitzhugh, "The Conservative Principle," *DBR*, 22 (1857), 458; Fitzhugh, "Reaction and the Administration," *DBR*, 25 (1858), 546–547; Fitzhugh, "Private and Public Luxury," *DBR*, 24 (1858), 49–52.

market questions. Thus southern jurists had little incentive to turn to southern political economists for guidance in preference to the more widely published northern. Proceeding – consciously or not – on the assumptions of a bifurcated legal system, southern political economists joined northern colleagues in supporting the modern theory of contract without offending their slaveholding and commercial constituents. And they divided among themselves on the issue that most dangerously threatened the planter-merchant alliance: the relation of federal to state jurisdiction over commercial law. For the merchants typically preferred federal to state courts. Federal courts increasingly supported developmental and pro-mercantile policies, whereas state courts, although not necessarily hostile, proved inconsistent and unreliable.[55]

Since most southern political economists rejected the labor theory of value, they tended toward views closer to Bailey's than to Ricardo's. The implicit shift opened the way to the overthrow of traditional notions of equity and to the enthronement of modern ideas of contract. Southern society required a moral defense of slavery based on a paternalistic rather than a market vision of the proper relation of capital to labor. The shift threatened an ideological debacle.[56]

Even in criminal cases, law and custom favored punishment of slaves by masters. Courts primarily took up cases of murder, arson, assaults on whites, and others not easily dealt with within the slaveholding household. The cases accepted by the courts as within their purview concerned relations between free men. The courts normally followed common-law procedures in cases of contract and tort, although the human nature of slave property constantly introduced theoretical contradictions and practical difficulties. We might therefore expect that those who espoused laissez-faire would have eagerly – if somewhat perversely – applied their favorite doctrine to justify the discretion of the master, so far as consistent with social safety, and to demand that the courts support the force of the market in all cases concerned with economic property. Time after time, however, political economists, like jurists, found that slavery

---

[55] Kilbourne, *Louisiana Commercial Law*. The central ideas of John Taylor of Caroline reverberated with increasing force in the South, although few read Taylor's largely unreadable books, which John Randolph prayed someone would translate into English. For whatever the purely economic arguments in favor of a national commercial law independent of the decisional law of the state courts (see, for example, *Riddle v. Mandeville* and *Bank of the United States v. Weisiger*), the constitutional and political implications looked more and more threatening to the South. See Horwitz, *Transformation of American Law*, 223. *Riddle* and *Weisiger* directly affected the slave states of Virginia and Kentucky, respectively. On the southerners' fear of federal judges, see especially John Taylor, *Construction Construed and Constitutions Vindicated* (Richmond, Va., 1820), and Calhoun, "Discourse of the Constitution," in Ross M. Lence, ed., *Union and Liberty: The Political Philosophy of John C. Calhoun* (Indianapolis, Ind., 1992).

[56] Conkin judges Cooper's reputed Ricardianism "ambivalent and confused": *Prophets of Prosperity*, 115. Conkin's criticism may be sustained by a comparison with Cooper's assertion, "Labour is the main or rather the only source of wealth," with his utilitarian theory of value and his attempt to reconcile his several contradictory formulations: *Lectures on Political Economy*, 37–40, 74–75, 78.

generated insurmountable difficulties. John Taylor of Caroline encountered them early. Property and natural interests, he argued, arise without the aid of municipal law. Indeed, that particular notion of property became the foundation of his political philosophy and political economy and led him to deny that ill-gained property should be considered property at all. He wrote, "*A transfer of property by law is aristocracy, and that aristocracy is a transfer of property by law.*" Since the paper money system Taylor hated was making slaves out of honest producers, the forms of property it generated lacked legitimacy.[57]

Louisa McCord

The ultimate irreconcilability of simultaneous dedication to economic science and to slave society appeared with special clarity in the work of Louisa McCord, whom the leading intellectuals of the South held in high esteem. Editors like De Bow, Simms, and James Henley Thornwell solicited her articles. Nathaniel Beverley Tucker spoke to Simms "in language of the highest compliment" of McCord's article on "The Right to Labor." Simms took her political opinions seriously. Edmund Ruffin visited her, receiving "much kind attention" from "a lady of fine mind & manners, & of no small note as an author." Hammond struck a sour note, although expressing regret for being ungallant. He thought her "Justice and Fraternity" old hat and not much better than stump oratory. Still, his remarks seemed complimentary when laid against his excoriation of an article by her husband on free trade.[58]

The well-read, acute Louisa McCord emerged as a caustic champion of slavery and opponent of the women's rights movement, which she considered a stalking horse for anarchism: "Universal equality! Fraternité extended even to womanhood! And why not? Up for your rights, ladies. What is the worth of a civilization which condemns one half of mankind to Helot submissiveness? Call ye this civilization, with such a stained and blurred blot upon it." With such displays of sarcasm, she joined a growing number of Southerners in repudiating the radical-egalitarian interpretation of the Declaration of Independence. She frankly averred that individuals and even some European nations – not merely the colored races – naturally fell into different stations in life. No man is born

---

[57] See especially T. D. Morris, "'As if the Injury Was Effected by the Natural Elements of Air or Fire': Slave Wrongs and the Liability of Masters," *Law and Society Review*, 16 (1981–1982), 569–599; John Taylor, *An Inquiry into the Principles and Policy of the Government of the United States*, ed. Loren Baritz (Indianapolis, Ind., 1969 [1814]), 103–104, 342.

[58] Nov. 12, 1860, *ERD*, 1:492; J. H. Hammond to W. G. Simms, July 9, 1849, in Mary C. Oliphant et al., eds., *The Letters of William Gilmore Simms*, 6 vols. (Columbia, S.C., 1952–1982), 2:532. Miss I. D. Martin visited the McCord plantation, "Old Lang Syne," in 1845, reporting, "It had been said of Mrs. McCord in her youth, that she had two grand passions – for her father [Langdon Cheves] and her State." "Sketch of Mrs. McCord by Miss I. D. Martin, in Louisa M. Smythe, ed., *For Old Lang Syne: Collected for My Children* (Charleston, S.C., 1900), 13; also, O'Neall, *Bench and Bar of South Carolina*, 2 vols. (Spartanburg, S.C., 1975 [1859]), 2:510.

free, she wrote, and no two individuals have ever been born equal. Slavery in varying degrees and forms existed everywhere: Nature fit individuals, nations, races, and women to labor for and seek the protection of more competent people.[59]

More an economic journalist than a political economist, she brushed off the gloomy projections of Ricardo and Malthus. For her, notwithstanding Carlyle's famous blast, political economy was no dismal science. She drew on ancient history and literature freely but cautioned against becoming imprisoned by them. She scoffed at notions of human perfectibility: "And yet we are of those who see in the present condition of the world, the working up of a new era." She exulted in an age of great advancement propelled by steam power and science and tempered by Christianity: "And yet the world is young!" The age was the greatest so far experienced, and the best was yet to come. The pro-market McCord tried to avoid difficulties by explicitly accepting a bifurcation between political economy (the science of the market) and labor relations (domestic affairs). Although she dismissed the notion that wage-labor constituted white slavery, she accepted some form of personal servitude as ubiquitous in world history. She rejected the doctrine "Right to Labor" because it threw all power to the state: "The individual becomes only the bold beggar, the claimant of governmental protection." So too she rejected the theory of an antagonism between capital and labor, warning that socialist ideas were gaining ground in the form of economic protectionism and assorted isms. Yet even she – at least when polemical purposes required – expressed sympathy for the miserable workers of Great Britain, calling on English ladies to stop worrying about well-cared-for and much-loved black slaves and to devote themselves to the care of their own white laboring poor. Her polemic ranked as standard fare in the propaganda war, but she ignored its implications for the classical political economy or the slave system, both of which she fervently espoused.[60]

McCord's ambiguous defense of slavery brought to the fore the dilemma of political economy in a slave society. Not only did she assault Harriet Beecher Stowe, socialists, abolitionists, and women's rights advocates but she also did not spare such defenders of slavery as Holmes and Fitzhugh, against whom she defended laissez-faire in uncompromising language. Like her hero Frédéric Bastiat, she wanted no government interference in the economy and only those few laws deemed absolutely necessary for social order. McCord commented on Bastiat's work in *Southern Quarterly Review*, especially applauding his book on the inefficacy of protectionism, which she translated into English.

---

[59] L. S. M. [McCord], "Diversity of the Races; Its Bearing upon Negro Slavery," *SQR*, 3 (1851), 416–417; McCord, "Enfranchisement of Women" in Richard C. Lounsbury, ed., *Louisa S. McCord: Political and Social Essays* (Charlottesville, Va., 1995), quoted at 106.

[60] L. S. M. [McCord], "Justice and Fraternity," *SQR*, 15 (1849), 356–374, quotes at 356, 357; L. S. M. [McCord], "Right to Labor," *SQR*, 16 (1849), 138–160; L. S. M. [McCord], "Carey on the Slave Trade," *SQR*, 9 (1854), 177; Lounsbury, ed., *McCord: Political and Social Essays*, 70, 88–89, 239–241, 377.

Her accolades notwithstanding, she implicitly contradicted Bastiat on a number of questions, most notably slavery, which Bastiat condemned.[61]

At first glance, McCord's defense of slavery appears to rest on no more than her racism, which ranked as extreme even in the Old South. She supported the pseudo-scientific theories of Samuel George Morton and Josiah Nott, who taught that blacks constituted a separate and inferior species. Her husband, David McCord, notwithstanding his being suspected of atheism, smugly argued that if God had not intended the black man to be inferior to the white, He would not have made him so. Like most white Southerners, the McCords considered emancipation a threat to the foundations of Western civilization and a provocation to a war of extermination against blacks. Louisa McCord rode down to the quarters daily to see after the sick, risking her life during epidemics. She had an operation performed to restore the ability to walk of a mentally deficient slave boy who would never earn his keep. But then, condescension was her style. A foreigner observed her attention to sick slaves: "She was a tall *queenly* looking woman, and a very queen at heart; motherly and kind. She treated me as though I were an over-grown boy."[62]

Had McCord left her defense of slavery on racial grounds, she might have argued that the science of political economy applied to the activities and talents of whites, whereas blacks lived and worked under different physical, moral, and social determinants. She might then have supported legislation to protect racial inferiors without doing violence to her opposition to legal interference in economic and social life. Instead, she aggressively pursued the social question in a many-sided way. Adhering to well-defined legal concepts, she refused to identify wage-labor with slavery, but she questioned the significance of her own purely formal legal concepts when asked whether starving free workers could really be considered free. Faithful to classical political economy, she refused to condemn free-labor societies, which she graciously credited with struggling with the social question as best they could. But her concession came immediately after a rebuke to English capitalists for abdicating responsibility toward their workers, which slaveholders accepted toward theirs.[63]

---

[61] On Frédéric Bastiat, see Schumpeter, *History of Economic Analysis*, 500; Francis Lieber's Introduction to Louisa McCord's translation of Bastiat's *Sophisms of the Protective Policy*. *SQR* devoted almost all of its six pages to excerpts from a work it pronounced "the very best of its class," adding, "The chapter on 'the balance of trade' is worth whole treatises": "Critical Notices," *SQR*, 14 (1848), 252–257, quotes at 252, 253.

[62] L. S. M. [McCord], "Diversity of the Races: Its Bearing upon Negro Slavery," *SQR*, 19 (1851), 392–419; D. J. McCord, "Africans at Home," *SQR*, 10 (1854), 70–96; on McCord's reputation as an atheist, see Robert Nicholas Olsberg, "A Government of Class and Race: William H. Trescot and the South Carolina Chivalry, 1860–1865" (Ph.D. diss., University of South Carolina, 1972), 29; Smythe, *For Old Lang Syne*, 4–5. For McCord's prediction of a race war see "Diversity of the Races; Its Bearing upon Negro Slavery," *SQR*, 19 (1851), 414; 20 (1851), 129. The McCords knew Josiah Nott personally, and David had been the law partner of Henry Junius Nott, Josiah's brother.

[63] L. S. M. [McCord], "Diversity of the Races; Its Bearing upon Negro Slavery," *SQR*, 19 (1851), 416–417; "Negro and White Slavery," *SQR*, 4 (1851), 129.

Implicitly, McCord advanced mutually exclusive theories of the proper function of the law. She praised political economy – all but equated with laissez-faire – as "alone with its great and simple truths" the carrier of a promise of "real regeneration." After a scornful slap at legal regulation of the market, she sneered, "Leave us to our old vulgar practices of 'buying and selling'" until you have something better to offer. But implicitly, she advocated the most sweeping legal protection of the laboring classes – the very view she explicitly denounced. Satisfied that southern masters loved and protected their slaves, she opposed further legal interference with the master-slave relation. Southern society, in her view, did not have perfect slavery, for its slaves had all the legal rights society dared offer. No, it was the workers of England and other free-labor societies who needed legal protection. She could not quite say as much without repudiating her radical laissez-faire doctrines – those specific theses of Bastiat on the law that she praised tirelessly. Yet what other conclusion could follow from her critique of labor conditions in England? She contrasted legal protection of the southern slaves with the lack of protection for the English workers in a way that left no doubt of her preference for the former. She specifically praised laws against child abuse under slavery and bled over the lack of them in England. McCord ended with a proud boast that slavery protected its laborers better than any alternative system.[64]

If these assertions, comparisons, and preferences did not add up to a call for legal intervention to protect the white laboring classes and to guarantee their minimum sustenance and security, what did they add up to? McCord had an answer of sorts. In her reply to Holmes, she retreated to racial ground and described a significant portion of the white race as uniquely fit for freedom. Her tough-minded attitude toward differences among individuals precociously projected a kind of Social Darwinism that could hardly aid and comfort proslavery theorists conscious of the need to offer a morally superior alternative to marketplace cannibalism. The implications of her solution were especially chilling for the laboring classes of the South, whom McCord seemed ready to have die off in a struggle of survival of the fittest.[65]

Allowing in 1851 that "the grand rule of Laissez Faire cannot cure all ills," McCord argued that the black slaves of the South fared much better than the white slaves of "great, proud, glorious England" who have "sunk far lower than they in the weltering abyss of misery and hopeless wretchedness." A southern slaveholder inescapably knew his responsibilities to his laborers. An English capitalist "may easily blind himself to them; he does not feel so intensely as

---

[64] L. S. M. [McCord], "The Right to Labor," *SQR*, 16 (1849), 141, 145; Frédéric Bastiat, *The Law*, trans. Dean Russell (Irvington-on-Hudson, n.d.); [L. S. McCord], "Carey on the Slave Trade," *SQR*, 9 (1854), 120, 179; "Uncle Tom's Cabin," *SQR*, 7 (1853), 87, 89.

[65] McCord's implicit position foreshadowed the explicit position of Friedrich Engels, who, during the War, predicted that the southern poor whites, whom he called a degenerate race, would die off once thrown into the marketplace created by a Union victory and the emancipation of the slaves. See Friedrich Engels to Karl Marx, July 15, 1865, in Marx and Engels, *The Civil War in the United States* (New York, 1937), 276–277.

the master of the negro (acknowledged) slave, the strong call for, the necessity of, curtailing his luxuries to supply the wants of his subordinate. . . . The poor victim of society, too, passes on, to toil, starve, and die – forgotten." The slaveholder had a "conscience" that eluded a capitalist who held de facto slaves: "We love our negroes. They form to us a more extended bond for human sympathies. We love our negroes; not as a miser loves his gold; but rather as a father loves his children. The tie, if not so close, is still of the same kind."[66]

Two years later, reviewing *Uncle Tom's Cabin*, McCord referred to the South's laws to protect slaves against cruelty but – citing child abuse in all societies – granted that cruelty did exist. Slavery worked better "for all classes" than any alternative, and nowhere were laborers as well off as in the South. Besides, slaves would murder brutal white men like Simon Legree. If Border-State slaveholders were beginning to view their slaves as mere property, it was because abolitionist agitators encouraged runaways, thereby undermining the paternalistic master-slave relation. She deplored the tendency, which remained slight but worrisome: "*This* is no longer the slavery we love to defend." Slavery, she concluded in utilitarian language, provided the greatest good for the greatest number: "Our system of slavery, left to itself, would rapidly develop its higher features, softening at once to servant and master."[67]

In 1854 McCord published an extended critique of Henry Carey's views on slavery, specifically of his remarks on the waste inherent in slave labor. She snarled "'*Waste labour*,' we have not to any important extent. We have an indulgent system of management which prevents us from forcing our negroes to an undue effort in labour." Blacks, unable to work as hard as whites, needed amusements. What Carey called wasteful was necessary to their well-being. Southerners took care of their young and old laborers: "Perhaps Mr. Carey may think this *wasteful*. He would have the decrepit grandmother forced to throw aside her crutch, and her grand child of six or eight called from its nursery pleasure to drudge beside her in the labours of a cotton mill." Asserting that some people must do the menial work, she challenged Carey to prove slavery an evil: "What is slavery? We answer *involuntary legal subjection* of any individual to another. This condition does *not* imply oppression on the part of the ruler, nor suffering on the ruled or slave." Southern slavery protected the slave's human rights: "*Perfect* freedom is, we repeat, incompatible with society. . . . In every government, and under every rule, woman has been placed in a position of slavery – actual legal slavery." McCord hurled back at Carey his account of the misery of the British working class, but she said too much. Carey, a protectionist, laid responsibility on the cruel workings of free trade. McCord, who endlessly recited the beauties of free trade, was writing a decade after repeal of the Corn Laws. No more than others could she square the circle.[68]

---

[66] L. S. M. [McCord], "Negro and White Slavery," *SQR*, 4 (1851), 118–132, words quoted from 119–121, 123.

[67] [L. S. McCord], "Uncle Tom's Cabin," *SQR*, 23 (1853), 81–120, words quoted from 87, 89, 108, 118–119.

[68] [L. S. McCord], "Carey on the Slave Trade," *SQR*, 9 (1854), 115–184, words quoted at 112.

Southern political economists faced a contradiction between their commitments to social science and to a slaveholding system based on antitheses of the principles that underlay the capitalist system and its prevalent economic theory. They produced ringing endorsements of slavery as an efficient labor system but only under specific conditions. They offered little hope for slavery's prospects in an industrial world. The clearer and more sophisticated the political economist, the more pessimistic he tended to be about slavery's future. By the 1840s the defense of slavery passed into the hands of moral and social philosophers, theologians, political scientists, and "sociologists" (as some were beginning to call themselves in the 1850s), who denigrated, repudiated, or ignored political economy.

Appendix

Political Economy as Taught in the South

Virginia led in the teaching of political economy, notably with Thomas Roderick Dew at William and Mary and George Tucker at the University of Virginia. See Michael J. L. O'Connor, *Origin of Academic Economics in the United States* (New York, 1944), 3; John K. Whitaker, "Early Flowering," in William J. Barber, ed., *Breaking the Academic Mould: Economists and American Higher Learning in the Nineteenth Century* (New Brunswick, N.J., 1993), 15–41. George Tucker's important books grew out of his lectures at the University of Virginia, and his *Theory of Money and Banks Investigated* (Boston, 1839) was assigned as a text in the 1840s.

In teaching the relation of moral philosophy to political economy, some southern colleges drew on Adam Smith's *Wealth of Nations* (1776). J. D. B. De Bow extolled the "deservedly immortalized" Adam Smith: "Some Thoughts on Political Economy and Government," *DBR*, 9 (1850), 259. At the University of Louisiana, De Bow also assigned J. R. McCullough, Jean-Baptiste Say, and Henry Vethake, as well as John Locke and Francis Lieber: See J. D. B. De Bow, *The Industrial Resources, Statistics, &c. of the United States and More Particularly of the Southern and Western State*s, 3rd ed., 3 vols. (New York, 1966 [1854]), 1:332. *Wealth of Nations* was assigned as a text at the College of William and Mary, although elsewhere it made its impact through excerpts or works that embraced its views. Smith, well known as the author of *The Theory of Moral Sentiments* (1759), proved especially attractive for his judicious balance of personal interest with justice and benevolence. The Methodist Reverend R. H. Rivers, however, complained that Smith, "one of the most ingenious writers on metaphysics," provided no yardstick except a vague and changeable "sympathy" to judge right from wrong: *Elements of Moral Philosophy* (Nashville, 1859), 135, 136, quote at 135. According to a writer in Charlottesville, had Adam Smith not written *Theory of Moral Sentiments* he probably would not have written *Wealth of Nations*: Q., "Metaphysics." *Virginia Literary Museum and Journal of Belles Lettres, Arts, Sciences, Etc.*, 1 (1830), 724, 727. See Henry F. May, *The Enlightenment in America* (New

York, 1976), 349, for Smith's impact in America and the steady vulgariza-
tion of his balance of competitive individualism with social responsibility. We
suggest that the South held to Smith's original stance much longer than the
North.

Not surprisingly, the antislavery Francis Lieber at South Carolina College
and the critical George Tucker at the University of Virginia assigned Say's *Treatise on Political Economy*, available in translation in 1821: Charles Mack and
Ilona S. Mack, ed., *Like a Sponge Thrown into Water: Francis Lieber's European Travel Journal of 1844–1845* (Columbia, S.C., 2002), 150. Surprisingly,
proslavery professors also used Say's *Treatise* despite its antislavery views.
Robert L. Dabney, who had been Tucker's student, assigned it to students until
the end of the century. Sean Michael Lucas has suggested that among other
virtues in Dabney's eyes, Say placed political economy in the Scottish empirical
tradition: *Robert Lewis Dabney: A Southern Presbyterian Life* (Phillipsburg,
Pa., 2005), 29. For a defense of Say's "Law of Markets" – supply creates its
own demand – see "Review of Thomas Cooper's Lectures on the Elements of
Political Economy," *SR*, 1 (1828), 197, 200, 209. Say's views became available
indirectly through Francis Wayland's text, which quoted Say liberally and supported his "law of markets," although warning of temporary gluts caused by
government interference and wars: Francis Wayland, *The Elements of Political
Economy*, 2nd. ed. (New York, 1838), 20–21, 183–184. In the 1850s Wayland was still assigned at the University of Alabama, Emory College, Emory
and Henry College, Furman University, Guilford College, Howard College,
Mississippi College (at Clinton), and the University of North Carolina. It was
discontinued at the University of Mississippi, Wake Forest, and Washington
College in the 1850s because of Wayland's antislavery views.

Some colleges, northern and southern, assigned Tucker's work. Other southern colleges assigned Thomas Roderick Dew, *Lectures on the Restrictive System
Delivered to the Senior Political Class of William and Mary College* (Richmond,
Va., 1829), which Senator William Smith of South Carolina called a crushing
blow to Henry Clay's American System: William Smith, Feb. 25, 1830, in Herman Belz, ed., *The Webster-Hayne Debate on the Nature of the Union*, 332.
For the assignment of Say, Dew, and Tucker, see O'Connor, *Origins of Academic Economics*, 51, 56, 121–122, 131, 153. *Southern Review* enlisted Say in
its opposition to tariffs and other measures, claiming his superiority to David
Ricardo and Thomas Malthus on matters on which they disagreed: 8 (1832),
492–511, esp. 496. *Southern Review* praised Thomas Cooper's *Elements of
Political Economy* for its lucidity and general soundness but took issue with its
adherence to Ricardo on rent and Malthus on population. In 1830, *Southern
Review*, reviewing the Webster-Hayne debate, scorned to deny that slavery lay
at the core of the South's greatness, and in 1832 a contributor dismissed as
erroneous criticisms of slavery by even the finest of British and French political
economists, recommending as a corrective "Dr. Cooper's excellent Lectures
on political economy." See *SR*, 1 (1828), 192–219; 6 (1830), 146–147; 8
(1832), 497. Holmes considered Cooper's *Manual of Political Economy* "one

of the most lucid and convenient expositions" of prevailing economic theory – more an endorsement of Cooper's talent than of his political economy as such: George Frederick Holmes, "Capital and Labor," *DBR*, 22 (1857), 251. Nathaniel Ware took protectionist ground but was barely heard among southern political economists: *Notes on Political Economy as Applicable to the United States* (New York, 1957 [1844]). Ware, born in Massachusetts in 1789, taught school in South Carolina and settled in Natchez, where he became a wealthy bank president and served as territorial secretary of Mississippi and acting governor in 1815–1816. He moved to Cincinnati and then to Philadelphia.

The Tucker Thesis

Northerners as well as Southerners prefigured George Tucker's thesis that capitalist development would end slavery. At the Federal Convention, Oliver Ellsworth decried attempts to pressure the southern states on slavery, arguing, "As population increases poor laborers will be so plenty as to render slaves useless. Slavery in time will not be a speck in our Country." See James Madison, *Notes of the Debates in the Federal Convention of 1787* (Athens, Oh., 1966), 504; also Smith to Horace Greeley, Jan. 29, 1844, in C. Peter Ripley et al., eds., *The Black Abolitionist Papers*, 5 vols. (Chapel Hill, N.C., 1985–1991), 3:432.

Building on Tucker's thesis, R. E. Cochrane argued against Fitzhugh that slavery would prove too expensive in Europe and that, therefore, its restoration was out of the question: "R. E. C." [Cochrane], "The Problem of Free Society – Part Two," *SLM*, 27 (1858), 12–13. See also "Slavery and Political Economy, in Richard C. Lounsbury, ed., *Louisa S. McCord: Political and Social Essays* (Charlottesville, Va., 1995), 428–429. Among prominent foreigners who endorsed the thesis, see Sir Charles Lyell, *Travels in North America, Canada, and Nova Scotia, with Geological Observations*, 2nd ed., 2 vols. (London, 1855), 1:192–193. Elias Peissner of New York turned Tucker's thesis against the abolitionists: *The American Question in Its National Aspect. Being also an Incidental Reply to H. R. Helper's "Compendium of the Impending Crisis of the South"* (New York, 1861), 103–104. Jefferson Davis, telling the U.S. Senate that slavery disappeared when it became unprofitable, offered his own version of the thesis: "Speech on the Oregon Bill," July 12, 1848, *JDP*, 3:357. John Fletcher of Louisiana implicitly followed suit but, believing in innate black inferiority, concluded that the future of slavery lay with the struggle for racial domination: *Studies on Slavery, in Easy Lessons* (Natchez, Miss., 1852), 381, 384. In Georgia, Samuel Galloway, author of *Ergonomy*, punted the tough question by declaring racially inferior blacks especially well fit for labor in tropical climates: Galloway to Calhoun, Jan. 27, 1846, in *JCCP*, 22:525–527. For a clerical argument that implicitly invoked the Tucker thesis, see R. Ryland, *The American Union: An Address Delivered before the Alumni Association of the Columbian College, D.C., June 23, 1857* (Richmond, Va.,

1857), 14. The argument that the North abolished slavery because it became unprofitable cannot be sustained; see Arthur Zilversmit, *The First Emancipation: The Abolition of Slavery in the North* (Chicago, 1967), 52–53.

In the early days of the Republic, John Taylor of Caroline affirmed that the elimination of slavery would destroy the South's social system. Although he paid lip service to schemes for the removal of the black population, his work on agricultural reform aimed to put slave labor to profitable use, not to offer a substitute labor system: *Arator: Being a Series of Agricultural Essays, Practical and Political: In Sixty-Four Numbers* (Indianapolis, Ind., 1977 [1818]), especially 111, 115–118, 356. Taylor's work was out of print by 1835, doubtless in part, as Arthur Schlesinger suggests [*The Age of Jackson* (Boston, 1946), 308], because of its turgid style, but we may also consider the effect of the radical implications of its Enlightenment premises since Taylor's *Arator* was much more readable than his verbose and difficult *An Inquiry into the Principles and Policy of the Government of the United States*, ed. Loren Baritz (Indianapolis, Ind., 1919 [1814]). More enigmatically, a contributor to *Russell's Magazine* suggested that the laws of political economy – understood as the laws of Providence – would determine the fate of slavery: "A Letter from Europe," *RM*, 6 (1860), 32.

Value Theory

For an erudite overview of the transatlantic debates, see Joseph A. Schumpeter's great *History of Economic Analysis*, ed. Elizabeth Boody Schumpeter (New York, 1954). Schumpeter does not mention Cardozo but pays tribute to Tucker as a rare antebellum American economist worthy of note; see 519. On the British debates, see Morton Paglin, *Malthus and Lauderdale: The Anti-Ricardian Tradition* (Clifton, N.J., 1973); on the American debates, see John Roscoe Turner, *The Ricardian Rent Theory in Early American Economics* (New York, 1921); Joseph Dorfman, *The Economic Mind in American Civilization*, 5 vols. (New York, 1966), 2:891; Francis Lieber, "Leading Truths in Political Economy," *DBR*, 15 (1853), 188; Jacob N. Cardozo, *Notes on Political Economy* (New York, 1972 [1826]), 67–68.

A critic at the University of Virginia defended Adam Smith against the innovations of Ricardo and McCullough, denouncing, in particular, Ricardo's theories of the origin of profits in labor, falling rate of profit, and immiseration of labor as "egregiously, palpably wrong": "Old School," "Ricardo's Theory of Profits," *Virginia Literary Museum and Journal of Belles Lettres, Arts, Sciences, Etc.*, 1 (1829), 273–276, quote at 273; also [H. R. M. Garnett], "Whateley's Lectures on Political Economy," *SQR*, 15 (1849), 4. Smith in fact had two labor theories of value to go along with another – incompatible – theory. Critics quarrel over Ricardo's theory, and some deny that he held a labor theory at all. In the South Ricardo's critics attributed a labor theory to him. Ricardian rent theory fared better in the South than did his putative theory of value. Henry Ruffner, for example, told his students at Washington College that Ricardo was the first to give "true meaning" to the concept of rent. See James S. Richeson, "Course of Lectures Delivered on Political Economy by Henry Ruffner," 68, in Henry Ruffner Papers.

Physiocracy had few followers anywhere in the United States; see Drew R. McCoy, *The Elusive Republic: Political Economy in Jeffersonian America* (New York, 1980), 45–46. The common attribution of Physiocracy to leading southern intellectuals received its primary sanction in Vernon Louis Parrington, *Main Currents in American Thought*, 3 vols. (New York, 1927), 2:14–19. It was carried to extraordinary lengths by William Appleman Williams, *Contours of American History* (Chicago, 1966). The attribution rests on no evidence but rather on an inaccurate understanding of Physiocracy. On Physiocracy and legal despotism, see Elizabeth Fox-Genovese, *The Origins of Physiocracy: Economic Revolution and Social Order in Eighteenth-Century France* (Ithaca, N.Y., 1976). There is no evidence of Physiocratic books in colonial American libraries: see George K. Smart, "Private Libraries in Colonial Virginia," *American Literature*, 10 (1938), 47, 50. In 1828, however, Francis Walker Gilmer of Virginia translated Quesnay's "Treatise on Natural Right": Gilmer, *Sketches, Essays and Translations*, 174–201.

5

The Appeal to Social Theory

> The cry about Emancipation, so well pleased with itself on Humanity Platforms, is but the keynote of that huge anarchic roar, now rising from all nations, for good reasons too – which tends to abolish all mastership and obedience whatsoever in this world, and to render society impossible among the sons of Adam!
> —Thomas Carlyle[1]

By the 1850s an emerging southern social theory – newly dubbed "sociology" – defended slavery on higher ground than political economy allowed for. The new social theorists included the eminent scientist Joseph Le Conte as well as theologians, moral philosophers, and political theorists. Their work exposed the ultimate irreconcilability of political economy with a social philosophy appropriate to slaveholding society. Slavery reappeared again and again as the foundation of a society incompatible with the transatlantic world that political economists qua political economists interpreted and extolled.

Socialism

Proslavery theorists had to combat the widespread assumption that the fledgling discipline of sociology preached socialism. Throughout the South applause for socialism's exposure of the ills of free-labor society accompanied dread of socialist movements. Southern clergymen and laymen condemned socialism's principal philosophical, psychological, and economic premises but drew heavily on its critique of the free-labor system, which by the 1850s was beginning to be called "capitalism." They also drew on radicals like William Godwin and Tories like Samuel Johnson to warn against the moral and physical dangers created by industrialization and the heavy concentration of population. Henry Theodore Tuckerman of Boston pictured Godwin in *Southern Literary Messenger* as a

---

[1] Thomas Carlyle to Nathaniel Beverley Tucker, Oct. 31, 1851, in Mrs. George P. Coleman, ed., *Virginia Silhouettes: Contemporary Letters Concerning Negro Slavery in the State of Virginia* (Richmond, Va., 1934), 48–49.

kind and upright man with pure motives, disinterested zeal, and an ardent love of truth who, like reformers generally, "exaggerated the acquired at the expense of the innate" and who "recognized nothing sacred in man but reason."[2]

South Carolinians led attempts to settle accounts with socialism. Rejecting expropriation of property as a cure for social ills, they quickly espied danger even in the reformist Workingman's Party, which in 1830 an alarmed *Southern Review* reported as growing stronger and more radical. Hugh Legaré observed that Robert Owen's Lanark and all attempts to remake human beings through social reconstruction constituted "a most pernicious error." A contributor to *Southern Quarterly Review* remarked, "Socialism will bring no blessing to mankind" because it overlooked "individual responsibility, duty, and condition." Edward J. Pringle "shuddered" at the doctrines of Louis Blanc and Etienne Cabet, which he feared had reached American shores. Pringle conceded that such captivating doctrines had "just enough of truth" to attract the masses. Similarly, a contributor to *Southern Quarterly Review* lumped Blanc with the radical nationalists Giuseppe Mazzini and Louis Kossuth as advocates of licentiousness disguised as liberty. The widely traveled James Johnston Pettigrew, discussing the national workshops created during the French Revolution of 1848, saw only a reward for the idle and dissolute and, worse, a spur to urban concentration: "The experience of our own country has shown that the great cities, with all their enlightenment, are very unsound depositories of political power." Pettigrew fell in love with Spain in no small part because of its resistance to modernity and the strength of its traditional communities. James M. Walker, accomplished legal scholar, quoted Chancellor Kent of New York as calling "fanciful" the notion that man ever held property in common and lived without a notion of separate property. For Walker, such theories were "wild reveries" and "sacrilege." The Presbyterian Reverend S. J. Cassells charged the "spurious benevolence" of the theological liberalism widespread in Europe and the North with creation of "a tendency to Socialism," an evil that threatens private property and the family as it "seeks the absolute submission of political and social institutions." Dr. Samuel Henry Dickson declared "ranters" like Frances Wright and Robert Owen "unworthy of notice or of reply."[3]

---

[2] Henry Theodore Tuckerman, "William Godwin," *SLM*, 16 (1850), 129–136, quotes at 131; for Godwin see, e.g., "A Virginian" [Lucian Minor], "Letters from New England – No. 4," *SLM*, 1 (1835), 273.

[3] *SR*, 6 (1830), 32; "Kent's Commentaries," *HLW*, 2:104; "Labor," *SQR*, 11 (1847), 84; Edward J. Pringle, "The People," *SQR*, n.s. 9 (1854), 33, 34; "Considerations on Some Recent Social Theories," *SQR*, n.s. 11 (1855), 253; [James Johnston Pettigrew], *Notes on Spain and the Spaniards in the Summer of 1850, with a Glance at Sardinia* (Charleston, S.C., 1861), 34; James M. Walker, *The Theory of the Common Law* (Boston, 1852), 110, and [Walker], "Distribution of Wealth" (review of Disraeli's *Young Duke*), *SR*, 8 (1831), 180; [James M. Walker?], "The Roman Law," *SQR*, n.s. 9 (1854), 348; [Cassells], "The Relation of Justice to Benevolence in the Conduct of Society," *SPR*, 7 (1853), 93; Samuel Henry Dickson, "Slavery in the French Colonies," *SLM*, 10 (1844), 269. For translation of a selection from Frédéric Bastiat's critique of the socialistic theories of Louis Blanc, Pierre-Joseph Proudhon, and Victor Prosper Considérant,

The Presbyterian Reverend Dr. James Henley Thornwell dismissed the idea that men had title to the fruits of their labor and a right to feel robbed, defrauded, and plundered when they get less: "Where is the maxim, in the sense in which it is interpreted, to be found in the Scriptures? Where, even in any respectable system of Moral Philosophy?" Only a few prominent southern educators took the position Thornwell condemned. Notably, the cautiously antislavery Henry St. George Tucker of Virginia – son of the antislavery St. George Tucker and brother of the proslavery Nathaniel Beverley Tucker – wrote in defense of natural rights: "Natural rights are a right to his life, limbs, and liberty; to the produce of his own labor; to the common use of air, light, and water, and of the common fruits of the earth aggregated by himself for his necessary use."[4]

Edgar Allan Poe of Virginia, extolling slavery as "the basis of all our institutions," labeled Charles Fourier and Horace Greeley "high priests" of a new philosophy that valued anything odd. Fourier sought to channel the natural passions of men constructively to produce social harmony. Poe found only one bond among these new philosophers: "Credulity – let us call it Insanity at once, and be done with it." In 1841, Professor John Blair Dabney of Richmond College doubtless had the socialists in mind when he viewed European politics as a confrontation of a party of established order against a party of destructive radicalism. Henry W. Miller of North Carolina's General Assembly, addressing students at the state university, singled out "Fourierism, with its train of leveling precepts and degrading purposes." He deplored the ability of socialists to win over not only the ignorant masses but "many of the best cultivated minds." In Alabama two gifted Catholic students at Spring Hill College – M. Thompson and Edward Bermudez, later chief justice of the Supreme Court of Louisiana – delivered addresses on the inherent tyranny of socialism and revolutionary movements. At the University of Alabama, Edward C. Bullock denounced both the free-labor system's oppression of labor and "those who boldly propose to remedy the evil by plunging headlong into the whirlpool of socialism, and, thus, as it were, terminate a miserable existence by a still more miserable suicide." The Presbyterian Reverend Joseph E. Wilson of Georgia recalled the Essenes as the abolitionists of biblical times who "inculcated unattainable notions of universal liberty." He maintained that Fourierism had once excited much attention but had palpably failed, along with all leveling attempts at obliterating the inequality grounded in the human condition. In agreement, Daniel Lee, editor of *Southern Cultivator*, called the socialist projects of Horace Greeley and others universally failures.[5]

which focused on the necessity for private property, see *RM*, 5 (1859), 193–212. When Cabet lectured on a transatlantic ship, J. H. Bills of Tennessee, in attendance, especially noted remarks on the misery of the European working classes: Bills Diary, June 2, 1851.

[4] *JHTW*, 4:389; Henry St. George Tucker, *A Few Lectures on Natural Law* (Charlottesville, Va., 1844), 52–53.

[5] [Edgar Allan Poe], "Critical Notices," *SLM*, 2 (1836), 337–339, quote at 337, and Poe, *Essays and Reviews* (New York, 1984), 1303; John Blair Dabney, "Capt. Marryatt and His Diary,"

Socialism and socialists nonetheless attracted some southern sympathy. Frances Wright's vigorous support for Martin Van Buren helped her reputation among some southern Democrats while provoking Henry A. Wise of Virginia and other opponents of the subtreasury to deprecate her as an irresponsible radical. The Presbyterian Reverend William S. Plumer of Virginia reviled Frances Wright, Robert Dale Owen, and "their compeers and imitators" for subverting the family and therefore all social order. Wright's radical Nashoba communitarian experiment in Tennessee drew plaudits from James Monroe. The planters reacted harshly, but most Tennesseans reserved judgment. Wright published her plans in the Memphis press, and a surprised Frances Trollope observed her reception as a celebrity in Memphis high society. Andrew Jackson, welcoming Wright to his home in Tennessee, wished her experiment well. As late as 1860 – after public opinion had turned against her because of Nashoba's promotion of miscegenation and free love – a contributor to *Southern Literary Messenger* cited her exposure of the dreadful labor conditions in the North. William E. Davis, brother of Jefferson Davis, who met and respected Wright and Robert Owen, saw socialist and communitarian theory as reinforcement for his sense that productivity as well as social order required persuasion and incentives more than exercise of raw power. He held out various inducements to his slaves, including authority to discipline malefactors. Here and there a peculiar case: At age fourteen, the Pennsylvania-born Thomas J. Durant, a self-described disciple of Thomas Jefferson and John Taylor of Caroline, went to New Orleans and stayed for some thirty-five years. An established printer and slaveholder, he supported the Democratic Party in the presidential election campaign of 1840, presiding over a rally of "workingmen." Afterward he came upon the writings of Charles Fourier, embraced socialism, and corresponded with planters and others interested in his views. After the War, Benjamin E. Green, the anticapitalist son of Duff Green, invoked John C. Calhoun and other proslavery theorists to support the struggle of Greenbackers, Populists, and labor reformers. With southern hopes long dead and big capital astride American politics, the Presbyterian Reverend Robert L. Dabney of Virginia demanded laws to encourage small property, curb monopoly, and strengthen the yeomanry as the basis of a free state.[6]

SLM, 7 (1841), 254; Henry W. Miller, *Address Delivered before the Philanthropic and Dialectic Societies of the University of North-Carolina* (Raleigh, 1857), 20; Joseph R. Wilson, *Mutual Relation of Masters and Slaves as Taught in the Bible* (Augusta, Ga., 1861), 9–10; Daniel Lee, "A Lecture on Labor," *Southern Cultivator*, 15 (1857), 43; for Bermudez and Thompson, see Michael Kenny, *Catholic Culture in Alabama: Centenary Story of Spring Hill College, 1830–1890* (New York, 1931), 146–149; Edward C. Bullock, *True and False Civilization: An Oration Delivered before the Erosophic and Philomathic Societies of the University of Alabama* (Tuscaloosa, Ala., 1858), 18.
[6] Celia Morris Eckhardt, *Fannie Wright: Rebel in America* (Cambridge, Mass., 1984), 109–110, 143–144, 163–166, ch. 6; on Wright, Van Buren, and Wise, see Sean Wilentz, *The Rise of American Democracy: Jefferson to Lincoln* (New York, 2005), 478, 482; William S. Plumer, *The Law of God, as Contained in the Ten Commandments, Explained and Enforced* (Harrisonburg, Va., 1996 [1864]), 459; Frances Trollope, *Domestic Manners of the Americans* (Gloucester,

Richmond had a German Social Democratic Association in 1851, and social democratic groups appeared in Baltimore, Louisville, and St. Louis. Germans who settled in the South early generally supported slavery, but those who fled the post-1848 reaction included antislavery socialists, radicals, and liberals. Walter Lenoir of North Carolina reported from Missouri that the Germans were not merely antislavery but "prone to all of the unhealthy isms of the day." St. Louis had diverse radical sects and publications, notably, the anti-Christian *Western Examiner*, which having anointed Thomas Paine as "the first American martyr to the promulgation of principle," celebrated the beauties of New Harmony, the socialitic Owenite community in Indiana. Lenoir notwithstanding, the German communities in Missouri and elsewhere were neither monolithic nor overwhelmingly radical. German settlers in Maryland and Texas initially accepted the southern view of slavery, but there too the European revolutionary wave of 1848 carried antislavery beliefs with it. Antislavery sentiment slowly waned, and most Germans accepted the Confederacy. North Carolina followed that pattern, but strong antislavery sentiment persisted down to the War. Although German immigrants in the North did not respond monolithically to slavery and the sectional crisis, the hard times of the 1850s radicalized German workers in New York, contributing to a growing apprehension that the United States would recapitulate the miseries of European industrialization.[7]

A few small Marxist groups appeared in Maryland, Kentucky, Missouri, Louisiana, and Texas, along with other socialist groups with other ideological tendencies. With an initial burst of enthusiasm Germans established a small communistic colony at Bettina, Texas, in 1847, but the colony petered out as the settlers did less and less work. Adolph Douai, after his imprisonment for participation in the Revolution of 1848, moved to America, became an abolitionist and labor reformer, and published the San Antonio *Zeitung* for a year before he had to flee Texas. *Deutsche Zeitung* appeared in New Orleans

Mass., 1974 [1832]), 24, 70–71, 183; "Horace Greeley's Lost Book," *SLM*, 31 (1860), 213; Janet Sharp Hermann, *Joseph E. Davis: Pioneer Patriarch* (Jackson, Miss., 1990), ch. 3, and her *Pursuit of a Dream* (Oxford, Miss., 1981), 3–6, 12, 17; Joseph G. Tregle, Jr., "Thomas J. Durant, Utopian Socialism, and the Failure of Presidential Reconstruction in Louisiana," *JSH*, 45 (1979), 485–512; Duff Green papers (Publ. microfilm, roll #17, frames 427–431); Robert L. Dabney, *The Practical Philosophy, Being the Philosophy of the Feelings, of the Will, and of the Conscience, with the Ascertainment of Particular Rights and Duties* (Harrisonburg, Va., 1984 [1897]), 476–477.

7 Walter Lenoir to Thomas I. Lenoir, Nov. 12, 1860, in Thomas Felix Hickerson, *Echoes of Happy Valley* (Durham, N.C., 1962), 55; "Thomas Paine," *Western Examiner*, 1 (1834), 57, "New Harmony, Indiana," *Western Examiner*, 1 (1834), 121; Randolph B. Campbell, *An Empire for Slavery: The Peculiar Institution in Texas, 1821–1865* (Baton Rouge, La., 1989), 215–218; for Maryland, see Mary Stoughton Locke, *Anti-Slavery in America: From the Introduction of African Slaves to the Prohibition of the Slave Trade (1619–1808)* (Gloucester, Mass., 1965 [1901]), 38–39, and Bart R. Talbert, *Maryland: The South's First Casualty* (Berryville, Va., 1997), 20–21; Bruce Levine, *The Spirit of 1848: German Immigrants, Labor Conflict, and the Coming of the Civil War* (Urbana, Ill., 1992), 80–82.

in 1856 and boldly supported Fremont. The hard road faced by social radicals became manifest in outbursts like that of Frank I. Wilson of North Carolina. Addressing the Wake County Working-Men's Association in 1860, he indignantly denounced allegations that working-class reformers sympathized with abolitionism and asserted that, to the contrary, they fully appreciated "the danger which threatens North-Carolina, as a sovereign slaveholding state." Then too, the southern-born Marx Edgeworth Lazarus, a social and political radical and exponent of free love, did a stint at Brook Farm, denounced slavery and marriage as twin despotisms, howled against secession, and wound up returning to his homeland to practice medicine as a loyal if disgruntled citizen of the Confederacy.[8]

It fell to George Frederick Holmes, born in British Guiana, to balance positive and negative appraisals of socialism. After practicing law in South Carolina, he served briefly as president of the University of Mississippi and then taught college in Virginia. He married Lavelette Floyd, daughter of Virginia governor John Floyd and a devout Catholic, and stopped just short of converting to Catholicism himself. Even during the 1840s, when he tended toward Enlightenment progressivism and admired Auguste Comte, he embraced social corporatism. Subsequently, a religious crisis and the revolutions of 1848 shook his confidence in science. Although his philosophical views changed, personal experiences reinforced his lifelong critique of bourgeois society and modernism.[9]

In 1851, Holmes complimented socialists for their exposure of the ills of modern society. He applauded the socialists' opposition to "the cry of the capitalists for the Laissez faire system" but dismissed their solutions as absurd. Identifying Fourier's ideas as the basis of Horace Greeley's radicalism, Holmes pronounced slavery – not socialism's "unmitigated Pandemonium" – a solution to the social question. In 1855, in a piece echoed in the *Richmond Enquirer*, he cited Robert DuVar's *History of the Working Classes* on the free-labor system's responsibility for the religious, moral, and material crisis in France but criticized DuVar for gross socialistic exaggerations that threatened the fabric of society. Consequently, Holmes regretted George Fitzhugh's identification of slavery with socialism, as encouragement for destructive visionaries. Holmes subsequently rebuked British economists for ignoring Pierre-Joseph Proudhon's work. He did not support Proudhon's theories or actions but did call for

[8] See Herbert Aptheker, *Abolitionism: A Revolutionary Movement* (Boston, Mass., 1989), 38–40; Walter Prescott Webb, ed., *The Handbook of Texas*, 3 vols. (Austin, Tex., 1952–1976), 1:153; W. Darrell Overdyke, *The Know-Nothing Party in the South* (Baton Rouge, La., 1950), 18; on Confederate Marxists in Texas, see Paul Marx, "Marx, Edgar von Westphalen, and Texas," *Southern Studies*, 22 (1983), 386–400; Frank I. Wilson, *Address Delivered before the Wake County Workingmen's Association: In the Court House at Raleigh, February 6, 1860* (Electronic ed.; Chapel Hill, N.C., 2000 [186?]), 5–6, quote at 21; John C. Spurlock, *Free Love: Marriage and Middle-Class Radicalism in America, 1825–1860* (New York, 1988), 67–68, 119, 171, 204.

[9] We are indebted to the many insights in Neal C. Gillespie, *The Collapse of Orthodoxy: The Intellectual Ordeal of George Frederick Holmes* (Charlottesville, Va., 1972).

a careful sorting out of his ideas. Shortly thereafter he called Proudhon "that most perverse and acute logician, and rabid innovator," and Fourier the spinner of "wild communist theories."[10]

Holmes's shifting tone on Proudhon illustrates the strains in proslavery efforts to evaluate the European Left's critique of capitalism. Unlike most European radicals, Proudhon supported slavery and the Confederacy. For Proudhon, the true benefactors of racially inferior blacks were "those who wish to keep them in servitude, yea to exploit them, but nevertheless to assure them of a livelihood, to raise their standard gradually through labor, and to increase their numbers through marriage." Proudhon fought against the socialists – not only against Marx but against Alexandre Ledru-Rollin and Louis Blanc – as fiercely as he fought against the financiers. He attacked the socialists for inciting undesirable class war. Notwithstanding his famous pronouncement, "Property is theft," he sought – in Salwyn Shapiro's words – "to preserve property rights and, at the same time abolish capitalism." No less to southern tastes, Proudhon staunchly defended the traditional family. A good many educated Southerners read Fourier and Owen, but most probably knew Proudhon through a reading of François Guizot. Among their number, William Gilmore Simms learned of the incoherence and failure of French attempts to establish a "social republic."[11]

Some defenders of slavery worried about polemical overkill in exposés of the free-labor system and northern social conditions. In 1835, William Hobby of Georgia, registering that Northerners reviled the South on the basis of reports of slavery's worst atrocities, urged Southerners to resist the temptation to revile the North for its treatment of white servants on the basis of similarly extreme and marginal cases of abuse. In 1851 in Tuscaloosa, Alabama, the northern-born F. A. P. Barnard delivered a strongly unionist speech on Independence Day. He ragged his audience about southern dependence on the northern economy and the tendency to blame the North for southern weaknesses. Barnard called on the South to realize its latent genius and match northern performance. He chided secessionists for preaching that Great Britain feared its industrial workers: "You say she fears the rabble of her unemployed operatives. What is to prevent her turning that rabble loose upon you?" Simms praised Charles

---

[10] [George Frederick Holmes], "Greeley on Reforms," *SLM*, 17 (1851), 257–280; [Holmes], "The Nineteenth Century," *SLM*, 17 (1851), 457–476, quote at 466; [Holmes], "Failure of Free Societies," *SLM*, 21 (1855), 136–138; [Holmes], "History of the Working Classes," *SLM*, 21 (1855), 193–203; Holmes, "Population and Capital," *DBR*, 21 (1856), 219; Holmes, "Theory of Political Individualism," *DBR*, 22 (1857), 135, quote at 146. For DuVar, see also *Richmond Enquirer*, May 2, 1856. For the "the bold avowal of the great French socialist that 'all property is robbery,'" see Edward C. Bullock, *True and False Civilization: An Oration Delivered before the Erosophic and Philomathic Societies of the University of Alabama* (Tuscaloosa, Ala., 1858), 20.

[11] J. Salwyn Shapiro, "Pierre Joseph Proudhon, Harbinger of Fascism," *American Historical Review*, 50 (1945), quotes at 729, 720; [William Simms], "Guizot's Democracy in France," *SQR*, 15 (1849), 139–141.

Kingsley, the Christian socialist author of *Alton Locke*, as a man of considerable talent but saw him as "measurably a communist." More pointedly, Simms viewed Warren Isham's *The Mud Cabin* as an amusing attempt to tell the British to take care of their own poor. But Simms, too, counseled against confusing miseries inherent in the human condition with those specific to a particular social system. A southern slaveholder, visiting New England, told northern reformers that exposés of the exploitation of factory workers in *Voice of Industry* – organ of the New England Labor Reform League – risked class war and violent rebellion: "It is true you have slavery here, but then such always has been and always will be."[12]

Corporatist Thought

The slaveholders' revolt against unbridled bourgeois individualism drove southern thought toward a concept of a corporate society adaptable to the exigencies of the modern world. As exponents of corporatism in the South, not even Fitzhugh or the more learned and subtle Holmes rivaled Henry Hughes of Mississippi. In idiosyncratic language he boldly projected a new social system. He rejected slavery (privately held "property in man") as an abomination and suggested that the southern system required changes to perfect its "warranteeism." For Hughes, the state held property, whereas individual masters held laborers in trust only so long as masters met their social responsibilities. He described capitalists and laborers as "economically affamilated" under warranteeism. The state consisted of families that include both: "The laborer and the capitalist belong to the same family. They have a home-association. The household is instituted. The head of the family is the capitalist. He warrants subsistence to all. This is his civil duty." Among the attendant joys: "The children of the laborer, are not dependent on the wages of their father or mother. They are dependent on the capital of the association." Under the free-labor system the worker had the impossible burden of providing for his children and aged parents, whereas under warranteeism he gained security.[13]

Hughes, a Democrat, spoke a language all his own – certainly not that of the eastern tidewater conservatives or of the Old School Presbyterian Church he attended. Maintaining that warranteeism recognized men as "born free and equal," he quickly dispelled misunderstandings: "Liberty is only freedom inside

[12] [William Hobby], *Remarks upon Slavery, Occasioned by Attempts Made to Circulate Improper Publications in the Southern States. By a Citizen of Georgia*, 2nd ed. (Augusta, Ga., 1835), 19; the text of Barnard's speech constitutes ch. 6 of John Fulton, ed., *Memoirs of Frederick A. P. Barnard* (New York, 1896), 112–140, quote at 138; [William Gilmore Simms], "Critical Notes," *SQR*, n.s. 9 (1854), 221–224; [William Gilmore Simms], "Critical Notes," *SQR*, n.s. 3 (1851), 289; slaveholder quoted in M. E., "Correspondence from Boston," *Voice of Industry* (May 28, 1847), republished in Philip Foner, ed., *The Factory Girls* (Urbana, Ill., 1977), 201.

[13] Henry Hughes, *Treatise on Sociology, Theoretical and Practical* (New York, 1968 [1854]), 186–188, quotes at 11, 186, 185–186, 187–188. (Compare Friedrich Engels's famous "Freedom is the recognition of necessity.")

of necessary order. This is freedom to do not what they would, but what they ought; and equality not of power but of justice." He followed corporatist logic and joined Thomas Cooper as – so far as we know – the only proslavery theorists with a good word for trade unions: "These unions are special mutual-insurance or warrantee associations. They are orderly; they both adapt and regulate themselves. The association, artificial body, or corporation, is the Warrantor; the associates, the Warrantees. Superordination and subordination are maintained."[14]

That was as much as Hughes chose to say. We may doubt that he supported the right to strike since he assailed the free-labor system precisely for its failure to capitalize labor. And although he considered warranteeism perfectly compatible with warrantees' civil liberty, he distinguished between an undefined civil liberty and political power, which must rest in the hands of the warrantor as representative of the entire household of dependent workers as well as kin. Hughes's unions apparently had the primary function of facilitating labor's mobility and discipline in the public interest, for he denounced as economically inefficient any excess of population. The state must regulate the supply of laborers to secure their existence, he wrote, and whenever a glut appeared, the state must move laborers to where they were needed. Since that move guaranteed laborers sustenance, they had a right to be subjected to it. Hughes, in his "Report on the African Apprentice System" (1859), elaborated his notion of warranteeism or "liberty labor": "The nature of the association is not private, like that of free and slave labor, but public. The servants' relation to the master, therefore, is not that of hirelings to the hirer, nor that of slaves to the owner, but that of magistrates. This has been judicially decided. By judicial decision the master is not a private but a public person." Association rested neither on desire nor on fear, but on duty. For God commands all to work, and masters work as deputies of the state. Hughes was doubtless cheered by the stance taken by southern "mechanics" associations, which included workers and the self-employed. The Wake County Working-Men's Association, petitioning for reform of North Carolina's tax structure, stated "emphatically" that it rejected class warfare and stressed its support for "domestic slavery": "The most industrious and unscrupulous demagogue can never, with us, succeed in bringing about any estrangement between the rich and the poor."[15]

In Port Gibson, Mississippi, the Presbyterian Reverend W. D. Moore, preaching Hughes's funeral sermon in 1862, hailed the *Treatise on Sociology, Theoretical and Practical* as "the most profound and original work on the subject of slavery, published in our time." Interpreting it for the faithful, Moore stressed the necessity of hierarchy – of ranks and classes, of governors

---

[14] Hughes, *Treatise on Sociology*, 102, 185, 196–197.
[15] "A Report on the African Apprentice System" (1859), in Stanford M. Lyman, ed., *Selected Writings of Henry Hughes: Antebellum Southerner, Slavocrat, Sociologist* (Jackson, Miss., 1985), 176–177; *Resolutions and Address of the Wake County Working-Men's Association* (Electronic ed.; Chapel Hill, N.C., 2002 [1859]), 2.

and governed. Hughes believed that free society was failing "in the lowest and most elementary object of society; namely, the subsistence of all its members." He extolled the miscalled southern system of slavery for steadily perfecting itself as warranteeism: It "eliminates all the suffering and crime arising from the tyranny of lawless and ungoverned capital in free societies." On this matter Hughes spoke for a wide range of Southerners. Among the more prominent, the Episcopalian Reverend James Warley Miles of Charleston, a theological liberal, did not mention Hughes but observed that Southerners had no proper word for their system and that blacks were not slaves in the usual sense.[16]

Holmes, having offered a balanced evaluation of socialism, performed the same feat with the unbridled individualism that Hughes and Fitzhugh denounced without restraint. In a positive review of Fitzhugh's *Sociology of the South*, Holmes rejected the dogmatism that censured free society as universally evil. He saw the evils of Europe as having roots in moral collapse rather than in the social system per se. Since all social systems perform in a manner better or worse, he conceded the possibility of salutary reform. Holmes emphatically agreed with Fitzhugh that free society had failed in northern Europe but chided him for ignoring the more favorable condition of the Mediterranean countries. His criticism startles. He might more sensibly have argued – as did James Johnston Pettigrew, who knew Spain and Italy well – that the Mediterranean countries had succeeded in curbing modern social antagonisms because they retained essentially corporate social systems. During the same year, 1855, Holmes assaulted capitalism for replacing personal slavery with "proletarianism" – a disguised and brutal form of public slavery. And he unceasingly located the roots of Europe's moral evils in a free-labor system that fostered egotistical individualism and assaulted the foundations of community.[17]

Although chary of Hughes's rigidities, Holmes advanced a comparable vision. Identifying laissez-faire with license, he favored a social order based on hierarchy and imposed social restraints. If necessary, the state must compel the propertied classes to guarantee a distribution of wealth that provided a decent standard of living for the people, thereby heading off revolutionary crises. He doubted the economic efficacy of slavery and ranged himself with prominent Southerners who demanded reforms that – despite ritual laissez-faire rhetoric – were markedly étatist. Nathaniel Beverley Tucker of Virginia

---

[16] "Life and Works of Colonel Henry Hughes: A Funeral Sermon Preached by the Rev. W. D. Moore, Port Gibson, Mississippi, October 26, 1862," in Lyman, ed., *Writings of Henry Hughes*, 215–218; James Warley Miles, *The Relation between the Races at the South* (Charleston, S.C., 1861), 4n. See Henry Hughes, *Treatise on Sociology, Theoretical and Practical* (New York, 1968 [1854]). We discuss the knotty theoretical issues and their practical applications of the denial that the South actually had slavery in *Fatal Self-Deception: Loyal and Loving Slaves in the Mind of Southern Slaveholders* (forthcoming).

[17] G. F. Holmes, "Fitzhugh's Sociology for the South," *QRMCS*, 9: (1855), 180–201; G. F. Holmes, "Ancient Slavery," *DBR*, 19 (1855), 559–578, quote at 565; [James Johnston Pettigrew], *Notes on Spain and the Spaniards in the Summer of 1859, with a Glance at Sardinia. By a Carolinian* (Charleston, S.C., 1861).

pointed to France as evidence that ruling classes had to tax themselves to take care of the poor or face lower-class insurrections. Tucker saw British parliamentary reports on the oppression of the laboring classes as an earnest of class war. C. G. Memminger of South Carolina – later secretary of the treasury in the Confederacy – aware of the radicalization of European and American workers, campaigned for public education designed to attach the loyalty of white workers.[18]

Sociology: The Science of Society

In 1857 the New Orleans *Daily Delta* taunted the North: "The truth is, no modern free society has yet worked out a sound social theory." W. S. Grayson of Mississippi and J. P. Holcombe of Virginia believed that a modern slave society could do so by fusing social theory with theology. "There is," Grayson wrote, "such a science as sociology – comprising the principles of social life." But it is a science of government, not of natural life, and it relies on the "Baconian method of observation" to discern the laws of nature, which have nothing to do with justice. For Grayson, sociology studied the division of labor in relation to property ownership. He denied that conscience and the human spirit flowed from natural law. Murder is contrary to law not because it is contrary to nature but because it is contrary to the laws of God. The civil law that upholds slavery follows Scripture. Holcombe, speaking in 1858 at an agricultural fair in Petersburg, affirmed that God does not ordain contradictions: "Men can derive no rights from him which are inconsistent with the duration and perfection of society." Since society establishes private property to promote civilization, the needs and circumstances of the community must determine the justice of slavery. Society established private property and thereby shut out the majority of mankind to promote civilization; hence, it could enslave some to serve others. The justice of slavery, "like other forms of involuntary restraint," rested on the community's needs and circumstances. Natural law dictates no natural rights in the political and social sphere; since it demonstrates the inferiority of the black race, it sanctions its enslavement.[19]

Southern theorists advanced several mutually exclusive positions on slavery. In contrast to Holcombe, William Gordon McCabe of Virginia defended slavery on grounds that slavery is just because unnatural – because man has the will and capacity to overcome nature to improve his lot. Man strives toward God, and slavery is a revealed right. Yet Edmund Ravenel, a respected scientist

[18] Nathaniel Beverley Tucker, "An Essay on the Moral and Political Effect of the Relation between the Caucasian and the African Slave," *SLM*, 10 (1844), 472–473; Henry D. Capers, *The Life and Times of C. G. Memminger* (Richmond, Va., 1893), 490–491.

[19] *New Orleans Daily Delta*, March 20, 1857; W. S. Grayson, "Natural Equality of Man," *DBR*, 26 (1859), 29–38; [William S. Grayson], "Civilization in Its Relations to Property and Social Life," *DBR*, 26 (1859), 164–165; Grayson, "Natural Equality of Man," *DBR*, 26 (1859), 29–38, quote at 30; also Grayson, "Slavery – Is It Natural or Unnatural," *SLM* 25 (1857), 321–329; J. P. Holcombe, "Is Slavery Consistent with Natural Law?" *SLM*, 27 (1858), 402–403, 407.

in Charleston, assailed the "Black Republicans" for not understanding that "physical laws cannot be altered by human skill & resources." In a series of articles and addresses in 1857, another nationally respected natural scientist, John McCrady of Charleston, contrasted the steady decline of Europe and the North with the rise of a South marked by a God-chosen "peculiar people." Although he insisted that slavery had been forced on the South, he hailed it as the foundation of southern virtue and prosperity, and – a polygenesist – he claimed that the application of the laws of the natural sciences to society justified white supremacy. The South was pioneering in a "philosophic sociology" that projected the white race as destined to subjugate the colored races on a world scale. Charleston's formidable scientific community rallied to the effort to render sociology scientific through application of the laws of nature to human development.[20]

Grayson, Holcombe, McCrady, and Ravenel, as well as Fitzhugh, Hughes, and Le Conte, lauded sociology as their favorite social science. Sociology emerged as a discipline from the Romantic revolt against atomistic liberalism and counterpoising corporatist collectivism. It viewed society as an organism with its own personality – with values apart from the subjective values of the individuals who inhabit it. Corporatist thought projected the community as more than the sum of its individual parts – as more than a composite of individual wills. The activities of citizens reveal the spirit of the community or nation, outside of which they have no meaning. Common purpose allows the individual to realize himself through self-discipline and subordination.[21]

Auguste Comte was not well known even in France until the mid-1850s. William Ellery Channing – perhaps the first distinguished American to take Comte seriously – thought him "the most thoroughly scientific intellect now on the planet." Edgar Allan Poe and John Reuben Thompson, among others, valued Comte's scientific work and advocacy of carefully guided social change to overcome social antagonisms. Most Southerners who commented

---

[20] "E. T." [William Gordon McCabe], "Slavery – Is It Natural or Unnatural," *SLM*, 25 (1857), 434–435; [John McCrady], "A Few Thoughts on Southern Civilization," *RM*, 1 (1857), 224–228, 338–349, 546–556; 2 (1857), 212–226; also John McCrady, *A System of Independent Research, the Chief Educational Want of the South* (Charleston, S.C., 1856), 9, and Lester D. Stephens, *Science, Race, and Religion in the American South: John Bachman and the Charleston Naturalists, 1845–1895* (Chapel Hill, N.C., 2000), 76–77, quote at 76 (Ravenel), 156–162 (McCrady). "E. T.," replying to Holcombe in *SLM*, 25 (1857), 434–435, also defended slavery as just because unnatural. For an earlier and weaker attempt to relate scientific developments to history, see Benjamin Faneuil Porter's lecture to the students at the University of Alabama: *The Past and the Present* (Tuscaloosa, 1845).

[21] "Thus," writes Roberto Mangabeira Unger, "it would be possible to view others as complementary rather than opposing wills": *Knowledge and Politics* (New York, 1984), 32, 83, quote at 220; see also Unger, *Law in Modern Society: Toward a Criticism of Social Theory* (New York, 1976), 19–34. For the relation of the emerging southern sociology to broader developments in the natural sciences and theology, see especially James Oscar Farmer, Jr., *The Metaphysical Confederacy: James Henley Thornwell and the Synthesis of Southern Values* (Macon, Ga., 1986), ch. 3.

on Comte read him in French; others settled for Harriet Martineau's translation and abridgement published as *Course of Positive Philosophy* (1853),
which attracted the attention of northern as well as British intellectuals.
Women appear to have contributed more than men to the spread of Comtean
positivism in the United States, notwithstanding Comte's slighting view of
women, which drew heavy fire from his English disciple John Stuart Mill. With
Martineau as the most important conduit, Lydia Maria Child and Julia Ward
Howe valued Comte's social theory as liberation from dogma. George Eliot
(Mary Ann Evans), who took the southern novel-reading public by storm in
the 1850s, contributed to Comte's influence. Ella Gertrude Clanton Thomas of
Georgia described *Adam Bede*, *The Mill on the Floss*, and Augusta Jane Evans's
Beulah as the "books which have created most sensation in the novel reading
portion of the country for some time." Eliot, notwithstanding Methodist roots,
became entranced with Comtean positivism as well as with the work of David
Friedrich Strauss, Ernest Renan, and the German Higher Criticism. In 1854
she translated Ludwig Feuerbach's *Das Wesens des Christentums* (The Essence
of Christianity), which made a splash in England and influenced Karl Marx.
Although Eliot looked Christian enough to the readers of *Adam Bede*, her later
works made clear that she considered Christianity primarily ethical doctrine.[22]

George Frederick Holmes's writings on Comte would fill a book of three
or four hundred pages. In essays published in 1850–1851, Holmes classified
Comte as a towering intellect with claims to equality with Aristotle, Descartes,
Bacon, Leibniz, and Kant. He applauded the "acute" Comte for his scientific contributions, penetrating analyses of modern society, and "strong and
accurate censures" on political morals. Holmes referred to "the great work
of Comte" and to the contribution of "the greatest of modern philosophers"
to the scientific dissection of the social ills that brought the Middle Ages to
a close. He doubtless was pleased that Comte – like Jean-Baptiste Say before
him and John Stuart Mill after him – rejected attempts to make sociology a
statistical science based on probability. Comte held that each science must have
a method appropriate to its subject matter. By 1853 or so, Holmes had doubts
about Comte, and thereafter he lost patience. Although still praising Comte for
properly identifying natural theology as the beginning of atheism, he assailed
Comte's own implicit atheism and social nostrums.[23]

---

[22] For Channing, Poe, and Thompson, see Richmond Laurin Hawkins, *Auguste Comte and the
United States (1816–1853)* (Cambridge, Mass., 1936), 26, 67, Channing quoted at 16; also
John R. Thompson, in *SLM*, 28 (1859), 319. E. G. C. Thomas, July 21, 1861, in Thomas
Papers; Sally Baxter Hampton to Anna Baxter, May 20, 1859, Ann Fripp Hampton, ed., *A
Divided Heart: Letters of Sally Baxter Hampton, 1853–1862* (Spartanburg, S.C., 1980), 61–
62; Margaret Leech, *Reveille in Washington* (New York, 1962), 22; Stephen Meats and Edwin
T. Arnold, eds., *The Writings of Benjamin F. Perry*, 3 vols. (Spartanburg, S.C., 1980), 1:474.
Matthew B. Grier warned that Harriet Martineau's translation of *Positive Philosophy* was less
a translation than her personal reconstruction of Comte's thought: Grier, "Positive Philosophy
of Auguste Comte," *SPR*, 9 (1855), 203.

[23] See the following signed and unsigned articles by George Frederick Holmes: "Morell's Philosophy of the Nineteenth Century," *SLM*, 16 (1850), quote at 385–396; "Latter-Day Pamphlets,"

Henry Hughes owed much to Thomas Carlyle, Victor Cousin, Charles Fourier, Jeremy Bentham, and John Stuart Mill in his quest for stability, order, and social guidance to avoid anarchy, but Douglas Ambrose demonstrates that Hughes owed less to Comte than widely asserted. Indirect evidence does, however, suggest that Comte reinforced the organicism of Le Conte, Simms, Mitchell King, and James H. Hammond, among others, encouraging the notion that social science could find a way to eradicate social antagonisms. On at least two matters Comte disturbed Southerners friendly to him. He respected the Catholic Church, which he had left as a young man, but despised Protestantism, which he considered ultra-individualistic, anti-authority, and anti-family. And he excoriated slavery as "une monstruosité sociale, émenée de l'infame oppression que la race intelligente exerça sur la race aimante" [a social monstruosity, emanating from the infamous oppression that an intelligent race imposed on a loving race].[24]

The Presbyterian Reverend Thomas Smyth of Charleston tempered sharp criticism of Comte with expressions of respect, but *Southern Literary Messenger* published an anything-but-respectful extended denunciation of Comtean philosophy as atheistic. A contributor to *Southern Quarterly Review* referred to Comte's embrace of religion after the death of Clotilde de Veaux – his mistress, whom he substituted for the Virgin Mary – as "the most absurd Fetischism [*sic*] of his own construction." The Baptist Reverend Edwin Theodore Winkler, commencement speaker at Wake Forest College, teased that even Comte's system required a veneer of religion. Winkler had sport with Comte's attempt to find room for religious worship in his brave new world despite his leading a "Punic War" against theology and metaphysics. More to the point, Dabney linked Comte to John Stuart Mill and Herbert Spencer as materialists. In *Southern Presbyterian Review*, Matthew B. Grier shrank from describing

SQR, n.s. 2 (1850), 324, also 335; "Cimon and Pericles," *SQR*, 3 (1851), 341; "Greeley on Reforms," *SLM*, 17 (1851), 260–261; "The Nineteenth Century," *SLM*, 17 (1851), 461; "The Positive Religion," *Methodist Magazine and Quarterly Review*, 4th series, 6 (1854), 334, 343. Despite hostility to Comte's project, Holmes admitted to having exaggerated the influence of St. Simon on positivism: Holmes to Comte, Oct. 30, 1852, in Hawkins, *Comte and United States*, 118–119. See also Stephen M. Stigler, *The History of Statistics: The Measurement of Uncertainty before 1900* (Cambridge, Mass., 1986), 194–195; Theodore M. Porter, *The Rise of Statistical Thinking, 1820–1900* (Princeton, N.J., 1986), 155–156. In 1856 a review of Comte's *Cours de philosophie positive* discussed the sciences without paying attention to Comte's own work: "The Nebular Hypothesis," *SQR*, 3rd ser., 1 (1856), 95–118. On Comte, compare the tone of "Some Thoughts on Social Philosophy," *SLM*, 22 (1856), 308, with that of "Lewes's Philosophy," *SLM*, 25 (1857), 408–411.

[24] Douglas Ambrose, *Henry Hughes and Proslavery Thought in the Old South* (Baton Rouge, La., 1996), 59–61, 72–73, 196; and for the affinity between the ideas of Hughes and Comte see 113; Drew Gilpin Faust, *James Henry Hammond and the Old South* (Baton Rouge, La., 1982), 263–265; Mitchell King, *A Discourse on the Qualifications and Duties of an Historian* (Savannah, Ga., 1843), 6; Joseph Le Conte, "Relation of Organic Science to Sociology," *SPR*, 13 (1860), 69–77. For Comte on Protestantism and slavery, see Richmond Laurin Hawkins, *Auguste Comte and the United States (1816–1853)* (Cambridge, Mass., 1936), especially ch. 1, Comte quoted at 12.

Comte as a socialist but noted his early association with the St. Simonians and Louis Blanc's mention of him as a social reformer. Grier was more troubled by the enthusiasm for Comte shown by scientific racists. The Episcopal Reverend W. N. Pendleton of Lexington, Virginia, complained of the influence of G. H. Lewes's *Biographical History of Philosophy*, arguing that too many knew Comte through Lewes and did not take the measure of the atheist materialism. Pendleton, expressing what others left implicit, denounced Comtean materialism for threatening "our Southern social organization."[25]

Le Conte, who taught at the University of Georgia and South Carolina College, applied the laws of nature to society. Specifically, Le Conte advanced an organic view of historical development that stressed the fragility and slow pace of change and fueled a conservative politics. He saw cycles of growth and decline in individual and social organisms but gave them a Christian and "progressive" twist in which each cycle prepared the way for another at a higher level. Le Conte delineated the relation of sociology to moral philosophy for the senior class at the College of South Carolina, significantly published in *Southern Presbyterian Review* in 1860. Sociology stood as the most important of the sciences: "All other sciences point as their final end and object, viz. the 'science of sociology' – the science of human society and human improvement." Sociology must develop as a distinct discipline but be founded on all the other sciences: "The fundamental idea and doctrines of Sociology are identical with those of Biology and Geology." But contrary to Comte and materialist philosophers, the methods of the organic sciences did not suffice, for "Man is spiritual as well as material."[26]

---

[25] "The Successful Merchant and the Lessons of His Life and Death," in *Complete Works of the Reverend Thomas Smyth, D. D.*, ed. J. William Flinn, 10 vols. (Columbia, S.C., 1908), 5:439–440; *SQR*, n.s. 10 (1854), 240; criticism of Comte is implicit in "Thoughts on Social Philosophy," *SLM*, 22 (1856), 308; "Lewes' Philosophy," *SLM*, 25 (1857), 408–415, esp. 411; "The Human Family," *SQR*, 11 (1855), 126; *DD*, 4:472–473; and "Positivism in England," 3:24–25; Robert L. Dabney, *The Sensualistic Philosophy of the Nineteenth Century Considered*, new and enl. ed. (New York, 1887), 103–104; Edwin Theodore Winkler, *The Pulpit and the Age* (Charleston, 1856), 10–11, and Winkler, "The Pulpit and the Age," *RM*, 2 (1858), 486; Sean Michael Lucas, *Robert Lewis Dabney: A Southern Presbyterian Life* (Phillipsburg, Pa., 2005), ch. 6; Matthew B. Grier, "Positive Philosophy of Auguste Comte," *SPR*, 9 (1855), 203–204, 210–214, 224; W. N. Pendleton, *Science: A Witness for the Bible* (Philadelphia, Pa., 1860), 73–75, quote at 75. For Comte's influence on American theology, see Charles D. Cashdollar, *The Transformation of Theology, 1830–1890: Positivism and Protestant Thought in Britain and America* (Princeton, N.J., 1989), 93–141. For the appalled reaction of orthodox Christians to Comte's positivism, see Theodore Dwight Bozeman, *Protestants in an Age of Science: The Baconian Ideal and Antebellum American Religious Thought* (Chapel Hill, N.C., 1977), 117; also, Bozeman, "Joseph Le Conte: Organic Science and a 'Sociology for the South,'" *JSH*, 39 (1973), 565–582.

[26] Joseph Le Conte, "Relation of Organic Science to Sociology," *SPR*, 13 (1860), 39–77, and for a critique of Schlegel, see 67; also Bozeman, "Joseph Le Conte: Organic Science and a 'Sociology for the South,'" *JSH*, 572. Le Conte's article appeared in six separate scientific journals in America, Canada, England, Scotland, and Ireland – and evoked widespread interest: Joseph Le Conte, "Correlation of Physical, Chemical and Vital Force," *Proceedings of the American Association for the Advancement of Science* (1859).

Thus sociology rested on science, moral philosophy, and history. In the end, Le Conte submits to the church, "for man primarily seeks God's truth." The increasing division of labor constituted a law of life that merged the individual into "the general life of the community by gradually increasing mutual dependence" in a process never complete. Le Conte identified "three fundamental corporations of the social body – three parts of the social being which, may, perhaps, be compared to the three parts of the human being, viz: the material, the intellectual and the moral natures." These corporations or organs of the social body are Guild, State, and Church: "the industrial organization." Organic Science connected "the political organization" through history, religious organization, and moral philosophy. Le Conte launched a critique of the dogmas of the French Revolution and revolutionary ideology and a defense of slavery: "The dogmas of universal liberty and equality, the right of self-government, of free inquiry, of free competition in labor, etc.; all ideas true in a certain sense and with certain limitations." Those limitations could be uncovered through comparisons of peoples and governments, which revealed that the current era wallowed in absolutes, dogmas, and anarchy. Comparison revealed "the relative nature of all human institutions" and "a clearer understanding of the place of slavery in human affairs."[27]

Race

For the new science of sociology to defend slavery and, in particular, Slavery in the Abstract, it had to confront race, doing more than asserting white superiority. In 1753, Jonathan Bryan of Georgia, planter and entrepreneur, thought about "the Special Providence of Almighty God, who has cast out so many Thousands of the Heathen before us" and created "a receptacle for the Professors of his Glorious Gospel and persecuted church in some parts of Europe." A century later, Henry Young Webb of Eutah, Alabama, paraphrased a sermon he had just heard from the Reverend Mr. Claghorn: "The law of Conquest has been recognized – from time immemorial – When a nation has been conquered – The lives & property of the vanquished are at the mercy of the Conqueror.... Or he buys a slave – He says do this – and expects and requires obedience – because the slave is his property." Webb thereupon reflected on

[27] See Bozeman, "Joseph Le Conte: Organic Science," *JSH*, 39 (1973), 565–582, especially 571. Bozeman writes that Le Conte, like many scientists of his day, worked in "a theological rather than utilitarian frame of reference." Showing no knowledge of the speculative sociology of Holmes, Fitzhugh, or Hughes, Le Conte was the first Southerner to attempt a scientific defense of slavery based on an organic sociology (579). Thornwell admired Le Conte's conservative sociology and solicited his article on "The Principles of a Liberal Education" for *SPR*, 12 (July, 1859): see Farmer, *Metaphysical Confederacy*, 106–109. For critical but respectful responses to Comte by Joseph Le Conte, William Gilmore Simms, the Presbyterian Reverend Thomas Smyth, and other Southerners, see Elizabeth Fox-Genovese and Eugene D. Genovese, *The Mind of the Master Class: History and Faith in the Southern Slaveholders' Worldview* (New York, 2005), ch. 19. Le Conte acknowledged a debt to Comte for relating biology to sociology.

man's slavery to God: "So we belong to God – we are bought with a price even the precious blood of the Son of God – and therefore we are bound to obey." In 1860 Sam Milligan of Tennessee wrote to Andrew Johnson, his close friend and political ally, that God ordained civilization through the workings of the laws of nature: "So that if the common interest require either the lands (as of the Indians) or the labor (as of the idle negro) of the vicious, the idle or unproductive, the laws of civilization can take them for the good of the whole." In much the same spirit, Louisa McCord of South Carolina viewed the white race as uniquely fit for liberty and destined to rule the inferior colored races.[28]

Racial categorization did not end with a dichotomy between whites and non-whites. Educated Southerners knew that the Greeks and Romans made quasi-racial distinctions among themselves while assuming that foreign "races" – Asians, notably, Scythians, Jews, Syrians – were born for slavery. E. A. Pollard of Virginia assailed the Romans for enslaving members of their own race and praised Southerners for uplifting an inferior race. Frederick Augustus Porcher of South Carolina, discussing the history of art, asserted that the Doric and Ionian Greeks fought each other in a racial war, and that Americans were "essentially members of a Northern Race." Porcher continued: "We call ourselves Americans, but we are not the less on that account, Saxons or Celts.... The races, as they now exist are characterized by essential differences in their moral and mental constitution – that these differences are so deeply rooted that education can do little more than modify them in individuals – that whenever the instinct of the race is touched, all conventional trainings disappear and nature asserts her dominion over the heart of man."[29]

Historians in Victorian England sang the praises of the Anglo-Saxon race and poured contempt on the Celts and other allegedly inferior European races. The notion grew that interracial mixture – say, of Celts and Teutons – produced infertility in offspring. Ideas of Nordic superiority arose unevenly among Europeans, thriving heartily among Mediterranean peoples, but whereas the Spanish nobility long prided itself on descent from the Goths, the Portuguese did not. Such ideas prevailed most notably among the French, who used the image of a vigorous people to the north as a weapon in their struggle against the decadence of their own peoples. Political ramifications of the racial classifications emerged directly. An article in *Russell's Magazine* noted that the Normans who conquered Britain claimed racial superiority: In 1860 a contributor to *Southern Literary Messenger* set forth an intriguing argument that found the origin of the sectional crisis in a racial difference between Northerners and

---

[28] [J. Bryan], Aug. 13, 1753, *Journal of a Visit to the Georgia Islands*, ed. Virginia Steele Wood and Mary R. Bullard (Macon, Ga., 1996), 20; Henry Young Webb Diary, May 1, 1858; Sam Milligan to Andrew Johnson, Feb. 8, 1860, *AJP*, 3:420. In *Louisa S. McCord: Political and Social Essays*, ed. Richard C. Lounsbury (Charlottesville, Va., 1995), see "Diversity of the Races," 173, and "British Philanthropy and American Slavery," 289–290, 317–318.

[29] Edward A. Pollard, *Black Diamonds Gathered in the Darkey Homes of the South* (New York, 1859), 82; F. A. Porcher, "Modern Art," in Michael O'Brien, ed., *All Clever Men, Who Make Their Way: Critical Discourse in the Old South* (Fayetteville, Ark., 1982), 313–314.

Southerners – in their descent from distinct white races. And during the War, J. Quitman Moore lauded the "superior" Norman race and its servile labor system, which avoided the destructive competitiveness that enfeebled its rivals.[30]

Fitzhugh dismissed the racial defense of slavery as an infidel procedure that contradicted the Bible by denying humanity's common ancestry and the suitability of slavery for whites as well as blacks. Educated Southerners knew that in ancient and medieval Europe whites enslaved whites and that the extreme brutality of punishments meted out to slaves marked the barrier between social classes and the "races" with which they often came to be identified. Unions between free men and slaves were considered unnatural and akin to the bestiality denounced in the Germanic legal codes. Scandinavian slaves were not "outsiders" set apart by religion or ethnicity, yet free men considered them morally deficient in ways that resembled racial stereotypes. Icelanders, and probably Norwegians, did not always judge dark skin a mark of racial difference, but did tend to view it as unattractive and a sign of foreign origin and moral inferiority. The chivalric literature of England and France identified the much-admired qualities of knighthood with genetic inheritance. By the eighteenth century Russian noblemen assumed that their authority stemmed from the inherent, implicitly racial, inferiority of serfs who needed special protection.[31]

Josiah Nott of Mobile, the South's leading scientific racist, argued that blacks and whites constituted separate species and that therefore environmental factors like climate did not determine their development. He considered colored races inferior to white; ranked the blacks as the lowest of all races; scorned American Indians; and notwithstanding a much better opinion of the Chinese, placed them below whites, whom he subdivided into many separate races with different levels of ability and accomplishment. Nott acknowledged much intermixture. He saw Jews as a purer race than most and criticized the Spanish,

---

[30] Peter J. Bowler, *The Invention of Progress: The Victorians and the Past* (London, 1989), 107–110; Jacques Barzun, *The French Race: Theories of Its Origins and Their Social and Political Implications Prior to the Revolution* (New York, 1932), 12, 19. See also Bruce Dain, *A Hideous Monster of the Mind: American Race Theory in the Early Republic* (Cambridge, Mass., 2002), especially 197–263; "Slavery in England," *RM*, 5 (1859), 21; "The Difference of Race between the Northern and Southern People," *SLM*, 30 (1860), 401–409; Moore, "Southern Civilization; or, The Norman in America," *DBR*, 32 (1862), 1–19; also, J. T. Wiswall, "Southern Society and British Critics," *DBR*, 32 (1862), 198. On the ambiguity in Southerners' use of "race," see Michael O'Brien, *Conjectures of Order: Intellectual Life and the American South, 1810–1860*, 2 vols. (Chapel Hill, N.C., 2004), 1:250.

[31] [George Frederick Holmes], "Grote's History of Greece," *SQR*, n.s. (3rd), 2 (1856), 113; George Fitzhugh, "Southern Thought," *DBR* 23 (1857), 338, 347; Peter Kolchin, "In Defense of Servitude: American Proslavery and Russian Proserfdom Arguments, 1760–1860," *American Historical Review*, 85 (1980), 811–813. See also M. I. Finley, *Ancient Slavery and Modern Ideology* (New York, 1989), 119. For medieval conditions, see Pierre Bonassie, *From Slavery to Feudalism in South Western Europe* (Cambridge, U.K., 1991), 21–22; Ruth Mazo Karras, *Slavery and Society in Medieval Scandinavia* (New Haven, Conn., 1988), 15–16, 64; Richard W. Kaeuper, *Chivalry and Violence in Medieval Europe* (New York, 1999), 190–191.

Portuguese, "and other dark races" for easily mixing with blacks. By "white races" he meant primarily Anglo-Saxons and Teutons: "The ancient Germans may be regarded as the parent stock from which the highest modern civilization has sprung. The best blood of France and England is German; the ruling caste in Russia is German; and look at the United States, and contrast our people with the dark-skinned Spaniards. It is clear that the dark-skinned Celts are fading away before the superior race, and that they must eventually be absorbed." In 1830 he expressed sympathy for the Irish poor. Later, he disparaged the Scots-Irish of the South, a majority of whom had become, through intermarriage, "stupid and debased in the extreme." Without subscribing to Nott's more peculiar views, Southerners used "race" to separate, say, the English and Germans from the French and Italians. Writing in 1872, W. H. Sparks of Georgia expressed an attitude that had been steadily advancing before the War. Viewing the European "races" differently, he praised the Celts for gallantry and damned the Saxons for cruelty. "There are many grades in the Caucasian race," he wrote. "The Anglo-Norman or Anglo-Celtic is certainly at the head. They rule wherever left to the conflict of mind and energy of soul."[32]

Before the French Revolution the proper delineation of "aristocrats" provoked controversy in Europe as aristocratic ranks expanded and claims of racial purity separated hereditary aristocrats from upstarts. In the South, even Hugh Legaré, who ignored the racially partisan anthropology of Lord Monboddo and Lord Kames, sought racial grounds for his distinction among Europeans between lords and villeins. Responding to the French Revolution of 1830, Legaré suggested that only Anglo-Saxons could support a government of laws and that the French were incapable of self-government. In a letter from Brussels to I. E. Holmes of South Carolina in 1832, he gushed that the Anglo-Saxons alone understood liberty: "What a race the English are! They are without exception, the highest specimen of civilization the world has ever seen – but don't tell them I say so."[33]

James Johnston Pettigrew wrote to his brother in 1850, "In Hungary the common people are but half civilized," but the nobles "are as much superior to their subordinates as we to our slaves." Beyond such generalizations went a decided preference for peoples of northwestern Europe. The Methodist Reverend W. J. Sasnett, a professor at Emory College, held that the Anglo-Saxon and Teutonic races complemented each other, the one disproportionately practical, the other disproportionately reflective or metaphysical, and their

[32] Nott, "Acclimation," in Josiah C. Nott and George R. Gliddon, *Indigenous Races of the Earth; or New Chapters of Ethnological Inquiry* (Philadelphia, 1857), ch. 4, quoted from 367–368; on the Jews, see 355; Josiah C. Nott, *Two Lectures on the Connection between the Biblical and Physical History of Man* (New York, 1849), 37; Nott quoted on the Scots-Irish in Reginald Horsman, *Josiah Nott: Southerner, Physician, and Racial Theorist* (Baton Rouge, La., 1987), 47; W. H. Sparks, *The Memories of Fifty Years* (Philadelphia, Pa., 1872), 106–108, quote at 122.
[33] "Constitutional History of Greece," in *HLW*, 1:375; Legaré to I. E. Holmes, Oct. 2, 1832; Legaré to Louis McLane, July 2, 1833, in *HLW*, 1:172, 204–205.

combination made Americans the greatest of races. In 1854 a contributor to *Quarterly Review of the Methodist Church, South* said nothing startling when he proclaimed in that racial differences lay at the root of the struggles between the English and Irish, the Austrians and Hungarians. Enigmatically, Albert Taylor Bledsoe of Virginia, defending racial stratification, described race as more than color. Not at all enigmatically, G. Norman Lieber of South Carolina asked how Portugal, which never learned to rule herself, could rule her colonies. Only Anglo-Saxons, he thought, had proven themselves capable of ruling others effectively. The Reverend William A. Scott of New Orleans extolled the races of Great Britain, America, and Germany as destined to rule the world and spread freedom. Henry Timrod, Charleston's celebrated poet, exclaimed that they combined in the southern mind to offer "that blending of the philosophic in thought with the enthusiastic in feeling, which makes a literary nation." J. S. Morris, a well-known attorney and soi-disant poet, wrote "Lines," a poem to be read at commencement at Oakland College, Mississippi, in 1858. It included:

> Of Anglo-Southern men, by whom t'is God's design
> To conquer, elevate and rule the heathen hosts,
> Who groan in pagan chains on Afric's torrid coast.[34]

The Presbyterian divines trod carefully. Thornwell made clear that the "Federal Theory" of original sin – a centerpiece of his Calvinist theology – compelled adherence to the doctrines of a common descent from Adam and of the unity of the human race, which he described as the rock of the family, the church, and society: "Christianity unquestionably binds the race together in ties unknown to nature. She establishes a sacred brotherhood in common origin, a common ruin, a common immortality, a common Saviour, which unites the descendants of Adam into one great family, and renders wars, discords, and jealousies as odious as they are hurtful." Those words did not contradict the observations

---

[34] Andreas A. M. Kinneging, *Aristocracy, Antiquity and History: Classicism in Political Thought* (New Brunswick, N.J., 1997), ch. 1; Pettigrew quoted in Clyde N. Wilson, *Carolina Cavalier: The Life and Mind of James Johnston Pettigrew* (Athens, Ga., 1990), 45. For Legaré and the anthropology of Lord Monboddo and Lord Kames, see Michael O'Brien, "Politics, Romanticism, and Hugh Legaré," in O'Brien and David Moltke-Hansen, eds., *Intellectual Life in Antebellum Charleston* (Knoxville, Tenn., 1986), 143; W. J. Sasnett, "German Philosophy," *QRMCS*, 12 (1858), 323–324; "Mrs. Sommerville's Physical Geography," *QRMCS*, 8 (1854), 520–521; Albert Taylor Bledsoe, "Liberty and Slavery," in E. N. Elliott, ed., *Cotton Is King and Pro-Slavery Arguments* (New York, 1969 [1860]), 332; G. Norman Lieber, "The Portuguese and Their Poet," *RM*, 4 (1858), 249–256; W. A. Scott, "The Progress of Civil Liberty," in Robert Gibbes Barnwell, ed., *The New-Orleans Book* (New Orleans, La., 1851); Edd Winfield Parks, ed., *The Essays of Henry Timrod* (Athens, Ga., 1942), 101; J. S. Morris, *Impromptu Lines Read before the Belles Lettres Society and Adelphic Institute of Oakland College* (Port Gibson, Miss., 1858). The North is Celtic and rebellious, the South Saxon and orderly: "Northern Mind and Character," *SLM*, 31 (1860), 343–349.

of two other high-powered southern Presbyterian divines. The Reverend Benjamin Morgan Palmer, acknowledging a debt to August von Schlegel, argued that every truly historic people had special traits and made a special contribution to civilization. Robert L. Dabney, in a memorial sermon on "The Christian Soldier," defined the duties of patriotism as natural, not scriptural or directly religious, but, nonetheless, consistent with Scripture: "The diversity of tongues, characters, races, and interests among mankind forbids their union in one universal commonwealth. The aggregation of men into separate nations is therefore necessary; and the authority of the governments instituted over them, to maintain internal order and external defence against aggression, is of divine appointment. Hence, to sustain our government with heart and hand is not only made by God our privilege, but our duty. Our best way to advance the well-being of the race is to advance that of the portion of our race associated with us in the same society. He who extends his philanthropy so broadly as to refuse a special attachment to the interests of his own people, will probably make it so thin as to be of no account to any people."[35]

Too bad Dabney never read Karl Marx. He might have saluted Marx's contemptuous reference to the "universal brotherhood swindle." Dabney and many other Southerners did read James Boswell's *The Life of Samuel Johnson* and Alexis de Tocqueville's *Democracy in America*. Johnson condemned the French as incapable of moral and political improvement and for living high amid a population of miserably poor people. Tocqueville commented that Americans took immense pride in their liberties but believed only a few nations capable of maintaining them. In *Democracy in America* he implied that which he made explicit in another book Americans did not know: The French were "unfit and unworthy to live a life of freedom." They were "always the same, as impatient, as thoughtless, as contemptuous of law and order, as easily led and cowardly in the presence of danger as [their] fathers were before them."[36]

During the 1840s and especially the 1850s, the southern press – from the prestigious *Southern Literary Messenger* to college publications – almost casually referred to the French as a race apart and to France as a nation of infidels and barbarous revolutions. Ignatius E. Shumate, in *Southern Repertory and College Review* of Emory and Henry College, referred to "France, that volcano

---

[35] In *JHTW*, see "The Office of Reason in Regard to Revelation" (3:183–220, quote at 211); "Nature of Our Interest in the Sin of Adam, Being a Review of Baird's Elohim Revealed" (1:527, 532, 552); also, "Moral Government" (1:257); "Original Sin" (1:349); "Religion Psychologically Considered" (3:134); for Palmer, see Stephen R. Haynes, *Noah's Curse: The Biblical Justification of American Slavery* (New York, 2002), 129–130; "The Christian Soldier," *DD*, 1:614–625, quoted from 615–616. For a cautious argument for white rule of colored peoples, see [A North Carolinian], *Slavery Considered on General Principles, Or, A Grapple with Abstractionists* (New York, 1861), 16–18, 24.

[36] Karl Marx, *The Eighteenth Brumaire of Louis Bonaparte* (New York, 1963), 116; James Boswell, *The Life of Samuel Johnson, L. L. D.* (New York, n.d.), 561; Alexis de Tocqueville, *Democracy in America*, 2 vols., tr. Henry Reeve (Boston, Mass., 1873), 2:268; J. P. Mayer, ed., *The Recollections of Alexis de Tocqueville* (London, 1948), 75.

of passion, that has ever belched forth billows of revolution." In 1845 Palmer considered the French the least religious of Europeans and the only ones capable of committing the atrocities of the Terror. Thornwell characterized France as an "unsettled country, which God seems to have made a striking example of the weakness, ignorance, and folly of man." Thirty years later Palmer published Thornwell's letter with the observation that nothing essential had changed. To Thornwell and Palmer, only liberty and Protestantism promised dignity and stability to a French character proven to be incapable of sustaining republican government, freedom, and peace. When the War came, Bishop Stephen Elliott of Georgia's Episcopal Church declared, "We are fighting to prevent ourselves from being transferred from American republicanism to French democracy." Similarly, prominent men like Bledsoe and the Presbyterian Reverend George D. Armstrong of Norfolk, considered the French unfit for self-government and in need of a strong leader. Bledsoe emphatically agreed with Napoleon that the French loved equality but cared little for liberty. Edmund Ruffin admired Giuseppe Garibaldi but thought Italy needed a constitutional monarchy. The Italians "are totally unfit for republican government." Reactions in the Southwest did not differ much from those in the Southeast.[37]

The Presbyterian Reverend Thomas Smyth regarded republicanism as the closest approximation of godly government but doubted its fitness for all: "The government which would prove a blessing to one community might prove no blessing to another." The Presbyterian Reverend S. J. Cassells publicly and Randal W. McGavock of Nashville privately, like Americans even before the Louisiana Purchase, concluded that the French could not sustain republican liberty. Freedom, for Cassells, was a blessing to those who became morally disciplined over time, whereas for those who had not, it produced only tyrants. Countless millions throughout the world were "no more fit for freedom than children or brute animals." The Reverend John Adger of South Carolina, who had spent many years in the Near East, told the Presbyterian General Assembly of 1857 that Presbyterians stood against mass democracy and for a "rational, regulated, constitutional freedom, the gift of God to but few of the nations." In 1848, William F. Hutson ridiculed the French as shallow philosophers for whom Reason is Revelation: "The French people, with a desire for conquest and

---

[37] *SLM*, 24 (1857), 248; Ignatius E. Shumate, "The Victim of Passion," *Southern Repertory and College Review*, 4 (1856), 218; Benjamin M. Palmer, *Influence of Religious Belief upon National Character: An Oration Delivered before the Demosthenian and Phi Kappa Societies of the University of Georgia* (Athens, Ga., 1845), 24–25; James Henley Thornwell to William H. Robbins, Aug. 27, 1842, in B. M. Palmer, *The Life and Letters of James Henley Thornwell* (Richmond, 1875), 233; Stephen Elliott, *God's Presence with the Confederate States* (Savannah, 1861), 21; Herschel Gower, et al., eds., *Pen and Sword: The Life and Journals of Randal W. McGavock, Colonel, C. S. A.* (Nashville, Tenn., 1959), ch. 13; Albert Taylor Bledsoe, *An Essay on Liberty and Slavery* (Philadelphia, Pa., 1856), 129; G. D. Armstrong, "Three Letters to a Conservative – Letter I," *Presbyterian Magazine* (1858), 12; *ERD*, 1:311. See also *VUM*, 2 (1858), 68; J. F. H. Claiborne, *Mississippi as a Province, Territory, and State, with Biographical Notices of Eminent Citizens* (Spartanburg, S.C., 1978 [1860]), 252–253. Among others, George Sawyer and J. A. Turner referred to the French as a race.

love of war, and that bigotry which has been their chief national characteristic, did pant after universal empire and universal plunder, as well as the universal acceptance of their creed at the point of the bayonet." He reminded his readers that twice the nations of Europe had to march to Paris to put down revolution and murder. Hutson suggested that the nations of Europe would have to do it again and that, the next time, they would either finish the French off or assume responsibility for the slaughter of millions. France, he concluded, was hopeless and must suffer endless barbarism or foreign bayonets.[38]

Southerners read Caesar's *Gallic Wars* in school and knew that he had taken no chances with the Gauls "for fear of their instability." They were, Caesar wrote, "capricious in choosing a course and prone to revolution." In reaction to the Reign of Terror even the Jeffersonian radical John Taylor of Caroline considered the French unfit for liberty. In the North, Judge Gould of the Litchfield Law School, at which Calhoun and other prominent Southerners studied, quipped, "Tell Mr. Beecher I am improving in [Calvinist] orthodoxy. I have got so far as this, that I believe in the total depravity of the whole French nation."[39]

In South Carolina nullifiers and unionists agreed on some things. The fiery nullifier George McDuffie did not veer far from the less flamboyant unionist Legaré in believing that only Anglo-Saxons could support a government of laws. Said McDuffie: "I rejoice that we have an English ancestry. The Anglo-Saxon, for sturdy and masculine national virtues, is unquestionably the best stock of modern times." For Calhoun, it was "a great mistake in supposing all people are capable of self-government." Only a people who had advanced "to a high state of moral and intellectual excellence" are so qualified. Francis Lieber cited with approbation the view of Barthold Niebuhr, the great German historian of ancient Rome, that the French lacked the cultural foundations for a republic. William Gilmore Simms described filibustering to William Porcher Miles as "the moral necessity of all Anglo Norman breed. It is the necessity of all pro-gressive races." Simms wrote to J. H. Hammond that an American-sponsored introduction of slavery would "civilize" Mexico. The dismal outcomes of the revolutions in France and Latin America strengthened the belief of Southerners, as well as Northerners, in the racial superiority of Anglo-Saxons and Teutons.[40]

---

[38] *Works of Thomas Smyth*, ed. Flinn, 6:22; Cassells, "Relation of Justice to Benevolence," *SPR*, 7 (1853), 98–99; John Adger, "The General Assembly of 1857," 10 (1857), 281–284; [William F. Hutson], "History of the Girondists," *SPR*, 2 (1848), 394, 396.

[39] Julius Caesar, *The Gallic War and Other Writings*, tr. Moses Hadas (New York, 1957), 76; Gould quoted in Charles Beecher, ed., *Autobiography, Correspondence, Etc. of Lyman Beecher*, 2 vols. (New York, 1871), 1:225; John Taylor, *Arator: Being a Series of Agricultural Essays, Practical and Political: In Sixty-Four Numbers* (Indianapolis, Ind., 1977 [1818]), 178.

[40] Gower et al., eds., *Pen and Sword: McGavock Journals*, ch. 13; John C. Calhoun, "From His Speech on His Resolutions in Reference to the War with Mexico," January 4, 1848, in Clyde N. Wilson, ed., *The Essential Calhoun: Selections from Writings, Speeches, and Letters* (New Brunswick, N.J., 1991), 114; Lieber, *Miscellaneous Writings: Selections from His Writings and Letters* (New Brunswick, N.J., 1991), 1:95; E. L. Green, ed., *Two Speeches of George McDuffie* (Columbia, S.C., 1905), 60–61; Michael O'Brien, *A Character of Hugh Legaré* (Knoxville,

Elsewhere, A. B. Meek of Alabama, historian and man of letters, taught the superiority of the "Anglo-Saxon race," especially crediting Protestantism for its formation. J. G. Baldwin wrote, "That political affairs require skill, judgment, intelligence, and integrity of character all concede, and we know that in the masses of the population of other countries, these qualities do not reside. The experiment of self-government has signally failed with them, whenever it has been tried." For increasing numbers of Southerners – and Northerners – God ordained the white race to rule the colored races and British and Germanic races to prevail above all. Matthew F. Maury, the influential oceanographer and frequent contributor to southern periodicals, repeatedly called for the eventual absorption of much of Latin America by the United States.[41]

The most influential southern ministers – those who drew large crowds everywhere they preached – stressed the common descent of humankind from Adam and Noah, and their congregations heard them loud and clear. While summering in Henderson County, North Carolina, Mitchell King – a Charleston intellectual luminary – was pleased to report that the Reverend Mr. Miles had preached from Acts, 17:22–29, noting especially verse 26: "He hath made of one blood all the nations of men for to dwell on the face of the earth." In Virginia, Bishop Meade cried out, "This whole world is but one large family, of which Almighty God is the Head and Master, providing food and shelter for all living creatures." The Methodist Reverend N. M. Crawford echoed the Lutheran Reverend John Bachman and the Presbyterian Thornwell in calling the Negro a "brother." Methodist Bishop George Foster Pierce, traveling among the Indians of the Southwest, wrote, "I felt that the religion of the Bible had obliterated the distinctions of color, race, and nation, and that a common salvation made us brethren in spirit." After the War orthodox Presbyterians and Catholics agreed in branding scientific racism a ploy to discredit the Bible. Dabney, although a white supremist, assailed the "half-scholars in natural science" who implied that the Church had no warrant to carry the Bible to blacks.

The divines' sincere, often passionate attacks on scientific racism had a grim side, for they unwittingly slipped into their own version of it. As men who believed in the compatibility of science with Scripture, they easily accepted as valid environmental and even biological arguments of black inferiority. Most divines stood with U.S. Representative James A. Stewart of Maryland, who spoke for the generality of opinion in the lower as well as upper South: "The negro race, although human, in all probability, is inferior and subordinate to the white race." Some defenders of slavery – Matthew Estes of Mississippi,

Tenn., 1985), 189–190. In Mary C. Oliphant et al., eds., *The Letters of William Gilmore Simms*, 6 vols. (Columbia, S.C., 1952–1982), see Simms to Hammond, June 15, 1854; Simms to Miles, Jan. 25, 1858 (2:332, 4:11), Simms to W. P. Miles, Feb. 22, 1861 (4:332).

[41] A. B. Meek, *Romantic Passages in Southwestern History* (New York, 1857, 64; Joseph Glover Baldwin, *Party Leaders: Sketches* (New York, 1868), 74. Ironically, "Gauls" is Latin for "Celts."

John Fletcher of Louisiana, the Presbyterian Reverend John Girardeau of South Carolina – considered blacks inferior in consequence of their particular historical evolution in which races as well as individuals may deteriorate and require protection against themselves.[42]

Scientific racism strengthened the especially dangerous strand of Slavery in the Abstract for which Hughes spoke most forcefully. A nuanced racism foreshadowed the ideologies of modern imperialism, promising to render the enslavement of whites more palatable to the tenderhearted. U.S. Representative Thomas Clingman of North Carolina, speaking on the Kansas-Nebraska Bill, acknowledged that the "revolutionary Fathers" had opposed slavery, but he said that science had undermined ideas of racial equality and reinforced biblical sanction of slavery. Hammond appealed to ethnography to justify the enslavement of blacks. He admitted that the jury was still out but clearly thought that the scientific racists were making their case. William J. Grayson, in his notes to "The Hireling and the Slave," quoted the *Westminster Review*:

Grant that the Negro is a distinct species, or even a metamorphosed orang, if you will, and what difference does it make to the social effect of the "domestic institution" – the ultimate ground upon which both moralist and legislator must take their stand in arguing either for or against it? We do not prosecute the drover or the cabman because we believe the poor, maltreated ox or horse to be our brother, a child of Adam and Eve, like ourselves, but because this and all other brutality is an evil to society – because it degrades the man who practices it, and increases the proclivity to crimes injurious to society in himself and others. And we are bound to put down the slaveholder for precisely the same reason, and not because of a hypothetical cousinhood with his victim, which may or may not exist.[43]

---

[42] Mitchell King Diary, Sept. 18, 1853, UNC; William Meade, *Sermons, Dialogues and Narratives for Servants, to Be Read to Them in Families* (Richmond, Va., 1831), 4; also Meade to Jefferson Davis, Jan. 21, 1862, in Dunbar Rowland, ed., *Jefferson Davis, Constitutionalist: His Letters, Papers and Speeches*, 10 vols. (Jackson, Miss., 1923), 5:186–188; N. M. C., "Southern View of Slavery," *Parlor Visitor*, 7 (1857), 414; George Foster Pierce, *Incidents of Western Travel: In a Series of Letters* (Nashville, Tenn., 1857), 50–51; James A. Stewart, *Powers of the Government of the United States – Federal, State, and Territorial* (Washington, D.C., 1856), 19; Matthew Estes to J. C. Calhoun, Aug. 30, 1845, in *JCCP*, 22:98–100; John Fletcher, *Studies on Slavery, in Easy Lessons* (Natchez, Miss., 1852), 504–505; J. B. Meek, "Work among Negroes," in George A. Blackburn, ed., *The Life Work of John L. Girardeau* (Columbia, S.C., 1916), Pt. 2:70–71. See generally Thomas V. Peterson, *Ham and Japheth: The Mythic World of Whites in the Antebellum South* (Lanham, Md., 1978), ch. 2. For postwar, see R. L. Dabney, *Systematic Theology* (Carlisle, Pa., 1985 [1878]), 292–293. "The Necessity and Nature of Christianity," *JHTW*, 2:64; Charles Hodge, *Systematic Theology*, 3 vols. (Grand Rapids, Mich., 1993 [1871]), 2:78–91, 4; Maria Genoino Caravaglios, *The Catholic Church and the Negro Problem in the XVIII–XIX Centuries* (Charleston, S.C., 1974), 203 (Verlot); Jaroslav Pelikan, *The Christian Tradition: A History of the Development of Doctrine*, 5 vols. (Chicago, 1989), 5:206, 209, 256.

[43] *Selections from the Writings and Speeches of Hon. Thomas L. Clingman of North Carolina* (Raleigh, N.C., 1877), 348–349; Faust, *J. H. Hammond*, 281; William J. Grayson, *The Hireling and Slave, Chicora, and Other Poems* (Charleston, S.C., 1856), 168.

Some religious and secular theorists pushed the doctrine of Slavery in the Abstract while justifying white lordship over the colored races. Pollard supported William Walker's filibustering in Central America, unabashedly identifying the cause as the extension of slavery into a world system. Wary Southerners, convinced that civilized society required slavery in some form, dismissed the idea that the North intended to emancipate black labor. In South Carolina in 1851, the Presbyterian Reverend J. C. Coit and the Episcopalian Reverend William O. Prentiss argued that the campaign to secure the territories for free labor did not aim to destroy slavery but to colonize and exploit southern labor by rendering slaveholders subservient to northern businessmen. In 1860 John Tyler, Jr., of Virginia, writing as "Python" in *De Bow's Review*, returned to a thesis he had advanced in 1857: The North had no intention of destroying black labor and its products by overthrowing slavery; rather, northern capital intended to subordinate black slave labor in a system of ruthless exploitation disguised as apprenticeship.[44]

A worldwide crusade for racial dictatorship did not sit well with conservatives, southern or northern, who saw it as a road to power at home for demagogues of all stripes. The Presbyterian Cassells and the Methodist Senator Henry W. Hilliard of Alabama agreed that imperialism turned a conquering country inward and destroyed its free institutions. The split between Southerners who favored American imperialism and those who opposed it threatened the unity necessary to defend slavery against outside attack. Whatever charm racial imperialism had for Southerners, they wanted it on the back burner politically and ideologically. American national expansion carried with it the danger of adding more free states to the Union or at least of immensely escalating the economic and political power of northern capitalists. Southerners remained chary of the siren calls from *Democratic Review* and other northern publications that advocated sectional cooperation to subjugate the colored races through an imperialism based upon free trade.[45]

The temptation to world dominion nonetheless remained strong even among the most fearful. Edmund Ruffin condemned the British for their unjust Opium War in China and called William Walker a piratical thug for his filibustering in Nicaragua. Yet Ruffin concluded – as he did in discussing the Sepoy

[44] Jack P. Maddex, Jr., *The Reconstruction of Edward A. Pollard: A Rebel's Conversion to Postbellum Unionism* (Chapel Hill, N.C., 1874), 25–29; J. C. Coit, *An Address Delivered to the Freemen of Chesterfield District* (Charleston, S.C., 1851), 32–33; William O. Prentiss, *A Sermon Preached at St. Peter's Church* (Charleston, S.C., 1860), 16. "Python" [John Tyler, Jr.], "The Issues of 1860," *DBR*, 28 (1860), 259–269; "Python," "The Secession of the South," *DBR*, 28 (1860), 367–392.

[45] Cassells, "Relation of Justice to Benevolence," *SPR*, 7 (1853), 89; Henry W. Hilliard, *Speeches and Addresses* (New York, 1855), 220; Kenneth M. Stampp, *America in 1857: A Nation on the Brink* (New York, 1990), 188–196. See the racial plea to Union and Confederacy by an exile from France's regime in Mexico, who wanted a reunited United States to carry the white man's burden: Alonzo Alvarez, *Progress and Intelligence of Americans, Whether in the Northern, Central, or Southern Portion of the Continent* (n.p., 1865).

mutiny – that the basically worthless colored races could advance to civilization only by succumbing to white rule, if they could advance at all. Ruffin's
views paralleled those of conservatives well removed from his secessionist politics – among them, William H. Holcombe of Mississippi, Daniel R. Hundley
of Alabama, J. B. Lindsley of Tennessee – whose proslavery commitments led
to similar thoughts about the destiny of the white race.[46]

With the collapse of the Confederacy and the end of slavery in Cuba (1886)
and Brazil (1888), the half-subdued imperialist tendency in the South ripened
into a new ideology that justified European world conquest. Yet no European
power reestablished slavery in other than disguised fashion or attempted to
re-create the master-slave relation as the basis for a colonial society. Consider
the career of the Presbyterian Reverend James Lyon of Mississippi, a leader
in the fight to humanize the slave codes – a unionist who defended slavery
while excoriating slaveholders for their un-Christian treatment of slaves. Lyon
believed that civilization required slavery "in some form" and predicted as late
as 1864 that the black race would perish if the South lost the War. As soon as
the War ended, he reconciled himself to a broader vision of a world order in
which the white race served as a surrogate master class. Before the War, even
Fitzhugh flirted with imperialism as a solution to the social question, projecting
the white race of Euro-America as a collective master of the colored peoples
of the world. After the War, like many others, he embraced a version of the
"people's imperialism" that provided white workers a secure place in a system
of worldwide conquest. Thus the growing tendency to embrace Slavery in the
Abstract and make race a special case of the social question ran into an impasse.
A way out appeared before the War but achieved centrality only afterward,
when the reunited Union plunged into imperialism and took up the white
man's burden on a world scale. Later in the century the antebellum stirrings,
previously stronger in the North than the South, became a loud all-American
shout. The white race, it seems, had a historic responsibility to rule the world,
civilize the heathens of Asia, Africa, and Latin America, and rightfully put them
to work for the master race.[47]

After the Confederacy and slavery collapsed, the pseudo-scientific racism
long popular in the North easily passed into the service of late nineteenth-
century imperialist ideology. Before the War the southern ideologues, led

---

[46] *ERD*, Jan. 30, 1857 (1:29); Feb. 14, 1857 (1:33); Aug. 10, 1857 (1:96–97); April 26, 1858
(1:181–182). William H. Holcombe, *The Alternative: A Separate Nationality or the African-
ization of the South* (New Orleans, La., 1860), 23–24; Daniel R. Hundley, *Social Relations in
Our Southern States* (Baton Rouge, La., 1979 [1860]), 316ff; J. B. Lindsley, Table Talk, May
16, 1862, in Lindsley Papers.

[47] For Lyon, see his report in *SPR*, 16 (July, 1863), 1–37, and Ernest Trice Thompson, *Presby-
terians in the South*, 3 vols. (Richmond, Va., 1963), 2:56; Iver Bernstein, *The New York City
Draft Riots: Their Significance for American Society and Politics in the Age of the Civil War*
(New York, 1990), 143; on Fitzhugh, see Genovese, *The World the Slaveholders Made: Two
Essays in Interpretation* (New York, 1969), Pt. 2, especially 209–210.

morally and to a considerable extent intellectually by an able and widely influential group of theologians, hewed to time-honored, conservative, Christian principles and thereby blocked the advance of the imperialist worldview that subsequently imposed unprecedented misery and mass slaughter on the world. Had the Confederacy won, the ideas of Nott, De Bow, and Hughes might have prevailed over those of Fitzhugh, Holmes, and Thornwell, once the issues between them were publicly joined. The defeat of the slaveholders, nonetheless, opened the floodgates to the global catastrophe their leading spokesmen had long warned was aborning.

"The Woman Question"

Proslavery efforts to contribute to a new social science or "sociology" faced another challenge. The much bedeviled "woman question" compelled clarification of assumptions and movement from abstract to concrete. "Man never suffers without murmuring and never relinquishes his rights without a struggle," President Thomas Roderick Dew of the College of William and Mary wrote. But woman's "physical weakness incapacitates her for combat; her sexual organization, and the part which she takes in bringing forth and nurturing the rising generation, render her necessarily domestic in her habits, and timid and patient in her sufferings." Man has the power to oppress women if he chooses. Louisa McCord formulated, as well as anyone, the slaveholding South's prevalent position on the rights, duties, and responsibilities of women. McCord, who admired Cornelia, mother of the Gracchi, and Joan of Arc, launched fierce assaults on the women's rights movement: "Wrath and power are hideous and fearful; wrath and weakness are hideous and contemptible." McCord did not question women's intellectual equality with men, but she feared that the grant of political and civic equality to physically inferior women would endanger them. Dr. J. M. Gaston agreed with McCord. Men's "athletic, robust frame is found associated with a stern, decisive spirit." He concluded an article on the physical basis of insanity: "Woman's body must have a woman's mind, else she is no longer that ornament to society, which virtue and chastity have ever made her."[48]

Hughes affirmed the physical theory of women's severe limitations, not to say inferiority, in his own special way. He ranked women with minors, lunatics, criminals, aliens, and blacks as mentally disqualified for participation in the

---

[48] "Professor Dew on Slavery," in *The Pro-Slavery Argument, as Maintained by the Most Distinguished Writers of the Southern States* (Charleston, S.C., 1852), 336–337; Thomas Roderick Dew, "Dissertation on the Characteristic Differences between the Sexes, and Women's Position and Influence in Society," *SLM*, 1 (1835), 493–512, 621–632, 672–691; "Enfranchisement of Woman, Lounsbury, ed., *L. S. McCord: Political and Social Essays*, 116, 117 (Joan of Arc), 119–120; J. McF. Gaston, "Action and Re-Action of Mind and Body as Affecting Insanity," *SPR*, 7 (1853), 200–201. For attitudes toward women, see also Fox-Genovese and Genovese, *Mind of the Master Class*, ch. 13.

affairs of state. He asserted that the South, unlike Europe and the North, appreciated women's virtues. Women, subordinate in Europe and coordinate in the North, were superordinate in the South – queens, not cooks and chambermaids. He meant white women, whom he championed as part of his campaign to reopen the African slave trade: "The African labor supply will take from the wash-tub, bake-oven, and scrub-broom, thousands of our tired and toiling wives, sisters, and daughters, and advance into the workplaces stout and willing negro wenches, to whom a civilized kitchen would be a Christian school and the pone they bake a foretaste of better bread."[49]

Le Conte applauded Comte's designation of Sociabilité over Personalité as the highest condition of society – "the mergence of the individual life into the general life." He quoted Comte's encomium to woman's superiority in Sociabilité, but he proceeded: "There are two ways in which the Personal may be subordinate to the Social, one through our material nature, and the other through our spiritual nature. The former is subordination through mutual dependence, resulting from our material wants; the latter is subordination through sympathy or love, resulting from our spiritual wants. The one annihilates the individual independence of life; the other only enhances the dignity of the individual life." Since man has a stronger material nature, he naturally rules church, state, and guilds – the three pillars of society. Woman subordinates herself: "Subordination of the Personal to the Social, through love – surely the highest attribute of humanity – this is the glory of woman."[50]

Le Conte must have blushed when he read the uses to which drivellers put his foray into psychobiology. We may settle for J. D. B. De Bow's puerile essay on "The Beautiful" in Simms's *The Charleston Book*: "Woman too – fair, beautiful woman! how she transports us, bewildered, to heaven – how she breaks the ice that congealed at the heart." *The Charleston Book* also included an essay on "Woman" by Charles R. Carroll, a planter and lawyer, which opened: "When we compare the present with the past condition of woman, we congratulate ourselves on the change in her disposition and the accomplishments of her mind." Women, he continued in self-congratulation, had become esteemed by men as moral agents, no longer mere objects of men's appetites. Men and women have different physical constitutions, appropriate to "the separate spheres in which they revolve." She is "timid, confiding, and submissive; he is bold, arrogant, and self-willed." Carroll concluded that for woman, love was not a burning passion. It is hard to believe that the worldly Simms did not laugh, but who knows? He wrote to Holmes, "Women, who are women at all and not children, have really cooler heads than men – are much less creatures of passion and impulse."[51]

[49] Lyman, ed., *Writings of Henry Hughes*, 101–102.

[50] For this and the following paragraph, see Le Conte, "Relation of Organic Science to Sociology," *SPR*, 13 (1860), 73–74.

[51] J. D. B. De Bow, "The Beautiful," and C. R. Carroll, "Woman," in William Gilmore Simms, ed., *The Charleston Book: A Miscellany in Prose and Verse* (Spartanburg, S.C., 1983 [1845]),

Leading divines strongly opposed movements for women's rights and accepted these biological and psychological arguments. But they distrusted arguments from women's alleged intellectual inferiority, if only because they could not readily separate the intellectual and moral dimensions of human character. God made "man" in His own image, wrote Dabney, but not in corporeal shape, "for of this God has none." Both Adam and Eve possessed "man's original moral perfection, the intelligence and rectitude of his conscience." The Episcopalian Reverend J. H. Linebaugh of Baton Rouge preached greater attention to women's education: "Our text declares that God created man in his own image – in the image of God created He him – male and female, created He them. The creation of man and woman in the image of God constitutes their great excellence and glory."[52]

The divines reminded congregants that when God expelled Adam and Eve from the Garden of Eden, He decreed that she should place herself at her husband's command. Simultaneously, the divines struggled to curb any abuse of power and stressed love in the marital relation. They had their hands full – and not only with the ungodly and vicious. A Virginian proposed a toast: "Woman – lovely Woman; if she brought death into the world, she produced everlasting life through a Saviour." Henry Hilliard, a Whig leader in Alabama, informed the young ladies of LaGrange Female College that God formed men for great exploits and women for home and as a helpmeet, and that it is becoming in man to achieve victories and becoming in woman to celebrate them. Hilliard proceeded to exalt the emergence of medieval chivalry and the Christian love of woman. Society proscribes woman from "the great affairs of life," not because she is inferior but because "she is far more beautiful in her own empire" and participation in public affairs "would unfit her for the gentler duties and those lovely offices which not even an angel could perform so well." The attitude of cultivated southern planters recalled that of European aristocrats who wanted the public role of women severely restricted but could not repress admiration for intellectually cultivated women. Gentlemen preferred women they could talk to and who had something to say. And they loved to show off intellectually accomplished wives and daughters.[53]

247, 134, 137–138; Simms to Holmes, March 15, 1849, in Oliphant et al., eds., *Letters of Simms*, 2, 494; also J. V. Ridgely, *William Gilmore Simms* (New York, 1962), 57.

[52] Robert L. Dabney, *Systematic Theology* (Carlisle, Pa., 1985 [1878]), 293–294; J. H. Linebaugh, *Education: A Discourse* (New Orleans, La., 1850), 8.

[53] A Virginian quoted in J. S. Buckingham, *The Slave States of America*, 2 vols. (New York, 1968 [1842]), 2:278; "Woman – Her True Sphere," in Hilliard, *Speeches and Addresses*, 481–483, 487–488, quote at 486; see also Mitchell King, Dec. 1, 1852, in King Papers; W. C. Preston and J. C. Calhoun to Maria Henrietta and Harriott Pinckney, Feb. 1835, in *JCCP*, 12:409. For contemporary biographical sketches, see, e.g., John Belton O'Neall, *Biographical Sketches of the Bench and Bar of South Carolina*, 2 vols. (Spartanburg, S.C., 1975 [1859]), and Stephen F. Miller, *The Bench and Bar of Georgia: Memoirs and Sketches*, 2 vols. (Philadelphia, Pa., 1858), which contain many favorable sketches of men who married intellectual women: 2:61, 187, 227, 294.

In 1857 at Mississippi's Presbyterian-sponsored Oakland College, "B. A. C." decried the long suppression of female intellect and paid tribute to great women politicians and warriors. And yet: "Woman cannot create like man; but by worshipping God in spirit and in truth, and thus showing forth her goodness and moral powers, she becomes the glory of man." The following year "N.," a self-proclaimed defender of women's rights, warned that women's-rights zealots were producing a reaction that would deprive women of any rights whatever. Women deserved "privileges" and had a right to an education; they were not intellectually inferior to men. "N." stood for women's rights but not as commonly understood: "We do not wish to be understood as advocating the claims of the gentler sex after the style of the so-called strong minded matrons and maidens of the present age, who, not contented with those privileges which the truly wise and good are assiduously laboring to ensure to them, must push themselves forward to take an active part in the great struggle of life, and display themselves as man's superior, not only in domestic economy, but would claim an equal share in governmental regulations." He put the question of woman's abilities aside: In any case, she should remain in her own exalted sphere uncontaminated by entrance into the masculine sphere of politics and public affairs.[54]

These student efforts suggest a broader current within an elite that could not wholly isolate itself from the emerging transatlantic struggle for women's rights. If nothing else, thoughtful Southerners began to view more critically centuries of male arrogance in the light of the principles of Christian chivalry. In 1805, Sterling Ruffin demanded that his son, Thomas, a student at Princeton, explain his disrespect for women: "Is it because tyrannical custom, added to the bitterness of the Ware [*sic*] which prohibits their being educated at Colleges and obtaining classical educations and obtaining diplomas that they are not to be regarded? or is it because they are really below the notice of a wise man? or what is the reason that your letters breath nothing but disgust agst. the whole sex?" A month later he reminded Thomas that God made women in His own image and endowed them as richly as He endowed men: "It is now owing to custom, tyrannical custom that they are generally inferior to Men in Moral, Civil and Political knowledge and usefulness." Sterling Ruffin did not speak for everyone. Dumas Malone, Thomas Jefferson's great biographer, remarked that Jefferson did not value his mother's counsel: "At no time in his life did he turn to women for serious advice." John Randolph admitted to valuing "female society" because without it, men, especially young men, would "degenerate into brutes." Still, in ruminating on these weighty matters, Randolph hoped

---

54 B. A. C., "Man and Woman: Intellectual Capacities and Mental Powers," *Oakland College Magazine*, 2 (1857), 49 (B. A. C. seems to have been C. A. Bridewell, the editor, who reversed his initials); N., "Women's Rights," *Oakland College Magazine*, 3 (1858), 11–12. For the argument that women were intellectually inferior to men, see, e.g., "The Female Mind" in *Randolph Macon Magazine*, 2 (1852), 77–83. See also David Alexander Barnes Diary, Feb. 15, 1840; L., "Woman's Rights and Woman's Wrongs," *SRCR*, 3 (1854), 233–243; quoted 231–232, 238.

that his young relative would not let fondness for the company of ladies "rob you of the time which ought to be devoted to reading and meditating on your profession."[55]

The inclination to respect, admire, and prefer women of intellect and to support educational opportunities for them went hand in hand with a fear of where it would all lead. David Outlaw much admired the intellectual qualities of his wife Emily, who apparently shared his social and political views. He wrote to her in 1850: "The meeting to which you refer in Ohio is certainly a very strange affair. These Yankees and their descendants have strange notions of propriety. Delicacy and modesty in women, which we esteem their highest ornaments are qualities they seem to attach but little importance." He added that Representative Robert C. Schenck of Ohio, who decided not to stand for reelection, jokingly remarked that he feared some lady might defeat him. No Southerner of note raised his voice in favor of women's rights – as understood today or as understood by English and northern reformers of their own day. Thomas Ritchie put his *Richmond Enquirer* behind the effort to improve the education of women, but even he did not express, except in the most gingerly way, his sympathy for women's suffrage.[56]

In the end, the effort to construct a proslavery and generally conservative sociology did not advance science, but it helped to render proslavery ideology modestly more consistent.

Thomas Carlyle

The need to project slavery as intellectually coherent and divinely and historically sanctioned via media between capitalism and socialism foundered on the slaveholders' inability to construct a social theory that could square the circles posed by political economy. The reception accorded Thomas Carlyle in the South illuminated the uniqueness of the southern defense of slavery and the gulf between southern and European conservatives; it also illuminated the difficulty in converting even the friendliest of European conservatives to Slavery in the Abstract. Still, Carlyle fared much better in the South than, among others, did August Vilmar, the conservative German Lutheran theologian. Although Southerners on balance responded negatively to the revolutions of 1848, they could not abide Vilmar's declaration that German Christians must repudiate "that Satanic thing, the sovereignty of the people" and rally to "the sovereignty of the prince." Southerners cut themselves off from Vilmar's social criticism, which they might have found attractive. He, too, condemned those "who reduce

---

[55] J. Sterling Ruffin to Thomas Ruffin, May 11, June 7, 1805, in J. G. deRoulhac Hamilton, ed., *The Papers of Thomas Ruffin*, 4 vols. (Raleigh, N.C., 1918), 1:78; *Letters of John Randolph to a Young Relative* (Philadelphia, Pa., 1834), 236 (Jan. 21, 1822); Dumas Malone, *Jefferson and His Time*, 6 vols. (Boston, Mass., 1962–1981), 1:37.

[56] David Outlaw to Emily Outlaw, May 15, 1850, in Outlaw Papers, UNC; Charles Henry Ambler, *Thomas Ritchie: A Study in Virginia Politics* (Richmond, Va., 1913), 120.

all property relationships to money" and appealed on behalf of "the industrial masses of today and the industrial slaves of tomorrow."[57]

"The spirit of Carlyle is abroad in the land," according to a contributor to *Southern Quarterly Review* who associated himself with Carlyle's dictum that history is at bottom the story of great men. The contributor identified as republican doctrine the belief that ordinary people wisely defer to superior minds and abilities. Ostensibly, republican institutions and free men provide the necessary framework for deference by retaining the power to resist the perversions and dangers of unbridled authority. Two years later Southerners emptied bookstores of *Latter-Day Pamphlets*, which steadily became more influential.[58]

Elite low-country youth grew up with Carlyle. *Sartor Resartus* made an especially big impression on the youthful Nathaniel Russell Middleton. The Unitarian Theodore Clapp of New Orleans met Carlyle in Britain and formed a lasting friendship with him. Carlyle also met and befriended the Presbyterian Reverend Moses Drury Hoge of Richmond. Some Southerners got their Carlyle indirectly through writers like Charles Dickens – a Carlyle admirer who, among other things, stood with Carlyle and Charles Kingsley in support of Governor Edward John Eyre of Jamaica when he crushed a black rising on Jamaica and executed some four hundred people. Frederick Douglass, J. Sella Martin, and other ex-slaves who addressed British audiences had their hands full in combating the proslavery influence of Carlyle, Kingsley, and others who indicted West Indian emancipation as a futile attempt to give freedom to people unfit for it and with the favorable reports of British travelers to the South.[59]

In the estimation of a contributor to *Southern Quarterly Review*, Southerners stood with Carlyle as "willing listeners to the cry of oppressed humanity, to the claims of the poor and the needy on the rich and the affluent." The Richmond *Enquirer* lauded Carlyle as proslavery and a resolute critic of capitalism and socialism. Carlyle appealed to the Virginians Dew, Fitzhugh, and Holmes and to the South Carolinians Hammond, Simms, Chancellor William Harper, and David Flavel Jamison because of his hostility to industrialism, democracy, and reform movements and his support for white supremacy. Fitzhugh described Carlyle as a "conservative socialist" – a formulation that invited

[57] Walter H. Conser, Jr., *Church and Confession: Conservative Theologians in Germany, England, and America, 1815–1866* (Macon, Ga., 1984), Vilmar quoted at 79, 81.

[58] "Carlyle's Works," *SQR* 14 (1848), 77–101, esp. 85–89, quote at 77; also, Gerald David Jaynes, *Branches without Roots: Genesis of the Black Working Class in the American South, 1862–1882* (New York, 1986), 12–13; Gerald M. Straka, "The Spirit of Carlyle in the Old South," *Historian*, 20 (1957), 39–57.

[59] "Reminiscences," in Alicia Hopton Middleton et al., *Life in Carolina and New England during the Nineteenth Century* (Bristol, R.I., 1929), 203; Henry Alexander White, *Southern Presbyterian Leaders* (New York, 1911), 437; Myron Magnet, *Dickens and the Social Order* (Philadelphia, Pa., 1985), 3–4; for Douglass and Martin, see R. J. M. Blackett, *Divided Hearts: Britain and the American Civil War* (Baton Rouge, La., 2001), 37–38, 91, 155–156. Frank Blair, among others, met Dickens on his American travels and found him a kindred democratic spirit: William E. Parrish, *Frank Blair: Lincoln's Conservative* (Columbia, Mo., 1998), 11.

the English observer James Stirling to cite Carlyle and Kingsley as Fitzhugh's "socialist collaborators." Jamison, citing Cicero, warned against society's tendency to create masses of men and to deprive them of their individuality. Cicero, Jamison recalled, did not have to face "the direful conflict between capital and labor, now going on in Europe, and portions of our own country, consequent on the abolition of the feudal tenures and villeinage, while nothing has been substituted in their place, but what Carlyle designates as, the very settlement of money wages, and then kicking the workman out of doors." Carlyle's famous critique of the "cash nexus" resounded across the South. "Virtue with the Romans meant courage," George H. Calvert of Maryland wrote in a book warmly praised in leading southern journals. "It now means cash." Appalled by the misery of the lower classes in France in the 1840s, Calvert sympathetically sketched Fourier, the socialists, and their dreams of remaking the social order.[60]

Carlyle's popularity in the North, where he influenced religious as well as secular intellectuals – not only conservatives but romantics of various hues – worried some Southerners. Ralph Waldo Emerson distrusted Carlyle's hero worship but was deeply influenced by him, as was Herman Melville. Horace Greeley described Carlyle's *Past and Present* as the greatest book of the century and referred to *Heroes and Hero Worship* as "glorious." In no small part, Johann Gottlieb Fichte, Johann Gottfried von Herder, Friedrich Schiller, and others came to the attention of Americans through Carlyle's efforts. His influence may also be gauged by the fire he drew: Walt Whitman wrote *Democratic Vistas* in part as a reply to *Shooting Niagara*.[61]

Southern divines, despite approval of Carlyle's social views, had trouble with the religious speculations of a "semi-infidel" – as the Episcopalian Reverend Henry Niles Pierce of Texas called him. The Baptist Reverend W. Carey Crane of Virginia, protesting against mere theories that passed for philosophy, derided "Carlyle mania." A contributor to *Southern Quarterly Review* paid a long tribute to Carlyle's genius: "Carlyle has none of the mysticism of Coleridge or Emerson." And Carlyle assailed Methodism as fervently as he assailed Puseyism. Not surprisingly, Sasnett and W. S. Grayson, both prominent Methodists, rebuked Carlyle for what Grayson called his "thinly clad"

---

[60] "Carlyle's Works," *SQR* 14 (1848), 77; *Richmond Enquirer*, June 19, 1855. George Fitzhugh, Centralization and Socialism," *DBR*, 20 (1856), 692–694; James Stirling, *Letters from the Slave States* (New York, 1968 [1857]), 113–114; D. F. Jamison, "Annual Address," in *Proceedings of the State Agricultural Society of South Carolina* (Charleston, S.C., 1856), 346; George H. Calvert, *Scenes and Thoughts in Europe*, 2nd series (New York, 1852), 8, 128–129, 135–137, 303, quote at 8; also, Edward C. Bullock, *True and False Civilization: An Oration Delivered before the Erosophic and Philomathic Societies of the University of Alabama* (Tuscaloosa, Ala., 1858), 24.

[61] F. O. Matthiessen, *American Renaissance: Art and Expression in the Age of Emerson and Whitman* (New York, 1941), 385, 632–633; Sydney E. Ahlstrom, *A Religious History of the American People* (New Haven, Conn., 1972), 596; G. G. Van Deusen, *Horace Greeley: Nineteenth-Century Crusader* (Philadelphia, Pa., 1953), 61, 74; Rollin G. Osterweis, *Romanticism and Nationalism in the Old South* (Baton Rouge, La., 1971), 33–34.

infidelity. Yet A. B. Stark, another Methodist, saluted Carlyle's views on the exploitation of free labor by capital: "American slavery is founded on the same political and social principles on which he bases his solution of this question of labor." Stark complimented Carlyle for his "earnest, truth-loving, high-gifted, reverent soul" and defended him against the charge of being anti-Christian. Stark sadly acknowledged that he "overlooks the Divine origin of Christianity, and views it simply as the highest attainment and development of human thought." W. H. Milburn, a northern Methodist preacher who read Carlyle while serving as a pastor in Montgomery, Alabama, admitted to having had his faith temporarily shaken by the force of Carlyle's "genius." Milburn expressed succinctly the conflicted view of many: "Mr. Carlyle's books had much the same power over me that Mephistopheles exercised over Faust." He added, "Yet for all that, I owe you more and love you better than any other author of the time." And despite much muttering about Carlyle's concessions to pantheism, Southerners applauded his emphasis on the Old Testament's God of Wrath.[62]

Secular critics who fancied themselves democrats found Carlyle hard to take. The strongly proslavery John Esten Cooke, Virginia's celebrated author, gagged on Carlyle's "political extravagance" and "wild doctrines." Among the less democratically inclined, Louisa McCord considered his obsession with the wretchedness of the masses an invitation to socialism. John Reuben Thompson, editor of *Southern Literary Messenger*, reviewing *Latter-Day Pamphlets*, dismissed Carlyle's views as "nonsense" and asked: "Most worshipful Sir Oracle, you tell us that we are but mice – that our so-called Liberty is a terrible cat, with claws and talons for our destruction – and that the only remedy is to put a bell upon her. Now, if you please, be good enough to teach us how to bell the cat." *Southern Literary Messenger* published Park Benjamin of New York, who dismissed *Latter-Day Pamphlets* as lacking the originality and power of his earlier work: Carlyle "has fallen entirely back into the slough of despond."[63]

Carlyle's prose offended reigning southern sensibilities. Edgar Allan Poe was among those Southerners who expressed contempt for Carlyle's hero worship. After dismissing Carlyle as "an ass," Poe wrote, "I have not the slightest faith

---

[62] Henry Niles Pierce, *Sermons Preached in St. John's Church, Mobile* (Mobile, Ala., 1861), 4; W. Carey Crane, "Speculative Philosophy, Cui Bono?" *SLM*, 10 (1844), 357. Also *Protestant Thought in the Nineteenth Century*, 2 vols. (New Haven, Conn., 1972, 1985), 1:187–188; "Carlyle's Works," *SQR*, 14 (1848), 83, 98; W. J. Sasnett, "German Philosophy," *QRMCS*, 12 (1858), 338; W. S. Grayson, "Cromwell and His Religion," *QRMCS*, 5 (1851), 62–64, quote at 77; A. B. Stark, "Thomas Carlyle," *QRMCS*, 15 (1861), 414, 404–405, quotes at 182, 405, 414; William Henry Milburn, *Ten Years of Preacher-Life: Chapters from an Autobiography* (New York, 1859), 291–292. For another defense of Carlyle against charges of infidelity, see "Carlyle and Macaulay," *SLM*, 14 (1848), 479.

[63] John Esten Cooke, "Thomas Carlyle and His Latter-Day Pamphlets," *SLM*, 16 (1850), 330–340; J. O. Beaty, *John Esten Cooke*, 23–24; L. S. McCord, "Right to Labor," *Political and Social Essays*, ed. Richard C. Lounsbury (Charlottesville, Va., 1995), 82; John R. Thompson, "Notice of New Works: Latter-day Pamphlets," *SLM*, 16 (1850), 255; Park Benjamin, "Letters from New York," *SLM*, 16 (1850), 317–318.

in Carlyle. In ten years – possibly in five – he will be remembered only as a butt for sarcasm." Poe focused primarily on Carlyle's obscure style, but he appears to have had severe if unclear criticisms of content. Daniel Whitaker, editor of *Southern Quarterly Review*, complained that Carlyle had abandoned his "pure and manly style" of the 1820s for a rude and unpolished notoriety-chasing style. Thompson hammered Carlyle's style in the 1850s, and *Southern Literary Messenger* continued its attacks under the editorship of George William Bagby. S. Teackle Wallis of Baltimore, another contributor to *Southern Literary Messenger*, spoke of Carlyle as "certainly a man of genius" who might, nonetheless, not seem so original or profound if his prose "were done out of German into English." Other contributors to *Southern Literary Messenger* referred to Carlyle's "crabbed and uncouth words, and involved constructions" and "misty jargon" and to him as "a philosophical day-dreamer." Only occasionally did a critic defend Carlyle's style. In 1852 the student editors of *North Carolina University Magazine* credited "the forcible style of a hard-thinking, vice hating Carlyle" with elevating and purifying literary taste. Usually, even favorable critics responded in the manner of Nathaniel Beverley Tucker and A. B. Stark, who defended Carlyle against detractors, but regretted his Germanic style. Paul Hamilton Hayne, expressing displeasure at Carlyle's "juggling tricks" with the English language, recommended that readers learn "Carlylese" to be rewarded by profound insights, grim humor, passion, and earnestness. Elsewhere, Hayne, echoing Carlyle, protested against the fashionable and disgraceful "pettifogging spirit" that denigrated great men.[64]

Holmes assumed the task of salvaging Carlyle despite his oddities and vices. Holmes reviewed those "singular and erratic productions," *Latter-Day Pamphlets*: "The strange extravagances, the grotesque utterance, the complicated and scrofulous style, the cloudy enthusiasm, the insane imagination, the elf-like humour, the unearthly antics, the quizzical grimaces, and the habitual buffooneries of the Latter-Day Pamphleteer, would have rendered perfectly intelligible to our minds the secret springs of that incredulity, with which the daughter of Priam was greeted." Besides, Carlyle insulted his readers as dolts and then expected them to heed him. After ten pages of abuse, including a rejection of Carlyle's religious views, Holmes got to the point: "*The*

---

[64] Edgar Allan Poe, *Essays and Reviews* (New York, 1984), quotes at 461, 1392, and for denigration of Carlyle, see also 460, 1040, 1176, 1310, 1321, 1392–1393, 1469; [Ernest Marchand], ed., "Poe as Social Critic," *American Literature*, 6 (1934), 33; [D. K. Whitaker], "Critical Notices," *SQR*, 9 (1846), 282. S. Teackle Wallis, *Leisure: Moral and Political Economy* (Baltimore, Md., 1859), 8. In *SLM* see [John R. Thompson], 16 (1850), 638; [Thompson], 27 (1858), 393; [George William Bagby], 31 (1860), 76–77; "The Dutch Republic," 27 (1858), 241; Thomas B. Holcombe, "Moral Tendency of Goethe's Writing," 22 (1856), 180; "Some Thoughts on Social Philosophy," 22 (1856), 309; *North Carolina University Magazine*, 1 (Electronic ed.; 1852), 5; N. B. Tucker, "The Present State of Europe," *SQR*, 16 (1850), 316; A. B. Stark, "Thomas Carlyle," *QRMCS*, 15 (1861), 183; [Paul Hamilton Hayne], "Review of Carlyle's History of Friedrich the Second," *RM*, 4 (1858), 276, 279, 286; also, E. D., "Carlyle's Miscellanies, *Magnolia*, n.s. 2 (1843), 96–100.

Latter-Day Pamphlets open with a sketch of the present time which is drawn with considerable power and artistic skill" and qualified as "truthful and condensed." Holmes lauded Carlyle's critique of the mass misery that had brought Europe to crisis, especially associating himself with Carlyle's contempt for both the economic nostrums of laissez-faire and the delusions of socialism. Holmes made clear his own intent in writing an unusually long review essay: "We have stripped Carlyle's propositions of their exaggeration and extravagance of expression; but we have incorporated his views."[65]

During the War, criticism of Carlyle, even from the clergy, gave way to appreciation of his expressions of sympathy for the Confederacy. A. W. Dillard denounced the "singularity" of Carlyle's style and the "uncouth address of his expressions" as probably the source of the widespread image of him as a profound thinker, yet Dillard too expressed gratitude for Carlyle's denunciation of abolitionism and defense of slavery. Bishop Elliott recalled "how grandly Carlyle strikes down this wretched materialism," which was draining confidence that a materially weaker South could prevail against the powerful Yankees. Mary Chesnut, who read Carlyle's *French Revolution* and other works, observed, "Carlyle does not hold up his hands in holy horror of us because of African slavery." The prominent Methodist Reverend Atticus Greene Haygood of Georgia and his sister read Carlyle avidly. Years later, when Carlyle died, Haygood commented, "Tens of thousands felt a sense of personal bereavement.... It cannot be questioned that he did much good; alas! it is equally certain that some minds were blighted under the fierce heats of his strange and imperious genius."[66]

In the end Carlyle disappointed the more radical of his southern admirers. De Bow, who recommended *Sartor Resartus* and *Heroes and Hero Worship* by "the original and eccentric" Carlyle, published an article from *Frazier's London Magazine*, attributed to Carlyle, which criticized West Indian emancipation but recommended a form of serfdom for blacks in place of slavery. That recommendation did not go down well with most proslavery Southerners. Replying to Nathaniel Beverley Tucker's call for support in 1851, Carlyle congratulated him for defending southern rights, white supremacy, and social order, adding, "Alas, the question is deep as the foundations of Society; and

65 [George Frederick Holmes], "Latter-Day Pamphlets," *SQR*, n.s. 2 (1850), 313–356, quotes at 313, 315, 323, 353.
66 A. W. Dillard, "Thomas Carlyle – His Philosophy and Style," *SLM*, 34 (1862), 290–296, quote at 290; Stephen Elliott, *Gideon's Water-Lappers: A Sermon Preached in Christ Church, Savannah* (Macon, Ga., 1864), 12; Mary Chesnut Diary, Aug. 27, 1861, June 4, 1865, Mar. 5, 1862, in C. Vann Woodward, ed., *Mary Chesnut's Civil War* (New Haven, Conn., 1981), 166, 298, 825, quote at 298; "Paul Hayne began with Carlyle, which led to Emerson": Chesnut Diary, June 13, 1862 (385). Atticus Greene Haygood, "Death of Carlyle," *Wesleyan Christian Advocate*, 3 (1881), 4; also, Harold W. Mann, *Atticus Greene Haygood: Methodist Bishop, Editor, and Educator* (Athens, Ga., 1965), 7. Among Carlyle's readers during the War: Lucy Wood Butler Diary, 1862–1863; May 4, 1865, in Robert T. Oliver, *A Faithful Heart: The Journals of Emmala Reed, 1865 and 1866* (Columbia, S.C., 2004), 72.

will not be settled this long while!" Carlyle thereupon preached, "The relation of the White man to the Black is not at present a just one, according to the Law of the Eternal." He inquired about the lack of a law of peculium, warning, "The Negro Question will be left in peace, when God Almighty's law about it is (with tolerable approximation) actually found out and practised; and never till then."[67]

---

[67] "The Publishing Business," *DBR*, 3 (1847), 92; "Carlyle on West India Emancipation," *DBR*, 8 (1850), 527–538; Carlyle to Tucker, Oct. 31, 1851, in Mrs. George P. Coleman, ed., *Virginia Silhouettes: Contemporary Letters Concerning Negro Slavery in the State of Virginia* (Richmond, Va., 1934), 48–49. For the complexities of Carlyle's views on slavery and abolition, especially as presented in *The Nigger Question* (1849) – and for the grounds of southern uneasiness – see David Alec Wilson, *Carlyle at His Zenith* (London, 1927), ch. 2, especially 216–217.

6

Perceptions and Realities

> How can a man be recalled to salvation, when he has none to restrain him, and all mankind to urge him on?
>
> —Seneca[1]

As self-anointed paternalists, slaveholders felt sorely put upon as scapegoats for the inevitable condition of laboring people. Arguing that no social system could be judged fairly by its accompanying evils, E. J. Pringle of South Carolina accused Harriet Beecher Stowe of being "unjust" to the South. No essential institution – neither Christian churches nor the family – could pass that test. Defenders of slavery appealed to Jesus: "The poor always ye have with you; but me ye have not always" (John, 12:8). Northerners and Southerners respected private property, but, Pringle asked, who could deny that its uses oppressed the poor? Man's inherent sinfulness marred every divinely sanctioned institution. Society would not need a criminal code if any system "could correct all the evil tendency of man's nature." In 1856 the Presbyterian Reverend Frederick A. Ross of Alabama described *Uncle Tom's Cabin* as "that splendid bad book" – "splendid in its genius over which I have wept, and laughed, and got mad." Ross told the New School General Assembly in New York in 1856 that bad theology, bad morals, and distortions of southern life were having a corrosive influence in the North and abroad. "Every fact in Uncle Tom's Cabin has occurred in the South," but there is greater cruelty toward women and the poor in New York and Boston than in the South. Another writer depicted Mrs. Stowe's "vital error": She treated the evils of slavery as if they were not evils of all social organization. Thus, she waged war on society's basic institutions.[2]

---

[1] "On the God within Us," in Seneca, *Epistles*, 3 vols., tr. Richard M. Gummere (Cambridge, Mass., LCL, 2002), 1:52 (Epistle 41).

[2] [E. J. Pringle], *Slavery in the Southern States, by a Carolinian* (Cambridge, Mass., 1852), 7–12, quote at 12; Frederick A. Ross, *Slavery Ordained of God* (Philadelphia, 1857), 16–17, 53, quotes at 16, 53; "Stowe's Key to Uncle Tom's Cabin," *SQR*, 8 (1853), 214–215, quote at 214.

Were, in fact, southern slaves better off materially than the workers and peasants of the world? Were they better fed, housed, and clothed? Did they have a shorter work day and an easier work load? To begin with, even if Southerners had grounds for self-congratulation for material conditions, the moral and psychological indictment of slavery remained. Man does not live by bread alone, although some slaveholders, while reading their Bible, acted as if they did not know as much. Harriett Martineau thought Southerners defined human rights as "sufficient subsistence in return for labor." There were exceptions. In 1820 a writer in the *Southern Recorder* of Milledgeville, Georgia, agreed that southern slaves probably lived better than many northern free men, but "Freedom is the same for the Negro as to the white man. Let us see whether we should not prefer freedom with poverty to the best condition of the slave."[3]

Material Conditions

Measurement of material conditions depends on specifics in time and place, but reliable statistics are often difficult to come by. Results of the most thorough statistical investigations differ widely when they focus on specifics – say, food or clothing. Slave children rarely went into fieldwork before the age of twelve, almost never before ten. They were then eased toward full-time work over a period of years and did not suffer the cruelties common to five- or six-year-old working-class children in England. All true. Yet a great many slave infants and small children suffered from poor health because of difficulties created by the attitude toward pregnant women. Masters assumed that pregnant women could withstand many more rigors than in fact they could, and their infants paid the price. The widespread "infant death syndrome" among slaves stemmed in large part from deprivation during the fetal period. Hence, slave mortality rates declined sharply after the age of five. Slaveholders did not have the benefit of proper medical instruction and were not acting mindlessly, much less sadistically. It remains unclear that except for the horrible threat of sale, slave children fared worse than peasant children elsewhere. What remains crystal clear is that slave children, like the children of the poor everywhere, suffered as no children should ever be made to suffer.[4]

On balance, modern historians sympathetic to the laboring classes and sensitive to the human suffering inherent in slavery have ruefully acknowledged

---

[3] Harriet Martineau, *Society in America*, 2 vols. (New York, 1837), 2:129; *Southern Recorder*, quoted in James C. Bonner, *Milledgeville: Georgia's Antebellum Capital* (Athens, Ga., 1978), 120.

[4] Richard Steckel in Robert William Fogel and Stanley L. Engerman, eds., *Without Consent or Contract: Technical Papers*, 2 vols. (New York, 1992), 2:489–507, also 369–392. European children, too, suffered conditions that provoked stunted growth and early death: Robert W. Fogel, *The Fourth Great Awakening and the Future of Egalitarianism* (Chicago, 2000), 75–78, 146–519. For dietary deficiency among slaves, see Leslie Owens, *This Species of Property: Slave Life and Culture in the Old South* (New York, 1976), 50–69.

the slaveholders' primary contention. Raimondo Luraghi – the eminent Italian historian of nineteenth-century America – has established that however awful the material conditions of southern slaves, they fared better – in physical conditions – than most peasants and agricultural workers in Russia, Poland, and Hungary. In particular, his comparison of labor conditions in the most economically advanced section of Italy and in the American South lends credence to proslavery charges. Charles Joyner, surveying the boast of the planters of Waccamaw, South Carolina, concedes substance to their boast that their slaves lived better than the peasants of Ireland, the miners of Scotland, and the laboring classes of most parts of the world. Forrest McDonald and Grady McWhiny have judged that slaves worked less and lived better than the free peasants of France, to say nothing of the serfs of Russia and Eastern Europe. Econometricians have established that during the course of a year, northern farmers worked ten percent more hours than southern slaves did.[5]

Although historians continue to argue over the living conditions of the English laboring classes, they can hardly gainsay the wretchedness of the agricultural laborers at the beginning of the nineteenth century who rose at 4 A.M. and worked until about 7 P.M. Mechanics and artisans outside London worked a twelve-hour day. "It would be easy," Eric Hobsbawm and George Rudé write of rural life in 1831, "to draw a horrifying picture of the poverty and degradation into which the English farm-labourer fell. From that day to this those who observed him, or studied his fate, have searched for words eloquent enough to do justice to his oppression." Southern travelers witnessed those conditions and reported back home. Meanwhile, the slaveholders were reading, if only in newspaper synopses, the lament of many an Englishman who strained for words "eloquent enough to do justice." In 1750, Britain had only two cities with more than 50,000 inhabitants, London and Edinburgh. In 1801 it had eight. By 1851, it had twenty-nine, including nine with more than 100,000, and more Britons lived in cities and towns than in the country. Hobsbawm: "And what cities!" Smoke hung over them, filth impregnated them, elementary public services and sanitation eluded them, and worse, the laboring poor had to wage a daily struggle to maintain a minimum level of decency and moral texture in their lives.[6]

5 Raimondo Luraghi, *Storia della guerra civile americana* (Milan, Italy, 1967), 57, 69; Raimondo Luraghi, "Wage Labor in the 'Rice Belt' of Northern Italy and Slave Labor in the American South – A First Approach," *Southern Studies*, 16 (1977), 109–127; Charles Joyner, *Down by the Riverside: A South Carolina Slave Community* (Urbana, Ill., 1984), 124–125; Forrest McDonald and Grady McWhiny, "The South from Self-Sufficiency to Peonage," *American Historical Review*, 85 (1980), 1103–1104; Robert W. Fogel, Ralph A. Gallantine, and Richard Manning, eds., *Without Consent or Contract: Evidence and Methods*, 2 vols. (New York, 1992), 34.

6 E. P. Thompson, "Time, Work Discipline, and Industrial Capitalism," *Past and Present*, 38 (1967), 77, 85; Eric Hobsbawm and George Rudé, *Captain Swing: A Social History of the Great English Agricultural Uprising of 1830* (New York, 1975), 52; E. J. Hobsbawm, *Industry and Empire: The Making of Modern English Society from 1750 to the Present Day* (New York, 1968), 67–68.

George Fitzhugh railed at the English Poor Law of 1834, which, in Hobsbawm's words, "made all relief 'less eligible' than the lowest wage outside, confined it to the jail-like workhouse, forcibly separating husbands, wives and children in order to punish the poor for their destitution, and discouraging them from the dangerous temptation of procreating further paupers." Until the 1850s, at least ten percent of the English population ranked as paupers. Eight and a half million Irish, mostly peasants, were "pauperized beyond belief," and almost a million starved to death during the great famine of 1846–1847. The condition of the peasantry, even in Germany, deteriorated markedly between 1810 and 1840, with more and more peasants driven from their land.[7]

We here bypass the debate over the standard of living of European workers and peasants and the extent to which undeniable horrors should be understood as part of the growing pains of an industrial society that, in time, generated the highest standard of living in world history for the mass of its population. Robert W. Fogel and others find that economic inequality began to recede in the eighteenth century and that the subsequent gains from economic development disproportionately favored the lower classes. Problems of measurement and qualitative judgment remain knotty, and Fogel acknowledges that during the nineteenth century the condition of British and American workers may have deteriorated in some respects. The social price of industrialization unquestionably reached frightful levels of human suffering. From the early Republic, the high average of American income resulted in a much better standard of living for the poor than that experienced by a substantial portion of the British laboring and lower middle classes. Yet with the coming of industrialization, pauperism emerged in the immigrant-swollen port cities of the Northeast. The apparent rise in real wages between 1790 and 1860 turns out to have been erroneous. Homelessness was worse during the middle of the nineteenth century than afterward. The figure of 0.4 percent of the population in 1990 fell well below the best estimates for the first half of the nineteenth century. Between 1830 and 1850, ten and twenty percent of the population of Britain and the continent went without shelter for substantial periods of time, and – the figures are less firm – the population of the large northern cities of the United States probably matched those. During 1810–1820, homelessness became increasingly evident in New York City, as wages declined and artisans were thrown into the proletariat. The solution? Frequent, usually ineffective, police sweeps designed to clear the streets of the homeless, prostitutes, poor blacks, and others classified as "vagrants." Charles Dickens took one look at Five Points and likened it to London's notorious East End.[8]

---

[7] Hobsbawm, *Industry and Empire*, 69–70, 73; E. J. Hobsbawm, *The Age of Revolution, Europe, 1789 to 1848* (New York, 1969), 205.

[8] Fogel, *The Fourth Great Awakening and the Future of Egalitarianism*, 110–113; Elizabeth Blackmar, *Manhattan for Rent, 1785–1850* (Ithaca, N.Y., 1991), 103–104, 170–171, 180. During most of the eighteenth and nineteenth centuries homeless workers accounted for between ten percent and twenty percent of the population of Britain and Western Europe. Paupers and wage-laborers probably accounted for half the English population at the end of the seventeenth

Southerners pounced on every report of misery in Europe. They had a lot to pounce on, including evidence provided by enemies of slavery. Assailing the slave trade in 1796, Samuel Taylor Coleridge ridiculed the argument that West Indian slaves fared as well as British peasants. He noted that Africans lived decently until dragged into the Atlantic slave trade and asked how Britons could condemn the French as a nation of atheists while enslaving Africans. "Now I appeal to common sense, whether to affirm that the slaves are as well off as our peasantry be not the same as to assert that our peasantry are as bad off as negro slaves? And whether if our peasantry believed it, they would not be inclined to rebel?"[9]

In the 1840s, Margaret Fuller, embracing socialism along with abolitionism, sent reports from Europe to Horace Greeley's New York *Tribune* that warmed the hearts of Southerners, a number of whom admired her intellect and character and forgave her radicalism. The look on the faces of the poor in Glasgow reminded her of the inscription over the gate to Dante's Inferno. With formidable stylistic power, she penned chilling descriptions of Manchester, London, and the cities of the Continent. Comparisons and contrasts did not prove slavery's superiority in material conditions and therefore did not establish a case for Slavery in the Abstract. But proslavery accounts of labor conditions in free societies provided a measure of plausibility.[10]

Surveying the Americas

Southern slaveholders maintained that they presided over the mildest slave system known to man – the only sizable slave society in world history in which slaves reproduced themselves. But since they defended slavery on principle and indicted the free-labor system, the more thoughtful shrank from savaging regimes under worldwide abolitionist attack. The exigencies of international politics reinforced their caution, particularly for those who hoped to annex Cuba as a slave state. Yet they had to dissociate themselves from the much publicized excesses of other slaveholding regimes, especially since some Southerners traveled to the Caribbean and brought back horror stories. Brazil, the world's second largest slaveholding country, attracted less attention than Cuba despite the efforts of Lt. Matthew Maury, who brought a powerful political and economic vision to his notable scientific excursions. In a typical early performance, *Western Review* and *Miscellaneous Magazine* of Lexington, Kentucky,

century: Christopher Hill, *Some Intellectual Consequences of the English Revolution* (Madison, Wisc., 1980), 35.

9 "On the Slave Trade," in *The Collected Works of Samuel Taylor Coleridge*, vol. 2: *The Watchman*, ed. Louis Patton (Princeton, N.J., 1970), 140.

10 Margaret Fuller, *"These Sad But Glorious Days"*: *Dispatches from Europe, 1846–1850*, ed. Larry J. Reynolds and Susan Belasco Smith (New Haven, Conn., 1991), 12, 79–80, 103, 211–212, 320. For southern admiration of Fuller, see Elizabeth Fox-Genovese and Eugene D. Genovese, *The Mind of the Master Class: History and Faith in the Southern Slaveholders' Worldview* (New York, 2005), Supplementary References: "Fuller."

reviewed Henry Koster's *Travels in Brazil, 1809–1815* and found the condition of slaves generally "comfortable and easy." During the 1850s interest in Brazil increased somewhat, especially at southern commercial conventions. As secession drew near, Southerners envisioned the Empire of Brazil as an ally for their own incipient independent republic, praising the political stability and economic prosperity they attributed to slavery. A contributor to *Russell's Magazine* wrote that in the Western Hemisphere only Brazil and the southern United States maintained a reputable place in the international community. Edward C. Bullock told students at the University of Alabama that slaveholding Brazil, despite bad government, showed vitality and progress, while nonslaveholding Mexico languished. In 1861 the *Richmond Examiner* asked, "How comes it that, except in Brazil, we are the only religious and conservative people in Christendom?"[11]

A number of Southerners, especially from the Southwest and the low country, knew Spanish, and some traveled to Cuba, which posed a difficult problem because of the political implications of its geographic proximity. Before British West Indian emancipation and pressure on the Spanish government to follow suit, Southerners tended to contrast the severity of Cuban slavery with the mildness of their own. Afterward, they did so with diminished vigor and with apologetics. In 1829 an anonymous reviewer of Abiel Abbot's Letter Written in the Interior of Cuba offered an epitome: "The Cuban planters exact the whole time of their slaves from day-break until dark (Except parts of Saturday and Sunday).... They have but two watches in the twenty-four hours, a severity of exaction, which we hope will never be introduced into the management of American plantations." He denounced Cuban practices as "not less impolitic than barbarous."[12]

In 1850, R. E. Caffrey, a planter in St. Mary's Parish, Louisiana, returned from Cuba with a mixed report that had the slaves as "generally barbarously treated" and "kept in subjection by the lash and bloodhounds." The politician

---

[11] "Travels in Brazil," *Western Review and Miscellaneous Magazine*, 4 (1821), 87; "Characteristics of Civilization" *RM*, 2 (1857), 109; Edward C. Bullock, *True and False Civilization: An Oration Delivered before the Erosophic and Philomathic Societies of the University of Alabama* (Tuscaloosa, Ala., 1858), 25; among M. F. Maury's works, see *The Amazon and the Atlantic Slopes of South America* (Washington, D.C., 1853); John G. Van Deusen, *The Ante-Bellum Southern Commercial Conventions* (Durham, N.C., 1926), 88–92; Edward B. Bryan, *The Rightful Remedy, Addressed to the Slaveholders of the South* (Charleston, S.C., 1850), 71; A. M. Clayton, "Advancement of the Agricultural Interests," *DBR*, 26 (1859), 226; J. R. H., "Slavery in Brazil," *DBR*, 28 (1860), 479–481; *Richmond Examiner*, July 17, 1861. For praise of the stability of slaveholding Brazil, see A. A. Porter, "North and South," *SPR*, 3 (1850), 357.

[12] *SR*, 4 (1829), 125. Mary Bayard Clarke of North Carolina and Texas lived in Cuba during 1854–1855. She published a series of "Reminiscences" under the pseudonym "Tenella," *SLM*, 21 (1855), 566, 593–597; and for context, see Terrell Armistead Crow and Mary Moulton Barden, eds., *Live Your Own Life: The Family Papers of Mary Bayard Clarke, 1854–1886* (Columbia, S.C., 2003), xxx–xxxiv. By 1846 some 1,000 North American expatriates were living in Cuba: Tom Chaffin, *Fatal Glory: Narciso López and the First Clandestine U.S. War against Cuba* (Charlottesville, Va., 1996), 17.

Thomas Caute Reynolds of Missouri suggested that American annexation of Cuba would guarantee the enforcement of laws to protect slaves against inhumane treatment and a staggering loss of life. George Walton Williams, a Charleston merchant, added another datum. Visiting Cuba in 1856, he came upon large numbers of miserable and virtually enslaved Chinese. The well-read Edmund Ruffin concluded that Cubans generally treated their slaves in a manner "most cruel." These judgments increasingly accompanied apologetics that portrayed even Cuban slavery preferable to the enormities attendant upon free labor, especially free black labor. J. S. Thrasher, in editorial notes to Alexander von Humboldt's book on Cuba, consoled himself that Cuba's black slaves fared much better than Haiti's free blacks, whom he said had relapsed into fetish worship, indolence, and barbarism. Southerners welcomed the voices of antislavery as well as proslavery men who reported southern slavery milder than Cuban. The French banker Salomon de Rothschild, on a business trip in 1861, judged the two hundred fifty slaves on J. M. Call's plantation in Louisiana much better off than the Cuban slaves he had seen, adding, "I confess frankly that they seem better fed and in better health and happier than many of our countrymen." Wiley P. Harris of Mississippi claimed that Gerrit Smith, the abolitionist, admitted favoring the annexation of Cuba in part to improve the condition of the slaves there: "You Southern people are better masters than the Spaniards, bad as you are and as all masters are."[13]

Apologists combined a defense of slavery wherever it existed with criticism of slaveholding regimes that fell short of southern standards. Noah B. Cloud, an influential agricultural editor, went much further than most – too far by a great deal – when he vented his spleen, apparently unaware of danger to the larger proslavery cause. Cloud furiously denied that southern slavery had much in common with the "inhumane and revolting" British West Indian slavery of earlier decades. For Cloud, the absentee-ridden British system lacked the softening day-to-day master-slave contact common in the South, and it worked slaves to death for the profit of far-off business interests. Others maintained – sometimes from personal experience in the Islands – that the blacks had done much better as slaves than they were doing as free men. After the War, Jefferson Davis called southern slavery "confessedly the mildest and most humane" form of slavery in world history. Charles Manigault wrote in the 1870s that unlike the planters of the West Indies, Southerners lived at least half the years with their slaves "to give them punctually their clothes, Blankets Etc, calling each by name & handing it to them." However southern slaveholders interpreted the

"Things in Cuba," *Planters' Banner,* 15 (Mar. 7, 1850), n.p.; [Thomas Caute Reynolds], "Cuba," *DBR,* 8 (1850), 313–323, esp. 320; E. Merton Coulter, *George Walton Williams: The Life of a Southern Merchant and Banker, 1820–1903* (Athens, Ga., 1976), 51–52; March 4, 1859, *ERD,* 1:290; Thrasher, ed., Alexander von Humboldt, *The Island of Cuba* (New York, 1856), 53–56, 208–209, 230–239 (Humboldt protested Thrasher's rendition as misleading and ideologically tendentious); Rothschild in Jacob Rader Marcus, ed., *Memoirs of American Jews,* 3 vols. (Philadelphia, Pa., 1955), 3:102; "Autobiography of Wiley P. Harris," in Dunbar Rowland, *Courts, Judges, and Lawyers of Mississippi, 1798–1935* (Jackson, Miss., 1935), 311.

record of other slaveholding countries, they congratulated themselves on their Christian virtue and the excellence of their peculiarly devised social system.[14]

Black inability to sustain freedom became a leading theme. Southerners pitted the happy lot of their slaves against the allegedly miserable lot of emancipated blacks in the West Indies. Excoriating West Indian emancipation, they interpreted the decline in sugar production as proof that blacks could not sustain freedom and were relapsing into barbarism. Abolitionists, with some notable exceptions, had little sympathy for the emergence of peasant self-sufficiency and were committed to market criteria. Thus, although the slaveholders viewed the economic problems in the British West Indies as confirmation of their worst fears, abolitionists denied that emancipation caused economic decline or attributed decline to continued coercion. Rejecting assertions of economic devolution, they celebrated the achievements of emancipation.[15]

Declaring emancipation misguided philanthropy, slaveholders drew blood from a vulnerable foe. William Gilmore Simms referred to "the insane and cruel act which set free the slaves of the British West Indies to the ruin of that region as well as themselves." Hammond reminded the British that Southerners based their criticism of free-labor social conditions largely on gloomy British assessments; he forgot to mention British challenges to those assessments. The negative evaluation of West Indian emancipation did not just come from the usual prejudiced sources. Although George Tucker, Virginia's formidable political economist, rejected doctrines of racial superiority and expected capitalist development to put an end to slavery, he conceded the aversion of Jamaican freedmen to wage-labor in the sugar fields and their preference for self-sufficiency.[16]

Poverty

Poverty at home and abroad took center stage. Although most of the world's peoples accepted poverty as inevitable, Americans considered it abnormal. Focusing on the cities and slums of the mid-nineteenth-century Northeast,

[14] Clud, "The Cotton Power, an American Power," *American Cotton Planter and Soil of the South*, n.s., 2 (1858), 331; Jefferson Davis, *The Rise and Fall of the Confederate Government*, 2 vols. (New York, 1958), 1:78; Charles Manigault, "Souvenir of Our Ancestor & of My Immediate Family" (ms.), Manigault Plantation Records. For the alleged deterioration of blacks under British emancipation, see T. R. R. Cobb, "Historical Sketch of Slavery," in *An Inquiry into the Law of Negro in the United States* (New York, 1968 [1858]), cxcvi–ccv; G. V. H. Forbes to St. John R. Liddell, Aug. 16, 1860, in Liddell Papers.
[15] For a balanced review of the debate, see Robert W. Fogel, *Without Consent or Contract: The Rise and Fall of American Slavery* (New York, 1991), 406–411; for the propaganda war in the North, see Louis Filler, *The Crusade against Slavery, 1830–1860* (New York, 1960), 140. In a forthcoming work – tentatively entitled *Fatal Self-Deception: Loyal and Loving Slaves in the Mind of Southern Slaveholders* – we examine at length the strength and significance of the view that emancipated blacks would replicate the fate of the Indians.
[16] Simms and Hammond in *The Pro-Slavery Argument, as Maintained by the Most Distinguished Writers of the Southern States* (Philadelphia, Pa., 1853), 197, 145; George Tucker, *Political Economy for the People* (Philadelphia, Pa., 1859), 84–85.

they treated poverty as a soluble problem. In truth, from the early days of the Republic, the high average level of American income resulted in a much higher standard of living for the poor than that experienced by a substantial portion of the British laboring and lower middle classes. Still, with the coming of industrialization, pauperism emerged in the immigrant-swollen port cities of the Northeast, and by 1830, ten percent of New York's population ranked as paupers.[17]

Foreign travelers to the early republic made much of the lack of poverty and paucity of beggars and criminals. By the 1820s their reports became clouded as unemployment and economic depression hit the large northern cities. In the late 1820s and 1830s, William Cobbett and Harriett Martineau agreed that the United States had few American-born paupers but many poverty-stricken European immigrants and free blacks. Yet, for long afterward, travelers who found little or no poverty hardly noticed immigrants and free blacks. Michael Chevalier, on a mission for the French government in the early 1830s, contrasted poverty-ravaged Europe to America: "There are no poor here, at least not in the Northern and Western States, which have protected themselves from the leprosy of slavery." Chevalier nevertheless compared the condition of slave laborers in Charleston favorably with that of free laborers of Europe. Two decades later, William Chambers similarly commented on the absence of beggars and ragged vagrants everywhere except in a few large cities. Travelers as keen as Richard Cobden, the English liberal, saw "no poor people or beggars" in Baltimore. Sir Charles Augustus Murray concurred during his travels through North and South.[18]

Southern ideologues, obsessed with evidence of terrible poverty in free-labor countries, were blind to poverty in Charleston, Nashville, and New Orleans. J. B. Ferguson of Nashville, Tennessee, announced that the South took better care of its laborers and had "comparatively no pauperism." A writer in *Southern Quarterly Review* denied that pauperism existed in the South, and another in *Southern Literary Messenger* drew on the antislavery Horace Greeley to state

[17] For changing attitudes toward poverty, see Gertrude Himmelfarb, *The Idea of Poverty: England in the Early Industrial Age* (New York, 1984); Robert H. Bremner, *From the Depths: The Discovery of Poverty in the United States* (New York, 1950); Fogel, *Fourth Great Awakening*, ch. 3; also, Daniel Bivona and Roger B. Henkle, *The Imagination of Class: Masculinity and the Victorian Urban Poor* (Columbus, Oh., 2006), Introduction.

[18] Jane Louise Mesick, *The English Traveller: in America, 1785–1835* (New York, 1922), 29–30, 109, 114; Max Berger, *The British Traveller in America, 1836–1860* (Gloucester, Mass., 1964), 165; Michael Chevalier, *Society, Manners, and Politics in the United States: Letters on North America*, ed. John William Ward (New York, 1961 [1835], William Chambers, *Things as They Are in America* (London, 1854), 341–344, quote at 107; P., "Southern Ladies" (1838), in Eugene L. Schwaab and Jacqueline Bull, eds., *Travels in the South: Selected from Periodicals of the Time*, 2 vols. (Lexington, Ky., 1973), 2:339; Sarah Mytton Maury, *An Englishwoman in America* (London, 1848), 214–215; Cobden Diary, June 11, 1835, in *The American Diaries of Richard Cobden*, ed. Elizabeth Hoon Cawley (Princeton, N.J., 1952), 93; Sir Charles Augustus Murray, *Travels in North America during the Years 1834, 1835 and 1836* (London, 1839), 2:297.

that New York had three times as many paupers as Ireland. Among others, Daniel Hundley of Alabama, who lived in Chicago for many years, announced that since the South had few paupers, it did not need a system of poor relief.[19]

In the typical southern view, poverty and related miseries arose from the free-labor system, whereas slavery gave its laborers cradle to grave security, if at a low level. Any able-bodied white man could support himself and his family. With a solid family structure embedded in extended kinship, home folks took care of their own, whether orphaned, old, or incapacitated. If they could not, churches and local authorities stepped in to provide support. John S. Wise looked back on conditions in late eighteenth-century Virginia: "Everybody on the Peninsula knows everybody else. Everybody there is kin to everybody else. Nobody is so poor that he is wretched; nobody is so rich that he is proud." Poorhouses had fallen into decay by the War: "When a man dies, his kin are sufficiently numerous to care for his family; and while he lives, there is no excuse for pauperism." Governor George Poindexter of Mississippi boasted in 1821, "The finger of want points not to the door of the humblest cottage in our country." The "miserable mendicant," Poindexter was sure, "is seldom seen among us, and if at all he is the itinerant stranger who seeks the aid of our munificence and hospitality." Governor George R. Gilmer of Georgia crowed in 1830, "We have no such class as the poor. Our lands are so cheap, and the absolute necessaries of life so easily obtained that the number of dependent poor are scarcely sufficient to give exercise to the virtues of charity in individuals. A beggar is almost as rare with us as a prince."[20]

The lack of beggars became a proud southern boast. In the 1840s Edmund Ruffin acknowledged "a most wretched & worthless population" in parts of southern South Carolina that eked out a living in part by stealing but rarely by begging from rich neighbors. Susan Dabney Smedes of Mississippi pronounced the piney woods people uneducated but decent, with well-kept homes and good manners. Travelers and sojourners, underscoring Ruffin and Smedes, found poor Southerners too proud to beg. Typical was the wartime account of J. L. Fremantle, an Englishman, who said that no Southerner – black or white, male or female – had ever asked him for alms. Calvin H. Wiley, North Carolina's educational reformer – hardly a Pollyanna – described eastern North Carolina in the 1830s as a region in which "without some

[19] J. B. Ferguson, *Address on the History, Authority and Influence of Slavery* (Nashville, Tenn., 1850), 21; "Horace Greeley and His Lost Book," *SLM*, 31 (1860), 212; "Domestic Histories of the South," *SQR*, 5 (1852), 511. For the extent of poverty in Charleston and the efforts to combat it, see Barbara L. Bellows, *Benevolence among Slaveholders: Assisting the Poor in Charleston, 1670–1860* (Baton Rouge, La., 1993).

[20] John S. Wise, *The End of an Era* (Boston, Mass., 1900), 16; Dunbar Rowland, ed., *Mississippi: Comprising Sketches of Counties, Towns, Events, Institutions, and Persons, Arranged in Cyclopedic Form*, 4 vols. (Spartanburg, S.C., 1976 [1907]), 2:448 (Poindexter); George Washington Paschal, *History of Wake Forest College*, 3 vols. (Wake Forest, N.C., 1935–1943), 1:3, n.2; Gilmer quoted in Elizabeth Wisner, *Social Welfare in the South, from Colonial Times to World War I* (Baton Rouge, La., 1970), 37.

great changes, beggary and starvation will never here be known." J. F. H. Claiborne of Mississippi insisted throughout his life that the South had "no great aggregations of capital, few monopolies, no oppression of labor, and no want and miseries," whereas in the North the "oppression of northern capitalists" produced "starving operatives."[21]

There was truth to these idylls, but not enough. The South had a right to boast that – relative to the North and Europe – it had few beggars, but beggars it did have. Beggars could expect to be given a meal at planters' homes and occasionally even a little money. As Kate Carney of Tennessee remarked when her parents invited a poor woman who had come to the door to the dinner table: "I felt quite sorry for her, for she certainly seemed to deserve the sympathy of mankind." More typical was the response of James Johnston, a planter who never turned beggars away but always put them up and fed them in an outbuilding rather than in the big house.[22]

With the intensification of the sectional struggle, claims of a povertyless South grew shriller. Elwood Fisher published a scathing critique of the poverty in Massachusetts and New York that engulfed twenty percent of their populations. In 1850, A. A. Porter reviewed Fisher: "This fearful curse and terrible burden is not felt at the South. We have scarcely one pauper for each county, and beggary is unknown, except by a few strolling foreigners." John Fletcher of New Orleans cried out that everyone knew of the condition of the beggars, thieves, and paupers of Europe: "The history of that community, in all free countries, is a monument and record of free labour." Breathing a sigh of relief, Fletcher was grateful that the South had no paupers. As late as 1923, I. Jenkins Mikell of South Carolina opened a chapter of his *Rumbling of the Chariot Wheels*, by maintaining, as his ancestors had before him, "A unique feature of life among us was that we had no poverty. Our slaves, if from no other policy than a business proposition, were well cared for. All enjoyed an abundance of means . . . to a greater or lesser degree." Porter, Fletcher, and Mikell received no few assists from conservative Northerners who, shocked by European conditions, thought the South a veritable Eden in comparison. Benjamin Silliman, Connecticut's distinguished scientist, expressed thanks that nothing like the

---

[21] William M. Mathew, ed., *Agriculture, Geology, and Society in Antebellum South Carolina: The Private Diary of Edmund Ruffin* (Athens, Ga., 1992), 182; Diary, July 7, 1863, in A. J. L. Fremantle, *Three Months in the Southern States: The 1863 Diary of an English Soldier, April–June 1863* (London, 1863), 296; Susan Dabney Smedes, *Memorials of a Southern Planter*, ed. Fletcher M. Green (New York, 1965 [1887]), 99; J. F. H. Claiborne, *Mississippi as a Province, Territory, and State, with Biographical Notices of Eminent Citizens* (Spartanburg, S.C., 1978 [1880]), 169–170; also, Kenneth R. Wesson, "Travelers' Accounts of the Southern Character: Antebellum and Early Postbellum Period," *Southern Studies*, 17 (1978), 313.

[22] Carney Diary, Mar. 4, 1859, also Apr. 21, 1859; Chalmers Gaston Davidson, *The Plantation World around Davidson* (Davidson, N.C., 1982), 27. "Gave a poor woman some flour": Greenlee Diary, Sept. 26, 1848. Black begging remains to be studied, but see T. Stephen Whitman, *The Price of Freedom: Slavery and Manumission in Baltimore and Early National Maryland* (Lexington, Ky., 2001), 90 and, generally, ch. 3.

poverty he saw in Britain existed in America, where "even a southern negro is better provided for" than a British worker.[23]

Yet credible reports of wretched poverty long persisted in some parts of the South. From colonial times poverty forced poor whites into one or another kind of enforced apprenticeship and quasi-servitude. In Virginia at the end of the eighteenth century Benjamin Henry Latrobe, the English-born architect and naturalist who settled in the South, found "hundreds of half-starved, miserably lodged, idle, besotted, and fever-smitten families that inhabit the country on the Potomac, and indeed all the back country of the slave States below the mountains." John Palmer of South Carolina wrote David Ramsay in 1808, "The settlers in our Pine woods make out but a very bad living. They might do better, but they are generally an idle set of people. Their principal living is by hunting." In 1813 the Methodist Reverend William Capers found the poor whites who eked out a living near Wilmington, North Carolina, lazy, dissolute, and beyond efforts at redemption.[24]

Writing from Fayetteville in 1828, Margaret Hunter Hall described the whites as worse in appearance and more degraded than the black slaves. She thought their houses more miserable, wretched, and squalid than those of the poorest peasants in Ireland. She knew that many were small slaveholders but did not reflect on their having a considerable amount of money to buy slaves. In 1831, Simms traveled up the Savannah River and reported, "Settlements are few, far between, and squalidly poor and unpromising in aspect." In 1839, Governor David Campbell reported to the legislature that Virginia had 40,000 children – twenty percent of all children between the ages of five and fifteen – whose families could not afford to send them to school. In 1852 the Literary Fund, which dispensed funds to the free schools, reported to the legislature that it had to care for many more children than those of the "dissolute and worthless." To the contrary: "The children of the industrious day laborer and helpless widow, the destitute orphans of respectable parents, form a large

[23] A. A. Porter, "North and South," *SPR*, 3 (1850), 356; John Fletcher, *Studies on Slavery, in Easy Lessons* (Natchez, Miss., 1852), 31–35, quote at 220; also, Wayne Gridley, *Slavery in the South: A Review of Hammond's and Fuller's Letters, and Chancellor Harper's Memoir* (Charleston, S.C., 1845), 17; I. Jenkins Mikell, *Rumbling of the Chariot Wheels* (Charleston, S.C., 1923), 199; Chandos M. Brown, *Benjamin Silliman: A Life in the Young Republic* (Princeton, N.J., 1989), 193. For another conservative Northerner who stressed the relative absence of poverty in the South, see [Anon.], *New Phase of the Subject of Slavery and Free Labor as Now Existing in the United States* (Newark, N.J., 1858), 21–22. For a critique of Fisher's statistics, see Osgood Mussey, *Review of Ellwood Fisher's Lecture on the North and the South* (Cincinnati, 1849), esp. 6, 28ff, 64, quote at 3. For southern praise of Fisher, see, e.g., [David J. McCord], "Barhydt's Industrial Exchanges," *SQR*, 15 (1849), 460, 472.

[24] *The Journal of Latrobe: Being the Notes and Sketches of an Architect, Naturalist and Traveler in the United States from 1796 to 1820* (New York, 1905), 34–36, quote at 34; John Palmer to David Ramsay, Dec. 3, 1808, in Ulrich B. Phillips, ed., *Plantation and Frontier Documents, 1649–1863*, 2 vols. (New York, 1969 [1910]), 166; William M. Wightman, *Life of William Capers, D. D., One of the Bishops of the Methodist Episcopal Church, South, Including an Autobiography* (Nashville, Tenn., 1902), 166–167.

proportion of the number receiving the patronage of the school commissioners." By 1850, T. M. Garrett, a student at the state university, still echoed the theme, finding the poor whites around Chapel Hill rude, filthy, shiftless, and degraded by their poverty. But he described the yeomanry to the west as good people who "live plentifully, liberally in their way, cultivate hardihood, energy and industry."[25]

Despite southern assertions that poverty plagued the free but not the slave states, Europeans did not like what they saw. In the 1830s the piney woods folks in Georgia struck Frances Kemble as tattered and filthy. In the 1840s, J. S. Buckingham remarked that South Carolina and Virginia seemed to have more paupers than the northern states. D. W. Mitchell reported that "a large proportion" of those who lived in the outskirts of Richmond congregated in "poor, mean, low neighborhoods." A few years later, Fredrika Bremer of Sweden came across clay-eating poor whites in the low country and piedmont of Georgia and South Carolina. Puzzled by the anomalies of their existence, she wrote that they "live in the woods, without churches, without schools, without hearths, and sometimes also without homes, but yet independent and proud in their own way." In the 1850s Charles Richard Weld, historian of the British Royal Society, charged that Virginia had many more paupers than Ohio. Even Ireland's stridently pro-southern John Mitchel described northwest Georgia and eastern Alabama as full of hungry and ragged people in small, rough, dingy log houses. Others commented on the how little the homes of the poorer whites differed from the cabins of the slaves in size and comfort.[26]

In the early 1850s, C. G. Parsons, an antislavery Northerner, asked slaveholders in northern Georgia how they felt about the many miserable poor whites he saw. Mrs. A. replied that slaveholders were hospitable to each other and to strangers but unconcerned about neighboring poor. In later years, J. S. C. Abbott, the popular historian, described the poor whites of eastern

---

[25] Margaret Hunter Hall to Sister Jane, Feb. 13, 1828, in Una Pope-Hennessey, ed., *The Aristocratic Journey: Letters of Mrs. Basil Hall Written during a Fourteen Months' Sojourn in the United States* (New York, 1931), 204; Simms, "To the City Gazette: Notes of a Small Tourist," 1831, in Mary C. Oliphant et al., eds., *The Letters of William Gilmore Simms*, 6 vols. (Columbia, S.C., 1952–1982), 1:19–20; in Edgar W. Knight, ed., *A Documentary History of Education in the South before 1860*, 5 vols. (Chapel Hill, N.C., 1949–1953), see "Report on the Literary Fund," 5:140–141, and "Governor David Campbell Tells the Legislature of Virginia about the Importance of Free Schools," 5:87; Thomas Miles Garrett Diary, Aug. 1, 1850.

[26] Frances Kemble, *Journal of a Residence on a Georgia Plantation in 1838–1839* (New York, 1863), 76; J. S. Buckingham, *The Slave States of America*, 2 vols. (New York, 1968 [1842]), 1:51, 2:537; D. W. Mitchell, *Ten Years in the United States: Being an Englishman's Views of Men and Things in the North and South* (London, 1862), 58; Fredrika Bremer, *Homes of the New World: Impressions of America*, 2 vols. (New York, 1853), 1:365; Charles Richard Weld, *A Vacation Tour in the United States and Canada* (London, 1855), 318; John Mitchel, "Tour in the South-West," *Southern Citizen*, Jan. 18, 1858; Buckingham, *Slave States*, 3:305; Avery O. Craven, "Poor Whites and Negroes in the Ante-Bellum South," *Journal of Negro History*, 15 (1930), 16.

Alabama and western Georgia as utterly degraded, although it is unclear how much he was testifying on his own experience and to what extent he was relying on the testimony of George M. Weston, author of the antislavery *Progress of Slavery in the United States*. Frederick Law Olmsted reported that many poor people in the Mississippi Pine Barrens stole to feed themselves properly and that many in western Virginia and North Carolina and eastern Tennessee went barefoot and scantily clad even in winter. Further south he spoke of "as much close packing, filth, and squalor in certain blocks, inhabited by laboring whites, in Charleston, as I have witnessed in any Northern town of its size; and greater evidence of brutality and ruffianly character." But he praised the good order in Savannah. Olmsted reported that the newspapers of the cities and larger towns rarely so much as mentioned rural poverty in the South, whereas those of the smaller towns commented frequently. A few years later, Britain's skeptical William Howard Russell called Olmsted's reports of southern cultural back-wardness and poverty "amusing": "I fear he c[oul]d draw pictures as strong of misery & ignorance among those in our land who are neither slaveowners nor slaves."[27]

With the coming of the railroads and then a mini-boom in manufacturing in the 1850s, the South felt some of the effects of economic swings. The yellow fever epidemic in Louisiana forced a cessation in railroad construction, and flooding along the Mississippi threw Irish laborers out of work. The *Federal Union* of Milledgeville, Georgia, described the number of workers reduced to penury as "incredible" and protested the callousness of their employers. Atlanta had no poorhouse, but a grand jury insisted in 1857 that the poor needed "consideration and action." As a gateway to the West, Atlanta attracted large numbers who could not support themselves or preferred an existence in idleness or vice. The grand jury recommended a poorhouse in which they could be made to support themselves. W. P. Harrison, missionary to the slaves, quoted C. W. Gooch of Henrico County, Virginia, as railing against degraded poor whites who traded with, plundered, and corrupted plantation slaves. Chief Justice J. H. Lumpkin of Georgia called for industrial development and jobs for Georgia's "poor, degraded, half-fed, half-clothed, and ignorant population." A state senator called the hill country of northern Alabama "so poor that a buzzard would have to carry provisions on his back or starve to death on his passage." Hundley described the typical abode of the "poor white trash" of the hill country as "a little hut of round logs," with chinks of space between them, wooden chimneys, puncheon floor, a few rickety chairs, a dirty bed or two, a spinning wheel, a few cooking utensils, and a rifle: One room for the entire

---

[27] C. G. Parsons, *An Inside View of Slavery: A Tour among the Planters* (Savannah, Ga., 1974 [1855]), 214–215; Frederick Law Olmsted, *A Journey in the Back Country* (New York, 1970 [1860]), 235; John S. C. Abbott, *South and North; or, Impressions Received during a Trip to Cuba and the South* (New York, 1969 [1860]), 142–145; Frederick Law Olmsted, *A Journey in the Seaboard Slave States* (New York, 1968 [1856]), 404–405, 707ff, quote at 404; W. H. Russell, March 5, 1861, in Martin Crawford, ed., *William Howard Russell's Civil War: Private Diary and Letters, 1861–1862* (Athens, Ga., 1992), 5.

family. In 1865, Eliza Frances Andrews of Georgia remarked on a Cracker "cabin that Brother Troup wouldn't put one of his negroes into."[28]

J. H. Hammond guessed the number of unemployed poor in South Carolina at 50,000; William Gregg at 50,000 in 1845 and 125,000 in 1851; James H. Taylor at 100,000. Well after the War, Tennessee's Confederate army veterans remembered substantial numbers of easily overlooked white poor in the interstices of the antebellum slave society. For one, Mrs. R. M. Grune, from middling slaveholders in Alabama, recalled that the local poor whites "were in a far more deplorable condition than the negro." A. J. Childers, a nonslaveholder in Tennessee, snarled that the planters treated poor whites no better than slaves. After the War some poor whites did say that they had lived almost as slaves, and that rich whites treated them as such. Henry Baker, who had been a slave in Alabama, reported on having heard a white preacher say after the War that he was glad the blacks were free "'cause de white man wuz a bigger slave dan de 'nigger' wuz."[29]

Some of the most damaging testimony on white poverty came from Southerners who, like E. A. Pollard of Virginia, recommended the reopening of the African slave trade in "the interests of the working classes and yeomanry," whose cause "cries to Heaven for justice." Pollard, after describing the loyalty of the laboring classes to the South, protested their being "treated with the most ungrateful and insulting consideration by their country, debarred from its social system, deprived of all share in the benefits of the institution of slavery, condemned to poverty, and even forced to bear the airs of superiority in black and beastly slaves! Is this not a spectacle to fire the heart?"[30]

Proslavery theorists, assuming that the social question plagued only free-labor countries, maintained that black slavery kept white labor from exploitation and despair. Southerners, despite a good deal of smugness, confirmed the

---

[28] S. E. McKinley in *Federal Union*, Jan. 9, 1855, reprinted in Phillips, ed., *Plantation and Frontier Documents*, 2:184; Franklin M. Garrett, *Atlanta and Environs: A Chronicle of Its People and Events* (Vol. 1: Athens, Ga., 1954), 1:428; Gooch quoted in William Pope Harrison, *The Gospel among the Slaves: A Short Account of Missionary Operations among African Slaves in the Southern United States* (Nashville, Tenn., 1893), 103; Paul De Forest Hicks, *Joseph Henry Lumpkin: Georgia's First Chief Justice* (Athens, Ga., 2002), 71; [Mary Gordon Duffee], *Duffee's Sketches of Alabama* (Tuscaloosa, Ala., 1970), 1; Daniel R. Hundley, *Social Relations in Our Southern States* (Baton Rouge, La., 1979 [1860]), 260, 265; Eliza Frances Andrews, *War-Time Journal of a Georgia Girl* (New York, 1907), 93; also Sidney Andrews, *South since the War*, 177–180, 182–183; Mark K. Bauman, "The Emergence of Jewish Social Service Agencies in Atlanta," *Georgia Historical Quarterly*, 69 (1985), 487–491.

[29] For Hammond and Gregg, see L. A. Cline, "Something Wrong in South Carolina: Antebellum Agricultural Tenancy and Primitive Accumulation in Three Districts" (M.A. thesis, University of South Carolina, 1996), 6–7; Mrs. R. M. Grune to H. C. Nixon, Mar. 21, 1913, in H. C. Nixon Collection; for the recollections of Confederate army veterans, see Coleen Morse Elliott and Louise Armstrong Moxley, eds., *The Tennessee Civil War Veterans Questionnaires*, 5 vols. (Easley, S.C., 1985), 2:691; 4:1316, 1332, 1711, Childers quoted at 2:503; also Bascom in John W. Blassingame, ed., *Slave Testimony: Two Centuries of Letters, Speeches, Interviews, and Autobiographies* (Baton Rouge, La., 1977), 661.

[30] Edward A. Pollard, *Black Diamonds Gathered in the Darkey Homes of the South* (New York, 1968 [1859]), 53.

existence of poverty in their midst – without necessarily considering it poverty. By "poverty," they usually meant destitution, hunger, and abject misery rather than a rock-bottom existence. In the 1780s the Marquis de Chastellux praised Virginians for their hospitality but lamented their lack of generosity in contributions to public causes. He could have said as much fifty years later. Indeed, Frances Trollope, writing about 1830, approved the absence of demoralizing poor laws in America but regretted the tight-fisted attitude of the wealthy and their lack of individual efforts for the poor: "I suppose there is less alms giving in America than in any other Christian country on the face of the globe. It is not the temper of the people either to give or to receive."[31]

Yet the great majority of southern preachers refused to stigmatize the poor. "Charity" was a common theme. The Reverend Franc Carmack of the Disciples of Christ said, "Charity, stands in the Bible sense of the term, at the head of the list of Christian virtues." The Presbyterian Reverend Robert L. Dabney of Virginia poured his wrath over a professing Christian who spent his wealth on self-indulgence and passed by "the hundreds of starving poor and degraded sinners around him." Instead of using his money to rescue them from hell-fire, he wasted it on a "strong, comfortable family carriage" and on keeping up with the Joneses. Dabney condemned "artificial luxuries and the costly refinements of fashionable life" – the conspicuous consumption and unnecessary expenditure that subverted Christian humility and spirituality. He charged Christians with the solemn duty to care for the helpless. The Presbyterian Reverend Dr. James Henley Thornwell of South Carolina, when a young man at Harvard, was "charmed" by the New England notion of universal philanthropy, but he preferred "the narrower circle of domestic affection and of private friendships." For, he explained, "The man who is careless of his own household is hardly able to take care of the world. . . . He is the best philanthropist who is the truest friend, the most faithful husband, the most tender parent, and affectionate neighbor." Episcopal Bishop James H. Otey of Tennessee told communicants that Christianity introduced the very idea of asylums to care for the afflicted.[32]

Long after the War, James C. Schofner, whose father had owned fifteen slaves, still maintained, "Poverty was no disgrace if the man was honorable." Few Southerners were ready to consider poverty as evidence of moral

---

[31] Marquis de Chastellux, *Travels in North America in the Years 1780,1781, and 1782*, 2 vols., rev. and tr. H. C. Rice, Jr. (Chapel Hill, N.C., 1963), 2:442; Frances Trollope, *Domestic Manners of the Americans* (Gloucester, Mass., 1974 [1832]), 118–119.

[32] Carmack Diary, Oct. 15, 1859; M. E. Carmichael Diary, Apr. 1, 1838; "Principles of Christian Economy," *DD*, 1:5 16–17, 27–28, quote at 9; J. H. Thornwell, to Alexander Pegues, Sept. 11, 1834, in Benjamin M. Palmer, *Life and Letters of James Henley Thornwell* (Richmond, Va., 1875), 123–124; Otey, "Address at the Annual Meeting of the Orphan Society of Natchez, 1836," in William Mercer Green, *Memoir of the Rt. Rev. James Hervey Otey, D. D., LL.D, the First Bishop of Tennessee* (New York, 1885), 188. Also Robert L. Dabney, *Systematic Theology* (Carlisle, Pa., 1985 [1871]), 530. On the preachers' attitude in general, see Kenneth M. Startup, *The Root of All Evil: The Protestant Clergy and the Economic Mind of the Old South* (Athens, Ga., 1997), ch. 6. For changing views of penitentiaries, poorhouses, and insane asylums in a democratizing society, see David J. Rothman, *The Discovery of the Asylum: Social Order in the New Republic*, 2nd ed. (Boston, Mass., 1990).

degradation rather than of unfortunate circumstances, and yet they did not easily resist making precisely that judgment. William Waller Carson, son of a Tennessean who owned two hundred slaves, said, "There, as always as everywhere, the fact that a man could do no better than make his living by manual labor was assumed to prove that he lacked brains, education, or money." The South, in this reading, had two kinds of poor whites: the "respectable" who did their best to work hard, attend church, and cooperate with their better-off neighbors; and the "trash" who formed a rural lumpenproletariat of asocials, antisocials, and criminals.[33]

Southern moral philosophers debated the Manchesterian notion that alms undermined the character of recipients. In 1826, Thomas Cooper and his associates at South Carolina College remarked in a report on primary and secondary education that America had no class of poor similar to that of Europe, where taxation oppressed the lower classes: "If any of our citizens approach this situation, except through sickness or personal disability, it is for the most part owing to a culpable want, either of industry or frugality." The Methodist Reverend W. S. Sasnett of Emory College warned that if the Church did not assume responsibility for orphans and the poor, the state would encourage poverty by rewarding idleness. Speaking in 1860 in opposition to a homestead bill, Senator Louis Wigfall of Texas denounced the poor as responsible for their own lot. The Reverend Thomas E. Peck of Richmond, Virginia, paraphrasing Thornwell on the evils of government charity, commented on the Presbyterian church's attitude toward the poor as formulated by the General Assembly of 1856: Work is a duty but poverty no disgrace. Those who could not work deserved alms. Peck insisted that support for the poor should come from the church and individual Christian effort, not from government. The Episcopalian Jasper Adams said much the same in his influential *Elements of Moral Philosophy.*[34]

"Men should be kind to each other," Henry Pinckney of Charleston told the Methodist Benevolent Society in 1835, "because man is essentially a dependent creature." His observation might just as easily have been uttered by a Bostonian or Philadelphian, but it had a special content for people committed to a concept of household extended to include slaves. Pinckney continued: "The whole social system is but a chain of reciprocal dependence, the poor hanging upon the rich, and the rich upon the poor." Pinckney's formulation invoked the master-slave relation and meant that, as William and Jane Pease put it, "at least half of Charleston's population was thus to be succored directly within the patriarchal

[33] Elliott and Moxley, eds., *Tennessee Civil War Veterans Questionnaires*, 5:1953 (Schofner); 2:465 (Carson).

[34] Thomas Cooper in Knight, ed., *Documentary History of Education in the South before 1860*, 5:25; William J. Sasnett, *Progress: Considered with Particular Reference to the Methodist Episcopal Church, South*, ed. T. O. Summers (Nashville, Tenn., 1855), 155–162; Alvy L. King, *Louis T. Wigfall: Southern Fire-eater* (Baton Rouge, La., 1970), 90–91; T. E. Peck, *Miscellanies*, ed. T. C. Johnson, 3 vols. (Richmond, Va., 1895–1897), 2:300–304; Jasper Adams, *Elements of Moral Philosophy* (Philadelphia, Pa., 1837), 239–250.

system rather than by any system of organized charity." Not that the New England attitude failed to appear among southern planters. Allen Tate caught it well in his novel *The Fathers*, when he portrayed George Posey – a parvenu, quasi-bourgeois slaveholder – as a man who would give an old woman beggar $10 but "won't pay his free labor enough to buy bacon and meal."[35]

Aid to the Distressed

In Texas the English-born Amelia E. H. Barr commented on wartime deprivation: "A poverty that is universal may be cheerfully borne; it is an individual poverty that is painful and humiliating." Southerners believed that charity begins at home, and the efforts of a concerned minority among the slaveholders were, despite all carping, impressive. First, they took care of their poorer relatives; then, poor folks in their own neighborhood. When drought struck the section of Georgia where Nancy Bostick DeSaussure's grandfather lived, he sent to Savannah for 2,000 bushels of corn to be distributed to his poor neighbors free of charge. His largesse did not contradict Cicero's warning – in a book Southerners read in college – that liberality must be tempered by a realistic estimate of resources, for the more people are helped, the more they will ask for help. We should be generous, Cicero taught, but we are not required to sacrifice our own interests to those of others. Thomas Jefferson extended charity to the poor he knew. He saw no point in contributing to the victims of far-off disasters, of which there were too many to do much about. During the War, Meta Morris Grimball of coastal South Carolina approved of her planter husband's efforts to aid the impoverished but reminded him that "he has first to consider his own family," which had fallen into straitened circumstances.[36]

The poor turned to the planters of the neighborhood in time of need, for in every neighborhood there would be some open-hearted planters, however many indifferent or hard-hearted ones there might also be. It is impossible to say how many planters replicated the wealthy Edmondstons – big planters in Halifax County, North Carolina – who built a house for a local poor woman. But widows insolvent or threatened by local bullies had protectors among the gentry. Planters provided schools for poor children and looked after them in various ways. They welcomed the children to play on the plantation, fed them,

---

[35] William Pease and Jane H. Pease, *The Web of Progress: Private Values and Public Styles in Boston and Charleston, 1828–1843* (New York, 1985), 144–145; Allen Tate, *The Fathers and Other Fiction*, rev. ed. (Baton Rouge, La., 1977), 82. For the southern concept of household as extended to include slaves, see Elizabeth Fox-Genovese, *Within the Plantation Household: Black and White Women of the Old South* (Chapel Hill, N.C., 1988).

[36] Amelia E. H. Barr, *All the Days of My Life: An Autobiography. The Red Leaves of a Human Heart* (New York, 1980 [1913]), 231; Nancy Bostick DeSaussure, *Old Plantation Days: Being Recollections of Southern Life before the War* (Electronic ed.; Chapel Hill, N.C., 1997 [1909]), 15; Cicero, *De Officiis*, tr. Walter Miller (Cambridge, Mass.: LCL, 1975), Bk. 2:15, Bk. 3:10; J. McLaughlin, *To His Exellency*, ed. n., 139; Meta Morris Grimball Journal, Oct. 24, 1862.

and took them in when their parents were ill or died. They sent their slaves to nurse sick yeoman neighbors.[37]

Poor free blacks depended on the charity of benevolent whites as well as the better-off of their own people. Individual whites usually dispensed largesse to individual blacks but on occasion made community efforts. Thomas F. Williams of Savannah raised money to establish America's first infirmary for aged and infirm blacks in 1832. Episcopalian planters like James Cuthbert of Beaufort, South Carolina, left generous bequests to church groups that cared for the white and black poor. William Boylan of Raleigh promoted the first county poorhouse in Wake County. Isaac Tuttle and his stepson Dr. Newton contributed substantially to the Augusta Orphan asylum, which the state government supplemented with a donation of railroad stock. The well-to-do claimed, with a romantic and self-serving flush, that they treated poor neighbors generously. And the recollections of former slaves reinforced those claims with expressions of admiration for the generosity of planters who distributed meat, vegetables, seed, and assorted supplies to poor neighbors in distress. Former slaves also recalled childless planter families that took in, reared, and educated the children of poor neighbors and recalled others who invited poor children to the plantation to play with their own children. Former slaves recalled planters who helped poor neighbors and other planters who did not.[38]

A poor man never knew what a planter would do when asked for help by a stranger. Martha Jackson's father would not share his wood with a poor man who badly needed it for his fireplace but did not object when his wife gave him supper and let him sleep on a cot in the dining room. John C. Calhoun's improvident son Andrew proved a benefactor of the poor but did not settle debts with peers. Linton Stephens turned a beggar away from his door. Why should he assist a big, strapping foreigner who could earn his own living? On second thought Stephens fretted: Suppose the beggar needed money for his children? A woman called upon Bishop Otey with a woeful tale of destitution, hunger, and an invalid husband: "I gave her $1.00 and told her told her to

---

[37] Oct. 6, 1862, in Beth G. Crabtree and James Welch Patton, eds., *"Journal of a Secesh Lady": The Diary of Ann Catherine Devereux Edmonston, 1860–1866* (Raleigh, N.C., 1979), 271; George C. Osborne, "Plantation Life in Central Mississippi, as Reflected in the Clay Sharkey Papers," *Journal of Mississippi History*, 3 (1941), 285; Smedes, *Memorials*, 78, 281. This neighborliness was general within and across class lines.

[38] On Williams, see E. Merton Coulter, *Wormsloe: Two Centuries of a Georgia Family* (Athens, Ga., 1955), 203. For a tribute to Cuthbert, see Louis M. De Saussure Plantation Record Book, Dec. 20, 1852; also William Capers's tribute to the Presbyterian Reverend Henry Kollock, "Autobiography," in William M. Wightman, *Life of William Capers, D. D., One of the Bishops of the Methodist Episcopal Church, South, Including an Autobiography* (Nashville, Tenn., 1902), 214; *DNCB*, 1:205 (Boylan); Charles C. Jones, in Jones and Dutcher, *Augusta*, 296–297; also John Belton O'Neall, *Biographical Sketches of the Bench and Bar of South Carolina*, 2 vols. (Charleston, S.C., 1859), 1:267; S. N. Hutchinson Journal, July 6, 1851. In George Rawick, ed., *The American Slave: A Composite Autobiography*, 19 vols. (Westport, Conn., 1972), see S. C., 2 (pt. 1), 105; 3 (pt. 3), 2, 119, 148; 3 (pt. 4), 39; (pt. 4), 121, 148; (pt. 4), 39; N. C., 15 (pt. 2), 345; Okla., 7 (pt. 1), 6.

bring me vouchers of his character & I would assist her more if she proved to be worthy."[39]

The wealthy were most likely to step in to care for widows, orphans, and afflicted men of their own class who had become indigent through no fault of their own, but they also reached out well beyond. Charleston had the oldest of the world's hundred or so chapters of the St. Andrew's Society, concerned primarily with helping the poor. By the 1790s Charleston had other such societies, most notably the St. George's Society, the South Carolina Society, the Fellowship Society, and the German Friendly Society. St. Andrews decided to focus on the education of poor children, financing its efforts through entrance fees, dues, rents on its hall, and some generous contributions.[40]

During the frequent and fearful epidemics, charitable organizations appeared out of nowhere to assist the stricken and to care for the poor. The well-to-do, in bursts of civic spirit, contributed money and paid the bills of the strapped, but, more impressively, some ministered to the sick in full knowledge of the risk. The well-to-do young men of the Harvard Club of Charleston made relief of the poor their special object during the epidemics. In Mobile, an organization of young physicians from affluent families worked without compensation during the frequent epidemics. In New Orleans, the ethnic associations, which usually attended to the needs of their own people, plunged into general relief work. John Duffy, historian of the epidemic of 1853, writes, "The percentage of middle and upper class citizens in New Orleans who assumed the responsibilities of brotherhood was almost unprecedented. They were not content with merely supplying financial and moral support for the impoverished sick but went into wretched hovels and tenements and actually nursed the occupants back to health."[41]

---

[39] M. R. Jackson Journal, July 17, 1833, in Jackson-Prince Papers; Ernest McPherson Lander, Jr., *The Calhoun Family and Thomas Green Clemson: The Decline of Southern Patriarchy* (Columbia, S.C., 1983), 23, 223; Otey Diary, Jan. 8, 1862; Linton Stephens to A. H. Stephens, Feb. 16, 1860, in James D. Waddell, *Biographical Sketch of Linton Stephens, Containing a Selection of His Letters, Speeches, State Papers, Etc.* (Atlanta, Ga., 1877), 208–209.

[40] Stephen Meats and Edwin T. Arnold, eds., *The Writings of Benjamin F. Perry*, 3 vols. (Spartanburg, S.C., 1980), 2:190; Henry W. Moncure et al. to Willie P. Mangum, March 4, 1846, in Henry Thomas Shanks, ed., *The Papers of Willie P. Mangum*, 5 vols. (Raleigh, N.C., 1955–1956), 4:400–401; O'Neall, *Bench and Bar of South Carolina*, 1:332; J. H. Easterby, *History of the St. Andrew's Society of Charleston, South Carolina, 1729–1929* (Charleston, S.C., 1929), 11, 34, 61, 89; George J. Gongaware, *The History of the German Friendly Society of Charleston, South Carolina, 1766–1916* (Richmond, 1935), especially 44–63.

[41] Edith Wyatt Moore, *Natchez Under-the-Hill* (Natchez, Miss., 1958), 80–83; Thomas McAdory Owens, *History of Alabama and Dictionary of Alabama Biography*, 4 vols. (Spartanburg, S.C., 1978 [1921]), 1:200–201; Clyde N. Wilson, *Carolina Cavalier: The Life and Mind of James Johnston Pettigrew* (Athens, Ga., 1990), 84; George D. Cummins, *A Sketch of the Life of the Rev. William M. Jackson* (Washington, D.C., 1856), 81 (Norfolk), 41; John Duffy, *Sword of Pestilence: The New Orleans Yellow Fever Epidemic of 1853* (Baton Rouge, La., 1966), 31, 44, 54–55, 70 (quoted), 128. Although many citizens rallied to care for the stricken, others seized the opportunity to mount waves of robberies: Thomas D. Cockrell and Michael B. Ballard,

In New Orleans some sixty or so wealthy young men formed the Howard Association to aid the poor during the epidemics; it won the hearts of the city by contributing substantial amounts of money to provide medical aid for the victims. During the epidemics of the 1850s, the Howard Association's young men risked their lives in New Orleans, Norfolk, and other cities to minister to black and white poor. In *Russell's Magazine* of Charleston, Simms offered a perspective on the Howard Association's heroic efforts to help the poor during the great epidemics in New Orleans: "Death has been said to equalize all conditions of mankind. In one sense this is true, but in another and more important sense, how utterly fallacious is the forlorn hope thus held out to the earth's suffering millions, 'the hewers of wood, and the drawers of water.'" Yet, more often than not, these young men had reputations not so much for their courageous community service but for their dissolute, devil-may-care behavior in ordinary times.[42]

Physicians improved their public image considerably by ministering to poor blacks and whites. Between epidemics most communities had physicians who worked pro bono. The cholera epidemic of 1833, J. D. Wright writes, showed the medical profession to be about as helpless as were the doctors who tried to combat the Black Death during the Middle Ages. Yet the prestige of the medical profession soared on the strength of its self-sacrificing work. True, some physicians slipped out of town during the epidemics, abandoning patients, but many others, including the eminent John Berrien Lindsley, performed heroically for blacks and whites. Physicians fell victim to the diseases and dropped from exhaustion; some, literally, died in the streets. Tallahassee, Florida, had a bad reputation as an unhealthful place in the wake of the cholera epidemic of 1841, but its citizens swore by their generally well-trained, college-educated physicians, whom they credited with holding down casualties. A few other illustrations from across the South: In Georgia, Dr. Henry Campbell, a neurologist of international reputation, and his brother Dr. Robert Campbell established a hospital for blacks in 1852. Louis Le Conte, father of Joseph and John, regularly attended to the medical needs of the poor in his region of Georgia, often without fee. On several occasions he took children chronically ill from malnutrition and inadequate care into his home for months at a time, nursing them back to health. During the frequent epidemics that raged across the South, physicians risked their lives to tend to all classes, including the poor, without remuneration. Carl Kohn, a merchant, knew it was time to leave New Orleans during the yellow fever epidemic of 1833 when he saw a half dozen physicians die at their post. Dr. James Holmes of Georgia lost two of his medical assistants to yellow fever in 1854 and almost lost a son and

eds., *A Mississippi Rebel in the Army of Northern Virginia: The Civil War Memoirs of Private David Holt* (Baton Rouge, La., 1995), 54–58.

42 [William Gilmore Simms?], "The Diary of a Samaritan," *RM*, 6 (1860), 574–575; also, John Reuben Thompson's poetic tribute, "To the Howard Association of New Orleans," *SLM*, 19 (1853), 462.

his own life. In Norfolk in 1855 physicians worked fervently during the epidemic, and nearly three-quarters of them succumbed. Dr. John Augustine Chilton of Fauquier County, Virginia, became locally renowned for his disinterested ministering to the poor. The socially prominent Charles A. Luzenberg of New Orleans, celebrated for his cataract operations and reputedly the highest paid surgeon in the United States, spent two hours a day serving the indigent. Southern physicians, especially those who ministered to the poor, maintained, as the Reverend Alexander Hewett did in South Carolina in 1779, that sick slaves received better medical care than did the poorest European laborers.[43]

The Catholic Church, like the medical profession, received widespread praise for its work with the poor and the sick. Priests and nuns earned the admiration of Protestants by performing selflessly during the frequent natural disasters and epidemics. The Church, which could ill afford to spare a single priest, lost a number to epidemics. In the 1840s the *Natchez Free Trader* lauded their ministrations to the sick and dying. Praise became general during the terrible yellow fever epidemic of 1853. In New Orleans the Presbyterian Reverend Benjamin Morgan Palmer and the Unitarian Reverend Theodore Clapp worked with priests and nuns during the epidemics, maintaining relations of mutual respect with the Catholic Church. Clapp, who had previously been aided by Stephen Poydras, a wealthy Catholic, especially praised the Catholics' work among poor residents and river boatmen and the courage of the priests and nuns who sacrificed their lives. The Methodist Bishop George Foster Pierce of Georgia returned from California full of praise for the disinterested zeal and good work of the Catholic clergy. Prominent Protestant laymen like Mitchell King and planters like J. H. Bills witnessed and never forgot the self-sacrifice of priests and nuns.[44]

---

[43] John D. Wright, Jr., *Transylvania: Tutor to the West* (Lexington, Ky., 1975), 86; Moore, *Natchez-Under-the-Hill*, 80–82; John Edwin Windrow, *John Berrien Lindsley: Educator, Physician, Social Philosopher* (Chapel Hill, N.C., 1938), 113; John Allison, *Notable Men of Tennessee: Personal and Genealogical*, 2 vols. (Atlanta, Ga., 1905), 1:104; Bertram H. Groene, *Ante-Bellum Tallahassee* (Tallahassee, Fla., 1971), 55. On the Campbells, see Charles C. Jones, Jr., and Salem Dutcher, *Memorial History of Augusta* (Syracuse, N.Y., 1890), Biographical Appendix, 4–16.

[44] Clapp, "Autobiographical Sketches," in John Duffy, ed., *Parson Clapp of the Strangers' Church of New Orleans* (Baton Rouge, La., 1957), 56, also v, 34; Thomas Cary Johnson, *The Life and Letters of Benjamin Morgan Palmer* (Richmond, Va., 1906), 174, 187, 188; James J. Pillar, *The Catholic Church in Mississippi, 1837–65* (New Orleans, La., 1964), 11, 15; Roger Baudier, *The Catholic Church in Louisiana* (New Orleans, La., 1939), 319–321, 374–376; Michael Allen, *Western Rivermen, 1763–1861: Ohio and Mississippi Boatmen and the Myth of the Alligator Horse* (Baton Rouge, La., 1990), 108; George G. Smith, *The Life and Times of George Foster Pierce, Bishop of the Methodist Church, South, with a Sketch of Lovick Pierce, D. D., His Father* (Sparta, Ga., 1888), 409; O'Neall, *Bench and Bar of South Carolina*, 1:351 (King); Bills Diary, July, 1845. For nuns with Confederate and Union armies, see Jean E. Schultz, *Women at the Front: Hospital Workers in Civil War America* (Chapel Hill, N.C., 2004).

The primary accomplishment of prominent Catholics who influenced the politics of early Washington, D.C., was work to relieve the distress of the poor. In Virginia the small Catholic community in firmly Presbyterian Lexington won acceptance in large part because of the dedicated work of communicants on behalf of the poor. Senator R. M. T. Hunter expressed the gratitude of many Virginians for the nuns' work during the epidemics and the War. Eliza Frances Andrews of Georgia was much impressed by the missionary work by Father Hamilton, a Catholic priest, for Yankee prisoners: "He has been working like a good Samaritan in those dens of filth and misery. It is shameful to us Protestants that we have let a Roman Catholic get so far ahead of us in this work of charity and mercy." In 1906 Myrta Lockett Avary, recalling the burning of the Ursuline convent in Columbia by Union troops, remarked on the splendid performance of the nuns in taking care of the poor, especially the children.[45]

In Protestant churches, ladies' groups carried much of the responsibility for ministering to the poor. Mahala Roach of Mississippi rose to the occasion during the yellow fever epidemic of 1853: She was nursing her infant but "sent out food to the sick as usual." She arranged for a doctor to see a poor sick woman and made the rounds in the neighborhood. Heroic women, like heroic men, were a minority of their class – the heroic always are – but they shaped the ethos of their class and impressed the poor. Eliza Clitherall of Mobile cried out in 1851, "Oh wou'd the rich and thoughtless squanderers of the bounties of the Almighty but allow their hearts to feel for the suffering of the poor, of the many whose crops have been destroy'd, whose all is lost – whose families are without even the hope of Provision, or the means to procure clothing or the simplest comfort – surely, surely, they wou'd supply the needy – retrench their superfluous expenses, & receive in return the blessing from on High promis'd to all those who 'delivereth the poor & needy.'"[46]

The comments of women who took their responsibilities seriously bared the extent of the suffering. Susan Nye Hutchinson berated herself for having a glass of wine at a pleasant visit with some ladies when her day would have been better spent "had I visited the poor, or the wretched!" She did her best to comfort "a great many very poor people" in Raleigh. "They receive me with pleasure, and listen with attention, but ah, I fear that I am not sufficiently anxious for the salvation of their immortal souls." On the eve of the War, Keziah Brevard cried out, "How much I feel for poor people who have large

45 William W. Warner, *At Peace with All Neighbors: Catholics and Catholicism in the National Capital, 1787–1860* (Washington, D.C., 1994), 159–160; Henry Boley, *Lexington in Old Virginia* (Richmond, Va., 1936), 31; on Hunter and the expressions of gratitude to the nuns of Richmond, see James Henry Bailey, II, *A History of the Diocese of Richmond: The Formative Years* (Richmond, 1956), 117–118; Jan. 1, 1865, in Andrews, *War-Time Diary*, 77; Myrta Lockett Avary, *Dixie after the War* (New York, 1918 [1906]), 4–5.
46 Roach Diary, Sept. 20–24, 1853, also Nov. 9, 1853, in Roach-Eggleston Papers; Clitherall, Aug. 6, 1851 (Clitherall's "Autobiography" [ms.] recounts a lifelong effort to relieve the poor). Also Carney Diary, Apr. 17, 1861; Charles M. Wiltse, *John C. Calhoun: Nationalist, 1782–1828* (Indianapolis, Ind., 1944), 267–268. Rowland, ed., *Mississippi*, 2:295.

families." The next day she reiterated her trust in God and her lack of trust in man: "Tomorrow I must perform my promise to one of my poor neighbors – send her four lb. of coffee." Out of the mouths of babes: In Arkansas in the mid-1850s, Nannie Cross, daughter of a state Supreme Court justice, contributed a school essay that berated the rich for enjoying a lovely winter without a thought for the suffering poor. Much of the effort of the rich went into raising money for foreign missions. Individually and in groups, the ladies took in stray orphans and placed them with suitable families. The Ladies Benevolent Society of Beaufort arose in 1815 to provide relief for distressed girls, and such groups appeared elsewhere. In Athens, Georgia, which had about thirty paupers in 1850, the Young Ladies Benevolent Society and the Athens Benevolent Society managed reasonably well, but their resources were strained when the number rose to fifty a decade later.[47]

Family members, neighbors, and friends delivered eulogies that praised the deceased's concern for the poor. Susan Catherine Bott of Virginia ranked as a veritable saint in the eyes of fellow Presbyterians for her attention to the white and black poor of Petersburg. On the eastern shore, Catherine Cooper Hopley, an English schoolteacher, celebrated the two maiden aunts of Senator R. M. T. Hunter as "highly educated and excellent ladies, who devoted their whole time and influence to the improvement and welfare of the poor white class of the neighborhood." In South Carolina, Elizabeth Witherspoon Williams, daughter of a prominent planter, helped the career of her husband, Governor David Williams, by indefatigable work among the poor. In the 1850s, Charleston toasted rich old Miss Pinckney for her public service and generosity. "Among the indigent," said Nathaniel Russell Middleton, "she was the first to come into their thoughts at time of need." Ministers' wives took the lead in church groups. Mary Jeffreys Bethell of North Carolina explained, "I love to visit the sick because God has commanded us to do it." In another instance: "I want to discharge my duty to these orphan children. I want to be a Mother to them, and lead them to the Savior. I hope to see them useful and Pious men." Being a "real Christian" in Savannah, Catherine Couper Lovell recalled, meant to help the poor. Everywhere, well-to-do women, as well as men, fed beggars, took in waifs, or extended charity to poor neighbors.[48]

47 S. N. Hutchinson Journal, July 1, 3, 1815; Keziah Brevard Diary, Dec. 22, 23, 1860; Nannie E. Cross, "Winter" (Nov. 10, 1856), in Edward Cross Papers; Ernest Trice Thompson, *Presbyterians in the South*, 3 vols. (Richmond, Va., 1963), 1:522–523; Sarah Eve Adams Diary, Feb. 14, 1814; Elizabeth Ruffin to Edmund Ruffin, Feb, 1, 1830, in Edmund Ruffin Papers; Lawrence S. Rowland et al., *The History of Beaufort County, South Carolina*, 2 vols. (Columbia, S.C., 1996), 287; Ernest C. Hynds, *Antebellum Athens and Clarke County, Georgia* (Athens, Ga., 1974), 37. For the female orphan asylum and the ladies who sustained it, see "The Savannah Female Assylum" [*sic*], *Georgia Analytical Repository*, 1 (1802), 68–74.

48 A. B. Van Zandt, *"The Elect Lady": A Memoir of Mrs. Susan Catherine Bott, of Petersburg, Va.* (Philadelphia, Pa., 1857), 134–135; Catherine Cooper Hopley, *Life in the South from the Commencement of the War*, 2 vols. (New York, 1971 [1863]), 1:101; Harvey Toliver Cook, *The Life and Legacy of David Rogerson Williams* (New York, 1916), 188; N. R. Middleton, in Alicia Hopton Middleton et al., *Life in Carolina and New England during the Nineteenth*

Elite men spurred efforts to care for the poor, the sick, and the insane, often in the teeth of heavy opposition from scoffers and tax-haters. Indigent immigrants poured into southern cities during the late 1840s and 1850s, placing a heavy burden on charity and contributing significantly to the rise of the Know Nothings. The Irish famine and European revolutions of 1848 sent thousands of emigrants to New Orleans, where admissions to the Charity Hospital ran to 18,000 a year during 1850–1852 – only 2,000 of whom were native-born and only 250 from Louisiana. Towns like Beaufort, South Carolina, bore the cost of providing for the poor until pressed by waves of indigent immigrants. At that, only some poor women received direct subsidies. The burdens on planters and their wives became unbearable during the War. Many did not try to help poorer neighbors, and those who did found themselves overwhelmed. Themselves strapped by wartime exigencies, they lacked the resources to take care of the needy. During the War, the upper classes in Virginia did much more than generally recognized to assist the poor, but increasingly they could do little to relieve the mounting suffering.[49]

Churches and secular associations assisted the poor, especially during epidemics, but their efforts fell short. Wayne Flynt concludes for Alabama: "Despite such efforts, the poor often fell through the cracks of this voluntary system of benevolence, especially if they belonged to no church." The churches worked hard for the poor, but despite some critical individual efforts, few Southerners – few rich planters – opened their purses to support organized efforts. In bad times, like the winter of 1830, citizens established committees to assist small farmers and others caught in an economic downturn. Yeoman communities rallied to people in difficulty: In the words of Bill Cecil-Fronsman, "The community was the family beyond the family." The churches kept the poor off the government rolls, but too often, church and planter efforts consisted largely of offering solace and distributing Bibles and religious tracts. Every denomination in every decade in every part of the South had a

---

Century (Bristol, R.I., 1929), 177; Clitherall Diary, 1810–1829; Hutchinson Journal, Oct. 2, 1831; John Walker Diary, Dec. 19, 1831; Sarah Gayle Journal, Apr. 29, 1833; M. Roach Diary, Nov. 9, 1853, in Roach-Eggleston Papers; Carney Diary, Mar. 14, 1859; J. A. Gilmer Diary, Sept. [?], 1861; Bethell Diary, July 29, 1863, Oct. [?], 1855, also, Mar. 10, 1862; Sept. 16, 1863. Also Caroline Couper Lovell, *The Light of Other Days* (Macon, Ga., 1995), 25–26.

49 Peter McCandless, *Moonlight, Magnolias, and Madness: Insanity in South Carolina from the Colonial Period to the Progressive Era* (Chapel Hill, N.C., 1996), ch. 2; Fletcher M. Green, *The Role of the Yankee in the Old South* (Athens, Ga., 1972), 128–131; W. Darrell Overdyke, *The Know-Nothing Party in the South* (Baton Rouge, La., 1950), 11, 16–17; Duffy, *Sword of Pestilence,* 4–5; Rowland et al., eds., *Beaufort County, S.C.,* 261–262. On the war years, see Richard N. Current, ed., *Encyclopedia of the Confederacy,* 4 vols. (New York, 1993), 3:1229–1230, 1425–1427; Charles W. Ramsdell, *Behind the Lines in the Southern Confederacy* (Baton Rouge, La., 1944), 23–29; William Alan Blair, *Virginia's Private War: Feeding Body and Soul in the Confederacy, 1861–1865* (New York, 1998); N. R. Middleton, Jr., "A Record," in Middleton et al., *Life in Carolina and New England,* 159–160; Meta Morris Grimball Journal, Nov. 28, 1862.

significant number of ministers who worked to alleviate the suffering of poor neighbors.[50]

Episcopalians, especially high-churchmen, used the pulpit to assist needy neighbors and raised a few dollars at a time to tide them over. Lay preachers and Sabbath school teachers proved indefatigable. In Alexandria, Virginia, students at the Episcopal theological seminary went house to house to distribute alms, devoting much time to the local fishermen, who appreciated their efforts but complained about having to hear apprentice preachers "practice" on their souls. Some big Episcopalian planters like James Cuthbert of Beaufort, South Carolina, left generous bequests to church groups that cared for poor whites and blacks. William Boylan of Raleigh, North Carolina, spurred efforts to build the first county poorhouse in Wake County.[51]

The high-church Episcopalian Reverend John Hamilton Cornish of Aiken, South Carolina, called on Mrs. B[lalock?], a transplanted New Yorker whose husband, a workingman, was away on a job. The poor woman was grieving as the life ebbed out of her only child, a ten-month-old infant. Cornish presided over the burial, which was attended by the local mechanics and a few of the neighborhood's ladies. Years later, Cornish administered the Blessed Sacrament to an ailing Sarah Blalock: "Many very poor people were gathered around the head of that poor sick girl in the hovel where she is lying. The scene was awfully solemn." A week later she died: "Many of her poor friends & acquaintances were assembled." Cornish led them in prayer and talked of her spirit departed in Jesus. For months he called on her family and paid the school dues of Eliza Blalock (presumably Sarah's daughter). Then, the Misses Timmons called on

---

[50] Wayne Flynt, *Alabama Baptists: Southern Baptists in the Heart of Dixie* (Tuscaloosa, Ala., 1998), 93; Bill Cecil-Fronsman, *Common Whites: Class and Culture in Antebellum North Carolina* (Lexington, Ky., 1992), 151–153, quote at 151; James C. Bonner, *A History of Georgia Agriculture, 1732–1860* (Athens, Ga., 1964), 56; Thompson, *Presbyterians in the South*, 1:292; Henry W. Malone to I. L. Brookes, March 18, 1826, and J. Dawson to Brookes, Aug. 13, 1849, in Iveson Brookes Papers; Edward Riley Crowther, *Southern Evangelicals and the Coming of the Civil War* (Lewiston, N.Y., 2000), 92; Charles D. Bates, *The Archives Tell a Story of the Government Street Presbyterian Church, Mobile, Alabama* (Mobile, Ala., 1959), 153; J. B. Cottrel Diary, Feb. 12, 1855; Walker Diary, May 31, 1830.

For the vigorous but disappointing efforts of cities and towns to protect the health of citizens, see David R. Goldfield, "The Business of Health Planning: Disease Prevention in the Old South," *JSH*, 42 (1976), 557–570. For the marginality of southern institutions that cared for the poor, see also Gail S. Murray, "Poverty and Its Relief in the Antebellum South: Perceptions and Realities in Three Selected Cities, Charleston, Nashville, and New Orleans" (Ph.D. diss., Memphis State University, 1991), chs. 3, 6, 8.

[51] George S. Yerger to J. H. Otey, July 1, 1848, and Otey Diary, Feb. 11, 1842, in Otey Papers; W. A. R. Goodwin, ed., *The History of the Theological Seminary in Virginia and Its Historical Background*, 2 vols. (New York, 1923), 1:178–179, 487–488; also, William Meade, *Sermons, Dialogues and Narratives for Servants, to Be Read to Them in Families* (Richmond, Va., 1831), 72; William Meade, *Old Churches, Ministers, and Families of Virginia*, 2 vols. (Berryville, Va., 1978 [1857]), 2:389–391. See the tribute to Cuthbert in L. M. DeSaussure Plantation Book, Dec. 20, 1852; *DNCB*, 1:205 (Boylan).

Cornish to inquire about H. Moseley's family. Ms. Moseley and ten children had nothing to eat. None of the children knew their own ages or could identify Jesus. In 1858, Cornish did what he could for Mr. and Mrs. Randall, both "very sick & destitute." They died. Cornish arranged for coffins and a proper burial. In 1860, at 6:30 A.M., Cornish took Miss Legaré and Miss Dawson to visit Mrs. Jordan and her poor family on Shaw's Creek some four miles away.[52]

Government Efforts

Public responsibility fell to each county, not to the state. The poorest counties with the scarcest resources had the most people to take care of. Without suitable public institutions, many counties used jails to care for the destitute. In colonial New England poor relief was a civil function, but in the South the Anglican Church assumed primary responsibility, especially for the all-too-many illegitimate children. With post-Revolutionary disestablishment and a growing population, county courts and other administrators took up the slack. Commissioners recruited the poor as laborers and assigned children to apprenticeships. The philanthropic Trustees of Georgia provided no government support for orphans and the destitute, relying on the church and the charity of individuals. Until secession, churches enlisted deacons to assist the poor, and by the late 1830s almost every southern city and town had a church-centered ladies' benevolent association. The results often disappointed for want of personnel as well as time and money. State efforts did not impress ministers and concerned citizens. The Methodist Reverend William Winans, visiting a poorhouse in Mississippi, found some twenty sick inmates crowded in two small rooms, sleeping on the floor under dirty single blankets without pillows. William D. Valentine, a lawyer, expressed relief that North Carolina had few paupers, for he doubted that poorhouses were worth much: "The destitute and diseased poor regard the Poorhouse as a Penitentiary. Well they may in some instances. It is a fact no doubt that they are unfeelingly, cruelly neglected."[53]

---

[52] Cornish Diary: April 10, 1842, April 23, 30, July 1, Dec. 7, 19, 1855, Jan. 16, 20, 1857, Oct. 27–29, 1858, April 23, 1860, Dec. 19, 1861. Cornish was a high-churchman. The Anglo-Catholics in the Church of England did missionary work in the slums of London and other cities, and many of their priests wore themselves out ministering to the poor. See John Shelton Reed, "'Ritualism Rampant in East London': Anglo-Catholicism and the Urban Poor," *Victorian Studies* 31 (1988), 375–377.

[53] Wisner, *Social Welfare in the South*, 11, 15–22; James Lowell Underwood, *The Constitution of South Carolina*, 4 vols. (Columbia, S.C., 1992–1994), 2:15–20; Clarence L. Ver Steeg, *Origins of a Southern Mosaic: Studies of Early Carolina and Georgia* (Athens, Ga., 1975), 101; William Holder, *William Winans: Methodist Leader in Antebellum Mississippi* (Jackson, Miss., 1977), 61; William D. Valentine Diaries; William Davidson Blanks, "Ideal and Practice: A Study of the Conception of the Christian Life Prevailing in the Presbyterian Churches of the South during the Nineteenth Century" (Th.D., Union Theological Seminary, 1960), 171–172; Startup, *Root of All Evil*, 96–117; Walter Brownlow Posey, *The Presbyterian Church in the Old Southwest, 1778–1838* (Richmond, Va., 1952), 16.

Counties gave a few dollars to an official to take care of the poor, but the courts, which had primary responsibility, spent much more time on the care of roads than the poor. Until 1824, South Carolina's Newberry District paid individuals to look after illegitimate children and the indigent; afterward, it levied a small tax at the disposal of a board of five commissioners, who farmed the children out as apprentices. Some mayors and town officials made strong efforts to attend to the needs of poor individuals. County courts had their hands full with orphans in the wake of frequent epidemics, bouts of personal violence, and bastardy. They indentured boys and girls to those considered respectable and responsible. A majority of the children probably received decent treatment, but no few became virtual slaves. Paupers in Mississippi and North Carolina often wound up auctioned to individual employers or convict farms, where at least they were housed and fed. Public support for the poor often became, in effect, private charity, for elected county supervisors of the poor were usually rich men who supplemented the paltry public funds out of their own pockets. Officials called on planters to supply firewood or other supplies to the needy. With or without being asked, prominent judges and lawyers as well as planters aided neighbors in distress. Lawyers worked pro bono for the local poor. James D. Watkinson writes that in poor and cash-poor counties like Lancaster County, Virginia, a thin line separated solvency from poverty. Some families lived near poverty. County government and courts stretched themselves to take care of the poor, giving special attention to children and orphans. Watkinson insists that compassion, not a thirst for social control, motivated efforts to sustain the poor, and his conclusion applies to much of the South.[54]

54 Wisner, *Social Welfare in the South*, 23, 24, 34–37, 43–47; Rhoda Coleman Ellison, *Bibb County, Alabama: The First Hundred Years, 1818–1918* (University, Ala., 1984), 30; Thomas H. Pope, *The History of Newberry County, South Carolina*, 2 vols. (Columbia, S.C., 1973), 1:164; Garrett, *Atlanta and Environs*, 1:53; see Feb. 25, Dec. 8, 1858, March 27, April 27, 1859, in Herschel Gower et al., eds., *Pen and Sword: The Life and Journals of Randal W. McGavock, Colonel, C. S. A.* (Nashville, Tenn., 1959), 457, 499, 513, 517; O'Neall, *Bench and Bar of South Carolina*, 2:166, 183, 199, 329, 481, 568; Fletcher M. Green, ed., *Ferry Hill Plantation Journal* (Chapel Hill, N.C., 1961), Nov. 20, 1838 (111); James D. Watkinson, "'Fit Objects of Charity': Community, Race, Faith, and Welfare in Antebellum Lancaster County, Virginia, 1817–1860," *Journal of the Early Republic*, 21 (2001), 41–75, quote at 55; Walter Prescott Webb, ed., *The Handbook of Texas*, 3 vols. (Austin, Tex., 1952–1976), 1:571; [Joseph Holt Ingraham], *The South-West. By a Yankee*, 2 vols. (n.p., 1966 [1835]), 2:190–191. For Dr. Mercer and St. Ann's Asylum for indigent women in New Orleans, see Pierce Butler, *The Unhurried Years: Memories of the Old Natchez Region* (Baton Rouge, La., 1948), 19. For Mobile, see Thomas McAdory Owens, *History of Alabama and Dictionary of Alabama Biography*, 4 vols. (Spartanburg, S.C., 1978 [1921]), 2:1005, 1209. For orphans in Richmond see [Joseph Francis Magri], *The Catholic Church in the City and Diocese of Richmond. By a Priest of the Diocese* (Richmond, Va., 1906), 77, 140–141. For Savannah, see Emily P. Burke, *Reminiscences of Georgia* (Oberlin, Oh., 1850), 36–37; George Gilman Smith, *The Story of Georgia and the Georgia People*, 2 vols. in 1 (Macon, Ga., 1900), 535; *Dictionary of Georgia Biography*, ed. Kenneth Coleman and Stephen Gurr, 2 vols. (Athens, Ga., 1983), 2:741 (Newton). For the orphan asylum in Columbus, see George White, *Statistics of the State of Georgia* (Savannah, Ga., 1849), 160, 444; Hodding Carter and Betty Werlein Carter, *So*

Notwithstanding widespread wariness of state intervention, ministers and reformers expected the state to support voluntary community efforts to build church-approved asylums, but they never formulated a coherent theory of the proper limits of state action. Charleston served as a model for the voluntary community efforts they had in mind. Indeed, Charlestonians took pride in their city's having led the way in the establishment of benevolent institutions, as the Scots, English, Irish, German, and French immigrants organized societies to care for their countrymen, as did the free coloreds in the Brown Fellowship Society. Visitors like J. S. Buckingham and prominent citizens like Jacob Cardozo and H. E. Ravenel sang their praises.[55]

Children, primarily orphans, attracted special attention. George Whitefield set a sterling example by building the Bethesda Orphanage in Georgia in 1740, which passed to the state a year later but as late as the 1850s depended heavily on the contributions of individuals like James Potter. In 1790 Charleston established America's first orphan asylum, which housed and educated between 2,000 and 3,000 children in the next seventy-six years. (New York's asylum came seventeen years later.) Jacob N. Cardozo wrote, "This noble charity is scarcely with a parallel anywhere. It had its commencement in the benefactions of all classes and denominations of our citizens. Among the contributors are Protestants of all sects, and Israelites." C. G. Memminger, who became the Confederacy's secretary of the treasury, ranked at the top of the gifted children to come out of the Charleston asylum, which Governor Thomas Bennett supported; and indeed, Bennett welcomed Memminger into his household and adopted him. He spent his early years there and came to the attention of powerful citizens who launched his career. James Stirling, a British traveler, struck a sour note. He thought the Orphan Hospital the most imposing building in Charleston – "physically unimpeachable, clean, airy, elegant" – but shook his head at the anomaly of so imposing a building amid the many wooden shanties of the immediate neighborhood. The pro-laissez-faire Stirling thought the project a case of self-defeating philanthropy and rebuked clergymen for inculcating "the Mohammedan virtue of indiscriminate almsgiving."[56]

Great a Good: A History of the Episcopal Church and of Christ Church Cathedral, 1805–1955 (Sewanee, Tenn., 1955), 95.

[55] Buckingham, *Slave States*, 1:51; J. N. Cardozo, *Reminiscences of Charleston* (Charleston, S.C., 1866), 62; Henry Edmund Ravenel, *Ravenel Records* (Atlanta, Ga., 1898), 56. These societies initially paid special attention to the care of children whose parents had died during the Atlantic crossing: George C. Rogers, Jr., *Charleston in the Age of the Pinckneys* (Columbia, S.C., 1962), 6.

[56] On the Bethesda Orphanage, see Henry Thompson Malone, *The Episcopal Church in Georgia, 1733–1957* (Atlanta, Ga., 1960), 37–38; on Whitefield's efforts for orphans, see Harry S. Stout, *The Divine Dramatist: George Whitefield and the Rise of Modern Evangelism* (Grand Rapids, Mich., 1991), 62–65, 84, 86, 99–100, 143–144; Mary Granger, ed., *Savannah River Plantations* (Spartanburg, S.C., 1983), 235; Cardozo, *Reminiscences of Charleston*, 19; Henry D. Capers, *The Life and Times of C. G. Memminger* (Richmond, Va., 1893), ch. 1; James Stirling, *Letters from the Slave States* (New York, 1968 [1857]), 252–254. The steam-heated Charleston Orphan House had 130 dormitory rooms.

Care of the mentally ill – like so much else – became a political pawn in the sectional war. Colonial Virginia, Maryland, South Carolina, and Kentucky established America's first asylums. In the 1820s South Carolina became the third state in the Union to establish a lunatic asylum; Georgia followed in 1844, North Carolina in 1856, and Alabama in 1860. But in 1849, *Southern Literary Messenger* stressed progress in the Northeast and pleaded with Virginians to provide for the "hundreds" of its insane men and women ("idiots"). Generally, families cared for the insane at home; county committees cared for the poor. In 1837 on the eve of the great financial crash, Georgia chartered a state asylum for "idiots, lunatics, and epileptics" but could not open it until the end of 1842. The charge was $100 per year, and family or friends had to supply clothing for the inmates; the state paid for paupers. By 1849, two hundred four patients had been admitted, of whom fifty-six had been discharged and fifty-three had died. North Carolina's asylum paid its director a modest annual salary of $1,200 in the 1850s. Success everywhere depended on the willingness of physicians to donate time to patients.[57]

The first U.S. Census of the insane projected the ratio of insane blacks to insane whites as eleven times higher in the free states than the slave. Calhoun and proslavery organs trumpeted the returns, which have not survived scrutiny. Still, at the end of the nineteenth century Judge Frank Alexander Montgomery of Mississippi repeated the common antebellum boast: "Insanity was as unknown among negroes before the war as homicides." In the 1850s a belief across the country and in scientific circles had insanity increasing in the crowded and crime-ridden cities of the Northeast. The insanity perceived for free blacks in the Northeast paralleled a perception of the Irish. Masters congratulated themselves on taking care of insane slaves. Meanwhile, South Carolina did not provide facilities for insane blacks until the abolition agitation pushed it into providing inferior facilities.[58]

---

[57] McCandless, *Moonlight, Magnolias, and Madness*, 3–8, 73; M. L. "The Education of Idiots," *SLM*, 15 (1849), 65–68; Matilda Freeman Dana, "Idiocy in Massachusetts," *SLM*, 15 (1849), 367–370; *Dictionary of Georgia Biography*, ed. Kenneth Coleman and Stephen Gurr, 2 vols. (Athens, Ga., 1983), 1:365; Pope, *Newberry District*, 1:164–165; also Smedes, *Memorials*, 30; George Gillman Smith, *The Story of Georgia and the Georgia People*, 2 vols. (Macon, Ga., 1900), 258–259; George White, *Statistics of the State of Georgia* (Savannah, Ga., 1849), 82–84; *DNCB*, 2:202; Thomas McAdory Owens, *History of Alabama and Dictionary of Alabama Biography*, 4 vols. (Spartanburg, S.C., 1978 [1921]), 2:778; Malcolm C. McMillan, *The Disintegration of a Confederate State: Three Governors and Alabama's Wartime Home Front, 1861–1865* (Macon, Ga., 1986), 10.

[58] C. B. Hayden, "On the Distribution of Insanity in the United States," *SLM*, 10 (1844), 178–181; Frank Alexander Montgomery, *Reminiscences of a Mississippian in War and Peace* (Electronic ed.; Chapel Hill, N.C., 1999 [1901]), 21. For scholarly critiques of the statistics, see Albert Deutsch, "The First U.S. Census of the Insane (1840) and Its Use as Pro-Slavery Propaganda," *Bulletin of the History of Medicine*, 15 (1944), 469–482. For a critique of statistics on black insanity, see also Norman Dain, *Concepts of Insanity in the United States, 1789–1865* (New Brunswick, N.J., 1964), 89–91, 104–108, 239, n. 91. For the effects of abolitionist attacks, see Ellen Mordecai, *Gleanings from Long Ago* (Raleigh, N.C., 1974), 37; McCandless, *Moonlight,*

John Jacobus Flournoy of Jackson, Georgia, a deaf-mute from a wealthy planter family, acquired a literary reputation and campaigned successfully for a state institution for education of the deaf. The Baptist Reverend Jesse Harrison Campbell served as state commissioner in the 1840s and convinced the legislature to establish a school for mutes to complement the school for the deaf at Cave Springs. North Carolina established separate schools for deaf whites and blacks in the mid-1840s. In 1848, state Senator A. C. McIntosh visited the asylum, praising it to relatives as splendid. In Mississippi, John Jones McRae made two splashes during his governorship in the 1850s: advocacy of the reopening of the African slave trade and establishment of an institution for the deaf and dumb. Mississippi's poorly financed state institution struggled to stay afloat. Texas opened a school for the deaf in 1857.[59]

The efforts of the churches and of countless caring individuals constitute a record of noble intentions and even impressive results but also a record of countless souls left unattended by a weak, hit-or-miss institutional structure. County governments confronted the limits of reliance on the private sector. A county government sometimes corrected the indifference of the individuals upon whom it preferred to rely. Thus Bibb County, Alabama, had trouble with people who were unwilling to care for aged parents and had to be compelled at law. The often splendid work of benevolent societies and well-to-do individuals accomplished just enough to convince communities that government action was unnecessary. The South paid the price in the crucible of the War. In 1861, individuals, churches, and community groups proved inadequate to care for the swelling number of dispossessed.[60]

Prostitution

Prostitution offered an illustration of the beneficial effects of slavery in contradistinction to the destructive effects of the free-labor system. Southerners

---

Magnolias, and Madness, 1–44, 151–160. John Minson Galt, II, the head of Virginia's prestigious Eastern State Hospital, admitted slaves since he, like other Southerners, thought there were too few in Virginia to justify a separate institution: Norman Dain, *Disordered Minds: The First Century of Eastern State Hospital in Williamsburg, Virginia, 1766–1866* (Williamsburg, Va., 1971), 109–110.

[59] *Dictionary of Georgia Biography*, ed. Coleman and Gurr, 1:158–1560; George Gillman Smith, *The Story of Georgia and the Georgia People*, 2 vols. (Macon, Ga., 1900), 223; *DNCB*, 4:193, 203; George White, *Statistics of the State of Georgia* (Savannah, Ga., 1849), 85; McIntosh, undated letter, 1848; Charles L. Coon, ed., *The Beginnings of Public Education in North Carolina: A Documentary History, 1790–1840*, 2 vols. (Raleigh, N.C., 1908), 1:379–382; Rowland, ed., *Mississippi*, 1:637–638; Walter Prescott Webb, ed., *The Handbook of Texas*, 3 vols. (Austin, Tex., 1952–1976), 2:759.

[60] Ellison, *Bibb County, Alabama*, 31. By the late Middle Ages the Scholastics recognized that unemployment was reaching proportions that private charity could not accommodate and that public efforts were needed: Joseph A. Schumpeter, *History of Economic Analysis*, ed. Elizabeth Boody Schumpeter (New York, 1954), 272, and, in general, Michel Mollat, *The Poor in the Middle Ages: An Essay in Social History*, tr. Arthur Goldhammer (New Haven, Conn., 1986), 192–193.

acknowledged the sexual frailties of both men and women and tolerated prostitution much more than they let on. But they did not tolerate the commonplace shenanigans in New York. Richmond, Charleston, Natchez, and New Orleans did not bristle with strip-joints and a pornographic penny press, and they did not take lightly abortion and homosexuality. Steven Pearl Andrews, preaching free love in the North, praised the South for promoting sexual freedom by refusing to recognize slave marriages. The crudest and most cynical of Southerners dared not speak that way.[61]

The subject of homosexuality in the South was taboo, and little may be said responsibly with the evidence now available. Educated Southerners knew that homosexuality flourished in ancient slave societies. In Sparta, homosexual relations between mature men and young boys, as well as between boys, constituted the basis for the lifelong bonds of affection that united the warrior class. The Romans took a stricter view of homosexuality than the Greeks. Yet Pierre Grimal writes, "This strictness was not applied indiscriminately to all homosexual affairs. Even in the very early times it would have occurred to no one to be shocked if a master conceived a passion for one of his male slaves." Homosexuality may have reached noticeable proportions in the army but was punished. Still, Southerners learned from Suetonius about Caesar's "evil reputation for both sodomy and adultery" and of Curio's calling Caesar "every woman's man and every man's woman."[62]

For the South we have only hints. In Arkansas, George Featherstonhaugh remarked with evident disgust upon the relation of a sinister-looking New Yorker to a Mr. Tunstall to whom he "seemed altogether devoted" and "in whose service perhaps he had consciously reached the lowest stage of human degradation." Georgia Baker remembered fondly Lordworth Stephens, a cousin of her master, Alexander H. Stephens: "Marsa Lordworth was a good man, but he didn't have no use for womans – he was a sissy." Male prostitutes were reported to be arriving in Richmond during the War, but who knows if they were Southerners or if the reports were accurate? Hints of scandals appeared in the Confederate Army, as when troops ran one of their comrades out of camp for "going to sleep with Captain Lowery's black man."[63]

Prostitution and pornography thrived in New York City in the 1820s; by the mid-1840s official estimates accounted for 10,000 prostitutes. An estimated

---

[61] S. P. Andrews to George Fitzhugh, Jan. 21, 1855, copy in G. F. Holmes Letterbook.

[62] Paul A. Rahe, *Republics, Ancient and Modern: Classical Republicanism and the American Revolution* (Chapel Hill, N.C., 1992), 133; Pierre Grimal, *Love in Ancient Rome*, tr. Arthur Train, Jr. (Norman, Okla., 1980), 103–104; Suetonius, *Lives of the Twelve Caesars*, tr. Joseph Cavore (New York, 1931), 31.

[63] George W. Featherstonhaugh, *Excursion through the Slave States* (New York, 1968 [1844]), 116; Georgia Baker in Ronald Killion and Charles Waller, eds., *Slavery Time When I was Chillun Down on Marster's Plantation* (Savannah, 1973), 9; Bell Irwin Riley, *The Common Soldier of the Confederacy* (Baton Rouge, La., 1978), 54; Confederate artilleryman quoted in Ervin L. Jordan, Jr., *Black Confederates and Afro-Yankees in Civil War Virginia* (Charlottesville, Va., 1995), 134. Thomas P. Lowry demonstrates that the evidence does not sustain recent exaggerations of homosexuality in the Union and Confederate armies or on the home front: see *The Story the Soldiers Wouldn't Tell* (Mechanicsburg, Pa., 1994), ch. 11.

200 brothels in the 1820s swelled to more than 600 by 1865. Nudity and illicit sexual relations disgraced the notorious Five Points and other neighborhoods. Between five and ten percent of New York's young women aged fifteen to thirty – some as young as ten – prostituted themselves at one time or another, often driven by severe economic pressure during recessions and depressions. The Irish bore the brunt of the criticism, but half the prostitutes were American farm girls. Prominent men like Isaac Singer of sewing machine fame and Daniel Sickles of political and later military notoriety flaunted their status as Johns. Some madams became celebrities.[64]

Southern revulsion revealed a dread that underlay discussions of white women's cohabitation with black men. Seventeenth-century Virginians, explaining their easy adoption of the principle of maternal descent for slaves, claimed – dubiously – that they had little fear of white women's voluntarily entering into sexual relations with black men. From then on, the story had such white women drawn solely from among poor whites. Poor white women who had babies by black men often endured childbirth alone and risked imprisonment. Yet, having no social standing to begin with, they likely received a modicum of kindness from communities that turned harshly on respectable women, who were supposed to know better. The poor-white story ran aground during the eighteenth and nineteenth centuries when at least a few free blacks had white wives across the South. In Virginia, scattered evidence suggests that more white women in all classes had mulatto babies than anyone wanted to talk about. William Ashworth, a rancher and the richest man of color in Texas, and several of his brothers had white wives. In South Carolina, which permitted interracial marriage, free coloreds married whites. Occasionally, a slaveholding white woman became a free black's lover and bore his children. George Patterson, an ex-slave, claimed that his grandmother was an Irish worker whom his master arranged to have "marry" his father. Richard Cobden, the English liberal, reported from Baltimore on gossip about white ladies with mulatto children. Blacks asserted that elite white women had illicit affairs with black men, some with issue. But when a white woman stood exposed for intercourse with a slave, she would be sorely tempted to charge rape.[65]

[64] See Timothy Gilfoyle, *City of Eros: New York City, Prostitution, and the Commercialization of Sex, 1790–1820* (New York, 1992), chs. 3, 5. Disgusted Southerners concluded, as Gilfoyle does: "Whenever a civilization relies upon the market to determine its major priorities, the social by-products are never 'free' or without cost" (20).

[65] James C. Ballagh, *A History of Slavery in Virginia* (Baltimore, Md., 1802), 43; Maria Bryan to Julia Ann Bryan Cumming, Nov. 13, 1830, in Carol Bleser, ed., *Tokens of Affection: The Letters of a Planter's Daughter in the Old South* (Athens, Ga., 1996), 125–127; for poor white women who fraternized with blacks, see also Charles C. Bolton, *Poor Whites of the Antebellum South: Tenants and Laborers in Central North Carolina and Northeast Mississippi* (Durham, N.C., 1994), ch. 3; James Hugo Johnston, *Race Relations in Virginia and Miscegenation in the South, 1776–1860* (Amherst, Mass., 1970), 254–255, 264–265; for Ashworth, see Loren Schweninger, *Black Property Owners in the South, 1790–1915* (Urbana, Ill., 1990), 135; Marina Wikramanayake, *A World in Shadow: The Free Black in Antebellum South Carolina* (Columbia, S.C., 1973), 76–77; for Patterson, see Rawick, ed., *American Slave: AS: S. C.,* 3 (pt. 3), 226;

Not remotely had John Rutledge of South Carolina ever seen as great a number of prostitutes in Charleston as in New York City in 1765. In the 1830s, Simms noted a report of the commissioners of the Magdalene Asylum in New York: There were 10,000 professional white prostitutes in New York City. The South, he stated, had prostitutes – black women and transplanted Northerners, who accounted for the dreadful evil. Chancellor William Harper, citing English sources, deplored the heartlessness of a free-labor system that forced working-class women to sell themselves. Southerners faced accusations of holding slave women as prostitutes, but "compare these prostitutes (if it is not an injustice to call them so) and their condition with those of other countries – the seventy thousand prostitutes of London, or of Paris, or the ten thousand of New York, or our other Northern cities."[66]

Rutledge, Simms, and Harper lived in South Carolina and surely knew that state authorities acknowledged serious problems with prostitution. Typically, eighteenth-century county courts regulated inns but closed them only in blatant cases of prostitution. Charles Woodmason, who strove to bring religion to the back country in the 1760s, discovered prostitutes everywhere and denounced corrupt officials for tolerating "lewd houses." Since Rutledge doubtless saw the many prostitutes who walked the streets of Charleston, he must have found New York very bad indeed. Prostitutes did good business with sailors in every seaport, including Charleston. In Virginia, George Mason drafted legislation in 1779 to curb the burgeoning "tippling houses" that were "encouraging Idleness, Drunkenness, and all manner of Vice and immorality." In Richmond and elsewhere during the following century, the racetrack drew more people than the theater and was no less open to the charge of providing a magnet for prostitutes.[67]

Criticism of New York and other northern cities carried into the 1850s, as Southerners replied to mounting abolitionist charges that – as the abolitionist

---

Cobden Diary, June 12, 1835, in *The American Diaries of Richard Cobden*, ed. Elizabeth Hoon Cawley (Princeton, N.J., 1952), 94; Rastus Nall, *Freeborn Slave: Diary of a Black Man in the South* (Birmingham, Ala., 1996), 1–2; Georgia Baker, in Killion and Waller, eds., *Slavery Time*, 11.

[66] Richard Barry, *Mr. Rutledge of South Carolina* (New York, 1942), 104. In *Pro-Slavery Argument, as Maintained by the Most Distinguished Writers of the Southern States*, see "Harper on Slavery," 40–45, and Sims, "The Morals of Slavery," 229–230; 104. In 1820, Paris had 163 licensed brothels and 2,653 licensed and more than 15,000 unlicensed prostitutes: Paul Johnson, *Birth of the Modern, 1815–1830* (London, 1992), 152.

[67] M. Eugene Sirmans, *Colonial South Carolina: A Political History* (Chapel Hill, N.C., 1966), 77; Paul M. McCain, *The County Court in North Carolina before 1750* (Durham, N.C., 1954), 140–141; *The Carolina Backcountry on the Eve of the Revolution: The Journal and Other Writings of Charles Woodmason, Anglican Itinerant*, ed. Richard J. Hooker (Chapel Hill, N.C., 1953), 24, 29, 129; "A Bill to Amend the Act Regulating Ordinaries and Tippling-Houses, Oct. 19, 1779," in Robert A. Rutland, ed., *The Papers of George Mason*, 3 vols. (Chapel Hill, N.C., 1970), 2:541; Harry M. Ward and Harold E. Greer, Jr., *Richmond during the Revolution, 1775–83* (Charlottesville, Va., 1977), 52, 114. J. W. Megginson barely mentions prostitution during the twentieth century and is silent on antebellum times: *African American Life in South Carolina's Upper Piedmont* (Columbia, S.C., 2006).

James Redpath put it – most married slaveholders had slave mistresses, and "every slave negress is a courtesan." Thomas Cobb of Georgia replied that naturally lewd black women found in bed with white men had doubtless invited them. Their ready availability took pressure off white women: "The poor white females of the slaveholding States are not subject to as great temptations and importunities as they would be under other circumstances." Southerners did not exaggerate the extent of prostitution in New York and other northern cities. Their charge that economic depressions turned thousands of northern working-class girls and young women into streetwalkers qualified as ideologically and politically self-serving, but for many it also qualified as a cri de coeur.[68]

A shortage of respectable women and the presence of seamen made the seaports and river ports centers of prostitution. The radical and antislavery German press in St. Louis protested the extent of prostitution there, insisting that "prostitution and mob have long been correlative concepts." Charleston proved no exception. Many of the women who serviced sailors wound up in the poorhouse with syphilis. During the 1850s Grace Peixotto operated a three-story brothel that featured prostitutes of every hue, patronized by gentlemen from prominent families. John Berkeley Grimball, among other low-country planters, took measures to restrain his slaves from patronizing brothels operated by white women. In Charleston, Winston, North Carolina, and other towns black prostitutes did a thriving business, servicing both white and black men. The mayor of Savannah acknowledged a ratio of one prostitute for every thirty-nine men in 1859 – rather an embarrassment since the ratio in New York was one to fifty-seven. He took some solace from knowledge that the principal clients were the sailors who filled the boardinghouses. In Savannah's brothels, black and white prostitutes serviced black and white clients. Most of the white prostitutes were Northerners or immigrants.[69]

---

[68] James Redpath, *The Roving Editor: Or, Talks with Slaves in the Southern States* (New York, 1859), 257, also 184, 228, 234, 258, 263; T. R. R. Cobb, *Law of Negro Slavery*, ccxix–ccxx, 40, 100, quote at ccxx. See also Lawrence M. Keitt, *Slavery and the Resources of the South* (Washington, D.C., 1857), 4; George Fitzhugh, *Sociology for the South, or, The Failure of Free Society* (New York, 1965 [1854]), 113 and ch. 20. For domestic service and prostitution, see Faye E. Dudden, *Serving Women: Household Service in Nineteenth-Century America* (Middletown, Conn., 1983), especially 94–96.

[69] *Anzeiger des Westens*, July 26, 1860, in Steven Rowan and James Neal Primm, eds., *Germans for a Free Missouri: Translations from the St. Louis Radical Press, 1857–1862* (Columbia, Mo., 1983), 121–122; Herbert Asbury, *Sucker's Progress: An Informal History of Gambling in America from the Colonies to Canfield* (New York, 1939), 128–129; Fraser, *Charleston! Charleston!*, 22, 104, 212, 235; Marina Wikramanayake, *A World in Shadow: The Free Black in Antebellum South Carolina* (Columbia, S.C., 1973), 104; W. H. Valentine Diary, July 23, 1853; Edward L. Ayers, *Vengeance and Justice: Crime and Punishment in the Nineteenth-Century South* (New York, 1984), 80; also, William B. Hayden, *The Institution of Slavery Viewed in the Light of Divine Truth* (Portland, Me., 1861), 39; Walter Fraser, Jr., *Savannah in the Old South* (Athens, Ga., 2003), 164, 288–289; Timothy James Lockley, *Lines in the Sand: Race and Class in Lowcountry Georgia, 1750–1860* (Athens, Ga., 2001), 54–56. Prostitutes regularly worked the boats on the Mississippi, usually in the company of professional gamblers: Allen, *Western Rivermen*, 126–130, 196; Fredrika Bremer, *Homes of the New World: Impressions of America,*

Grand juries in Charleston and Columbia called prostitution "an increasing influence" and carefully identified prostitutes by name so as to shame them. The prostitutes did not mind, treating public listing as advertisements. In the 1830s the seventeen-year-old J. D. B. De Bow raged about the noisy and vulgar prostitute-ridden streets of Charleston. In 1835, Captain M. C. Shaffer of the Town Guard denounced as exaggeration the widespread criticism of Columbia; it had, he said, no more than its share of the brothels that infested every town. In Mississippi, Natchez-Under-the-Hill got an early start under the Spanish during the eighteenth century when it became known as the Sodom and Gomorrah of the lower Mississippi Valley. Polished courtesans and street-walkers operated openly. The self-styled Madam Aivoges carried herself like a lady, operating a house considered the most elegant ever to grace Under-the-Hill – well appointed with fine rugs, satin brocade curtains, and a spinet imported from Lisbon. Her lovely and well-mannered blonde working girls were often taken as daughters of Nabobs. His Excellency, the Spanish governor, availed himself of their pleasures, and a ferocious bouncer made sure that clients behaved like gentlemen. After the Americans took control in the nineteenth century, brothels sprang up in abundance, especially to service men on the move from Kentucky and northward. In Vicksburg, notwithstanding its famous purge of social undesirables during the 1830s, prostitution remained a public nuisance and ran wild during the War. Belle Forrest's bordello stood out but had rivals. A tavern-qua-bawdy-house enlivened Memphis in 1830; by 1850 it had many competitors. In Nashville the waterfront had a section called "The Jungle," which housed brothels, saloons, and assorted hideouts for criminals. It became impossible for a gentleman to walk the area without being accosted by prostitutes, although less fastidious gentlemen became patrons. In Louisville in 1839, William Reynolds, a northern merchant, expressed astonishment at the loose morals: "Couretzans allmost flock the Streets."[70]

2 vols. (New York, 1853), 2:477. For prostitution in wartime Memphis and Nashville, see Lowry, *Story the Soldiers Wouldn't Tell*, ch. 7.

[70] Thanet Aphornsuvan, "James D. B. De Bow and the Political Economy of the Old South" (Ph.D. diss., State University of New York at Binghamton, 1991), 54; Jack Kenny Williams, *Vogues in Villainy: Crime and Retribution in Ante-Bellum South Carolina* (Columbia, S.C., 1959), 57–58; Moore, *Natchez Under-the-Hill*, 9, 44–45, 105–106; [Joseph Holt Ingraham], *The South-West. By a Yankee*, 2 vols. (Ann Arbor, Mich., 1966 [1835]), 2:59; William C. Davis, *A Way through the Wilderness: The Natchez Trace and the Civilization of the Southern Frontier* (New York, 1995), 247; James T. Currie, *Enclave: Vicksburg and Her Plantations, 1863–1870* (Jackson, Miss., 1980), 21, 28–29; John Hebron Moore, *The Emergence of the Cotton Kingdom in Old Southwest: Mississippi, 1770–1860* (Baton Rouge, La., 1988), 255; Gerald M. Capers, Jr., *The Biography of a River Town. Memphis: Its Heroic Age* (Chapel Hill, N.C., 1939), 62, 133; William Kingsford, *Impressions of the West and South* (Toronto, Ont., 1858), 46. For hints of promiscuous young women and of prostitution in a Mississippi village, see Walker Diary, Aug. 2, 25, 1850, in Lynette Boney Wrenn, ed., *A Bachelor's Life in Antebellum Mississippi: The Diary of Dr. Elijah Millington Walker, 1849–1852* (Knoxville, Tenn., 2004), 71, 77.

Respectable women, especially widows, operated a good many taverns in a society that considered few occupations for women respectable. They had to be careful to avoid suspicion

New Orleans, with its theaters and public balls, became a powerful magnet for prostitutes from New York and other northern cities, and the authorities, despite occasional bouts of reformist zeal, remained unable to curb a mushrooming industry. Despite howls from the clergy, the "Girod Street Swamp" featured a dozen blocks of brothels, bars, and gambling houses, and the short Gallatin Street had a concentration of brothels. During the 1840s and 1850s, unemployment propelled significant numbers of young women into prostitution. Public ballrooms notoriously promoted prostitution under the protection of politicians and the police. Landlords and housing speculators made big money by renting property to brothel keepers, and small businessmen had a vested interest in selling goods to brothels and prostitutes. The medical community's warnings against the ravages of venereal disease evoked little response.[71]

State capitals, like ports, attracted prostitutes. Richmond had extensive problems with brothels during the Revolutionary era, even before it became Virginia's capital. Between the Revolution and the War for Southern Independence red-light districts were kept under control – if barely. In the 1850s interracial prostitution reached noticeable proportions despite tenacious attempts to suppress it. In Georgia, Milledgeville's town marshal counted only fifteen prostitutes, all white, in his census of 1828, but they constituted about ten percent of the white women between the ages of fifteen and forty. Principally, they accommodated the legislators who assembled every year to regulate community morals. As in other southern towns, both the authorities and the proprietors tried to keep brothels out of sight. Milledgeville's district existed only two blocks from the governor's mansion but in a mosquito-ridden swamp. Usually, the authorities cracked down only when neighbors complained, so it made sense to locate in an isolated spot. Interior cities had their own troubles, especially in earlier days. Poor Mrs. Erwin had Susan Nye Hutchinson's sympathy when the man she had recently married had his throat cut in a brothel. Even after crusaders started to clean up the rough frontier town of Atlanta in the 1850s, the authorities had trouble closing brothels in lower-class districts or in getting "painted women" off the streets. Still, in contrast to state capitals and ports,

of running brothels. For women's inns as brothels, see John Randolph to Dr. Brokenbrough, May 30, 1828, in K. Shorey, ed., *Collected Letters of John Randolph of Roanoke to Dr. John Brockenbrough, 1812–1833* (New Brunswick, N.J., 1988), 106; *DNCB*, 2:49; Charles C. Bolton, *Poor Whites of the Antebellum South: Tenants and Laborers in Central North Carolina and Northeast Mississippi* (Durham, N.C., 1994), 63.

[71] Henry A. Kmen, *Music in New Orleans: The Formative Years, 1791–1841* (Baton Rouge, La., 1966), 31–32, 196; Thomas Ewing Dabney, *One Hundred Great Years: The Story of the Times-Picayune from Its Founding to 1940* (Baton Rouge, La., 1940), 11; Richard Tansey, "Prostitution and Politics in Antebellum New Orleans," *Southern Studies*, 18 (1979), 449–479. Despite a bad reputation, eighteenth-century New Orleans was not especially vice-ridden by contemporary standards. How vice-ridden it became by the 1850s remains debatable: see Christina Vella, *Intimate Enemies: The Two Worlds of the Baroness de Pontalba* (Baton Rouge, La., 1997), 29 and ch. 9.

Atlanta identified only forty-nine prostitutes in 1860 in a total population of 7,741.[72]

Promoters sought to situate colleges away from towns or to insulate those in or near towns. But boys will be boys. Occasional crackdowns helped but did not suffice. South Carolina College and the University of Virginia disciplined students for patronizing brothels run by local blacks and for having prostitutes in their dormitories. In the late 1820s a free black from Philadelphia joined with a white woman to run a brothel frequented by students in Charlottesville. In 1850, President Basil Manly of the University of Alabama suspected that Morgan, a college servant, was pimping Professor Frederick A. P. Barnard's slaves to students. Denominational colleges, too, had problems. Mr. Crowder, the printer, had to leave town after he got caught with one of the prostitutes near the Associate Presbyterians' Erskine College in Due West, South Carolina. Apparently, she suffered nothing worse than expulsion from the premises by an irate Mrs. Hawthorne, who owned the boardinghouse at which Crowder and some students stayed. The prostitute enjoyed the scene, shouting that she "had burned some fellow's ass."[73]

From the eighteenth century, free and slave women worked as prostitutes, and most appear to have been white. In one town after another the authorities harassed black prostitutes a good deal more than they harassed white. When American troops occupied Florida in 1818, they stumbled upon brothels in Fernandina that provided prostitutes of both colors to young bachelors, cheating husbands, and visiting sailors. Tallahassee, a city about forty percent black, had four brothels all worked by illiterate poor white women, one of whom was gamely putting two of her four children through school. In scattered cases, masters pimped their slaves, especially in towns in which slaves could hire their own

---

[72] Joshua D. Rothman, *Notorious in the Neighborhood: Sex and Families across the Color Line in Virginia, 1787–1861* (Chapel Hill, N.C., 2003), ch. 3; also Harry M. Ward and Harold E. Greer, Jr., *Richmond during the Revolution, 1775–83* (Charlottesville, Va., 1977), 52, 109, 122; Gregg D. Kimball, *American City, Southern Place: A Cultural History of Antebellum Richmond* (Athens, Ga., 2003) 48, 250; Virginius Dabney, *Richmond: Story of a City* (Garden City, N.Y., 1976), 163, 182–183. James C. Bonner, *Milledgeville: Georgia's Antebellum Capital* (Athens, Ga., 1978), 71, 94; Hutchinson Diary, Sept. 30, 1840; Harold W. Mann, *Atticus Haygood: Methodist Bishop, Editor, and Educator* (Athens, Ga., 1965), 9; Garrett, *Atlanta and Environs,* 2:265, 488, 491; James Michael Russell, *Atlanta, 1847–1890: City Building in the Old South and the New* (Baton Rouge, La., 1988), 73–74.

[73] Hynds, *Antebellum Athens,* 10, 49–50; faculty meeting reports for South Carolina College in Edward W. Knight, ed., *Documentary History of Education in the South before 1860,* 5 vols. (Chapel Hill, N.C., 1949–1953), 3:91, 95; Charles Coleman Wall, Jr., "Students and Student Life at the University of Virginia, 1825–1861" (Ph.D. diss., University of Virginia, 1978), 277–278; Phillip Alexander Bruce, *History of the University of Virginia, 1819–1919: The Lengthening Shadow of One Man,* 5 vols. (New York, 1920–1922), 2:273–274; James B. Sellers, *History of the University of Alabama,* 2 vols. (University, Ala., 1953), 1:236; Agnew Diary, April 28, 1851 (Crowder). For college students' patronizing of prostitutes and venereal disease on southern campuses, see Robert F. Pace, *Halls of Honor: College Men in the Old South* (Baton Rouge, La., 2004), 78–79.

time. During the 1850s, newspapers in New Orleans and Baton Rouge complained of white men who lived with black women they pimped for $8 to $10 an
encounter. Especially galling were the capital gains from ensuing pregnancies.[74]

North Carolina took a surprisingly benign view of prostitutes. A student
at the University of North Carolina was acquitted of murder when a jury
accepted his plea of self-defense. His principal supporting witness was a well-
known prostitute whose reputation for veracity was sworn to by prominent
citizens, including a justice of the peace. In Rutherford, when a Dr. Scheifflin
was recovering from an unsuccessful suicide attempt, many sympathetic people
came to cheer him up, including Caty Dean, the town prostitute, whom he
joshed about seeing in hell. A decade later a seamstress in Raleigh gained fame
as a veritable "belle-of-the-ball" prostitute. Ministers opened their churches to
local prostitutes. The sermons of the young John Girardeau of South Carolina –
on his way to becoming a formidable theologian – attracted a number of
prostitutes in Columbia in the mid-1840s.[75]

Prominent southern gentlemen invested in brothels. John McDonogh of New
Orleans – an eccentric, unmarried multimillionaire – left much of his estate for
the education of black as well as white children. Reputedly, he made good
money with saloons and brothels on Girod Street. More curious was the scene
in Milledgeville where Farish Carter – big planter, businessman, and philanthropist – bankrolled the establishment of Phoebe Brown, the most notable of
local madams. Her liquor license cost only $10 but required a $300 bond as
security against disorderly conduct. Carter paid it, thereby guaranteeing her an
enormous advantage over her dry competitors. We cannot ascertain whether
he extended an interest-bearing loan or had a disreputable motive or exercised a raised gender consciousness by encouraging female entrepreneurship.
While Phoebe Brown prospered, Carter manifested his philanthropic interest
in young women by sponsoring the education of the more pious residents of

---

74 Ward and Greer, *Richmond During the Revolution*, 122; Bonner, *Milledgeville*, 71, 94, 346;
   Groene, *Ante-Bellum Tallahassee*, 109; Rembert W. Patrick, *Aristocrat in Uniform: General
   Duncan L. Clinch* (Gainesville, Fla., 1963), 42; Rembert W. Patrick, *Florida Fiasco: Rampant
   Rebels on the Georgia-Florida Border, 1810–1815* (Athens, Ga., 1954), 46–48; Richard C.
   Wade, *Slavery in the Cities: The South, 1820–1860* (New York, 1967), 23–25, 28, 122, 260;
   Robert Reinders, "Slavery in New Orleans in the Decade before the Civil War," *Mid-America*
   44 (1962), 211–221; William L. Richter, "Slavery in Baton Rouge, 1820–1860," *Louisiana
   History* (1969), 10 (1969), 125–145. The practice of pimping one's slaves had a long history
   in Europe; see, e.g., Pierre Bonnassie, *From Slavery to Feudalism in South-Western Europe*, tr.
   Jean Birrell (Cambridge, U.K., 1991), 78.
75 Kemp P. Battle, *University of North Carolina*, 2 vols. (Spartanburg, S.C., 1974 [1907]), 1:690;
   James Graham to W. A. Graham, June 18, 1832, in J. G. DeRoulhac Hamilton, ed., *The Papers
   of William Alexander Graham*, 5 vols. (Raleigh, N.C., 1957–1973), 1:239 (Scheifflin); William
   Hooper Haigh Diary and Letters, Aug. 10, 1844; George A. Blackburn, ed., *The Life Work of
   John L. Girardeau* (Columbia, S.C., 1916), 25. Sherman's troops found a half dozen brothels
   on a half block of Gervais Street: Charles Royster, *The Destructive War: William Tecumseh
   Sherman, Stonewall Jackson, and the Americans* (New York, 1991), 19.

Milledgeville. In Mobile, Dr. Josiah Nott, the South's leading scientific racist, did not invest in brothels but did find them socially useful. He used prostitutes as well as slaves as guinea pigs for his experimental cures for yellow fever and women's diseases. Four madams in Mobile prospered with "female lodging houses," stocked largely with Northern and foreign prostitutes.[76]

William D. Valentine – a lawyer and planter's son who lived in a boarding-house in Bethel, North Carolina – left an account of his adventure-of-sorts in a bawdy house in 1837. Out on an evening stroll, he passed a house of ill repute. He heard a friend's voice. To gratify his curiosity he decided to investigate, since information "was sometimes gained in the very sinks of iniquity." He trusted "conscience and my honor" to save him from temptation by "so indecent a company." Valentine, describing himself as "a man of the world in pursuit of Knowledge," recoiled: "men, women and cards and shocking obscenity." Several of his "respectable acquaintances" greeted him cordially. "Modesty and morals were here put to the blush. Low Life, wretched indeed." Valentine was not prepared for the pièce de résistance: "The head of this seraglio was in every way a beautiful girl to look at. Although regrettably devoid of virtue, she had an impressively 'strong mind.'" Curiosity satisfied by the "detestable, revolting odium," Valentine left with his chastity intact, but returned briefly to recover a book he had left behind. Valentine had doubtless read the Satyricon, for his pompous account recalls Petronius's uproarious account of two gentlemen who ran into each other in a bisexual brothel and fumbled to explain themselves to each other and to themselves.[77]

Prostitution in the countryside did not reach proportions that the authorities deemed serious. An exception: prostitution thrived in the gambling houses and saloons open day and night in the gold mining regions of Georgia, in which blacks, free and slave, contributed significantly to the labor force. And native Southerners and foreign travelers alike were disgusted at conditions in parts of North Carolina in the 1850s, where in the words of future senator Augustus S. Merrimon, drunken women and "dirty, filthy strumpets" marked the "brutal debauchery" of the area. Planters reluctantly hired poor white girls to help their wives with sewing or quilting, worrying if they were prostitutes. A Virginian told Olmsted what others did not care to discuss with strangers – that the poor, miserable creatures sold themselves to blacks and were responsible for many of the mulatto children about. Chaste poor white girls, therefore, refused to work as servants for planters, no matter how straitened, since those who did were taken for prostitutes. In New Orleans and Mobile, Irish and German

[76] Robert Douthat Meade, *Judah P. Benjamin: Confederate Statesman* (New York, 1943), 68–69; Bonner, *Milledgeville*, 94–95; Reginald Horsman, *Josiah Nott: Southerner, Physician, and Racial Theorist* (Baton Rouge, La., 1987), 158; Harriet Elizabeth Amos, "Social Life in an Antebellum Cotton Port: Mobile, Alabama, 1820–1860" (Ph.D. diss., University of Alabama, 1976), 150, 260.

[77] Valentine Diaries, March 26, 1837; Petronius, *The Satyricon*, tr. P. G. Walsh (Oxford, U.K., 1996), 5–6.

women supplemented or even replaced blacks as favored domestics, but their reputation for sexual looseness proved difficult to overcome.[78]

There were occasional horror stories. In Louisa County, Virginia, Richard Sandridge, with the cooperation of his slave Sydnor, killed a slave woman who refused to sleep with him, much less with his friends. Occasionally, outraged masters learned that their drivers were sending women slaves to service white neighbors – often but by no means always poor men. John Cocke uncovered a ring on his Alabama plantation: George, his excellent driver, rented out his own two daughters to local gentlemen. Cocke sold the daughters, describing them as "incorrigible strumpets." John Walker, a devout Methodist planter in Virginia, found, to his dismay, that his driver had been pimping young slave women to Benjamin Pollard, a powerful local politician. To make matters worse, a few, including a wet nurse, contracted venereal disease, and several deaths resulted.[79]

Northern abolitionists dwelt on the market in "fancy girls," no doubt in large part because they were so light-skinned as to seem white – beautiful octoroons and quadroons. Solomon Northup, who had been a slave in Louisiana in the 1840s, described Maria as "a rather genteel looking colored girl, with a faultless form, but ignorant and extremely vain." Maria "entertained an extravagantly high opinion of her own attractions." She liked the idea of going to New Orleans. "Assuming a haughty mien, she declared to her companions, that immediately on our arrival in New Orleans, she had no doubt, some wealthy single gentleman of good taste would purchase her at once!" Mary Reynolds, who had been a slave on a cotton plantation, recalled, "Once Massa goes to Baton Rouge and brung back a yaller gal dressed in fine style. She was a seamster nigger. He builds her a house 'way from the quarters, and she done fine sewing for the whites." Reynolds described her master as promiscuous with both white and black women and the father of illegitimate children. "This yaller

---

[78] David Williams, "Georgia's Forgotten Miners: African-Americans and the Georgia Gold Rush," *Georgia Historical Quarterly*, 75 (1991), 79; Merrimon quoted in John C. Inscoe, *Mountain Masters, Slavery, and the Sectional Crisis in Western North Carolina* (Knoxville, Tenn., 1989), 35, which also cites Featherstonhaugh; for the area near Raleigh, see Hutchinson Journal, July 22, 1815; Olmsted, *Seaboard Slave States*, 83–84, 507–509; Olmsted, *Back Country*, 276; Abbott, *South and North*, 210. Also Rawick, ed., *American Slave: Ark.*, 9 (Pt. 4), 56.

[79] Philip J. Schwarz, *Twice Condemned: Slaves and the Criminal Law of Virginia, 1705–1865* (Baton Rouge, La., 1988), 245; Reinders, "Slavery in New Orleans," 219; Judith K. Schafer, *Slavery, the Civil Law, and the Supreme Court of Louisiana* (Baton Rouge, La., 1994), 238–239; Timothy F. Reilly, "Robert L. Stanton, Abolitionist of the Old South," *Journal of Presbyterian History*, 53 (1975), 41; for Cocke, see Randall M. Miller, ed., *"Dear Master": Letters of a Slave Family* (Ithaca, N.Y., 1978), 149–151; Barrow Diary, ed., Sept. 4, 1837, in Edwin Adams Davis, ed., *Plantation Life in the Florida Parishes of Louisiana, 1836–1846, as Reflected in the Diary of Bennet H. Barrow* (New York, 1943), 98, 46 n.; Walker Diary for 1834, and Claudia L. Bushman, *In Old Virginia: Slavery, Farming, and Society in the Journal of John Walker* (Baltimore, Md., 2002), 96–97. Low country planters suspected female slaves of whoring for poor white neighbors: William Dusinberre, *Them Dark Days: Slavery in the American Rice Swamps* (New York, 1996), 112.

gal breeds so fast and gits a mess of young-uns. She larnt them fine manners and combs out they hair." Her mistress did not take it well, but her husband denied everything and kept her in finery. Lexington, Kentucky, with its wealthy horse-breeding planters and notorious speculators, ranked next to New Orleans as a fancy-girl market. Prices could be staggering: They always had been in slave societies. In Renaissance Italy, comely young slaves from Eastern Europe went at "prezzo d'affezione" (a heavy premium), and in nineteenth-century Russia, so implacable a foe of serfdom as Ivan Turgenev spent seven hundred rubles on a beauty when ordinary housemaids cost fifty.[80]

In New Orleans in the 1830s some young women sold at prices ten times greater than they would have sold for ordinary purposes, and in the 1850s a woman went for an astonishing $1,700 at a time when a prime male field hand was selling for hundreds of dollars less. Fredrika Bremer saw twelve-year-old girls sold in Augusta, Georgia, for $1,500. In Virginia, South Carolina, and Georgia, Bremer observed the sale of lovely young women at prices so high as to leave no doubt they were slated for the bedroom. In Memphis, the *Eagle and Enquirer* reported that the master of a beautiful slave up for sale had refused an offer of $5,000.[81]

The War created a new situation for which slavery was not responsible: Prostitutes flocked into cities and army camps. Richmond became the brothel capital of the South, attracting prostitutes from every direction, although it could not match Washington's 450 bordellos and 7,000 streetwalkers. Swarms of prostitutes greeted Union troops in Richmond, Nashville, and the port cities. In Nashville, "Cyprians" ranged from streetwalkers to sophisticated concubines. Large numbers of prostitutes had recently arrived from New England. Venereal disease spread so widely in occupied Nashville that the Union army rounded up between 150 and 300 prostitutes and shipped them north. Not surprisingly, the authorities at their appointed destinations often refused to let them disembark. Army officers in Nashville thereupon set up America's first legal red-light district, requiring regular medical inspections and other measures to control the trade and render it less destructive.[82]

---

[80] Solomon Northup, *Twelve Years a Slave* (New York, 1970 [1854]), 65; Benjamin A. Botkin, ed., *Lay My Burden Down* (Chicago, 1945), 122–123; J. Winston Coleman, *Slavery in Kentucky* (Chapel Hill, N.C., 1940), 131; Frederick Bancroft, *Slave Trading in the Old South* (New York, 1959), 159. For Italy, see Iris Origo, "'The Domestic Enemy': The Eastern Slaves in Tuscany in the Fourteenth and Fifteenth Centuries," *Speculum*, 30 (1955), 321–366; and for Russia, see Jerome Blum, *Lord and Peasant in Russia, from the Ninth to the Nineteenth Century* (Princeton, N.J., 1961), 426.

[81] Lyle Saxon et al., *Gumbo Ya-Ya: A Collection of Louisiana Folk Tales* (New York, 1945), 225–226; Joe Gray Taylor, *Negro Slavery in Louisiana* (Baton Rouge, La., 1963), 87; Bremer, *Homes*, 1:373, 2:535. Taylor found Conrad's $8,000 astonishing and suspected the erroneous addition of an extra zero. But such prices were in fact known.

[82] Emory M. Thomas, *The Confederate State of Richmond: A Biography of the Capital* (Austin, Tex., 1971), 39, 68; Catherine Clinton, "Prostitution," in Current, ed., *Encyclopedia of the Confederacy*, 4 vols. (New York, 1993), 3:1276; Bell I. Wiley, *The Life of Billy Yank: The Common Soldier of the Union* (Baton Rouge, La., 1978), 258–261; also, Wiley, *Life of Johnny*

Proslavery men who declared the "general absence" of prostitutes in the South tested the limits of "general." They knew that southern towns housed prostitutes – probably, more whites than blacks – and that the countryside had many more than recorded. Yet the South did not match the enormous numbers posted in the big cities of the North. And that was the point. Sin-conscious Southerners were not surprised to encounter prostitutes everywhere. Substantial numbers of prostitutes populated big cities, and except for New Orleans, there were few cities of even medium size south of Baltimore. To the extent that slavery inhibited urbanization, its advocates could take credit for keeping prostitution within tolerable limits. The South suffered more prostitution than its ideologues admitted but did not suffer the wholesale commercialization of sexuality common in the North. Baltimore came close, but it was in Maryland, which seemed to be on its way to conversion to free labor. The ideologues' rhetoric offered little solace to southern white girls and young women whom poverty lured into prostitution, much less to black slaves forced into it. As Amy Dru Stanley aptly observes in *From Bondage to Contract*, after the War, "more than any other figure, the prostitute evoked the nightmare of freedom envisioned in the Old South."[83]

Marriage and Divorce

Marriage and divorce provided a side issue in the southern indictment of northern sexual misbehavior. Southerners imbibed a traditional version of marriage that stressed centrality of the family to society. The Methodist Protestant Reverends Charles W. Jacobs and A. A. Lipscomb recalled that even pre-Christian heathens had family gods. Educated Southerners appreciated the Romans for treating marriage as a firmly grounded institution, and modern historians attributed much of Rome's decadence and eventual decline to erosion of respect for an institution long judged sacred. Defenders of slavery celebrated the stability of southern marriages and pounced on the high rate of divorce in the free states, ascribing it in part to the influence of social and political radicalism, with Fourierist socialism a prime culprit. The frequency of divorce in the

---

Reb, 50–55; Ayers, *Vengeance and Justice*, 148. On Nashville, see Steven V. Ash, *When the Yankees Came: Conflict and Chaos in the Occupied South, 1861–1865* (Chapel Hill, N.C., 1995), 85–86. For venereal disease in the Union and Confederacy, see Lowry, *Story the Soldiers Wouldn't Tell*, 99–108.

[83] Amy Dru Stanley, *From Bondage to Contract: Wage Labor, Marriage, and the Market in the Age of Slave Emancipation* (New York, 1998), 218, and for elaboration see ch. 6. The causeway in Baltimore's second ward was notorious for its brothels, rowdies, and Know Nothing hoodlums: Jean H. Baker, *Ambivalent Americans: The Know-Nothing Party in Maryland* (Baltimore, Md., 1977), 129. Thomas R. R. Cobb of Georgia acknowledged that large, densely peopled cities spawned progress but warned of the high social price: *Educational Wants of Georgia: An Address Delivered before the Society of the Alumni of Franklin College* (Athens, Ga., 1857), 13–14.

free states, especially in the Northwest, distressed churchmen. Indiana ranked as a divorce haven, much as Nevada would later.[84]

In 1831 the *Carolina Law Journal*, edited by Abram Blanding and David J. McCord, boasted that South Carolina stood alone among the civilized nations of the world in prohibiting divorce. During the early decades of the nineteenth century, the legislature received petitions for divorce on grounds of fraud, adultery, and cruelty but refused relief. Nor would South Carolina recognize foreign divorces – a category that included other states of the Union. Knowing that separations and illicit living arrangements resulted, the authorities discreetly refused to prosecute fornicators and adulterers. For decades grand juries, complaining of this "growing evil," demanded proscription only to be rebuffed. The legislature protected the economic security of wives and legitimate children, limiting to one-quarter of an estate the amount left to concubines and bastards. As J. S. Buckingham grasped, South Carolina's legislators and jurists believed that they would do less evil to society by denying a few releases from unpleasant marriages than by encouraging carelessness and incaution in formation of marriages. They thereby made the stern Presbyterian Church look wishy-washy, for the Church, in good Calvinist fashion, sanctioned divorce for adultery and willful desertion. After the War, Benjamin Perry, leader of the up country unionists, reasserted the official antebellum view: "Divorces were never allowed in South Carolina for two hundred years until the State was dishonored by a carpet-bag and scalawag and negro government. The religious and moral sentiment of public opinion now demands that this disgraceful Act should be erased from our statutes." Some prominent northern conservatives approved South Carolina's course. New York's own strict divorce laws won the approval of U.S. Supreme Court Justice Joseph Story, who put in a good if grudging word for South Carolina's outright prohibition.[85]

---

[84] A. A. Lipscomb, *The Social Spirit of Christianity, Presented in the Form of Essays* (Philadelphia, 1846), 15, 45–47; "Stowe's Key to Uncle Tom's Cabin," *SQR*, 8 (1853), 251–252; Frederick A. Ross, *Slavery Ordained of God* (Philadelphia, 1857), 55; Wesley Norton, *Religious Newspapers in the Old Northwest to 1861: A History, Bibliography, and Record of Opinion* (Athens, Oh., 1977), 83. John Tyler, Jr. ["Python"], ended a two-part historical discussion of sexual morals, marriage, and divorce from ancient times to the present by blistering the North and its free-labor system: "The Relative Moral Status of the North and South," *DBR*, 22 (1857), 246–248 and, generally, 113–132, 227–248. American divorce provoked European debates over the causes; see Carole Shammas, *A History of Household Government in America* (Charlottesville, Va., 2002), 107. In keeping with currently fashionable sensibilities, Pierre Grimal has questioned the general decadence and specific decline: *Love in Ancient Rome*, 26.

[85] "The Effect of Foreign Divorces on South Carolina Marriages," *Carolina Law Journal*, 1 (1831), 377–383; Sarah Leverette, "The *Carolina Law Journal* of 1830," *South Carolina Law Quarterly*, 12 (1960), 199; Michael Stephen Hindus, *Prison and Plantation: Crime, Justice, and Authority in Massachusetts and South Carolina, 1767–1878* (Chapel Hill, N.C., 1980), 51–52; Buckingham, *Slave States of America*, 1:77; Girardeau, "Family Religion," in George A. Blackburn, ed., *Sermons by John L. Girardeau* (Columbia, S.C., 1907), 145; generally, Blanks, "Ideal and Practice," 54–55; Meats and Arnold, eds., *Writings of B. F. Perry*, 2:71; Joseph Story, *Commentaries on the Constitution of the United States*, 2nd ed., ed. W. W. Story, 2 vols.

South Carolina's model did not prove useful in newer regions. Legislatures and courts bent, lest they break. Not only early Tennessee and mid-century Texas, but also Georgia, which retained frontier flavor, struggled to formulate policies that public opinion would support. The closer a state remained to the frontier, the more liberal its divorce laws. Florida became a divorce haven under territorial governor John Eaton, who saw no point in holding together couples that could not get along. A surprised Matilda Charlotte Houstoun found that a declaration of incompatibility was about all it took in the Republic of Texas. In Tennessee the legislature maintained concurrent jurisdiction but followed New England in promulgating a judicial divorce act before 1800. Grounds for divorce included adultery, willful and malicious desertion, impotence, bigamy, and conviction for a felony. In 1824, Governor Troup pleaded with the Georgia state legislature to "discourage divorces," which seldom did credit to either party and indicated "a depraved state of society." Until 1835 divorce could be obtained in Georgia only by petitioning the legislature, which granted 291 between 1798 and 1835, ten percent of them in 1833. Thereupon, divorces were transferred to the courts. Eugenius A. Nisbet, the intellectual jewel of Georgia's Supreme Court, said that the legislature wanted to curb its own abuses by handing power to a reliably conservative judiciary. Relaxation of divorce laws and procedures were formal concessions to the democratic temper of the times but did not imply laxness toward the permanence and solidity of the family. Nisbet expressed alarm over the ease with which Georgia granted divorces between 1798 and 1835: "How fearful was the ratio of increase! Well might the patriot, the Christian, and the Moralist look about him for some device to stay this swelling tide of demoralization. The facts prove one of two things incontestably, either I am right that divorces were granted for any and all causes, or society in Georgia was deplorably rude and licentious."[86]

Riots

Since the South had no poverty it had no riots: Such became the refrain. Mayor Richard D. Arnold of Savannah may have dissented: He barely escaped death at the hands of a mob in the 1840s. Southern cities had election-day riots in the

(Boston, Mass., 1851), 2:95–128; "Natural Law," in W. W. Story, ed., *The Miscellaneous Writings of Joseph Story* (Boston, Mass., 1852), 315–316.

[86] For territorial Florida, see John Marszalek, *Petticoat Affair: Manners, Mutiny and Sex in Andrew Jackson's White House* (Baton Rouge, La., 2000), 212, and *The Autobiography of Peggy Eaton* (New York, 1932), 171–173; Mrs. [Matilda Charlotte] Houstoun, *Texas and the Gulf of Mexico; or Yachting in the New World* (Austin, Tex., 1968 [1845]), 252; Cornelia Anne Clark, "Justice on the Tennessee Frontier: The Williamson County Circuit Court, 1810–1820," *Vanderbilt Law Review*, 22 (1979), 433–435. For Georgia, see Maxwell Bloomfield, *American Lawyers in a Changing Society, 1776–1876* (Cambridge, Mass., 1976), 121–122; Troup, "First Annual Message to the State Legislature of Georgia" (1824), in Edward J. Harden, *The Life of George M. Troup* (Savannah, Ga., 1859), 239; *Head v. Head*, 2 Ga., 190, quoted in Bond Almond, "History of the Supreme Court of Georgia: The First Hundred Years," *Georgia Bar Journal*, 6 (1944), 187.

1850s, especially after the rise of the Know Nothings. Anti-Catholic violence occurred occasionally in Baltimore, Louisville, and other Border State cities. Louisville suffered an ethnic riot that left twenty dead and hundreds hurt. Senator Henry S. Foote of Mississippi acknowledged as much when, in a postwar retrospective, he praised bench and bar of the Southwest for suppressing the "evils of disorder and anarchical lawlessness."[87]

Frequent and bloody riots in northern cities far outstripped anything suffered in the South. In the 1830s serious mob violence against Masons, with some Masonic counter-violence, occurred in northern but not southern cities. Between 1790 and 1830, in the wake of mass immigration, the population of northeastern cities tripled and quadrupled and that of New York ballooned from 30,000 to 200,000. In 1835, Massachusetts, when it abolished capital punishment, toughened its stand against rioters. And no wonder. During the summer of 1834, an anti-Catholic, anti-Irish mob burned the Ursuline convent in Boston, and an antiabolition riot in New York lasted for a week. The urban lower classes of America, Alexis de Tocqueville wrote in the early 1830s – his eye primarily on blacks and recent immigrants – "constitute a rabble even more formidable than the populace of European towns." He predicted steady worsening and the advent of standing armies to keep order. During the 1820s and 1830s, the propertied classes in northern cities did not disguise their terror at mob actions and public disturbances. Newspapers – increasingly cheap and aimed at a mass audience – reported disturbances and began to campaign for tougher police measures. Yet Southerners questioned whether "rabble" alone caused the violence in northern cities. They had heard of the participation of Boston's firemen – drawn from "respectable" elements across class lines – in the burning of the Ursuline convent. Anti-Catholic mobs accounted for much of the rioting in 1834 and 1837 and some in the 1850s. Hooligans had a grand time in the 1830s, attacking Catholic convents in upstate New York, burning blacks out of their homes in Philadelphia and Boston, breaking up Masonic meetings, and assaulting abolitionists across the country. Endless reports of riots in the brothels of New York entertained Southerners. By 1830 a class of pimps had arisen, protected by corrupt policemen, who subjected prostitutes to physical violence – a pastime that sometimes provoked retaliatory violence from chivalrous working-class toughs.[88]

[87] R. D. Arnold to John W. Forney, Dec. 18, 1850, in Richard H. Shryock, ed., *Letters of Richard D. Arnold, M. D., 1808–1876* (Durham, N.C., 1929), 47; Henry S. Foote, *The Bench and Bar of the South and Southwest* (St. Louis, 1876), 13; Henry Bailey, II, *A History of the Diocese of Richmond: The Formative Years* (Richmond, 1956), 121–123; Kenneth M. Stampp, *America in 1857: A Nation on the Brink* (New York, 1990), 37–38; Richard J. Carwardine, *Evangelicals and Politics in Antebellum America* (New Haven, Conn., 1993), 233.

[88] Steven C. Bullock, *Revolutionary Brotherhood: Freemasonry and the Transformation of the American Social Order, 1730–1840* (Chapel Hill, N.C., 1996), 277–301; Alexis de Tocqueville, *Democracy in America*, 2 vols., tr. Henry Reeve (Boston, Mass., 1873), 1: 342, n. 1; Louis P. Masur, *Rites of Execution: Capital Punishment and the Transformation of American Culture, 1776–1865* (New York, 1989), 100–102; Daniel A. Cohen, "Passing the Torch: Boston

The responsibility of antislavery men for anti-Catholic violence became a favorite proslavery theme. Augustus Baldwin Longstreet portrayed the abolitionist: "He shrieks out at slavery, and calls on the Catholic to help him crush it. He shrieks out at Popery, and calls on the slaveholder to help him crush it – then hurls a firebrand into the habitation of the one, and the Church of the other." A disgusted William J. Grayson commented on the burning of Catholic convents in his famous *The Hireling and the Slave*. John Fletcher of New Orleans joined William Ellery Channing in deploring the burning of Freedom Hall in Philadelphia but asked why antislavery men said little about the convent-burning by Channing's "own townsmen, the good people of Boston." In the 1850s, Alexander Stephens carried the banner against the Know Nothings in Georgia: "Of all the Christian denominations in the United States, the Catholics are the last that southern people should join in attempting to put under the ban of civil proscription. For as a church Catholics have never warred against us or our peculiar institutions." Stephens regretted that he could not say the same for northern Protestants.[89]

Southerners took riots that stemmed from the economic hardships as normal wherever free labor prevailed, and they took anti-Catholic riots as confirmation that the North reeked of religious bigotry. The depression that

Firemen, 'Tea Party' Patriots, and the Burning of the Charlestown Convent," *Journal of the Early Republic*, 24 (2004), 527–586; Ronald G. Walters, *American Reformers, 1815–1860* (New York, 1978), 9–10; Pease and Pease, *Web of Progress*, 153–170; James Brewer Stewart, *Holy Warriors: The Abolitionists and American Society* (New York, 1976), 64–73; on brothel riots, see Gilfoyle, *City of Eros*, ch. 4. Urban rioting did not rise to dangerous proportions until the 1830s; by 1840 more than 125 people had been killed in riots: David Grimstead, "Rioting in a Jacksonian Setting," *American Historical Review*, 77 (1972), 362–364.

   Lyman Beecher denied that his anti-Catholic fulminations had inspired the mob that burned the Ursuline convent in Boston in 1834, but he concentrated his outrage on the Catholics he alleged to have threatened mob action in retaliation: Charles Beecher, ed., *Autobiography, Correspondence, Etc. of Lyman Beecher*, 2 vols. (New York, 1871), 2:335. The antislavery Harriet Martineau considered him a bigot and held him partly responsible for the burning in Boston: *Retrospect of Western Travel*, 2 vols. (London, 1838), 2:55, 212. Vincent Harding writes in his generally sympathetic biography of Beecher: "Though Beecher had not helped to incite this particular mob, it is doubtless that the spirit he represented was influential in the genesis of such an act." *A Certain Magnificence: Lyman Beecher and the Transformation of American Protestantism, 1775–1863* (Brooklyn, N.Y., 1991), 361; see also Nancy Lusignan Schultz, *Fire and Roses: The Burning of the Charlestown Convent, 1834* (New York, 2000). For an overview and interpretation of American rioting, see Paul A. Gilje, *Rioting in America* (Bloomington, Ind., 1996), and for Beecher's responsibility for the events in Charlestown, see 83, 116–117, 160.

[89] [Augustus Baldwin Longstreet], *A Voice from the South: Comprising Letters from Georgia to Massachusetts, and to the Southern States* (Baltimore, Md., 1847), 22; William J. Grayson, *The Hireling and the Slave, Chicora, and Other Poems* (Charleston, S.C., 1856), 163, n. 32; John Fletcher, *Studies on Slavery, in Easy Lessons* (Natchez, Miss., 1852), 214; A. H. Stephens to T. W. Thomas, May 9, 1855, in Henry Cleveland, *Alexander H. Stephens in Public and Private. With Letters and Speeches before, during, and since the War* (Philadelphia, Pa., 1866), 464. Robert Toombs, who denounced Know Nothingism as "imbecility," contributed money to the Catholic Church as well as to Protestant churches. Pleasant A. Stovall, *Robert Toombs: Statesman, Speaker, Soldier, Sage* (New York, 1892), 122, 124–125.

followed the crash of 1837 provoked "flour riots" and widespread disorder in northern cities, which alarmed politicians, journalists, and foreign observers alike. Hezekiah Niles and Orestes Brownson, among prominent Northerners, depicted workers in an insurrectionary mood. Brownson, then attached to the radical left, sounded like Calhoun in denouncing capital as inherently antagonistic to labor. Twenty years later, riots still wracked New York with outright class warfare.[90]

In 1844 the moderately antislavery unionist Henry St. George Tucker drew the attention of his law school students at the University of Virginia to the riots and social disorders of Europe, relating them to the miserable condition of the laboring classes. He hoped that with a sparse population and enormous stretches of land, the United States could avoid Europe's fate. Tucker might hope, but that very year a riot in Philadelphia left twelve dead, and another at New York's Astor Place left twenty-two dead. The anti-Catholic violence of 1844 and the consequent necessity to impose martial law shocked the Middletons of South Carolina, among wealthy Southerners who lived in Philadelphia. Thomas Butler King of Georgia understood that riots over bread and jobs were of a piece with the riots over religious antagonisms. A society that made a fetish of freedom and confused it with license was suffering a breakdown of law and order. When King spoke to an audience of thousands in New York in 1844, news arrived of a riot in Philadelphia in which Know Nothings and Catholics were killing each other. His audience stayed put but afterward poured out to take vengeance on local Catholics. King thought that some twenty or thirty people were killed and churches burned during the next few days. An irate Simms assailed the anti-Catholic riots in Massachusetts and Pennsylvania as "evil deeds of a fanaticism" and manifestations of lynch law.[91]

Slaveholders laid responsibility for the chronic disorder in northern cities at the feet of the radical democracy engendered by the free-labor system. Almost every year between 1840 and 1861, John Tyler read with dismay reports in *Niles' Register* of riots and tumults in northern cities. Tyler, who sometimes wondered if slavery were in fact a great blessing, saw the horrible scenes in northern society as goading Southerners to harden their commitment. The news of Dorr's rebellion in Rhode Island threw him into a tizzy. His secretary of state and fellow Virginian, Abel Upshur, wrote to Nathaniel Beverley Tucker, "This is the very madness of democracy, and a fine illustration of the workings of the majority principle.... This comes of giving the government of the country to those who do not own the country.... The end will be a revolution, but not in my time or yours." Calhoun commented to Henry Wise on the

[90] Arthur M. Schlesinger, Jr., *Age of Jackson* (Boston, Mass., 1946), 210–211, 218–221, 274, 299–300; Stampp, *America in 1857*, ch. 8.
[91] Henry St. George Tucker, *Lectures on Government* (Charlottesville, Va., 1844), 157; Eliza Middleton Fisher to Mary Herring Middleton, May 10, 1844, in Eliza Cope Harrison, ed., *Best Companions: Letters of Eliza Middleton Fisher and Her Mother, Mary Hering Middleton, from Charleston, Philadelphia, and Newport, 1839–1846* (Columbia, S.C., 2001) 380; Thomas Butler King to Anna M. King, May 11, 1844; [William Gilmore Simms], *SWMR*, 2 (1845), 221.

Irish-Nativist riot in Philadelphia in 1844: "the legitimate fruit of fanaticism & the spoils principle & that of the numerical majority." The "growth and power of mobs in New York" did not surprise Representative William Russell Smith of Alabama. What should you expect from 100,000 "floating" and easily manipulated aliens who "never go to church" and prefer to frequent New York's 9,000 grog shops? In 1858, Thornwell got an earful from Nathaniel Hewitt of Connecticut on the distressing rise of New York's crime rate and on a riot on Staten Island.[92]

Southerners did not condone rioting but "understood" it when outraged, respectable, decent citizens confronted abolitionist agitators. Rioters also assaulted blacks, and Southerners reiterated that northern whites, unlike southern, hated blacks and wanted them dead. What may have been the worst anti-black riot in antebellum America occurred in Cincinnati in 1841. The blows fell on a thrifty, hardworking black community that fought back. A riot against abolitionists and blacks killed people of both races.[93]

Northerners charged proslavery men with demagogy for harping on the terrible exploitation of northern workers during the prosperous and booming 1850s. But the general prosperity disguised a hidden depression of catastrophic proportions for the working class. In the 1840s and 1850s, workers suffered from epidemics, falling wages, deteriorating housing, and an increasingly unhealthful environment. Working-class conditions declined between 1830 and 1860. In the 1850s, New York City's crime rate rose more than four times the increase in population. The moral unraveling – marked by vagrant children, prostitution, widespread drunkenness – shocked visitors, dismayed ministers,

---

[92] Upshur to Tucker, Aug. 20, 1842, in Lyon Gardiner Tyler, *The Letters and Times of the Tylers*, 3 vols. (Williamsburg, Va., 1884–1896), 2:198; see 2, 192–199, 468 on John Tyler's reactions; J. C. Calhoun to H. A. Wise, May 11, 1844, in *JCCP*, 18:491; W. R. Smith quoted in William Garrett, *Reminiscences of Public Men in Alabama for Thirty Years* (Atlanta, Ga., 1872), 561; Nathaniel Hewitt to J. H. Thornwell, Sept. 8, 1858, in Thornwell Papers. George McDuffie of South Carolina denied turbulence and violence in American elections: E. L. Green, ed., "On the Election of the President and Vice President of the United States," in *Two Speeches of George McDuffie* (Columbia, S.C., 1905), 38–39. On violence in Richmond, see Peter C. Hoffer, "Disorder and Deference," in David J. Bodenhamer and James W. Ely, eds., *Ambivalent Legacy: A Legal History of the South* (Jackson, Miss., 1984), 188, 190–191, 195–199. On Dorr, Marvin E. Gettleman, *The Dorr Rebellion: A Study in American Radicalism, 1833–1849* (New York, 1973), 17–18, 43–49, 129–130, 145; and for the political impact of the Dorr War beyond Rhode Island, see Sean Wilentz, *The Rise of American Democracy: Jefferson to Jackson* (New York, 2005), 559–556; also "The Influence of Civil Government on Religion," in Richard Newman, ed., *Black Preacher to White America: The Collected Writings of Lemuel Haynes, 1774–1833* (Brooklyn, N.Y., 1990), 65–76.

[93] Daniel Aaron, *Cincinnati: Queen City of the West, 1819–1838* (Columbus, Oh., 1992), 294–314; William Cheek and Aimee Lee Cheek, *John Mercer Langston and the Fight for Black Freedom, 1829–65* (Urbana, Ill., 1989), 63–67. In Boston, Utica, New York, and other northern cities, the abolitionists took a fearful beating in the mid-1830s. Leading newspaper editors called for their suppression, and mobs broke up their meetings and physically assaulted speakers: William Lee Miller, *Arguing about Slavery: The Great Battle in the United States Congress* (New York, 1996), ch. 6.

and terrified the middle class. Workers responded with union organization, strikes, political action, campaigns for homesteads – and riots. Native workers often directed their anger and frustration against immigrants.[94]

During the secession crisis Southerners alternately taunted and assured northern friends about the greater safety of life among slaves. Indeed, in 1813 John Adams wrote to Jefferson that Virginians had never felt the rebellions and riots that threatened the North with Jacobinism and a reign of terror. Among many Southerners in the 1850s, J. F. H. Claiborne railed against the riots and disorder in the northern cities. George Washington Mordecai of Raleigh wrote a northern Republican in 1860, "I would much sooner trust myself alone on my plantation, surrounded by my slaves, than in one of your large manufacturing towns when your labourers are discharged from employment and crying for bread for themselves and their little ones." In Georgia, a year later, a sarcastic planter on Skidaway Island assured his northern mother-in-law, "We believe our negroes as reliable as the mobs of the Northern cities." In Louisiana, Braxton Bragg, sugar planter and future Confederate general, wrote to his friend William Tecumseh Sherman, "We have a large class of our population in subordination, [which is] just and necessary. Where do we find the fewest mutinies, revolts, and rebellions? In the best disciplined commands. Human nature is the same throughout the world. Give us all disciplined masters, managers, and assistants, and we shall never hear of insurrection – unless as an exception."[95]

Corruption

In 1834, John C. Calhoun assaulted Andrew Jackson's administration for unprecedented corruption: "The time has gone by when office is bestowed as the reward of merit. Neither capacity, honesty, nor passed [*sic*] services are now in the least regarded." He told the Senate in February 1835, "The only cohesive principle which binds together the powerful party rallied under the name of General Jackson is official patronage." A month later he cried out, "Things are now not only tolerated, but are scarcely noticed, which, at any other period, would have prostrated the Administration of Washington himself." Calhoun proposed a reduction in government expenditure and income and an end to

[94] Fogel, *Without Consent or Contract*, 355–364, 469 n. 80; also N. Ware, *The Industrial Worker, 1840–1860: The Reaction of American Industrial Society to the Advance of the Industrial Revolution* (Boston, Mass., 1924), 6–7, 78.

[95] John Adams to Jefferson, 2:346–348 (June 13, 1813), 2:371 (Sept. 2, 1813), Jefferson to Adams, 2:388–389 (Oct., 28, 1813), in Lester Cappon, ed., *The Adams-Jefferson Letters: The Complete Correspondence between Thomas Jefferson and John and Abigail Adams*, 2 vols. (Chapel Hill, N.C., 1959); Claiborne, *Mississippi*, 168–169; Mordecai quoted in Clement Eaton, *The Freedom-of-Thought Struggle in the Old South* (New York, 1964), 252; the planter from Skidaway quoted in Clarence C. Mohr, *On the Threshold of Freedom: Masters and Slaves in Civil War Georgia* (Athens, Ga., 1986), 311, n. 87; Grady McWhiney, *Braxton Bragg and Confederate Defeat* (New York, 1969), 143.

efforts to provoke war with France. He could denounce corruption freely, for even so severe a political opponent as Thomas Hart Benton of Missouri acknowledged that his "character placed him above the suspicion of venal motive."[96]

As the federal payroll swelled, so did good old-fashioned stealing. The 1850s prefigured the Gilded Age. Washington and state capitals swarmed with lobbyists. In Wisconsin the governor and leading politicians shamelessly feathered their own nests and those of railroad promoters. Their crime in the new era was to have gotten caught. Dishonest contractors and politicians on the take bilked northern cities. Even the political machines had internal scandals. Isaac Fowler, the leader of New York's Tammany Hall, absconded with $150,000 of the party's money in 1858, and throughout the North leaders of the shiny new Republican Party, no less than the Democratic, stole money, rigged elections, and shilled for the railroads and other business interests.[97]

In earlier decades Martin Van Buren, Thomas Hart Benton, and Thurlow Weed were considered "spoilsmen"; by 1850 they were vehemently protesting a wave of corruption that made them fear for the Republic. Steam magnates received lavish mail subsidies. Railroad promoters and allied bankers, having bought legislators, got lush subsidies. Street gangs terrorized election day, and

---

[96] Thomas Hart Benton, *Thirty Years' View; or, A History of the Working of the American Government for Thirty Years, from 1820 to 1850*, 2 vols. (New York, 1854), 1:414–415. John Quincy Adams faced an outcry when his administration appointed a relative of Henry Clay postmaster of Nashville: Charles M. Wiltse, *John C. Calhoun*, 3 vols. (Indianapolis, Ind., 1944–1951), 1:20, 2:332.

In teaching the classics, southern colleges strongly emphasized the role of corruption in destroying ancient republics, but, then, so did Princeton, which a good many Southerners attended down to secession: see Woodward and Craven, ed., *Princetonians, 1784–1790* (Princeton, N.J., 1991), and Looney and Woodward, eds., *Princetonians, 1791–1994* (Princeton, N.J., 1991). The common assumption, shared by Southerners, that high taxation ruined a corrupt and dysfunctional ancient Rome has been challenged: Ramsay MacMullen, *Corruption and the Decline of Rome* (New Haven, Conn., 1988), 41–42.

[97] See especially Mark W. Summers, *The Plundering Generation: Corruption and the Crisis of the Union, 1849–1861* (New York, 1987), which not only provides an extensive overview and a detailed account of the chicanery but shrewdly analyzes its bearing on the slavery controversy. Also Arthur C. Cole, *The Irrepressible Conflict, 1850–1865* (New York, 1934), 28–30; William C. Wright, *The Secession Movement in Middle Atlantic States* (Rutherford, N.J., 1973), 167; Kenneth M. Stampp, *America in 1857: A Nation on the Brink* (New York, 1990), ch. 9.

Many southern politicians succumbed to the temptation to fight for control of the federal patronage. See, e.g., J. Mills Thornton, *Power and Politics in a Slave Society: Alabama, 1800–1860* (Baton Rouge, La., 1978), 302–304, 312; Louis Martin Sears, *John Slidell* (Durham, N.C., 1925), 44; William H. Pease and Jane H. Pease, *James Louis Petigru: Southern Conservative, Southern Dissenter* (Athens, Ga., 1995), 27; H. A. Trexler, "Jefferson Davis and Confederate Patronage," *South Atlantic Quarterly*, 28 (1929), 45–58. For northern views on the links between corruption, slavery, and universal suffrage, see Paul E. Johnson and Sean Wilentz, *The Kingdom and Matthias* (New York, 1994), ch. 4; Louis S. Gerteis, *Morality and Utility in American Antislavery Reform* (Chapel Hill, N.C., 1987), 12.9. The abolitionist George Cheever returned to the attack on universal suffrage in 1865 in *The Wanderings of a Pilgrim in the Shadow of Mont Blanc and the Jungfrau Alp* (Glasgow, U.K., 1865), 284.

well-oiled party machines recorded the votes of dead men. The dishonesty of the press hurt. The prize went to the New York *Tribune*, which in 1852 reported on a violent primary day that featured ballot stuffing and the organized voting of prostitutes, aliens, and drunks. Good story. But, alas, none of it happened since the primary had been postponed for a week. Still, when primary day did arrive, the invented disgrace did occur. The public's democratic insistence upon low salaries for government officials claimed a high price. Officials compensated for inadequate salaries. The sheriff of San Francisco County wound up with a yearly income four times that of the president of the United States, and no one knows how much the collector of the Port of New York pocketed, although we may assume that he broke all records.

Southern critics linked expansion of the federal government to corruption in states and localities. Access to big money led through Washington. Despite southern demands for low tariffs and a reduction in federal expenditures, Southerners competed with Northerners for funds for naval bases and other goodies. The railroad boom invited massive corruption, from which the southern states were hardly free. In Georgia, the Western & Atlantic Railroad operatives intervened to prevent Howell Cobb's election to the Senate. In Texas, a legislator protested against the "general mania" for railroad charters across the South. Alabama increased public expenditures and taxes enormously during the 1850s. In Louisiana, John Slidell brought New Orleans $400,000 in federal money for a new customs house and for harbor improvement. Electoral corruption and hooliganism spread in the southern cities and even in such sedate towns as Hillsboro, North Carolina. J. L. Petigru, as attorney-general of South Carolina, occasionally prosecuted public officials for embezzlement, and every other state had a scandal or two. The taste for spoils remained to plague Jefferson Davis's efforts to manage the Confederate government.[98]

Abolitionists and free-soilers tried, with considerable success, to turn the corruption issue against the South. Somehow, the slaveocracy – morally corrupt by definition – bore responsibility. After all, did not the South exercise disproportionate power in the federal government through the apportionment of Senate seats and the three-fifths clause of the Constitution? The Republican Party, notwithstanding its own corruption, rose on popular disgust with the unprecedented corruption of Democrats and Whigs. Thus the South found itself in a no-win position, vainly fighting to roll back federal patronage as part of its larger effort to return substantial power to the states.

Yet corruption did thrive in the North much more than in the South – at least outside Louisiana – and it affected cities much more than towns and

[98] Thornton, *Power and Politics in a Slave Society*, 302–304, 312; Louis Martin Sears, *John Slidell* (Durham, N.C., 1925), 44; Pease and Pease, *James Louis Petigru*, 27; H. A. Trexler, "Jefferson Davis and Confederate Patronage," *South Atlantic Quarterly*, 28 (1929), 45–58. For public corruption and scandals, see, e.g., Edgar W. Knight, *Public Education in the South* (Boston, Mass., 1922), 164–167; *DNCB*, 3:87; Dunbar Rowland, ed., *Mississippi: Comprising Sketches of Counties, Towns, Events, Institutions, and Persons, Arranged in Cyclopedic Form*, 4 vols. (Spartanburg, S.C., 1976 [1907]), 1:795–796.

villages. In 1852, James M. Walker of South Carolina wrote that "corruption was undermining private property and its political influence and would increase as population became denser." Corruption troubled the slave states more than Southerners wished to admit. On balance, however, the South, especially the plantation South, avoided the worst and had grounds for identifying the wave of national corruption with the ascendancy of business interests in the North. In 1841, Willie P. Mangum of North Carolina wrote to William A. Graham, a fellow Whig, about his fears of the "old Fed. clique to the North, which differs from anything we see in the South." Even in the turbulent 1850s, Mark W. Summers writes in *Plundering Generation*, "Republicans had to acknowledge the South's reputation for probity where money was concerned.... No one seriously suggested that Southern congressmen could be bought to resist the Kansas-Nebraska bill, as Northerners reputedly were. When Southerners believed in something, they stood by it. That was what made them so dangerous."[99]

The relation of corruption to republican government, democracy, and social stability hovered over the great nineteenth-century political struggles. By the 1840s, northern clergymen, alarmed over countless scandals, blamed the advent of popular democracy for the proliferation of suspicious religious cults, sex murders, and a perceived moral degeneration. Northerners, too, railed at corruption but with a different view of its roots. Abolitionists in particular had a swelling audience for their charge that the excesses of democracy were of a piece with the aggressions of the "Slave Power." Southerners insisted that the degeneration of constitutionally sanctioned republican politics into democratic demagoguery opened the way to the looting of the public domain. Their proposed cure lay in power to the people, which most Southerners interpreted as the devolution of federal power to the states. Joseph Hodgson of Mobile reflected in 1875: "There was no official dishonesty in those days. To be suspected even of selfishness in office was to be discarded from public favor."[100]

Southerners fought a two-front war – against a corrupt northern politics hostile to the South and against those in their own ranks who partook of the spirit of the age. As old-fashioned Christians, they accepted sin as a fact of life and therefore expected political and economic corruption. Notwithstanding occasional holier-than-thou polemical fireworks, they rested their case not on their own innate morality but on the superiority of a social system that discouraged evildoing. Despite the railroad boom and the rising pressure for expenditures on education and social projects, the southern states remained relatively lean and restricted opportunities for the looting of their treasuries.

[99] James M. Walker, *The Theory of the Common Law* (Boston, 1852), 117; W. P. Mangum to W. A. Graham, March 27, 1841, in Henry Thomas Shanks, ed., *The Papers of Willie P. Mangum*, 5 vols. (Raleigh, N.C., 1955–1956), 2:129; Summers, *Plundering Generation*, 217; and for the southern reaction to corruption, see Kenneth S. Greenberg, *Masters and Statesmen: The Political Culture of American Slavery* (Baltimore, Md., 1985).

[100] Joseph Hodgson, *The Cradle of the Confederacy: Or, The Times of Troup, Quitman, and Yancey* (Spartanburg, S.C., 1975), 176, 16.

Temptations remained and even grew stronger, but so did the resistance. As Calhoun had long preached, slavery, states' rights, and inexpensive, minimal government at home as well as in Washington formed one great cause. The southern reaction to Lincoln's election in part reflected the insight that the corruption of human nature, manifested in the distribution of federal patronage in the South, would lay the foundations for an antislavery party. In 1860 the Charleston *Mercury* warned of the threat inherent in the appointment to federal offices of opportunistic Southerners: "The Brownlows and Botts, in the South, will multiply. They will organize; and from being a Union Party, to support an Abolition Government, they will become, like the Government they support, Abolitionists. . . . The contest for slavery will no longer be one between the North and the South. It will be in the South, between the people of the South."[101]

[101] "The Terrors of Submission," *Charleston Mercury*, Oct. 11, 1860, in Dwight Lowell Dumond, ed., *Southern Editorials on Secession* (Gloucester, Mass., 1964), 179.

Afterword

You are not obliged to complete the work, but neither are you free to evade it.
—Rabbi Tarfon[1]

The long gestating doctrine of Slavery in the Abstract had deep roots in the Old South. Its branches spread widely if unevenly. George Fitzhugh of Virginia alone offered the extraordinary if ultimately utopian insight that to prevail, a slaveholding world had to destroy the world market and dismantle the capitalist system. Henry Hughes of Mississippi advanced a more practical view that pointed toward twentieth-century doctrines of the corporate state. Despite a common defense of Slavery in the Abstract, their specific formulations pointed in opposite directions: the one backward, the other forward. Yet Fitzhugh, Hughes, Thomas Roderick Dew, and George Holmes shared with the South's leading theologians, social theorists, and political spokesmen certain convictions: Free society had failed; the laboring classes needed to be subjected to personal servitude; and corporatism, not individualism, was the lesson of the past and the wave of the future. They projected a new world order based on the subjugation of labor to individual masters, however much they implicitly disagreed about the proper relation of those masters to the state.

Were we to credit postwar pronouncements, we might wonder how slavery survived so long with so few adherents. But those who issued disclaimers were kind enough to leave behind their antebellum writings, speeches, and – much more revealing – their private diaries and letters, which tell a different story. Were postwar Southerners lying? If so, they were lying to themselves. Few ever wallowed in guilt over ownership of slaves, but they faced a rising tide of transatlantic public opinion that kept doubt alive. And since the divine sanction at the root of their conviction appeared withdrawn at Appomattox, they distanced themselves as much as possible from their original convictions.

No one in the South – nary a soul – advocated the enslavement of white men. Albert Taylor Bledsoe announced in *Liberty and Slavery*, "No one here

---

[1] *Mishnah: Avot,* 2:16 (first century A.D.).

contends for the subjection to slavery of any portion of the civilized world." Bledsoe wrote those words while living in the Virginia of Fitzhugh, Holmes, George Armstrong, John Mitchel, Edward A. Pollard, and others of whom he could hardly have been unaware. And we may wonder what he thought of the *Richmond Examiner*'s rave review of *Liberty and Slavery*, which declared it an admirable contribution to "the doctrine of slavery in the abstract." Yet in a sense Bledsoe may have been right. For most proslavery men were, after all, saying only that society required some form of slavery; that white workers would be better off under it; and that they would sooner or later have to face it in any society that did not have slaves of a supposedly inferior race. All of which did not, as a matter of logical necessity, mean that they advocated what they deemed inevitable.[2]

After the War few Southerners admitted to having ever believed in Slavery in the Abstract, but then, few admitted to having ever much liked black slavery either. They even forgot the straightforward sentiments they uttered at the end of the War. An example: "The admirable order system of labor which had hitherto existed in the cultivation of these valuable plantations," Arthur Middleton Manigault of South Carolina lamented in 1865, "could not be restored." The collapse of the Union led the old Whig Unionist William Cabell Rives of Virginia, a persistent critic of slavery, to assert that slavery provided the only viable solution to the social question and protected society from anarchy or despotism. In the twentieth century William Alexander Percy of the Mississippi Delta harked back to the proslavery argument, declaring that the paternalism supposedly inherent in the relation of landlord to cropper and tenant provided a moral foundation for capital-labor relations in a post-slavery world. The early postwar planters dreamed in vain, writes Harold D. Woodman: "Master-slave relations would become employer-employee relations with the fewest possible alterations in both the organization of production and control of the work force."[3]

The length to which honest and sensible men went to deny that they were saying what they plainly were saying inspires awe – or laughter. Southerners who sought to avoid charges of extremism in their defense of slavery especially

---

[2] Albert Taylor Bledsoe, *An Essay on Liberty and Slavery* (Philadelphia, Pa., 1857 ed.), 140; *Richmond Examiner*, July 25, 1856. That severe castigation of working conditions in free-labor countries did not necessarily lead to espousal of Slavery in the Abstract is stressed in Michael Wayne, *Death of an Overseer: Reopening a Murder Investigation from the Plantation South* (New York, 2001), 149.

[3] R. Lockwood Tower, ed., *A Carolinian Goes to War: The Civil War Narrative of Arthur Middleton Manigault* (Columbia, S.C., 1983), 14; William Alexander Percy, *Lanterns on the Levee: Recollections of a Planter's Son* (Baton Rouge, La., 1973), 280–282. See Harold D. Woodman, *New South – New Law: The Legal Foundations of Credit and Labor Relations in the Postbellum Agricultural South* (Baton Rouge, La., 1995), 62, 67–68, quote at 62, 3–94. For postwar remnants of paternalism, see Jay Mandle, *Not Slave, Not Free: The African American Economic Experience* (Durham, N.C., 1992), ch. 5; Bruce Levine, *Half Slave and Half Free: The Roots of Civil War* (New York, 1992), ch. 1; and Jeffrey R. Kerr-Ritchie, *Freedpeople in the Tobacco South: Virginia, 1860–1900* (Chapel Hill, N.C., 1993).

denied advocacy of Slavery in the Abstract. It is comical to observe the intellectual gyrations that some went through before the War in an effort to deny that they were advocating any such concept. Technically, they were correct, for with few exceptions, they predicted rather than advocated. Their prediction flowed from a combination of theology, political economy, and historical interpretation. They read historical trends as pointing toward a restoration of slavery – or, more precisely, of various forms of personal servitude – for the laboring classes of Europe and eventually of the North too. William J. Grayson emphatically denied that he advocated any slavery other than black slavery, but his polemical writings and his famous poem, *The Hireling and the Slave*, did not merely praise the southern slave system as more humane than the northern free-labor system; they specifically condemned the free-labor system as an atrocious offense against Christianity and decency.[4]

Brought up in a democratic republic and confirmed believers in black inferiority, Southerners could not easily swallow the idea of enslaving whites. Almost all of the foreign and northern critics of capitalism rejected any such idea, although they supported the southern notion that the slaves fared better than most of the world's wage-workers and peasants. Holmes rebuked Fitzhugh for that very confusion of realms. Wilhelm Steinert, a German traveler to Texas, illustrated Holmes's point. He admitted that the slaves ate better than many laborers in Germany and quoted German laborers in Texas as calling themselves "white slaves." Steinert nevertheless rejected slavery since "man does not live by bread alone."[5]

Unquestionably, Southerners preferred racial grounds and shrank at the thought of reenslaving whites. They hoped against hope that reenslavement would not be necessary; that some way could be found to overcome the antagonism between capital and labor. But they feared the worst. Politicians with national aspirations and alliances, intellectuals with national and international connections, even ordinary citizens who did not wish to antagonize fellow Americans tried desperately to hold to an agnostic position, especially since convinced that the North, unlike Europe, might be able to postpone the inevitable for centuries. Their political philosophy made them wary of trying to tell others what to do. They analyzed the course of Western civilization's development and warned of an impending catastrophe. They were not trying to dictate solutions to people who had a right to work out their own solutions to their own problems. They did not recognize the right of Yankees to intervene

[4] For further discussion of Grayson's views, see Eugene D. Genovese, *The Slaveholders' Dilemma: Freedom and Progress in Southern Conservative Thought, 1820–1860* (Columbia, S.C., 1991) and Genovese, Foreword to Richard J. Calhoun, ed., *Witness to Sorrow: The Antebellum Autobiography of William J. Grayson* (Columbia, S.C., 1990).

[5] Holmes, "Fitzhugh's Sociology for the South," *QRMCS*, 9 (April, 1855), 180–201; Gilbert J. Jordan, ed. and trans., "W. Steinert's View of Texas in 1849," *Southwestern Historical Quarterly*, 81 (1977–1978), 57–58, 65. See also Max Berger, *The British Traveller in America, 1836–1860* (Gloucester, Mass., 1964), 118.

in the internal affairs of the South and did not claim the right to interfere in the internal affairs of the North.

The War and the defeat of the Confederacy challenged those who had promoted Slavery in the Abstract, whether openly or sotto voce, to envision a world without slavery. What kind of social relations would have come out of the War if the Confederacy had scored a last-minute victory? Those most committed to the basic ideas of Slavery in the Abstract simply assumed that slavery without personal masters, even if disguised as wage labor or peonage, would run wild. But as the War wound down, those Southerners who grappled with the prospect of an end of their social system left few hints about where they thought it would end. "The mutual hatred of the North & South now is too deep, too eradicable," John Preston Sheffey, C. S. A., wrote to his fiancée in 1861. Continuation in the Union "would be too degrading, too disgraceful to be endured by the proud Slaveocracy of the gallant South." But would the "proud Slaveocracy" have survived as a slaveholding class? In October 1863, Linton Stephens wrote to his brother Alexander, "I believe the institution of slavery is already so undermined and demoralized as never to be much use to us, even if we had peace and independence to-day. The institution has received a terrible shock, which is tending to its disintegration and ruin!" And in December 1864 Col. Alexander Fleet of Virginia, a planter's son, still hoped for victory but did not expect slavery to survive. Reaffirming slavery as neither morally not politically an evil, he added, "I consider it a divine institution as we have it here in Virginia, but not I have been surprised to see in South Carolina." In short, after four years of devastating war could slavery have survived as a viable social system?

In the wake of Confederate defeat, E. A. Pollard of Virginia lashed out at "the slaveholding interest, in its usual narrow spirit – in its old character of a greedy, vulgar, insolent aristocracy." Yet he simultaneously praised the slaveholders' "singularly pure type of civilization" and poured scorn over the free-state aristocracy of money. Slavery, he insisted, introduced order, conservatism, and true democracy, which outweighed the vulgar elements he had been denouncing.[6]

The slaveholders erred badly in underestimating the desire for freedom among the downtrodden. They erred no less badly in projecting an ultimate outcome onto short-term trends, which, to be sure, lasted long enough to impart much human misery. When Southerners surveyed the social costs of European and northern capitalist development, they knew what they saw, but

---

[6] John Preston Sheffey to Josephine Spiller, Mar. 23, 1861, in James I. Robertson, ed., *Soldier of Southwestern Virginia: The Civil War Letters of Captain John Preston Sheffey* (Baton Rouge, La., 2004), 15; Linton Stephens to Alexander H. Stephens, Oct. 3, 1863, in James D. Waddell, *Biographical Sketch of Linton Stephens, Containing a Selection of His Letters, Speeches, State Papers, Etc.* (Atlanta, Ga., 1877), 263; Alexander Fleet to his father, Dec. 9, 1864, in Betsey Fleet and John D. P. Fuller, eds., *Green Mount: A Virginia Plantation Family during the War* (Charlottesville, Va., 1962), 349; E. A. Pollard, *Southern History of the War*, 2 vols. (New York, 1866), 2:472, 568.

their proslavery "solution" to the evils of the day could not be borne. The proslavery side scored hits on free-state institutions and practices but not without embarrassments. As time went on, the South grew more conservative in attitude, legislation, and – up to a point – practice. The free states suffered the liberal direction of development rather than some wholesale plunge into loose living. And therein lay the southern embarrassment. Notwithstanding South Carolina's intransigence and bold defense of slavery as a bulwark against moral decay, southern wavering raised fears of a similar drift. The acid test would have come had the South won its independence. It did not come, although the proslavery side continued to claim its moral superiority.

Only the most thoughtful Southerners worried about the ultimate logic of the proslavery argument. Like people everywhere and in all ages, they lived with myriad contradictory thoughts. Yet to one extent or another and with varying degrees of consistency, they slowly forged a worldview critical of the deepest assumptions of a bourgeoisie that was making an apparently irresistible – and ultimately victorious – bid for world power. The slaveholders steadfastly yet fretfully defended the remnants of a passing age while offering a doomed vision of a sinister future.

Index